Street by Street

GLOUCESTERSHIRE

PLUS BRISTOL, CHEPSTOW, CRICKLADE, LEDBURY, MALMESBURY, SHIPSTON-ON-STOUR

Enlarged Areas Cheltenham, Gloucester

Ist edition May 2001

© Automobile Association Developments Limited 2001

Published by AA Publishing (a trading name of Automobile Association Developments Limited, whose registered office is Norfolk House, Priestley Road, Basingstoke, Hampshire, RG24 9NY. Registered number 1878835).

Mapping produced by the Cartographic Department of The Automobile Association.

A CIP Catalogue record for this book is available from the British Library.

Printed by in Italy by Printer Trento srl

Key to map pages — ii-iii

Key to map symbols — iv-1

Enlarged scale pages — 2-7

Street by Street — 8-353

Index – towns & villages — 354-356

Index – streets — 356-385

Index – featured places — 385-390

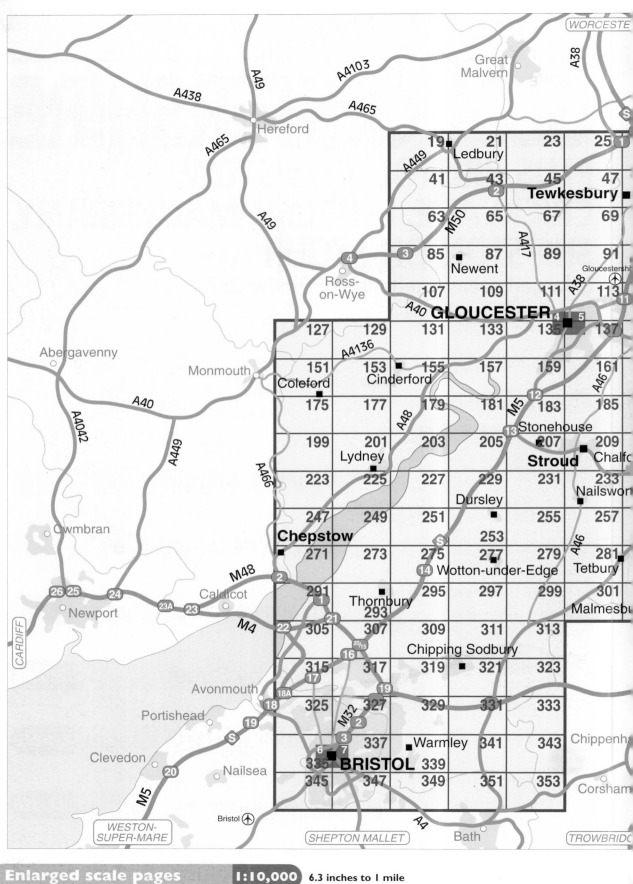

Enlarged scale pages **1:10,000** 6.3 inches to 1 mile

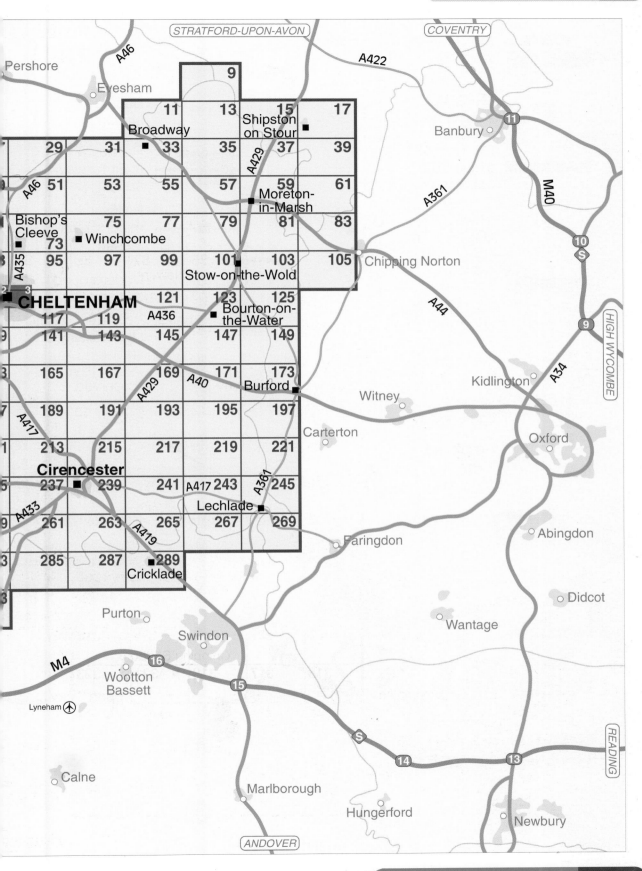

STRATFORD-UPON-AVON

COVENTRY

Pershore

A46

A422

Evesham

9

11   **13**   **15**   **17**

Broadway   Shipston on Stour

Banbury

11

29   **31**   **33**   **35**   **37**   **39**

A429

M40

51   **53**   **55**   **57**   **59**   **61**

A46

Moreton-in-Marsh

A361

10
S

Bishop's Cleeve   **75**   **77**   **79**   **81**   **83**

73   Winchcombe

A435

95   **97**   **99**   **101**   **103**   **105**

Chipping Norton

9

HIGH WYCOMBE

Stow-on-the-Wold

2
3

CHELTENHAM   **121**   **123**   **125**

117   **119**   A436   Bourton-on-the-Water

A44

141   **143**   **145**   **147**   **149**

A34

165   **167**   **169**   **171**   **173**

A429   A40   Burford

Kidlington

Witney

189   **191**   **193**   **195**   **197**

A417

Carterton

Oxford

213   **215**   **217**   **219**   **221**

Cirencester

237   **239**   **241**   A417 **243**   **245**

A361

A433   Lechlade

261   **263**   **265**   **267**   **269**

A419

Faringdon

Abingdon

285   **287**   **289**

Cricklade

Didcot

Purton

Swindon

Wantage

M4

16

Wootton Bassett

15

Lyneham ✈

S

READING

14   **13**

Calne

Marlborough

Newbury

Hungerford

ANDOVER

3.6 inches to 1 mile   **Scale of main map pages   1:17,500**

0   1/2   miles   1

0   1/2   1   kilometres   1 1/2   2

Junction 9	Motorway & junction
Services	Motorway service area
	Primary road single/dual carriageway
Services	Primary road service area
	A road single/dual carriageway
	B road single/dual carriageway
	Other road single/dual carriageway
	Restricted road
	Private road
← ←	One way street
	Pedestrian street
	Track/footpath
	Road under construction
	Road tunnel
P	Parking

P+	Park & Ride
	Bus/coach station
	Railway & main railway station
	Railway & minor railway station
	Underground station
	Light railway & station
+++++++++++	Preserved private railway
LC	Level crossing
•–•–•–•–•	Tramway
- - - - - -	Ferry route
··············	Airport runway
– · – · – · –	Boundaries- borough/district
∧∧∧∧∧∧∧	Mounds
93	Page continuation 1:17,500
7	Page continuation to enlarged scale 1:10,000

River/canal lake, pier

Aqueduct lock, weir

465
▲
Winter Hill
Peak (with height in metres)

Beach

Coniferous woodland

Broadleaved woodland

Mixed woodland

Park

Cemetery

Built-up area

Featured building

City wall

A&E
Accident & Emergency hospital

Toilet

Toilet with disabled facilities

Petrol station

PH Public house

PO Post Office

Public library

i Tourist Information Centre

Castle

Historic house/ building

Wakehurst Place NT
National Trust property

M Museum/ art gallery

† Church/chapel

Country park

Theatre/ performing arts

Cinema

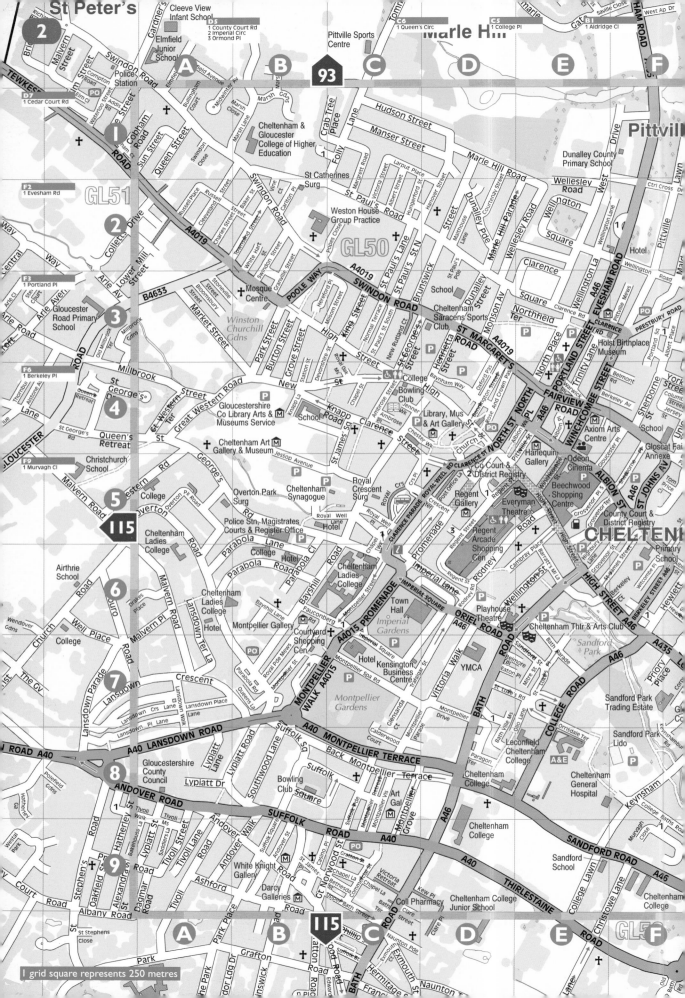

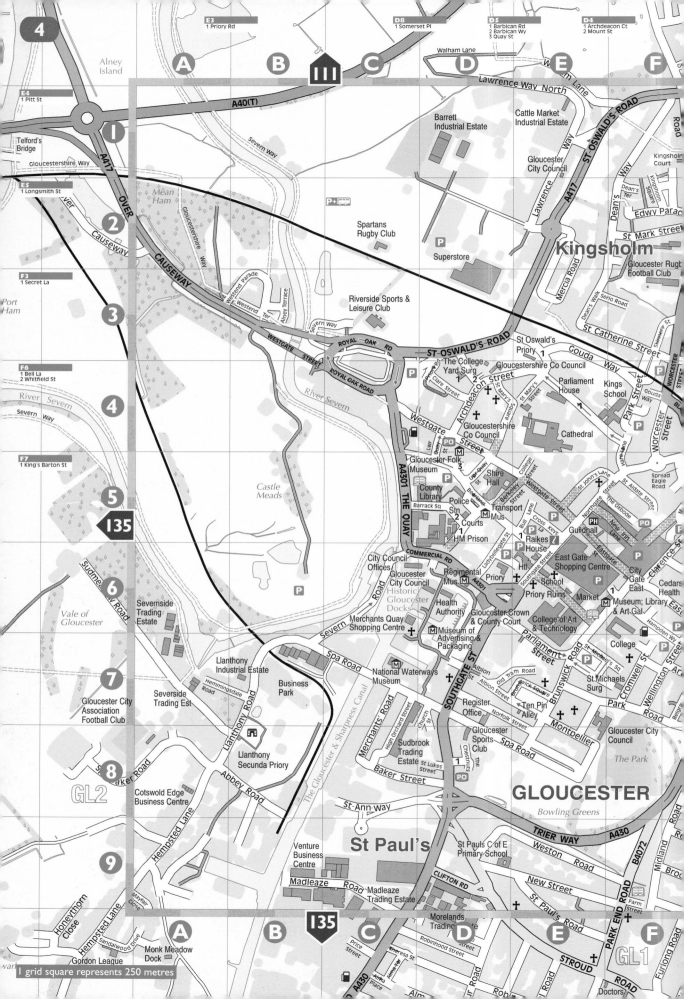

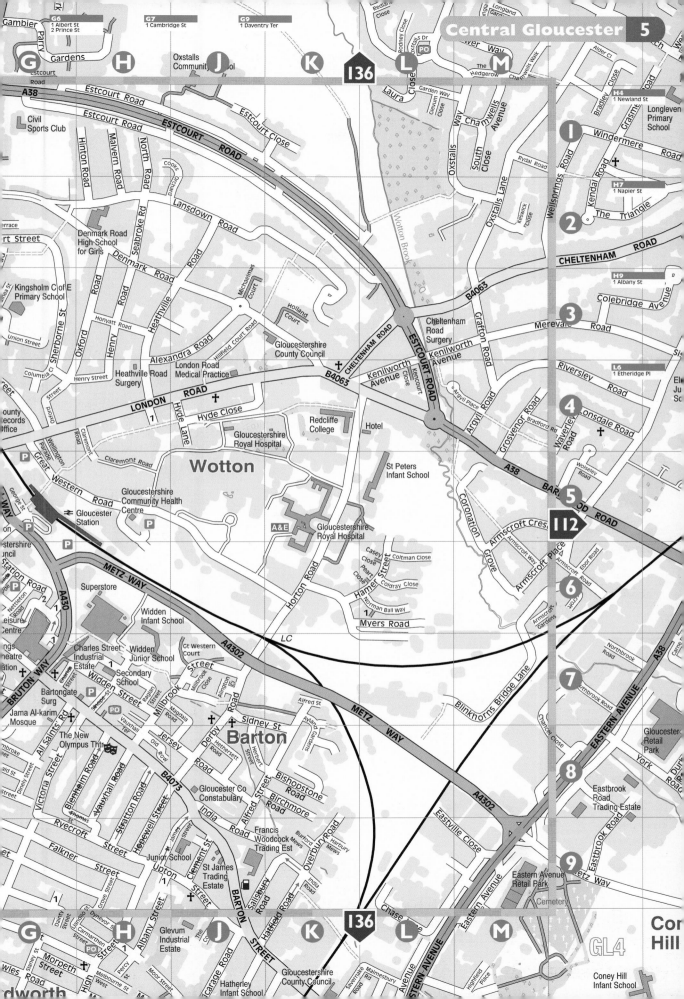

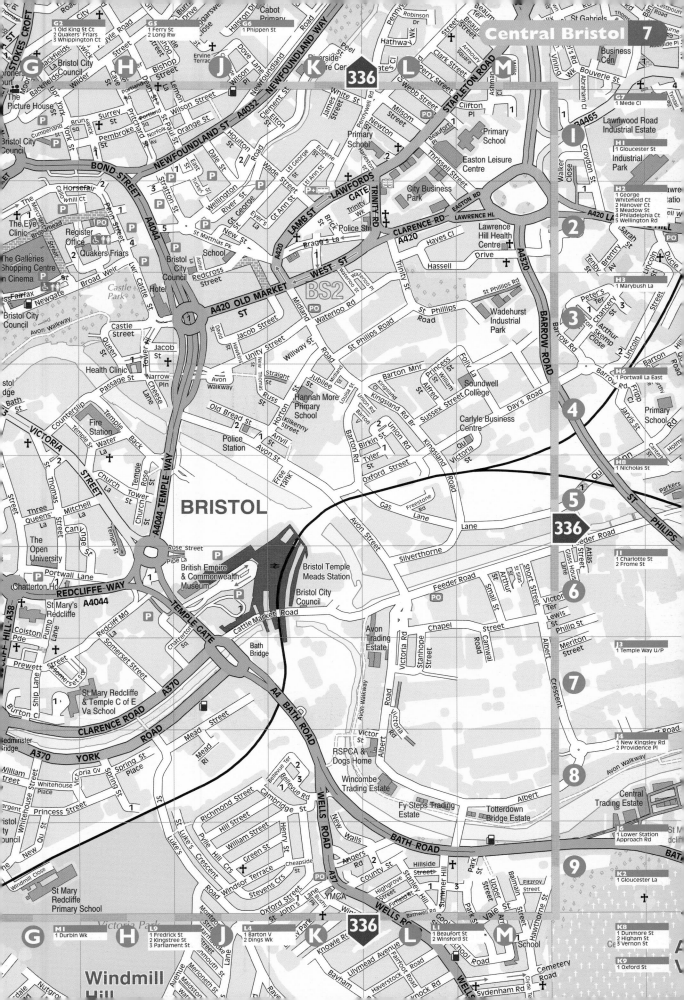

G
H
J
K
L
M

G6
1 Orchard Cl

Boundary R
Road

Sharry
Lane

B4632

Infant
School
The
Surgery
Park

Magdale Cl
St Swithin's
The Close
Ct
Aylstone
Dr

Main Road
Friday
St
The Firs

Thackeray
Cl
Stileman
Cl
Bastyan Av

1

Tailor's
Lane
Lane

Edmonds
Rd
Dobie Rd

Hill Lane
Goose Lane
Meon Close

Meon Lane

**Upper
Quinton**

2

Monarch's Way

Lower
Meon

3

CAMPDEN ROAD

**Lower
Clopton**

Meon Hall

Heart of England Way

4

ROAD

Meon
House

Monarch's Way

Admington Lane

Admin
Farm

5

Heart of England Way

**Upper
Clopton**

Coleman's
Hill

6

B4632

Meon Road

Nursery
Cl
Granbrook
Lane

Lane

Warwickshire County
Gloucestershire County

Monarch's Way

Hidcote
Combe

7

Cedar Road

GRANBROOK LANE

B4632

Mickleton

Old Mnr Gdns

Mickleton Wood
Farm

8

Cemetery

aker's Hill

Kiftsgate
Gardens

Hidcote
Garden (N

**Hidcote
Bartrim**

Gloucestershire County
Warwickshire County

G7
1 Frampton Dr

G8
1 Jordans Cl

H7
1 Church St

G H J K L M

Weston Road

I
2
3

WESTON ROAD

B4035

Larkborough
Farm

Honeybourne Airfield
Industrial Estate

Worcestershire County
Gloucestershire County

Honeybourne Road

Poden Lane

Saintbury
Grounds

Buckle Street

Weston-
sub-Edge
4

PO

Cidermill
Orch

Dover's Vw

12

Parsons Lane

Chapel Lane

B4632

5

†

6

Top Farm

Willersey
Industrial
Estate

B4632

Saintbury

7

Park Farm

Timms
Green

PO

Willersey
School

†

1

MAIN STREET

Colin Close

Hays
Close

Willersey

B4632

†

Fields Lane

Willow Road

BROADWAY ROAD

Campden Lane

Buckle Street

Weston
Park

8

G H J K L M

33

Gloucestershire County
Worcestershire County

Foxhill

The Narr

Cemetery

G H J K L M

Kiftsgate Gardens

9

Hidcote Manor
Garden (NT)

**Hidcote
Bartrim**

Monarch's Way

Nebsworth Lane

I

2

3

Heart Of England Way

**Hidcote
Boyce**

Longlands
Farm

Furze Lane

Hidcote Road

4

14

GL55

Mickleton Hills
Farm

5

Nash's Lane

Ebrington

6

Nash's Lane

Elm Grove Road

New Road

Campden   Road

†

LC

May   Lane

Battledene
Farm

7

Station Road

Castle
Gardens

THE CAM   B4035

8

G H J K L M

35

B4035   PU   IT LANE

14

A B C D E F

Stoke

Campden Pitch
Campden Street
Frog La
Grump Street
Foxcote Hill
X
1

Harolds Farm

Woodmeadow
Farm

I

Nebsworth Lane

Nebsworth

2

SWO... e

The Downs
House

Campden

Foxcote Hi

Avenue

3

Foxcote Farm

Southfield
Farm

Cathole

4

13

Gloucestershire County
Warwickshire County

5

Hoarston

Compton
Scorpion Manor

Nash's Lane

Longmoor
House

6

Elm Grove
Lane

New
Road

7

Hotel

B4035

Charingworth

Charingworth
Grange

8

Braxfield
House

B4035

Gloucestershire County
Warwickshire County

A B C **36** D E F

Cottage
Farm

1 grid square represents 500 metres

Man...long
Farm

B4479

Tankards Hill

B5
1 High St
2 Horsefair
3 Husbandmans Cl
4 Market Pl
5 Norluck Ct
6 Pound Cl

B4
1 Badgers Crs

A6
1 Costard Av
2 Hanson Av

A5
1 Farm Cl

A B C D E F

Hill Clumps

Honington

Granby Road

River Stour

A3400

Fell Mill Lane

Centenary Way

Fell Mill Lane

Fell Mill Farm

Centenary Way

A3400

Mayo Rd

Shipston Medical Cen

Donnington Rd

STRATFORD ROAD

River Way

station

The Drive

Shipston Industrial Estate

Tilemans La

Brickhill Cl

Junior & Infant School

Watery La

The Ellen Badger Hospital

Shipston-on-Stour

Fell Mill Lane

Stour Valley Community School

Darlingscote Rd

Ivy Meadow

Greenway Road

Oxway Cl

Mundy La

Glen Cl

The

Warwick Pl

Berry Cl

Telegraph St

Berry Avenue

Sheep St

PO

WEST ST

4 PH

1

NEW STREET

River Stour

Pittway Av

Queens Av

Clark

ROAD

Green Lane

Old Rd

Gerrards Rd

5

PH

Oldbutt Rd

Campden Rd

Hanson Av

Marshall Av

The Hobbins

The Malders

2

CAMPDEN

Simpson Rd

Parsons Cl

Callaways Rd

Greenfields Cl

4

Callaways Rd

Bostley Cl

Keyte Rd

Springfield Road

Springfield

Fulready Meadow

Banister

FURZE HILL ROAD

LONDON ROAD

Hawthorn Way

Ashgrove

Holly Rd

Elm Rd

Cemetery

Barcheston

B4035

Willington

Pig Brook

Horseleys Farm

A B C D E F

B6
1 A3400
2 Green Lane Cl
3 Orchard Cl
4 South Lynn Gdns
5 Stour Ct

River Stour

CV36

1 grid square represents 500 metres

G H J K L M

I
2
3
4
5
6
7
8

Centenary Way

nary Way

Littleworth
Farm

Aylesmore
Farm

St Dennis

Tus Brook

Tusbrook
Farm

nolland's Farm

B4035

Barcheston
Ground Farm

Roundhill Farm

Castle Hill

FANT HILL

Bells
Lane

Hill
Lane

Gillett's
Lane

**Upper
Brailes**

Castle Hill Lane

Braies C of E
Primary School

Famington
Farm

Highwall
Spinney

Hendrook Lane

**Grove
End**

Jeffs
Close

Sutton Lane

G H J K L M

39

L2
1 Abercrombie Cl
2 Drinkwater Cl
3 Northdown Cl
4 Sunshine Cl

L3
1 Massey Rd

M1
1 Challen Cl
2 The Garth
3 Plaister's End

G   H   J   A458   K   L   M

ROAD

B4214

I

Grovesend

New
Mills

Saxon
Way

Ledbury
Station

Station
Industrial Estate

2

Orchard
Business
Park

The Hops
Business
Park

HEREFORD ROAD

BUSH
PITCH

Callow End

Knapp La

Upperfields

Wallhills

Yeoman

Viking

Target

Northmead

The Langland

Newbury
Park

THE HOMEND

Homend Crescent

Upr Hall

Hillfield Drive

A438

Falcon Lane

A417 LEADON WAY

John Lee Rd

Pt Rupert Rd

Frost Rd

New Mills Way

Gibson Rd

Frome Brook
Road

Loden
Brook

Preston
Brook
Close

LEDBURY

Primary
School

The Mews

Belle Orch

Belle Orch La

Orchard La

Station
Industrial
Est

Shell Ho
Gallery

Upr Hall
Close

2
3

Church St

Margaret Rd

Long Acres

Lawnside Rd

Queen's Wy

Bye St

PO

PH

St Katherines St

3

Flights
Farm

Bridge   Street

Barnett Pl

Barnett
Close

Woodleigh
Close

Woodleigh Rd

Oatleys Crs

Oatleys Ter

Ledbury
Market Surg

Queen's Ct

Ledbury
Mkt Theatre

St Katherines
Surg

Market St

Hotel

B4216

PH

THE SOUTH

A449

Lower Road

Victoria Road

Albert Road

Oatleys
Road

Churchill Mnr

NEW
STREET

Pound Meadow

Pound
Pde

4

20

Little
Marcle
Road

Bankside
Industrial
Estate

Egar Cl

Barracks
Rd

Chestnut
Cl

Elmsdale
Rd

Birch
Close

John
Masefield
High School

Oakland Dr

Cemetery

Oakland Drive

Aston

Martins
Wy

Villa Wy

Russet
Cl

Bramley

Orchard

Blenheim
Dr

5

Old Lilly
Hall

Rowland's
Green

Ledbury Town
Football Club

Woodfield

Fernbank

Biddulph

Shepherds

Spring Gv

Hazle
Cl

Old Wharf
Industrial Estate

Old
Wharf

LEADON   WAY

6

Lilly Hall Lane

Hill House

A449

Robinscroft

Orlham
Lane

B4216

River Leadon

Hazel
Farm

7

Ludstock

A449

Orlham
Farm

Siddington
Farm

Argus
Farm

8

Orlham Lane

County of Herefordshire
Gloucestershire County

B4216

Dinchall

Oldfields

Poets
Path

Herrow

Poets Path

M5
1 Furlong Ct
2 Miller Craddock
Wy

M2
1 Kempley Brook
Dr

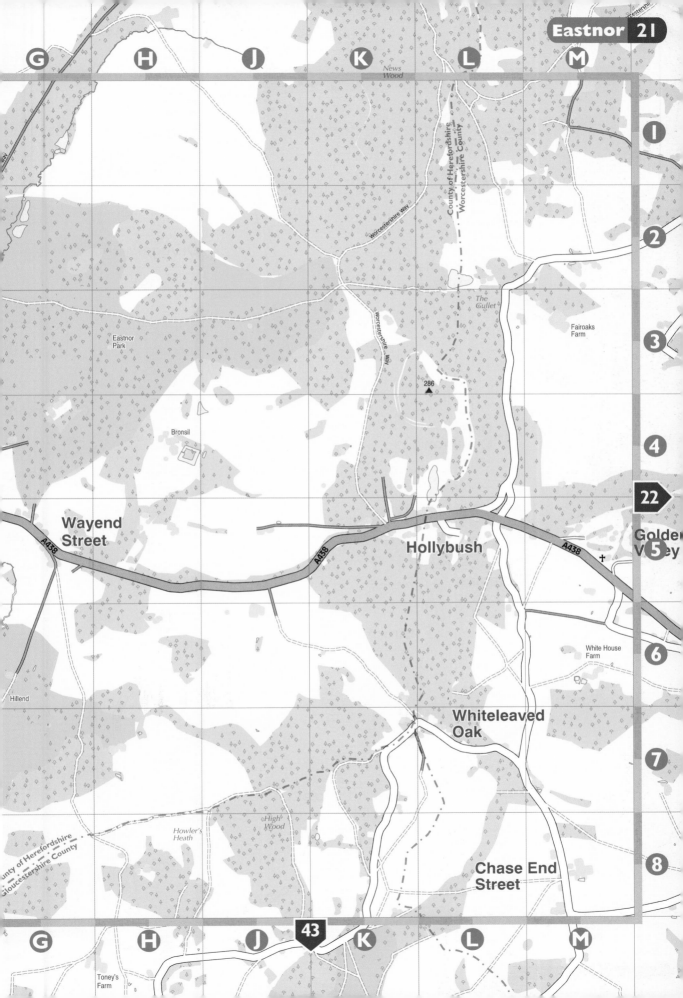

G H J K L M

News
Wood

I

2

County of Herefordshire
Worcestershire County

3

Worcestershire Way

The
Gullet

Fairoaks
Farm

▲ 286

4

22

Eastnor
Park

Golden
Valley 5

Worcestershire Way

Bronsil

**Wayend
Street**

A438

Hollybush

A438

†

White House
Farm

Hillend

6

**Whiteleaved
Oak**

7

County of Herefordshire
Gloucestershire County

Howler's
Heath

High
Wood

**Chase End
Street**

8

G H J 43 K L M

Toney's
Farm

A   B   C   D   E   F

1

New Road

Eight Oaks
Farm

Sansome
Farm

2

Druggers End

Drugger's End Lane

**Chandler's
Cross**

B4208

Biddle's
Farm

3

oaks

Rough Chase

Castlemorto

4

**Hollybed
Common**

B4208

Mill Farm

Castlemorton
School

✝

21

**Golden
Valley**

5

**Coombegreen
Common**

Miller's
Court

Miller's   Court   Road

6

White
Farm

B4208

✝

Birts Street

◁PH

7

A438

Rye
Court

**Rye
Street**

8

**Camer's
Green**

B4208

A438

A   B   C   D   E   F

Whiting
Farms

1 grid square represents 500 metres

G H J K L M

I

2

3

4

24

5

6

7

8

Welland Stone

Little Welland

Longdon Hill End

Walk Farm

Drinkwater's Farm

Hillend Court

Cutler's Farm

Birtsmorton

Longdon Marsh

Longdon Brook

Marsh End

The Hill

Red House

Worcestershire Way Link

Worcestershire Way Link

Locker Lane

Rye Way Link

er's Court Road

G H J K L M

45

A438

Pendock Moor

G H J K L M

River Seve

1 The Cross

Saxon's Lode

Stratford

A38(T)

Phelp's Farm

I

Uckinghall

A38(T)

2

Brockeridge Common

Ripple

Station   Road

Ferry   Lane

Bow Lane

Gubberhill Farm

3

Junction

Ripple Brook

The Twittocks

4

M50

26

Puckrup

Cherry Orchar

A38

5

Lane

Puckrup

Bow Farm

Page's

6

Church End

River Severn

Severn Way

Abb

7

Shuthonger

A38

Bredon School

8

Windmill Tump

Shuthonger Common

G H J K L M

Worcestershire Link

47

Worcestershire Way

HS
1 Bricknell Av
2 The Croftlands
3 Glebeland Dr
4 Gravel Pits Cl
5 Homestead Cl
6 Plantation Crs
7 Russet Cl

G   H   J   K   L   M

Bredon's Norton

Rectory Farm

B4080

Mill End

Moreton Lane

Severn Sailing Club

Westmancote

Chapel Lane

Farm Lane

Hill Cl

Lower Westmancote

Kemerton Road

Bayliss Road

Wing Lane

Kemerton

PO   Job's Lane

The Priory

28

Kinsham Lane

First School

PH
PO
Church St
Back La
Derwell Cl
The Dell

KEMERTON ROAD

HIGH ST
Bredon
Farm La
Oak Lane

Station Dr
Jubilee Dr
Cotswold Cl
Blenheim
Drive
Poppins Rd
Waterloo Wy
Orchard Cl
Queensmead

4   6   5   1   3   2

Dock Lane

CHELTENHAM ROAD

Kinsham

Chapel Lane

B4079

Kinsham Lane

1
2
3
4
5
6
7
8

G   H   J   K   L   M

49

Carrant Brook

Worcestershire
Gloucestershire

G H J K L M

Sandfield Farm

I

Holcomb Nap

Wood La

Gorse Hl

Cornfield Wy

PO

Hillside

Elmley Road

Cotton's Lane

Wychavon Way

Carrant Brook Farm

2

A46(T)

Baker's Lane

Ashton under Hill

Ashton under Hill Primary School

Station Road

3

Beckford Road

Willow Cl

4

Grafton

Wychavon Wy

A46(T)

30

Carrant Brook

5

Wychavon Way

6

eckford

Didcot Farm

7

A46(T)

Worcestershire County

Gloucestershire County

8

Hill Farm

Pleasant

G2
1 Old Hall Cl

H2
1 Woodland Cl

G H J K L M

I

2

3

4

32

5

6

7

8

Glebe Rd

School Rd

PO

Broadway Road

1

7

Church Rd

✝

lle

Buckland
Fields

Worcestershire County
Gloucestershire County

Hinto   d

B4632

Wormington

Leasow
House

Stanton
Fields

G H J K L M

53

Wormington
Grange

B

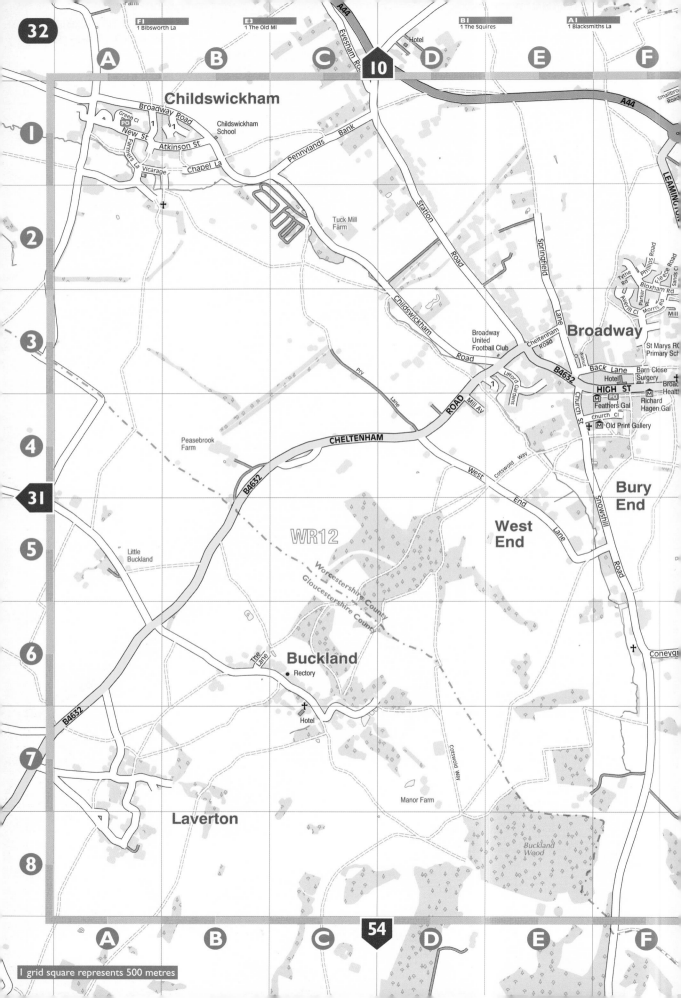

G2
1 Bridgemans Cl

G3
1 Bredon Vw
2 Daston Cl
3 High St

G H J II K L M

Fields
Lane

BROADWAY ROAD
Willow Road

Gloucestershire County
Worcestershire County

Foxhill
Manor

Golf Course

I Iarrow

Buckle Street

den Lane

Bibsworth
Farm

Lane

A44

Hotel

2

rt Av
y School
1

Bibsworth Gardens

Collett's Cl

King Cole Ct

Fields

Anderson Gallery
otswold Teddy-Bear-Mus 3

Kirtlands
Preparatory
School

Farncombe
House

Cotswold Way

3

Bibsworth Lane

Fish Hill

FISH HILL

Cotswold Way

Buckle Street

4

Cotswold Way

Tilbury
Hollow

34

Coombe
Farm

5

Cotswold Way

Peter's
Farm

A44

6

Broadway
Tower

Broadway Tower
Country Park

Springhill
Industrial
Estate

7

Dor
Knap

Buckle Street

Kite's
Nest

Middle
Hill House

Heath Farm

8

Worcestershire County
Gloucestershire C

Dur
Woo

G H J 55 K L M

Seven
Wells

A **B** **C** **D** **E** **F**

Weston
Park

The Narrows

Cotswold Way

I

2

Campden
House

3

4

Coombe
Farm

5

B4081

Lapstone Farm

6

Springhill
Industrial
Estate

7

A44

FIVE MILE DRIVE

8

Littleworth

The
Medical Centre
Primary
School

1 Pear Tree Cl

Town
Hall

High St
LWR HIGH ST
PH

Police
Court 1 Izod's Cl
Police Court

Westington

Park Road

Blind Lane

The Meadows

Pollards
Close

B4081

Hoo
Lane

Littleworth
Lane

Dyer's
Lane

SHEEP
STREET

Shepherd's
Close

CONDUIT HILL

Coldicotts

Haysum's

Cherry
Orchard

Cherry
Close

George
Lane

Federated Primary Schools of
Ebrington & St James

The
Green

Catbrook
Close

HIGH ST LEYS

CHURCH
STREET

Monarch's Way

Swimming Pool

PH

Broad
Campden

B4081

Monarch's Way

Campden Hill
Farm

Monarch's Way

Hangman's H
Farm

Monarch's Way

Northwick
Hill

Holt
Farm

Dovedale Farm

A **B** **C** **D** **E** **F**

Upton Wold
Farm

1 grid square represents 500 metres

A B4035
B
C A4035
14
D
E
F

Braxfield House

Charingworth Gran C7
1 Church Farm La

1

Marfurlong Farm
B4479

Gloucestershire County
Warwickshire County

Cottage Farm

Tankards Hill

2
B4479

Blackdowns

Stretto on-Fos

Paxford
3

Middle Ditchford

4

Knee Brook

35
Stapenhill Farm

Ditchford Hill

5
Neighbrook

6
Knee Brook

7
Church vw
†
Aston Magna

Aston Hale
A429

8

Dorn Hill
A
B
C
58
D
E
F

G H J 15 K L M

Rowborough

Horseleys Farm

I

2

Carson Cl
Chapel Gate
Belcony

3

Paddle Brook
A429
High Furze

Ditchford Frary Village

4

38

Lower Ditchford Village
Lower Farm
5

Becket Cl

stone Br
6

Todenham

Gloucestershire County
Warwickshire County
7

Oldborough Farm

8

G H J 59 K L M

Wolford Road

Geat Wolf

Mount Sorrell
The Green

Famington
Farm

North
Farm

Famington
nge

Cherington
Butts

Highwall
Spinney

New House
Farm

Brailes
Golf Club

Church
Farm

Sutton Lane

Tommy's Turn Lane

Sutton Lane

Sutton Lane

Jeffs
Close

Sutton-under-Brailes

† **Stourton**

St John's
Road

St John's
Cl

Featherbed Lane

Cherington

Wood
Lane

Steels
La

Berrills Lane

Sutton Mill

Lanes End
Farm

Stourton Hill

Margett's
Hill

Weston
Park

G H J 17 K L M

1
2
3
4
5
6
7
8

G H J 61 K L M

G H Oldfields J **19** K L M

County of Herefordshire
Gloucestershire County

Henberrow

Leddington

Mirabels Farm

Dinchall Farm

Poets Path

Poets Path

Path

1

2

Donnin

3

Tillputsend Cott

Donnington Hall

Rosehill

Poets Path

Greenway
PO

4

42

Tillers' Green

Great Netherton

B4215

Preston Brook

Poets Path

Ockington Farm

5

Poets

B4024

Windcross Farm

Wilton Place

6

Poets Path

Hill Ash

7

Shakesfield

B4215

B4216

Poets Path No 2

Dymock

Poets Path No 1

Poets Path No 2

8

Allums

Poets Path No 1

Daffodil Way

PO
Western Way

Crowfield

Lane

The Pound

The Old Rock

Daffodil Way

Daffodil Way

B4215

G H J **63** K L M

42

A   B   C   20   D   E Clencher's   F
                                   Mill

Dingwood Park
Farm

1

A417

Woodfields Farm

Pepper
Mill

2

Glynch Brook

Donnington

Noad
Farm

A417

Brookend

3

Haffield

The Vineyard

Dyke House Lane

4

Grove
House

Donnington
Hall

PO

Bell Lane

41

Sandfield

Broom's
Green

Bromsberrow Heath
Business Park

M50

5

Bromsberrow
Heath

Ockington
Farm

Poets' Path No 2

The Hill

6

Ryton

Poets' Path No 1

7

Poets' Path No 2

M50

M50

8

Poets' Path No 1

Callow
Farm

The
Pound

A   Crowfield   B   C   64   D Ketford   E   F

River Leadon

Poets' Path No 1

M50

1 grid square represents 500 metres

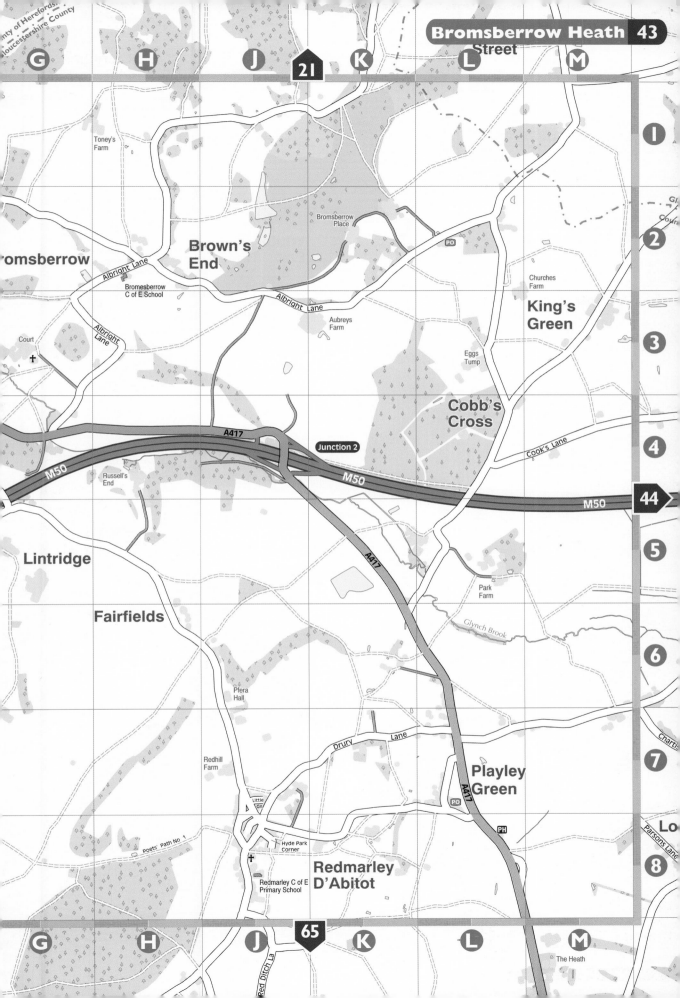

Street

County of Herefordshire
Gloucestershire County

G H J 21 K L M

I

Toney's Farm

Bromsberrow Place

2

Brown's End

Bromsberrow

PO

Churches Farm

King's Green

Albright Lane

Bromesberrow C of E School

3

Albright Lane

Court

†

Albright Lane

Aubreys Farm

Eggs Tump

Cobb's Cross

4

A417

Junction 2

Cook's Lane

M50

M50

M50

44

Russell's End

5

Lintridge

Park Farm

A417

Glynch Brook

Fairfields

6

Pfera Hall

Drury Lane

7

Redhill Farm

Playley Green

Little Gn

PO

Chart...

Poets' Path No 1

Hyde Park Corner

A417

PH

Lo...

Parsons Lane

†

Redmarley D'Abitot

8

Redmarley C of E Primary School

G H J 65 K L M

Red Ditch La

The Heath

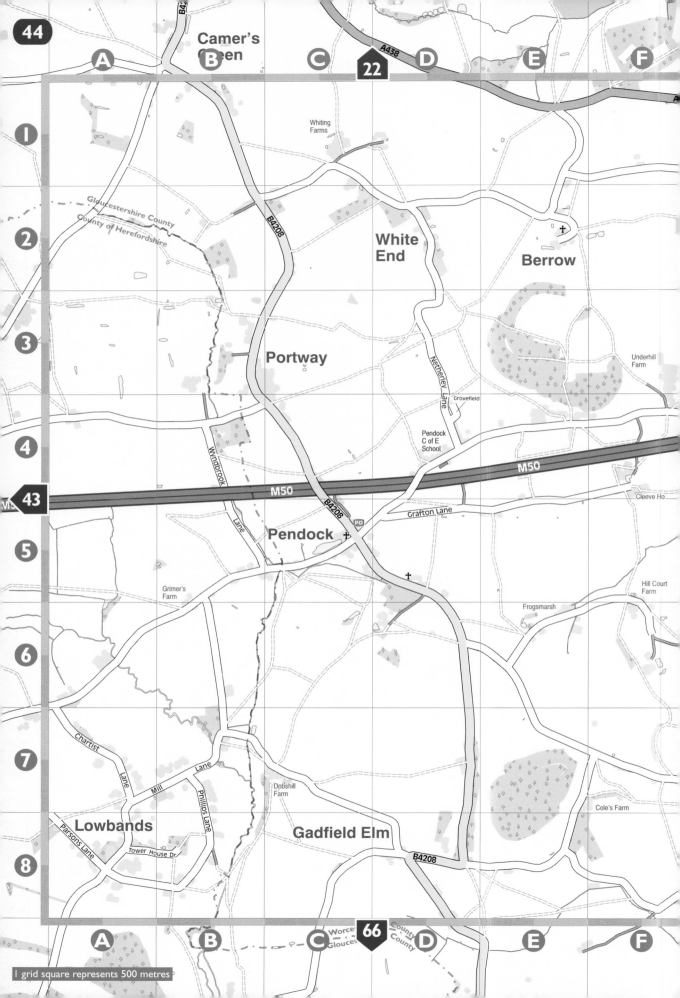

44

A   B   C   **22**   D   E   F

A438

Camer's Green

1

Whiting Farms

2

Gloucestershire County
County of Herefordshire

White End

Berrow

B4208

3

Portway

Netherley Lane

Grovefield

Underhill Farm

4

Wyndbrook Lane

Pendock C of E School

M50

M50

Cleeve Ho

43

M5

M50

B4208

Grafton Lane

5

PO

Pendock ✝

✝

Grimer's Farm

✝

Hill Court Farm

Frogsmarsh

6

7

Chartist Lane

Lane

Mill

Phillips Lane

Dobshill Farm

Cole's Farm

8

Lowbands

Parsons Lane

Tower House Dr

Gadfield Elm

B4208

A   B   C   **66**   D   E   F

Worce'
Glouces

County
County

1 grid square represents 500 metres

J2
1 Crofts Fld

M5
1 Mill St

M7
1 Theocs Cl

G H J 25 K L M

Windmill Tump

Bushley Green

Worcestershire Way Link

Worcestershire Way Link

Severn Way

River Severn

Bushley

Wood Street

Stokes Road

Wood Street

A438

A438

A438

Bushley Park

Upper Lode

Severn Way

48

Lane

Alcock's Farm

Worcestershire County
Gloucestershire County

Severn Ham

Millcot Gallery

Hotel

Hotel

St Mary's Rd

St Mary's La

Church St

8 Abbey School

The John M Museum

TEWKESBURY

Tewkesbury Abbey

Bishop's Walk

Home Farm

Forthampton Court

Bishop's Walk

Bishop's Walk

Lode Lane

Lower Lode

Severn Way

Council Offices

Cemetery

Lincoln Cl

Battle Rd

Gloucester Road

Lower Lode

Lower Lode

Tewkesbury Park

Battle 1471

Lincoln Green Lane

Hotel

River Severn

Severn Way

Golf Course

Club House

Southwick Park

I 1

Th My

2

3

4

5

6

7

8

G1
1 Tug Wilson Close

G2
1 The Apple Orch
2 Bevan Gdns
3 Cromers Cl
4 George Dowty Dr
5 Monkey Meadow
6 The Pear Orch
7 Redwood Ct
8 Wheatstone Cl

G H J **27** K L M

I

Aston on Carrant

Worcestershire
Gloucestershire

Carrant Brook

2

Gould Dr
Sinderberry Dr
Bowler Rd

Carrant Brook
Junior School

Grange Road

LC

3

The Sandfield

Northway Lane
Grange Ct

Virginia Rd
Cedar
Elm
Steward Rd
Lee Rd
Ash Rd
Fairway

Northway
Infant School

Northway

† Aston
Cross

A46(T)

A46(T)

3

North Av

St Davids Road
St Georges Road
South Av

Austin Road

Title Brook

Pamington

Ellendene Dr

B4079

4

Northway Trading Est

Northway
Trading
Estate

Ashchurch for
Tewkesbury
Station

St Davids Rd
St Andrews
St Patricks Rd

Fitzhamon Pk
Tredoroos Gra
St Barbara's Cl

Ashchurch
County
Primary School

A46(T)

Ashchurch

50

5

Natton

LC

6

Homedowns
Business
Park

edowns

B4079

7

A435

Claydon

8

ddington

Monks Lane

G H J **71** K L M

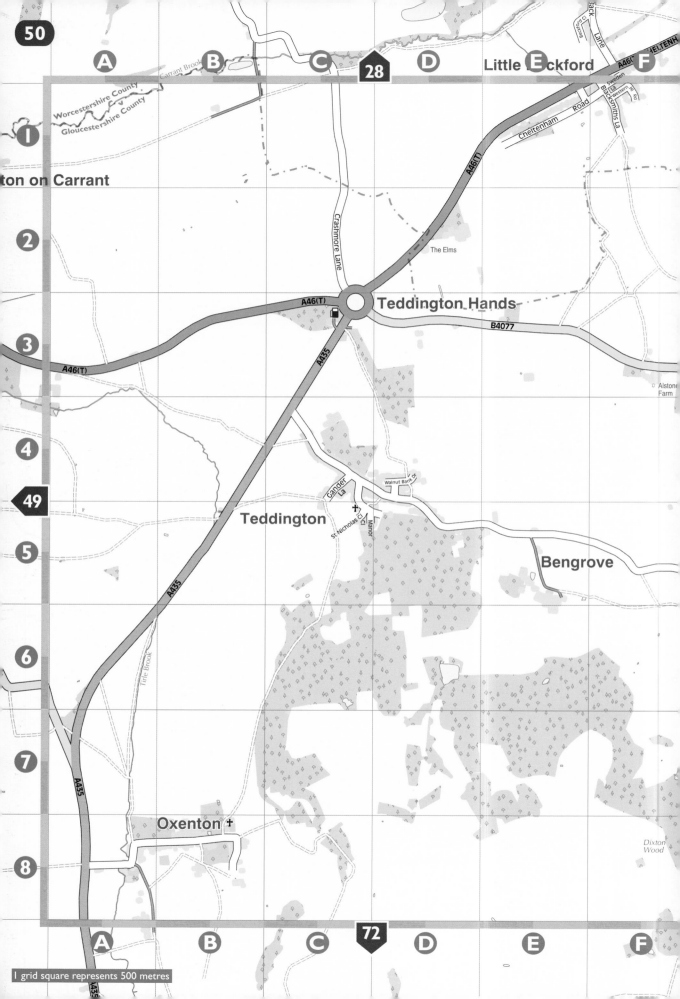

A B C **28** D Little **E**ckford F

I

Worcestershire County
Gloucestershire County

ton on Carrant

2

The Elms

Cheltenham Road

A46(T)

3

A46(T)

A46(T)

A435

A46(T)

B4077

Teddington Hands

Alstone
Farm

4

Gander La

Walnut Bank Dr

49

Teddington

St Nicholas Cl

Manor Cl

Bengrove

5

A435

6

Titte Brook

7

A435

Oxenton ✝

Dixton
Wood

8

A B C **72** D E F

G H J **29** K L M

I

2

3

Hill Farm

Wychavon Way

Great
Washbourne

Little
Washbourne

B4077

Alstone

Beckford Road

Blenheim Cl

Ellenor
Dr

St Margarets Rd

PO

St Margarets
Dr

Willow Bank Road

B4077

Primary
School

Orchard
Rd

School
Rd

Harcsmiths Rd

Church Rd

Brookside

Dibden Lane

Alderton

4

52

5

B4077

**Alderton
Fields**

Frampton
Court

6

**Gretton
Fields**

7

Lower
Farm

8

A B C **32** D E F

I

Stanton

2

3

53

4

5

6

7

8

Buckland Wood

Cotswold Way

Great Brockhampton Farm

Snowshill

Snowshill Manor (NT)

Cotswold Way

Papermill Farm

Lidcombe Wood

Stanway Ash Wood

Field Barn

Taddington

Lower Coscs

B4077

A B C **76** D E F

I grid square represents 500 metres

A B C D E F

Dovedale Farm

1

Upton Wold
Farm

Campden
Ashes

2

FIVE MILE DRIVE

3

Far Upton
Wold Farm

4

A44

5

Highland
Lodge

A424

Bourton
Far Hill Farm

Kildanes
Bottom

6

Bourton
Hill House

7

Wav
Stud

8

Sezincote
Warren

A B C D E F

Hinchwick
Hill Barn

1 grid square represents 500 metres

G H J **35** K L M

...kley
C of E School
Police Station
1 Chantry Gdns
Sleepy Hollow Farm Park ●
Winter...
Summerne
Map Hale
Millview
Bell Bank
Hotel
PO
PH
Chapel Lane
High
School Lane
LOWER ST
B4479
Brook La
Donkey La
Pasture Lane
Dovedale
Park Farm
Monarch's Way

Dorn Hill
I

2

B4479

Downs Farm
Pasture Farm

Hailstone Farm

Batsford ✝
Batsford
3

Arboretum ●
Batsford Park

Bourton Woods

Monarch's Way
Falconry Centre ●
4

B4479

58

A44

Monarch's Way
5

Bourton-on-the-Hill

1 ✝
Fernhill Close
A44
6

Hill Top House

7

8

Sezincote

Sezincote House & Ga...
Icenouse Lane

G H J **79** K L M

A   B   C   36   D   E   F

D5
1 The Green

C7
1 Bowes Lyon Cl
2 St Edwards Ct
3 St James Ct
4 St Pauls Ct
5 St Peters Ct

C6
1 Jameson Ct
2 University Farm

C5
1 Bowling Green Ct
2 High St

Hale

Dorn
Hill

Lower
Lemingt

1

2

Dorn

Batsford

3

Lemington
Grange

4

57

Boram Home
Farm

5

Moreton-
in-Marsh
Hospital

Police
Station

Fosse Way
Business
Cen

MORETON-
IN-MARSH

Dormer House
PNEU School

Moreton-in-
Marsh Station

Nursery Ct

Hospital Road

HIGH ST

New Road

PO

Council
Offices

Davies
Road
Errington

Mosedale

Duiverton

Corder's
La

Doctors
Surg

OXFORD
ST

Cemetery

Close Court

Prim

Stockwells

6

Monarch's Way

A44

BOURTON ROAD

A429

Swan Close

Parkers La

2

St Davids
Primary
School

East St

Hotel

Church st

Gray's
La

St George's

Warneford

Croft Holm

Catsmore Close

Evenlode

Cemetery
Moreton Wanderers
Football Club

Wellington
Rd
Evenlode
Gdns

Road

GL56

Cotswold
Cdns

Tinker's

Fosseway Dr

Keble
Rd

Sankey

Oriel

Redesdale
Place
Hotel

STOW ROAD

3
2
5
1
4

A429

Keble
Av

Avenue

FOSSEWAY

7

Upper Fields
Farm

Monarch's

Fosseway
Farm

Monarch's Way

8

Coldicote
Farm

A   B   80   C   D   E   F

Lower
Rye Farm

D6
1 Oxford St

A429

E6
1 The Grove
2 Radburn Cl

Frogmore
Farm

1 grid square represents 500 metres

G H J 37 K L M

Geat Wolf

Mount Sorrell

The Green

PO

PH

Woodhills Farm

Upper Lemington Village

Wolford Wood

Old Covert

60

Gravels Coppice

Fire Service Technical College

The Four Shire Stone

A44

Wells Folly

Gloucestershire County

Oxfordshire County

Kitebrook

A44

Brookend House

G H J 81 K L M

Middle Brookend

1
2
3
4
5
6
7
8

G H J **39** K L M

Margett's Hill

Weston Park

Whichford

I

Ascott

Whichford Wood

Roman Rd

Akeman Way

2

HacK Lane

Long Compton Woods

Macmillan Way

3

Macmillan Way

SHIPSTON ROAD

Compton Ct

Crockwell St

Long Compton

4

Burway Lane

Malthouse La

Vicarage Lane

PO

Broad Street

Back Lane

5

East Street

Weston Ct

School Cl

Butlers Cl

Long Compton Junior & Infant School

Butlers La

A3400

Barncroft

Butlers Road

Coombe Farm

6

Clarks Lane

Oxfordshire County

Warwickshire County

Butlers Road Farm

7

Macmillan Way

Butlers Road

The Hollows

Butlers Hill Farm

South Hill Farm

A3400

8

G H J **83** K L M

Kings Men

Whispering Knights

Warwickshire County

Oxfordshire

Lyne
Down

A   B   40   C   D   E   F

1

Bickerton
Court

County of Herefordshire

Gloucestershire County

Daffodil Way

St Mary's
Church

Kempley
Court

Brookland

2

Whittocks
End

Daffodil Way

3

Kempley

4

Woodhouse
Farm

Fishpool

Kempley Green

Daffodil Way

5

6

Upton
Court

Daubies
Farm

Linton
Wood

7

Queen's
Wood

8

Upton
Bishop

pton
rews

Tedgewood

A   B   84   C   D   E   M50   F

The Pound

Crowfield

Poets' Path No 1

Callow Farm

River Leadon

Ketford

42

Cutmill

Dur Far

Poets' Path No 1

M50

Welsh House

Welsh House Lane

Welsh House Lane

Little Woodend Farm

Welsh House Lane

B4215

Paunt House

Castletump

Aylesmore

Vineyard

Hayes Farm

Poolhill

Pauntley C of E Primary School

63

Compton Green

The Parks

Birches Lane

B4215

Botloe's Green

Scarr Road

Brand Green

Orchard Rd

The Scarr

Newbarn Farm

Holder's Farm

GL18

Coldharbour Lane

Ford House Road

Ford House Farm

Three Ashes Lane

B4215 LAMBS BARN PITCH

Three Ashes

86

Littleford

Tewkesbury Road

Stream

Lane

A B C D E F

1 grid square represents 500 metres

G H J 43 K L M

Redmarley C of E Primary School

Hyde Park Corner

Redmarley D'Abitot

Poets' Path NE

Red Ditch La

Scar Farm

Durbridge Road

Chapel Lane

Murrell's End

Payford Bridge

River Leadon

Chapel Farm

Innerstone Lane

Innerstone La

Hawcross

Chapel Lane

The Heath

The Down House

A417

Roundbush

Sacksfield Farm

A417

Pauntley Court Drive

Pauntley Court

Everess Farm

66

Sladbrook

Collinpark Wood

Eden's Hill

Gloucester

Carswalls Manor

v Road

Forge Lane

G H J 87 K L M

Upleadon

Upleadon Court

I

2

3

4

5

6

7

8

44

A B C D E F

DS
1 Johnstone Cl

I

Tower House Dr

The Down
House

2

Roundbush

Mill Lane

3

Mill Lane

Hethelpit Cross

Staunton

The Hill

The Moat

Moat Lane

B4208

Pillows
Green

Pillows green Road

Worcestershire County
Gloucestershire County

A417

A417

Ledbury Road Crescent

B4213 STRAIGHT LANE

PO

MALVERN ROAD

Staunton & Corse C of E
Aided School

4

†

Staunton Court
Business Park

Staunton
Court

Cullingham Close

Key Cl

Corse

Chartist Way

Chartist Piece

Sovereign

Cha

GLOUCESTER RD

Corse
Surgery

65

Prince

Hatfield Close

Compton

Crescent

Police Station

School Crescent

5

Sladbrook

Brierley Grange

The stone Rd

Boundary Pl

1

Corse

Snig's
End

6

Pitt's
Mill

7

Stanbrook Farm

Corse House
Farm

Oridge Street

Lawn Farm

Oridge Street

8

Grove
Farm

Oridge Street

Old Field
Top

Crosshands
Farm

WORCESTER ROAD

A417

The Tailors

Sto
Ho

A B C D E F

88

I grid square represents 500 metres

Linkend

Linkend Rd
B4211

A
B
C
46
D
E
F

Eldersfield
Lawn School

Corse
Lawn

I

Hotel

1 Cotswold Vw
B5

Chaceley
Hole

Hillend

Rock Street

C

B4211

2

Rye Cou
Farm

3

Hawker's
Farm

Sandpits

Cumberwood
Farm

River Severn

4

Town
Street

67

Josend
Crescent

5

Tirley

Cabb Lane

B4213

Tirley St

6

B4213

Haw Bridge

Court

7

Great House

Ham Road

The Haw

Apperley
Court

8

B4213

Greyhill
Farm

Walnlode Lane

A
B
C
90
D
E
F

A · B · C · D · E · F

48

I
2
3
4
69
5
6
7
8

Southwick Park

Hotel

Stonehouse Farm

Southw Farm

Hoo Lane

Southend Farm

GLOUCESTER ROAD A38

GLOUCESTER ROAD A38

Highfield Farm

Rudgeway Farm

Tredington

River Swilgate

M5

M5

M5

Phillant Farm

Walton Hill Farm

Cursey Lane

Rudgeway Farm

Cursey Lane

Archers

A38

Copse Green Farm

Hardwicke

A38

Knightsbridge Business Centre

A · B · C · D · E · F

92

...ightsbridge

Colman's Farm

Dukes Way 1

Vine Way

Malmsey Cl

Mowbray Av 2

5

Courtne... Cl

A   **B**   **C**   **D**   **E**   **F**

50

Daston Wood

1

A435

Woolstone La

Woolstone

2

Tirle Brook

Gretton Road

Gretton Road

Cranha La

Malleson Road

Gotherington

3

Gotherington Fields

Shutter La

Aggs La

Ashmead Dr

The Lawns

Manor Lane

Manor Farm

Long Furlong

Cleeve Road

4

71

5

Homelands Farm

Gotherington Lane

Gloucestershire & Warwickshire Railway

Butt's Lane

Bushcomb

6

Dean Farm

A435

Honeysuckle Wy

Evesham Road

Nottingham Rd

Berwick Rd

Wellbrook Road

Foster Cl

Oldacre Drive

Ltl Acorns

Blackberry Gv

Bramble Cha

Selborne Rd

Sandoun Rd

Hardy Road

Millham Road

Barbers Leys

Hayfield Way

Acacia Pk

Wheatsheaf Dr

The Cornfields

Hertford Rd

Sedgley Rd

Station Road

Oxmead

Woodmancote CP School

7

Cutsdean Cl

Jardine Dr

Hunters Rd

Chiltern Av

Stoke Cl

The Withers

GL52

Greyholme Surgery

Church Road

The Surg

Priory Lane

Pine Bank

Celandine Bk

Greenway

Beverley Gdns

Aesops Orch

Stoke Road

Lindley Cha

Meadow Bank

Snowshill Dr

Bishops Cleeve Primary School

Churchfields

School Road

Feldgate Rd

Pecked Lane

Birchfield Road

Withyfield Rd

Ashfield Cl

Longlands Road

The Rowans

Cotswold Vw

Meade-King Gv

Chapel La

8

A435

Kingscote Dr

The Highgrove

Foxwell Dr

Furlong La

La Grange Dr

Cheltenham Road

Hart Cl

Bishops Drive

Orchard

Woodmans Wy

Hemming Wy

Kingswood

Croom

Dale Wk

Courtiers

St Michaels Av

Minetts Avenue

Meads

Tobyfield

Linworth Road

Hyatts Way

Jesson Road

Whitenouse Wy

Keepers Mill

Willow

Bella Vis

Cable Point

New Road

Potters Field Road

Stockwell Lane

Manor House

Hillside Gardens

Woodmancote

Two Hedges Road

Sunnycroft

Cleeve Sch

94

Cemetery

A   **B**   **C**   **D**   **E**   **F**

1 grid square represents 500 metres

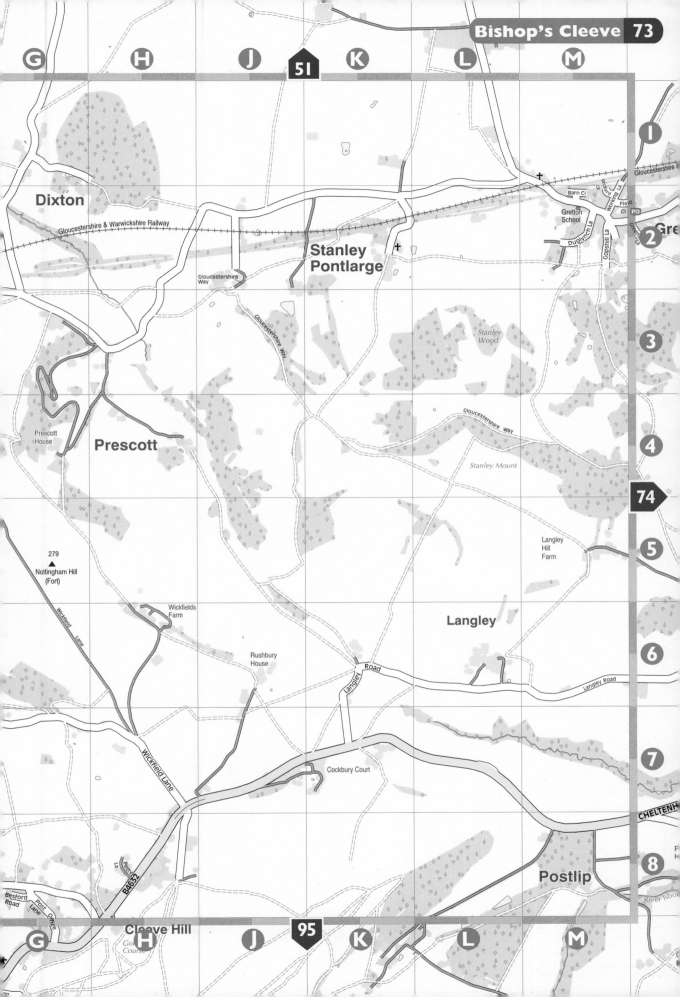

G H J 51 K L M

I

Dixton

Gloucestershire & Warwickshire Railway

Stanley
Pontlarge

Gloucestershire
Way

Gloucestershire Way

Barn Cl

Gretton
School

Duglynch La

Godshill La

Green La

PO

Gre

2

Stanley
Wood

3

Prescott
House

Prescott

Stanley Mount

4

74

Langley
Hill
Farm

5

279
▲
Nottingham Hill
(Fort)

Wickfield Lane

Wickfields
Farm

Langley

6

Rushbury
House

Langley Road

Langley Road

Wickfield Lane

Cockbury Court

7

CHELTENH

Besford
Road

Post Office La

B4632

Perry La

Postlip

8

River Isbo

Cleeve Hill

Golf
Course

Stanway

Didbrook

G H J K L M

53

Millhampost Farm

B4632

Lower Cosco

I

2

Salter's Lane

Hailes

Hailes Abbey (NT)

Hailes Wood

3

Cotswold Way

4

Farmcote

76

Salter's Lane

5

Little Farmcote

Salter's

6

Gloucestershire Way

7

Lynes Barn Farm

8

deley ge

Farmcote Wood Farm

97

G H J K L M

76

A   B   C   Taddington   D   E   F

54

1

Lower
Coscombe

B4077

Stumps
Cross

2

Upper
Coscombe

PO

Cutsdean

3

Jackdaws Cast

B4077

4

PH

Ford

Gloucestershire Way

75

B4077

5

Slade Barn
Farm

Hyde

6

Manor
Farm

Temple
Guiting

The Sherry

Pinnock
Farm

PO

7

Temple Guiting
School

8

A   B   C   D   E   F

98

I grid square represents 500 metres

G H J K L M

55

Scarborough Farm

I

Ford Hill Farm

Gloucestershire Way

Gloucestershire Way

Gloucestershire Way

2

3

Trafalgar Farm

4

78

B4077

5

B4077

6

7

Kinetonhill Farm

8

igh ood

Bemborough Farm

Cotswold F..k

99

G H J K L M

A B C 56 D E F

I
2
3
4
77
5
6
7
8

A B C 100 D E F

Hinchwick Hill Barn

Sezincote Warren

E6
1 Church Vw
2 Close Gdns

The Warren

Hinchwick

Gloucestershire way

Guitinghill Farm

Hinchwick Manor Farm

Condicote

2
1
†

Fox Farm

Condicote Lane

B4077

Kinetonhill Farm

well Wold m

1 grid square represents 500 metres

G   H   J   K   L   M

K3
1 Orchard Ri

K4
1 Old Rectory Gdns

Se **57** ote

Sezincote
House & Gardens

Icehouse Lane

Monarch's Way

1

2

3

Bean Hl

Charlesway

PO

Ganborough   Road

Longborough C of E
Primary School

1

High Street

Longborough

4

80

Banks Fee La

PH

Ganborough

Luckley
Farm

Banks Fee

5

Monarch's Way

Banks Fee
Farm

Donnington 6

A424

Duncombe House

7

ne Farm

8

B4077

101

G   H   J   K   **Upper Swe**   L   M

A424

Ⓐ Ⓑ Ⓒ Ⓓ Ⓔ Ⓕ

58

Coldicote
Farm

Ⓘ

Lower
Rye Farm

Frogmore
Farm

⓶

⓷

River Evenlode

**Little
Barrow**

⓸

Heath
Barn

79

⓹

North Rye
House

Cownham
Farm

D❻nington

Monarch's Way

Monarch's Way

Kennel Lane

Quinmoor
Farm

⓻

Manor
House

Monarch's Way

Foxes
Row

Millbrook Ley

Chapel Street

Broadwell

A429

⓼

Ⓐ Ⓑ Ⓒ Ⓓ Ⓔ Ⓕ

102

Broadwell

G H J **59** K L M

Broc[...] House

I

Middle Brookend Farm

Grove Farm

2

Chasleton Glebe

3

Oxfordshire County
Gloucestershire County

The Lane

4

Chastleton House (NT)

82

Chastleton

5

Horn Farm

Horn Lane

Horn Lane

Evenlode

Church Lane

Green Lane

Peasewell Wood

Macmillan Way

6

Fern Farm

Coomb Wood

7

Hillside Farm

Evenlode Grounds Farm

Sydenham Farm

River Evenlode

Macmillan Way

8

Back Rw

Schooler's Lane

Main Street

PO

Adlestrop

G H **103** J K L M

Upton
Bishop

ton
ews

A B C 62 D E F

I

2

B4221

M50

3

Fording Lane

Shutton

PO

Linton

The
Fording

Fording Lane

Rudhall Brook

4

Tedgewood

F3
1 Dalebrook
2 Springdale
3 Sugar Tump

E3
1 Gorsley Gdns
2 Sundale

Linton
Wood

M50

Gorsley Goffs
C of E
Primary School

Bound
Farm
La

B4221

Ivy House Lane

The
Manse
La

FORTY'S PITCH

PO

Cockatoos
La

Cothar's
Pitch

Chapel
Lane

Quarry La

Lovers
Walk

Junction 3

Ross-on-Wye
Golf Club

Frowens Lane
1 2 2 1

Gorsley
Common

3 Prospect Row Lir

Woodend Lane

Woodend Lane

Woodend
Farms

Linton Hill

The
Line

Lane

Darnell's

Sargent's Lane

Darnell's
Farm

Beavan's
Hill

5

Pinford Lane

ding Lane

6

Cut Throat Lane

Burton
Court

Withymoor
Farm

7

Cut
Throat
Lane

B4224

Eccleswall
Court

Aston
Crews

8

Warren Lane

A B C 106 D Aston
Mills E F

Warren Lane

G   H   J   63   K   L   M

Hay Wood

Peter's

I

Pitch

Haywood

Hawthorne Hill

White House

Hawthorne Hill

2

Whitehouse

Lane

Blue Lane

Lower House

Crooke's Farm

B4221

Sterrys

Road

Gorsley

Blue La Blue La

Kews

Lane

B4221

Conigree Court

3

Old Lane (Simmonds Lane)

Place Hill

Ford Farm

Ford   Lane

B4221

Kilcot

4

Stoney

Lane

Wood   Lane

Kilcot Wood

Common Fields

86

Shotts

Darks Road

Little Gorsley

B4222

Briery Hill

5

Gypsy Lane

Mill   Lane

Bouls

Ravenshill

Acorn Wood

6

Reslaw Wood

National Birds of Prey Centre

B4222

7

Aston Bank

Aston Ingham

The Green

Oaks Lane

Woodgate

8

Chapel Pitch

Southall Ter

Clifford's Mesne

G   New House Farm   H   J   107   K   L   M

64
108
85

C2
1 Friar's Wk

B4
1 Connemara Cl

B3
1 Gardeners Wy

B2
1 Greenaways

A3
1 Bradfords Ct

A   B   C   D   E   F

Littleford

Ford Hou

Ford House

I

Oxenhall

Three
Ashes

Stream
Lane

2

Picklenash

ROSS ROAD

Furnace Lane

Ell Brook

Horsefair

Lane

Old Station
Rd

BRIDGE ST

B4215 LAMBS BARN PITCH

Three

Cottage Pitch

Hopyard Lane

Tewkesbury Road

Hill Top Lane

Tewkesbury Road

Cleeve Mill

B4215

Cleeve Mill Lane

Croft Rd

B4215

Lake Side

Court Rd

NEWENT

Glebe Infant School

Glebe Cl

Glebe Ct

Glebe
Way

HIGH ST

Holts Road

Holts Health Centre

Police Stn

Court La

Church street

Church La

Shambles Museum

The B

Church Wy

Gloucester Street

Broad St

PO

Cowdy Gallery

West View

Vauxhall

Bradfords

The Tythings

Akermans Orch

Watery Lane

John Stone Road

Brookside

Winthing

Craddock Rd

Cemetery

Newent Town Council

Newent Sports Centre

Newent Community School

Knights Way

Knight Crs

Tythings

Bury Bar

Foley Rd

Ach The

Russell

Perry Cl

Weaverst Rd

Onslow

Foley

Road

Cooper's

Onslow Rd

3

Nelfields

Coxmore Fa

Watery Lane

Common Fields

CULVER STREET

B4216

Southend

Southend Lane

Southend Farm

4

5

Boulsdon

The Moat

6

Caerwents

7

Anthony's Cross

Anthony's Cross

Normans

The Green

Woodgate

Cugley

B4216

8

A   B   C   D   E   F

C3
1 America Gdns
2 Peacock Cl
3 Peacock Gdns
4 St Bartholomews

C4
1 Cherry Bank

D3
1 Ayland Cl
2 Blenheim Dr
3 Cleeve Rl
4 The Crease
5 Pippin Cl

D2
1 Croft Cl

Ploddy House

1 grid square represents 500 metres

G   H   J   65   K   L   M

Garswalls Manor

Upleadon Court

Eden's Hill

Gloucester Road

Upleadon

Forge Lane

Middletown

1

2

River Leadon

3

Buttersend

Hook's Lane

Okle Green

Okle Clifford

Ell Brook

Football Club

4

Malswick

B4215

Hay Farm

88

Ell Brook

Rymes Place Farm

B4215

5

Red Hill Farm

Highlea Court

The Alderleys

6

Moat Farm

B4215

7

Park

Drews

...nt's Green

Taynton Pound Farm

High...

8

Taynton Court Farm

New Hall

B4215

A   B   C   D   E   F

Old Field Top

66

The Tailors

Crosshands Farm

Stone End House

1

Corse Court Farm

2

Prestberries Farm

Hill House Farm

3

Buttersend

Blackwells End Green

Corsend Farm

Corsend Road

4

Hartpury

87

Limbury

Buttersend Lane

Danford Lane

5

Highleadon Court

6

Tweenhills Farm

7

Park Road

Home Farm

Drews Farm

Highleadon

River Leadon

Moor End

8

B4215   A   B   C   D   E   F

110

ury College

Laughton's Farm

A417

WO

Dent's

1 grid square represents 500 metres

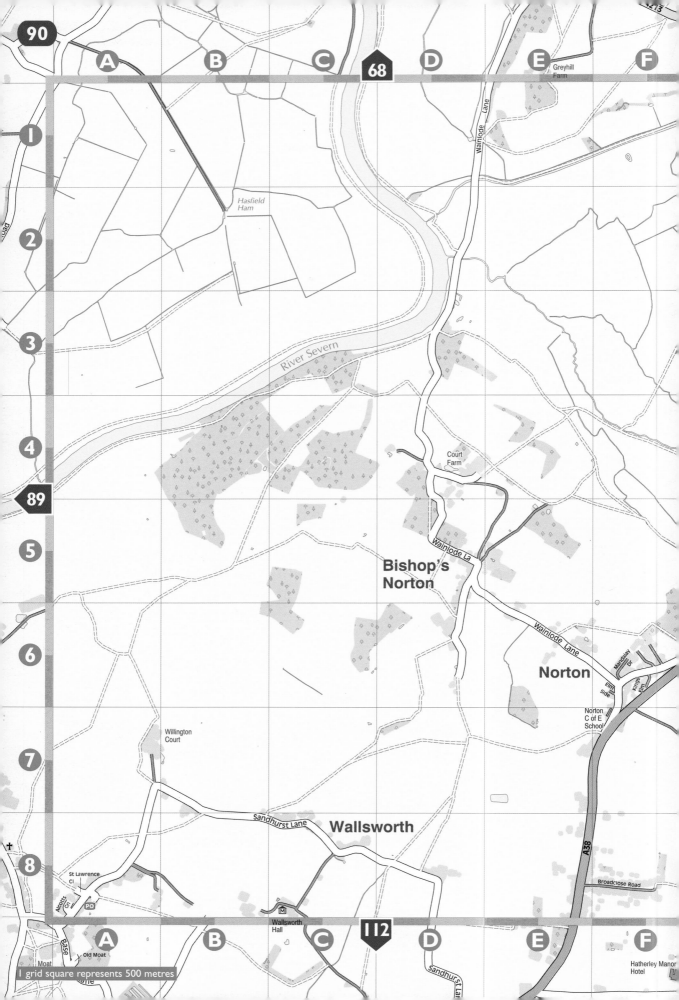

G   H   J   **69**   K   L   M   A3

The Leigh

igh End

Beckett's Farm

Pancake Lane

Blacksmith La

A38

Church   Lane

Leigh House

Leigh Brook

A38

River Chelt

Barrow

92

Norton Court Farm

A38

Prior's Norton

e   of   Gloucester

Brock Farm

The Cherry Orch

I

2

3

4

5

6

7

8

own Hatherley

Lane

ood

G H J **73** K L M

1
2
3
4
96
5
6
7
8

Cleve Hill

Golf Course

The Ring

Cleeve Cloud

Cleeve Common

Cotswold Way

erswood

Wontley Farm

Upper Hill Farm

Lower Hill Farm

Cotswold Way

West Down

Drypool Farm

Piccadilly Farm

Cotswold Way

G H J **117** K L M

The Hewletts

B4632

Ostlip

River Isbourne

Ruckham

96

A   B   C   74   D   E   F

I   Postlip House
     Corndean Farm

2   Corndean Hall
     Corndean Lane
     Cotswold Way
     Wadfield Farm
     Cotswold Way

3   Waterha

4   Cotswold Way   Belas Knap
     Humblebee

95

5   ntley Farm
     Goldwell Farm
     Holt Farm

6   West Down   West Wood   Charlton Abbots   †

7

8   Whitehall Farm   118   Cotehay
     A   B   C   D   E   F
     Brockhampton Park
     Puckham

River Isb
Beesmoo Brook

I grid square represents 500 metres

G H J **75** K L M

1

2

3

4

98

5

6

7

8

Farmcote Wood Farm

Parks Farm

Wardens' Way

Deadmanbury Gate

Camoden La

Wardens' Way

Guiting Wood

Spoonley Farm

Roel Hill Farm

Camoden Lane

Roel Gate

Windrush Way

Wine

Whitehill Farm

Hawling †

G H J **119** K L † M

G H J **77** K L M

Bemborough Farm

Cotswold Farm Park

Farm

1

2

3

4

100

5

Guiting Stud

Summerhill

6

Wardens' Way

Grange Hill Farm

Wardens' Way

7

Naunton

Village Av

PO

PH

Wardens' Way

Wardens' Way

Dale St

Brockhill Barm

8

B4068

Naunton Downs Golf Club

G H J **121** K L B4068 Hari[...]dge M

Lower

G H J K L M

I

2

3

4

102

5

6

7

8

79

Upper Swell

Gloucestershire Wy

B4077 TEWKESBURY ROAD

Abbotswood

A424 EVESHAM ROAD

Bowl Farm

B4068

Buildings

St Mary's Close

Whittlestone Hollow

Lower Swell

Swell Primary School

Rectory Cl

Mill Lane

STOW-ON-THE-WOLD

Talbot Sq

High St

Hotel

Hotel

Church Street Gallery

Walton Ho Gallery

PO

SHEEP

Back

Well

Cemetery

Nether Swell Manor

Monarch's Way

A429

Fir Farm

Monarch's Way

Macmillan Way

Hyde Mill

Hotel

Kirkham Farm

Monarch's Way

River Dikler

Meadow Farm

A429

A424

Copsehill Road

Macmillan Way

Mill La

The Old Mill Museum

Stow Bridge

Lower Slaughter

Copse Hill

Heath Hill

J3 1 Whittlestone Cl

J4 1 Stonehouse Ct

B4077

B3
1 Mount Pleasant
Cl

A4
1 Fisher Cl

A3
1 Church St
2 Digbeth St
3 Glebe Cl
4 Market Sq

A2
1 Fosse Folly
2 Fosse La

A B C 80 D E F

I

2

EVESHAM ROAD

Broadwell
Hill

Monarch's Way

Stow
Well

High St
Well
Doctors Surgery
Talbot
Sq
Hotel
Hotel
White Hart
La
Camp Gdns
Shepherds Wy
Chapel St
Primary
School
Griffin Cl
Kg
St Edwards
Drive
Sterling
Cl
Georges
Field

3
Hotel
Church Street Gallery
Walton Ho Gallery
PO M M John Blockley Gal
SHEEP ST
Back Walls
Union St
Hti
ODDINGTON RD
A436
A436

Cemetery
The Park
Chamberayne
Cl
Bartletts
Park
Maugersbury Pk
Lower Pk
A436
B4450
Martin's
Hill

4

A429

101

Chapel
Street
Maugersbury
Manor
Macmillan Way
Cotswold Crest
Farm

5

6

Hotel

Oxleaze
Farm

Ash
Farm

A424

7

Smenham
Farm

8

Wyckhill
Farm

A B C 124 D E F

A424

1 grid square represents 500 metres

G3
1 Embrook

Syder Farm

G

H

J

81

K

Schooler's Lane
Back Rw
PO

L

M

A436

A436

Adlestrop

I

Macmillan Way

Adlestrop Park

2

Broadwell Road

Home C

Sawpits La

PH

PO

Church Place

Lower Oddington

Church Road

Daylesford

3

New Farm

Back Lane

Brins Lane

Upper Oddington

River Evenlode

4

104

5

Bledington Heath

6

Bledington Grounds

B4450

7

Jay Farm

Mickland's Hill

8

B4450

River Evenlode

G

H

Pebbly Hill Farm

J

125

K

STOW ROAD

L

Chapel Street

M

PH

Chapel St

Church

MAIN STREET

Old Forge Close

New Road

Lower Farm

104

A   B   C   82 Cornwell   D   E   F

Glebe Farm

Cornwell Manor

1

Daylesford Hill Farm

Daylesford House

2

The Dell

Gloucestershire County

Oxfordshire County

Kingham Hill School

Kingham Hill Farm

3

w Farm

Slade Farm

Kingham Hill School

103

Sarsden Halt

4

5

Kingham County Primary School

Churchill Road

6

The Moat

West Street

The Green

Manor Farm Close

Chapel Lane

West End

Cozens Lane

The Gra

Church St

PO

Kingham

Fowler's Road

7

Orchard Way

✝

Coxmoor Cl

Meadow Way

New Road

Station Road

Field Road

Hotel

Station Road

8

River Evenlode

B4450

A   B   C   D   E   F

Kingham Station

Rynehill Farm

ROAD

1 grid square represents 500 metres

A44

Primsdown
Industrial
Estate

Cemetery

WORCESTER ROAD

WORCESTER ROAD   NEW STREET

Discala La

83

Kennel Lane

Cox Lane

Toy Lane

Common Lane

Lewis Road

Station Road

Webb Crescent

Dunstan Avenue

3

Withers Wy

Bliss

The Leys

Cross Leys

WEST END

Leys Approach

Alexandra
Square

WEST

St M
Prim

Lords Piece

Tilsley Road

Road

CHURCHHILL ROAD

Halley Avenue

1

2

3

I

Meads
Farm

Cornish Road

Halley Road

South Rd

Walter L

2

Chipping Norton
Football Club

B4450

3

Churchill
Grounds Farm

Boulter's Barn

4

Besbury   Lane

B4450

5

Sarsgrove
Farm

Sarsgrove
Wood

6

Hill

Road

Churchill

Langston Cl

ers La

B4450

TON ROAD

Sarsden
Glebe Farm

Iron
Buildings

A361

7

Sars Brook

8

Sarsden

Sarsden
House

CREWS

D3
1 Rudhall Vw

C3
1 Millbrook Gdns
2 Saunders Cl

B4
1 The Acorns
2 Norden Dr

B3
1 The Brambles

84

1

Aston
Mills

Crews Hill

2

A40(T)

B4224

Warren Lane

Green Lane

Adam's
Cottage

3

Lea C of E
County
Primary School

Lea

A40(T)

PO

B4222

Coach
Rd

Knightshill

High
Hope

B4222

A40(T)

Lea Line

4

Hoovers Lane

Watery Lane

Orchard

B4224

County of Herefordshire
Gloucestershire County

5

East
Dean

A40(T)

Boxbus

Lyndors
Farm

6

Bradley
Court

7

B4224

Bilbut
Farm

8

ROSS ROAD

Ash Grove

The Crescent

Hollywell

CARISBROOK RD

Old Dean Rd

Deansway

Close

Court Farm Lane

TOWNSEND ST

BRAD

130

A   B   C   D   E   F

Poly
Stn

Brook St

Churchill Way

PO

Mitcheldean
Surgery

I grid square represents 500 metres

High

B4215

G H J K L M

87

133

Tibberton

Bulley

Lower Farm

Bovone

Tibberton Primary School

Old Ct Dr

Orchard

Phelps Way

Rise

Muzzle Patch

Bovone Lane

Court Farm

Court Farm

Meredith

The Grove

Birdsend

Whitehall Lane

Whitehall Farm

110

Morse's Farm

Rundlesshill

Collier's Elm

Woodgreen

Bulley Lane

Churcham House

Lake Lane

Bulley Lane

Bulley Lane

Spring Dale

A40(T)

Churcham School

A40(T)

Farm

Court

I
2
3
4
5
6
7
8

G5
1 Poppy Fld
2 Woodleigh Fld

G6
1 Clayburn Cl
2 Gordon Cl
3 Peters Fld
4 Popes Meade
5 Stoney Fld

L8
1 Alney Ter
2 Westend Ter

Sandhurst

G

H

J

89

K

L

M

Spring Hill

Overton

Maisemore
Park

River Severn

Moat
Farm

Old Moat

I

Gardiner's
Farm

2

Abbot's
Lodge

3

Steadings
Business Centre
Maisemore Court

Maisemore

Old Road

Church Road

The Rudge

Church
Rise

Abloads
Court

4

Blacksmiths Lane

The Ridings

Stanleigh
Ter

Bridge Farm

112

Persh Lane

Persh Farm

West Channel

East Channel

5

Base Lane

Maisemore
Ham

A417

Sandhurst Lane

Walham

A4

6

Alney
Island

A40(T)

4

Lawrence
North

Cattle Market
Ind Est

Gloucester
City Council

7

Over

A40(T)

Telford's
Bridge

Mean
Ham

Severn Wy

Over Causeway

OVER CAUSEWAY

Gloucestershire Wy

Barrett
Industrial Est

Spartans
Rugby Club

Superstore

St Oswald's

Lawrence Way

ST OSW

Road

Riverside
Sports &
Leisure Club

8

Port
Ham

Royal Oak Wy

Western Parade

A417

ROYAL OAK RD

ROYAL OAK ROAD

The College
Yard Surg

St Oswald's
Priory

Co Council

Parliamen
House
Cath

Lower
Parting

135

River Severn

THE QUAY

Gloucester
Folk Mus

County Library
County Co

Shire Hall

College St

G

H

J

K

L

M

G H J **95** K L M

I

2

3

4 W

118

5

6

7

8

The Hewletts

Piccadilly Farm

Woodlands Farm

Puckham Woods

Aggs Hill

Northfield Farm

Puckham Farm

Whalley Farm

Ham Hill

Ham Road

Cotswold Way

Woodlands

Colgate Farm

Dowdeswell Wood

A40

River Chelt

The Barlands

LONDON ROAD

Cotswold Way

Dowdeswell Reservoir

A40

Lower Dowdeswell

Rossley Manor

Upper Dowdeswell

Lineover Wood

Cotswold Way

Sandy Park

PH

C8
1 Crossfields

C7
1 Huntsmans Meet

A   B   C   96   D   E   F

1

Whitehall
Farm

Puckham
Woods

odlands
rm

Cotehay

Brockhampton
Park

Park Lane

PO

Broc

2

Nash
Barn

3

Church Lane

Sevenhamp

4

Whittington

5

6

Sandywell
Park

Syreford

7

Station

PO

Hunter's
Way

A40

Waterside
Close

Road

Ossage

A436

A436

Andoversford

8

Sports
Club

Primary
School

PH

Templefields

Andoversford
Industrial Estate

Andoversford
Link

GLOUCESTER ROAD

A436

Andoversford
Industrial Estate

A   B   C   **142**   D   E   F

Shipton
Solers

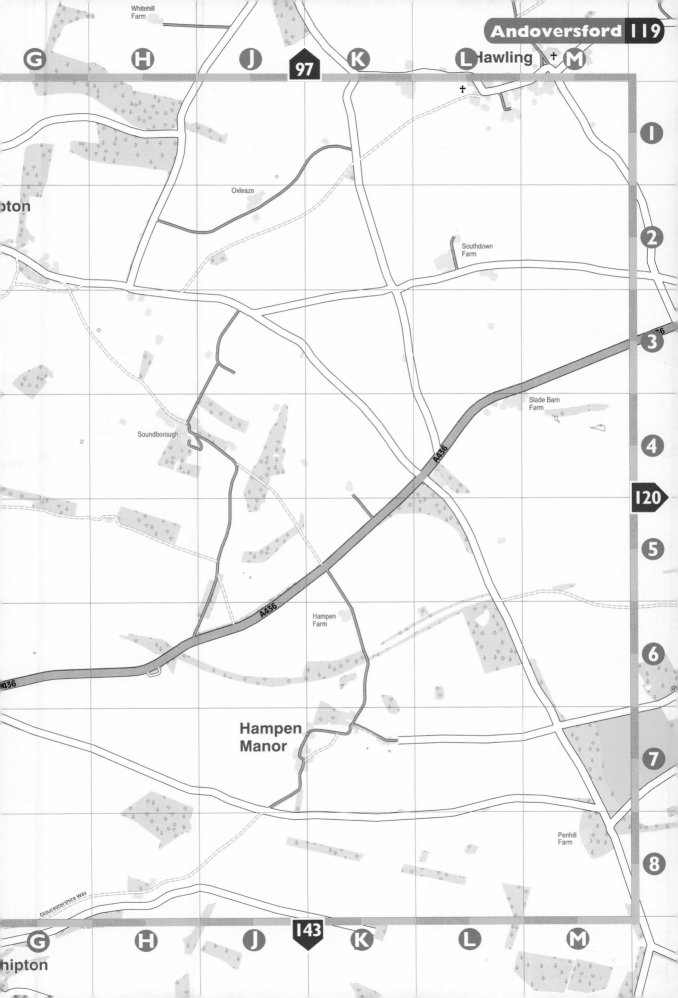

G H J **97** K L Hawling M

I

Whitehill
Farm

Oxleaze

2

Southdown
Farm

3

Slade Barn
Farm

A436

4

Soundborough

120

5

A436

6

A436

Hampen
Farm

Hampen
Manor

7

Penhill
Farm

8

Gloucestershire Way

hipton

G   H   J   99   K   L   M

B4068

B4068   Harford Bridge

1

Lower
Harford Farm

Windrush Way

2

Windrush

Windrush Way

Roundhill Farm

3

Aylworth

Windrush Way

Windrush Way

Hill Farm

Upper
Harford

4   A436

A436

122

Folly
Farm

5

6

Notgrove

PO

Gloucestershire   Way

Cold Aston

Gloucestershire   Way

Cold Aston C of E
Primary School

7

PH

Chapel La

Aston

Lane

Macmillan   Way

Bangup
Barn

Bangup

Grove
Farm

8

G   H   J   145   K   L   M

Pountwell

Aston
Grove

Shewhill

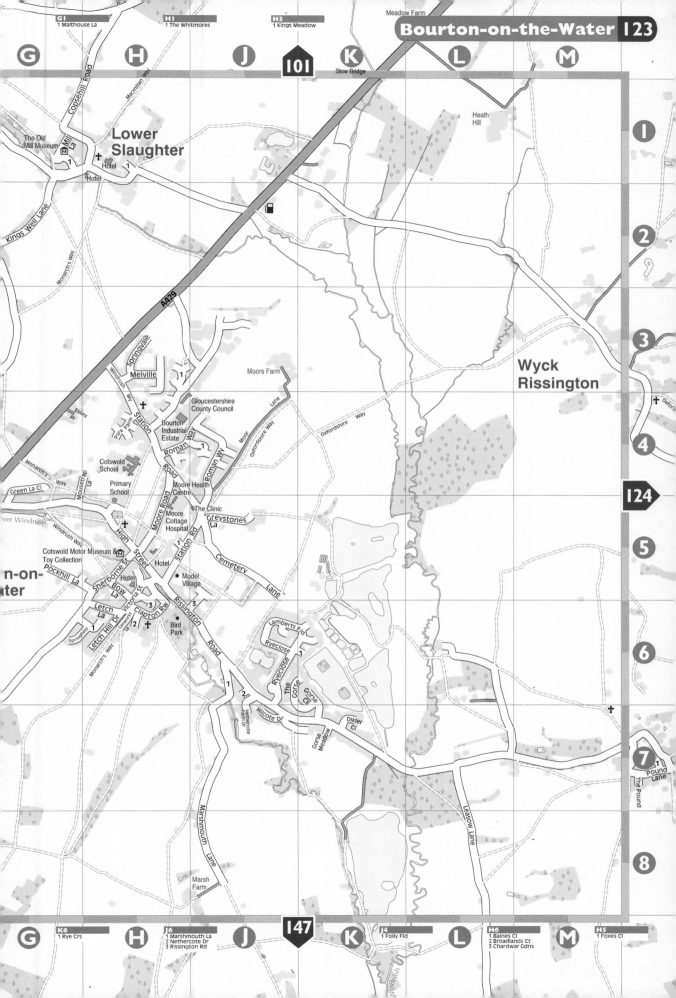

Meadow Farm

Stow Bridge

The Old
Mill Museum
Lower
Slaughter
Hotel
Hotel

Heath
Hill

Kings Well Lane

Monarch's Way

Macmillan Way

Copsehill Road

Mill La

I

2

Wyck
Rissington

A429

3

Oxford

4

Springvale
Melville
Moors Farm

124

Gloucestershire
County Council
Bourton
Industrial
Estate

Oxfordshire Way

Oxfordshire Way

Windrush Wy

Essex Pl

Park Farm

Station

Roman Way

Roman Wy

Moor Lane

5

Cotswold
School
Primary
School
Moore Health
Centre
The Clinic
Greystones
Moore
Cottage
Hospital

Moore Road

Station Rd

Greystones La

Monarch's Way

Green La Cl

Mousetrap La

River Windrush
Windrush Way
Cotswold Motor Museum &
Toy Collection

High Street

Hotel
Hotel
Model
Village

Cemetery Lane

Pockhill La

n-on-
ater

Sherborne
Bow La

Letch La
Letch Hill Dr

Victoria Ct

Clapton Rw

Rissington

Bird
Park

Springfield

Monarch's Way

5

Lamberts Fld
Ryeclose
Ryeclose

The Gorse
Gorse Cl

6

Road

Hilcote Dr

Nethercote Farm Dr

Gorse Meadow

Dikler Cl

7
Pound
Lane
The Pound

Marshmouth Lane

Leasow Lane

8

Marsh
Farm

K6
1 Rye Crs

J6
1 Marshmouth La
2 Nethercote Dr
3 Rissington Rd

J4
1 Folly Fld

H6
1 Baines Cl
2 Broadlands Ct
3 Chardwar Gdns

H5
1 Foxes Cl

G   H   J   147   K   L   M

C7
1 Blenheim Cl
2 Harris Gdns
3 Snipe Rd

A7
1 Manor Farm

A B C **102** D E F

1

Wye Farm

Hill Farm

Icomb †

2

Hotel

3

† Oxfordshire Way

A424

Gawcombe

Oxfordshire Way

4

123

Wyck Beacon

Oxfordshire Way

A424

5

6

Bobble Barn

Siskin Road
Sopwith Rd
Wright Cl
Wright Road
Folland Dr
Bristol Road
Vickers Rd
Hamilton Rd
Avro Road

Upper Rissington

Hawker Sq
Dodd Drive
Smith Barry Crescent

7

Sandy Lane

Farman Cl
Bleriot Road
Grebe Square
3
Hawker Sq
Smith Barry Crs
Smith Barry Rd
†

The Pound
1 Pound Lane
†

Little Rissington

2
1
Wellington Rd
Gerrard Rd
Longmore Rd
Fulton Road
Longmore Av
Kirby Road
Road
A P Ellis Rd
Lichterdale
Road

8

Lithgow Road
Randall

Little Rissington Airfield

A B C **148** D E F

G H J 103 K B4450 L M

I

Mickland's Hill

Pebbly Hill Farm

STOW ROAD

CHAPEL ST
PO
PH
MAIN STREET
Chapel Street
Church Street
Old Forge Close
First Cl
New Road
OLD BURFORD ROAD
Bledington County Primary School

Lower Farm

Oxfordshire Way

2

Bledington

B4450

Westcote Brook

Gloucestershire County
Oxfordshire County

3

Foscot

4

Oxfordshire Way

Nature Reserve

5

Church Westcote

Bould

6

ther stcote

A424

Church St

Herbert's Heath

7

Idbury

Spring Lane

Gloucestershire County
Oxfordshire County

8

G H A424 J 149 K Fifield L M

High St
Church Street

ymouth Road

Llangrove
C of E
Primary
Green

A Llan**A**ove   **B**   **C**   **D**   **E** Marstow   **F**

E6 1 Horse Pool La

E5 1 Leaping Stocks Rd

D4 1 Norton Cl

A4137

1

Hill Farm

Little Trewen Lane

Trewen

2

The Tump Farm

A40(T)

Greenway Farm

Ridgeway Crescent

3

Whitchurch

Whitchurch Valley School

Grange Park

PO

B4164

4

Lewstone

A40(T)

A40(T)

Pulrodd Pool Lane

Sawpitts Lane

Ashes Lane

Sandyway Lane

5

Crocker's Ash

Great Doward

Wye

Meeks Well Lane

Brook Road

B4164

6

Little Doward

Leaping Stocks Rd

May Bush Lane

View Lane

Symonds Yat

Mine Pitts Lane

A40(T)

7

Wyastone Leys

Wye Valley Walk

Seven Sisters Rocks

8

Far Hearkening Rock

Lord's Wood

Wye Valley Walk

Hadnock Road

A   **B**   **C**   150   **D**   **E**   **F**

1 grid square represents 500 metres

Hadnock Court

The Biblins

K8
1 Redhouse La

G   H   J   K   L   M

PO
Castle
Lane
B4229

Goodrich
Cross

B4234

Kne Bridge

Old Forge

A40(T)

B4229

River Wye
Wye Valle

1

2
Thomas
Wood

Rocklands
Farm

3

Mainoaks

Baynhams

Wye Valley Walk

Upper Stowfield
Road

4

Huntsham
Court

The Green

County of Herefordshire

Gloucestershire County

128

5

Wye valley Walk

Probertsbarn

6

Wye Valley Walk

Common Grove

Symond's Yat
Rock

PH

English Bicknor
C of E
Primary School

7

Hotel

Coldwell
Rocks

Bicknor
Court

Redinhorne

orchard
Ct

**English
Bicknor**

8

Redhouse Lane

Holly
Barn

Murrells
Road

Smithy
Close

Eastbach
Court

Ancient Road

G   H   J   **151**   K   L   M

Dryslade
Farm

A B C D E F

1

2

3

◄ **127**

4

5

6

7

8

Bishop's
Wood

Home
Farm

Drybrook
House

River Wye
Wye Valley Walk
PO
B4234

Thomas
Wood

Great Marstow
Farm

Cash
Hill

Cindern

High

Townsend

Rua
Prim

+Welsh
Bicknor

Courtfield

Upper Stowfield
Road

Wye Valley Walk

B4234

Wye Valley Walk

B4234

Vention

Lane

Smithers
Cross

Coppice Road

**Joy's
Green**

Eddys

Lane

Probertsbarn   Lane

Forge   Hill

Rocks Road

1 2

Orchard Rd

Joys Green
CP School

School Road

PO

Readings

**The
Pludds**

Greenfield Road

Highbeech Road

High

Street

Ash Dene
Road

Royal Oak Road

**Lower
Lydbrook**

B4234

Forge

Hill

Edwards Close

Joys
Green
Road

Horslea

**Upper
Lydbrook**

B4234

PO

Uphill Rd

Lydbrook
Health Cen

Church Rd

Church Hill

Forest Rise

New Road

School La

Holbrook

Lydbrook
CP School

B4234

8 Eastbach
Court

A B C D E F

Worrall

G
1 Belle Vue Rd
2 Boxtree Cl

H3
1 Crooked End Pl

H5
1 Roebuck Mdw

Cowles House

G   H   J   K   L   M

County of Herefordshire

Hom Grove Farm

Puddlebrook

Hawthorns Road

Hillside Road

County of Herefordshire
Gloucestershire County

Vain Farm

Woodland Road

Mannings Rd

Hazel Road   West Av   Morgan Close
North Av   Street
High   Drybrook Rugby Football Club

St. Margaret's Road

Varnister Road
Park Vw   Varnister
St John's Rd   Highfield Road
Morse Lane   Morse Lane   Whitehill Lane   PO   Street

Crooked End

Ruardean
Turner's Tump   Morse Road   Well Lane   Swish Lane   Quabbs Lane   Drybrook Surgery   Drybrook Primary School   Drybrook

Meend Lane   Spout Lane   Spout Lane   Morse Road   130   Dean's Walk   Woodend Rd

Ruardean Hill   The Hollow   Drybrook Road   Mount Cl   Trinity   Harrow H

Ruardean Woodside   Bakers Piece Road   Highview   Millers Gn   Road   Greenbank Cl   Larksfield   Sycamore Road   Eastwood Road

Lane   The Patches   Farm Road   PO   Morgans   Ashfield Rd   Bridge Road   Road

Wesley Rd   Duttons La   Baptist Way

Forest Road   Denehurst Road   A4136

Brierley Road   Woodside CP School   A4136   Nailbridge

The Branch   A4151

STEAM   Steam Mills School   Steam Mills Road

MILLS   Steam Mills

Brierley   Brierley Banks   A4136   Gloucestershire Way   ROAD   Newtown Road   Broadmoor Park   A4151

HIGH STREET   A4136   Gloucestershire Way   Pavilion Business Park   roa

BROADMOOR ROAD   Corinium Business Park   Whimsey Rd

Serridge Green   Birch   Whimsey   Whimsey Industrial Estate

FOREST   Estate

M5   M3
1 Eastwood Rd   1 Sunnymead Cl
2 Oakland Rd

G   H   J   153   K   L   M

130

A   B   C   **106**   D   E   F

I

2

GL17

3

Mitcheldean

Stenders Business Park

Stenders Business Cen

The Stenders

New Street

CROSS ROAD

The Crescent

CARISBRO
RD

Hollywell Rd

Old Dean Rd

Deans

BRADLEY

Brook St

TOWNSEND

Police Stn

Court Farm
Lane

Churchill Way

St Michael's Close

PO

High St

Mitcheldean Surgery

Eastern Avenue

Parks Road

GLOUCESTER RD

A4136

BARTON HILL

Ladygrove Business Park

Brl
Hill

Orchard
Cl

Stenders Rd

Primary School

May Meadow

Colchester Cl

Winters

Bayhnham Rd

Wayley
Close

NEW ROAD

Silver Street

Anns
Wk

Meadow
Close

Folly Farm

Dene Magna Community School

RFC
Football Club

Mannings Rd

Merrion
Close

Street

1 Oakhill Rd
C1

4

129

5

Walk

Road

Road

Harksfield
W

Eastwood Road

Harrow Hill

2

S W

A4136

A4136

Plump Hill

Dockins Hill Way

Way

Glencoe Lane

Jubilee Road

A4136

Gloucestershire Way

Gloucestershire Way

Abenhall

Plump Hill County Primary School

6

Nailbridge

7

n Mills

Steam Mills Road

MILL'S ROAD

The Rookery

Jubilee Road

Shapridg

8

ADMOOR

Newtown

A4151

Broadmoor Park

Pavilion Business Park

Whimsey Rd

Broadmoor

rinium usiness rk

Whimsey Industrial Estate

A41

Boey's Pike

Green Bottom

154

A   B   C   D   E   F

1 grid square represents 500 metres

Heywood Sports Centre

Lane

Collafield

G H J 107 K L M

I

Chessgro
Chessgrove Lane
HI 1 The Bramleys
2 Latchen Orch
3 Nupend Gdns

Gloucestershire Way
Nupend Lane
The Nappi
Spring
The Wend The Willows
PO
Station Lane
Hope Est
Hobbs Lane

Longhope

Latchen
Barthams
3
2
The Temple
Old Monmouth Rd
Mill Lane
Velthouse Lane
Old Hill
A4136
Royal Spring
Hopes Hill Primary School
Chapel Lane
A4136
Chapel Lane
Hinders Lane
Blaisdon Lane

Little London

A4136

2

Nottwood Hill

Stanley House

3

Hope Wood

Longhope Brook

Blaisdon Wood

Velthouse

✝

4

132

Gaulet

Blaisdon

✝

5

Flaxley Woods

6

Monk Hill Farm

7

Boseley Court

nbury d

Flaxley

✝

8

Grove Farm

G H J 155 K L M

Broughtons

Dene's

G   H   J   **109**   K   L   M

I

Birdwood   A40(T)   Churcham School   A40(T)   Church Lane   **Churcha**

2

Hill Farm   Church La   Court

Sainthill   **Oakle Street**   3

Old Ley Court

Ley Brook   4

Gloucestershire Way   A4

134

LC   Ley Road   Duni Farm   River Severn   Severn Way   5

Ley Court   Hooks Farm   Gloucestershire Wy   A48(T)   Severn Way

6   Lake Street

Ley Road   Severn Way

A48(T)

Lower Ley   Ley Road   7   Lake Street

The Flat

PO   A48(T)   Severn Way   **Farleys End**   8

more Common   A48(T)

G   H   J   **157**   K   Bridgemacote   Severn Way   L   M

Walmore Hill Primary School   Broadway Lane

G   **H**   **J**   **K**   **L**   **M**

K5
1 Waters Reach

L2
1 Hemmingsdale Rd

L7
1 Stratford Cl

M1
Street names for this grid square are listed at the back of the index

1

I

2

GLOUCE

3

St Paul's

4

136

5

Linden

6

Podsmead

7

8

Hempsted

Rea

Lower Rea

Newark

Vale of Gloucester

River Severn

Severn Way

Lower Tuffley

G   **H**   **J**   **K**   **L**   **M**

M8
1 Blakeney Cl
2 Foley Cl

M6
1 Thornhill Cl

159

M4
1 Philip St
2 Theresa St

M3
1 The Chestnuts
2 St Lukes St
3 Somerset Pl

M2
1 Church St
2 High Orchard St
3 Ladybellegate St
4 Merchants' Rd

M5
1 Talbot Ms

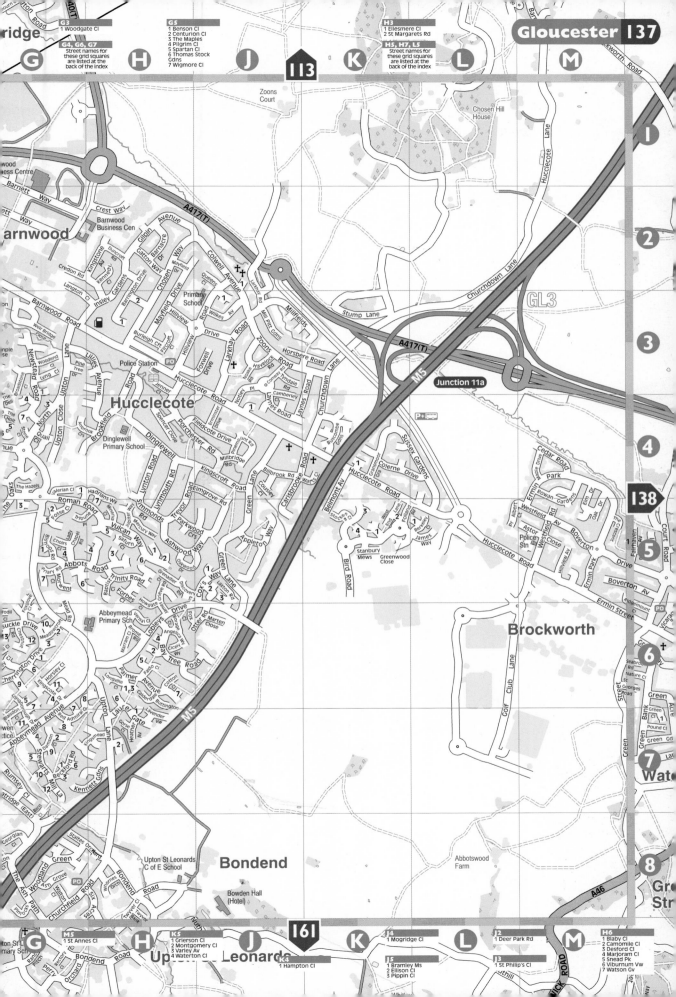

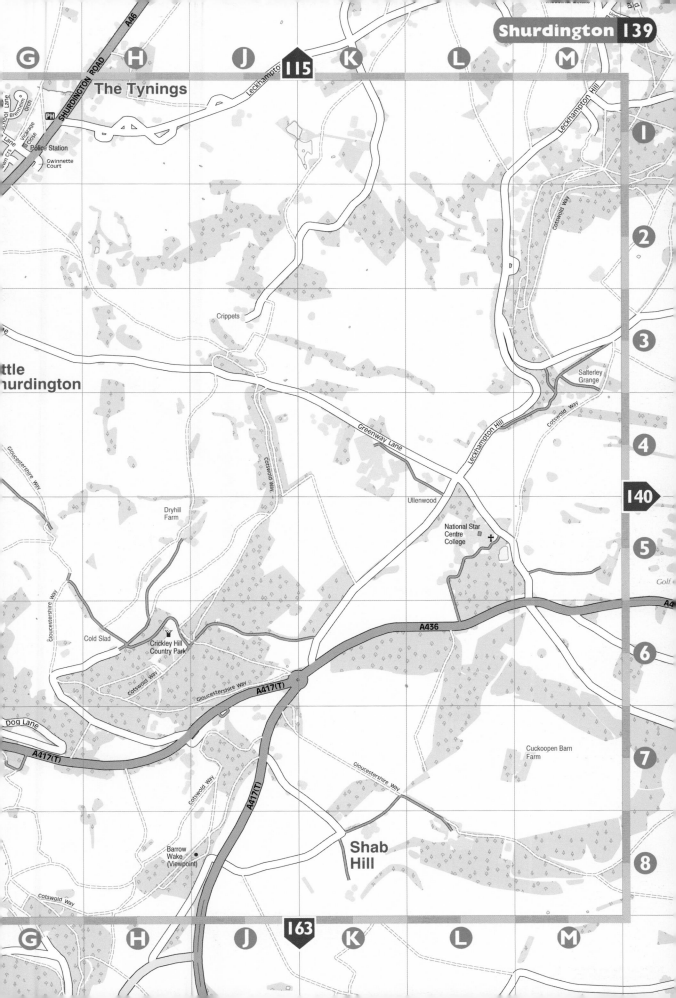

G   H   J   115   K   L   M

The Tynings

I

2

3

Crippets

Salterley
Grange

ttle
hurdington

Greenway Lane

4

Gloucestershire Way

Dryhill
Farm

Ullenwood

140

National Star
Centre
College

5

Golf

A4

Cold Slad

Crickley Hill
Country Park

A436

6

Gloucestershire Way

Cotswold Way

A417(T)

Dog Lane

A417(T)

7

Cuckoopen Barn
Farm

Gloucestershire Way

Cotswold Way

A417(T)

Barrow
Wake
(Viewpoint)

Shab
Hill

8

Cotswold Way

A   B   C   D   E   F

Manor

Golf Course

Cotswold Way

Charlton Kings Common

Cotswold Way

Daisybank Road

Sandy Lane

CIRENCESTER ROAD

Cotsbill Road

mbe Lane

Vineyards Farm

1

2

Hartley Farm

3

Salterley Grange

A436

A435

Chatcombe Wood

Cotswold Way

4

Hartley Bottom

Seven Springs

Way

5

Golf Course

A436

A436

Cotswold Way

New Farm

A435

6

Dowman's Farm

Coberley School

PO

7

Coberley

Close Farm

+

Gloucestershire Way

Gloucestershire Way

8

Coldwell Bottom

A   B   C   D   E   F

Cowley

Gt D B

A435

+

G H J **117** K L M

I

Kilkenny

PH

A436

A436

Pegglesworth

St Paul's
Epistle

2

Gloucestershire Way

3

Foxcote Hill
Farm

Ratshill
Bank

4

142

Pinchley
Wood

Gloucestershire Way

5

Needlehole

Shornhill
Farm

6

Hilcot Wood

stershire Way

Hilcot

pper
oberley

A436

7

Hilcot Brook

Mercombe
Wood

8

Pinswell
Plantation

Lyde
Bank

A   B   GLOUCESTER ROAD   C   D   E   F

Templefields
Club

Andoverford Link

Industrial Estate

118

Andover
Industrial Estate

A40

1   PH

Shipton
Solers

School Lane

Sh
Ol

†   †   †

1

Foxcote

A436

PH

A40 (T)

Kilham Lane

2

Cleevely
Wood

3

Northfield
Farm

4

Thorndale

141

5

6

Upcote
Farm

Harnham Lane

7

Withington
C of E School

†

Bras
Gdn

Withington
Primary School

The Farthings

Withington

High Street

PH

Kings Head La

8

A   B   C   166   D   E   F

Woodbridge Lane

Staple

G H J 119 K L M

I

2

3

Hill
Barn

A40(T)

Springhill

Manor
Farm

144

5

Compton
Abdale

†

Compton
Grove

Ravenswell
Farm

6

7

8

Cassey Compton

Gloucestershire way

pton

River
Coln

Star
Wood

G H J **121** K L M

I
2
3
4
146
5
6
7
8

Pountwell

Shewhill
Barn

Macmillan Way

Aston
Grove

Smith's
Barn

Broadwater
Bottom

✝
Turkdean

Barn

Leygore
Manor

A429

A429

A40(T)

Northleach
Downs

Hill House
Farm

Prison
Copse

Monarch's Way

Monarch's Way

A429

Heritage
Centre

Old Coalyard
Farm Est.
West

Grace Dr
Graveney Rd
Ward
May's
Jesson Dr
Quggle La
Shepherds Wy
Antelope
Paddock
End
Police Stn
Hotel
Mac Arthur Rd
Fortey Road
Farmington Road

169

Oldhill

Northleach

A40(T)

G H J **169** K L M

G   H   J   123   K   L   M

I

2

3   Leasow Lane

4   at
Rissi

148

5

6

7

8

River Windrush

Clapton-on-
the-Hill

Marsh
Farm

Broadmoor
Farm

The Fork

Upper
Broadmoor

Sandy Hill
Farm

Crookmoor
Ash

Sherborne
Common

Northfield
Barn

Sherborne Br

Cemetery

G   H   171   J   K   L   M

A B C 124 D E F

1

2

Leasow Lane

3

The Barn
Business
Centre

Lane End

Green's
Cl

Little Rissington
Airfield

B4
1 Orchard Bank

PH

4

Great
Rissington

Sherborne Lane

147

Great
Rissington
CP School

The
Follies

5

Barrington
Bushes

6

7

Miletree
Clump

8

A B C 172 D E F

Horseclo
Copse

Bicknor

15	J8	K5
1 Bracelands Dr	1 Buchanan Cl	1 Bath Pl
2 The Horsepool	2 Sunny Bank	2 Coverham Cl
3 Tudor Wk	3 Sunnybank Rd	

G   H   J   127   K   L   M

1
Carter

2

3

Dryslade
Farm

Folly   Lane

Hillersland

Hoarthorns
Farm

4

Shortstanding

Joyford

152

Picnic
Site

Christchurch

Ninewells

5

Broom   Hill

Coleford
CP Sch

Berry Hill

Berry Hill
R F C

**Five
Acres**

Leisure
Centre

Lakers
School

6

Marian
Inclosure

**Lower Berry
Hill**

LOWER ROAD

WOODGATE ROAD

Mil
En

7

A4136

Forest
Hills
Golf Club

Crossways

Lark
Rise

Buchanan

Greenfield
Road

Coombs Road

**Baker's
Hill**

GL16

B4226 POOLWAY ROAD

Broad

8

Scowles

St Johns
School

Cemetery

M8	M7	K8
1 Ambrose La	1 Owls Eye Cl	1 Wynols Hill La
2 Broadwell Br		
3 Stafford Cl		

Police Stn

Bells Hotel & The Royal
Forest of Dean
Golf Club

Fox's Lane

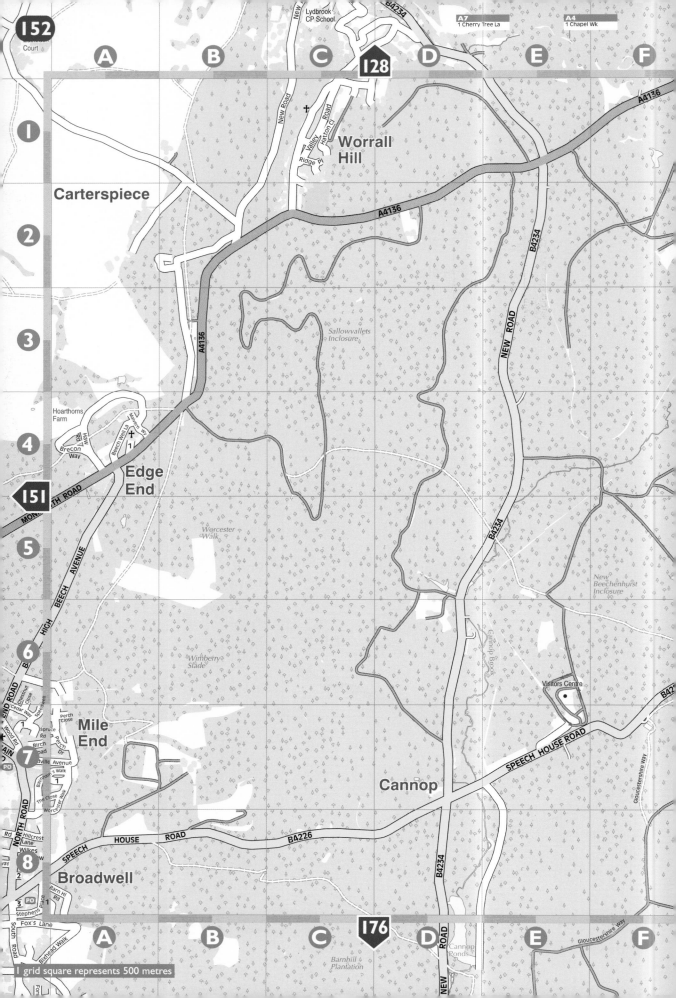

Brierley

G HIGH STREET A4136 **H** **J** 129 **K** **L** **M**

Serridge Green

Birch Wood

Gloucestershire Way

FOREST VALE ROAD

Whimsey Industrial Estate

Whimsey Road

Business Park

I

Gloucestershire Way

Serridge Enclosure

Birchwood Close

Crabtree Road

Laymore Road

Brookside Rd

Forest Vale Road

Hollyhill Road

B4227

Foxes Bridge Rd

Bilson Gre

2

English Estates Workshops

Rothdean Trading Estate

Gloucestershire Way

B4227

3

4

Business Par

154

5

Dilke Memorial Hospital

SPEECH HOUSE ROAD

Speech House Hotel

B4226

Cemetery

Railway

Peacock La

6

Cullimore Vw

PO

Kibble Lane

Bells Pl

Eastern Way

Hudso

Ruspidge Road

7

Fir View Road

Tramway Road

Speech House Walk

Gloucestershire Way

Spruce Ride

Forest of Dean

Spruce Ride

G **H** **J** 177 **K** **L** **M**

Speech House Inclosure

G   H   J   **131**   K   L   M

I

2

3

4

156

5

6

7

8

H7
1 Harrison Cl
2 The Mertons

I7
1 Beeches Rd
2 Brightlands
3 St Peter's Cl
4 Smithyman Ct

Grove
Farm

Broughtons

Pope's
Hill

Peglar's
Farm

The Slad

Upper
Hall

A48(T)

Elton Court

A4151

Elton

Westbury-o

ELTON ROAD

ELTON ROAD

A48(T)

Pound
Farm

GL14

Wyncoll's

The
Grove

Broadoak

River Severn

Arlingham
Warth

Little
Hyde

Hyde
Farm

Severn Way

Stears

Newnham
C of E School

Station Road

Hyde
La

Hyde
Lane

Unlawater Lane

A48(T)

Kings Mead

Dean Road

Orchard Rise

Allsopp Cl

Queen's
ACRE

HIGH ST

High St

Newnham
Surg

The
Surgery

Police
Stn

Back
Street

War Lane

The Culver
House

Severn
St

PO

The Green

Church Road

Newnham

High Street

Friday Street

Bell Orch

Vale
Bank

A48(T)

Severn Way

Passage Road

Ruddle

Arlingham

PO

The Ct Gdns
Road

G H J K L M

133

Severn Way

Bridgemacote

I

ore Common

Broadway Lane

Walmore Hill
Primary
School

A48(T)

Goose Lane

Chaxhill

River Severn

Waterend

Wicks Green
Farm

2

Crowgate
Lane

Goose Lane

Goose

Bollow

Downend

3

Road

Castle End
Farm

4

Boxbush

158

Severn Way

Ellis's
Farm

Longney

5

Cowley's
Elm

Longney

Longney C of E
Primary School

Manor
Farm

6

River Severn

Lynch
Farm

7

Rodley

Bury Court
Road

Upper
Dumball

8

Severn Way

Epney

Farleys
158

Elmore
Court

Elmore

F3
1 Bekdale Cl
2 Waterdale Cl

F2
1 Ferry Gdns
2 Kingfisher Ri
3 Merchants Mead
4 Millers Dyke
5 Sandpiper Cl
6 Watermans Ct
7 Waterside Cl

A B C **134** D E F

I

Barhouse

Kenton Green

Severn Way

Elmore Lane

Stonebench

2

Velthouse Farm

Hollow Farm

Moorhen Ct
Pochard Ct
Dunlin Ct
Teal
Whimbrel Rd
The Mallard
Shelduck Rd
Millers Dyke
Ardea
7 6 3
Pintail Close
Turnstone Dr

3

Springdale Cl
Arkendale Dr
Wharfdale Wy

Hardwicke Farm

4

Clarke's Farm

Sellars Road

157

Madam's End Farm

School Farm

5

Stank Lane

Church Lane

6

Laynes Farm

Pound Lane

Southfield Farm

7

Hardwicke Court

A38

Road Farm

8

Oakey Farm

Gloucester and Sharpness Canal

A B C **182** D E F

Hiltmead

Parkend Bridge

Green Lane

1 grid square represents 500 metres

Lower
Rea

G

G1
1 Brockeridge Cl
2 Longfield

G3
Street names for
this grid square are
listed at the back of
the index

H

Elmore
Lane

J

G2
1 Blackthorn Gdns
2 Camellia Wk
3 Magnolia Wk
4 Pendock Cl
5 Silver Birch Cl

135

G4
1 Catkin Cl
2 Chestnut Cl

K

G5
1 Ploughmans Wy

Goodridge
Trading Est

Shepherd
Rd

Central
Tra

Holmleigh Road

Junior
Sch

L

St George's
Way

Grange
Infant Sch

M

Police
Station

I

STROUD

A4173

Merlin
Drive

Highclere
Road

Severnvale
Drive

Saddlers
Road

Carters
Orchard

Farriers
End

coopers
Elm

Park

A38

Hendingham
Close

Beaufort
Community
School

PO

Lower
Tuffley

Robert Raikes

Whittle Avenue

Evenlode Road

Bourton Rd

Charlton Rd

Quedgeley

Severn Vale
Secondary School

Beech Green
CP School

St James
Hlth Cen

Park Drive

St James

Church Drive

B4008

BRISTOL ROAD

A38

Highcliffe
Dr

Field Court C of E
Junior & Infant Sch

Giles Cox

The Dawes

Holly End

Daniels Brook

Manor
Farm

Nuttley

Windsor
Drive

Junior &
Infant Sch

Harewood Cl

Denham Cl

Sulgrave Cl

Arundel Cl

Bodiam
Avenue

Dunster Close

Warwick Av

Longleat Av

Vincent Avenue

Glencairn
Avenue

Thoresby
Avenue

Petworth
Avenue

Charlecote Av

Tuffley
Farm

Grange
Road

2

3

Chiltern
Road

The Holly

Naas Lane

Hunts Grove
View

Weogham
Av

160

4

Waterwells
Farm

Naas
Farm

Naas Lane

5

Hardwicke

A38

Four Mile
Elm

Haresfield
Lane

Police
Station

Colethrop
Farm

M5

Naas Lane

Chambers'
Farm

6 Broo

7

Pool Farm

M5

8

G

B4008

M2
1 Bateman Cl
2 Enborne Cl
3 Harwell Cl
4 Headlam Cl
5 Linsley Wy
6 Westcote Rd

H

M1
1 Holmwood Cl
2 Jewson Cl
3 Robert Raikes Av
4 Voyce Cl

J

183

L1
1 Pearwood Wy
2 Windsor Dr

K

H4
1 Mansfield Ms
2 Meerbrook Wy

L

Colethrop

H2
1 Laburnum Gdns
2 The Moat

M

H1
1 Lion Cl
2 Taylors Gnd
3 Weavers Rd

Bondend

Upton St Leonards C of E School

1 Sanatorium Rd

St Leonards ry Sch

Bondend Road

High Street

The Stanley

Stanley Walk

Upton St Leonards

Whitley Court

Nuthill

PAINSWICK ROAD

Nuthill

Pincott Farm

Nature Reserve

Brockworth Wood

Cotswold Way

Cotswold Way

High E the

oorend

Watery Lane

Portway

Valley Lane

Prinknash Abbey

A46

Nature Reserve

Bird Park

Portway

PAINSWICK ROAD

A46

1

Buckholt Road

162

Cotswold Way

Cotswold Way

Mill Lane

Mill Lane

Simmond's Hall Farm

Kimsbury House

Pope's Wood

Castle End

B4073

Fort

A46

Cotswold Way

Beacon Close

Olivers

Painswick Stream

Batch Farm

Castle Godwyn

Paradise

Golf Course

Cotswold Way

B4073

Cem

Course Road

A46

Rococo

Damsells Cross

A46

Green
Street

A   **B**   **C**   **138**   **D**   **E**   **F**

Droys
Court

Witcombe
Reservoir

**Great
Witcombe**

†

Witcombe
Park

1

Green Street

Cotswold Way

Nature
Reserve

2

Cotswold Way

*Brockworth
Wood*

Cotswold way

Witcombe
Wood

**High
Brotheridge**

3

The Buckholt

Cotswold Way

Buckholt   Road

Cotswold Way

Buckholt   Road

Buckholt Road

*Buckholt
Wood*

*Buckle
Wood*

Buckholt Road

4

161

PO

PH

†

Cranham

*Cranham
Wood*

*Hazel H
Wood*

B4070

5

Mill Lane

Simmond's Hall
Farm

*Cranham
Common*

6

†

Overtown

Climperwell
Farm

B4070

7

Batch
Farm

8

B4070

Calf Way

Wateredge
Farm

A   **B**   **C**   **186**   lf Way   **D**   **E**   **F**

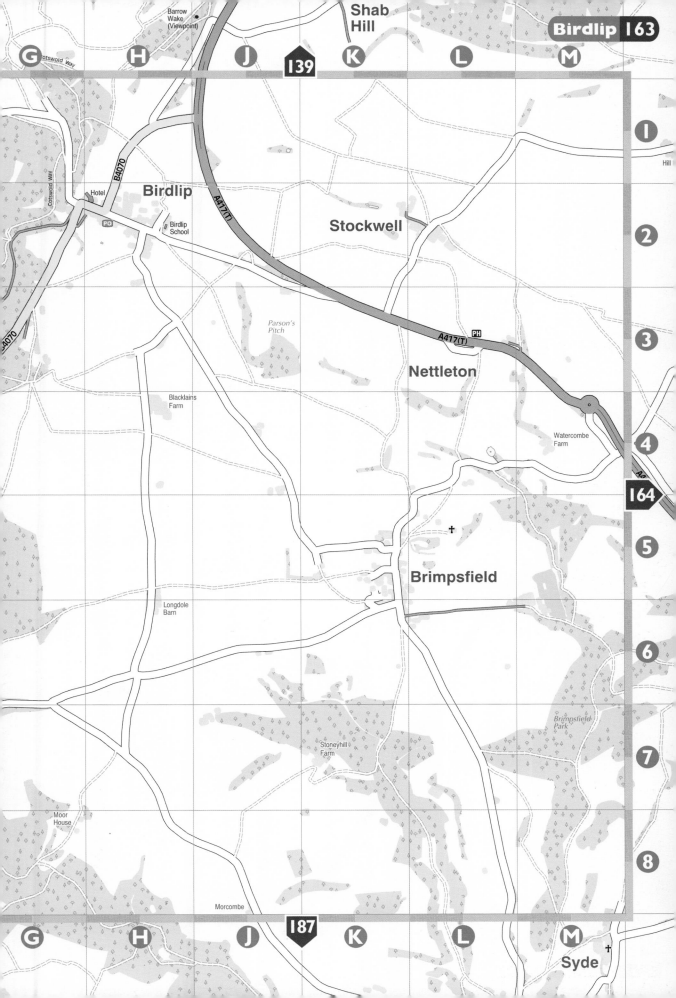

Shab
Hill

Barrow
Wake
(Viewpoint)

G
Cotswold Way
H
J
139
K
L
M

1
Hill

Birdlip
Hotel
B4070
PO
Birdlip
School
A417(T)

Stockwell

2

A4070

Parson's
Pitch

A417(T)
PH

Nettleton

3

Blacklains
Farm

Watercombe
Farm

4

A4

164

Brimpsfield

5

Longdole
Barn

6

Brimpsfield
Park

Stoneyhill
Farm

7

Moor
House

8

Morcombe

G
H
J
187
K
L
M
Syde

A **B** **C** **D** **E** **F**

140

1

Cowley

GL53

A435

2

Cockleford

Tomtit's
Bottom

River Churn
A435

Harcombe
Bottom

Cockleford
Farm

3

Cowley
Wood

Bubb's
Hill

4

High Cross

A477(T)

163

5

Highgate
Farm

Elkstone

Sparrowt

combe

6

A477(T)

field

Sadlers
Farm

7

Gloucester
Beeches

Elkstone
Farm

8

Harcombe
Farm

A477(T)

188

A **B** **C** **D** **E** **F**

Water
Farm

rde

1 grid square represents 500 metres

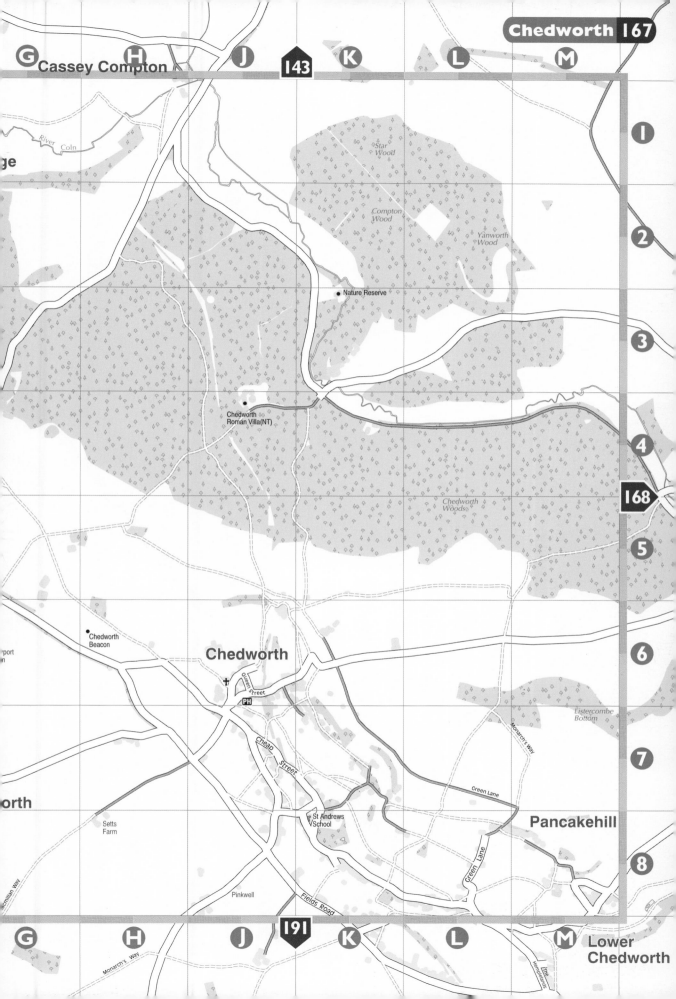

G Cassey Compton

H

J **143**

K

L

M

1

2

River Coln

Star Wood

Compton Wood

Yanworth Wood

3

• Nature Reserve

4

Chedworth Roman Villa(NT)

168

Chedworth Woods

5

• Chedworth Beacon

Chedworth

†

Queen Street

PH

6

Listercombe Bottom

Monarch's Way

Cheap Street

Green Lane

7

Setts Farm

St Andrews School

Pancakehill

Green Lane

8

Macmillan Way

Pinkwell

Fields Road

H

Monarch's Way

J **191**

K

L

M **Lower Chedworth**

The Homelands

168

A   B   C   **144**   D   E   F

Hangman's Stone

Oaks Bottom

1

Way

Macmillan

Monarch's Way

Cowlease Grove

2

Oxpens Farm

Monarch's Way

3

☩

Yanworth

Stowell Grove

4

A429

Stowell

☩

167

Monarch's Way

Stowell Park

5

A429

6

Raybrook Barn

Listercombe Bottom

7

A429

8

Hotel

A429

PH

Fossebridge

Lower Chedworth

A   B   C   **192** ☩   D   **Coln St Denms**   E   F

1 grid square represents 500 metres

G **H** **J** **145** **K** **L** **M**

J1
1 Barnett Wy
2 Bettenson Ri
3 Hammond Dr

Prison Copse **K1**
1 Farmington Ri

A40(T) **K2**
1 Short Hedges Cl

I

2

Heritage Centre

Oldhill Barn

Old Coalyard Farm Est

Monarch's Way

A429

Shepherds Wy

West End

Antelope Paddock

Mill View

Mill End

All Alone

Police Stn

PO

Hotel

Jesson Dr

Gracel Dr

Gravenley Rd

Mount Rd

Tayler Rd

Guggle La

Ward Pk

May's Cl

May's Ct

MacArthur Rd

Fortey Road

High St

East End

Dutton Leys

Gall Vw

Walkers Garden

Farmington Road

Brook

Fallows Rd

Eastington Rd

Bassett Road

Ashwin

Nostle Rd

Northleach

Upper End

A40(T)

3

Winterwell Barn

Cats Abbey Farm

Winterwell Farm

4

170 **Easti**

Trinder's Barn

5

Crickley Barrow Farm

6

Broadfield Covert

Trowel Covert

7

Sheep House Farm

Broadfield Farm

8

G Saltway Farm **H** Calcot Peak Farm **J** **193** **K** **L** **M**

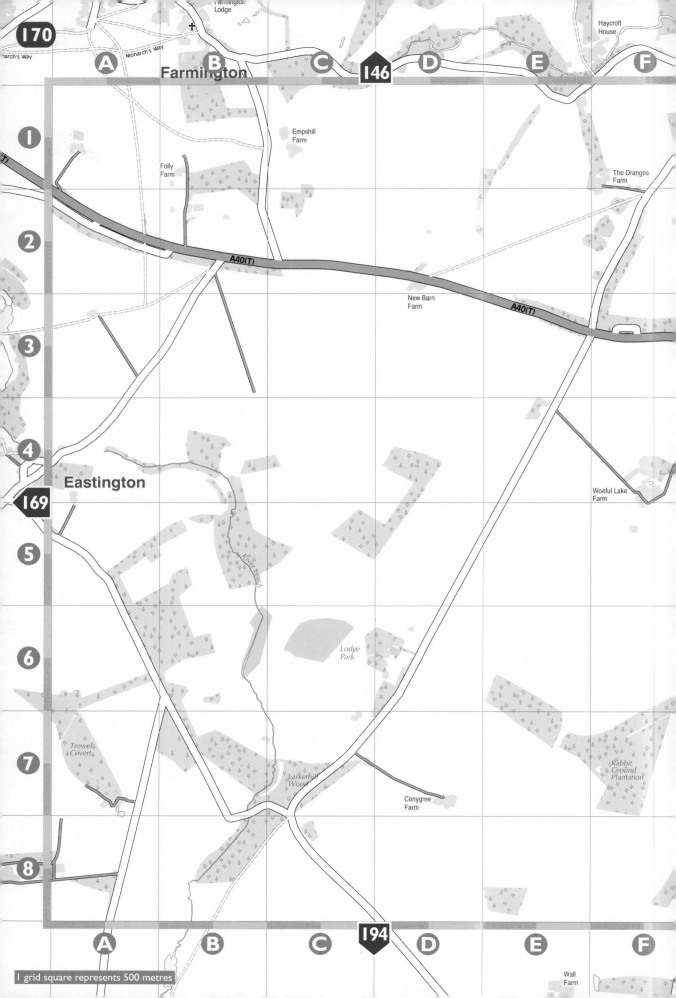

G H J **147** K L M

I

2

3

River Windrush

4

Windrush

172

5

6

7

8

Sherborne Brook

Cemetery

Sherborne

PO

Sherborne Park

Home Farm

A40(T)

A40(T)

A40(T)

Snowbottom Belt

Camp Barn

Budgehill Wood

Northmoor Barn

G H J **195** K L M

Blackpits

A B C 150 D E F

B3
1 Tinmans Gn

1

REDBROOK ROAD

Washing's Lane

River Wye

2

A466

Redbrook

Duffield's Lane

+ Primary School
French Lane

PH

3

REDBROOK ROAD

1 Tinmans Green

Highbury Road

PH

Newland

+ Almshouses
Road

Savage Hill

4

Lone Lane

Highbury
Farm

French
La

Laundry Road

5

Wye Valley Walk

A466

Offa's Dyke Path

Glyn
Farm

6

The
Grove

7

Hael
Woods

Offa's Dyke Path

Lodges
Farm

Cau
Farm

8

River Wye

A466

Coxbury
Farm

Coxbury And Wyegate Lane

Lodges
Barn

A B C 198 D E F

Wyeseal
Farm

Offa's Dyke Path

Gloucester

Wye Lane

1 grid square represents 500 metres

NOR

Hillcrest Lane
Wilkes

SPEECH HOUSE ROAD
B4226
B4234

176

Broadwell

A B C **152** D E F

3 PO

Stephen's Place

Fox's Lane

South Road

New Road

Old Road

Birch Park

Baxhead Walk

Forsdene Walk

Cannop Ponds

NEW ROAD

Russell's Inclosure

Gloucestershire Way

1

Coalway

Prosper Lane

Parkend Road

Parkend Walk

Cannop Ponds

2

Gloucestershire Way

3

RSPB Site

Nagshead Plantation

Barnhill Plantation

B4234

4

175

NEW ROAD

Nature Reserve

5

Smiths Hill

Gloucestershire Way

CANNOP ROAD

Woodland Rise

Fern Road

Ellwood

Ellwood County Primary School

Ellwood Football Club

6

Hughes Terrace

B4234

Parkend

Holly Lane

Bromley Road

Gloucestershire Way

Crown La

PO

Church W

7

Little Drybrook

Parkend Walk

Dean Forest Railway

8

Parkhill Inclosure

NEW ROAD

A B C **200** D E F

Knockley Patch

BOW

B4221

1 grid square represents 500 metres

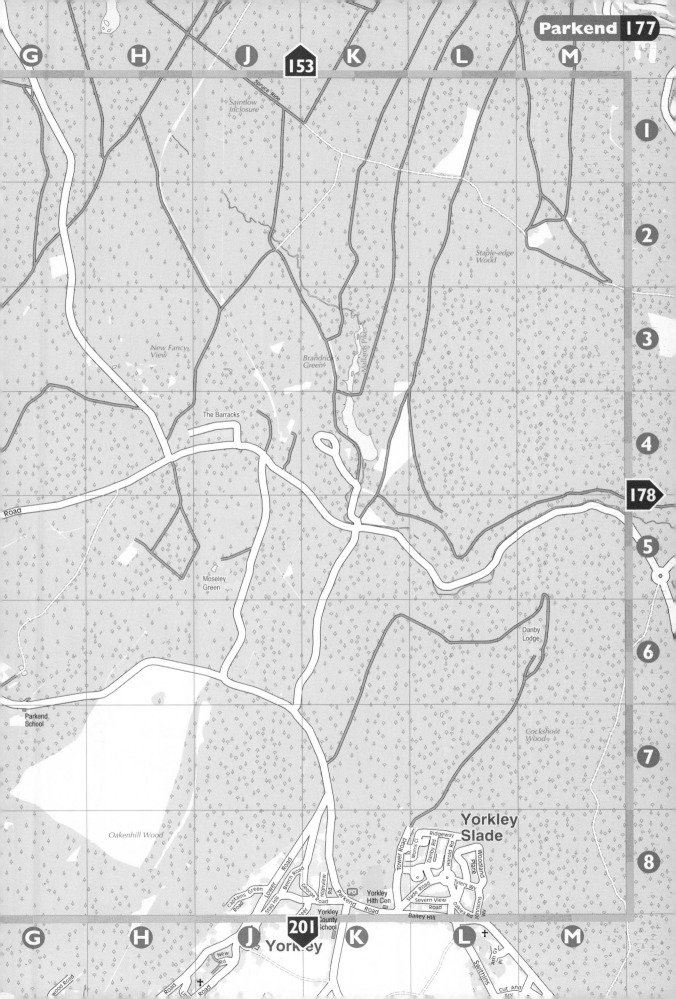

G H J **153** K L M

Spruce Ride

Saintlow
Inclosure

I

2

Staple-edge
Wood

3

New Fancy
View

Brandrick's
Green

Millards Pike

The Barracks

4

178

5

Moseley
Green

Danby
Lodge

6

Road

Parkend
School

Cockshoot
Wood

7

Oakenhill Wood

Yorkley
Slade

Ridgeway

8

Tower Road

Morris Cl

Danby Rd

Harold Rd

Woodland
Place

Captains Green

Lower
Road

Beech Road

Stany Hill

Highview
Rd

George Road

Parkend Road

PO

Yorkley
Hlth Cen

Slade Road

Severn View

Tylers Wy

Johnsons Wy

Yorkley
County
School

Oakea Rd

Bailey Hill

Severn View
Road

G H J **201** K L M

Yorkley

New
Rd

Swithins La

Ash Gv
Pl

Cut Ang
Spr

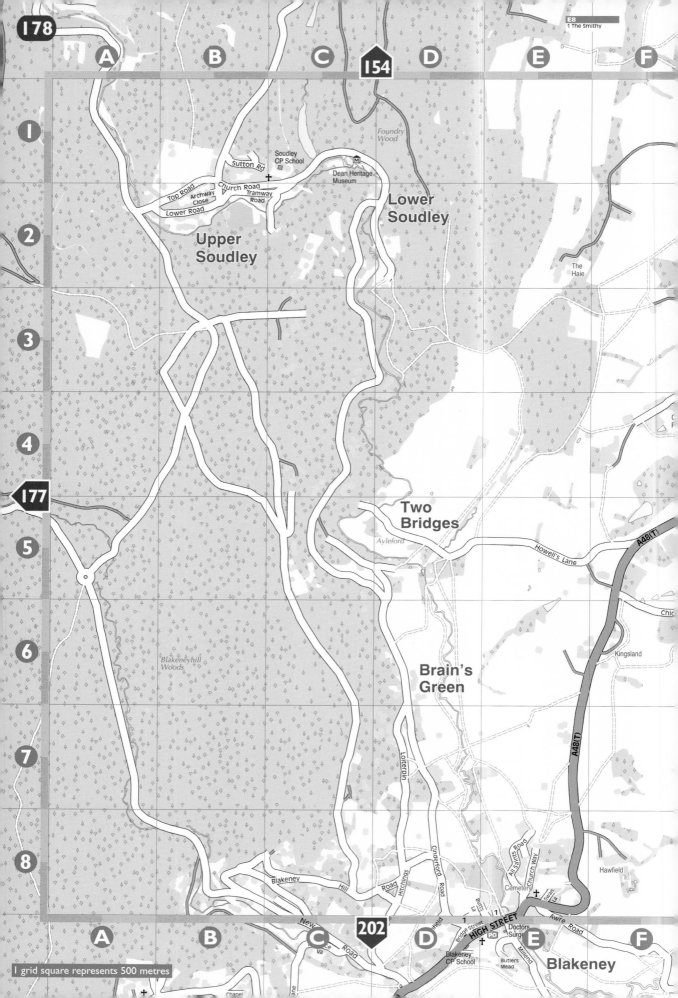

F G dle   H   J   155   K   P   Road   L   M   High   Friday   Street

Bell Orch   Vale Bank

Arlingham   PO   I

The Ct Cotts

Vicarage Lane   Church Road   Pound Lane   2

Portlands Nab

Severn Way

A48(T)

Bullo   3

River Severn

4

The Priory   180

Northington   Northington Lane   5

Box Farm   6

Lane   Awre   ✝

Bledisloe Farm   Fieldhouse   PO   PH   Woodend Lane   7

Hall Farm   8

Little Box   LC

G   H   J   203   K   L   M

Poulton Court

A B 156 C D E F

Milton
End

Overton

Overton Lane

Overton
Farm

Fretherne

The
Reddings

Hock
Cliff

Severn Way

Severn Way

Severn Way

179

River Severn

204

A B C D E F

1 grid square represents 500 metres

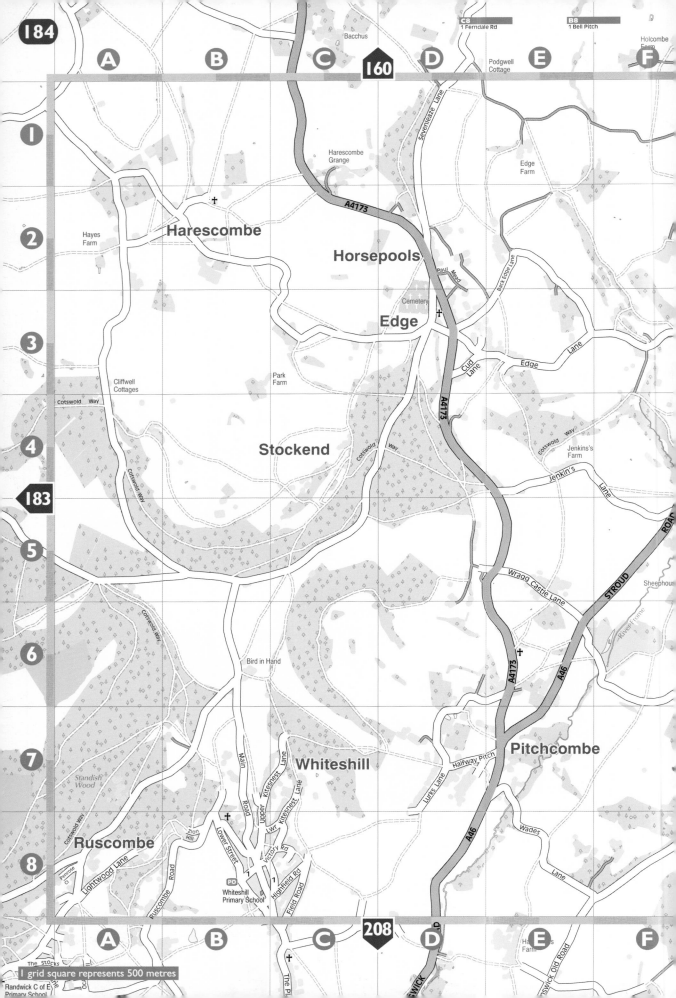

| H3 |
1 Ashwell Hyett Cl
2 Berry Cl
3 Bisley St
4 Friday St
5 George Ct
6 Hollyhock La
7 St Mary's St
8 Victoria St
9 White Horse La

| H4 |
1 Castle Cl
2 Randalls Fld
3 Woodborough Cl

G   H   J | 161 | K   L   M

Rococo
Painswick House

Damsells Cross

The Park

Cem

GLOUCESTER ROAD
Gyde Road
Canton Acre
Butt Green
PULLENS RD
Golf Course Road
CHELTENHAM ROAD
A46
Upper Washell
Lower Washell La
Police Station

Jack's Green

Cockshoot

Croft Primary School
Churchill Way
Blakewell Md
Hambutts Md
Hambutts Dr
Kingsmead
Road
Way

Town Hall
PO
PH
NEW STREET
Orchard Ct
The
Knap Lane
Stamage's Lane
Queenshead
Cotswold Md
Vicarage Street

Beech Lane

Longbridge

B4070

Dell Farm

Hotel Tibbiwell Lane
Hale La
Kemps Lane
Orchard Md
Randalls Field
Greenhouse Lane

ainswick

Painswick Valley

The Beacon Medical Practice

Skinner's Mill Farm

Mill Lane
Stepping Stone Lane

Greenhouse Court

Yokehouse Lane

Bulls Cross

| 186 |

B4070
SLAD ROAD

Down Farm

Wick Street

Folly Lane

Slad

B4070

ck Street

Catswood Farm
Catswood Lane
Elcombe

Anstea Farm

Nature Reserve

Slad
Knapp

186

A   B   C   162   D   E   Calf Way   F

Waterledge Farm

1

Calf Way

Bidfield Farm

B4070

County Primary Sch

2

Sheepscombe

ack's reen

†

Hazle Manor

B4070

Wisha

3

SLAD ROAD

The Camp

B4070

Down Barn Farm

4

Calf Way

185

Dillay

5

Southmead Lane

6

The Scrubs

Upper Southmead Farm

Piedmont   Sydenhams

7

GL6

Ansteads Farm

8

Calfway Farm

Catswood Lane

Calf Way

A   Stancombe Farm   B   Calf Way   C   210   D   E   rds Farm   F

Bisley Road

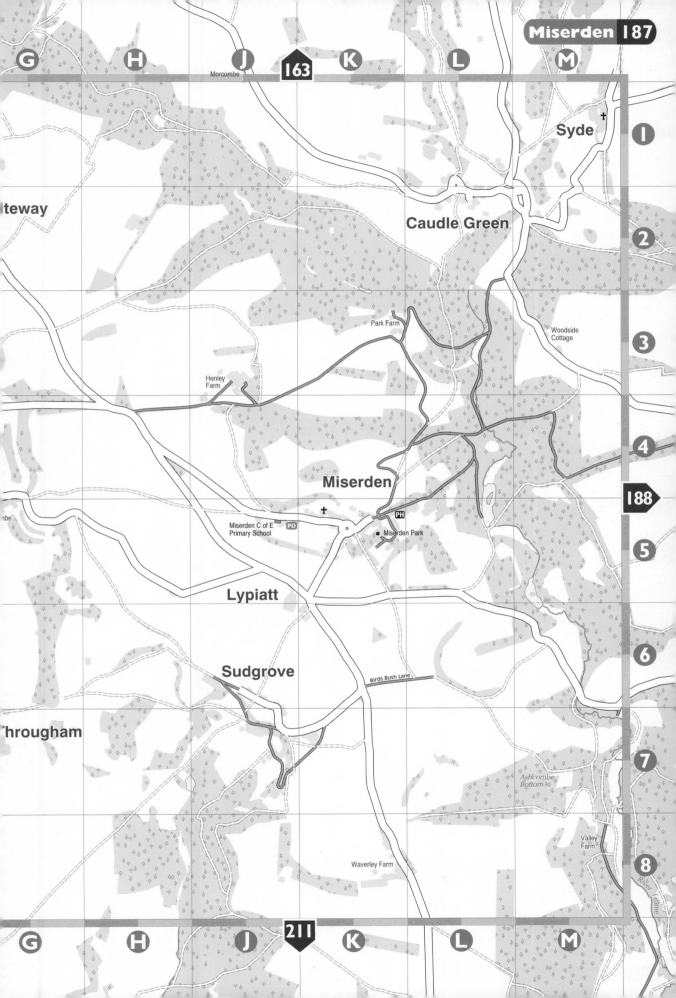

G H J **163** K L M

Morcombe

Syde

teway

Caudle Green

I

2

Park Farm

Woodside
Cottage

3

Henley
Farm

4

Miserden

188

Miserden C of E
Primary School **PO**

● Miserden Park **PH**

5

Lypiatt

6

Sudgrove

Birds Bush Lane

7

Ashcombe
Bottom

hrougham

Valley
Farm

8

Waverley Farm

River Frome

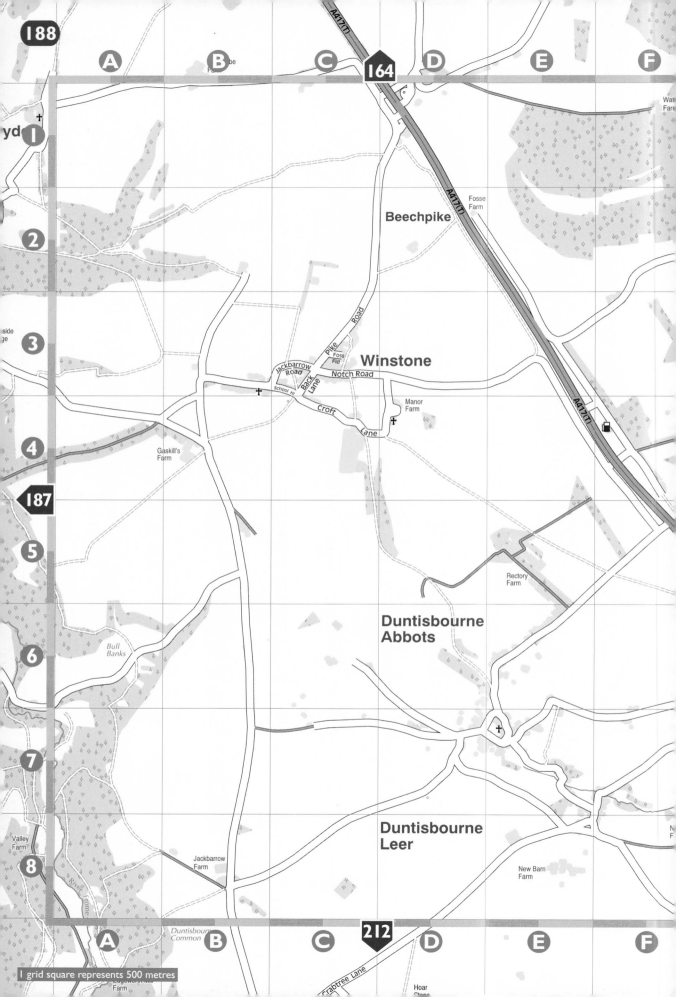

L4
1 Woodland Vw

G   H   J   K   L   M

Rapsg
Park   165

Eycot
Wood

1

Shewel
Wood

Aycote
Farm
2

3

Cotswold
Park

Cotswold
rm.

Hobbs Lane

Robinson
Lane

Macmillan Way

4

Burcombe Lane

Hayes
Lane

Woodmancot 190

Burcombe   Lane

5

Field's
Farm

Moor
Wood

Burcombe Lane

6

A417(T)

Voxhills
Farm

Macmillan Wy

7

Macmillan   Way

Dartley
Farm

8

Merchants'
Downs

G   H   J   K   L   M

213

Welsh Way

Bag

G H J **167** K L M

Green Lane

Lower Chedworth

I

Monarch's Way

The Hempelands

Denfurlong Farm
(Farm Trail)

2

Ashwell
Lodge

A429

3

Fosse
Cross **PH**

4

Fosse Cross
Industrial
Estate

192

Dark Lane

Calmsden

STOW ROAD

A429

5

6

Colnp
Copse

7

Hollow Fosse
Farm

STOW ROAD A429

Barnsley
Wold

8

G H oney Down J **215** K L M

G H J K L M

Broad
Farm

169

I

2

3

4

194

5

6

7

8

Saltway
Farm

Calcot Peak
Farm

Oldwalls
Farm

Prehistoric
Monument

River

Ablington

Potlicker's Lane

Bibury
Farm

B4425

217

G H J K L M

Arlington

Police
Station

Arl... Mill
Museum

B4425

PH

Hawkers Hill

Awkward
Hill

The Diane
Breen Gallery

M

Horse Lane

Bibury

dowlands
...n

194

A   B   C   170   D   E   F

1

Wall
Farm

2   Cocklebarrow
Farm

PO

3

4   Kilkenny
Farm

193   B4425   Swyre
Farm

5

6   Kilkenny
Cottages

Bratch
Copse

7

Johnmans
Barn

8

River Leach

A   B   C   218   D   E   F

Knoll
Barn

1 grid square represents 500 metres

G H J **171** K L M

1
2
3
196
5
6
7
8

Blackpits
Copse

B4425

B4425

Barrington Downs
Farm

Ladbarrow
Farm

No
Pla

Dean Farm

Macaroni Downs
Farm

River Leach

Lappingwell
Wood

Coltsmoor
Farm

G H J **219** K L M

Tyning
Wood

196

A   B   C   172   D   E   F

1

2

B4425

gton Downs

3

Downs
Farm

4

195

No Man's Land
Plantation

Westwell
Copse

5

Holwell Downs
Farm

6

Eastleach
Downs Farm

Oxfordshire County
Gloucestershire County

7

8

Broughtondowns
Plantation

A   B   C   220   D   E   F

1 grid square represents 500 metres

LS
1 Clissard Wy

G   H   J   173   Signet Hill   K   L   M   A361

1

Signet

Job's Lane

Job's Lane

2

A361

3

Westwell

4

Hawthorn Dr
Birch Dr
Acer Ct
1
Woodside Drive

Holwell

5

A361

6
Bradwell Grove
Woodside Farm
Wildlife Park

Home Farm

7
Bradwell Grove Wood

8
Filkins Down Farm

Furze Ground

G   H   J   221   K   L   M

G6
1 St Bruel's Cl

175

G H J K L M

Clements End

Drybr

Stowe Green

Trow
Green

Stowe

Longley
Farm

Noxon
Farm

Noxon
Park

B4228

B4228

BREAM

AVENUE

231

Slade Bottom

Bearse
Common

B4228

Br
Cro

Bearse
Farm

Roads
Farm

200

Briavels

B4228

The Great
Hoggins Farm

Close Turf
Farm

Gloucestershire Way

Willsbury
Farm

ELL LANE

Smithville
Place

Smithville
Close

St Briavels
Surg

Bream Road

Townsend
Close

Bream Road

Severn View
Farm

Gloucestershire Way

The Warren

Park
Farm

Great
Dunkilns

Rodmore
Farm

Aylesmore
Court

Highgrove
Farm

223

G H J K L M

Clanna
Lodge

1
2
3
4
5
6
7
8

A   B   C   178   D   E   F

I

New Road

Blakeney

Furnace Va

Pollards Lane

Swithins Road

Chapel Rd

Meadow Cl

Pine Tree Way

Church Walk

PO

✝

Viney Hill

Nibley

Viney

A48(T)

Hitchings

Clark's Lane

Cinderford Road

Highfield

Bridge Street

Butts

High Street

HIGH STREET

PO

✝

Blakeney CP School

Doctors Surgery

Butlers Mead

All Saints Road

Cemetery

Church Way

Shan La

Awre Road

1 Orchard Ga

Hawnfield

Millend

Blakeney

Oatfie Farm

2

Holly Tree

Brierley Wy

PI

St

Oldcroft

3

Hayes

Etloe

Gatcombe

4

The Purlieu

A48(T)

Lensbrook

201

Hill Farm

5

Gurshill Farm

Purton

6

The Wards

7

Hurst Farm

Wellhouse Bay

River Severn

8

Severn Way

A   B   C   226   D   E   F

T(T)

Cliff Farm

Sharpness

G H J **179** K L M

1

2

3

4

204

5

6

7

8

Little Box

LC

Poulton Court

Hagloe

Hagloe House

Tites Point

Purton

Severn Way

Severn Way

ter and Sharpness Canal

Kingshill Farm

inton

Red Wood

G H J **181** K L M
Fromebridge

Vicarage Lane

Severn Way

The S

Lane

Glebe Close

†

latt
dge

**Church
End**

Nastfield
Farm

B4071

CLAYPITS HILL

A38

1

2

Claypits

ess Canal

M5

3

Puddleworth

The
Marshes

Park's
Farm

Alke

4

River Cam

206

Wicksters Brook

A38

5

use

Ryalls Lane

Elm
Farm

Capehall
Farm

M5

6

Hillhouse
Farm

urt

Ryalls Lane

A38

Beechmeadow
Farm

7

Cambridge

BRISTOL ROAD

Elmcote
Farms

M5

Slimbridge

Narles Road

8

White
House

River Cam

Slimbridge
CP School

Wisloe Rd

Wisloe Road

Road

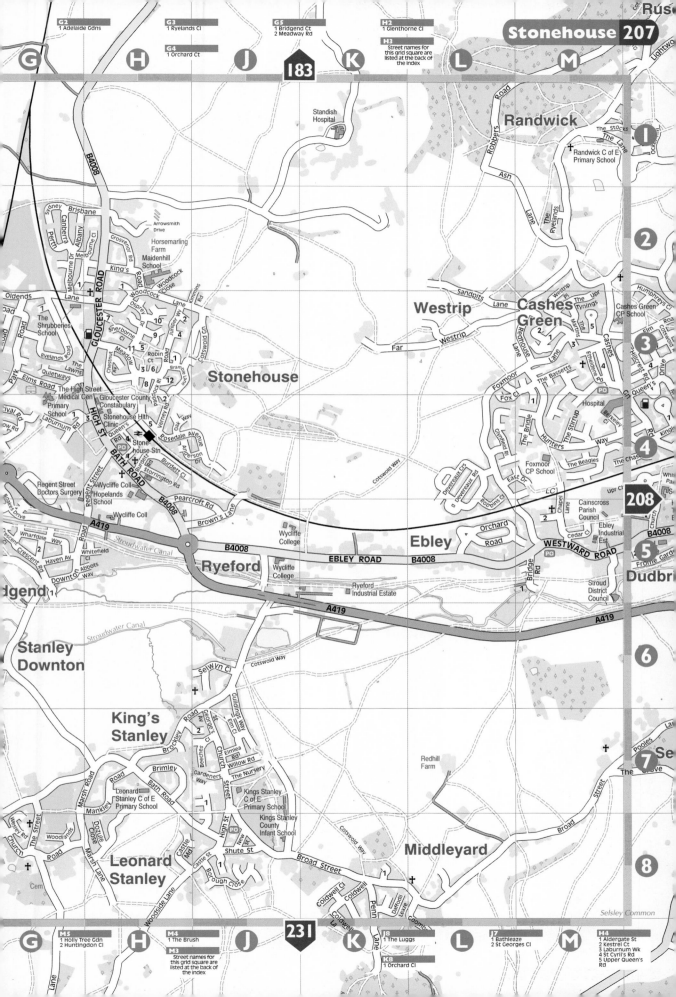

183
208
231

G   H   J   K   L   M

G2
1 Adelaide Gdns

G3
1 Ryelands Cl

G4
1 Orchard Ct

G5
1 Bridgend Ct
2 Meadway Rd

H2
1 Glenthorne Cl

H3
Street names for
this grid square are
listed at the back of
the index

Rus

Standish
Hospital

Randwick

The Stocks
The Lane

Randwick C of E
Primary School

Robbers Road

Ash Lane

The Ryelands

Sandpits Lane

Westrip

Cashes Green

Westrip Pl

The Upr Tynings

St Martins

Cashes Green CP School

Humphries Cl

Cotswold Rd

Elm

Sydney
Brisbane
Canberra
Albany
Perth
Melbourne Dr
Melbourne Cl

King's Lane

Grosvenor Rd

Woodcock Cl

Woodcock Close

Arrowsmith Drive

Horsemarling Farm

Maidenhill School

Oldends

The Shrubberies School

Ryelands Road

Quietways

The Lawns

Elms Road

The High Street

Medical Cen

Laburnum Rd

School

Primary School

Gloucester County Constabulary

Stonehouse Hlth Clinic

Stone-house Stn

Woodcock Lane

Kimmins Rd

Osprey

Sherborne

Junior Way

Robin Ct

Chestnut

Meadow

Bramble

Patrick Rd

Verney Rd

Queen's Rd

Posedale Avenue

Anderson Dr

Burdett Cl

Storrington Rd

Cotswold Gn

Stonehouse

Westrip Lane

Far

Redhouse Lane

Foxmoor Lane

Fox Cl

The Bridge

Chinfield Rd

The Bassetts

Ethelrede Rd

Foxmoor CP School

East Dr

Devereaux Cres

Devereaux Rd

Robbins Way

Hospital

Berkeley Cl

The Stirrup

Hunters Way

The Beagles

The Chas

Queen's

Cashes

Chapel Lane

Cedar Cl

Cainscross Parish Council

Ebley Industrial Est

LC

Upr Ct

Whit Par

GLOUCESTER ROAD

BATH ROAD

HIGH ST

Regent Street

Regent Street Doctors Surgery

Wycliffe Coll Hopelands School

Wycliffe Coll

B4008

Pearcroft Rd

Brown's Lane

Wycliffe College

Stroudwater Canal

A419

Wharfdale Way

Crescent

Haven Av

Abbots Way

Downton Way

Bingend

Whitefield

B4008

EBLEY ROAD   B4008

Ebley

Ryeford

Wycliffe College

Ryeford Industrial Estate

Orchard Road

Bridge Rd

WESTWARD ROAD

PO

Stroud District Council

Dudbri

Frome Gard

208

B4008

Stroudwater Canal

A419

Stanley Downton

Cotswold Way

Selwyn Cl

King's Stanley

Brockey Cl

George's Rd

Guildings Way

Elm Cl

Elmlea Rd

Willow Rd

The Nursery

Beeches

Gardeners Way

Church St

Leonard Stanley C of E Primary School

Brimley

Bath Road

Marsh Road

Mankley

Dozule Close

Marsh Road

Westley Rd

Woodlands

The Street

Kings Stanley C of E Primary School

Kings Stanley County Infant School

High St

PO

New St

Castle Md

Castle St

Bough Close

Shute St

Broad Street

Cotswold Way

Redhill Farm

Middleyard

Coaley Cl

Coaley Cl

Penn La

Coaley La

Daffodil Leaze

Coomb

Pooles La

The

Broad Street

Se

Selsley Common

Leonard Stanley

Church Road

Cem

G   H   J   K   L   M

M5
1 Holly Tree Gdn
2 Huntingdon Cl

M4
1 The Brush

M3
Street names for
this grid square are
listed at the back of
the index

J8
1 The Luggs

K8
1 Orchard Cl

J7
1 Bathleaze
2 St Georges Cl

M4
1 Aldergate St
2 Kestrel Ct
3 Laburnum Wk
4 St Cyril's Rd
5 Upper Queen's Rd

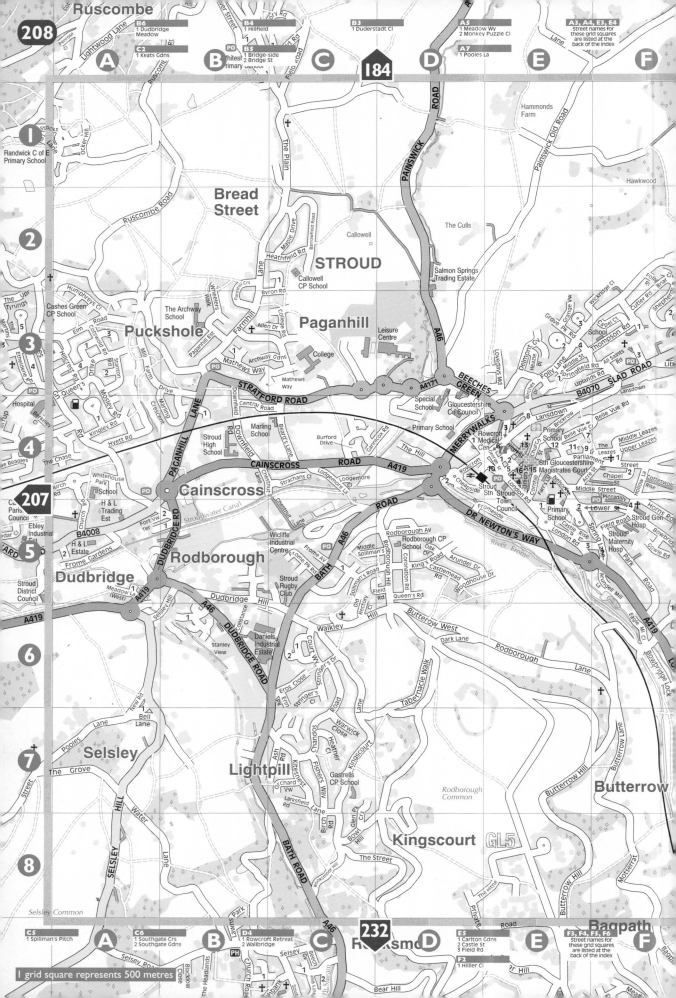

186

A **B** **C** **D** **E** **F**

C3
1 Church Hl

A8
1 Robin Cl

A7
1 Bluebell Cha

Ansteads
Farm

Calfway
Farm

Derryards
Farm

Stancombe
Farm

Parlour
Farm

Bisley Road

Calf Way

Calf Way

Bisley Road

Bisley Road

Cheltenham Road

Stroud Road

Manor
Street

Van Der Breen St

Bisley

Hayhedge Lane

PH

George
St

PO

Back
Lane

Bisley
Blue Coat
School

Wells Rd

Far Wells Road

Wells Road

High
St

Rectory
Farm

Holloway

Road

Limekiln Lane

Nashend

Copsegrove
Farm

Kitlye

Fidges
Lane

Eastcombe

PO

School

Dr Crouch's Road

Bracelands

Brockley Acres

Thomas Keble
School

**Bournes
Green**

Moon's
Lane

Baker's
Farm

Farmcote Cl

Bussage C of E
Primary School

Gardiner
Close

Stonecote Rd

Common

Foxes

Water Wy

Bluebell Rd

Pagin Close

Middle

The
Frithwood
Way

Surg

Gerald Way

Police
Station

Frith

Abnash

Frith

Neighbourhood

Old

Down
Vw

Hill

Aston Vw

Tyler's Way

Highfield

Way

Upr
Lynch

Lynch
Road

Road

Sturmyes
Road

Hillside

PH

PO

Oakridge
Parochial
School

The Broadway

Oakridge

France Lynch

Middle Hl
Crs

Abbenesse

Burcombe
Way

Road

Burcombe

Midway

Brantwood
Rd

Randall's Green

Lynch

Keble Road

Road

PO

Chalford

234

A **B** **C** **D** **E** **F**

Primary
School

Stony
Riding

Coppice Hl

School

Dark
Lane

Mule
Hill

Commercial

I grid square represents 500 metres

1
2
3
4
5
6
7
8

187

G H J K L M

1

2 Edgeworth

3

Frand
Woo

4

Gloucester
Beeches

212

5

6 River Fron

7

8 Sapperton

Waverley Farm

Farm

Ashletts Road

Farm Road

School Lane

combe

Rookwoods

terlane

The
Trench

King's
Farm

Tunley

Far
Oakridge

Hillhouse
Farm

Dane Lane

iedown

Trillis
Cottage

Daneway

Sapperton
C of E
School

Church

The
Glebe

Cemetery

River Trome

235

G H J K L M

Broad Ride

Frampton

Leer

A   B   C   188   D   E   F

I

Edgeworth Mill
Farm

Duntisbourne
Common

Jackbarrow
Farm

New Barn
Farm

Crabtree Lane

Hoar
Stone

2

Edgeworth

Duntisbourne
Hotel

Macmillan Way

Longhill Road

Knightswood
Common

3

Francombe
Wood

Longhill
Farm

Overley
Wood

4

Gloucester
Beeches

211

5

6

River Frome

The
Leasowes

Park
Corner

Overley Road

7

Dagiingworth Path

Haines
Ash
Bottom

8

Sapperton

Overley
Ride

Alfred's
Hall

Oakley
Wood

A   B   C   236   D   E   F

Ten
Rides

G H J **189** K L M

Merchants'
Downs

Welsh Way

**Middle
Duntisbourne**

Welsh Way

Upper
End

Bagendon
Downs

A417(T)

Macmillan Way

ntisbourne
use

A417(T)

Itlay

Lane

Dowers' Lane

i Road

Dowers'
Lane

Daglingworth

Overley
Farm

**Lower
End**

214

Wellhill
Plantation

Cemetery

Stratto

Barn

Cirencester
Park

2
3
4
5
6
7
8

Ba

G　H　J　**193**　K　L　M

I

2

3

4

218

5

6

7

8

G　H　J　**241**　K　L　M

Arlington

Arlington Mill
Museum

Police
Station

The Quarry

Hawkers Hill

Awkward Hill

B4425

Hotel

Packhorse Lane

The Diane
Breen Gallery

Cemetery Lane
Bibury C of E
Primary School

Church Road

Hotel

Bibury

The
Grove

River Coin

Quarry Hill
Farm

dowlands

Furzey
Barn Farm

**Ready
Token**

Welsh Way

Coneygar
Wood

Hartwell
Farm

Poulton
Grange

Welsh Way

Poulton
Fields

Sunhill

G   H   J   195   K   L   M

1

Tyning Wood

2
Deer Furl
Buildings

Williamstrip
Farm

East Leach
Folly

3

Macaroni
Farm

4

220

Macaroni
Wood

5

6

Barrow Elm
Farm

Homeleaze
Farm

Hammersmith Bottom

7

Tiltup

8

G   H   Farhill
Farm   J   243   K   L   M

Coltsmoor
Farm

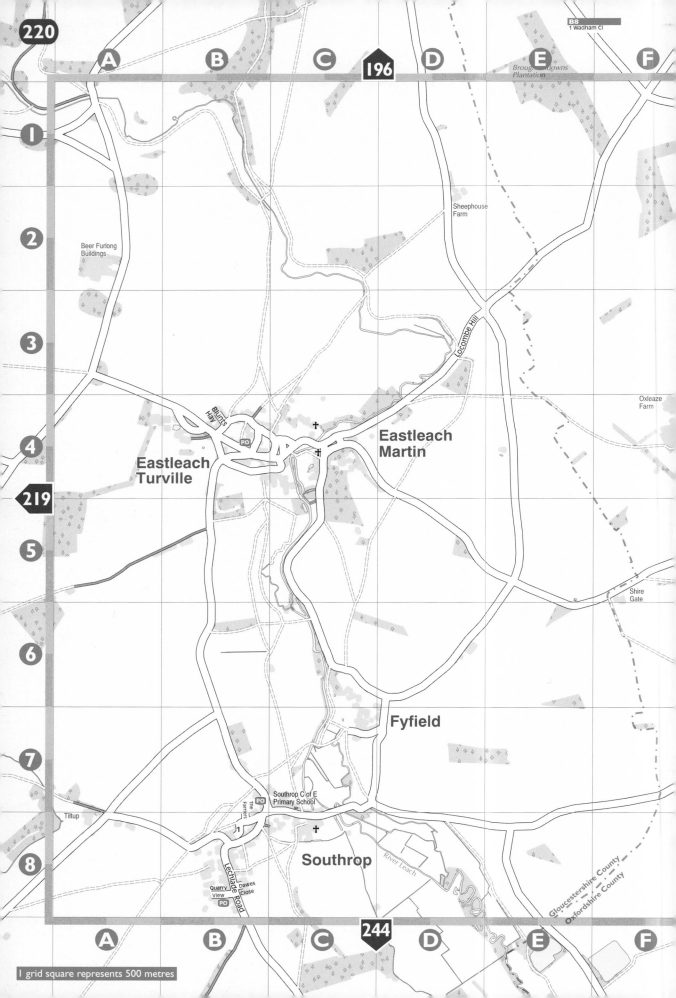

A B C 196 D E F

I

2

3

4

219

5

6

7

8

A B C 244 D E F

B8
1 Wadham Cl

Brough Downs
Plantation

Sheephouse
Farm

Beer Furlong
Buildings

Oxleaze
Farm

Blunts Hav

PO

Eastleach
Martin

Eastleach
Turville

Shire
Gate

Fyfield

Tiltup

Southrop C of E
Primary School

The Farriers

PO

Southrop

River Leach

Quarry View

Dawes Close

Lechlade Road

PO

Gloucestershire County
Oxfordshire County

Locombe Hill

G H J **197** K L M

I
2
3
4
5
6
7
8

Filkins Down
Farm

College
Farm

Kencot Hill
Farm

Furzey Hall
Farm

A361

Filkins
Farm

The
Pills

A361

Cross
Tree
La

Woollen
Mill

Filkins

Rouses
La

PO

Hazells
La

PH

Kings

Lane

Manor
Farm

PH

Manor
Farm

**Broughton
Poggs**

Broadwell

Colston House
Tennis Club

Langford Downs
Farm

A361

Brook

Filkins

Broadwell   Road

G H J **245** K L M

Road

Road

Lang

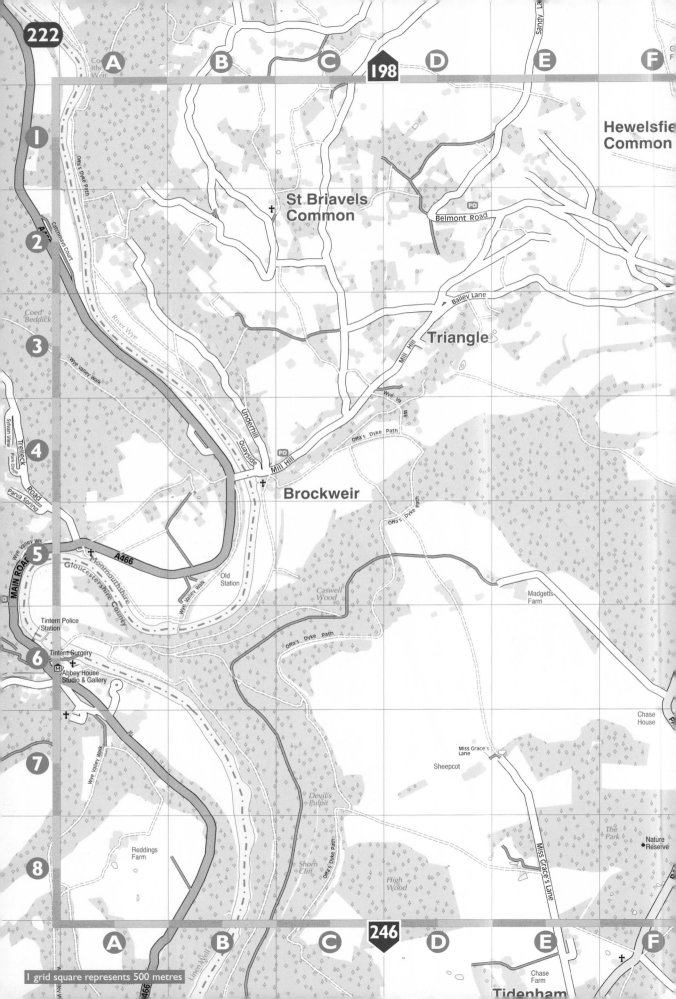

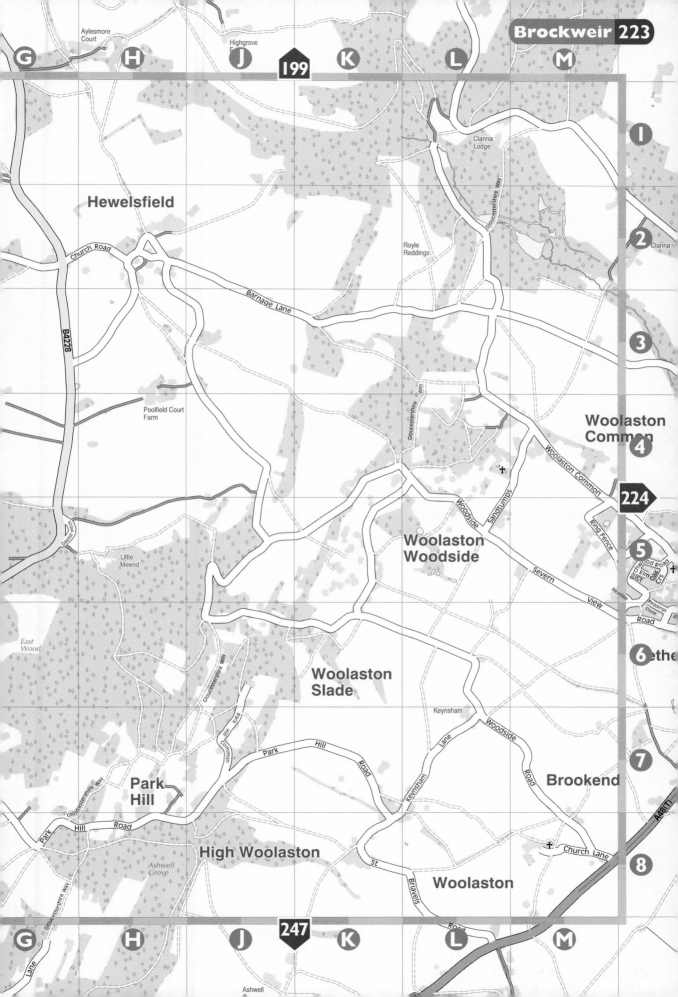

G H J **199** K L M

I

2

3

Clanna

Clanna Lodge

Royle
Reddings

**Woolaston
Common**
4

224

5

6

ethe

7

8

Aylesmore
Court

Highgrove
F

Hewelsfield

Church Road

B4228

Barnage Lane

Poolfield Court
Farm

Gloucestershire Way

Gloucestershire Way

Little
Meend

Cockshill PICO

East
Wood

**Woolaston
Woodside**

Woodside

Sandtrumps

Woolaston Common

Ring Fence

Severn

View

Pinedale

Birchwood Road

Elm
Cl

Oak
Cl

Reddings
Close

Road

**Woolaston
Slade**

Keynsham

Keynsham Lane

Woodside

Road

Brookend

Gloucestershire Way

Park
Hill

**Park
Hill**

Common

Park

Hill

Road

Park   Hill   Road

Gloucestershire Way

Park

Hill   Road

High Woolaston

Ashwell
Grove

Keynsham Lane

St

Brravels

Road

Church Lane

Woolaston

A48(T)

A48(T)

G H J **247** K L M

Lane

Ashwell

Redhill
House

1 Darters Cl
2 Herbert Howells
Cl
3 Steeple Vw

1 Chantry Cl
2 Vicarage Cl

Stonebury
Day Hospital

Lydney
C of E School

Lydney
Hlth Cen

Severn Banks
Primary
School

B4234

Newerne

Bath
Pl

Bracken Dr

G

H

J

201

K

L

M

Lydney
Rugby Football
Club

Kionodyke Av

Steel
Av

Jubilee Road

Rodley
Manor
Rd

Severnbank

Shepherdine

A48(T)

I

Lydney

Tutnalls

Pylers Way

Rushyleaze

Severn
Road

Harrison Way

Purton
Pl

Mount Pleasant

Orchard
Rd

Valley
Rd

Hopes
Rd

Ridger
Road

Avenue

Mary's
Sq

2

Naas
Court

High Street

Town
Hall

Whitecross
School

Whitecross
Business
Park

Town
Hall

CHURCH RD

B4231

Lych Ga
Mws

3

7   2

Swimming
Pool

Cemetery

Church Rd

LC

Church
Gdns

Cricket
Club

Station Road

Summerleaze

Summerleaze
Dr

Lakeside

Cambourne

Lydney
Golf Club

A48(T)

LC

Naas Lane

LC

3

Naas House

Lydney
Industrial Estate

Lydney
Yacht Club

Park Farm

A48(T)

Mead
Lane

Mead Lane
Industrial
Estate

Ward Industrial
Estate

LC

LC

Lydney
Station

Harbour Road

Lydney
Harbour

Naas Lane

4

226

5

New Grounds

6

7

8

Severn Way

A B C 202 D E F

D2
1 Great Western Rd

1

A447

Cliff
Farm

LC

2

Naas
Court

3

Naas House

Naas Lane

Lydney
Yacht Club

4

225

5

The
Paddock

6

Severn Way

7

Berkeley Pill

8

Hamfield Farm

Severn Way

Sharpness

Bridge Road

Dock Road

PO

Bridge

Road

Oldminster Road

Oakfield Way

Severn Road

Severn Way

Newtown

The
Crescent

New St

Jubilee Wy

Baylands

Bays Hill

PO

Gloucester
Rd

Sharpness
Primary
School

B4066

Saniger Lane

Saniger
Farm

Oakhunger
Farm

Westfield
Brake

Hook Street

Oakhunger La

Lynch

A B C 250 D E F

Severn Way

Severn Way

Hamfield Lane

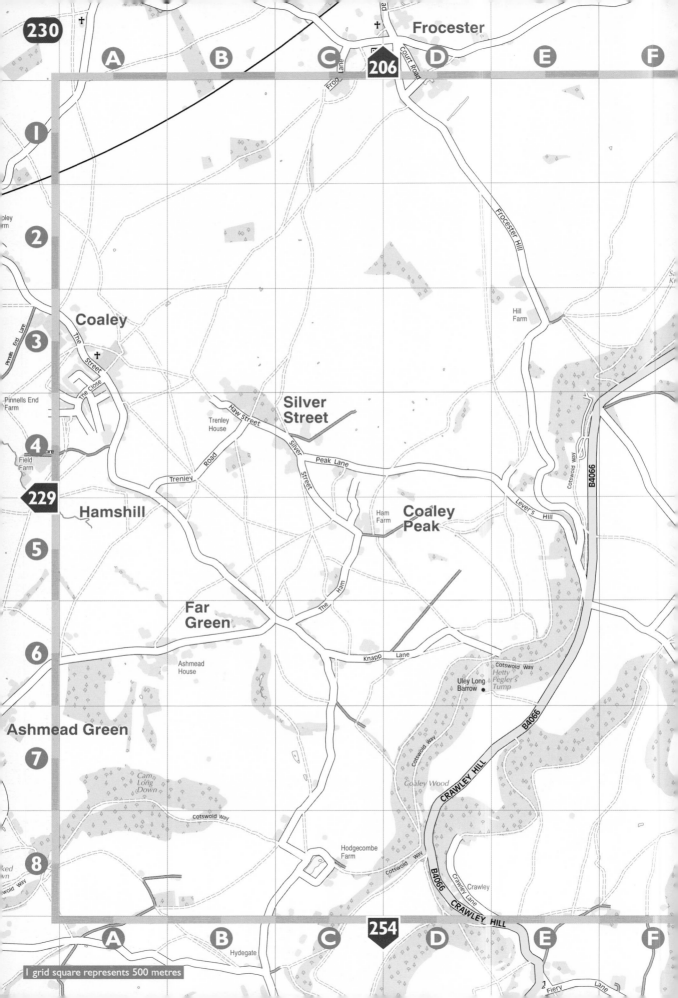

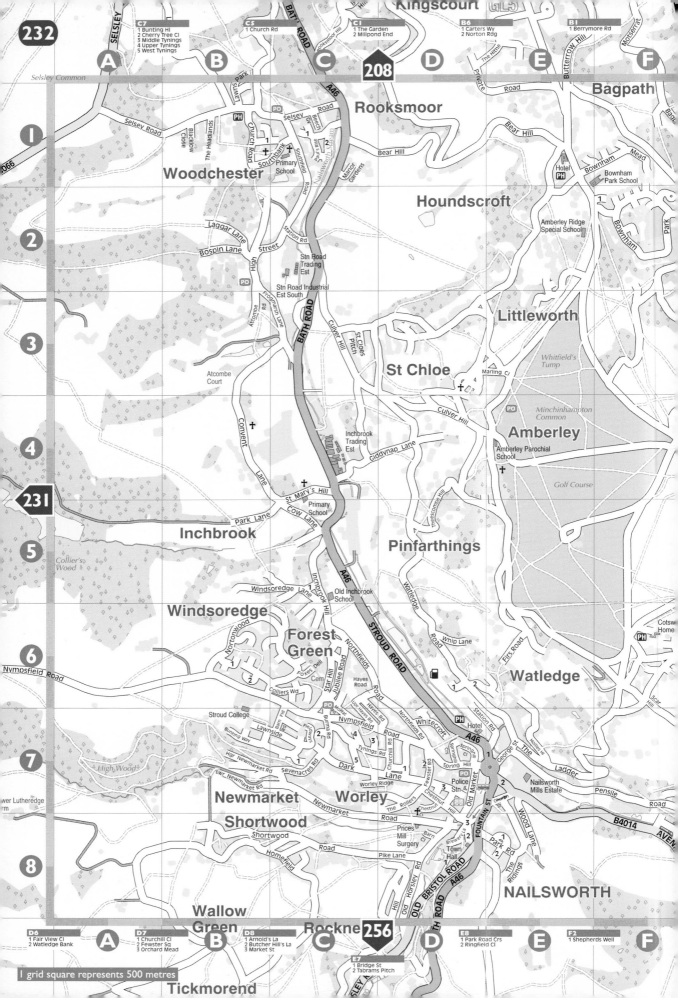

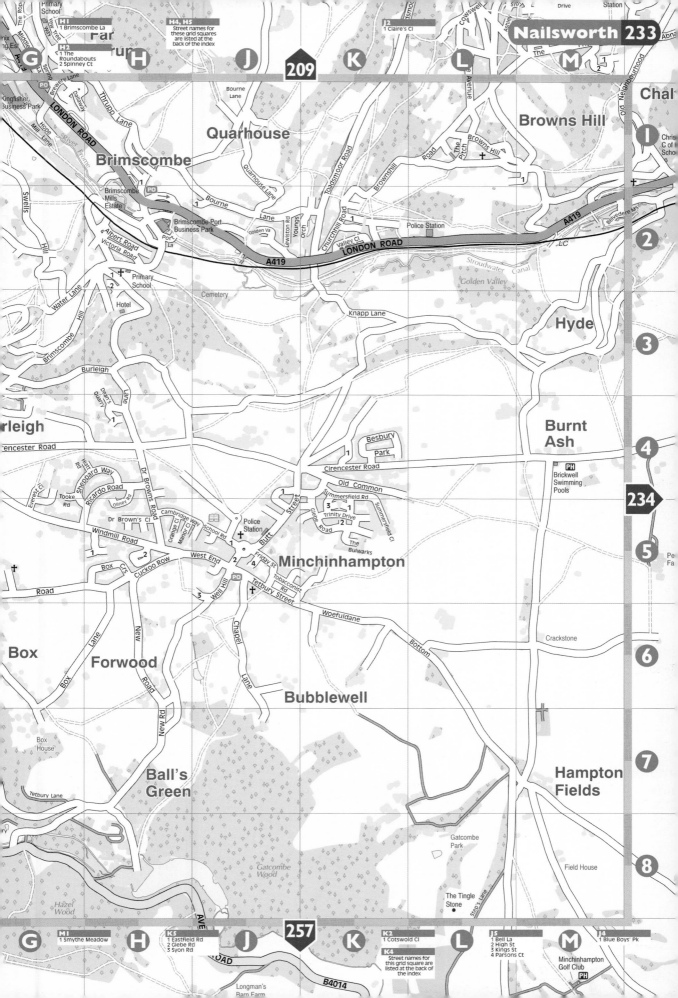

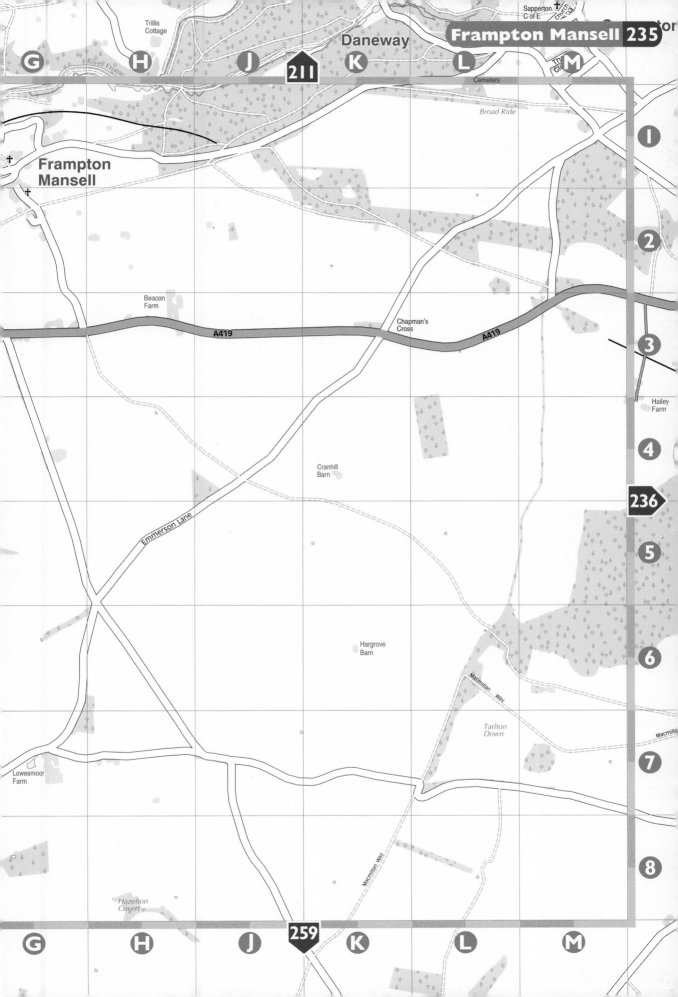

G H J **211** K L M

Sapperton
C of E
Church

Daneway

Cemetery

Broad Ride

I

Frampton
Mansell

2

Beacon
Farm

Chapman's
Cross

A419   A419

3

Hailey
Farm

4

Cranhill
Barn

236

Emmerson Lane

5

Hargrove
Barn

6

Macmillan Way

Tarlton
Down

Macmilla

7

Lowesmoor
Farm

Macmillan Way

8

Hazelton
Covert

River Frome

Trillis
Cottage

G H J 213 K L M

I

2

3

4

238

5

6

7

8

Cirencester Park

Ivy Lodge

Ewe Pens

Pope's Seat

A419 STROUD ROAD A419

A419

Cirencester Comprehensive School

Cirenc

Cirenc FC

TETBURY ROAD

Monarch's Way

Bledisloe

Monarch's Way

Field Barn

A429

A429

Swallow Copse

rton tion

Source of the River Thames

A433

Thames Path

Thames Head

G H J 261 K L M

Field Farm

G8
1 Hambledon Cl

M2
1 The Pleydells

B4425

215

Norcote

LONDON ROAD

A417(T)

Witpit Lane

A417(T)

Witpit Lane

Ampney Park

Ampney Crucis

Allotment Lane

School Lane

PH Hotel

Waterton House

A417

Preston

St Augustine Farm

Church Lane

Manor House

Harnhill

240

Ildington House

A419

Gray Rd

Thompson Rd

Hannah Road

Jackson Road

Aaron Road

Mottershead Road

CIRENCESTER ROAD

Ermin Farm

A417(T)

Trenchard Gardens

1

263

Airfield

Driffield Cross Roads

...ster Road

G H J K L M

A   B   C   216   D   E   F

GL7

1

2 Ampney
Crucis

Hilcot
End

Ampney
St Mary

Allotment Lane

School Lane

The Donkey Field

Hotel 3

A417

Ampney Brook

A417

Eastington
House

Ampney
St Peter

4

5

Church Lane

Manor
House

6

Priory
Farm

Poulton
Priory

7

Driffield

8

Edward

St

A   Manor Farm B   C   264   D   E   F

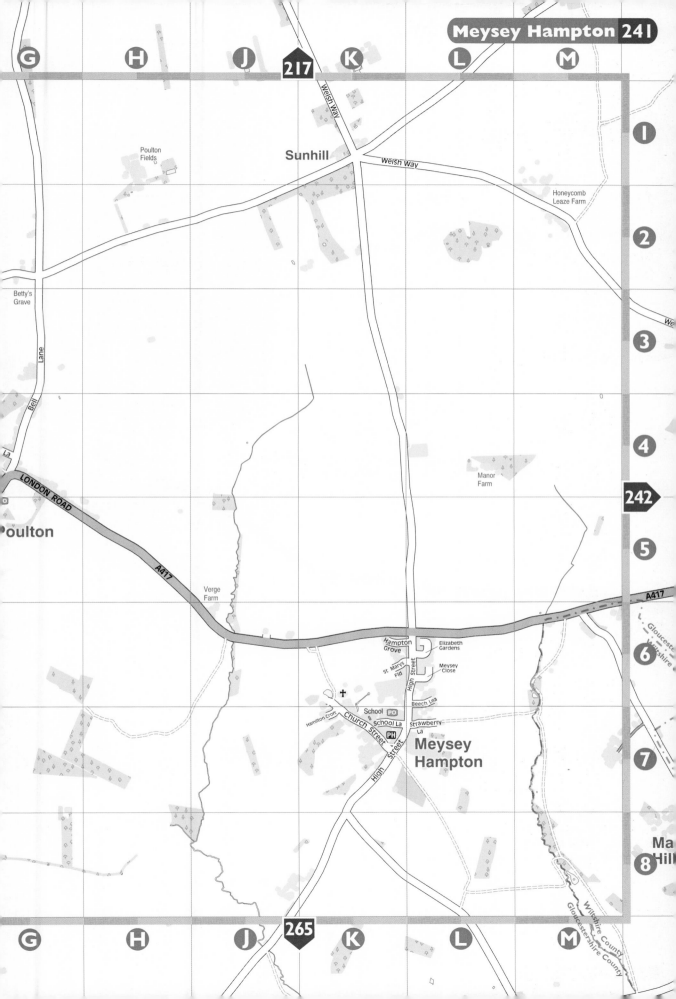

G H J **217** K L M

I

2

3

4

242

5

6

7

8

Poulton Fields

Sunhill

Welsh Way

Welsh Way

Honeycomb Leaze Farm

Betty's Grave

Bell Lane

La

LONDON ROAD

Poulton

A417

Verge Farm

Manor Farm

A417

Gloucester Wiltshire

Hampton Grove

Elizabeth Gardens

St. Marys Fld

Meysey Close

High Street

Beech Lea

Hamilton Croft

School La

Strawberry La

School

PO

Church Street

PH

Meysey Hampton

High Street

Ma Hill

Wiltshire County
Gloucestershire County

G H J **265** K L M

G   H   J   219   K   L   M

I

2

3

4

244

5

6

7

8

Farhill
Farm

South Farm

Snowstorm
Gorse

Stanford
Hall

Kidsworth Rd

Fairford
FC

A417

Claydon
Fields

Thornhill Farm

Cotsworld
Water Park

Cotswold
Water Park

G   H   267   J   K   L   M

Whelford

River C

G H J **221** K L M

I

Lang

Filkins Road

Tennis Club

Lechlade Road

The Elms

St Christophers
C of E School

1 Church La

Rectory
Farm

Hooks
Close

2

A361

Hulse Grounds
Farm

3

Langford
House

Langford Brook

4

Horseshoe
Lake

5

6

7

Mill Lane

River Leach

Paradise Farm

Oxfordshire County
Gloucestershire County

Kelmscot

8

PH

PH

G H J **269** K L M

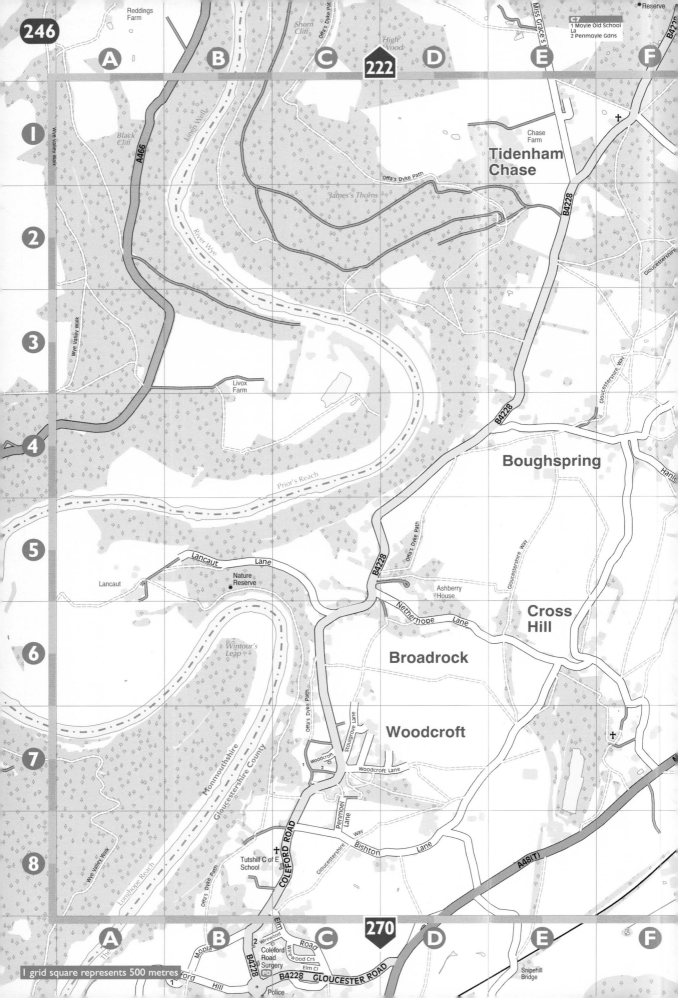

High Woolaston

Woolaston

Church

St Briavels Road

G H J **223** K L M

I

Ashwell Grove

Gloucestershire Way

Sully Lane

Ashwell Grange

Woolaston Grange

2

A48(T)

3

Stroat

Rosemary Lane

4

Wibdon

248

5

Hanley House

A48(T)

6

7

denham

Pill House

8

Plusterwine

A   **B**   **C**   **224**   **D**   **E**   **F**

Road

LC

1

Woolaston
Grange

River Severn

2

3

4

5

Gloucestershire County
South Gloucestershire

Chapel House

6

7

Shepperdi

8

A   **B**   **C**   **272**   **D**   **E**   Jobsgreen   **F**
                                                            Farm

1 grid square represents 500 metres

G H J 225 K L M

1

2 Severn

3 Worldser

Severn
House Farm

4 Worldser

County of Gloucestershire
South Gloucestershire

250

Severn Way

5

Dayhouse Farm

6

Nupdown

Tranton Lane

7

rels

Hill
Court

Scotlands
Farm

8

Nupdown Road

Hill Lane

Nupdown Road

Hill

Woodend Lane

Church
Wood

A B C D E F

226

1
Severn Way

Hamfield Farm   Severn Way   Hamfield Lane

Har

Fl
Fa

Hamfield L

2
Severn Lane   Woodlands Lane   Woodlands Farm   Blackhall Cott

3
Worldsend   Willis Elm

Lane   Park Farm

Worldsend Farm

4   Park House

Whitcliff Park
(Deer Park)

Pedington Elm

249

Bevington   Bevington Lane

5   Pedington Farm

6   **Hystfield**

Upper Hill

Appleridge Farm   Appleridge Lane

7   Gloucestershire County
South Gloucestershire

Hill
Court

8   Newpark Farm

II

A   B   C   D   E   F

274

Church hill
Wood   **Lower
Stone**

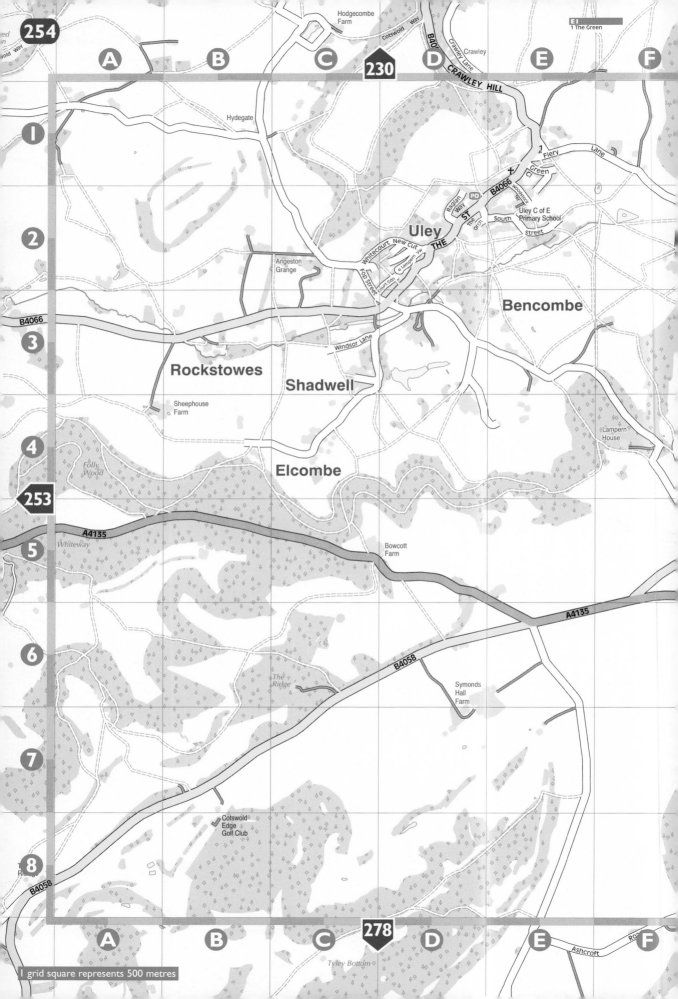

A   B   C   **230**   D   E   F

EI
1 The Green

Crawley

Crawley Lane

CRAWLEY HILL

B40

Cotswold Way

Hodgecombe
Farm

Hydegate

I

Fiery   Lane

Green
Cl

Woodrock

B4066

PO

Raglan Way

Uley C of E
Primary School

2

Uley

The
orch

South
Street

ST
THE

Whitecourt

New Cut

Angeston
Grange

FOP Street

Lampern Vw

court cdn

Bencombe

B4066

3

Windsor Lane

Rockstowes

Shadwell

Sheephouse
Farm

Lampern
House

4

Folly
Wood

Elcombe

253

A4135

Whiteway

5

Bowcott
Farm

A4135

6

The
Ridge

B4058

Symonds
Hall
Farm

7

Cotswold
Edge
Golf Club

8

Rie

B4058

A   B   C   **278**   D   E   F

Ashcroft   Ro

Tyley Bottom

1 grid square represents 500 metres

G   H   J   231   K   L   M

Woodcock

I

Upper Lutheredge
Farm

Sallywood
Farm

B4058

Nu

2

Boscombe

3

Woodleaze
Farm

wlpen

Kingscote
Wood

4

Binley
Farm

B4058

256

5

PO

A4135

6

Lower
Hazelcote

Kingscote

Ashel Barn

7

Barnhill
Farm

A4135

8

G   H   J   279   K   L   M

Bagpath

Newington

G H J **233** K L M

K2 1 Woodstock Cl
L2 1 Church St
L3 1 Orchard Fld
2 Pound Hl

Gatcombe Wood

AVENING ROAD

B4014

Longman's Barn Farm

Minchinhampton Golf Club PH

Hill Farm

I

Nag's Head 2

Hampton

Brandhouse Farm

Avening House

The Sunground

Hill

Lawrence Rd

Old Hill

Rectory Lane

Macmillan

1

HIGH ST

Woodstock Lane

Avening School

1

Sandford

PO

Leaze

Powls Lane

Macmillan Way

Mays Lane

Macmillan 3

Avening Court

New Inn

New La

Farm Hl

Point Rd

The Grove

2

Avening Park

Westfield Barn

West End

Macmillan Way

TETBURY HILL

Avening

B4014

4

258

Star Lane

Star Farm 5

Longtree Bottom

Macmillan Way

6

7

Chavenage Green

B4014

Chavenage House

Lodge Farm

Tetbury Upton

Upton Grove 8

Lowfield Farm

Macmillan Way

G H **281** J K L M

G H J 235 K L M

1
2
3
4
260
5
6
7
8

Hazel Cover

Macmillan Way

Macmillan Way

Hazelton
Manor Farm

Hocberry

PO ✝

St. Peter's Close

Rodmarton
School

Rodmarton

Oathill Lane

Monarch's Way

Rodmarton
Manor

*Windmill
Tump*

Long Borrow •

*Tump
Plantation*

Irongate
Farm

Monarch's Way

Trull
House

A433

A433

Holt
Farm

Culkerton

Oxleaze
Road

Manor
Farm

New
Barn

Purley
Covert

Gloucestershire County
Wiltshire County

G H J 283 K L M

✝

Manor **Ashley**

A   B   C   236   D   E   F

1

2

3

4

259

5

6

7

8

A   B   C   284   D   E   F

Sandpool Lane

Monarch's Way

Mountpleasant Plantation

Monarch's Way

HARESDOWN HILL

A433

A433

Jackaments Bottom

A429

Kemble Airfield

Kemble Wood

Gloucestershire County
Wiltshire County

Morgans Tynings

A429

Woodlands

H4
1 The Oaks
2 Tamesis Dr

Thames Head

G H J **237** K L M

I

Thames Path

2

3

Field Farm

Kemble Station

Windmill Road

Clayfurlong Farm

Thames Path

Thames Path

Hotel

PO

Glebe La

Clayfurlong

A429

Kemble

Kemble County Primary School

Ewen

PH

Station Road

School Road

Lane

West

Limes Road

Old Vicarage La

Church Road

262

River Thames Or Isis

Thames Path

Kemble House

4

5

6

Glebe Farm

7

Kemble Wick

Poole Keynes

Thames Path

8

G H J **239** K L M

1 Boxbush Cl

Trenchard Gardens

I

Airfield

Driffield
Cross Roads

Northmoor Lane

Cirencester Road

A419(T)

2

Northmoor Lane

Northmoor

Sisters
Farm

3

Cirencester

Silver Street

WOW

BOW

River Churn

**South
Cerney**

Timbrells
School Lane
Church La

The Close

Boxbush Road
Field Cl

Lakeside

4

264

River Way

Phoenix
Surgery

PO

Police
Station

Mill

The Lennards

Robert Franklin Way

Wildmoorway Lane

River Way
Meadow

Church Way

Station Road

Willow Gv

Huxley

Station Road

Langett
Jubilee Cl
High Street

Berkeley Cl

Sudeley
Drive

Horn Lane

Station Road

SPINE ROAD (EAST)

5

Upper Up

Broadway Lane

York Way

Cerney Wick Lane

Ann Edwards
School

The
Leaze

Beaverstone Cl

Beverstone Rd

Evergreen
Industrial
Estate

B4696

6

Broadway
Trading Estate

Broadway Lane

Cotswold
Water
Park

Broadway Lane

7

Wickwater Lane

Whitefriars Lane

SPINE ROAD (EAST)

8

B4696

Fridays

G H **287** J K L M

North End

Clayhill

Ham Lane

Cleveland
Farm

A   B   C   D   E   F

240

I

2

3

4

263

5

6

7

8

Manor
Farm

Poulton
Hill Farm

The
Folly

Ampney Brook

Vines
Brake

Cirencester Road

Fosse
Farm

Dukes
Brake

Chestnut
Cl   7   Suffolk
Pl

Down   Ampney Road

Manor
Farm

Down Ampney Road

Cirencester Road

Cerney Wick Lane

Lane

Westfield
Farm

Cirencester Road

Croft   Lane

Cerney
Wick

The   Street

Gosditch

Upcott

Lowcott

Latton

Riding
School

A419(T)

A419(T)

Gloucestershire County
Wilts County

Thames   Path

North
Meadow

A   B   C   D   E   F

288

Ma
Hil

G   H   J   241   K   L   M

I

2

3

Castle Hill
Farm

Broadleaze

mpney C of E
School

4

The Thesaurry

Down Ampney

The Street

Marston
Mevsey

266

Oak

Road

5

The Street

6

Oak

Road

7

Gloucestershire County
Wiltshire County

ppen Bridge

8

Alex
Farm

G H J **243** K L M

I

2

3

4

268

5

6

7

8

Whelford

River Coln

Ham
Barn

Lane

River Thames or Isis

Gloucestershire County
Swindon

Thames Path

Hannington
Bridge

Thames Path

Blackford
Farm

North Lea
Farm

Manor
Farm

**Hannington
Wick**

G H J K L M

Box Hedge
Farm

A   B   C   244   D   E   F

1

2

Dudgrove Farm

3

4

5

6

7

8

Inglesham

Gloucestershire County
Swindon

Thames Path

A361

River Cole

Oxfordshire County
Swindon

Weston Farm

LECHLADE ROAD A361

Thames Path

Upper Inglesham

Lynt Road

College Farm

North Leaze Farm

A361

Thames Path

or Isis

THE STREET

River Thames or Is

River Cole

C of E School

A   B   C   D   E   F

I grid square represents 500 metres

245

G · PH
H
J · e Farm
K
Oxfordshire County
Gloucestershire County
L
M · PH

I

River Leach

Thames · path

River Thames or Isis

2

LECHLADE ROAD · A417

✝

Buscot

PO

Kilmester's Farm

3

Snowswick Lane

LECHLADE ROAD A417

4

Buscot Park (NT)

5

Broadleaze Farm

Bushy Heath

Heath Farm

6

Oldfield

Snowswick Farm

7

Pennyswick Farm

Brimstone Farm

8

G
H
J
K · Middle Leaze Farm
L
M

G   H   J   **247**   K   L   M

1

2

3

4

272

5

6

7

8

Gloucestershire County
South Gloucestershire

River Severn

Severn Way

Severn Way

Littleton
Warth

G   H   J   **291**   K   L   M

A　　B　　C　**248**　D　　E　　F

1

Oldbury Power Station
Visitors Centre

Jobsgreen
Farm

Knight's
Farm

Shepperdine Road

2

3

Oldbury
Naite

4

Ham Lane

Oldbury
House

5

Westend Lane

W End

Camp Road

Westend

The Naite

Oldbury-on-Severn

Featherbed Lane

PO

✝

Chapel

Road

Picked

PH

6

Westmarsh Lane

**Pullens
Green**

Kington Road

Oldbury-on-Severn
C of E School

✝

7

Severn Way

Church Road

Pillhead
Gout

Chu
Far

Cowhill

8

Littleton
Warth

St Arild's

A　　B　　C　**292**　D　　E　　F

Lower Corston
Farm

G   H   J   **249**   K   L   M

K8
1 Kempton Cl

L8
1 Pittville Cl

Scotland
Farm

Court

Church
Wood

I

2

3

Lodge Farm

4

274

5

Duckhole

PO **Newton**

6

Horse Lane

**Lower
Morton**

7

Oldbury Lane

U
M

GLOUCESTER ROAD

8

Hill Lane

Foss Lane

Rockhampton Rhine

Parkmill
Farm

Kington Road

Park Farm

Manor Wk
Queens Wk
Dyrham Cl
Parkland Way
Rossiter
Wy
Charles Cl
Victoria
Cl
Hyde Av
Alexandra
Wy
Regents Cl
Oaksworth Rd
Manor
Brook
School

Butt
Lane

Morton
Street

Swallow Park

Morton
Way

Osprey Park

Morton

G   H   J   **293**   K   L   M

The
Castle
School

Park Road

Dean Av
Milfield

North Road
Eastland Av
Park

Seven View Rd
Squires
Teaze

Dewpads
Mallow

Finch
Cl
Nightingale
Wy
Falcon Wy

Hotel

Chantry Rd

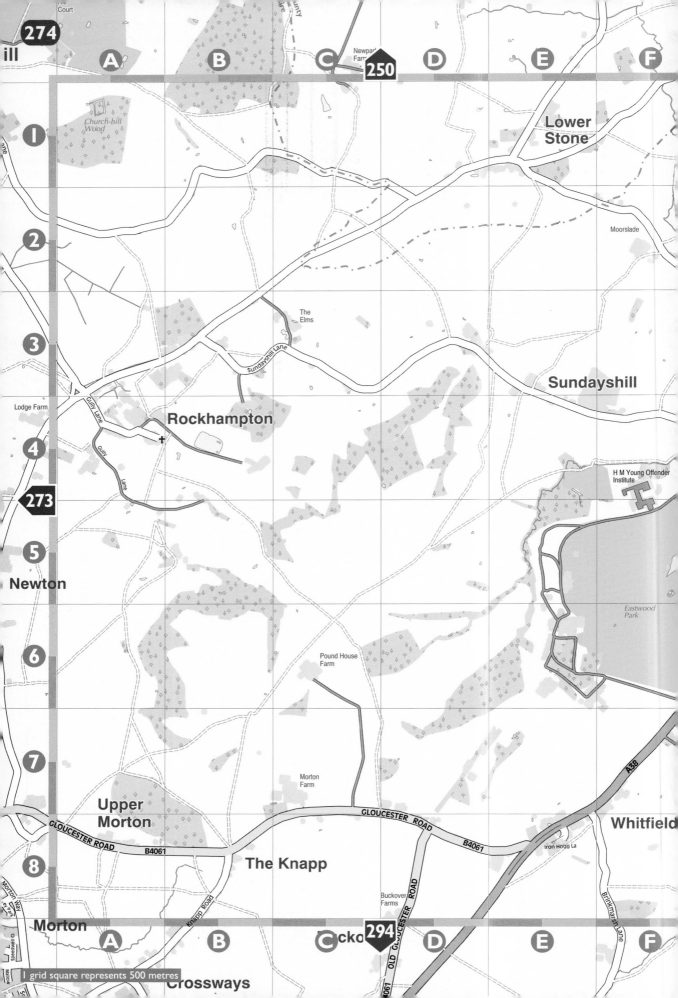

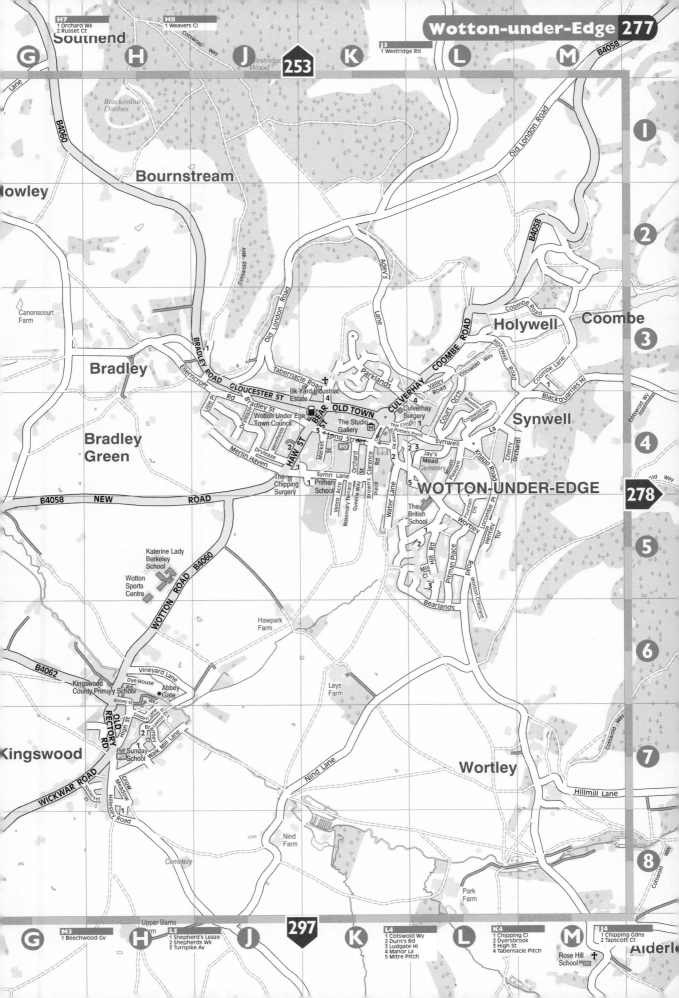

G H J 253 K L M

H7
1 Orchard Wk
2 Russet Ct

H8
1 Weavers Cl

Soutnend

J3
1 Westridge Rd

B4058

I

2

B4058

3

Coombe

Holywell

Coombe Road

Bournstream

Cotswold Way

Old London Road

Canonscourt Farm

Brackenbury Ditches

Iowley

Lane

B4060

Coombe Road

Coombe Lane

Black Quarries Hl

Cotswold Wy

Adey's Lane

Holywell Road

Parklands

Tabernacle Road

Bk Yard Industrial Estate

COOMBE ROAD

CULVERHAY

Valley Road

Culverhay Surgery

Court Orch

Meadow Gdns

Cotswold Gdns

Synwell

4

Bradley

BRADLEY ROAD

GLOUCESTER ST

Ellerncroft Rd

Bradley St

Isle Pl

Dryleaze

Westfields

Wotton Under Ege Town Council

BEAR ST

HAW ST

Market St

Long Street

The Studio Gallery

The Cloud

R Potters Pond

Orchard St

Clarence Rd

Jay's Mead Cemetery

Synwell La

Mount Pleasant

Knapp Road

Cherry Orchard

Cotswold Way

278

Bradley Green

Merlin Haven

Dryleaze

The Chipping Surgery

Symn Lane

Primary School

Venns Acre

Rosemary Terrace

Queens Way

Brown's Piece

Water Lane

The British School

Wortley

Fountain Cl

Hill Rd

Locombe Cr

Hentley Tor

5

B4058 NEW ROAD

WOTTON ROAD B4060

Katerine Lady Berkeley School

Wotton Sports Centre

Pitman Place

Mill Cl

Bearlands

Wotton Crescent

6

B4062

Vineyard Lane

Dye House Rd

Kingswood County Primary School

Abbey Gate

Hawpark Farm

Leys Farm

7

Kingswood

OLD RECTORY RD

Abbey St

Golden Lane

Braxton Dr

High St

Sunday School

PO

Walk

Mill Lane

Nind Lane

Wortley

Hillmill Lane

WICKWAR ROAD

Crow Meadow

Somerset

Hillesley Road

Cotswold Way

8

Nind Farm

Cemetery

Park Farm

297

G H J K L M **Aiderle**

M3
1 Beechwood Gv

H5 Upper Barns
1 Shepherd's Leaze
2 Shepherds Wk
3 Turnpike Av

L5
1 Cotswold Wy
2 Durn's Rd
3 Ludgate Hl
4 Manor La
5 Mitre Pitch

K4
1 Chipping Cl
2 Dyersbrook
3 High St
4 Tabernacle Pitch

J4
1 Chipping Gdns
2 Tapscott Ct

Rose Hill School

A4135

G **H** **J** 255 **K** **L** **M**

I

Bagpath

Newington
Bagpath

Lasborough **2**

Scrubbett's Lane

† **3**
Boxxxown Road

Scrubbett's
Farm

Lasborough
Park

A46

Goss **4**

Long
Covert

280

West Wood **5**

Monarch's Way

Boxwell **6**

Haymead

Boxwell

Lane

Road

7
Cross Roads
Lodge

Whitewater
Farm

Whitewater

Road

Stonehill
Wood

8
Boxwell Road

Leighterton
County
Primary School

PO

Tetbury Lane

Leighterton

Back Lane

Farm

The Street

The Meads

Cem

G **H** **J** 299 **K** **L** Monarch's Way **M**

Glentworth
Farm

Bath Road

G   H   J   257   Tetbury Upton   L   M   Lowfield Farm

L2
1 Webb Rd

L3
1 Newleaze Gdns
2 Romney Rd

M2
1 Woodward Cl

Lodge Farm

Upton Grove

I

2

Sir William Romn Sch

Hampton Street Industrial Estate

Hermit's Cave

B4014

Beverston

GL8

Macmillan Way

Longtree Cl
Upton Gdns
grove gdns
Berkeley Wy
Northands Wy
Conygar Road
Bartley Crt

Wheat Hill
Windsor
Chavenage Lane
Quail Mdw
Linfoot Road
Sherwood Road
Holder Cl

St Mary's Road
St Marys C of E Primary Sch
Magdalen Road
Field Ct

HAMPTON STREET
B4014
A433
LONG L

3

A4135

Charlton House

CHARLTON ROAD
NEW CHURCH ST
Romney Ho Surgery
Close Gdns
The Hlth Clinic
West Street
Cotton's Lane
Cutwell

Hotel
Long Street
Conn Gal
4
Hill
Tetbu
PO M 4
5
Fight Be

4

282

Hookshouse Lane

Oldown

Hookshouse Lane

The Berrells
Berrells Rd
Southfield

Old Qua Industria

5

Long Furlong Lane

BATH ROAD

6

Macmillan Way

Hookshouse

Elmestree House

Monarch's Way

Highgrove House

Close Farm

7

A433

Charlton Down

Doughton

8

Monarch's Way

G   H   J   301   K   L   M   BATH ROAD

A433

M4
1 Monarch's Wy
2 Old Brewery La

M3
1 Alexander Gdns
2 Chestnut Cl
3 Elizabeth Gdns
4 Five Trees Ct
5 London Rd
6 Malthouse Wk

G H J **259** K L M

I
2
3
4
284
5
6
7
8

Ashley

Manor
Farm

Monarch's Way

Fosse
Gate

Stadborough
Copse

Gloucestershire County
Wiltshire County

West
Crudwell

Chedglow

Idridge
arm

Crudwell Lane

Tetbury

Tuners Lane
The
Ridge
The
Oakney's
Lane
PO
The
Butts
The STREET
Ridge
Meadow
Gooselands

A429

Murco

Marsh
Farm

Bishoper
Farm

A   B   C   260   D   E   F

A5
1 Brookside

Woodland

Morgans
Tynings

I

Chelworth
Lawns

2

Laynes
Farm

The Grove

Chelworth

3

A429

4

Days
Ct
Hotel

Tetbury

Tuners Lane

The
Ridgeway

Crudwell C of E
Primary School

5

The
Dawney's
Lane

PO

Crudwell

Ea

The
Butts

oselands

THE STREET

Meadow

6

A429

Murcott

7

Rookery
Farm

8

A429

Hankerton Field
Farm

FollyField

A   B   C   D   E   **Hankerton**   F

Church La

el La

Poole
Keynes

G H J **261** K L M

I

2

Dean
Plantation

Dean
Farm

Lowfield
Farm

Oaksey Moor
Farm

3

Lower Moor
Farm

Wick
Road

The Street

Chapel
La
PO
Earls Cnr

The Street

Court
Farm

† **Oaksey**

Bendy
Bow

The Green

Challinger

4

Flintham
House

286

5

Park
Farm

Minety Lane

Stert
Farm

6

Lyngrove
Farm

7

Braydon Brook
Farm

Oaksey
Nursery

Oaksey
Road

Flisteridge
Wood

Flisteridge Road

**Upper
Minety**

†

8

St Leonard's

G H J K L M
PO

Cloatley
End

oatley

Hankerton Road

Somerford
Keynes

262

West

Thames
Path

Neigh Bridge
Country Park

Spine   Road

Thames Path

1

2

3

Clattinger
Farm

Swill Brook

4

Swillbrook
Farm

Pike
Corner

285

5

Cooles
Farm

6

Rigsby's
Lane

LC

7

Brandier

Flower's
Farm

Field
Farm

8

Lower Moor

Minety C of E
School

Sawyers
Hill

Chapel La

Sawyers
Ct

Silver

Oakleaze

SAMBOURNE
ROAD

1 grid square represents 500 metres

1 Milling Cl
2 Park End

1 Ashfield

SPINE ROAD (EAST)

B4696

263

G H J K L M

Clayhill Copse

North End

I

Cleveland Farm

Cox's

Hill

† **Ashton Keynes**

Kent End

2

Street

Back

The Leaze

Church Wk

PO

†

Richmond Ct

Fore Street

Fridays Ham Lane

Ashton Keynes C of E School

1

Eastfield

Kent End

Harris Rd

Dairy Farm

Gosditch

Thames Pl

2

Birch Cld

1

The Lords

Park Vw

Four Acre Cl

Thames Path

3

Derry Fields

Road

The Mdw

Derry

The

Thames Path

Manor Farm

River Thames or Isis

Waterhay Bridge

4

Waterhay

288

B4696

High Bridge

†

Archer's Farm

ASHTON

5

Glebe Farm

Derry Brook

Grove Farm

Cove House Farm

Swan Lane

Leigh

Leigh C of E School

†

Swan Lane

6

ROAD

Swan Lane

Hillside

MALMESBURY ROAD

B4040

B4696

†

7

B4040 MALMESBURY ROAD

Greenacres

8

G H J K L M

en Bridge
1 Hammonds

G3

G H J 265 K L M

1

Alex
Farm

Eysey

River Thames or Isis

2

Thames Path

Thames Path

A419(T)

Thames Path

3

Red
Lion
Lane

ington Ct

Thames Lane

Farm

Water Eaton
House

Thames Path

Lane

Manor
Orch

CALCUTT

CRICKLADE

ary School

SWINDON ROAD

Calcutt

A419(T)

4

ark

Spital

ST

ce
mon

5

Seven Bridges
Farm

Kingshill
Farm

Ox House
Farm

6

Farfield
Farm

Farfield Lane

Headlands
Farm

Wiltshire County
Swindon

Farfield Lane

7

Lower Widhill
Farm

A419(T)

River Ray

Chapel
Farm

8

Hayes Oak
Farm

more

G H J K L M

Hayes

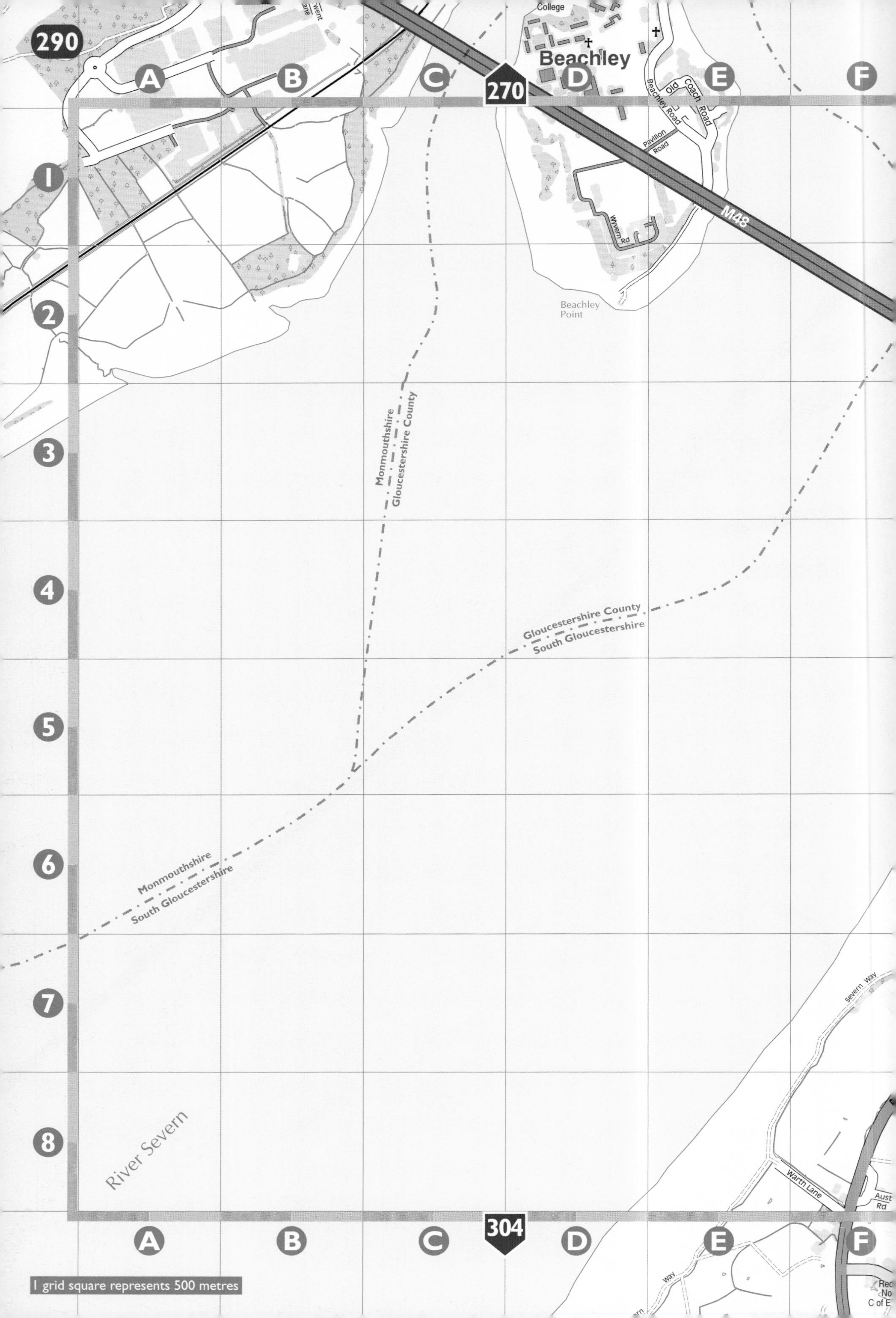

A B C **270** D E F

I

2

3

Monmouthshire
Gloucestershire County

4

Beachley
Point

Beachley

College

Old Coach Road

Beachley Road

Pavillion Road

Wyvern Rd

M48

Gloucestershire County
South Gloucestershire

5

6

Monmouthshire
South Gloucestershire

7

Severn Way

8

River Severn

Warth Lane

Aust Rd

Way

C of E

A B C **304** D E F

J4
1 Orchard Dr

G   H   J   271   K   L   M

I

Littleto
upon-

2

Severn Way

Rusholme   Jubilee Way

Jubilee Way

3

Severn Way

Cote
Farm

Severn View Service Area

Toll

Severn Way

M48

B4461

Manor
Farm

Junction 1

4

292

Sandy
Lane

The Rw

PH

A403

Old Passage

Aust

B4461

5

Severn Way

Red
Hill

REDHIL

Aust Ro

A403

6

Cake Pill
Gout

Old Splott Rhine

Ingst

7

Valley Farm

Ingst Road

Ingst

M48

8

Bilsham
Farm

Bilsham Lane

Rhine Ingst

rthwick

Mead   Lane

Holm

The Knapp

A

B

C

274

D

E

F

Morton

Buckover

Crossways

I

OLD GLOUCESTER ROAD

B4061

A38

Whitewall

Lane

Milbury Heath

Horseshoe Farm

Chapel La

Clay Lane

2

School

Hacket Lane

Cumbria Cl

Morton Way

Green La

Crossways Road

Cleveland Cl

Cheviot Dr

Pentland Av

The Hacket

Hope Farm

Jubilee Dr

Elizabeth Cl

Chiltern Pk

Hacket Lane

Hacket Hill

Curtisheath Road

3

Main

Morton Way

Corbets

Waterford

4

Avon Way

Grovesend Road

Grovesend

M5

5

Abbey Lane

Itchington Road

Tytherington Road

New Road

Stow Hill Road

Stowell Hill Road

Baden Hill Road

6

Itchington Road

The Castle

The Orch

West Street

Street

PO

Studcot Lane

Duck

The Nurserie

Tytherington

7

M5

Jubilee Way

Jubilee Way

Itchington Road

Itchington Road

Owlsnest Farm

8

Field Lane

Moorleaze

A

B

C

308

D

E

F

Conygre Farm

Itchington

Lower Farm

1 grid square represents 500 metres

G H J 275 B'stone L M

I

B4058

Abbotside
Farm

Sodam
Mill

PO

Talbot's
End

Cromhall Lane

Church Lane

Townwell

St Andrews C of E
VC Primary School

BRISTOL ROAD

Priest
Wood

Rectory Lane

Cromhall

2

The Burtons

Farleigh Lane

The
Green

Heath
End

3

Jubilee Lane

Cromhall
Common

4

Cowship Lane

296

Cowship
Farm

BRISTOL

Stidcot

5

Cowship Lane

ROAD

Ashworthy Farm

Rag

6

Stidcote Lane

Lane

Barber's Court
Farm

BAGSTONE ROAD

7

B4058

Oldclose
Farm

Bagstone

8

Wixoldbury
Farm

Hall
End

G H J 309 K L M

BAGSTONE ROAD

Limekiln Rd

Jubilee Way

M3
1 St Giles Barton
2 Vicarage La

G H J 277 K L M

Nind Farm

Cemetery

Alderle

Rose Hill School

1

Upper Barns Farm

2

Folly Farm

Alderley Road

New

3

Haroldsfield Farm

Lower Witheymore Farm

Farmcote

Kingswood Road

Killcott Road

Day House Lane

Day House Farm

2

Hillesley

High Street

Chapel Lane

1

Primary Sch

Mounteney's Farm

Gloucestershire County

South Gloucestershire

Assley Common

4

298

Splatt's

5

Inglestone Farm

South Moon Ridings

Lovetts Wood Farm

Lance Coppice

Oxleaze Farm

Hawkesbury Road

6

Lower Woods Lodge

Inglestone Common

7

Lower Wetmoor

Littley Wood

Hawkesbury Knott

8

Newhouse Farm

Burnt Wood

Hawkesbury Common

G H J 311 K L M Hawkesbury

G H J **279** K L M

Stonehill
Wood

Leighterton
County
Primary School

PO

Tetbury Lane

The Meads

Cem

Monarch's Way

Glentworth
Farm

Back

Farm

The Street

I

Bath Rd

A46

Bath Road

2

Sadlenwood
Manor

3

Waste
Barn

A46

4

Park
Wood

300

5

**Oldbury on
the Hill**

6

Woodhayes
House

A433

Creephole

7

Gloucestershire Co
Wilts

Didmarton

Bertha's Fld

St Arild's
Rd

PH

Chapel Wk

THE STREET

A433

ch Lane

8

Folly Farm

A433

G H J **313** K L M

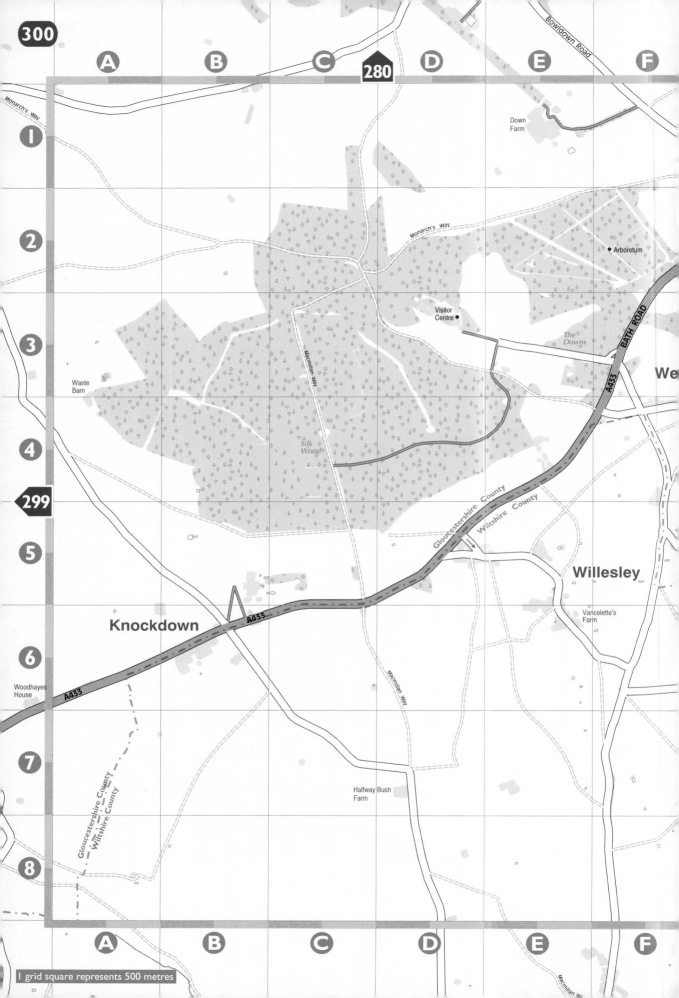

G H J K L M

BATH ROAD 281

A433

Monarch's Way

Monarch's Way

Hotel

Bowldown Road

Home Farm

Tanner's

Westonbirt School

Eagle Lodge

Whitehouse Lane

The Street

Whitehouse Lane

Hillcourt

Pond Farm

Golf Course

Hedgeditch Lane

PO

SH
Mc

302

Elmleaze Barn

Cranmore Farm

Gloucestershire County
Wiltshire County

Church Farm

Pinkney Court

HILL

Easton Grey House

B4040

Easton Grey

BRANSDOWN

River Avon (Sherston

kney G H J K L M

1
2
3
4
5
6
7
8

A B C D E F

282

I

Shipton Wood

Estcourt House

B4014

Bell Farm

Eagle Lodge

Manor Farm

2

Whitenouse Lane

River Avon (Tetbury Branch)

The Street

3

Hodges Farm

Fosse Tilery Farm

✝

Shipton Moyne

PO

Southside

Gloucestershire County

Wiltshire County

Church Lane ✝

4

Brokenborough

301

Fosse Farm

5

Cranmore Farm

cestershire County
Wiltsh...ounty

6

Boakley Farm

B4040

7

B4040

B4040

B4040

Twatley Manor Farm

8

Hyam Wood

Hyam Farm

River Avon (Sherston Branch)

A B C D E F

1 grid square represents 500 metres

River Severn

A   B   C   **290**   D   E   F

Warth Lane

Aust Rd

Red Nor C of E S

1
2
3
4
5
6
7
8

Way

Severn

Worthy Farms

SEVERN ROAD

M4

New Passage

Junction 22

REDWICK

Redwick Rd

Redwick Rd

M4

Shaft Road

Green Lane

B4064

Redwick

ROAD B4064

Wick Rd

SEVERN ROAD B4064

B4055

Pilr

Beach Road

Osborne Rd

BEACH AVENUE

Road

Little Green Lane

Whitehouse Rd

Keen's

The Vicarage Rd

Redwick Gdns

7

The Glebe

PO

CROSS HANDS ROAD

MAR

Covet

Gorse Cover Rd

Wainbridge Crs

Cranmoor Gn

Severn Wy

Gorse

Church Road

PO

Church Road

Road

Severn Beach CP School

Severn Beach

Whitehouse Farm

M49

A403

South Gloucestersh Council

Beach

Station Road

PO

Riverside Park

2

Severn Beach Stn

Albert Rd

Victoria Crs

Appleton

Denny Isle Dr

Prospect Rd

Lane

Abbott Rd

Severnwood Gdns

SEVERN ROAD

A403

Ableton

Lane

Dyer's Common

SEVERN ROAD

A403

Central

Avenue

Avlon Works

Farm Lane

South Gloucester City of Bris

314

A   B   C   D   E   F

Severnside Works

1 grid square represents 500 metres

G H J 297 K L M

Hawkesbury

1

2

3

4

312

5

6

7

8

Newhouse
Farm

Hawke
Common

Burnt
Wood

nybridge
ood

Haskin's
Farm

Cat
Cottage

Lower Chalkley
Farm

Upper Chalkley
Farm

Wood

Lane

King Lane

orwood
iding

Vinney Lane

Springfield
Farm

Vinney Lane

Bix
Farm

Tylers Green
Farm

Mapleridge

King Lane

Horton
Bushes

Bushes
Lane

Mapleridge Lane

Horton Road

Horton Hill

Horton

Horton Primary
School

Highfield Lane

Hall Lane

Totteroak

Horton Road

Horton Court (NT)

Widdenhill
Farm

Horton Hill

Crowshall Barn
Farm

Sodbury
Common

tle
dbury End

Monarch's Way

New Tyning Lane

Monarch's Way

Great House
Farm

Little Sodbury

G H J 321 K L M

Harwoodgate
Farm

Portway Lane

G H J 299 K L M

I

Folly Farm

A433

Hinnegar

Bullpark
Wood

PO

Church La

2
✝ **Sopworth**

3

Badminton
Down

4

Luckley
Farm

South Gloucestershire
Wiltshire County

Wick
Farm

5

North End
Farm

Little
Badminton

Cherry
Orchard

Cherry Orchard Lane

Cherry Orchard Lane

6
Primary
School

✝ Church La

Well Lane

Hermit's
Cell

Allengrove
Farm

Allengrove Lane

Luckington
7

Badminton
Park

• Badminton
Show Jumping
Circuit

Allengrove Lane

OL ROAD

8

• Giant's Cave

G
Shop La

Kennel La

PO

High Street

Haye's

✝ H

Great
Badminton

J 323 K L M

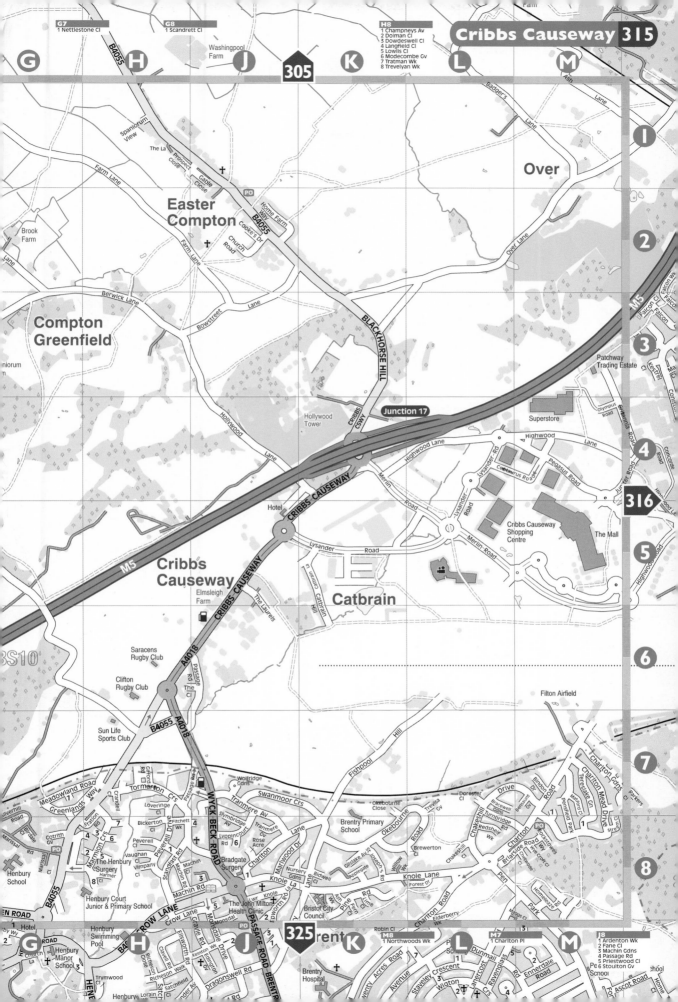

B4
1 Common Rd
2 Crossley Cl

C3
1 Thornhayes Cl

B3
1 Prospect La

A7
1 Cairn Gdns
2 Prospect Cl

A6
1 Burghley Ct

A4
1 Dawley Cl

A · B · C · D · E · F

308

BRIST OAD

Algars Manor

Frome Valley Walkway

1

Cog Mill Farm

Perrinpit Farm

2

North Corner

BRISTOL ROAD

Perrinpit Road

Conifer Cl

Church Road

Mill Lane

Frampton End Rd

3

Robel Av
Western Av
Robel Road
School
Frampton Cotterell C of E School
Stanford Close
Camberley Dr
Court

Rectory Rd
Beaufort Rd
Foxe Rd
Rectory Road
Brookside Dr
Meadow Rd
Bridge Wy
Church Cl
Church Road

Park Row
Rectory Rd
Clyde Rd
Doctors Surg

St Peter's Crs
South View
Rockside Gardens

Crossdale Rd
Upr Stone Cl
Stone Cl

PO

Highcroft Junior School

Frampton En

4

York Gdns
Mount Cl
Rylestone Close
Road

Park Lane
Sunnyside
Woodend
Footes La
Brockridge La
Rivercroft Road

Infant School

Meadow View
Blademoor Cl
Watermore Cl

The Cswy
Rushton Av
Wavleaze

Silverhill School

B4058

Bourne Cl
Watley's
Carrolls Cl
Star Barn Rd
Lewton
End
North Road
Manor La
Beaver Cl
Factory Rd
The Gully

Harris Barton
Frome Vw
Park La
Wayside Ct

West Rdg
Upr Chapel La
Lower Chapel La
Landtmann Cl

Chapel La
Hillside

The Rdg
Main Rd
Boundary Rd
Ridgeway
Heathcote Rd

Alexandra Dr

A432
Rose Oak La
Barcombe

5

317

HIGH STREET

St Michael's

Nicholls
Park Avenue
Sallys Wy
Masons Wy
Saint Francis Drive

Medway Dr
Heather Av
Kelbra Cl

Lower Bell
Park Av

Newlands Av
Oldlands Av

South Vw
South Cl

Doctors Surg Vw

Coalpit

Winterbourne

Elm Park School
Friary Grange Park
Abbeydale
St Francis Dr

Parkside Av
Ridings High School

Cloisters Road

Beesmoor Rd
St Saviours Rise
The Ridings
Manor Cl
The Cl Rd
Bell

Manor C of E School

6

M

PO

Flaxpits
Green Dragon Rd
Bradley Av
Bradford Cl

Heath Orchard Cl
Linden Cl
Burrows La
Hicks Lane
Common Road

Hicks Common

Frome Vale

River Frome
Frome Valley Walkway

Nightingale close

Park Lane

Rathbone Close

Henfield Road

Ram Hill

Harcombe Road
Mount Crs
Cedar Wy
Barton Cl
Crossman Av
Matford Cl
Pendock Rd
Avenue
Frome Wy
Deacon Cl

Doctors Surgery

A432

Serridge House

7

Dragon Road
Marsh La
Sandstone Rise
Colston Close
Station Road
Rose La
Harcombe Hill
Quarry La
Down Road

Frome Valley Walkway

Winterbourne Down

Badminton Road
Huckford La
Park La

Ruffet Road

Henfield Road

Ram Hill

Camp View
Church Road
PO
Frome Gln
Stone Lane
The Dingle

Down Road

Kendleshire

Hollows

Cooks Lane

8

orner

Norre

Bury Hill

Cuckoo

Badminton Road

Coalsack Lane

M4

A · B · C · D · E · F

328

C4
1 Nightingale La

D3
1 Barley Cl
2 Downfield Dr
3 Winchcombe Rd

D4
1 The Spinney

E4
1 Gladstone La
2 Hillside La

E5
1 Church La
2 Willow Wy

F4
1 Fire Engine La
2 Larkfield
3 Oakleaze
4 Orchard Rd
5 Rose Oak Dr
6 Rose Oak Gdns

1 grid square represents 500 metres

322

A **B** Gricks Farm **C** **D** 312 **E** **F**

I

Beech Copse

Castle Barn Tyning The
Lime Av Roach's Lane

2

3 Lyegrove House Lyegrove Farm Lime Avenue Old Down Road

4

321 040 Newhouse Farm B4040

5 Oakes

6 Lane

7 Old Warren
Sheepcot Barn Parks Farm

8

A **B** **C** 332 **D** **E** **F**

I grid square represents 500 metres

G H J `313` K L M

I

2

3

4

5

6

7

8

Great
Badminton

shop La

Kennel Drive

PO

High Street

Hayes La

School La

The Limes

Station Road

Cape
Farm

B4040

Hebden
Farm

Macmillan Way

Station-Approach
Industrial Estate

B4040

Wiltshire County
South Gloucestershire

Alderton Road

B4040

Acton Turville

B4039

Chapel La

Hollybush Cl

Trinity
C of E
School

Macmillan Way

Police
Station

BURTON ROAD

Road

ormarton

Road

Viner's La

B4039

Littleton Drew

Marsh Lane

M4

South Gloucestershire

Wiltshire County

M4

B4039

B4039

M4

Top Down Way

PH

Burton

Horsedown

The
Meads

Nettleton Road

Edgecorner Lane

Macmillan Way

G H J `333` K L M

Westfield
Farm

G H J 321 K L A46 ROAD BATH M

Sands Court

Old Farm

PH
Hotel

Dodington Ash

B4465

1 rm

Laddown Lane

Springs Farm

Junction 18

2 A4

Marshfield

Lower Lapdown Farm

Cotswold Way

3

West Littleton Down

4

A46(T)

332

5

Field Lane

Lane

Wallsend

6

Dunsdown Lane

Dyrham Park (NT)

7

Butts Lane

Camp Lane

West Littleton

8

nds Hill

A46(T)

332

Ⓐ   Ⓑ   Ⓒ   **322**   Ⓓ   Ⓔ   Ⓕ

Ⓘ Tormarton

Lapdown Lane

②
M4
Marshfield Road

South Gloucestershire
Wiltshire County

Lower Lapdown
Farm

Kingto
Farm

③

Shire Hill

West ⸻n
Down

④   Down
Farm

331

⑤   Rownham
Farm

Broadmead Brook

Broadmead Brook

⑥   Tormarton Road   Shirehill
Farm

⑦   Harcombe
Farm

⑧   Downthorns
Farm

West Little⸻
Road   ⸻shmead Lane

Ⓐ   Ⓑ   Ⓒ   **342**   Ⓓ   Ⓔ   Ⓕ

Martor
Industrial
Est
Culverslade

Down Road

⸻th Gloucester⸻
⸻e Wiltshire County

1 grid square represents 500 metres

G　H　J　323　K　L　M

1

Westfield
Farm

2

Nettleton
Green　PO

Lugbury
Farm

The Meads

Fleton Road

Corner Lane

Macmillan Way

3

†

Wood Lane

Nettleton
Shrub

Holloway Hill

Macmillan Way

4

†

Drifton　Hill

West
Kington

†

Smith Street

Broadmead Brook

5

West Kington
Wick

6

7

Fosse
Farm

Mountain
Bower

8

†

G　H　J　343　K　L　M

North Wraxall

Old　Coach　Road

A420

†

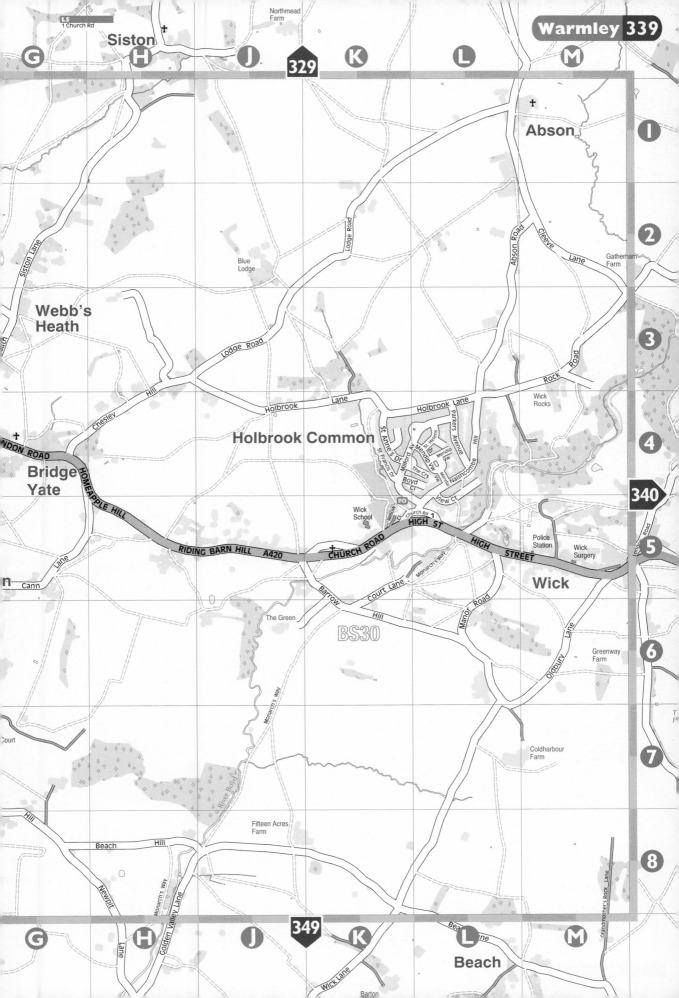

340

A   B   C   330   D   E   F

Doynton   339

350

Lower Hamswell

I grid square represents 500 metres

G   H   J   **331**   K   L   M

West
Littleto

West Litt

I Road

Castle

1

Springs
Farm

Middledown
House

Castle
Farm

2

Westend Town
Farm

Bond's Lane

Middledown Road

Bond's
Lane

Gorse Lane

3

A46(T)

Oldfield
Farm

Cotswold Way

A420

4

Pennsylvania

342

5

Beek's Lane

**The
Folly**

Hyde's Lane

**Cold
Ashton**

Limestone Link

6

Slough Lane

A46(T)

Limestone Link

7

Nimlet

Henley
Tyning
Farm

Leigh Lane

Beek's
Farm

8

Monkswood
Reservoir

Beek's Lane

Limestone Link

Hall Lane

St Catherines End
House

Lane

G   H   J   **351**   K   L   M

G H J K L M

333

H5
1 Holly Dr

J6
1 Ash Rd
2 Cherry Rd
3 Rowan Cl

J8
1 Green La
2 Nursery Rd

I

2

3

4

5

6

7

8

North Wraxall

Upper
Wraxall

A420

The
Shoe

A420

Old   Coach   Road

Bury Camp

Doncombe Hill

Pinewood
Way

Doncombe Lane

Walnut Drive
Fir Road
Linden
Close

Larch Road

Cypress
Walk

Laurel Drive

Oak   Road

Palm Rd

Lime Close

Poplar

Elm Road

Hazel
Way

3

2

1

Way

PO

Barracks

Redwood   Way

Beech Rd

Lucknam
Park

Hotel

Woodlea

Hillcrest
Fairview

Valley
Way

Thickwood   Lane

Thickwood

Eastrip

Doncombe Lane

Airfield

Colerne C of E
Primary School

Totts La

Forester Green

Quarry   Lane

Martins Croft

Trimnells

Colerne

Eastrip   Lane

Colerne Rugby
Football
Club

The Firs
Surgery

Round Barrow
Close

Causeway

Silver   Street

High St

Rockfield

2

3

1

2

Cleeves Av

Chapel
Close

Box
View

Market   Pl

Tutton

Vicarage

Chapel

The Bank

Watergates

PO

353

G H J K L M

Washmeres

Bath

B3128

xtor Grammar
School

Pill
Grove

CLARKEN

D1
1 Ridgeview
2 Westward Gdns

C2
1 Providence Vw

B3
1 Paulman Gdns

B5128

B2
1 Birdwell La
2 Lovelinch Gdns

ASHTON ROAD

A   **B**   **C**   **334**   **D**   **E**   **F**

A370

Church
La

I

Golf
Course

Folleigh
Cl

Folleigh Dr

Lodge
Dr

Glebe
Cl

Long Ashton Road

Parsonage
Rd

Providence Lane

Monarch's Way

Heath Ridge

Short Lane

Highlands Rd

Kempe's
Cl

Estrune Wk

Folleigh
Lane

North
Leaze

Primary
School

Cattley
Cl

Hillside
Rd

Parsonage
Rd

Glebe Rd

Warren Lane

Cherry
Rd

Orchard
Road

Keedwell Hl

Cedar Cl

Willow

Keith's La

Ridgeway

Chestnut Rd

**LONG
ASHTON**

Long Ashton Road

Theynes Croft

CV

Ryecroft
Cl

Brook

2

Fenswood
Md

Fenswood
Rd

Ravens Cross Road

Surgery

Weston Road

PO

Birdwell Rd

Yeomeads

Lampton

Unbrook

Well Cl

Lyveston Vw

Coprord La

Warren La

Bradville Gdns

Raymore Rd

Howls La

Hollis Cl

Birdwell Primary
School

Fenshurst Gdns

1

Yanley La

Yanley

3

Road

A370

Wildcountry Lane

Yanley Lane

4

dwood
rm

A370

A370

Monarch's Way

Barrow
Hospital

Yanley Lane

BRIDGWATER ROAD

5

Barrow
Wood

Yanleigh
Cl

BS41

Lane

6

**Barrow
Gurney**

Wildcountry Lane

Colliter's Brook

hool La

PO

STREET

Hern Lane

Reservoir

7

Barns
Close

B3130

Dundry Lane

Monarch's Wy

Hobbs Lane

Reservoir

Barrow
Common

Monarch's Way

Highridge Road

Highri

Lane

8

A38

Reservoir

Dundry Lane

Ham Lane

Highridge Road

Church Road

ATER ROAD

A

Gle
Farm

B3130

B   **C**   **D**   **E**   **F**

Lane

Caste
Farm

Dundry
Primary
School

PO

The
Md

Castle

Dundry

1 grid square represents 500 metres

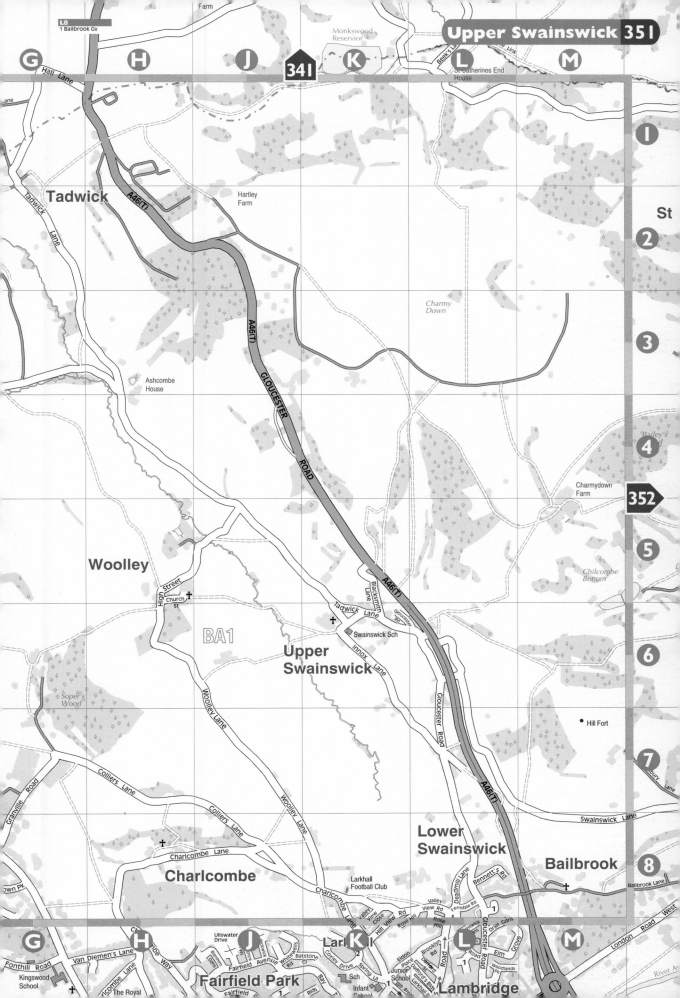

L8
1 Bailbrook Gv

G   H   J   341   K   L   M

I

St

2

3

Tadwick

A46(T)

Hartley
Farm

Monkswood
Reservoir

Beek's La

St Catherines End
House

Charmy
Down

4

352

5

Ashcombe
House

GLOUCESTER ROAD

A46(T)

Charmydown
Farm

Chilcombe
Bottom

Woolley

High Street

Church
St

BA1

Blacksmith Lane

Tadwick Lane

Innox Lane

Swainswick Sch

Gloucester Rd

Upper
Swainswick

6

Soper's
Wood

Woolley Lane

Gloucester Road

Hill Fort

7

Colliers Lane

Colliers Lane

Woolley Rd

Granville Road

Fonthill Road

Kingswood
School

Charlcombe Lane

Charlcombe

Lower
Swainswick

Swainswick Lane

A46(T)

Bailbrook

Bailbrook Lane

8

Van Diemen's Lane

Uliswater
Drive

Fairfield Avenue

Charlcombe Lane

Larkhall
Football Club

Valley
View Close

Hill View Rd

Rose Hill

Deadmill Lane

Bennett's Rd

Brooklyn Rd

Gloucester Road

Oriel Gdns

Elm Grove

Woodlands

London Road West

River Av

The Royal

Fairfield Park

Fairfield

Brookleaze

Winifred's

Batstone Cl

Coxley Drive

Spring La

Bay

Bladud's Bldgs

Eldon Place

Dafford's Bldgs

Larkhall

Knox's

Junior
School

Infant
School

Lambridge

G   H   J   Lark   K   L   M

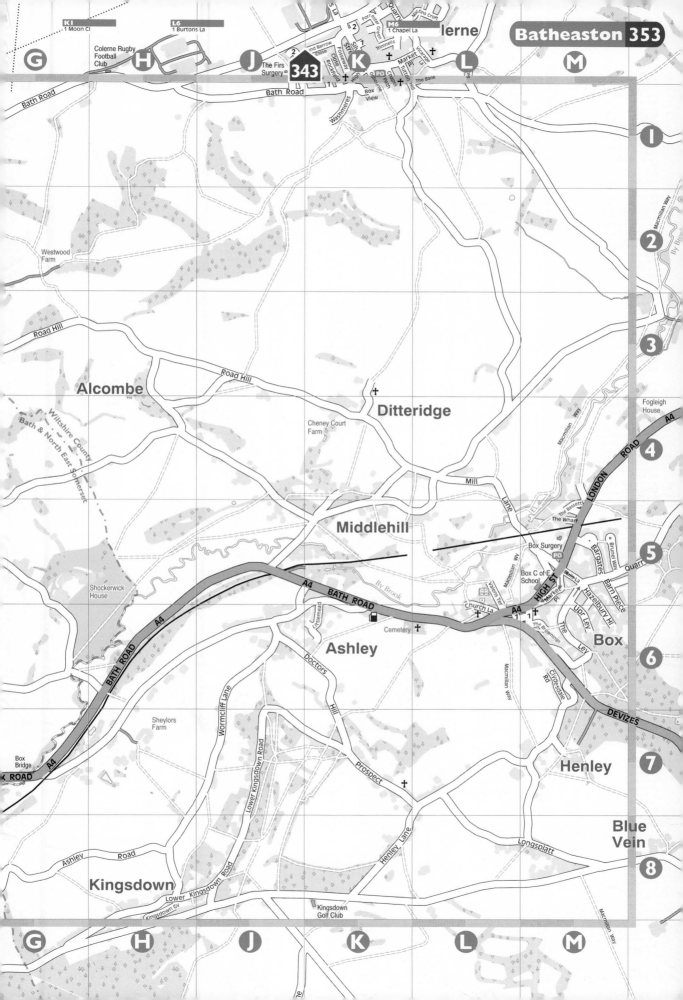

K1 1 Moon Cl
L6 1 Burtons La

G
Colerne Rugby
Football
Club
H
The Firs
Surgery
J
343
Bath Road
Bath Road
Box
View
lerne
Forester Green
Quarr
Martins Croft
Barrow Close
M6 1 Chapel La
Trinmells
Fosse Way
Rochfield
Wasmere
Market Pl
K
Chapel
PO
High St
Box Path
Tutton Hill
Vicarage La
L
The Bank
M

I

2
Macmillan Way

Westwood
Farm

3

Road Hill

Alcombe

Road Hill

Ditteridge

Cheney Court
Farm

Fogleigh
House

A4

LONDON ROAD

4

Mill Lane

Middlehill

The Bassetts
The Wharf

Box Surgery
PO

Brunel Way

Bargates

5

Shockerwick
House

A4

BATH ROAD

By Brook

Macmillan Way

Box C of E
School

HIGH ST

Market Pl

Barn Piece

Quarr

Hazelbury Hl

Upr Ley

Barn
Piece

Littlemead

Cemetery

Valens Ter

Church La

A4

The Brownings

The Ley

Box

6

Ashley

Doctors Hill

Macmillan Way

Clydesdale Rd

DEVIZES

7

Sheylors
Farm

BATH ROAD

A4

Box
Bridge

K ROAD

Wormcliff Lane

Lower Kingsdown Road

Prospect

Henley Lane

Henley

Blue
Vein

Longsplatt

8

Kingsdown

Ashley Road

Lower Kingsdown Road

Kingsdown Gv

Kingsdown
Golf Club

Macmillan Way

G
H
J
K
L
M

Place	Page	Grid
Abbeydale	136	E7
Abbots Leigh	334	C3
Abenhall	130	E4
Ablington	193	H7
Abson	339	M1
Acton Turville	323	G5
Adlestrop	103	M1
Alcombe	353	G3
Alderley	298	A1
Alderton	51	L4
Alderton Fields	51	L6
Aldsworth	194	F2
Alkerton	206	A4
Allaston	201	K5
Almondsbury	306	E7
Alstone	51	G6
Alstone	115	J1
Alveston	293	H6
Alveston Down	292	F6
Alvington	224	C5
Amberley	232	E4
Ampney Crucis	239	M2
Ampney St Mary	240	D2
Ampney St Peter	240	C4
Andoversford	118	D7
Andrews Corner	198	F5
Anthony's Cross	86	C7
Apperley	69	H6
Arle	93	J7
Arlebrook	183	H6
Arlingham	179	L1
Arlington	217	H1
Arno's Vale	336	D7
Ashchurch	49	H4
Ashleworth	89	J3
Ashley	283	J1
Ashley	353	K6
Ashley Down	326	B7
Ashmead Green	229	M7
Ashton Gate	335	H7
Ashton Keynes	287	G2
Ashton under Hill	29	H3
Ashton Vale	345	H1
Aston Crews	84	E8
Aston Cross	49	L3
Aston Ingham	85	H7
Aston Magna	36	A7
Aston on Carrant	49	M1
Aston Somerville	30	F2
Aston Subedge	12	C3
Aust	291	K5
Avening	257	L3
Avening Green	276	A3
Awkley	305	M3
Awre	179	L6
Aylburton	224	F3
Aylburton Common	224	D2
Aylton	18	B3
Aylworth	121	H2
Aztec West	316	C1
Badgeworth	114	D8
Badsey	10	A1
Bagendon	214	A1
Bagpath	232	E1
Bagpath	279	H1
Bagstone	295	H7
Bailbrook	351	M8
Baker's Hill	151	L8
Ball's Green	233	H7
Bamfurlong	114	A3
Barcheston	16	C7
Barnsley	216	B4
Barnwood	137	G2
Barrow	91	L5
Barrow Common	344	D1
Barrow Gurney	344	A6
Barton	5	J8
Barton	98	F3
Barton End	256	F4
Barton Hill	336	E5
Barton-on-the-Heath	60	B5
The Batch	338	D6
Batheaston	352	F1
Batsford	57	M3
Battledown	3	L7
Battlescombe	210	F2
Baunton	214	C5
Beach	349	L1
Beachley	270	D8
Beavan's Hill	84	F5
Beckford	29	G7
Bedminster	335	K8
Bedminster Down	345	K3
The Beeches	238	F2
Beechpike	188	D2
Bencombe	254	E3
Bengrove	50	E5
Benhall	115	G3
Bentham	138	F6
Berkeley	227	H8
Berkeley Heath	227	J8
Berkeley Road	228	B6
Berrow	44	E2
Berry Hill	151	J5
Berwick	314	F5
Beverston	281	G3
Bevington	250	A5
Bibstone	275	K8
Bibury	217	L1
Bilson Green	153	M2
Birdlip	163	H2
Birdwood	133	G3
Birtsmorton	23	G7
Birts Street	22	C6
Bishop's Cleeve	71	M8
Bishop's Norton	90	D5
Bishopston	325	M7
Bishopsworth	345	H6
Bisley	210	D2
Bitton	349	H3
Blackhorse	328	B4
Blaisdon	131	L5
Blaise Hamlet	324	F1
Blakeney	202	E1
Bledington	125	L2
Blockley	34	F8
Blue Vein	353	M8
Boddington	92	A4
Bollow	157	H3
Bondend	137	J8
Botloe's Green	64	C6
Boughspring	246	E4
Bould	125	L5
Boulsdon	86	A5
Bournes Green	210	D6
Bournside	115	J4
Bournstream	277	H1
Bourton-on-the-Hill	57	K5
Bourton-on-the-Water	122	F5
Bowbridge	208	F6
Bower Ashton	334	F7
Bowling Green	238	D1
Box	233	G6
Box	353	M6
Boxbush	106	F5
Boxbush	157	H4
Boxwell	279	J6
Bradley	277	H3
Bradley Green	277	H4
Bradley Stoke	317	G3
Bradlow	20	B1
Brain's Green	178	D6
Brand Green	64	F6
Breadstone	227	M5
Bread Street	208	B2
Bream	200	C3
Bream's Meend	200	B2
Bredon	27	G5
Bredon's Hardwick	26	E8
Bredon's Norton	27	J1
Brentry	325	K1
Bridge End	45	H7
Bridgend	207	G5
Bridge Yate	339	G4
Brierley	129	G8
Brimpsfield	163	L5
Brimps Hill	130	F7
Brimscombe	233	H1
Brislington	337	G8
Bristol	7	J5
Britain Bottom	312	D2
Broad Campden	34	F3
Broad Marston	8	B2
Broad Moor	130	A8
Broadoak	155	L4
Broadrock	246	D6
Broadway	32	E3
Broadwell	80	E7
Broadwell	152	A8
Brockham End	350	A3
Brockhampton	93	L2
Brockhampton	118	F2
Brockhollands	200	D4
Brockweir	222	C4
Brockworth	137	L6
Brokenborough	302	E4
Bromley Heath	327	L1
Bromsberrow	43	G2
Bromsberrow Heath	42	E5
Brookend	223	M7
Brookend	227	G2
Brookthorpe	160	A6
Broomhill	327	G5
Broom Hill	337	J7
Broom's Green	42	A5
Broughton Poggs	221	K7
Brown's End	43	H2
Browns Hill	233	M1
Bubblewell	233	J6
Bubb's Hill	164	D4
Buckbury	46	D2
Buckland	32	C6
Buckover	294	C1
Bulley	109	L7
Bullo	179	H3
Bulwark	270	A6
Burleigh	233	G4
Burmington	38	C2
Burnt Ash	233	M4
Burton	323	K8
Bury End	32	F4
Buscot	269	J3
Bushley	47	K2
Bushley Green	47	G1
Bussage	209	M7
Butterrow	208	F7
Cadbury Heath	338	C6
Cainscross	208	B4
Calcot	192	E2
Calcott's Green	134	C5
Calcutt	289	J4
Calmsden	191	H5
Cam	229	H7
Cambridge	205	J7
Camer's Green	22	B8
The Camp	186	E4
Cannop	152	D7
Carterspiece	152	A2
Cashes Green	207	M3
Cassey Compton	143	G8
Castle Eaton	266	D7
Castlemorton	22	F4
Castletump	64	A4
Catbrain	315	K5
Caudle Green	187	L2
Cerney Wick	264	B7
Chaceley	68	F1
Chaceley Hole	68	C1
Chaceley Stock	69	G3
Chalford	234	A1
Chandler's Cross	22	B2
Chapel Hill	224	E3
Charfield	276	B6
Charfield Green	276	D6
Charfield Hill	276	B6
Chargrove	115	H7
Charingworth	14	C7
Charlcombe	351	H8
Charlton Abbots	96	D6
Charlton Kings	116	E5
Charlton Park	116	B4
Chase End Street	21	L8
Chase Hill	296	F5
Chastleton	81	L3
Chavenage Green	257	G7
Chaxhill	157	H2
Chedglow	283	K4
Chedworth	167	J6
Chedworth Laines	166	F7
Cheltenham	2	E5
Chelworth	284	E2
Chelworth Lower Green	288	B5
Chelworth Upper Green	288	D5
Cherington	39	H5
Cherington	258	D1
Chesterton	238	A5
Childswickham	32	B1
Chipmans Platt	206	B2
Chipping Campden	12	D7
Chipping Sodbury	320	F2
Christchurch	151	J5
Churcham	133	M2
Church Down	113	M5
Churchdown	114	A7
Church End	25	M6
Church End	205	G1
Churchend	206	C3
Churchend	276	B8
Churchill	105	H6
Church Westcote	125	G5
Cinderford	154	B5
Cirencester	238	E4
Clapton-on-the-Hill	147	H2
Claydon	49	J8
Clay Hill	337	H1
Claypits	205	M2
Clearwell	175	H7
Cleeve	156	C5
Cleeve Hill	95	H1
Clements End	199	M1
Clencher's Mill	20	E8
Clifford's Mesne	107	L1
Clifton	335	H3
Coaley	230	A3
Coaley Peak	230	D5
Coalpit Heath	318	F5
Coalway	176	A2
Coates	236	E5
Cobb's Cross	43	L4
Coberley	140	B7
Cockleford	164	C2
Codrington	330	C1
Cold Ashton	341	J5
Cold Aston	121	L7
Colt's Green	321	G3
Compton Abdale	143	L5
Compton Green	64	F5
Compton Greenfield	315	G3
Conderton	28	D4
Condicote	78	E5
Coney Hill	136	E4
Conham	337	J6
Coombe	277	M3
Coombe Dingle	324	E3
Coombegreen Common	22	A5
Coomb's End	321	J5
Cornwell	82	D8
Corse	66	D5
Corse Lawn	68	A1
Cotham	335	L2
Cotswold Community	262	F7
Cowhill	272	C8
Cowhorn Hill	338	E7
Cowley	164	C1
Cranham	162	B5
Cress Green	206	C5
Crews Hill	106	E2
Crew's Hole	337	H4
Cribbs Causeway	315	H5
Cricklade	289	G4
Crocker's Ash	126	C5
Cromhall	295	J2
Cromhall Common	295	J4
Crooked End	129	H3
Cross Hill	246	E6
Crossways	151	G8
Crossways	294	B1
Crudwell	284	A5
Culkerton	259	J6
Cutsdean	76	D2
Daglingworth	213	J4
Damery	276	A2
Daneway	211	K8
Darlingscott	15	H2
Daylesford	103	M3
Deerhurst	69	J3
Deerhurst Walton	69	L6
Derry Fields	287	G3
Didbrook	53	K8
Didmarton	299	J7
Ditteridge	353	K4
Dixton	73	G2
Dodington	321	G6
Donnington	42	A3
Donnington	79	M6
Dorn	58	D7
Doughton	281	K8
Down Ampney	265	G2
Downend	256	B2
Downend	327	M4
Down Hatherley	113	G1
Doynton	340	D2
Draycott	35	L7
Draycott	229	H3
Driffield	240	A7
Druggers End	22	E2
Drybrook	129	M4
Duckhole	273	L5
Dudbridge	208	A5
Dumbleton	30	B6
Dunfield	266	C3
Dunkirk	312	D3
Duntisbourne Abbots	188	D6
Duntisbourne Leer	188	D8
Duntisbourne Rouse	212	F2
Dursley	253	K1
Dursley Cross	107	J6
Dyer's Common	304	E8
Dymock	41	K8
Dyrham	330	E7
Earthcott Green	308	B4
Eastcombe	210	A6
Eastcourt	284	F5
East Dean	106	A5
East End	242	F5
East End	342	D3
Easter Compton	315	H2
Eastfield	325	K4
Eastington	170	A4
Eastington	206	B3
Eastleach Martin	220	L1
Eastleach Turville	220	A4
Eastnor	20	E4
Easton	336	E2
Easton Grey	301	L7
Eastrip	343	M7
Eastville	326	E8
The Eaves	200	E2
Ebley	207	L5
Ebrington	13	L6
Edge	184	D3
Edge End	152	A4
Edgeworth	211	M2
Elberton	292	C6
Elcombe	254	C4
Eldersfield	45	G8
Elkstone	164	E5
Ellwood	176	A6
Elmbridge	112	F8
Elmore	134	D8
Elmore Back	134	A5
Elmstone Hardwicke	93	G2
Elton	155	L2
Emerson's Green	328	E5
Engine Common	309	K6
English Bicknor	127	K8
Epney	157	L8
Etloe	202	E3
Evenlode	81	G5
Ewen	261	M4
Fairfields	43	H6
Fairford	242	A4
Fairview	2	F4
Falfield	275	G4
Far Green	230	B6
Farleys End	133	M8
Farmcote	75	L4
Farmington	146	B8
Far Oakridge	211	H7
Far Thrupp	209	H8
The Fence	198	D3
Fiddington	48	F8
Fiddler's Green	114	E1
Fifield	149	K1
Filands	303	J5
Filkins	221	L6
Filton	316	D8
Filwood Park	346	B3
Fishponds	327	H6
Fishpool	62	D4
Five Acres	151	L5
The Flat	133	J7
Flaxley	131	J8
The Folly	341	H5
Footbridge	74	E5
Ford	76	D4
The Fording	84	A4
Forest Green	232	C6
Forthampton	46	E3
Forthay	253	G5
Forwood	233	H6
Foscot	125	M3
Fossebridge	168	A8
Four Mile Elm	159	H6
Four Oaks	63	K5
Foxcote	142	A2
Frampton Cotterell	318	C4
Frampton End	318	E3
Frampton Mansell	235	G1
Frampton on Severn	181	M6
France Lynch	210	D8
Frenchay	327	K3
Fretherne	180	F4
Frocester	206	D8
Frogland Cross	307	L7
Frombridge	181	M8
Fyfield	220	D7
Gadfield Elm	44	C8
Ganborough	79	H4
Ganders Green	107	L6
Gatwick	156	E3
Gaunt's Earthcott	307	K6
Gawcombe	124	E4
Geat Wolford	60	A1
Glasshouse	107	L4
Gloucester	4	E8
Golden Hill	325	M5
Golden Valley	22	A5
Golden Valley	114	C1
Goodrich	127	J1
Goose Green	309	M6
Goose Green	338	E2
Gorsley	85	G3
Gorsley Common	84	D3
Gossington	228	F2
Gotherington	72	C3
Grafton	29	G4
Grange Village	154	F6
Great Badminton	323	H1
Great Barrington	172	E3
Great Doward	126	D5
Great Rissington	148	A4
Great Stoke	317	J6
Great Washbourne	51	H2
Great Witcombe	162	D1
Green Bottom	130	E8
Green Street	138	A8
Green Street	229	L5
Greenway	41	L4
Greet	74	D2
Gretton	74	A2
Gretton Fields	51	L7
Grove End	17	M8
Grovesend	294	
Guiting Power	98	
Guller's End	24	
The Hacket	294	
Hagloe	203	
Hailes	75	
Hailey	314	
Hallen	210	
Hall End	295	
Hallwood Green	40	
Halmore	227	
Ham	116	
Ham	250	
Hambrook	327	
Ham Green	324	
Hampen Manor	119	
Hampnett	144	
Hampton Fields	233	
Hamshill	230	
Hanham	337	
Hanham Green	337	
Hannington Wick	267	
Hardwicke	70	
Hardwicke	158	
Hardwicke	159	
Hardwick Green	45	
Harescombe	184	
Haresfield	183	
Harleywood	256	
Harnhill	239	
Harrow Hill	130	
Harry Stoke	327	
Hartcliffe	345	
Hartpury	111	
Hasfield	67	
Hatherley	114	
Hatherop	218	
Hawcross	65	
Hawkesbury	311	
Hawkesbury Upton	312	
Hawling	97	
Hayden	92	
Hazleton	144	
Headley Park	345	
Heath End	295	
Heathfield	251	
Hempsted	135	
Henbury	325	
Henfield	318	
Hengrove	346	
Hengrove Park	346	
Henleaze	325	
Henley	138	
Henley	353	
Hester's Way	93	
Hethelpit Cross	66	
Hewelsfield	223	
Hewelsfield Common	222	
Hicks Gate	347	
Hidcote Bartrim	13	
Hidcote Boyce	13	
High Brotheridge	162	
Highfield	201	
Highfields	253	
Highleadon	88	
Highnam	110	
Highnam Green	110	
High Nash	175	
Highridge	344	
High Woolaston	223	
Hilcot	141	
Hilcot End	240	
Hill	249	
Hill End	26	
Hillend Green	63	
Hillersland	151	
Hillesley	297	
Hillfields	327	
Hinchwick	78	
Hinnegar	313	
Hinton	203	
Hinton	330	
Holbrook Common	339	
Holdfast	24	
Hollybed Common	22	
Hollybush	21	
Holwell	197	
Holywell	277	
Homedowns	48	
Honington	16	
Hook Street	226	
Horcott	242	
Horfield	326	
Horsedown	323	
Horsepools	184	
Horsey Down	288	
Horsley	256	
Horton	311	
Horwood Riding	311	
Hotwells	335	
Houndscroft	232	
Howley	277	
Hucclecote	137	
Hudnalls	198	
Huntingford	276	
Huntley	108	
Hyde	76	
Hyde	233	
Hystfield	250	
Icomb	124	
Idbury	125	
Inchbrook	232	
Inglesham	268	
Ingst §	291	
Innsworth	113	
Iron Acton	308	
Itchington	308	
Jackaments Bottom	260	
Jack's Green	185	
Joy's Green	128	
Kelmscot	245	
Kelston	349	
Kemble	261	
Kemble Wick	261	
Kemerton	27	
Kempley	62	
Kempley Green	62	
Kempsford	266	
Kendleshire	318	

...nton Green ... 158 B1
...t's Green ... 87 G7
...ford ... 64 D1
...ynsham ... 348 C6
...cot ... 85 K4
...kenny ... 141 L1
...eton ... 98 E1
...gham ... 104 C7
...gscote ... 255 J6
...gscourt ... 208 D8
...gsditch ... 93 J6
...gsdown ... 353 H8
...g's Green ... 43 M3
...gs Hill ... 238 F3
...gshill ... 253 J1
...gsholm ... 4 E2
...g's Stanley ... 207 H7
...gswood ... 277 G7
...gswood ... 338 A3
...gton ... 293 G2
...sham ... 27 J7
...ebrook ... 59 M8
...lye ... 210 A5
e Knapp ... 274 B8
...ightsbridge ... 92 A1
...ockdown ... 300 A6
...owle ... 346 C2
...gley ... 73 L6
...ngridge ... 350 F3
...nsdown ... 115 J3
...nsdown ... 350 D5
...borough ... 279 L2
...teridge ... 308 D5
...ton ... 264 F7
...verton ... 32 B8
...rence Weston ... 324 C1
...a ... 106 B3
...a Line ... 106 E4
...athern Bottle ... 228 D6
...chlade ... 244 F7
...khampton ... 115 L7
...bury ... 19 L3
...ddington ... 41 J1
...gh ... 287 L6
...ghterton ... 279 M8
e Leigh ... 91 G2
...gh Woods ... 334 E5
...nard Stanley ... 207 H8
...wstone ... 126 B4
...hill ... 275 K6
...htpill ... 208 B7
...ne Street ... 67 J2
...den ... 135 M6
...kend ... 45 M8
...ton ... 84 C4
...ton Hill ... 84 D5
...tridge ... 43 J5
...tle Badminton ... 313 G6
...tle Barrington ... 172 D5
...tle Barrow ... 80 C4
...tle Beckford ... 28 E8
...tle Bristol ... 276 D8
...tle Compton ... 82 D2
...ledean ... 154 E3
...ledean Hill ... 154 D2
...tle Doward ... 126 C6
...tle Drybrook ... 176 A8
...tle Faringdon ... 245 H3
...tleford ... 86 E1
...tle Gorsley ... 85 J5
...tle Haresfield ... 183 G4
...tle Herbert's ... 116 K7
...tle London ... 131 L2
...tle Marcle ... 18 D5
...tle Rissington ... 124 A7
...tle Rollright ... 83 J2
...tle Shurdington ... 139 G3
...tle Sodbury ... 311 J8
...tle Sodbury End ... 311 G7
...tle Stoke ... 316 F4
...tleton Drew ... 323 M6
...tleton-upon-Severn ... 292 A2
...tle Washbourne ... 51 J3
...tle Welland ... 23 H2
...tle Witcombe ... 138 E7
...tle Wolford ... 38 D7
...tleworth ... 12 C8
...tleworth ... 232 E3
...ckleaze ... 326 K4
...g Ashton ... 344 C2
...gborough ... 79 L4
...g Compton ... 61 J4
...gdon ... 24 A6
...gdon Heath ... 24 C1
...gdon Hill End ... 23 L2
...gford ... 112 A5
...g Green ... 46 C4
...nghope ... 131 J1
...g Newnton ... 282 E6
...gney ... 157 L5
...gridge ... 185 L4
...gridge End ... 89 H6
...gwell Green ... 338 A8
...wbands ... 44 A8
...wer Apperley ... 69 G7
...wer Berry Hill ... 151 H7
...wer Cam ... 229 G6
...wer Chedworth ... 191 M1
...wer Clopton ... 9 H3
...wer Dowdeswell ... 117 L7
...wer End ... 213 K5
...wer Hamswell ... 340 D8
...wer Hazel ... 293 G8
...wer Kilcott ... 298 C4
...wer Knowle ... 346 A2
...wer Lemington ... 58 F2
...wer Ley ... 133 H7
...wer Lode ... 47 L7
...wer Lydbrook ... 128 B6
...wer Meend ... 198 D6
...wer Moor ... 286 D8
...wer Morton ... 273 M7
...wer Oddington ... 103 H3
...wer Rea ... 135 G8
...wer Slaughter ... 123 H1
...wer Soudley ... 178 D2
...wer Stone ... 274 E1
...wer Swainswick ... 351 L8

Lower Swell ... 101 K4
Lower Tuffley ... 159 L1
Lower Westmancote ... 27 K4
Lower Wick ... 252 A5
Luckington ... 313 M7
Ludgrove ... 19 H7
Ludstock ... 19 H7
Luxley ... 107 G3
Lyde Green ... 329 G3
Lydney ... 225 K1
Lynworth ... 3 K2
Lynworth ... 94 C7
Lypiatt ... 187 J5
Maisemore ... 111 J4
Malmesbury ... 303 J7
Malswick ... 87 G4
Mangotsfield ... 328 B6
Marle Hill ... 93 M7
Marsden ... 166 A7
Marsh Common ... 305 C7
Marsh End ... 23 K8
Marshfield ... 342 A3
Marsh Lane ... 175 M7
Marston Hill ... 242 A8
Marston Meysey ... 265 M4
Matson ... 136 E8
Mayshill ... 319 G2
Mead Riding ... 310 E8
Meysey Hampton ... 241 L7
Mickleton ... 9 G7
Middle Duntisbourne ... 213 H1
Middlehill ... 353 K5
Middle Street ... 206 A5
Middle Wick ... 252 B6
Middle Yard ... 207 K8
Milbourne ... 303 M7
Milbury Heath ... 294 D2
Mile End ... 152 A7
Milkwall ... 175 M4
Mill End ... 169 H2
Millend ... 175 H4
Millend ... 206 C4
Millend ... 253 J6
Mill Hill ... 200 C2
Milton End ... 180 B1
Milton End ... 242 C4
Minchinhampton ... 233 J5
Minsterworth ... 134 A4
Miserden ... 187 K4
Mitcheldean ... 130 B1
Mitton ... 48 D3
Montpelier ... 336 A1
Moor End ... 116 B6
Moorend ... 161 G3
Moorend ... 228 D1
Moorend ... 328 A1
Moreton-in-Marsh ... 58 E5
Moreton Valence ... 182 D3
Mork ... 198 F4
Morton ... 293 M1
Mountain Bower ... 333 H7
Mount Hill ... 338 A5
Much Marcle ... 40 B5
Murcott ... 284 A7
Murrell's End ... 65 G2
Murrell's End ... 110 D2
Nag's Head ... 258 A2
Nailbridge ... 129 M6
Nailsworth ... 232 E8
Nashend ... 210 C4
Nastend ... 206 D2
Natton ... 49 H5
Naunton ... 99 K7
Nebsworth ... 14 B1
Netham ... 336 E5
Netherend ... 224 A6
Netherton ... 218 E5
Nether Westcote ... 125 G6
Nettleton ... 163 L3
Nettleton Green ... 333 J2
Nettleton Shrub ... 333 K3
New Cheltenham ... 338 B2
Newent ... 86 B3
Newerne ... 201 J8
New Grounds ... 204 D3
Newington Bagpath ... 279 K1
Newland ... 174 F3
Newmarket ... 232 B7
New Mills ... 19 L1
New Mills ... 201 J6
New Mills ... 238 F3
Newnham ... 155 J7
New Passage ... 304 C2
Newport ... 251 K3
Newton ... 273 M5
Newtown ... 48 E5
New Town ... 53 G6
New Town ... 82 C3
Newtown ... 206 D7
Newtown ... 226 F2
Nibley ... 202 C1
Nibley ... 319 J2
Nibley Green ... 252 E6
Nimlet ... 341 G8
Ninewells ... 151 L4
Norcote ... 239 H1
Norman Hill ... 229 J8
North Cerney ... 190 C7
North Common ... 338 F5
North Corner ... 318 B2
North End ... 287 H1
Northend ... 352 C6
Northington ... 179 K5
Northleach ... 169 K1
North Nibley ... 252 F7
North Stoke ... 349 L4
Northway ... 49 G1
Northwick ... 305 G1
Northwood Green ... 132 B6
North Wraxall ... 343 K1
Norton ... 90 E6
Notgrove ... 121 J6
Nottwood Hill ... 131 M7
Novers Park ... 345 M3
Noverton ... 94 F8
Nupdown ... 249 H6
Nupend ... 206 D1
Nupend ... 256 A2
Nuppend ... 224 C4

Nympsfield ... 231 G6
Oakle Street ... 133 K3
Oakley ... 116 E1
Oakridge ... 210 F8
Oaksey ... 285 H3
Okle Green ... 87 K3
Oldbury Naite ... 272 F4
Oldbury-on-Severn ... 272 E5
Oldbury on the Hill ... 299 K6
Oldcroft ... 202 A3
Old Down ... 292 E8
Oldend ... 206 F2
Old Forge ... 127 G1
Oldland ... 338 C8
Oldland Common ... 338 F8
Old Passage ... 291 H5
Old Sodbury ... 321 K4
Old Wharf ... 19 M5
Olveston ... 292 C8
Oridge Street ... 66 D7
Over ... 111 J7
Over ... 315 M1
Overbury ... 28 B3
Overton ... 180 D2
Owlpen ... 255 G2
Oxenhall ... 86 A1
Oxenton ... 50 B8
Ozleworth ... 278 E3
Paganhill ... 208 C3
Painswick ... 185 G4
Palmer's Flat ... 175 L3
Pamington ... 49 K4
Pancakehill ... 167 M8
Paradise ... 161 J8
Parkend ... 176 F6
Parkend ... 182 E1
Parkfield ... 329 J4
Park Hill ... 223 H7
The Park ... 115 K5
Parkway ... 20 B7
Patchway ... 316 C2
Paxford ... 35 M3
Pebworth ... 8 B1
Pendock ... 44 C5
Pennsylvania ... 341 H4
Perrott's Brook ... 214 B3
Petty France ... 312 C4
Picklenash ... 86 A2
Piff's Elm ... 92 C2
Pilley ... 116 A7
Pillowell ... 201 H2
Pillows Green ... 66 F3
Pilning ... 304 F4
Pinfarthings ... 232 D5
Piper's End ... 46 C1
Pitchcombe ... 184 E7
Pitt Court ... 253 J6
Pittville ... 2 F1
Pixley ... 18 C1
Playley Green ... 43 L7
The Pludds ... 128 F6
Plump Hill ... 130 C4
Plusterwine ... 224 A8
Podsmead ... 135 M7
Poole Keynes ... 261 L8
Poolhill ... 64 E4
Pope's Hill ... 155 H1
Portway ... 44 C3
Postlip ... 73 M8
Poulton ... 241 G5
The Pound ... 63 M1
Prescott ... 73 H4
Prestbury ... 94 D6
Preston ... 18 E8
Preston ... 41 G1
Preston ... 239 H5
Prior's Norton ... 91 H6
Priors Park ... 48 B6
Pucklechurch ... 329 J6
Puckrup ... 25 L5
Puckshole ... 208 A3
Pullens Green ... 272 E6
Purton ... 202 D5
Putley Green ... 18 A3
Putloe ... 182 C3
Pye Corner ... 317 M8
Quarhouse ... 233 J1
The Quarry ... 228 F7
Quedgeley ... 159 G2
Queenhill ... 24 F5
Quenington ... 218 C6
Ram Hill ... 318 F7
The Rampings ... 46 E2
Randwick ... 207 L1
Rangeworthy ... 309 J2
Rea ... 135 H7
Readings ... 128 E6
Ready Token ... 217 G5
Redbrook ... 174 B2
The Reddings ... 114 C4
Redland ... 325 L8
Redmarley D'Abitot ... 43 K8
Redwick ... 304 D3
Rendcomb ... 190 B3
Ridgeway ... 327 H8
Ripple ... 25 J3
Rockhampton ... 274 B4
Rockness ... 256 C1
The Rocks ... 310 B6
Rockstowes ... 254 B3
Rodborough ... 208 B5
Rodley ... 157 H7
Rodmarton ... 259 L3
Rooksmoor ... 232 C1
Rowanfield ... 115 H1
Rowland's Green ... 19 H5
Ruardean ... 129 G4
Ruardean Hill ... 129 J4
Ruardean Woodside ... 129 G5
Ruddle ... 155 G8
Rudford ... 110 A4
Rudgeway ... 307 H2
Ruscombe ... 184 A2
Ruspidge ... 154 A6
Ryeford ... 207 J5
Rye Street ... 22 C7
Ryeworth ... 116 K4
Ryton ... 42 D6

Nympsfield ... 231 G6
St Anne's Park ... 337 G5
St Briavels ... 199 G5
St Briavels Common ... 222 C2
Saintbridge ... 136 D5
Saintbury ... 11 J7
St Catherine ... 352 A2
St Chloe ... 232 D3
St George ... 337 J4
St Mark's ... 115 H2
St Paul's ... 4 C9
St Peter's ... 93 K8
Salford ... 83 J6
Salperton ... 120 B6
Salperton Park ... 120 B7
Sandhurst ... 89 L8
Sandpits ... 68 A3
Sapperton ... 211 M8
Sarsden ... 105 J8
Sarsden Halt ... 104 F5
Saul ... 181 H4
The Scarr ... 64 C7
Scowles ... 175 G1
Sea Mills ... 324 E6
Sedbury ... 270 D4
Sedgeberrow ... 30 C1
Selsley ... 208 A7
Sevenhampton ... 118 F3
Seven Springs ... 140 C4
Severn Beach ... 304 D5
Sezincote ... 57 J8
Shab Hill ... 139 K8
Shadwell ... 254 C3
Shakesfield ... 41 J7
Shapridge ... 130 F6
Sharpness ... 226 D1
Shaw Common ... 63 J7
Sheepscombe ... 186 A2
Shepherd's Patch ... 204 D6
Shepperdine ... 248 F8
Sherborne ... 171 J1
Shipston-on-Stour ... 16 B5
Shipton ... 142 E1
Shipton Moyne ... 302 A3
Shipton Oliffe ... 143 G1
Shipton Solers ... 142 E1
Shirehampton ... 324 A4
The Shoe ... 343 J2
Shorncote ... 262 D5
Shortstanding ... 151 G4
Shortwood ... 232 B8
Shortwood ... 328 F7
Shurdington ... 138 F1
Shuthonger ... 25 M7
Shutton ... 84 A3
Siddington ... 238 F7
Signet ... 197 M2
Signet Hill ... 173 K8
Silver Street ... 230 C4
Siston ... 329 H8
Siston Common ... 338 C2
Slad ... 185 J7
Sladbrook ... 65 M5
Slades Green ... 46 E1
Sledge Green ... 45 J2
Slimbridge ... 205 G7
Sling ... 175 L7
Smallbrook ... 224 B5
Sneyd Park ... 324 F7
Snig's End ... 66 E5
Snowshill ... 54 E3
Somerdale ... 348 A4
Somerford Keynes ... 262 C8
Sopworth ... 313 M2
Soundwell ... 328 A8
Southam ... 94 D3
South Cerney ... 263 H4
Southend ... 253 G8
Southmead ... 325 K2
Southrop ... 220 C8
Speedwell ... 337 J1
Springbank ... 92 F8
Standish ... 183 G6
Stanley Downton ... 207 G6
Stanley Pontlarge ... 73 K2
Stanton ... 54 A2
Stantway ... 156 D3
Stanway ... 53 K6
Staple Hill ... 328 A4
Stapleton ... 326 E6
Starveall ... 298 F7
Staunton ... 66 C4
Staunton ... 150 E5
Staverton ... 92 A7
Steam Mills ... 129 M7
Stinchcombe ... 252 D2
Stockend ... 184 B4
Stockwell ... 163 K2
Stockwood ... 346 F5
Stockwood Vale ... 347 K5
Stoke Bishop ... 324 F7
Stoke Gifford ... 316 F6
Stoke Orchard ... 71 G5
Stone ... 251 G8
Stone Hill ... 338 A7
Stonehouse ... 207 J3
Stourton ... 39 K5
Stourton Hill ... 39 L7
Stowe ... 199 G1
Stowe Green ... 199 H1
Stowell ... 168 C4
Stow-on-the-Wold ... 101 M3
Strand ... 156 B4
Stratford ... 25 L1
Stratton ... 214 A7
Stretton-on-Fosse ... 36 F2
Stroat ... 247 J3
Stroud ... 208 C2
Stroud Green ... 183 H7
Stub Riding ... 310 D8
Stumps Cross ... 76 B2
Sudgrove ... 187 J6
Sundayshill ... 274 A2
Sunhill ... 241 J1
Sutton-under-Brailes ... 39 L4
Swanley ... 251 L6
Swindon ... 93 K8
Swineford ... 349 J4

Syde ... 187 M1
Symonds Yat ... 126 F6
Synwell ... 277 L4
Syreford ... 118 D6
Taddington ... 54 C8
Tadwick ... 351 G2
Talbot's End ... 295 L1
Tarlton ... 236 B7
Taynton ... 108 D3
Taynton ... 173 K3
Teddington ... 50 B5
Teddington Hands ... 50 D3
Temple Guiting ... 76 E6
Tetbury ... 282 A4
Tetbury Upton ... 257 K8
Tewkesbury ... 47 M6
Thames Head ... 237 H8
The Mythe ... 48 A2
Thickwood ... 343 L6
Thornbury ... 293 K2
Througham ... 187 G7
Thrupp ... 209 G7
Tibberton ... 109 K3
Tickmorend ... 256 B1
Tidenham ... 247 G7
Tidenham Chase ... 246 E1
Tidmington ... 38 A2
Tillers' Green ... 41 J5
Tilsdown ... 229 H7
Tiltups End ... 256 D4
Tirley ... 68 B5
Tirley Knowle ... 67 L3
Tockington ... 306 C2
Toddington ... 52 F5
Todenham ... 37 L6
Tormarton ... 332 A1
Tortworth ... 275 L4
Totteroak ... 311 G6
Town Street ... 68 B4
Townwell ... 295 K2
Tredington ... 70 C3
Tredworth ... 136 B4
Tresham ... 278 E8
Trewen ... 126 A2
Triangle ... 222 D3
Trow Green ... 199 L1
Tuffley ... 136 A8
Tumpy Green ... 228 C3
Tunley ... 211 J2
Turkdean ... 145 H4
Tutnalls ... 225 L1
Tutshill ... 270 B2
Twigworth ... 112 C2
The Twittocks ... 25 M4
Two Bridges ... 178 D5
Two Mile Hill ... 337 K2
Twyning ... 26 B5
Twyning Green ... 26 C5
The Tynings ... 139 H1
Tytherington ... 294 E6
Uckinghall ... 25 H2
Uckington ... 92 F5
Uley ... 254 D2
Up Hatherley ... 114 F6
Uplands ... 209 G2
Upleadon ... 87 H1
Upleadon Court ... 87 M1
Upper Brailes ... 17 L3
Upper Cam ... 229 K7
Upper Coberley ... 141 G7
Upper Dowdeswell ... 117 K3
Upper End ... 169 L3
Upper End ... 213 M1
Upper Framilode ... 181 G2
Upper Hill ... 250 A6
Upper Inglesham ... 268 D6
Upper Kilcott ... 298 F6
Upper Ley ... 132 E3
Upper Lode ... 47 L4
Upper Lydbrook ... 128 D7
Upper Minety ... 285 L8
Upper Morton ... 274 A7
Upper Oddington ... 103 G4
Upper Quinton ... 9 J2
Upper Rissington ... 124 D7
Upper Siddington ... 238 D7
Upper Slaughter ... 100 F7
Upper Soudley ... 178 B2
Upper Swainswick ... 351 J6
Upper Swell ... 101 K1
Upper Up ... 263 G5
Upper Weston ... 350 D8
Upper Wick ... 252 B5
Upper Wraxall ... 343 G2
Upthorpe ... 229 K6
Upton ... 173 L5
Upton Bishop ... 62 A8
Upton Cheyney ... 349 K3
Upton St Leonards ... 161 H1
Viney Hill ... 202 B2
Vinney Green ... 328 C4
Walham ... 111 M6
Wallow Green ... 232 B8
Wallsworth ... 90 C8
Walton Cardiff ... 48 C6
Wanswell ... 226 F4
Wapley ... 320 A7
Warden Hill ... 115 H6
Warmley ... 338 D4
Warmley Hill ... 338 B3
Warmley Tower ... 338 D5
Waterend ... 157 J2
Waterhay ... 287 L4
Waterlane ... 210 F5
Watermead ... 138 A7
Watermoor ... 238 D4
Watledge ... 232 E6
Watley's End ... 318 C4
Wayend Street ... 21 G5
Webb's Heath ... 339 G3
Welland ... 23 K1
Welland Stone ... 23 J1
Welsh Bicknor ... 128 A3
Westbury-on-Severn ... 155 M3
Westbury on Trym ... 325 G5
Westbury Park ... 325 K7
West Crudwell ... 283 M4
West End ... 32 E5
Westend ... 206 B1

West End	257 K3	Whichford	61 M1	Wickhamford	10 A4	Withington	142 C7	Woolstone	72
Westend	272 D5	Whitchurch	126 E5	Wickridge Street	67 J8	Withywood	345 H7	Worley	232
West End	296 A5	Whitchurch	346 F7	Wick Street	185 H7	Woodbridge	166 F1	Wormington	31
Westerleigh	319 J7	Whitebrook	198 B1	Wickwar	296 C6	Woodchester	232 B1	Worrall Hill	152
Westerleigh Hill	319 M8	Whitecliff	175 H2	Wiggold	215 H5	Woodcroft	246 D7	Wortley	277
Westington	34 C1	Whitecroft	200 F2	Willersey	11 H7	Woodfield	229 G8	Wotton	5
West Kington	333 G4	White End	44 D2	Willesley	300 E5	Woodfield	251 J7	Wotton-under-Edge	277
West Kington Wick	333 K5	Whitehall	336 E2	Willington	16 E8	Woodhouse Down	306 F4	Wyck Rissington	123
West Littleton	331 L8	Whiteleaved Oak	21 L7	Willsbridge	348 L1	Woodmancote	72 D8	Wyegate Green	198
Westmancote	27 L3	Whiteshill	184 C7	Winchcombe	74 B5	Woodmancote	189 M4	Wymans Brook	93
Westonbirt	300 F3	Whiteshill	317 L8	Windmill Hill	336 A8	Woodmancote	253 J3	Yanley	344
Weston-sub-Edge	11 M4	Whiteway	187 G2	Windrush	172 A5	Wood Stanway	53 M8	Yanworth	168
Westrip	207 L3	Whiteway	256 B1	Windsoredge	232 B6	Woolaston	223 L8	Yate	319
Westwell	197 G2	Whitfield	274 F8	Winson	192 D5	Woolaston Common	223 M4	Yate Rocks	310
Whaddon	3 K3	Whitminster	181 M6	Winstone	188 C3	Woolaston Slade	223 K6	Yorkley	201
Whaddon	160 B3	Whittington	118 A4	Winterbourne	317 M5	Woolaston Woodside	223 L5	Yorkley Slade	177
Wheatenhurst	181 L5	Wibdon	247 H4	Winterbourne Down	318 B7	Woolley	351 H5	
Whelford	267 J1	Wick	339 M5	Wishanger	186 F3	Woolridge	89 H7	

USING THE STREET INDEX

Street names are listed alphabetically. Each street name is followed by its postal town or area locality, the Postcode District, the page number, and the reference to the square in which the name is found.

Example: **Abbey Ct** *BRSG/KWL/STAPK* BS4 .... **337** H6 🔟

Some entries are followed by a number in a blue box. This number indicates the location of the street within the referenced grid square. The full street name is listed at the side of the map page

GENERAL ABBREVIATIONS

ACC	ACCESS	CTYD	COURTYARD	HLS	HILLS	MWY	MOTORWAY	SE	SOUTH E
ALY	ALLEY	CUTT	CUTTINGS	HO	HOUSE	N	NORTH	SER	SERVICE A
AP	APPROACH	CV	COVE	HOL	HOLLOW	NE	NORTH EAST	SH	SH
AR	ARCADE	CYN	CANYON	HOSP	HOSPITAL	NW	NORTH WEST	SHOP	SHOPP
ASS	ASSOCIATION	DEPT	DEPARTMENT	HRB	HARBOUR	O/P	OVERPASS	SKWY	SKY
AV	AVENUE	DL	DALE	HTH	HEATH	OFF	OFFICE	SMT	SUM
BCH	BEACH	DM	DAM	HTS	HEIGHTS	ORCH	ORCHARD	SOC	SOCI
BLDS	BUILDINGS	DR	DRIVE	HVN	HAVEN	OV	OVAL	SP	SI
BND	BEND	DRO	DROVE	HWY	HIGHWAY	PAL	PALACE	SPR	SPR
BNK	BANK	DRY	DRIVEWAY	IMP	IMPERIAL	PAS	PASSAGE	SQ	SQU
BR	BRIDGE	DWGS	DWELLINGS	IN	INLET	PAV	PAVILION	ST	STR
BRK	BROOK	E	EAST	IND EST	INDUSTRIAL ESTATE	PDE	PARADE	STN	STAT
BTM	BOTTOM	EMB	EMBANKMENT	INF	INFIRMARY	PH	PUBLIC HOUSE	STR	STRE
BUS	BUSINESS	EMBY	EMBASSY	INFO	INFORMATION	PK	PARK	STRD	STRA
BVD	BOULEVARD	ESP	ESPLANADE	INT	INTERCHANGE	PKWY	PARKWAY	SW	SOUTH W
BY	BYPASS	EST	ESTATE	IS	ISLAND	PL	PLACE	TDG	TRAD
CATH	CATHEDRAL	EX	EXCHANGE	JCT	JUNCTION	PLN	PLAIN	TER	TERRA
CEM	CEMETERY	EXPY	EXPRESSWAY	JTY	JETTY	PLNS	PLAINS	THWY	THROUGHW
CEN	CENTRE	EXT	EXTENSION	KG	KING	PLZ	PLAZA	TNL	TUNN
CFT	CROFT	F/O	FLYOVER	KNL	KNOLL	POL	POLICE STATION	TOLL	TOLLW
CH	CHURCH	FC	FOOTBALL CLUB	L	LAKE	PR	PRINCE	TPK	TURNP
CHA	CHASE	FLD	FIELD	LA	LANE	PREC	PRECINCT	TR	TRA
CHYD	CHURCHYARD	FLDS	FIELDS	LDG	LODGE	PREP	PREPARATORY	TRL	TR
CIR	CIRCLE	FLS	FALLS	LGT	LIGHT	PRIM	PRIMARY	TWR	TOW
CIRC	CIRCUS	FM	FARM	LK	LOCK	PROM	PROMENADE	U/P	UNDERP
CL	CLOSE	FT	FORT	LKS	LAKES	PRS	PRINCESS	UNI	UNIVERS
CLFS	CLIFFS	FWY	FREEWAY	LNDG	LANDING	PRT	PORT	UPR	UPF
CMP	CAMP	FY	FERRY	LTL	LITTLE	PT	POINT	V	V
CNR	CORNER	GA	GATE	LWR	LOWER	PTH	PATH	VA	VAL
CO	COUNTY	GAL	GALLERY	MAG	MAGISTRATE	PZ	PIAZZA	VIAD	VIADU
COLL	COLLEGE	GDN	GARDEN	MAN	MANSIONS	QD	QUADRANT	VIL	VI
COM	COMMON	GDNS	GARDENS	MD	MEAD	QU	QUEEN	VIS	VI
COMM	COMMISSION	GLD	GLADE	MDW	MEADOWS	QY	QUAY	VLG	VILLA
CON	CONVENT	GLN	GLEN	MEM	MEMORIAL	R	RIVER	VLS	VIL
COT	COTTAGE	GN	GREEN	MKT	MARKET	RBT	ROUNDABOUT	VW	V
COTS	COTTAGES	GND	GROUND	MKTS	MARKETS	RD	ROAD	W	W
CP	CAPE	GRA	GRANGE	ML	MALL	RDG	RIDGE	WD	WD
CPS	COPSE	GRG	GARAGE	ML	MILL	REP	REPUBLIC	WHF	WHA
CR	CREEK	GT	GREAT	MNR	MANOR	RES	RESERVOIR	WK	WK
CREM	CREMATORIUM	GTWY	GATEWAY	MS	MEWS	RFC	RUGBY FOOTBALL CLUB	WKS	WA
CRS	CRESCENT	GV	GROVE	MSN	MISSION	RI	RISE	WLS	WE
CSWY	CAUSEWAY	HGR	HIGHER	MT	MOUNT	RP	RAMP	WY	WY
CT	COURT	HL	HILL	MTN	MOUNTAIN	RW	ROW	YD	YA
CTRL	CENTRAL			MTS	MOUNTAINS	S	SOUTH	YHA	YOUTH HOS
CTS	COURTS			MUS	MUSEUM	SCH	SCHOOL		

POSTCODE TOWNS AND AREA ABBREVIATIONS

ALMDB	Almondsbury	CBRISNE	Central Bristol north & east	EVE	Evesham	LYD	Lydney	RTEWK/TIB	Rural Tewkesbu
AVONM	Avonmouth	CFTN/FAIL	Clifton/Failand	EVILLE/WHL	Eastville/Whitehall	MALM	Malmesbury		Tibber
BAD	Badminton	CHCAM	Chipping Campden	FGDN	Faringdon	MANG/FISH	Mangotsfield/Fishponds	RWYE	Ross-on-W
BATHSE	Bath south & east	CHELT	Cheltenham	FRCTL/WBN	Frampton Cotterell/	MIM	Moreton-in-Marsh	SHPSTR	Shipston-on-Sto
BBLUN	Broad Blunsdon	CHELTE/BC	Cheltenham east/		Winterbourne	MONM	Monmouth	STNHO	Stonehou
BDWAY	Broadway		Bishop's Cleeve	GL	Gloucester	MTCHDN	Mitcheldean	STRAT	Stratford-upon-A
BMSTR	Bedminster	CHELTS	Cheltenham south	GLE	Gloucester east	NAIL	Nailsea	STROUD	Stro
BMSTRD/HC/WWD	Bedminster Down/	CHELTW	Cheltenham west	HGHW	Highworth	NWNT	Newent	SWDNW	Swindon west/Puri
	Hartcliffe/Withywood	CHEP	Chepstow	HGRV/WHIT	Hengrove/Whitchurch	OLD/WMLY/WICK	Oldland/	TET	Tetb
BRKLY	Berkeley	CHNTN	Chipping Norton	HNBRY/STHM	Henbury/Southmead		Warmley/Wick	TEWK	Tewkesbu
BRSG/KWL/STAPK	Brislington/Knowle/	CHPMW/MSHF	Chippenham west/	HNLZ/SM/SNYPK/WT	Henleaze/	PER	Pershore	THNB/SVB	Thornbury/Severn Be
	St Anne's Park		Marshfield		Sea Mills/Sneyd Park/	PTSHD/EG	Portishead/	UUSV	Upton upon Sev
BRSTK/PCHW	Bradley Stoke/Patchway	CIND	Cinderford		Westbury-on-Trym		Easton-in-Gordano	VGL	Vale of Glouces
BUR/CRTN	Burford/Carterton	CIR	Cirencester	HORF/LLZ	Horfield/Lockleaze	RBANSW	Rural Banbury south & west	WUE	Wotton-under-E
BWTH/CHD	Brockworth/Churchdown	CLFD	Coleford	KEYN	Keynsham	RDLND/MONT	Redland/Montpelier	YATE/CS	Yate/Chipping Sodb
CBATH/BATHN	Central Bath/Bath north	COR/BOX	Corsham/Box	KGWD/HNM	Kingswood/Hanham	RGTMLV	Rural Great Malvern		
CBRIS/FH	Central Bristol/	COTS	Cotswolds	LED	Ledbury	RSTROUD/NAIL	Rural Stroud/Nailsworth		
	Floating Harbour	DSLY	Dursley	LGASH	Long Ashton				

Aar - Alb

A

Aaron Rd *CIR* GL7	239 H7
Abbenesse *RSTROUD/NAIL* GL6	210 A8
Abbey Ct	
BRSG/KWL/STAPK BS4	337 H6 🔟
Abbeydale *FRCTL/WBN* BS36	318 A5
Abbey La *THNB/SVB* BS35	293 M5
Abbeymead Av *GLE* GL4	136 F4
Abbey Meadow *TEWK* GL20	48 B8 🔟
Abbey Pk *KEYN* BS31	348 B5
Abbey Rd	
HNLZ/SM/SNYPK/WT BS9	325 H5
VGL GL2	4 A8
Abbey Rw *MALM* SN16	303 J8
Abbey St *CIND* GL14	154 B3
WUE GL12	277 H6
Abbey Wy *CIR* GL7	238 B1
Abbeywood Dr	
HNLZ/SM/SNYPK/WT BS9	324 E6 🔟
Abbots Av *KGWD/HNM* BS15	337 L7
Abbots Cl *CHELT* GL50	115 K6
HGRV/WHIT BS14	346 C8
Abbots Court Dr *TEWK* GL20	26 A6
Abbotsford Rd	
RDLND/MONT BS6	335 K2
Abbots Leigh Rd *CFTN/FAIL* BS8	334 D4
Abbots Leys Rd *COTS* GL54	74 B6
Abbots Ms *CHELTE/BC* GL52	94 A1
Abbots Rd *CIR* GL7	238 E3 🔟
GLE GL4	137 G5
KGWD/HNM BS15	347 L1
TEWK GL20	48 A7
Abbots Vw *CIND* GL14	154 B6
Abbots Wk *CIR* GL7	244 F1
Abbots Wy	
HNLZ/SM/SNYPK/WT BS9	325 H1
STNHO GL10	207 G5
Abbotswood	
KGWD/HNM BS15	337 M4 🔟
YATE/CS BS37	319 M4 🔟
Abbotswood Cl *GLE* GL4	135 M8
Abbotswood Rd	
BWTH/CHD GL3	138 A6
Abbott Rd *THNB/SVB* BS35	304 C6
Abbotts Gdn *MALM* SN16	303 J8
Abercrombie Cl *LED* HR8	19 L2 🔟
Aberdeen Rd	
RDLND/MONT BS6	335 K2
Abingdon Court La *HCHW* SN6	289 G3
Abingdon Rd *MANG/FISH* BS16	327 J8
Ableton La *HNBRY/STHM* BS10	314 B3
THNB/SVB BS35	304 C5
Ableton Wk	
HNLZ/SM/SNYPK/WT BS9	324 E6 🔟
Abnash *RSTROUD/NAIL* GL6	210 A8
Abraham Cl *EVILLE/WHL* BS5	336 D3 🔟
Abson Rd *MANG/FISH* BS16	329 K6
OLD/WMLY/WICK BS30	339 L2
Acacia Av *MANG/FISH* BS16	327 L7
Acacia Cl *CHELTE/BC* GL52	94 C6
LYD GL15	200 D3 🔟
MANG/FISH BS16	327 L8 🔟
Acacia Ct *KEYN* BS31	347 L2 🔟
Acacia Dr *DSLY* GL11	229 J8
Acacia Pk *CHELTE/BC* GL52	71 M6
Acacia Rd *MANG/FISH* BS16	327 M8
Acer Cl *BUR/CRTN* OX18	197 M4
Acer Gv *VGL* GL2	159 G1
Acomb Crs *CHELTE/BC* GL52	116 D5 🔟
Acorn Gv	
BMSTRD/HC/WWD BS13	345 G5
The Acorns *RWYE* HR9	106 B4 🔟
Acraman's Rd *BMSTR* BS3	6 D8
Acresbush Cl	
BMSTRD/HC/WWD BS13	345 J6
Acre St *STROUD* GL5	208 E4
Acton Rd *MANG/FISH* BS16	327 J8 🔟
Adams Hay	
BRSG/KWL/STAPK BS4	346 F2 🔟
Adams Wy *CLFD* GL16	151 J5
Adderly Ga *MANG/FISH* BS16	328 D4
Addiscombe Rd	
HGRV/WHIT BS14	346 D6
Addison Rd *BMSTR* BS3	336 A8
Addis Rd *CHELTW* GL51	93 K8 🔟
Addymore *DSLY* GL11	229 H6 🔟
Adelaide Gdns *STNHO* GL10	207 G2 🔟
Adelaide Pl *EVILLE/WHL* BS5	336 D3 🔟
MANG/FISH BS16	327 H7 🔟
Adelaide St *GL* GL1	136 C4
Adey's La *WUE* GL12	277 K2
Admington La *SHPSTR* CV36	9 M5
Admiral Cl *CHELTW* GL51	114 F1
Admirals Cl *LYD* GL15	200 D2 🔟
Aesops Orch *CHELTE/BC* GL52	72 E8
Agate St *BMSTR* BS3	335 K8
Aggs Hl *CHELTE/BC* GL52	116
Aggs La *CHELTE/BC* GL52	72
Aiken St *EVILLE/WHL* BS5	336
Air Balloon Rd *EVILLE/WHL* BS5	337
Aintree Dr *MANG/FISH* BS16	328
Airport Rd *HGRV/WHIT* BS14	346
Aisne Rd *LYD* GL15	201
Akeman Rd *CIR* GL7	238
Akermans Orch *NWNT* GL18	86
Alard Rd *BRSG/KWL/STAPK* BS4	346
Albany *STNHO* GL10	207
Albany Ga *BRSTK/PCHW* BS34	317
Albany Rd *CHELT* GL50	115
RDLND/MONT BS6	336 B
Albany St *GL* GL1	5 H
GL GL1	136
KGWD/HNM BS15	337
Albany Wy	
OLD/WMLY/WICK BS30	338
Albemarle Ga *CHELT* GL50	93
Albemarle Rd *BWTH/CHD* GL3	113
Albermarle Rw	
CFTN/FAIL BS8	335 H
Albert Crs *CBRISNE* BS2	7
Albert Dr *CHELTE/BC* GL52	94

ert Gv EVILLE/WHL BS5 ...... 337 H3
erton Rd MANG/FISH BS16 ..... 327 H5
ert Pde EVILLE/WHL BS5 ...... 336 E3
ert Pk RDLND/MONT BS6 .. 336 B2
　RDLND/MONT BS6 .... 336 A2
ert Pl CHELTE/BC GL52 .... 2 E1
　NLZ/SM/SNYPK/WT BS9..... 325 J4
ert Rd CBRISNE BS2 .... 7 M8
　BRISNE BS2 .... 336 D7
　HELTE/BC GL52 .... 3 C2
　HELTE/BC GL52 .... 94 A7
　ND GL4 .... 154 A4
　LFD GL16 .... 175 J1
　EYN BS31 .... 348 A6
　GWD/HNM BS15 .... 337 M6
　D HR8 .... 19 L4
　ANG/FISH BS16 .... 328 A7
　ROUD GL5 .... 233 H2
　HNB/SVB BS35 .... 304 C5
ert St CHELT GL50 .... 2 C6
　t GL1 .... 5 G6
　GL15 .... 201 J7
ert Ter MANG/FISH BS16 ...... 327 H7
on Cl MANG/FISH BS16 .... 328 B6
on Pl CHELTE/BC GL52 .... 2 E4
on Rd CIND GL14 .... 154 B1
on St CHELTE/BC GL52 .... 2 E5
　GL7 .... 214 B8
　VILLE/WHL BS5 .... 336 E3
　GL1 .... 4 D7
on Wk CHELTE/BC GL52 .... 2 D4
ght La LED HR8 .... 43 H3
tts Gn VGL GL2 .... 90 A8
ve Rd MANG/FISH BS16 ...... 327 G8
er Cl VGL GL2 .... 112 E7
rcombe Rd
　NLZ/SM/SNYPK/WT BS9..... 324 A3
rdale LYD GL15 .... 201 K7
rdown Cl AVONM BS11 .... 324 C3
er Dr EVILLE/WHL BS5 .... 337 G2
rgate St STNHO GL10 .... 207 H4
rley Rd WUE GL12 .... 297 M2
rmoor Wy
　OLD/WMLY/WICK BS30 .... 338 A7
rnay Av
　NLZ/SM/SNYPK/WT BS9..... 337 H7
rs Gn VGL GL2 .... 112 D6
t Alders CHELTS GL53 .... 115 K7
rton Cl GLE GL4 .... 137 G7
rton Rd CHELTW GL51 .... 115 G3
ORF/LLZ BS7 .... 326 A3
er Wy RSTROUD/NAIL GL6 ..... 210 A7
ridge Cl CHELT GL50 .... 2 B1
sworth Cl CIR GL7 .... 243 G4
wick Av
　MSTRD/HC/WWD BS13 .... 345 L8
kander Dr CIR GL7 .... 238 B5
kander Gdns TET GL8 .... 281 M3
kander Rd MALM SN16 .... 303 G6
ANG/FISH BS16 .... 327 M7
kandra Gdns
　MANG/FISH BS16 .... 327 M7
kandra Pk MANG/FISH BS16 .. 327 H7
DLND/MONT BS6 .... 335 L1
kandra Pl MANG/FISH BS16 .. 327 M7
kandra Rd
　MSTRD/HC/WWD BS13 .... 345 H4
FTN/FAIL BS8 .... 335 K3
kandra Sq CHNTN OX7 .... 105 M1
kandra St CHELT GL50 .... 115 K4
kandra Wy TEWK GL20 .... 48 F4
HNB/SVB BS35 .... 273 K8
rd Rd
　RSG/KWL/STAPK BS4 .... 346 E1
ed Hl CBRISNE BS2 .... 6 E1
ed Pde CBRISNE BS2 .... 6 E1
ed Pl CBRISNE BS2 .... 335 L3
ed Rd BMSTR BS3 .... 335 M8
DLND/MONT BS6 .... 325 J7
ed St CBRISNE BS2 .... 7 L4
VILLE/WHL BS5 .... 336 E3
t GL1 .... 5 J9
ers St BMSTR BS3 .... 335 M8
e Crs CHEP NP16 .... 270 C7
gton Cl GL1 .... 5 J7
gton Rd STNHO GL10 .... 206 B4
lone COTS GL54 .... 169 H2
nmead Rd
　GRV/WHIT BS14 .... 346 D3
ston Rd LYD GL15 .... 201 K5
ndale LYD GL15 .... 112 E7
n Dr STROUD GL5 .... 208 B3
nfield Rd CHELTS GL53 ...... 115 L6
ngrove La
　HPMW/MSHF SN14 .... 313 L8
rton Crs HGRV/WHIT BS14 ... 346 F4
rton Gdns HGRV/WHIT BS14.. 346 D6
rton Rd HGRV/WHIT BS14 ... 346 C7
oxton Rd HORF/LLZ BS7 ..... 326 C8
allows Rd
　VILLE/WHL BS5 .... 336 D3
gton Dr
　OLD/WMLY/WICK BS30 .... 338 B7
ngton Rd BMSTR BS3 .... 6 C7
on Av
　RSG/KWL/STAPK BS4 .... 337 G7
on Rd
　RSG/KWL/STAPK BS4 .... 337 G8
tment La CIR GL7 .... 240 F2
aints' La CBRIS/FH BS1 ...... 6 F4
aints' Rd CFTN/FAIL BS8..... 335 J4
HELTE/BC GL52 .... 3 G5
t GL1 .... 5 G8
TROUD GL5 .... 208 F3
aints' Ter CHELTE/BC GL52... 3 H4
aints' Villas Rd
　HELTE/BC GL52 .... 3 C4
opp Cl CIND GL14 .... 155 H7

Alma Cl CHELTW GL51 .... 115 H4
Alma Pl GL GL1 .... 135 M4
Alma Rd CFTN/FAIL BS8 ...... 335 J3
　CHELTW GL51 .... 115 H5
　KGWD/HNM BS15 .... 338 A3
Alma Road Av CFTN/FAIL BS8 .. 335 K3
Alma Ter GL GL1 .... 135 M4
Alma Vale Rd CFTN/FAIL BS8.. 335 J3
Almeda Rd EVILLE/WHL BS5.... 337 J5
Almond Cl GLE GL4 .... 136 F8
Almond Wk LYD GL15 .... 201 K7
Almorah Rd BMSTR BS3 ...... 336 A8
Almshouses Rd CLFD GL16 .... 174 E4
Alney Ter GL GL1 .... 4 B3
Alpha Cl TEWK GL20 .... 48 C4
Alpha Rd BMSTR BS3 .... 6 E8
Alpine Cl GLE GL4 .... 136 D5
Alpine Rd EVILLE/WHL BS5 .... 336 E2
Alsop Rd KGWD/HNM BS15 .... 337 M3
Alstone Av CHELTW GL51 ..... 115 K1
Alstone Cft CHELTW GL51 .... 115 K1
Alstone La CHELTW GL51 ..... 115 J1
Althorp Cl GL GL1 .... 159 K1
Alton Rd HORF/LLZ BS7 ...... 326 B5
Altringham Rd
　EVILLE/WHL BS5 .... 336 F3
Alverstoke Rd HGRV/WHIT BS14 .. 346 B4
Alverton Dr CHELTE/BC GL52 .. 94 A1
Alveston Gra CAM GL55 ...... 8 F8
Alveston Hl THNB/SVB BS35 ... 293 J5
Alveston Rd ALMDB BS32 ..... 292 E8
Alveston Wk
　HNLZ/SM/SNYPK/WT BS9'.... 324 D4
Alvin St GL GL1 .... 4 F4
Alwins Ct
　OLD/WMLY/WICK BS30 .... 338 B7
Amaranth Wy CHELTW GL51 ... 115 H6
Amberley Cl KEYN BS31 .... 348 A1
　MANG/FISH 327 M4
Amberley Rd
　BRSTK/PCHW BS34 .... 316 D3
　CHELTW GL51 .... 115 G1
　GLE GL4 .... 136 D6
　MANG/FISH 327 M4
Amberley Wy WUE GL12 ...... 296 D6
Amble Cl KGWD/HNM BS15 .... 338 B4
Ambleside Av
　HNBRY/STHM BS10 .... 325 K2
Ambra V CFTN/FAIL BS8 ...... 335 J5
Ambra V East CFTN/FAIL BS8 .. 335 J5
Ambra V South
　CFTN/FAIL BS8 .... 335 J5
Ambra V West CFTN/FAIL BS8.. 335 J5
Ambrose Cl CLFD GL16 .... 151 M8
Ambrose Pl CHELT GL50....... 2 C4
Ambrose Rd CFTN/FAIL BS8 ... 335 J5
Ambrose St CHELT GL50 ...... 2 C4
Amercombe Wk
　HGRV/WHIT BS14 .... 346 F4
America Gdns NWNT GL18 .... 86 C3
Ampney La CIND GL14 .... 132 B5
Anbrook Crs GLE GL4 .... 137 G4
Anchor Rd CBRIS/FH BS1 ..... 6 B5
　KGWD/HNM BS15 .... 338 C2
Ancient Rd CLFD GL16 .... 151 H1
Andereach Cl HGRV/WHIT BS14 .. 346 D4
Anderson Cl CHELTE/BC GL52 . 72 D8
Anderson Dr STNHO GL10 .... 207 H4
Andorra Wy BWTH/CHD GL3 .. 113 K5
Andover Cl
　BRSG/KWL/STAPK BS4 .... 346 B1
CHELT GL50 .... 2 A8
CHELT GL50 .... 115 K3
Andover Rd
　BRSG/KWL/STAPK BS4 .... 346 B1
Andoversford Link COTS GL54 .. 118 C8
Andover Wk CHELT GL50 ..... 2 B9
Andover Wk CHELT GL50 ..... 2 A9
Andrew's Cl GLE GL4 .... 160 B6
Angel Fld CLFD GL16 .... 175 J1
Angelica Wy GLE GL4 .... 137 H6
Angels Gnd
　BRSG/KWL/STAPK BS4 .... 337 H5
Angers Rd BRSG/KWL/STAPK BS4 .. 7 K9
Anglesea Pl CFTN/FAIL BS8 ... 335 J1
Anne Hathaway Dr
　BWTH/CHD GL3 .... 114 A6
Anns Wk MTCHDN GL17 ...... 130 C3
Ann Wicks Rd VGL GL2 .... 181 J6
Ansdell Dr BWTH/CHD GL3 ... 138 A5
Ansell Cl CHELTW GL51 ...... 115 H6
Anstey's Cl KGWD/HNM BS15 .. 337 K6
Anstey St EVILLE/WHL BS5 .... 336 D2
Antelope Paddock COTS GL54 .. 169 J1
Anthea Rd EVILLE/WHL BS5 ... 337 G1
Anthony's Cross NWNT GL18 .. 86 C7
Antrim Rd
　HNLZ/SM/SNYPK/WT BS9..... 325 K5
Anvil St CBRISNE BS2 .... 7 K4
A P Ellis Rd COTS GL54 ...... 124 D8
Apperley Cl YATE/CS BS37 .... 319 M3
Apperley Dr VGL GL2 .... 159 G2
Apperley Pk RTEWK/TIB L19... 69 G5
Appleby Wk
　BRSG/KWL/STAPK BS4 .... 345 M4
Apple Cl CHELTE/BC GL52 .... 94 C6
Appledore Cl HGRV/WHIT BS14 .. 346 D3
Applegate HNBRY/STHM BS10 .. 315 K8
Apple Orch CHELTE/BC GL52 .. 94 C6
The Apple Orch TEWK GL20 .. 49 G2
Appleridge La BRKLY GL13 ... 250 E7
Appleton Av CHELTW GL51 ... 114 D5
Appleton Wy BWTH/CHD GL3 . 137 J5
Apple Tree Cl BWTH/CHD GL3 .. 113 J4
　CHELTE/BC GL52 .... 94 E1
　GLE GL4 .... 137 G2
April Cl DSLY GL11 .... 253 J3
Apsleys Md ALMDB BS32....... 316 E1
Apsley Cl CIR GL7 .... 238 B4
Apsley Rd CFTN/FAIL BS8..... 335 J2
　CIR GL7 .... 238 B5
Apsley St EVILLE/WHL BS5 .... 336 E1
Aragon Wy BWTH/CHD GL3 .. 113 H4
Arbutus Dr
　HNLZ/SM/SNYPK/WT BS9..... 324 E4
Archdeacon Ct GL GL1 .... 4 D4
Archdeacon St GL GL1 .... 4 D4

Archer Ct
　OLD/WMLY/WICK BS30 .... 338 B8
Archers La CHELTE/BC GL52 ... 70 F6
Archer Wk HGRV/WHIT BS14 .. 347 G5
Archery Rd CIR GL7 .... 238 D5
Archibald St GL GL1 .... 5 G8
Archway Cl CIND GL14 .... 178 B2
Archway Gdns STROUD GL5 ... 208 B3
Ardea Cl VGL GL2 .... 158 E2
Arden Cl ALMDB BS32 .... 317 G5
Arden Rd CHELTS GL53 .... 115 L6
Ardenton Wk
　HNBRY/STHM BS10 .... 315 J8
Ardern Cl
　HNLZ/SM/SNYPK/WT BS9..... 324 D3
Ardmore Cl GLE GL4 .... 136 A8
Argus Rd BMSTR BS3 .... 335 L8
Argyle Cl CFTN/FAIL BS8 ..... 335 J5
Argyle Pl CFTN/FAIL BS8 ..... 335 J5
Argyle Rd CBRISNE BS2 ...... 336 A3
　MANG/FISH 337 K1
Argyle St BMSTR BS3 .... 336 C6
　EVILLE/WHL BS5 .... 336 E1
Argyll Pl VGL GL2 .... 5 L4
Argyll Rd CHELTS GL53 .... 2 F8
　VGL GL2 .... 112 E7
Ariel Lodge Rd CHELTE/BC GL52.. 3 H4
Arkells Ct WUE GL12 .... 296 C5
Arkendale Dr VGL GL2 .... 158 F3
Arkle Cl CHELT GL50 .... 93 L6
Arle Av CHELTW GL51 .... 115 K1
Arle Cl CHELTW GL51 .... 115 K1
Arle Dr CHELTW GL51 .... 115 J1
Arle Gdns CHELTW GL51 ...... 115 J1
Arle Rd CHELTW GL51 .... 93 J8
Arley Cottages
　RDLND/MONT BS6 .... 335 M2
Arley Hl RDLND/MONT BS6 .... 335 M2
Arley Pk RDLND/MONT BS6 ... 335 M2
Arley Ter EVILLE/WHL BS5 .... 337 G2
Arlingham CHELTW GL51 ..... 115 G6
Arlingham Wy
　BRSTK/PCHW BS34 .... 316 A3
Arlingham Rd GL GL1 .... 135 M7
Arlingham Wy
　BRSTK/PCHW BS34 .... 316 A3
Arlington Ct CHEP NP16 ..... 270 C3
Arlington Rd
　BRSG/KWL/STAPK BS4 .... 336 F5
Arlington Vls CFTN/FAIL BS8 .. 335 J4
Armada Cl BWTH/CHD GL3 ... 113 H4
Armada Pl CBRIS/FH BS1 ..... 6 F3
Armidale Av
　RDLND/MONT BS6 .... 336 A2
Armoury Sq EVILLE/WHL BS5 .. 336 C3
Armscroft Ct VGL GL2 .... 136 E2
Armscroft Gdns VGL GL2 ..... 5 M6
Armscroft Pl VGL GL2 .... 5 M6
Armscroft Rd VGL GL2 .... 136 E2
Armscroft Wy VGL GL2 ...... 5 M5
Armstrong Cl
　THNB/SVB BS35 .... 293 M4
Armstrong Dr
　OLD/WMLY/WICK BS30 .... 338 D6
Armstrong Wy YATE/CS BS37... 309 L8
Arnall Dr HNBRY/STHM BS10 .. 325 L2
Arneside Rd HNBRY/STHM BS10 .. 325 M3
Arnold's La
　RSTROUD/NAIL GL6 .... 232 D8
Arnolds Wy CIR GL7 .... 238 E2
Arreton Av GLE GL4 .... 136 E5
Arrowhead Cl GLE GL4 .... 136 D7
Arrowsmith Dr STNHO GL10 .. 207 H2
Arthur Skemp Cl
　EVILLE/WHL BS5 .... 336 D4
Arthur St CBRISNE BS2 .... 7 M6
　EVILLE/WHL BS5 .... 336 E3
　GL GL1 .... 4 F7
Arthurswood Rd
　BMSTRD/HC/WWD BS13 ...... 345 J7
Arundel Cl
　BMSTRD/HC/WWD BS13 ...... 345 J7
　GL GL1 .... 159 L2
Arundel Dr STROUD GL5 ..... 208 D3
Arundel Mill La STROUD GL5 .. 208 F5
Arundel Rd HORF/LLZ BS7 .... 325 M9
　TEWK GL20 .... 48 C3
Ascot Cl MANG/FISH BS16 .... 328 B2
Ascot Rd HNBRY/STHM BS10 .. 325 M1
Ashbourne Cl
　OLD/WMLY/WICK BS30 .... 338 E5
Ashbrook La CIR GL7 .... 241 C7
Ashburton Rd
　HNBRY/STHM BS10 .... 325 L2
Ashbury Cl CHELTW GL51 .... 138 F1
Ash Cl BRSTK/PCHW BS34 .... 316 F4
　CHELTS GL53 .... 116 A6
　CHEP NP16 .... 270 A6
　DSLY GL11 .... 229 J7
　LYD GL15 .... 201 K7
　YATE/CS BS37 .... 309 M8
Ashcombe Cl
　OLD/WMLY/WICK BS30 .... 338 E5
Ashcombe Crs
　OLD/WMLY/WICK BS30 .... 338 F5
Ashcot Ms CHELTW GL51 ..... 115 G6
Ashcott HGRV/WHIT BS14 ..... 346 B5
Ashcroft Av KEYN BS31 ...... 347 M6
Ashcroft Rd CIR GL7 .... 238 C3
Ashcroft Rd GLE GL4 .... 160 F1
　HNLZ/SM/SNYPK/WT BS9..... 324 E4
　WUE GL12 .... 278 C1
Ashdale Cl COTS GL54 .... 194 F2
Ashdene Av EVILLE/WHL BS5 .. 326 F8
Ash Dene Rd MTCHDN GL17 .. 128 F6
Asher La CBRISNE BS2 .... 7 J2
Ashes La RWYE HR9 .... 126 E5
Ashfield Cl CHELTE/BC GL52 .. 72 C8
Ashfield Pl
　RDLND/MONT BS6 .... 336 B2
Ashfield Rd BMSTR BS3 ...... 335 K8
　MTCHDN GL17 .... 129 K5
Ashford Rd BRSTK/PCHW BS34.. 316 C4
　CHELT GL50 .... 2 A9
Ash Gv GLE GL4 .... 137 G3
　MANG/FISH 327 L8

MTCHDN GL17 .... 106 C8
Ashgrove CHELTS GL53 .... 116 D7
　SHPSTR CV36 .... 16 B7
　THNB/SVB BS35 .... 293 L2
Ashgrove Av CFTN/FAIL BS8 .. 334 D4
　GLE GL4 .... 136 E5
　HORF/LLZ BS7 .... 326 C8
Ashgrove Cl VGL GL2 .... 159 G4
Ash Grove Pl LYD GL15 ...... 201 L1
Ashgrove Wy GLE GL4 .... 136 E5
Ashland Rd
　BMSTRD/HC/WWD BS13 ...... 345 J7
Ashlands Cl CHELTW GL51 .... 93 G8
Ashlands Rd CHELTW GL51 ... 93 G8
Ash La ALMDB BS32 .... 305 M8
　STNHO GL10 .... 207 L1
　VGL GL2 .... 112 C5
Ashlea Mdw CHELTE/BC GL52 .. 71 M7
Ashleigh La CHELTE/BC GL52 .. 94 F2
Ashletts Rd RSTROUD/NAIL GL6 .. 211 L3
Ashleworth Gdns VGL GL2 ... 159 G3
Ashley KGWD/HNM BS15 ...... 338 B3
Ashley Cl CHELTE/BC GL52 ... 116 D4
　HORF/LLZ BS7 .... 326 B7
Ashley Court Rd
　RDLND/MONT BS6 .... 336 B1
Ashley Down Rd HORF/LLZ BS7 .. 326 A6
Ashley Dr RSTROUD/NAIL GL6 .. 209 L8
Ashley Grove Rd
　CBRISNE BS2 .... 336 B1
　CBRISNE BS2 .... 336 C2
Ashley Hl RDLND/MONT BS6 .. 326 A8
Ashley Pde CBRISNE BS2 ..... 336 B1
Ashley Pk RDLND/MONT BS6 .. 326 B8
Ash Rd CBATH/BATHN BA1 .... 553 C8
　CHELTE/BC GL52 .... 3 L9
　RDLND/MONT BS6 .... 336 A1
Ashley St CBRISNE BS2 ...... 336 C2
Ashman Cl EVILLE/WHL BS5 ... 7 M1
Ashmead VGL GL2 .... 112 D6
Ashmead Dr CHELTE/BC GL52 . 72 C3
Ashmead Rd CIND GL14 ...... 154 B4
　KEYN BS31 .... 348 D6
Ashmead Wy CBRIS/FH BS1 .. 335 H6
Ashmore Rd GLE GL4 .... 136 E7
The Ash Pth GLE GL4 .... 137 G8
Ash Ridge Rd ALMDB BS32 ... 306 D8
Ash Rd CHPMW/MSHF SN14 .. 343 G6
　HORF/LLZ BS7 .... 326 A6
　STROUD GL5 .... 208 C7
　TEWK GL20 .... 49 G3
Ashton Av CBRIS/FH BS1 ..... 335 J6
Ashton Cl CHELTW GL51 ...... 137 G8
Ashton Dr BMSTR BS3 .... 345 G2
Ashton Gate Rd BMSTR BS3 .. 335 J7
Ashton Gate Ter BMSTR BS3 . 335 J7
Ashton Rd BMSTR BS3 .... 335 H8
　CIR GL7 .... 238 E8
　CIR GL7 .... 262 E1
　LGASH BS41 .... 334 E8
　MALM SN16 .... 287 H5
　TEWK GL20 .... 28 F6
Ashton Vale Rd BMSTR BS3 .. 335 G8
Ashton Wy KEYN BS31 .... 348 A5
Ash Tree Cl NWNT GL18 ..... 86 C5
Ashville Rd BMSTR BS3 ...... 335 J7
　VGL GL2 .... 135 K6
Ash Wk HNBRY/STHM BS10 ... 315 K8
Ashway COTS GL54 .... 169 K1
　LYD GL15 .... 224 B6
Ashwell Cl HGRV/WHIT BS14 .. 347 G5
Ashwell Hyett Cl
　RSTROUD/NAIL GL6 .... 185 H3
Ashwicke HGRV/WHIT BS14 ... 346 B5
Ashwicke Rd
　CHPMW/MSHF SN14 .... 342 B6
Askwith Rd GLE GL4 .... 136 D5
Askwith Rd GLE GL4 .... 136 D5
Aspen Dr VGL GL2 .... 159 C1
Asquith Rd CHELTS GL53 ..... 116 A5
Assembly Rooms La
　CBRIS/FH BS1 .... 6 E5
Aston Bank RWYE HR9 .... 85 C7
Aston Bridge Rd MTCHDN GL17.. 128 F6
Aston Cl CLFD GL16 .... 151 K6
　LED HR8 .... 19 M5
Aston Gv CHELTW GL51 ...... 114 F1
　COTS GL54 .... 121 M7
Aston Rd CHCAM GL55 .... 12 E7
Aston Vw RSTROUD/NAIL GL6.. 210 B8
Astor Cl BWTH/CHD GL3 ..... 137 M5
Astridge Rd BWTH/CHD GL3 .. 138 C7
Astry Cl AVONM BS11 .... 324 C2
Atchley St EVILLE/WHL BS5 ... 336 D4
Atcombe Rd STROUD GL5 .... 232 B3
Athelney Wy CHELTE/BC GL52 . 3 H7
Athelstan Rd MALM SN16 .... 303 H7
Atherston
　OLD/WMLY/WICK BS30 .... 338 E6
Atherstone Cl CHELTW GL51 .. 92 B8
Atherton Cl CHELTW GL51 .... 138 F1
Athlone Wk
　BRSG/KWL/STAPK BS4 .... 346 A2
Atkins Cl HGRV/WHIT BS14 ... 347 G5
Atkinson Cl BDWAY WR12 .... 32 A1
Atlas Cl EVILLE/WHL BS5 ..... 337 J1
Atlas Rd BMSTR BS3 .... 336 A8
Atlas St CBRISNE BS2 .... 336 D6
Attwood Cl CHELTW GL51 .... 93 H6
Atwell Dr ALMDB BS32 .... 316 D2
Atwood Dr AVONM BS11 ...... 324 D1
Aubrey Meads
　OLD/WMLY/WICK BS30 .... 349 G3
Aubrey Ri MALM SN16 .... 303 J6
Aubrey Rd BMSTR BS3 .... 335 K8
Auburn Av
　OLD/WMLY/WICK BS30 .... 338 D6
Auburn Rd RDLND/MONT BS6 . 335 K1
Auden Crs LED HR8 .... 19 L2
Audley Cft LED HR8 .... 19 M2
Audrey Wk
　HNLZ/SM/SNYPK/WT BS9..... 325 M5
Augustine Wy
　BWTH/CHD GL3 .... 137 H5
Augustus Wy LYD GL15 ...... 201 K6
Aust Crs CHEP NP16 .... 270 C4

Austen Gv HORF/LLZ BS7 ..... 326 C3
Austin Dr VGL GL2 .... 112 B5
Austin Rd CIR GL7 .... 238 E3
　TEWK GL20 .... 49 J3
Aust Rd THNB/SVB BS35 ...... 290 F8
　THNB/SVB BS35 .... 292 A6
Avalon Rd EVILLE/WHL BS5 ... 337 K5
Avebury Cl GL GL1 .... 159 K1
Avebury Rd BMSTR BS3 ...... 345 G1
Avenall Pde CHELTS GL53 .... 3 G8
Avening Rd GLE GL4 .... 136 B6
　KGWD/HNM BS15 .... 337 J3
　RSTROUD/NAIL GL6 .... 232 F8
Avenue Rd UUSV WR8 .... 24 C1
The Avenue BRSTK/PCHW BS34.. 316 C5
　BWTH/CHD GL3 .... 113 L6
　CFTN/FAIL BS8 .... 335 J2
　CHELTS GL53 .... 116 A6
　CIR GL7 .... 238 D3
　DSLY GL11 .... 228 F8
　EVILLE/WHL BS5 .... 337 H4
　HNLZ/SM/SNYPK/WT BS9..... 334 F1
　KEYN BS31 .... 348 A4
　MANG/FISH BS16 .... 327 G2
　RDLND/MONT BS6 .... 326 A8
　RSTROUD/NAIL GL6 .... 209 L8
　VGL GL2 .... 112 E7
　YATE/CS BS37 .... 319 M2
Averay Rd MANG/FISH BS16 .. 326 E7
Averill Cl BDWAY WR12 ...... 32 F3
Avon Cl BRSG/KWL/STAPK BS4 .. 337 H5
　KEYN BS31 .... 348 B5
Avon Ct CBATH/BATHN BA1.... 352 C7
Avon Crs BWTH/CHD BS3 ..... 138 B6
　CBRIS/FH BS1 .... 335 J6
　WUE GL12 .... 296 D5
Avondale Pl
　CBATH/BATHN BA1 .... 352 B8
Avondown Cl
　HNBRY/STHM BS10 .... 325 M1
Avon Gv
　HNLZ/SM/SNYPK/WT BS9..... 334 F1
Avon La KEYN BS31 .... 349 H6
Avonlea KGWD/HNM BS15 .... 337 L6
Avonleaze
　HNLZ/SM/SNYPK/WT BS9..... 324 D6
Avonleigh Rd BMSTR BS3 .... 345 K1
Avon Mill La KEYN BS31 ...... 348 B5
Avon Pk EVILLE/WHL BS5 ..... 336 F4
Avon Rd
　BMSTRD/HC/WWD BS13 ...... 345 J5
　CHELTE/BC GL52 .... 3 K4
　KEYN BS31 .... 348 B5
　MALM SN16 .... 303 H7
　WUE GL12 .... 276 C7
Avonside Rd CBRISNE BS2 .... 336 E5
Avonside Wy
　BRSG/KWL/STAPK BS4 .... 337 H5
Avon St CBRISNE BS2 .... 7 J4
Avon V
　HNLZ/SM/SNYPK/WT BS9..... 324 F7
Avonvale Rd EVILLE/WHL BS5 .. 336 E4
Avon Vw KGWD/HNM BS15 .... 337 K8
　TEWK GL20 .... 48 C3
Avon Walkway
　OLD/WMLY/WICK BS30 .... 348 E5
Avon Wy HNBRY/STHM BS10 .. 325 M3
　HNLZ/SM/SNYPK/WT BS9..... 324 E6
　THNB/SVB BS35 .... 293 L3
Avonwood Cl AVONM BS11 .... 324 A5
Avro Rd COTS GL54 .... 124 D6
Awdelett Cl AVONM BS11 .... 324 D2
Awdry Wy GLE GL4 .... 159 M1
Awebridge Wy GLE GL4 ...... 136 E7
Awkley La THNB/SVB BS35 .... 306 A2
Awkward Hl CIR GL7 .... 217 J1
Awre Rd LYD GL15 .... 202 E1
Axbridge Rd
　BRSG/KWL/STAPK BS4 .... 346 B1
Aycote Cl GLE GL4 .... 136 D6
Ayford La CHPMW/MSHF SN14 . 342 F2
Ayland Cl NWNT GL18 .... 86 D3
Ayland Gdns GL GL1 .... 5 K7
Aylesbury Crs BMSTR BS3 .... 345 K2
Aylesbury Rd BMSTR BS3 .... 345 K2
Aylmer Crs HGRV/WHIT BS14 .. 346 D5
Aylminton Wk AVONM BS11 ... 324 D1
Aylton Cl CHELTW GL51 ...... 114 F5
Aysgarth Av CHELTW GL51 ... 115 G6
Azalea Dr CHELTW GL51 ...... 115 H6
Azalea Gdns VGL GL2 .... 159 G1

B

Back Albert Pl CHELTE/BC GL52 .. 2 F3
Back Br MALM SN16 .... 303 G6
Back Edge La
　RSTROUD/NAIL GL6 .... 184 E3
Back Ends CHCAM GL55 ...... 12 D8
Backfields CBRISNE BS2 ...... 7 G1
Backfields La CBRISNE BS2 ... 336 A3
Back La BDWAY WR12 .... 32 E3
　CHCAM GL55 .... 8 F7
　CHPMW/MSHF SN14 .... 342 B3
　CIR GL7 .... 188 C3
　CIR GL7 .... 242 C5
　COTS GL54 .... 74 B6
　KEYN BS31 .... 348 A5
　MANG/FISH BS16 .... 329 L7
　MIM GL56 .... 103 G3
　MTCHDN GL17 .... 129 L3
　RSTROUD/NAIL GL6 .... 210 C3
　SHPSTR CV36 .... 61 J5
　TET GL8 .... 279 L8
　TEWK GL20 .... 27 G4
　TEWK GL20 .... 28 E8
　WUE GL12 .... 296 C5
Back Montpellier Ter CHELT GL50 .. 2 B8
Back of Avon TEWK GL20 .... 48 A5
Back of Kingsdown Pde
　RDLND/MONT BS6 .... 335 M3
Back of Mount Pleasant
　TEWK GL20 .... 48 B5
Back Rd BMSTR BS3 .... 335 J7
Back Rw MIM GL56 .... 81 L8

Back Stoke La
 HNLZ/SM/SNYPK/WT BS9 .... **325** H5
Back St *BAD* GL9 .... **298** C8
 CIND GL14 .... **155** J7
 HGHW SN6 .... **287** H2
The Back *CHEP* NP16 .... **270** B2
Back Walls *COTS* GL54 .... **102** A3
Backwell Wk
 BMSTRD/HC/WWD BS13 .... **345** H3
Baden Hill Rd *WUE* GL12 .... **294** E6
Baden Rd *EVILLE/WHL* BS5 ...... **336** E4
 KGWD/HNM BS15 .... **338** C4
Bader Av *BWTH/CHD* GL3 .... **113** L6
Bader Cl *YATE/CS* BS37 .... **309** M8
Badger Cl *GLE* GL4 .... **136** F8
Badgers Cl *ALMDB* BS32 .... **306** F8
Badgers Crs *SHPSTR* CV36 ...... **16** B4
Badger's La *ALMDB* BS32 .... **315** L1
Badgers Wk
 BRSG/KWL/STAPK BS4 .... **346** F1
Badgers Wy *LYD* GL15 .... **200** D2
Badger Vale Ct *GL* GL1 .... **135** L6
Badgeworth *YATE/CS* BS37 ...... **319** M5
Badgeworth La *CHELTW* GL51 .. **138** E2
Badgeworth Rd *CHELTW* GL51 .. **114** C6
The Badhams *TEWK* GL20 .... **24** B6
Badmington Rd
 MANG/FISH BS16 .... **328** B3
Badminton Cl *CHELTS* GL53 .... **115** M5
Badminton Rd *CBRISNE* BS2 .... **336** B2
 FRCTL/WBN BS36 .... **318** C8
 GLE GL4 .... **136** D6
 MANG/FISH BS16 .... **328** A4
 YATE/CS BS37 .... **319** K1
 YATE/CS BS37 .... **321** C3
Badsey La *EVE* WR11 .... **10** E4
Bafford Ap *CHELTS* GL53 .... **116** B7
Bafford Gv *CHELTS* GL53 .... **116** B7
Bafford La *CHELTS* GL53 .... **116** C6
Baglyn Av *KGWD/HNM* BS15 .... **328** B8
Bagnell Cl *HGRV/WHIT* BS14 .... **347** G6
Bagnell Rd *HGRV/WHIT* BS14 .. **347** G6
Bagpath La *STROUD* GL5 .... **232** F1
Bagstone Rd *WUE* GL12 .... **295** J6
Bagworth Dr
 OLD/WMLY/WICK BS30 .... **338** B8
Bailbrook Gv
 CBATH/BATHN BA1 .... **351** L8
Bailbrook La
 CBATH/BATHN BA1 .... **352** A8
Bailey Hl *LYD* GL15 .... **201** K1
Bailey La *LYD* GL15 .... **222** D3
Bailey Rd *STRAT* CV37 .... **8** F1
Baileys Court Rd *ALMDB* BS32 . **317** C5
Baileys Mead Rd
 MANG/FISH BS16 .... **326** E6
Bailiffe Piece *HGHW* SN6 .... **288** F2
Baines Cl *COTS* GL54 .... **123** H6
Bakehouse La *CHELT* GL50 ...... **115** K4
Bakersfield
 OLD/WMLY/WICK BS30 .... **338** C6
Bakers Gnd
 BRSTK/PCHW BS34 .... **317** H6
 CLFD GL16 .... **151** L8
Baker's Hl *CHCAM* GL55 .... **9** G8
Baker's La *EVE* WR11 .... **29** K2
 RTEWK/TIB GL19 .... **88** F5
Bakers Piece Rd *MTCHDN* GL17 . **129** H5
Baker St *CHELTW* GL51 .... **2** B2
 GL GL1 .... **4** C8
Balaclava Rd
 MANG/FISH BS16 .... **327** H8
Bala Rd *CHELTW* GL51 .... **115** H5
Balcarras *CHELTS* GL53 .... **116** E6
Balcarras Gdns *CHELTS* GL53 .. **116** E6
Balcarras Retreat
 CHELTS GL53 .... **116** E6
Balcarras Rd *CHELTS* GL53 ...... **116** E6
Baldwin St *CBRIS/FH* BS1 .... **6** F4
Balfour Rd *BMSTR* BS3 .... **335** K8
 GL GL1 .... **135** M4
Ballards Cl *CHCAM* GL55 .... **8** F8
Ballinode Cl *CHELTW* GL51 ...... **93** K6
Ballinska Ms *VGL* GL2 .... **112** F6
Balmain St *BRSG/KWL/STAPK* BS4 .. **7** M9
Balmoral Cl
 BRSTK/PCHW BS34 .... **316** F7
Balmoral Ct
 MANG/FISH BS16 .... **328** C6
Balmoral Rd *KEYN* BS31 .... **348** A7
 OLD/WMLY/WICK BS30 .... **348** B1
 RDLND/MONT BS6 .... **336** B1
Bamfield *HGRV/WHIT* BS14 ...... **346** B4
Bamfurlong La *CHELTW* GL51 .... **114** A2
Bampton Cl
 BMSTRD/HC/WWD BS13 ...... **345** K4
Bampton Dr
 MANG/FISH BS16 .... **327** M2
Banady La *CHELTE/BC* GL52 ...... **71** G6
Baneberry Rd *GLE* GL4 .... **136** C6
Banfield Cl *AVONM* BS11 .... **324** C3
Bangor Gv
 BRSG/KWL/STAPK BS4 .... **337** H6
Bangup La *COTS* GL54 .... **121** M8
Bangrove Wk *AVONM* BS11 ...... **324** A3
Bank Crs *LED* HR8 .... **20** A2
Bank Rd *KGWD/HNM* BS15 ...... **337** M3
 THNB/SVB BS35 .... **304** F4
Banks Fee La *MIM* GL56 .... **79** K4
Bankside *MANG/FISH* BS16 ...... **328** B7
Bankside Rd
 BRSG/KWL/STAPK BS4 .... **336** F8
Bank Sq *CHEP* NP16 .... **270** A3
Bank St *CHEP* NP16 .... **270** A3
 CLFD GL16 .... **175** J1
The Bank *CHELTE/BC* GL52 ...... **94** E7
 CHPMW/MSHF SN14 .... **343** L8
Bannerdown Cl
 CBATH/BATHN BA1 .... **352** D7
Bannerdown Dr
 CBATH/BATHN BA1 .... **352** C7
Bannerdown Rd
 CBATH/BATHN BA1 .... **352** C8
Bannerleigh La
 CFTN/FAIL BS8 .... **335** G5
Bannerleigh Rd *CFTN/FAIL* BS8 .. **335** G4

Bannerman Rd
 EVILLE/WHL BS5 .... **336** D3
Banner Rd *RDLND/MONT* BS6 .. **336** A2
Bannetts Tree Crs
 THNB/SVB BS35 .... **293** J6
Bantry Rd
 BRSG/KWL/STAPK BS4 .... **346** A3
Banwell Cl
 BMSTRD/HC/WWD BS13 ...... **345** J3
Banwell Rd *BMSTR* BS3 .... **335** J8
Baptist Cl *GLE* GL4 .... **137** H5
Baptist St *EVILLE/WHL* BS5 ...... **336** C2
Baptist Wy *MTCHDN* GL17 ...... **129** K5
Barbican Cl *GL* GL1 .... **4** D5
Barbican Wy *GL* GL1 .... **4** D5
Barbour Gdns *BMSTRD/HC/WWD* BS13 .. **345** M8
Barbour Rd
 BMSTRD/HC/WWD BS13 ...... **345** M8
Barbridge Rd *CHELTW* GL51 ...... **93** G8
Barcroft Cl *KGWD/HNM* BS15 ... **337** L3
Baregains La *LED* HR8 .... **18** F2
Bargates *CBRISNE* BS2 .... **353** M5
Barker Pl *CIR* GL7 .... **242** F4
Barker's Leys *CHELTE/BC* GL52 .. **72** C7
Barkers Md *YATE/CS* BS37 ...... **310** B7
Barkleys Hl *MANG/FISH* BS16 .. **326** E6
Barksdale *COTS* GL54 .... **74** B6
The Barlands *CHELTE/BC* GL52 . **117** G7
Barley Cl *CHELTW* GL51 .... **92** F6
 FRCTL/WBN BS36 .... **318** D3
 MANG/FISH BS16 .... **328** C5
 VGL GL2 .... **159** G5
Barley Cft
 HNLZ/SM/SNYPK/WT BS9 .... **325** H6
Barleycroft Cl *GLE* GL4 .... **160** F1
Barlow Cl *STNHO* GL10 .... **207** G4
Barlow Rd *CHELTW* GL51 .... **93** H7
Barnabas St *CBRISNE* BS2 ...... **336** A2
Barnaby Cl *GL* GL1 .... **136** B4
Barnacre Dr *GLE* GL4 .... **137** H2
Barnage La *LYD* GL15 .... **223** J3
Barnard Wy *KEYN* BS31 .... **347** M7
Barn Cl *COTS* GL54 .... **73** M2
 GLE GL4 .... **137** G7
 RSTROUD/NAIL GL6 .... **232** D8
Barncroft *SHPSTR* CV36 .... **61** H6
Barn End *CHPMW/MSHF* SN14 .. **342** C7
Barnes St *EVILLE/WHL* BS5 ...... **336** F4
Barnes Wallis Wy
 BWTH/CHD CL3 .... **113** L6
Barnett Av *LED* HR8 .... **19** L3
Barnett Cl *CHELTW* GL51 .... **93** G6
Barnetts Cl *LED* HR8 .... **19** L3
Barnett Wy *COTS* GL54 .... **169** J1
 GLE GL4 .... **137** G2
Barn Field Rd
 RSTROUD/NAIL GL6 .... **232** C7
Barnfield Wy
 CBATH/BATHN BA1 .... **352** D7
Barn Gnd *VGL* GL2 .... **110** F6
Barnhay *BWTH/CHD* GL3 .... **113** L7
Barn Hill Rd *CLFD* GL16 .... **151** M8
Barnhill Rd *YATE/CS* BS37 ...... **320** D2
Barn La *BUR/CRTN* OX18 .... **173** M6
 EVE WR11 .... **30** B2
 MTCHDN GL17 .... **129** G5
Barnmeadow Rd *COTS* GL54 .... **74** C5
Barn Owl Wy
 BRSTK/PCHW BS34 .... **317** H6
Barn Piece *COR/BOX* SN13 ...... **353** M5
Barns Cl *NAIL* BS48 .... **344** A7
Barnstaple Rd
 BRSG/KWL/STAPK BS4 .... **346** A3
Barnstaple Wk
 BRSG/KWL/STAPK BS4 .... **346** B3
Barn Wy *CIR* GL7 .... **214** A8
Barnwood Av *GLE* GL4 .... **136** F3
Barnwood Rd *GLE* GL4 .... **137** G3
 VGL GL2 .... **5** M5
 YATE/CS BS37 .... **319** L4
Barossa Pl *CBRIS/FH* BS1 .... **6** F6
Barrack Sq *GL* GL1 .... **4** C5
Barratt's Mill La *CHELT* GL50 .... **2** E6
Barratt St *EVILLE/WHL* BS5 ...... **336** D2
Barrington Av *CHELTW* GL51 .... **114** D1
Barrington Ct
 KGWD/HNM BS15 .... **338** A2
Barrington Dr *GLE* GL4 .... **137** H3
Barrow Cl *VGL* GL2 .... **159** H3
Barrowfield Rd *STROUD* GL5 .... **208** C2
Barrow Hl *BWTH/CHD* GL3 ...... **113** M8
 OLD/WMLY/WICK BS30 .... **339** K5
Barrowmead Dr *AVONM* BS11 .. **324** B3
Barrow Rd *EVILLE/WHL* BS5 ...... **7** M3
 EVILLE/WHL BS5 .... **336** D4
Barrs Court Av
 OLD/WMLY/WICK BS30 .... **338** C6
Barrs Court Rd
 OLD/WMLY/WICK BS30 .... **338** C6
Barrs La *DSLY* GL11 .... **253** C7
Barry Cl
 OLD/WMLY/WICK BS30 .... **348** E2
Barry Rd
 OLD/WMLY/WICK BS30 .... **348** E1
Bartletts Pk *COTS* GL54 .... **102** A4
Bartlett's Rd *BMSTR* BS3 .... **345** L1
Bartley Cft *TET* GL8 .... **282** A3
Bartley St *BMSTR* BS3 .... **6** E9
Barton Cl
 BRSG/KWL/STAPK BS4 .... **337** H5
 CHELTS GL53 .... **116** C7
 FRCTL/WBN BS36 .... **318** A6
 THNB/SVB BS35 .... **293** J6
Barton Ct *EVILLE/WHL* BS5 ...... **336** E5
Bartonend La
 RSTROUD/NAIL GL6 .... **256** C2
Barton Hl *MTCHDN* GL17 .... **130** D1
Barton Hill Rd *EVILLE/WHL* BS5 . **336** D5
Bartonia Gv
 BRSG/KWL/STAPK BS4 .... **346** F2
Barton La *CIR* GL7 .... **238** B2
Barton Mnr *CBRISNE* BS2 .... **7** L4
Barton Ms *TEWK* GL20 .... **48** B5
Barton Rd *CBRISNE* BS2 .... **7** K4

SHPSTR CV36 .... **60** D4
TEWK GL20 .... **48** A5
Barton St *CBRIS/FH* BS1 .... **6** F1
 GL GL1 .... **5** J9
The Barton *KGWD/HNM* BS15 .. **337** K7
Barton V *CBRISNE* BS2 .... **7** L4
Barton Wy *CHELTW* GL51 .... **115** C5
Barwick Rd *CHELTW* GL51 ...... **115** H6
Barwood Cl
 KGWD/HNM BS15 .... **338** B3
Base La *VGL* GL2 .... **111** M3
Basil Cl *GLE* GL4 .... **136** F7
Bassett Cl *COTS* GL54 .... **74** C5
Bassett Rd *COTS* GL54 .... **169** K2
The Bassetts *COR/BOX* SN13 .... **353** M5
 STROUD GL5 .... **207** M3
Batchfield La *YATE/CS* BS37 .... **329** L3
Bateman Cl *GLE* GL4 .... **159** M2
Bates Cl *EVILLE/WHL* BS5 .... **336** C3
Bathams Rd *MTCHDN* GL17 ...... **131** H1
Bath Br *BRSG/KWL/STAPK* BS4 . **7** J7
Bath Buildings
 RDLND/MONT BS6 .... **336** A2
Bath Crs *LYD* GL15 .... **201** C2
Bath Hl *KEYN* BS31 .... **348** B6
Bathleaze *STNHO* GL10 .... **207** J7
Bath Pde *CHELTS* GL53 .... **2** E7
Bath Pl *CLFD* GL16 .... **151** K5
 LYD GL15 .... **201** K8
Bath Rd *BAD* GL9 .... **331** L1
 BRSG/KWL/STAPK BS4 .... **7** K7
 BRSG/KWL/STAPK BS4 .... **347** H2
 CHELT GL50 .... **2** D7
 CHELTS GL53 .... **115** M4
 CHPMW/MSHF SN14 .... **353** C1
 COR/BOX SN13 .... **353** H6
 HGHW SN6 .... **288** F3
 KEYN BS31 .... **347** K3
 OLD/WMLY/WICK BS30 .... **338** F5
 OLD/WMLY/WICK BS30 .... **340** A8
 OLD/WMLY/WICK BS30 .... **348** F3
 RSTROUD/NAIL GL6 .... **256** D4
 STNHO GL10 .... **206** B5
 STNHO GL10 .... **207** H4
 STROUD GL5 .... **208** C5
 TET GL8 .... **299** K1
 THNB/SVB BS35 .... **293** K3
 WUE GL12 .... **299** H2
 YATE/CS BS37 .... **321** L6
Bath Road Brislington Hl
 BRSG/KWL/STAPK BS4 .... **347** G1
Bath St *BMSTR* BS3 .... **335** J7
 CBRIS/FH BS1 .... **7** C4
 MANG/FISH BS16 .... **328** A7
Bath Ter *CHELT* GL50 .... **2** C9
Bathurst Pde *CBRIS/FH* BS1 .... **6** F7
Bathurst Park Rd *LYD* GL15 .... **201** J8
Bathurst Rd *CIR* GL7 .... **238** B4
 GLE GL4 .... **136** B5
Bath Ville Rd *CHELTS* GL53 ...... **2** D8
Bathwell Rd
 BRSG/KWL/STAPK BS4 .... **336** C8
Batley Ct
 OLD/WMLY/WICK BS30 .... **338** F7
Battenburg Rd
 EVILLE/WHL BS5 .... **337** J3
Batten Ct *YATE/CS* BS37 .... **320** F2
Batten's La *EVILLE/WHL* BS5 .... **337** J5
Battens Rd *EVILLE/WHL* BS5 .... **337** K4
Battersby Wy
 HNBRY/STHM BS10 .... **325** C1
Battersea Rd *EVILLE/WHL* BS5 .. **336** E3
Battledown Ap *CHELTE/BC* GL52 . **3** J7
Battledown Cl *CHELTE/BC* GL52 .. **3** J6
Battledown Dr *CHELTE/BC* GL52 . **3** K7
Battledown Md *CHELTE/BC* GL52 . **3** K1
Battle Rd *TEWK* GL20 .... **47** M7
Battson Rd *HGRV/WHIT* BS14 .. **347** G7
Baugh Gdns *MANG/FISH* BS16 . **328** A2
Baunton La *CIR* GL7 .... **214** A6
Baxter Cl *KGWD/HNM* BS15 .... **338** B3
Bay Gdns *EVILLE/WHL* BS5 ...... **336** E1
Bayham Rd
 BRSG/KWL/STAPK BS4 .... **336** B8
Baylands *BRKLY* GL13 .... **226** F3
Bayleys Dr *KGWD/HNM* BS15 .. **337** L5
Bayliss Rd *TEWK* GL20 .... **27** M4
Baynard Rd *MTCHDN* GL17 ...... **130** C2
Baynham's Wk *CLFD* GL16 ...... **151** M7
Baynton Rd *BMSTR* BS3 .... **335** J7
Bays HI *BRKLY* GL13 .... **226** F3
Bayshill La *CHELT* GL50 .... **2** B6
Bayshill Rd *CHELT* GL50 .... **2** B6
Bayswater Av
 RDLND/MONT BS6 .... **325** K7
Bayswater Rd *HORF/LLZ* BS7 ... **326** B4
Bay Tree Cl *BRSTK/PCHW* BS34 . **316** B4
Bay Tree Rd *GLE* GL4 .... **137** H6
Bazeley Rd *GLE* GL4 .... **160** D1
Beach Av *THNB/SVB* BS35 ...... **304** C4
Beachgrove Gdns
 MANG/FISH BS16 .... **327** L7
Beachgrove Rd
 MANG/FISH BS16 .... **327** K7
Beach Hl
 OLD/WMLY/WICK BS30 .... **339** H8
Beach La
 OLD/WMLY/WICK BS30 .... **349** L1
Beachley Rd *CHEP* NP16 .... **270** C3
Beach Rd *THNB/SVB* BS35 ...... **304** B4
Beacon Cl *RSTROUD/NAIL* GL6 . **161** J6
Beacon La *MANG/FISH* BS16 .... **317** K6
Beaconlea *KGWD/HNM* BS15 ... **337** M5
Beacon Rd *GLE* GL4 .... **136** D8
Beaconsfield Rd
 BRSG/KWL/STAPK BS4 .... **336** D8
 CFTN/FAIL BS8 .... **335** J2
 EVILLE/WHL BS5 .... **337** C3
Beaconsfield St
 EVILLE/WHL BS5 .... **336** D5
Beacons View Rd *CIND* GL14 .... **154** C2
The Beagles *STROUD* GL5 .... **207** M4
Beale Cl *HGRV/WHIT* BS14 ...... **347** G5
 RSTROUD/NAIL GL6 .... **209** M7
Beale Rd *CHELTW* GL51 .... **92** F8
Beam St *EVILLE/WHL* BS5 .... **336** E4
Bean Hl *MIM* GL56 .... **79** L3

Beanhill Crs *THNB/SVB* BS35 .... **293** J6
Bean St *EVILLE/WHL* BS5 .... **336** C2
Bearbridge Rd
 BMSTRD/HC/WWD BS13 ...... **345** H7
Bearcroft Gdn *CHCAM* GL55 .... **8** F7
Beard's La *STROUD* GL5 .... **208** C4
Bearland *GL* GL1 .... **4** D5
Bearlands *WUE* GL12 .... **277** L6
Bear La *TEWK* GL20 .... **24** B7
Bear St *WUE* GL12 .... **277** K4
Beauchamp Cl *CIR* GL7 .... **242** F4
Beauchamp Meadow *LYD* GL15 . **201** L7
Beauchamp Rd *EVILLE/WHL* BS5 . **336** F4
Beaufort Ct *CIR* GL7 .... **238** C4
Beaufort Crs
 BRSTK/PCHW BS34 .... **317** G7
Beaufort Dr *CIR* GL7 .... **225** K1
Beaufort Pl *CHEP* NP16 .... **270** A3
 EVILLE/WHL BS5 .... **7** L1
 EVILLE/WHL BS5 .... **336** F4
Beaufort Rd *CFTN/FAIL* BS8 .... **335** J2
 CHELTE/BC GL52 .... **3** J9
 EVILLE/WHL BS5 .... **336** F4
 FRCTL/WBN BS36 .... **318** C3
 GLE GL4 .... **136** B6
 HORF/LLZ BS7 .... **326** A2
 KGWD/HNM BS15 .... **337** K2
 MANG/FISH BS16 .... **328** A7
 YATE/CS BS37 .... **319** M1
Beaufort St *BMSTR* BS3 .... **345** L1
 EVILLE/WHL BS5 .... **7** L1
Beaufort Wy
 HNBRY/STHM BS10 .... **325** M3
Beaufort Wk *BMSTR* BS3 .... **6** B8
Beauley Rd *BMSTR* BS3 .... **6** B8
Beaumont Cl
 OLD/WMLY/WICK BS30 .... **338** C8
Beaumont Dr *CHELTW* GL51 .... **92** F7
Beaumont Pl *LYD* GL15 .... **201** J8
Beaumont Rd *CHELTW* GL51 .... **92** F7
 VGL GL2 .... **112** E6
Beaumont St
 EVILLE/WHL BS5 .... **336** C3
Beaumont Ter
 EVILLE/WHL BS5 .... **336** C3
Beaumoor Pl *CIR* GL7 .... **242** F5
Beaver Cl *FRCTL/WBN* BS36 .... **318** B4
Beaverstone Cl *CIR* GL7 .... **263** H5
Beazer Cl *MANG/FISH* BS16 .... **327** M8
Becket Cl *MIM* GL56 .... **37** L6
Becket Ct *MANG/FISH* BS16 .... **329** K6
Becketts La *COTS* GL54 .... **74** D3
Beckfordcl *TEWK* GL20 .... **28** E8
Beckford Gdns
 HGRV/WHIT BS14 .... **346** C8
Beckford Rd *EVE* WR11 .... **29** K4
 GLE GL4 .... **137** C2
 TEWK GL20 .... **51** K4
Beckington Rd *BMSTR* BS3 ...... **346** B1
Beckington Wk *BMSTR* BS3 .... **346** B1
Beckspool Rd
 MANG/FISH BS16 .... **327** L3
Becky Hl *COTS* GL54 .... **122** F1
Bedford Av *CHELTW* GL51 ...... **115** H1
Bedford Crs *HORF/LLZ* BS7 ...... **326** B6
Bedford St *GL* GL1 .... **5** G6
 STROUD GL5 .... **208** A3
Bedminster Br *BMSTR* BS3 ...... **7** G8
Bedminster Down Rd
 BMSTR BS3 .... **345** K1
 BMSTRD/HC/WWD BS13 ...... **345** K4
Bedminster Pde *BMSTR* BS3 .... **6** F8
Bedminster Pl *BMSTR* BS3 ...... **6** E8
Bedminster Rd *BMSTR* BS3 ...... **345** L1
Beech Av *CLFD* GL16 .... **151** L6
Beech Cl *CHELTE/BC* GL52 ...... **94** E7
 OLD/WMLY/WICK BS30 .... **338** C6
 THNB/SVB BS35 .... **293** J6
 VGL GL2 .... **110** F7
 VGL GL2 .... **159** G4
Beechcroft Rd *VGL* GL2 .... **112** C6
Beechcroft Wk *HORF/LLZ* BS7 .. **326** C3
Beechen Dr *MANG/FISH* BS16 .. **337** K1
Beeches Gn *STROUD* GL5 .... **208** B3
Beeches Gv
 BRSG/KWL/STAPK BS4 .... **346** F1
Beeches La *CHELTS* GL53 .... **116** D7
 CIND GL14 .... **155** J7
 CIR GL7 .... **238** C3
The Beeches *ALMDB* BS32 ...... **316** F3
 BRSG/KWL/STAPK BS4 .... **337** G6
 OLD/WMLY/WICK BS30 .... **348** E1
Beechfield Cl *LGASH* BS41 ...... **344** E1
Beech Gv *CIR* GL7 .... **238** E2
 STROUD GL5 .... **232** C1
Beech La *RSTROUD/NAIL* GL6 .. **185** K3
Beech Lea *CIR* GL7 .... **241** L6
Beech Leaze *THNB/SVB* BS35 .. **293** J6
Beechmore Dr *CHELTW* GL51 ... **115** G6
Beechmount Gv
 HGRV/WHIT BS14 .... **346** D8
Beech Rd *CHPMW/MSHF* SN14 . **343** J6
 HORF/LLZ BS7 .... **326** A6
 KEYN BS31 .... **349** G8
 STROUD GL5 .... **177** J8
Beechurst Av *CHELTE/BC* GL52 .. **3** H5
Beechurst Wy
 CHELTE/BC GL52 .... **71** M7
Beech Wy *CIND* GL14 .... **154** D3
 LYD GL15 .... **200** C3
Beech Well La *CLFD* GL16 ...... **152** A4
Beechwood Av
 KGWD/HNM BS15 .... **337** M6
Beechwood Cl *CHELTE/BC* GL52 . **3** M7
 HGRV/WHIT BS14 .... **346** E3
Beechwood Dr
 RSTROUD/NAIL GL6 .... **209** M8
Beechwood Gv *GLE* GL4 .... **136** A8
 WUE GL12 .... **277** M3
Beechwood Ri *DSLY* GL11 ...... **253** H1
Beechwood Rd
 MANG/FISH BS16 .... **327** G4
Beek's La *CBATH/BATHN* BA1 ... **341** L8
 CHPMW/MSHF SN14 .... **341** M5
Beesmoor Rd *FRCTL/WBN* BS36 . **318** D4

Begbrook Dr *MANG/FISH* BS16 . **32**
Begbrook La *MANG/FISH* BS16 . **32**
Begbrook Pk *MANG/FISH* BS16 . **32**
Beggarswell Cl *CBRISNE* BS2 .... **336**
Bekdale Cl *VGL* GL2 .... **158**
Belcony *MIM* GL56 ....
Belfast Wk
 BRSG/KWL/STAPK BS4 .... **346**
Belfry Cl *GLE* GL4 .... **13**
Belgrave Hl *CFTN/FAIL* BS8 ...... **335**
Belgrave Pl *CFTN/FAIL* BS8 ...... **335**
Belgrave Rd *CFTN/FAIL* BS8 ...... **33**
 GL GL1 ....
Bellamy Av
 BMSTRD/HC/WWD BS13 ...... **34**
Bellamy Cl *KGWD/HNM* BS15 ... **33**
Belland Dr *CHELTS* GL53 .... **11**
 HGRV/WHIT BS14 .... **34**
Bella Vis *CHELTE/BC* GL52 ...... **7**
Bell Bank *MIM* GL56 ....
Bell Barn Rd
 HNLZ/SM/SNYPK/WT BS9 .... **32**
Bell Cl *HNBRY/STHM* BS10 ...... **32**
Belle Orch *LED* HR8 ....
Belle Orchard Cl *LED* HR8 ......
Bellevue *CFTN/FAIL* BS8 ....
Bellevue Cl *KGWD/HNM* BS15 . **338**
Belle Vue Cl *STROUD* GL5 ...... **20**
Bellevue Crs *CFTN/FAIL* BS8 ....
Bellevue Pk
 BRSG/KWL/STAPK BS4 .... **346**
Belle Vue Rd *CIND* GL14 .... **15**
 EVILLE/WHL BS5 ....
 MTCHDN GL17 .... **129**
 STROUD GL5 ....
Bellevue Rd
 BRSG/KWL/STAPK BS4 .... **33**
 EVILLE/WHL BS5 ....
 KGWD/HNM BS15 .... **33**
Bellevue Ter *BMSTR* BS3 ....
 BRSG/KWL/STAPK BS4 .... **346**
Bell Hl *MANG/FISH* BS16 .... **32**
Bell Hill Rd *EVILLE/WHL* BS5 .... **33**
Bellhouse Wk *AVONM* BS11 .... **324**
Bell La *CBRIS/FH* BS1 ....
 CIR GL7 .... **24**
 CIR GL7 .... **24**
 GL GL1 .... **4**
 LED HR8 ....
 RSTROUD/NAIL GL6 .... **233**
 STROUD GL5 ....
Bell Orch *VGL* GL2 .... **15**
Bell Pitch *RSTROUD/NAIL* GL6 . **184**
Bell Rd *FRCTL/WBN* BS36 ......
Bells La *RBANSW* OX15 ....
Bells Pl *CIND* GL14 .... **15**
 CLFD GL16 .... **17**
Belluton Rd
 BRSG/KWL/STAPK BS4 .... **33**
Belmont Av *BWTH/CHD* GL3 .... **13**
Belmont Dr *BRSTK/PCHW* BS34 . **3**
Belmont La *CLFD* GL16 .... **15**
Belmont Rd
 BRSG/KWL/STAPK BS4 .... **336**
 CHELTE/BC GL52 ....
 LYD GL15 .... **2**
 RDLND/MONT BS6 .... **33**
 STROUD GL5 .... **209**
Belmont St *EVILLE/WHL* BS5 .... **33**
Belmore Pl *CHELT* GL50 ....
Beloe Rd *HORF/LLZ* BS7 .... **32**
Belroyal Av
 BRSG/KWL/STAPK BS4 .... **33**
Belsher Dr *KGWD/HNM* BS15 ... **33**
Belstone Wk
 BRSG/KWL/STAPK BS4 .... **34**
Belton Rd *EVILLE/WHL* BS5 ...... **337**
Belvedere Ms
 RSTROUD/NAIL GL6 .... **23**
Belvedere Rd
 RDLND/MONT BS6 .... **33**
Belworth Dr *CHELTW* GL51 ...... **11**
Bence Ct *KGWD/HNM* BS15 .... **337**
Bendy Bow *MALM* SN16 .... **28**
Benford Cl *MANG/FISH* BS16 ... **32**
Benhall Av *CHELTW* GL51 .... **1**
Bennett Cl *EVILLE/WHL* BS5 .... **337**
Bennett's Ct *YATE/CS* BS37 .... **32**
Bennett's Rd
 CBATH/BATHN BA1 ....
Bennington St *CHELT* GL50 ......
Bensaunt Gv
 HNBRY/STHM BS10 .... **3**
Benson Cl *GLE* GL4 .... **137**
 VGL GL2 .... **1**
Bentley La *CHELTE/BC* GL52 ....
Benton Ct *STNHO* GL10 .... **20**
Benville Av
 HNLZ/SM/SNYPK/WT BS9 .... **3**
Berenda Dr
 OLD/WMLY/WICK BS30 .... **33**
Beresford Gdns
 CBATH/BATHN BA1 .... **350**
Berkeley Av *CFTN/FAIL* BS8 ....
 CHELTE/BC GL52 ....
 HORF/LLZ BS7 .... **32**
Berkeley Cl *BWTH/CHD* GL3 .... **13**
 CIR GL7 .... **2**
 MANG/FISH BS16 .... **32**
 STROUD GL5 .... **20**
 WUE GL12 .... **2**
Berkeley Ct *VGL* GL2 .... **20**
Berkeley Crs *LYD* GL15 .... **20**
Berkeley Gdns *KEYN* BS31 ......
Berkeley Gn *EVILLE/WHL* BS5 .. **336**
 MANG/FISH BS16 .... **327**
Berkeley Gv *EVILLE/WHL* BS5 .. **336**
Berkeley Md *ALMDB* BS32 ...... **3**
Berkeley Pl *CHELTE/BC* GL52 ....
Berkeley Rd *CIR* GL7 ....
 HORF/LLZ BS7 .... **32**
 KGWD/HNM BS15 .... **338**
 MANG/FISH BS16 .... **32**
 RDLND/MONT BS6 .... **32**
Berkeley Sq *CFTN/FAIL* BS8 ....

keley St CHELTE/BC GL52 .... 2 F6
VILLE/WHL BS5 .... 326 E8
L GL1 .... 4 D5
ketey Wy MANG/FISH BS16 .... 328 D4
ET GL8 .... 282 A2
kshire Rd HORF/LLZ BS7 .... 325 M8
rrells Rd TET GL8 .... 281 M5
Berrells TET GL8 .... 281 M5
rills La SHPSTR CV36 .... 39 J6
rrington Rd CHCAM GL55 .... 13 G8
row NK BMSTR BS3 .... 346 A1
ry Av SHPSTR CV36 .... 16 A5
ry Cl RSTROUD/NAIL GL6 .... 185 H3 🖪
HPSTR CV36 .... 16 A5
ryfield Gld
WTH/CHD GL3 .... 113 J5 🖪
ry Hill Crs CIR GL7 .... 214 C8
ry Hill Rd CIR GL7 .... 214 C8
ry La HORF/LLZ BS7 .... 326 C5
ry Lawn GLE GL4 .... 136 F8
rymore Rd STROUD GL5 .... 232 B1 🖪
tha's Fld BAD GL9 .... 299 K7
ry Vw EVILLE/WHL BS5 .... 337 H3
nel Rd EVILLE/WHL BS5 .... 337 H3
a Cl GL20 .... 48 E3
semer Cl CLFD GL16 .... 175 K2 🖪
hesda St CHELT GL50 .... 2 C9
lleman Cl VGL GL2 .... 135 L7
lleman Ct
LD/WMLY/WICK BS30 .... 338 C6 🖪
tenson Ri COTS GL54 .... 169 J1 🖪
tertons Cl CIR GL7 .... 242 D4
an Ct BRSTK/PCHW BS34 .... 326 B1
an Gdns TEWK GL20 .... 49 G2 🖪
erley Av MANG/FISH BS16 .... 328 B2
erley Cl EVILLE/WHL BS5 .... 337 K5 🖪
erley Cft CHELTW GL51 .... 114 E1 🖪
erley Gdns CHELTE/BC GL52 .. 72 C8
NLZ/SM/SNYPK/WT BS9 ...... 324 F4
erstone
GWD/HNM BS15 .... 337 L3 🖪
erstone Rd CIR GL7 .... 263 H6
erston Gdns
/ONM BS11 .... 324 D1 🖪
ington Cl
RSTK/PCHW BS34 .... 316 A1
ington Wk BRKLY GL13 .... 250 B5
ington Wk
RSTK/PCHW BS34 .... 316 A2
ley Wy BWTH/CHD GL3 .... 113 J6
ley Rd MANG/FISH BS16 .... 328 B2
on Dr DSLY GL11 .... 229 H5 🖪
stone KGWD/HNM BS15 .... 338 C3
sworth Av BDWAY WR12 .... 33 G3
sworth La BDWAY WR12 .... 32 F1 🖪
iry Av BRSTK/PCHW BS34 ...... 316 D3
ry Av
NLZ/SM/SNYPK/WT BS9 ...... 325 M4
iry Crs
NLZ/SM/SNYPK/WT BS9 ...... 325 M4
GWD/HNM BS15 .... 337 C8
iry Rd CHELTW GL51 .... 115 C3
LE GL4 .... 136 B5
erton Cl
NBRY/STHM BS10 .... 315 H8
ford Cl
LD/WMLY/WICK BS30 .... 338 C5
ley Cl KGWD/HNM BS15 .... 347 L1 🖪
nor St CLFD GL16 .... 151 K4
estone Rd HORF/LLZ BS7 ...... 326 A3
dulph Wy LED HR8 .... 19 M5
eford Crs
RSG/KWL/STAPK BS4 .... 346 B5
well Cl HNBRY/STHM BS10 ... 315 K8
eld Cl HGRV/WHIT BS14 .... 347 L6
eld Gdns HGRV/WHIT BS14 ... 347 L6
eld Rd HGRV/WHIT BS14 .... 347 H6
stone Gv CHEP NP16 .... 270 C1
wood La CBRIS/FH BS1 .... 6 C4
erry Cl GLE GL4 .... 137 H7 🖪
NLZ/SM/SNYPK/WT BS9 ...... 324 E3 🖪
ie Cl HNBRY/STHM BS10 .... 325 M5
nd Cl
MSTRD/HC/WWD BS13 .... 345 G8
rook Rd BWTH/CHD GL3 .... 137 J4
ry Cl GLE GL4 .... 136 D5
ngs Wy CHELT GL50 .... 115 K5
ham La THNB/SVB BS35 .... 305 C1
on Dr HNBRY/STHM BS10 ...... 315 M7
ey Gv HGRV/WHIT BS14 .... 346 F6
mead Gdns
MSTRD/HC/WWD BS13 .... 345 K7 🖪
von Cl EVE WR11 .... 10 A1
von Rd COTS GL54 .... 74 B6
eck Rd
NLZ/SM/SNYPK/WT BS9 ...... 325 G6
hall Av GLE GL4 .... 160 C1
hall Rd RDLND/MONT BS6 ..... 325 L7
h Av GLE GL4 .... 136 D5
h Cl BRSTK/PCHW BS34 .... 316 A4
HELTS GL53 .... 116 E7 🖪
ED HR8 .... 19 M4
h Ct KEYN BS31 .... 347 L1 🖪
h Cft HGRV/WHIT BS14 .... 346 D8 🖪
hdale Rd HGRV/WHIT BS14 ... 346 C3
h Dr BUR/CRTN OX18 .... 197 L4
ANG/FISH BS16 .... 329 K6
HNB/SVB BS35 .... 293 H7
hes Cl STROUD GL5 .... 208 E3 🖪
hes Dr STROUD GL5 .... 208 E4
hes La NWNT GL18 .... 66 A8
hfield Rd CHELTE/BC GL52 .. 72 C7 🖪
h Gld HGHW SN6 .... 287 H3
hley Rd CHELTE/BC GL52 .... 3 K7
hmore Rd GL GL1 .... 5 K8
h Pk CLFD GL16 .... 175 M2
h Rd BMSTR BS3 .... 6 A8
FD GL11 .... 151 M7
SLY GL11 .... 229 J7

KGWD/HNM BS15 .... 328 A8
STROUD GL5 .... 208 C8
YATE/CS BS37 .... 319 M1
Birchwood Cl CIND GL14 .... 153 M2
Birchwood Flds GLE GL4 .... 135 M8
Birchwood Rd
BRSG/KWL/STAPK BS4 .... 337 D2
LYD GL15 .... 224 A5
Birdale Cl HNBRY/STHM BS10 .. 315 G8
Bird Rd BWTH/CHD GL3 .... 137 K5
Birds Bush La
RSTROUD/NAIL GL6 .... 187 K6
Birdwell La LGASH BS41 .... 344 B2 🖪
Birdwell Rd LGASH BS41 .... 344 B2
Birdwood KGWD/HNM BS15 ... 337 M5
Birdwood Cl GLE GL4 .... 137 G7 🖪
Birgage Rd BAD GL9 .... 312 B1
Birkdale OLD/WMLY/WICK BS30 . 338 D5
YATE/CS BS37 .... 320 A3
Birkin St CBRISNE BS2 .... 7 K4
Bishop Manor Rd
HNBRY/STHM BS10 .... 325 M4
Bishop Rd CHELTW GL51 .... 139 G1
HORF/LLZ BS7 .... 325 L7
Bishops Cl CHELTE/BC GL52 .. 72 C8 🖪
CHEP NP16 .... 270 B7 🖪
HNLZ/SM/SNYPK/WT BS9 .... 325 G8
Bishops Cove
BMSTRD/HC/WWD BS13 ..... 345 H6 🖪
Bishops Dr CHELTE/BC GL52 .. 72 B8
Bishopsfield HGHW SN6 .... 288 E4 🖪
Bishops Ga LYD GL15 .... 225 J1
Bishops Knoll
HNLZ/SM/SNYPK/WT BS9 .... 324 E8
Bishops Meadow
CHELTE/BC GL52 .... 72 A7 🖪
Bishops Rd GLE GL4 .... 137 C5
Bishopstone Cl CHELTW GL51 . 114 E2 🖪
Bishopstone Rd GL GL1 .... 5 K8
Bishop St CBRISNE BS2 .... 336 A3
Bishop's Wk RTEWK/TIB GL19 .. 46 D5
Bishop's Wd ALMDB BS32 .... 306 E5
Bishopsworth
BMSTRD/HC/WWD BS13 ..... 345 J4
Bishopthorpe Rd
HNBRY/STHM BS10 .... 325 M4
Bishport Av
BMSTRD/HC/WWD BS13 ..... 345 J4
Bishport Cl
BMSTRD/HC/WWD BS13 ..... 345 K7
Bishton La CHEP NP16 .... 246 C8
Bisley Cl YATE/CS BS37 .... 319 L4
Bisley Old Rd STROUD GL5 ..... 208 F4
Bisley Rd CHELTW GL51 .... 115 G3
GLE GL4 .... 160 A2
RSTROUD/NAIL GL6 .... 210 B1
STROUD GL5 .... 208 F5
Bisley St RSTROUD/NAIL GL6 .. 185 H3 🖪
Bissex Md MANG/FISH BS16 ... 328 D6
Bittern Av GLE GL4 .... 136 F5
Bitterwell Cl FRCTL/WBN BS36 . 318 F8
Bixhead Wk CLFD GL16 .... 175 M1
Blaby Cl GLE GL4 .... 137 H6 🖪
Blackacre HGRV/WHIT BS14 ... 346 E8
Blackberry Av
MANG/FISH BS16 .... 327 G6 🖪
Blackberry Cl GLE GL4 .... 137 G7 🖪
Black Berry Fld CHELTE/BC GL52 .. 94 E8
Blackberry Gv CHELTE/BC GL52 . 72 A7
Blackberry Hl MANG/FISH BS16 . 327 G6
Blackbird Ct STNHO GL10 .... 207 H3 🖪
Blackboys DSLY GL11 .... 229 J8
Black Dog Wy GL GL1 .... 4 F4
Blackdown Ct
HGRV/WHIT BS14 .... 346 D6 🖪
Blackford La HGHW SN6 .... 266 E7
Blackfriars CBRIS/FH BS1 .... 6 F2 🖪
Blackhorse Hl THNB/SVB BS35 . 315 K3
Blackhorse La MANG/FISH BS16 . 328 C3
Blackhorse Pl
MANG/FISH BS16 .... 328 C5 🖪
Blackhorse Rd
KGWD/HNM BS15 .... 337 M3
MANG/FISH BS16 .... 328 C5
Black Jack St CIR GL7 .... 238 C2 🖪
Blacklow Cl STROUD GL5 .... 208 F5
Blackmoor Rd CFTN/FAIL BS8 .. 334 A1
Blackmoors La BMSTR BS3 ...... 335 G8
Blackquarries Hl WUE GL12 .... 277 M4
Blacksmith Hl WUE GL12 .... 278 E4
Blacksmith La BWTH/CHD GL3 . 113 M7
CBATH/BATHN BA1 .... 351 K5
RTEWK/TIB GL19 .... 91 K2
Blacksmiths Cl EVE WR11 .... 30 C2
Blacksmiths Gnd VGL GL2 .... 110 F6 🖪
Blacksmiths La BDWAY WR12 .. 32 A1 🖪
CHELTE/BC GL52 .... 94 D7
EVE WR11 .... 30 B6
TEWK GL20 .... 50 F1
VGL GL2 .... 111 H4
Blacksmiths Rd TEWK GL20 .... 51 L4
Blackswarth Rd
EVILLE/WHL BS5 .... 336 E1 🖪
Blackthorn Cl
BMSTRD/HC/WWD BS13 ..... 345 M6
Blackthorn Dr ALMDB BS32 ..... 316 F4 🖪
Blackthorn Gdns VGL GL2 .... 159 G2 🖪
Blackthorn Rd
BMSTRD/HC/WWD BS13 ..... 345 M6
Blackthorn Wk
KGWD/HNM BS15 .... 338 A1 🖪
Blackwater Wy VGL GL2 .... 113 G6
Black Wls DSLY GL11 .... 253 K4 🖪
Bladon Ms CHELTW GL51 .... 114 D4 🖪
Blagdon La MTCHDN GL17 ..... 131 M2 🖪
Blagrove Wy CHELTW GL51 ...... 93 G6
Blaise Wk
BMSTRD/HC/WWD BS13 ..... 345 G7 🖪
Blake Cft CHELTW GL51 .... 93 G7 🖪
Blake Hill Wy GLE GL4 .... 136 F4 🖪

Blakeney Cl GL1 .... 135 M8 🖪
Blakeney Hill Rd LYD GL15 ..... 178 C8
Blakeney Mills YATE/CS BS37 .. 319 M2 🖪
Blakeney Rd
BRSTK/PCHW BS34 .... 316 A2
HORF/LLZ BS7 .... 326 C4
Blake Rd CIR GL7 .... 238 C2
HORF/LLZ BS7 .... 326 D5
Blakes Rd THNB/SVB BS35 ...... 293 K2
Blakewell Md
RSTROUD/NAIL GL6 .... 185 C3
Blanchards YATE/CS BS37 .... 320 E3
Blandford Cl
HNLZ/SM/SNYPK/WT BS9 .... 325 K5 🖪
Blenheim Cl COTS GL54 .... 124 C7 🖪
TEWK GL20 .... 51 K4
Blenheim Ct COTS GL54 .... 74 C5
Blenheim Dr
BRSTK/PCHW BS34 .... 316 D7
LED HR8 .... 20 A5
NWNT GL18 .... 86 D3 🖪
TEWK GL20 .... 27 H5
YATE/CS BS37 .... 309 L8
Blenheim Orch CHELTW GL51 . 139 G1
Blenheim Rd GL GL1 .... 5 G8
RDLND/MONT BS6 .... 325 K8
Blenheim Sq CHELTW GL51 ...... 93 G8 🖪
Blenman Cl MANG/FISH BS16 .. 327 J4 🖪
Bleriot Rd COTS GL54 .... 124 C7
Blethwin Cl HNBRY/STHM BS10 . 325 H2
Blicks Hl MALM SN16 .... 303 H8 🖪
Blimeshire LYD GL15 .... 201 H2
Blind La CHCAM GL55 .... 34 D1
Blinkhorns Bridge La VGL GL2 .... 5 M7
Bloomfield Rd
BRSG/KWL/STAPK BS4 .... 336 E7
GL GL1 .... 135 M5
Bloomfield Road Link
BRSG/KWL/STAPK BS4 .... 336 E7
Bloomfield Ter GL GL1 .... 135 M5
Bloomsbury St CHELTW GL51 .... 2 A3
Bloxham Rd BDWAY WR12 .... 32 F2
Bloxhams Orch RTEWK/TIB GL19 . 89 J3
Bloy St EVILLE/WHL BS5 .... 336 E2
Bluebell Cha
RSTROUD/NAIL GL6 .... 210 A7 🖪
Bluebell Cl GLE GL4 .... 136 F6 🖪
THNB/SVB BS35 .... 293 M1
Bluebell Dr CHEP NP16 .... 270 B6
Bluebell Gv CHELTW GL51 .... 115 H6
Bluebell Ri RSTROUD/NAIL GL6 .. 210 A7
The Bluebells ALMDB BS32 ..... 317 G4
ALMDB BS32 .... 317 H4 🖪
Blue Boys' Pk
RSTROUD/NAIL GL6 .... 233 J4 🖪
Blue La NWNT GL18 .... 85 K3
Blue Quarry Rd CIR GL7 .... 238 E2 🖪
Blue Rock Crs LYD GL15 .... 200 D2
Blunts Hay CIR GL7 .... 220 B4
Boakes Dr STNHO GL10 .... 207 C4
Bockenem Cl
THNB/SVB BS35 .... 293 M4 🖪
Bodey Cl
OLD/WMLY/WICK BS30 .... 338 C6
Bodham Rd CHELTW GL51 .... 93 G7
Bodiam Av GL GL1 .... 159 K2
Bodmin Wk
BRSG/KWL/STAPK BS4 .... 346 B3 🖪
Bodyce Rd THNB/SVB BS35 .... 293 J6 🖪
Boleyn Cl BWTH/CHD GL3 ...... 113 H4
Bolton Rd HORF/LLZ BS7 .... 326 A8
Bondend Rd GLE GL4 .... 161 G1
Bond's La CHPMW/MSHF SN14 . 341 M2
Bond St CBRIS/FH BS1 .... 7 H1
Bonners Cl MALM SN16 .... 303 J7
Bonnington Wk HORF/LLZ BS7 . 326 D4
Bonville Rd
BRSG/KWL/STAPK BS4 .... 347 G2
Bootenhay Rd
CHELTE/BC GL52 .... 72 C7 🖪
Booth Rd BMSTR BS3 .... 6 D9 🖪
Boot La BMSTR BS3 .... 6 F8
Borage Cl BWTH/CHD GL3 ...... 137 H6
Bordesley Rd HGRV/WHIT BS14 . 346 C8
Borleyton Wk
BMSTRD/HC/WWD BS13 ..... 345 H7 🖪
Borough Cl STNHO GL10 .... 207 J8
Borver Gv
BMSTRD/HC/WWD BS13 ..... 345 K7
Boscombe Crs
MANG/FISH BS16 .... 328 B4 🖪
Boscombe La
RSTROUD/NAIL GL6 .... 256 A3
Bosley Cl SHPSTR CV36 .... 16 A7
Bospin La STROUD GL5 .... 232 B2
Boswell St EVILLE/WHL BS5 .... 336 E1 🖪
Botham Dr
BRSG/KWL/STAPK BS4 .... 347 G2 🖪
Bottom Cl HGRV/WHIT BS14 ... 346 C5
Boucher Pl CBRISNE BS2 .... 336 C1 🖪
Boulters Rd
BMSTRD/HC/WWD BS13 ..... 345 L7 🖪
Boulton La DSLY GL11 .... 253 K3
Boulton Rd CHELT GL50 .... 93 M6
Boulton's Rd KGWD/HNM BS15 . 337 M3
Bouncer's La CHELTE/BC GL52 . 3 M2
Boundary Pl RTEWK/TIB GL19 .. 66 D5
Boundary Rd FRCTL/WBN BS36 . 318 F4
Bourchier Gdns
BMSTRD/HC/WWD BS13 ..... 345 M8
Bourne Cl FRCTL/WBN BS36 ... 318 A4
KGWD/HNM BS15 .... 337 K3
Bourne Lake Pk HGHW SN6 .... 288 A5
Bourne La STROUD GL5 .... 233 J2
Bourne Rd KGWD/HNM BS15 .. 337 J3
Bourneville Rd
EVILLE/WHL BS5 .... 336 F3 🖪
Bournside Cl CHELTW GL51 .... 115 J4
Bournside Dr CHELTW GL51 ... 115 J4
Bournside Rd CHELTW GL51 ... 115 J4
Boursland Cl ALMDB BS32 .... 316 F1 🖪
Bourton Av BRSTK/PCHW BS34 . 316 E3
Bourton Cl BRSTK/PCHW BS34 . 316 E3
Bourton Rd GLE GL4 .... 160 A1
MIM SN56 .... 58 C6
Bourton Wk
BMSTRD/HC/WWD BS13 ..... 345 J3 🖪

Boverton Av BWTH/CHD GL3 .. 137 M5
Boverton Dr BWTH/CHD GL3 .. 137 M5
Boverton Rd
BRSTK/PCHW BS34 .... 316 D8
Bovone La VGL GL2 .... 109 M3
Bowbridge La CHELTE/BC GL52 . 94 D6
STROUD GL5 .... 208 F5
Bowbridge Lock STROUD GL5 .. 208 F6
Bowden Cl
HNLZ/SM/SNYPK/WT BS9 .... 324 E3
Bowden Pl MANG/FISH BS16 ... 328 B4 🖪
Bowden Rd EVILLE/WHL BS5 ... 337 G2 🖪
Bowen Cl CHELTE/BC GL52 .... 3 K1
CHELTE/BC GL52 .... 94 C7
Bowen's Hl CLFD GL16 .... 175 J1
Bowen's Hill Rd CLFD GL16 .... 175 J1
Bowerleaze
HNLZ/SM/SNYPK/WT BS9 .... 324 D6
Bower Rd BMSTR BS3 .... 335 J8
Bower Wk BMSTR BS3 .... 336 A4
Bowes Lyon Cl MIM SN56 .... 58 C7 🖪
Bow La COTS GL54 .... 123 H5
TEWK GL20 .... 25 J3
Bowldown Rd TET GL8 .... 280 E8
Bowler Rd TEWK GL20 .... 49 G2
Bowl Hl STROUD GL5 .... 208 C8
Bowling Green Av GL GL7 ...... 238 C1
Bowling Green Ct MIM SN56 ..... 58 C7 🖪
Bowling Green La CIR GL7 .... 238 C1
Bowling Green Rd CIR GL7 ...... 238 C1
Bowling Hl YATE/CS BS37 .... 320 C2
Bowling Hill Rd YATE/CS BS37 . 320 D3
Bowly Crs CIR GL7 .... 238 E7
Bowly Rd CIR GL7 .... 238 E5
GL GL1 .... 135 M5
Bownham Md STROUD GL5 ..... 232 E1
Bownham Pk STROUD GL5 ...... 232 F2
Bowring Cl
BMSTRD/HC/WWD BS13 ..... 345 L6
Bowsland Wy ALMDB BS32 ...... 316 F1 🖪
Bowson Rd LYD GL15 .... 200 D1
Bowstreet La THNB/SVB BS35 .. 315 J3
Bow Wow CIR GL7 .... 263 J4
Boxbush Cl CIR GL7 .... 263 J4 🖪
Boxbush Rd CIR GL7 .... 263 J4
CLFD GL16 .... 175 J1
Box Crs RSTROUD/NAIL GL6 ... 233 H5 🖪
Boxhedge Farm La
FRCTL/WBN BS36 .... 319 G8
Box La RSTROUD/NAIL GL6 ...... 233 C6
Box Rd CBATH/BATHN BA1 ...... 352 E8
DSLY GL11 .... 229 J3
Box Road Av DSLY GL11 .... 229 H3
Boxtree Cl MTCHDN GL17 .... 129 C3 🖪
Box Vw CHPMW/MSHF SN14 ... 353 G7
Boxwell Rd TET GL8 .... 279 L8
Boyce Dr CBRISNE BS2 .... 336 C1 🖪
Boyce's Av CFTN/FAIL BS8 ...... 335 J4 🖪
Boyd Cl OLD/WMLY/WICK BS30 . 339 K4
Boyd Rd KEYN BS31 .... 348 F8
Brabazon Rd
BRSTK/PCHW BS34 .... 326 D1
Bracelands RSTROUD/NAIL GL6 . 209 M6
Bracelands Dr CLFD GL16 .... 151 J5 🖪
Bracewell Gdns
HNBRY/STHM BS10 .... 315 L7
Bracey Dr MANG/FISH BS16 .... 327 L5 🖪
Brackenbury Dr
BRSTK/PCHW BS34 .... 317 C6
Bracken Cl LYD GL15 .... 201 L8
Brackendene ALMDB BS32 ...... 316 E2 🖪
Bracken Dr LYD GL15 .... 201 K8
Bracton Dr HGRV/WHIT BS14 .. 346 C7
Bradeston Gv MANG/FISH BS16 . 327 J4
Bradford Rd VGL GL2 .... 5 M4
Bradfords Cl NWNT GL18 .... 86 A3 🖪
Bradfords Ct NWNT GL18 .... 86 A3 🖪
Bradfords La NWNT GL18 .... 86 A3
Bradhurst St
EVILLE/WHL BS5 .... 336 D5 🖪
Bradley Av AVONM BS11 .... 324 A5
Bradley Crs AVONM BS11 .... 324 A5
Bradley Rd BRSTK/PCHW BS34 . 316 B3
CHELTS GL53 .... 116 C7
WUE GL12 .... 277 J3
Bradley Court Rd
MTCHDN GL17 .... 130 C1
Bradley Crs AVONM BS11 .... 324 A5
Bradley St WUE GL12 .... 277 J4
Bradley Stoke Wy ALMDB BS32 . 316 E1
Bradshaw Cl VGL GL2 .... 113 G6 🖪
Bradstone Rd
FRCTL/WBN BS36 .... 317 M6 🖪
Bradville Gdns LGASH BS41 .... 344 B3
Bradwell Gv HNBRY/STHM BS10 . 325 G3
Braemar Av HORF/LLZ BS7 ...... 326 B2
Braemar Crs HORF/LLZ BS7 .... 326 B2
Brae Wk GLE GL4 .... 136 F7
Bragg's La CBRISNE BS2 .... 7 K2
Braikenridge Rd
BRSG/KWL/STAPK BS4 .... 336 F7
Brainsfield
HNLZ/SM/SNYPK/WT BS9 .... 325 H5
Brake Cl ALMDB BS32 .... 317 G5
KGWD/HNM BS15 .... 338 B4 🖪
The Brake FRCTL/WBN BS36 ... 318 E6
YATE/CS BS37 .... 310 A6
Bramble Cha CHELTE/BC GL52 . 72 A6 🖪
Bramble Dr DSLY GL11 .... 229 J3
HNLZ/SM/SNYPK/WT BS9 .... 324 E8
Bramble La
HNLZ/SM/SNYPK/WT BS9 .... 324 E8
STNHO GL10 .... 207 H3
Bramble Lawn GLE GL4 .... 136 F8
Bramble Ri CHELTE/BC GL52 ..... 94 E8
Bramble Rd CLFD GL16 .... 175 J4
The Brambles BRKLY GL13 ...... 227 G7 🖪
KEYN BS31 .... 347 M8
RWYE HR9 .... 106 B3 🖪
Brambling Wk
MANG/FISH BS16 .... 327 H5
Bramley Cl LED HR8 .... 19 M5
THNB/SVB BS35 .... 292 C8
WUE GL12 .... 277 H7

Bramley Ct
OLD/WMLY/WICK BS30 .... 338 B7 🖪
Bramley Dr RTEWK/TIB GL19 .. 108 D7
Bramley Ms BWTH/CHD GL3 ... 137 J5 🖪
Bramley Rd CHELTW GL51 .... 93 G8
TEWK GL20 .... 48 B4
The Bramleys MTCHDN GL17 .. 131 H1 🖪
Branche Gv
BMSTRD/HC/WWD BS13 ..... 345 M6
Branch Hill Ri CHELTS GL53 ... 116 C7
Branch Rd CHELTW GL51 .... 114 D4
The Branch CIND GL14 .... 129 M6
Brandash Rd YATE/CS BS37 .... 320 E2
Branders CHGW SN6 .... 288 F3
Brandon Cl BWTH/CHD GL3 .... 113 J3
Brandon Pl CHELT GL50 .... 115 L4 🖪
Brandon Steep CBRIS/FH BS1 ... 6 C4 🖪
Brandon St CBRIS/FH BS1 .... 6 C5 🖪
Brangwyn Gv HORF/LLZ BS7 .. 326 D5
Branksome Crs
BRSTK/PCHW BS34 .... 316 D8 🖪
Branksome Dr
BRSTK/PCHW BS34 .... 316 D8
FRCTL/WBN BS36 .... 318 A5
Branksome Rd
RDLND/MONT BS6 .... 325 K8 🖪
Branscombe Rd
HNLZ/SM/SNYPK/WT BS9 .... 324 E7
Bransdown Hl MALM SN16 ...... 301 J8
Brans La MIM SN56 .... 103 G3
Brantwood Rd
RSTROUD/NAIL GL6 .... 210 B8
Branwhite Cl HORF/LLZ BS7 ... 326 D4 🖪
Brasenose Rd TEWK GL20 .... 27 C5
Brassington Gdns COTS GL54 .. 142 F7
The Bratches CHCAM GL55 .... 12 E6
Bratton Rd
BRSG/KWL/STAPK BS4 .... 345 M4 🖪
Braunton Rd BMSTR BS3 .... 335 L8
Bray Av LED HR8 .... 20 A4
Braydon Av BRSTK/PCHW BS34 . 316 F3
Braydon La HGHW SN6 .... 288 B6
Brayne Ct
OLD/WMLY/WICK BS30 .... 338 C5
Breaches Ga ALMDB BS32 .... 317 H5
Breach Rd BMSTR BS3 .... 335 J8
Bream Av CLFD GL16 .... 199 M2
Bream Rd LYD GL15 .... 199 J6
Brean Down Av
HNLZ/SM/SNYPK/WT BS9 .... 325 K6
Brecknock Rd
BRSG/KWL/STAPK BS4 .... 336 C3
Brecon Cl VGL GL2 .... 159 G3
Brecon Rd
HNLZ/SM/SNYPK/WT BS9 .... 325 J5
Brecon Wy CLFD GL16 .... 152 A4
Bredon Cl KGWD/HNM BS15 ... 338 B4 🖪
Bredon Nook Rd
HNBRY/STHM BS10 .... 325 L4 🖪
Bredon Rd TEWK GL20 .... 48 B4
Bredon Vw BDWAY WR12 .... 33 G3 🖪
Bregawn Cl CHELTE/BC GL52 ... 94 A1
Breinton Wy VGL GL2 .... 112 F6
Bremilham Ri MALM SN16 ...... 303 G8
Bremilham Rd MALM SN16 ..... 303 H7
Brendon Cl
OLD/WMLY/WICK BS30 .... 338 D7
Brendon Rd BMSTR BS3 .... 335 M8 🖪
Brenner St EVILLE/WHL BS5 ... 336 D1
Brensham Rd TEWK GL20 .... 48 D4 🖪
Brent Rd HORF/LLZ BS7 .... 326 B6
Brentry Av EVILLE/WHL BS5 .... 336 D4
Brentry La HNBRY/STHM BS10 . 325 J1
Brentry Rd MANG/FISH BS16 ... 327 C7
Brereton Wy
OLD/WMLY/WICK BS30 .... 338 D7
Brewerton Cl
HNBRY/STHM BS10 .... 315 L8
Brewery Hl
OLD/WMLY/WICK BS30 .... 349 H3
Brewery La RSTROUD/NAIL GL6 . 232 D8
STROUD GL5 .... 233 C1
Briarbank Ri CHELTE/BC GL52 . 116 E4
Briar Cl STROUD GL5 .... 208 F2
Briarfield Av
KGWD/HNM BS15 .... 337 L6 🖪
Briar Lawn GLE GL4 .... 136 F8
Briarleaze THNB/SVB BS35 ..... 307 H1
Briars Cl BWTH/CHD GL3 .... 113 J5
Briarside Rd
HNBRY/STHM BS10 .... 315 L8
Briar Wk CHELTE/BC GL52 .... 94 E8
MANG/FISH BS16 .... 327 L8
Briar Wy MANG/FISH BS16 ..... 327 K7
Briarwood
HNLZ/SM/SNYPK/WT BS9 .... 325 H5
Briary Rd CIR GL7 .... 244 F5
Briavels Gv RDLND/MONT BS6 . 326 B1
Brickhill Cl SHPSTR CV36 .... 16 A5
Brickrow STROUD GL5 .... 208 E4
Brick St CBRISNE BS2 .... 7 K2
Bridewell Dr EVE WR11 .... 30 B2
Bridewell St CBRIS/FH BS1 .... 6 F2 🖪
Bridge Cl CIR GL7 .... 238 D5 🖪
HGRV/WHIT BS14 .... 346 D7 🖪
VGL GL2 .... 135 K5
Bridge End CIR GL7 .... 238 D4
Bridge Farm VGL GL2 .... 111 K4
Bridge Farm Cl
HGRV/WHIT BS14 .... 346 D7 🖪
Bridgeleap Rd
MANG/FISH BS16 .... 328 B3
Bridgemans Cl BDWAY WR12 ... 33 G2 🖪
Bridge Meadow Cl EVE WR11 ... 30 C1
Bridgend Ct STNHO GL10 .... 207 G5 🖪
Bridgend Rd CHELTW GL51 .... 114 E4 🖪
Bridge Rd BRKLY GL13 .... 226 E1 🖪
CFTN/FAIL BS8 .... 334 F5
CIR GL7 .... 238 D5
EVILLE/WHL BS5 .... 326 D8 🖪
KGWD/HNM BS15 .... 328 B8
MANG/FISH BS16 .... 328 B2
MTCHDN GL17 .... 129 M5
STROUD GL5 .... 207 M5
VGL GL2 .... 181 H6
YATE/CS BS37 .... 319 J1

Bridges Ct *MANG/FISH* BS16 .... 327 K7 🔢
Bridges Dr *MANG/FISH* BS16 ...... 327 L5 🔢
Bridge-side *STROUD* GL5 .... 208 B5 🔢
Bridge St *CBRIS/FH* BS1 .... 6 F4
  CHELTW GL51 .... 93 K7
  CHEP NP16 .... 270 A2
  CIR GL7 .... 242 E4
  EVILLE/WHL BS5 .... 336 F1 🔢
  LED HR8 .... 19 L3
  LYD GL15 .... 202 D1
  NWNT GL18 .... 86 C2
  RSTROUD/NAIL GL6 .... 232 E7 🔢
  STROUD GL5 .... 208 B5 🔢
Bridget Dr *CHEP* NP16 .... 270 C4
Bridge Valley Rd *CFTN/FAIL* BS8.. 335 G3
Bridge Wk *HORF/LLZ* BS7 .... 326 C3
Bridge Wy *FRCTL/WBN* BS36...... 318 D3
Bridgman Gv
  BRSTK/PCHW BS34 .... 316 D8
Bridgwater Rd
  BMSTRD/HC/WWD BS13...... 345 H3
  NAIL BS48 .... 344 C7
The Bridle *THNB/SVB* BS35....... 293 H7
Bridle Wy *THNB/SVB* BS35......... 293 H7
Briercliffe Rd
  HNLZ/SM/SNYPK/WT BS9.... 324 F4
Brierley Banks *MTCHDN* GL17.. 129 H8
Brierley Cl *GLE* GL4 .... 137 G6 🔢
Brierley Rd *MTCHDN* GL17....... 129 H6
Brierley Wy *LYD* GL15......... 201 M2
Brierly Furlong
  BRSTK/PCHW BS34 .... 316 F8
Briery Leaze Rd
  HGRV/WHIT BS14 .... 346 C6
Brightlands *CIND* GL14 .... 155 J7 🔢
Brighton Crs *BMSTR* BS3........ 345 K1 🔢
Brighton Pk *EVILLE/WHL* BS5 .. 336 D5 🔢
Brighton Pl
  KGWD/HNM BS15 .... 337 M2 🔢
Brighton Rd
  BRSTK/PCHW BS34 .... 316 B3
  CHELTE/BC GL52 .... 3 G5
  RDLND/MONT BS6 .... 335 L2
Brighton St *CBRISNE* BS2 ...... 336 A3
Brighton Ter *BMSTR* BS3 .... 345 K1 🔢
Bright St *EVILLE/WHL* BS5 ..... 336 D4 🔢
  KGWD/HNM BS15 .... 337 M3
Brigstocke Rd *CBRISNE* BS2 .... 336 A2
Brimbles *HORF/LLZ* BS7 .... 326 D1
Brimley *STNHO* GL10 .... 207 H7
Brimscombe HI *STROUD* GL5 .... 233 J3
Brimscombe La *STROUD* GL5 .. 233 H1 🔢
Brimsome Meadow *VGL* GL2 .... 110 F6
Brindle Cl *GLE* GL4 .... 136 E7 🔢
Brinkmarsh La *WUE* GL12 ...... 274 F8
Brinkworthy Rd
  MANG/FISH BS16 .... 326 F5
Brinmead Wk
  BMSTRD/HC/WWD BS13...... 345 H8 🔢
Brins Cl *BRSTK/PCHW* BS34.... 317 H7
Brinsham La *YATE/CS* BS37 ..... 310 C5
Brionne Wy *VGL* GL2 .... 112 D6
Brisbane *STNHO* GL10 .... 207 G2
Briscoes Av
  BMSTRD/HC/WWD BS13 ..... 345 L7
Bristol Br *CBRIS/FH* BS1........... 7 G4
Bristol HI *BRSG/KWL/STAPK* BS4.. 346 F1
Bristol Rd *CIR* GL7 .... 238 D4
  COTS GL54.................. 124 D7
  FRCTL/WBN BS36 .... 318 B3
  GL GL1 .... 135 M4
  HGRV/WHIT BS14 .... 346 E8
  KEYN BS31................. 347 N5
  MANG/FISH BS16 .... 327 K3
  STNHO GL10 .... 206 F4
  THNB/SVB BS35........... 293 K4
  VGL GL2 .... 159 H3
  VGL GL2 .... 205 H8
  WUE GL12 .... 295 J5
Bristol St *MALM* SN16 .... 303 H8
Britannia Crs
  BRSTK/PCHW BS34 .... 316 F6
Britannia Rd
  BRSTK/PCHW BS34 .... 315 M4
  EVILLE/WHL BS5 .... 336 D2
  KGWD/HNM BS15 .... 337 L3
Britannia Wy *CHELTE/BC* GL52 ... 72 D8
British Rd *BMSTR* BS3 .... 335 L8
Britten Ct
  OLD/WMLY/WICK BS30 ..... 338 B7 🔢
Brixham Rd *BMSTR* BS3 .... 345 L1
Brixton Rd *EVILLE/WHL* BS5 ... 336 D3
Brizen La *CHELTS* GL53 .... 115 J7
Broadbury Rd
  BRSG/KWL/STAPK BS4...... 346 A3
Broadclose Rd *VGL* GL2 .... 90 F8
Broad Cft *ALMDB* BS32....... 316 E1 🔢
Broadfield Av
  KGWD/HNM BS15 .... 337 L3
Broadfield Rd
  BRSG/KWL/STAPK BS4...... 346 C2
  STNHO GL10 .... 206 B4
Broadlands Av *KEYN* BS31..... 347 M5
Broadlands Ct *COTS* GL54 .... 123 H6 🔢
Broadlands Dr *AVONM* BS11.... 324 C2
Broad La *FRCTL/WBN* BS36 .... 318 F6
  YATE/CS BS37 .... 309 L1
  YATE/CS BS37 .... 319 J7
Broadleas
  BMSTRD/HC/WWD BS13...... 345 K4
Broadleaze *AVONM* BS11....... 324 A4 🔢
  CIR GL7 .... 265 G3
Broadleys Av
  HNLZ/SM/SNYPK/WT BS9.... 325 K4
Broad Leys Rd *GLE* GL4 .... 136 F4
Broad Marston Rd *CHCAM* GL55 ... 8 E5
Broadmead La *KEYN* BS31 ..... 348 C5
Broadmere Cl *DSLY* GL11...... 229 G8
Broadmoor La
  CBATH/BATHN BA1 .... 350 B7 🔢
  SHPSTR CV36................. 38 C7
Broadmoor Pk *CIND* GL14...... 129 M8
Broadmoor Rd *CIND* GL14...... 129 M8
Broadmoor V
  CBATH/BATHN BA1 .... 350 C8
Broad Oak Rd
  BMSTRD/HC/WWD BS13....... 345 H7

Broad Oaks *CFTN/FAIL* BS8 ..... 335 G5 🔢
Broadoak Wk *MANG/FISH* BS16 ... 327 K7
Broad Oak Wy *CHELTW* GL51 .... 115 G5
Broad Quay *CBRIS/FH* BS1 .... 6 E4
Broad Rd *KGWD/HNM* BS15 ..... 337 L2
Broadstone Cl *GLE* GL4 .... 137 G4
Broadstone Wk
  BMSTRD/HC/WWD BS13...... 345 M6
Broad St *CBRIS/FH* BS1 .... 6 F3
  CIND GL14.................. 154 D3
  MANG/FISH BS16 .... 328 A7
  NWNT GL18 .... 86 C3
  RTEWK/TIB BS19 .... 89 G5
  SHPSTR CV36................ 61 H5
  STNHO GL10 .... 207 J8
  STROUD GL5 .... 207 M8
  YATE/CS BS37 .... 320 D2
Broad Wk
  BRSG/KWL/STAPK BS4....... 346 B1
  YATE/CS BS37 .... 320 B1 🔢
Broadway *KEYN* BS31 .... 348 F8 🔢
Broadway Av *CIR* GL7 .... 266 F5
Broadway La *CIND* GL14 .... 157 J1
  CIR GL7 .... 263 H5
Broadway Rd *BDWAY* WR12...... 11 G8
  BDWAY WR12................. 31 H2
  BMSTRD/HC/WWD BS13 ..... 345 H6 🔢
  CHCAM GL55 .... 8 E8
  COTS GL54.................. 53 H6
  HORF/LLZ BS7 .... 325 M8
Broadways Dr
  MANG/FISH BS16 .... 327 H4 🔢
The Broadway *DSLY* GL11 ...... 253 H3
  RSTROUD/NAIL GL6 .... 210 E7
Broad Weir *CBRIS/FH* BS1 .... 7 H3
Broadwell Br *CLFD* GL16 .... 151 M8 🔢
Broadwell Cl *GLE* GL4 .... 137 G6 🔢
Broadwell Rd *CIR* GL7 .... 221 M8
  MIM GL56 .... 103 H2
Brock Cl *CHELTW* GL51 .... 114 D5
Brockeridge Ct *VGL* GL2 .... 159 G1 🔢
Brockeridge Rd *TEWK* GL20 ..... 26 C5 🔢
Brockhollands Rd *LYD* GL15 .. 200 D3
Brockhurst Gdns
  KGWD/HNM BS15 .... 337 J3
Brockhurst Rd
  KGWD/HNM BS15 .... 337 J3
Brockley Acres
  RSTROUD/NAIL GL6 .... 210 A6
Brockley Cl
  BRSTK/PCHW BS34 .... 316 E4 🔢
Brockley Rd *KEYN* BS31 .... 348 F8 🔢
  STNHO GL10 .... 207 H7
Brockley Wk
  BMSTRD/HC/WWD BS13 ..... 345 J3 🔢
Brockmoor La *NWNT* GL18...... 85 H3
Brockridge La
  FRCTL/WBN BS36 .... 318 E4
Brocks Rd
  BMSTRD/HC/WWD BS13...... 345 L8
Brockworth *YATE/CS* BS37 ..... 319 L5
Brockworth Crs
  MANG/FISH BS16 .... 327 H5
Brockworth Rd *BWTH/CHD* GL3... 113 M8
Brome Rd *GLE* GL4 .... 137 H6
Bromfield Wk
  MANG/FISH BS16 .... 328 D4 🔢
Bromley Dr *MANG/FISH* BS16 ... 327 M3
Bromley Heath Av
  MANG/FISH BS16 .... 327 M3
Bromley Heath Rd
  MANG/FISH BS16 .... 327 M3 🔢
Bromley Rd *CLFD* GL16 .... 176 A6
  HORF/LLZ BS7 .... 326 B6
Brompton Cl *KGWD/HNM* BS15 .. 338 B3
Bronncsea Rd *HORF/LLZ* BS7 .. 326 B2
Bronte Cl *CHELTW* GL51 .... 115 H4 🔢
Brook Cl *COTS* GL54 .... 74 B7
  COTS GL54.................. 169 K2
  LGASH BS41 .... 344 D2
Brookcote Dr
  BRSTK/PCHW BS34 .... 316 F5
Brook Ct *CHELT* GL50 .... 115 K5
Brookdale Rd
  BMSTRD/HC/WWD BS13...... 345 K5
Brooke Rd *CIR* GL7 .... 238 B5
  LED HR8 .... 19 L2
Brookfield Av *HORF/LLZ* BS7 .. 325 M8 🔢
Brookfield Cl *YATE/CS* BS37 ... 320 C3
Brookfield La *BWTH/CHD* GL3... 114 A6
  RDLND/MONT BS6 .... 335 M1 🔢
Brookfield Rd
  BRSTK/PCHW BS34 .... 316 D3
  BWTH/CHD GL3 .... 114 A6
  GLE GL4 .... 137 H4
  RDLND/MONT BS6 .... 335 M1 🔢
Brookfield Wk
  OLD/WMLY/WICK BS30 ..... 338 E8 🔢
Brook Ga *BMSTR* BS3 .... 345 G2
Brook HI *RDLND/MONT* BS6 .... 336 A2
Brookland Rd
  RDLND/MONT BS6 .... 325 M6 🔢
Brooklands Pk *VGL* GL2 .... 112 E6
Brook La *MANG/FISH* BS16 .... 327 G5
  MIM GL56 .... 57 G1
  RDLND/MONT BS6 .... 336 B2 🔢
  VGL GL2 .... 112 E2
Brooklea
  OLD/WMLY/WICK BS30 ..... 338 D7
Brookleaze
  HNLZ/SM/SNYPK/WT BS9.... 324 E6
Brook Lintons
  BRSG/KWL/STAPK BS4...... 336 F8 🔢
Brooklyn Cl *CHELTW* GL51 ..... 93 H8 🔢
Brooklyn Gdns *CHELTW* GL51 ... 93 J8
Brooklyn Rd
  BMSTRD/HC/WWD BS13...... 345 K3
  CHELTW GL51 .... 115 H1
Brookmead *THNB/SVB* BS35 ... 293 M4 🔢
Brook Rd *BMSTR* BS3 .... 6 E8 🔢
  CHELTW GL51 .... 93 J7
  EVILLE/WHL BS5............ 337 G2
  KGWD/HNM BS15 .... 338 C3 🔢
  MANG/FISH BS16 .... 327 J7
  RDLND/MONT BS6 .... 336 B2

Brooksdale La *CHELTS* GL53 .... 115 L5 🔢
Brookside *MALM* SN16 .... 284 A5 🔢
  MIM GL56 .... 35 L4
  NWNT GL18 .... 86 C3
  TEWK GL20 .... 48 C3
  TEWK GL20 .... 51 L4
Brookside Cl
  CBATH/BATHN BA1 .... 352 B6
Brookside Dr *FRCTL/WBN* BS36.. 318 D3
Brookside Rd
  BRSG/KWL/STAPK BS4....... 347 G5
  CIND GL14 .... 153 M2
Brook St *EVILLE/WHL* BS5 ..... 336 E4 🔢
  GL GL1 .... 4 F9
  MTCHDN GL17 .... 130 C1
  YATE/CS BS37 .... 320 C2
Brookthorpe *YATE/CS* BS37 .... 319 M3
Brookthorpe Av *AVONM* BS11 .. 324 C3
Brookthorpe Cl *GLE* GL4....... 135 M8
Brook V *CHELTE/BC* GL52 .... 3 J9
Brookview Wk
  BMSTRD/HC/WWD BS13...... 345 K4
Brook Wy *ALMDB* BS32 .... 316 E2
Brookway Dr *CHELTS* GL53 ..... 116 C5
Brookway Rd *CHELTS* GL53.... 116 C5
Broom Bungalows *GLE* GL4 ... 136 C6 🔢
Broom HI *CLFD* GL16 .... 151 H5
  MANG/FISH BS16 .... 327 C6
Broomhill Rd
  BRSG/KWL/STAPK BS4....... 337 H8
The Brooms *MANG/FISH* BS16 .. 328 C1
Brow HI *CBATH/BATHN* BA1 .... 352 B8
Brown Cl *CHELTW* GL51 .... 93 G8 🔢
Browning Ct *HORF/LLZ* BS7 ... 326 D3 🔢
Browning Ms *CHELTW* GL51 ... 115 H4 🔢
The Brownings *CHELTW* GL51 .. 115 H4 🔢
The Brownings *COR/BOX* SN13 .. 353 M6
Browns HI *RSTROUD/NAIL* GL6.. 233 L1
Brownshill Rd
  RSTROUD/NAIL GL6 .... 233 K2
Brown's La *STNHO* GL10 .... 207 J5
Brown's Piece *WUE* GL12 ...... 277 K5
Broxholme Wk *AVONM* BS11 ... 324 B3 🔢
Bruce Av *EVILLE/WHL* BS5 ..... 336 E2
Bruce Rd *EVILLE/WHL* BS5 ..... 336 E2
Brummels Dr *CLFD* GL16 ...... 151 J5
Brunel Cl
  OLD/WMLY/WICK BS30 ..... 338 C4
Brunel Lock Rd *CBRIS/FH* BS1 .. 335 H6
Brunel Rd
  BMSTRD/HC/WWD BS13...... 345 H3
  CHEP NP16 .... 270 A2
Brunel Wy *BMSTR* BS3 .... 335 G8
  COR/BOX SN13 .... 353 M5
  STNHO GL10 .... 206 E3
  THNB/SVB BS35 .... 293 K4
Brunswick Pl *CBRIS/FH* BS1 ... 335 H6 🔢
Brunswick Rd *GL* GL1 .... 4 E7
Brunswick Sq *CBRISNE* BS2 ...... 7 G1
  GL GL1 .... 4 E7
Brunswick St *CBRISNE* BS2 .... 336 A3
  CHELT GL50 .... 2 C3
  EVILLE/WHL BS5 .... 336 E4 🔢
The Brush *STROUD* GL5 .... 207 M4 🔢
Bruton Cl *EVILLE/WHL* BS5 .... 337 H3 🔢
Bruton Wy *GL* GL1 .... 5 J2
Bryansons Cl
  MANG/FISH BS16 .... 326 F5 🔢
Bryant's HI *EVILLE/WHL* BS5 ... 337 K5
Bryaston Cl *CHELTW* GL51 ..... 115 J1
Bryerland Rd *CHELTW* GL51 ... 138 C7
Brymore Av *CHELTE/BC* GL52 ... 94 C6
Brymore Cl *CHELTE/BC* GL52 ... 94 C6
Brynland Av *HORF/LLZ* BS7 .... 326 A7
Bryony Bank *CHELTS* GL53 .... 115 K7 🔢
Bryworth La *CIR* GL7 .... 244 C5
Buchanan Av *CLFD* GL16....... 151 J8 🔢
Buchanan Cl *CLFD* GL16 ...... 151 J8 🔢
Buckholt Rd *GLE* GL4 .... 161 M4
Buckholt Wy *BWTH/CHD* GL3 ... 115 H1
Buckingham Cl *STNHO* GL10 ... 206 A3
Buckingham Dr
  BRSTK/PCHW BS34 .... 316 F7
  BWTH/CHD GL3 .... 113 J4 🔢
Buckingham Gdns
  MANG/FISH BS16 .... 328 A5
Buckingham Pl
  MANG/FISH BS16 .... 328 A5 🔢
Buckingham Rd
  BRSG/KWL/STAPK BS4....... 336 F6 🔢
Buckingham St *BMSTR* BS3 .... 345 L1 🔢
Buckingham V
  CFTN/FAIL BS8 .... 335 J3 🔢
Buckland Cl *CHELTE/BC* GL52 ... 72 B7 🔢
Buckles Cl *CHELTS* GL53 ...... 116 D6
Buckle St *BDWAY* WR12 .... 33 J7
  CHCAM GL55 .... 11 L4
Buckshaft Rd *CIND* GL14 ..... 154 A7
Buckstone Cl *CLFD* GL16 ..... 151 M6
Budding Ct *STNHO* GL10 ...... 206 A3
The Budding *STROUD* GL5 ..... 209 G2
Buddleia Cl *GLE* GL4 .... 137 H7 🔢
Bude Av *EVILLE/WHL* BS5 ...... 337 J3
Bude Rd *BRSTK/PCHW* BS34 ... 316 D8
Buettell Wy *MALM* SN16 ...... 303 H6
Buller Rd *BRSG/KWL/STAPK* BS4.. 346 E1
Bulley La *VGL* GL2 .... 109 G8
Bullfinch Rd *GLE* GL4 .... 136 C5
Bullfinch Wy *VGL* GL2 .... 112 F4 🔢
Bullingham Ct *CHELTW* GL51 ..... 2 A1
Bull La *COTS* GL54 .... 74 D6
  EVILLE/WHL BS5............ 337 H5
  GL GL1 .... 4 E5
Bull Pitch *DSLY* GL11 .... 253 K2
Bulls La *COR/BOX* SN13 .... 353 M5
Bully La *YATE/CS* BS37 .... 309 M3
Bulwark Av *CHEP* NP16 .... 270 B5
Bulwark Rd *CHEP* NP16 .... 270 A4
The Bulwarks
  RSTROUD/NAIL GL6 .... 233 K5
Bunting HI
  RSTROUD/NAIL GL6 .... 232 C7 🔢
Bunting Wy
  RSTROUD/NAIL GL6 .... 232 B7
Burbank Cl
  OLD/WMLY/WICK BS30 ..... 338 C8

Burchells Green Cl
  KGWD/HNM BS15 .... 337 K3
Burchells Green Rd
  KGWD/HNM BS15 .... 337 K2
Burcombe La *CIR* GL7 .... 189 H6
Burcombe Rd
  RSTROUD/NAIL GL6 .... 210 A8
Burcombe Wy
  RSTROUD/NAIL GL6 .... 210 B8
Burden Cl *ALMDB* BS32........ 317 G5
Burdett Cl *STNHO* GL10 .... 207 H4
Burdett Rd *STNHO* GL10 ...... 207 H4
Burfoote Gdns
  HGRV/WHIT BS14 .... 347 G7
Burfoot Rd *HGRV/WHIT* BS14 .. 347 G7
Burford Dr *STROUD* GL5 ...... 208 C4
Burford Gv *AVONM* BS11....... 324 B6
Burford Ms *GL* GL1 .... 5 K9
Burford Rd *CIR* GL7 .... 238 C2
Burford St *CIR* GL7 .... 244 E7
Burgage Cl *YATE/CS* BS37 ..... 320 D3 🔢
The Burgage *CHELTE/BC* GL52 .. 94 D6
Burgess Green Cl
  BRSG/KWL/STAPK BS4....... 337 G4 🔢
Burghill Rd *HNBRY/STHM* BS10 .. 325 J2
Burghley Ct
  FRCTL/WBN BS36 .... 318 A6 🔢
Burghley Rd *RDLND/MONT* BS6.. 336 A1
Burgis Rd *HGRV/WHIT* BS14 ... 346 F5 🔢
Burleigh Cft *GLE* GL4 .... 137 H3
Burleigh La *STROUD* GL5 ...... 233 G3
Burleigh Tor *STROUD* GL5 ..... 233 H4 🔢
Burleigh Vw
  RSTROUD/NAIL GL6 .... 209 M7
Burleigh Wy *WUE* GL12 .... 296 D6
Burley Av *MANG/FISH* BS16..... 328 B6
Burley Crest *MANG/FISH* BS16 .. 328 B5
Burley Gv *MANG/FISH* BS16 ... 328 B5
Burlington Rd
  RDLND/MONT BS6 .... 335 K1
The Burltons *CHELTE/BC* GL52 .. 72 G7
Burma Av *CHELTE/BC* GL52 .... 3 L3
Burma Rd *RSTROUD/NAIL* GL6 .. 232 C7
Burnbush Cl *HGRV/WHIT* BS14.. 347 G5
Burnell Dr *CBRISNE* BS2 .... 336 B3
Burneside Cl
  HNBRY/STHM BS10 .... 325 L1 🔢
Burnet Cl *GLE* GL4 .... 136 C7
Burney Wy
  OLD/WMLY/WICK BS30 ..... 338 C8
Burnham Cl
  KGWD/HNM BS15 .... 338 B2 🔢
Burnham Dr *KGWD/HNM* BS15... 338 B2 🔢
Burnham Rd *MALM* SN16 ...... 303 H7
Burnham Rd *MALM* SN16 ...... 303 J8
Burnivale *MALM* SN16 .... 303 H8
Burns Av *VGL* GL2 .... 135 L7
Burnt Barn Rd *CHEP* NP16 .... 270 A6
Burnt Oak *DSLY* GL11 .... 253 J2
Burrington Wk
  BMSTRD/HC/WWD BS13 ..... 345 J3 🔢
Burrough Wy *FRCTL/WBN* BS36.. 318 A6
Burrups La *RWYE* HR9 .... 84 F2
Burton Cl *CBRIS/FH* BS1 .... 7 G7
Burton Ct *CFTN/FAIL* BS8 .... 6 A3 🔢
Burton Rd *BAD* GL9 .... 323 H5
Burtons La *COR/BOX* SN13 .... 353 L6 🔢
Burton St *CHELT* GL50 .... 2 B4
Burwalls Rd *CFTN/FAIL* BS8 .... 335 G5
Bury Bar La *NWNT* GL18......... 86 C3
Burycourt Cl *AVONM* BS11 .... 324 C2 🔢
Bury Court Rd *CIND* GL14 ..... 157 G8
Bury HI *MANG/FISH* BS16 ...... 318 A8
Bury Hill La *YATE/CS* BS37 .... 310 C3
Bury La *OLD/WMLY/WICK* BS30 .. 340 B2
  VGL GL2 .... 134 A4
Buryway La *SHPSTR* CV36........ 61 H4
Buscombe Gdns
  BWTH/CHD GL3 .... 137 K4
Bush Av *BRSTK/PCHW* BS34 ... 316 E6
Bush Cl *STNHO* GL10 .... 206 B3
Bushcombe Cl *CHELTE/BC* GL52 .. 72 E8
Bushcombe La *CHELTE/BC* GL52 .. 72 F7
Bushes La *YATE/CS* BS37 ...... 311 J5
Bush Hay *BWTH/CHD* GL3 ..... 113 K6
Bush Pitch *LED* HR8 .... 19 L1
Bushy Pk *BRSG/KWL/STAPK* BS4 ... 7 K9
Bushy Wy *CHELTW* GL51 .... 92 F6
Bussage HI *RSTROUD/NAIL* GL6.. 209 L7
Butcher Hill's La
  RSTROUD/NAIL GL6 .... 232 D8 🔢
Butcombe Wk
  HGRV/WHIT BS14 .... 346 D6
Butlers Cl *EVILLE/WHL* BS5 .... 337 H4
Butlers La *SHPSTR* CV36......... 61 J5
Butler's Fld *CIR* GL7 .... 244 E6
Butlers La *SHPSTR* CV36......... 61 H6
Butlers Md *LYD* GL15 .... 202 E1
Butlers Rd *SHPSTR* CV36........ 61 J5
Buttercross La *CHELTE/BC* GL52 .. 94 F8
Buttercup Lawn *GLE* GL4 ...... 160 F1
Butterfield Cl
  HNBRY/STHM BS10 .... 326 A4
Butterfield Rd
  HNBRY/STHM BS10 .... 326 A4
Buttermere Cl *CHELTW* GL51 ... 115 G5
Buttermilk La *BWTH/CHD* GL3 .. 113 K5
Butterow West *STROUD* GL5 .. 208 D6
Butterrow HI *STROUD* GL5 ..... 208 E8
Butterrow La *STROUD* GL5 .... 208 F7
Butterworth La *RTEWK/TIB* BS19.. 88 C5
Butterworth Rd
  BRSG/KWL/STAPK BS4....... 345 M4 🔢
Butt Gn *RSTROUD/NAIL* GL6 ... 185 G2
Buttington Cl *GLE* GL4 .... 137 H6
Buttington HI *CHEP* NP16 ..... 270 D4
Buttington Rd *CHEP* NP16 .... 270 C3 🔢
Buttington Ter *CHEP* NP16 .... 270 D5
Butt La *THNB/SVB* BS35 .... 273 L8
Butt's La *CHELTE/BC* GL52 ...... 72 G6
  CHPMW/MSHF SN14 .... 331 K7
  LYD GL15 .... 178 D8
The Butts *GLE* GL4 .... 136 C7
  MALM SN16 .... 284 A5
  NWNT GL18 .... 86 D3
Butt St *RSTROUD/NAIL* GL6 ... 233 J5
Buxton Wk *HORF/LLZ* BS7 ..... 326 C3

Byard Rd *VGL* GL2 13
Bybrook Gdns *GLE* GL4 15
Bybrook Rd *GLE* GL4 15
Bye Md *MANG/FISH* BS16 15
Bye St *LED* HR8 2
Byfield Cl *CHELTE/BC* GL52 9
Byfords Cl *RTEWK/TIB* GL19 ... 108
Byfords Rd *RTEWK/TIB* GL19 ... 10
Byron Av *VGL* GL2 13
Byron Pl *CFTN/FAIL* BS8 6
  MANG/FISH BS16 328
Byron Rd *CHELTW* GL51 11
  DSLY GL11 25
  STROUD GL5 20
Byron St *CBRISNE* BS2 336
  EVILLE/WHL BS5 336

C

Cabot Cl *YATE/CS* BS37......... 32
Cabot Wy *CFTN/FAIL* BS8 33
Cadbury Heath Rd
  OLD/WMLY/WICK BS30 33
Caddick Cl *KGWD/HNM* BS15 ... 33
Cade Cl *BRSTK/PCHW* BS34 31
  KGWD/HNM BS15 33
Cadogan Rd *HGRV/WHIT* BS14 .. 34
Caen Rd *BMSTR* BS3 34
Caernarvon Cl *CHELTW* GL51 ... 11
Caernarvon Rd *CHELTW* GL51 ... 11
  KEYN BS31................. 34
Caerwent La *CHEP* NP16 27
Caesar Rd *VGL* GL2 13
Caesars Cl *LYD* GL15 201
Caine Rd *HORF/LLZ* BS7 326
Cains Cl *KGWD/HNM* BS15 33
Cainscross Rd *STROUD* GL5 ... 20
Caird St *CHEP* NP16 27
Cairn Gdns *FRCTL/WBN* BS36 .. 31
Cairns' Crs *CBRISNE* BS2 336
Cairns Rd *RDLND/MONT* BS6 ... 33
Cakebridge Pl *CHELTE/BC* GL52 ... 9
Cakebridge Rd *CHELTE/BC* GL52 .. 9
Calcott Rd
  BRSG/KWL/STAPK BS4....... 33
Calcutt St *HGHW* SN6........... 28
Caldbeck Cl
  HNBRY/STHM BS10 325
Calder Cl *KEYN* BS31 34
Calderdale *GLE* GL4 13
Calderwood Cl *CHELT* GL50 11
Caldicot Cl *AVONM* BS11 324
  OLD/WMLY/WICK BS30 33
Caledonian Rd *GL* GL1 4
Caledonia Pl *CFTN/FAIL* BS8 ... 33
Calf's La *CHCAM* GL55.......... 1
Calf Wy *RSTROUD/NAIL* GL6 ... 18
  RSTROUD/NAIL GL6 20
California Rd
  OLD/WMLY/WICK BS30 338
Callaways Rd *SHPSTR* CV36 6
Callicroft Rd
  BRSTK/PCHW BS34 31
Callington Rd
  BRSG/KWL/STAPK BS4....... 34
  HGRV/WHIT BS14 34
Callow End *LED* HR8 1
Callowhill Ct *CBRIS/FH* BS1 7
Calspick Wy *VGL* GL2 112
Calton Rd *GL* GL1 13
Calverley Ms *CHELTW* GL51 ... 115
Camberley Cl *BWTH/CHD* GL3... 11
Camberley Dr
  FRCTL/WBN BS36............ 31
Camberley Rd
  BRSG/KWL/STAPK BS4....... 345
Camberwell Rd *CHELTW* GL51 .. 11
Camborne Rd *HORF/LLZ* BS7 ... 32
Cambourne Pl *LYD* GL15 22
Cambray Pl *CHELT* GL50........
Cambrian Dr *YATE/CS* BS37 31
Cambrian Rd *TEWK* GL20 ......
Cambridge Av *CHELTW* GL51.... 11
  DSLY GL11 ....
Cambridge Crs
  HNLZ/SM/SNYPK/WT BS9.... 32
Cambridge Pk
  RDLND/MONT BS6 32
Cambridge Rd *HORF/LLZ* BS7 .. 32
Cambridge St *BMSTR* BS3 .....
  EVILLE/WHL BS5 336
  GL GL1 5
Cambridge Wy
  RSTROUD/NAIL GL6 23
Camden Cl *MIM* GL56 ....
Camden Rd *BMSTR* BS3 ....
Camden Ter *CFTN/FAIL* BS8 335
Camelford Rd
  EVILLE/WHL BS5 336
Camellia Cl *CHELTW* GL51 115
Camellia Wk *VGL* GL2 159
Cameron Wk *HORF/LLZ* BS7 ... 326
Cameroons Cl *KEYN* BS31 34
Camerton Cl *KEYN* BS31 349
Camerton Rd
  EVILLE/WHL BS5............ 336
Cam Gn *DSLY* GL11 137
Camomile Cl *GLE* GL4 13
Campbell Cl *BWTH/CHD* GL3 ... 113
Campbell Farm Dr
  AVONM BS11.................
Campbell Rd *CLFD* GL16........ 15
Campden Av *SHPSTR* CV36 3
Campden La *BDWAY* WR12 9
  COTS GL54................... 9
Campden Pitch *SHPSTR* CV36 ...
Campden Rd *CHCAM* GL55 ......
  CHELTW GL51 11
  GLE GL4 13
  SHPSTR CV36 ....
  STRAT CV37.................
Camp Gdns *COTS* GL54 9
Campion Cl *GLE* GL4 13
  THNB/SVB BS35 ....
Campion Dr *ALMDB* BS32 316

mpion Pk CHELTW GL51 ...... 115 H7
m Pitch DSLY GL11 .... 229 H6
mp La CHPMW/MSHF SN14 .... 331 L7
mp Rd CFTN/FAIL BS8 .... 335 H4
CHELTE/BC GL52 .... 3 M6
CHEP NP16 .... 270 B5
THNB/SVB BS35 .... 272 D5
m Rd CHELTE/BC GL52 .... 3 L2
ms Gnd VGL2 .... 110 F5 🔲
e Cam CHCAM GL55 .... 13 H8
mwal Rd CBRISNE BS2........... 7 M6
nada W FRCTL/WBN BS1 .... 335 J6
nberra STNHO GL10 .... 207 G2
nberra Gv BRSTK/PCHW BS34 316 D7
nford La HNLZ/SM/SNYPK/WT BS9 325 H3
nford Rd HNLZ/SM/SNYPK/WT BS9 525 H3
nnans Cl FRCTL/WBN BS36 .... 318 A3
nning Rd VGL2 .... 113 G6 🔲
nnon La OLD/WMLY/WICK BS30 ... 339 C5
nnon St BMSTR BS3 .... 6 D9
CBRIS/FH BS1 .... 6 F2
nnop Rd LYD GL15 .... 176 E5
nonbury St BRKLY GL13 ...... 227 H8
non Pk BRKLY GL13 .... 227 C7
non's Wk KGWD/HNM BS15 ... 338 A1
nowie Rd RDLND/MONT BS6 .. 325 K8
ntell Gv HGRV/WHIT BS14 .... 347 H6 🔲
nterbury Cl YATE/CS BS37.... 310 A8
nterbury Leys TEWK GL20 .... 48 C4
nterbury St
EVILLE/WHL BS5 .... 336 D5 🔲
nterbury Wk CHELTW GL51 ... 115 H6 🔲
nters Leaze WUE GL12 .... 296 D7
nton Acre
RSTROUD/NAIL GL6 .... 185 H2
ntors Cl CHELTE/BC GL52 .... 94 B1 🔲
ntors Dr CHELTE/BC GL52 .... 94 A1
nvey Cl
HNBRY/STHM BS10 .... 326 A4 🔲
nynge Rd CFTN/FAIL BS8...... 335 H3
nynge Sq CFTN/FAIL BS8...... 335 H3
nynge St CBRIS/FH BS1 .... 7 C5
pel Cl KGWD/HNM BS15....... 338 D1
pel Ct STROUD GL5 .... 208 F3
pel Rd AVONM BS11 .... 324 C2
GLE GL4 .... 160 E1
grave Cl
BRSG/KWL/STAPK BS4...... 337 J8
grave Crs
BRSG/KWL/STAPK BS4...... 337 J8
ptain Barton Cl STROUD GL5 . 209 C3
ptains Green Rd LYD GL15 .... 177 J8
raway Gdns
EVILLE/WHL BS5 .... 336 E1 🔲
rdigan Rd
HNLZ/SM/SNYPK/WT BS9.... 325 K5
rdill Cl
BMSTRD/HC/WWD BS13...... 345 J3
res Cl CHELTE/BC GL52 .... 72 C7 🔲
risbrooke Dr
CHELTE/BC GL52 .... 116 E4 🔲
risbrooke Rd
BRSG/KWL/STAPK BS4....... 345 M3
BWTH/CHD GL3 .... 137 J5
risbrook Rd MTCHDN GL17 ... 106 C8
rlow Rd
BRSG/KWL/STAPK BS4....... 346 A3
riton Gdns STROUD GL5 ..... 208 E1 🔲
riton Pk EVILLE/WHL BS5 ..... 336 E3
riton Pl CHELTW GL51 .... 2 B2
riton Rd CHELTE/BC GL52 ...... 3 C6
rlyle Gv CHELTW GL51 .... 92 F7 🔲
rlyle Rd EVILLE/WHL BS5....... 336 E2
rmarthen Cl YATE/CS BS37 .. 310 B7 🔲
rmarthen Gv
OLD/WMLY/WICK BS30 .... 348 D2 🔲
rmarthen Rd CHELTW GL51 .. 114 F5
HNLZ/SM/SNYPK/WT BS9 .... 325 J6 🔲
rnarvon Rd
RDLND/MONT BS6 .... 335 L1
rne Pl GLE GL4 .... 136 C2
roline Cl KEYN BS31 .... 347 L7
YATE/CS BS37 .... 320 D1 🔲
KEYN BS31 .... 348 A6
rrant Rd TEWK GL20............ 48 B4
rrington Rd BMSTR BS3 ...... 335 J7
rrol Gv CHELTW GL51 .... 92 F7
rson Cl MIM GL56 .... 37 C2
rsons Rd MANG/FISH BS16 ... 328 D8
rter Rd CHELTW GL51 .... 93 H6
rters Orch VGL2 .... 159 H1
rters Wy
RSTROUD/NAIL GL6 .... 232 B6 🔲
rter Wk ALMDB BS32 .... 316 F3 🔲
rtledge Rd
EVILLE/WHL BS5 .... 336 E2 🔲
rtway Gn CIND GL14 .... 154 A3
sey Cl VGL2 .... 5 L6
shes Green Rd STROUD GL5 . 207 M3
sh Hl MTCHDN GL17 .... 128 F3
sino Pl CHELT GL50.............. 2 B9
ssell Rd MANG/FISH BS16 ... 327 L6
ssey Bottom La
EVILLE/WHL BS5 .... 337 J4 🔲
stle Cl HNBRY/STHM BS10... 325 G1
stle Coombe RSTROUD/NAIL GL6 ... 185 H4 🔲
stle Coombe THNB/SVB BS35. 293 L1
stle Ct BRSG/KWL/STAPK BS4 . 336 E7
THNB/SVB BS35 .... 293 L1
stle Crs LYD GL15 .... 198 F6
stle End RSTROUD/NAIL GL6 . 161 G4
stle Farm Rd
KGWD/HNM BS15 .... 347 L1
stlefields Av
CHELTE/BC GL52 .... 116 E5
stlefields Dr CHELTE/BC GL52.. 116 E5 🔲
CHELTE/BC GL52 .... 116 E5
stleford Gdns CHEP NP16 ... 270 B1 🔲
stleford Hl CHEP NP16 .... 270 A1

Castle Gdns CHCAM GL55 ..... 13 G8
Castle Hl RBANSW OX15 .... 17 M6
Castle Hill Dr BWTH/CHD GL3 . 138 B7
Castle Hill La RBANSW OX15 . 17 M7
Castle La CHPMW/MSHF SN14 . 342 A2
VGL2 .... 181 M1
Castlemaine Dr CHELTW GL51 . 114 E3
Castle Md STNHO GL10 .... 207 H8
Castlemead Rd STROUD GL5 .. 208 D5
Castle Ri STROUD GL5 .... 208 E5
Castle Rd KGWD/HNM BS15 .. 337 L1
MANG/FISH BS16 .... 329 L5
OLD/WMLY/WICK BS30 ...... 338 E8
Castle St CBRISNE BS2 .... 7 H3
CIR GL7 .... 238 C3
COTS GL54 .... 74 D6
STNHO GL10 .... 207 K3
STROUD GL5 .... 208 E5 🔲
THNB/SVB BS35 .... 293 J1
Castleton Rd GLE GL4 .... 136 F4
Castlett St COTS GL54 .... 98 E4
Castle Vw CHEP NP16 .... 270 C5
Catbrain Hl HNBRY/STHM BS10 . 315 K5
Catbrain La HNBRY/STHM BS10.. 315 K5
Catbrook Cl CHCAM GL55 ...... 34 E2
Catchpot La YATE/CS BS37 ... 321 J5
Cater Rd
BMSTRD/HC/WWD BS13 ..... 345 K5
Catherine Hl THNB/SVB BS35 . 306 B1
Catherine Mead St BMSTR BS3 . 6 D9
Catherine Wy
CBATH/BATHN BA1 .... 352 B4
Catkin Cl VGL2 .... 159 L4 🔲
Catley Gv LGASH BS41 .... 344 D2
Catswood Ct STROUD GL5 .... 209 G2
Catswood La
RSTROUD/NAIL GL6 .... 185 K8
Cattistock Dr EVILLE/WHL BS5 . 337 J5
Cattle Market Rd CBRIS/FH BS1 . 7 J6
Cattybrook Rd
MANG/FISH BS16 .... 328 F6
Cattybrook St
EVILLE/WHL BS5 .... 336 D3 🔲
Caudle Hl MTCHDN GL17 ..... 128 F3 🔲
Caudle La MTCHDN GL17 ..... 128 F4
Causeway Rd CIND GL14 ...... 154 B1
The Causeway
FRCTL/WBN BS36............. 318 E4
VGL2 .... 158 F2
Causley Dr
OLD/WMLY/WICK BS30 ...... 338 B6
Cavan Wk
BRSG/KWL/STAPK BS4........ 345 M2
Cave Dr MANG/FISH BS16 .... 327 M5
Cave Gv MANG/FISH BS16 .... 328 D4
Cavendish Av BWTH/CHD GL3 . 113 M6
Cavendish Gdns
HNLZ/SM/SNYPK/WT BS9.... 324 E7
Cavendish Rd
BRSTK/PCHW BS34............ 316 B3
HNLZ/SM/SNYPK/WT BS9.... 325 A6
St CBRISNE BS2 .... 336 A3
Cecil Av EVILLE/WHL BS5 ..... 337 H2
Cecil Rd CFTN/FAIL BS8 ...... 335 H3
GL GL1 .... 135 M4
KGWD/HNM BS15 .... 337 M3
Cecily Hl CIR GL7 .... 238 B2
Cedar Cl BRSTK/PCHW BS34 .. 316 B4
CHELTS GL53 .... 116 D6 🔲
LGASH BS41 .... 344 B2
OLD/WMLY/WICK BS30 ...... 338 D7 🔲
STROUD GL5 .... 207 M5
Cedar Ct LED HR8 .... 20 A3
Cedar Court Rd CHELT GL50 .... 2 D7 🔲
Cedar Dr DSLY GL11 .... 253 J2
KEYN BS31 .... 347 M7
Cedar Gdns STNHO GL10 ..... 207 H3 🔲
Cedar Gv COTS GL54 .... 74 C5
HNLZ/SM/SNYPK/WT BS9.... 324 F6
Cedar Pk
HNLZ/SM/SNYPK/WT BS9.... 324 F6
Cedar Rd BWTH/CHD GL3 .... 137 M4
CHCAM GL55 .... 9 G7
TEWK GL20 .... 49 C3
Cedar Wy CLFD GL16 .... 151 M7
FRCTL/WBN BS36............. 317 M4
MANG/FISH BS16 .... 329 K6
Cedarwood Dr GLE GL4 ...... 136 A8
Celandine Bank
CHELTE/BC GL52 .... 72 D7 🔲
Celandine Cl THNB/SVB BS35 . 293 M1
Celestine Rd YATE/CS BS37 .. 309 L8
Celia Ter
BRSG/KWL/STAPK BS4........ 337 H5 🔲
Cemetery La CIR GL7 .... 217 K1
COTS GL54 .... 123 J5
Cemetery Rd
BRSG/KWL/STAPK BS4........ 336 C8
GLE GL4 .... 136 C5
Cennick Av KGWD/HNM BS15 . 338 A2
Centaurus Rd
BRSTK/PCHW BS34............ 315 L4
Central Av HNBRY/STHM BS10.. 304 C8
KGWD/HNM BS15 .... 337 H7
Central Cross Dr CHELTE/BC GL52 .. 2 F2
Central Rd GL GL1 .... 136 A4
STROUD GL5 .... 208 B4
Central Wy CHELTW GL51 .... 115 K1
Centurion Cl GLE GL4 .... 137 G5 🔲
Centurion Rd LYD GL15 .... 201 L7
Centurions Wk CLFD GL16 ... 175 K2 🔲
Ceres Cl OLD/WMLY/WICK BS30 . 348 B1
Cerimon Ga
BRSTK/PCHW BS34............ 317 G6 🔲
Cerney La AVONM BS11 .... 324 A6
Cerney Wick La CIND GL14 ... 263 M6
Cesson Ct YATE/CS BS37 ...... 320 E2
Chaceley Cl GLE GL4 .... 137 G6 🔲
VGL2 .... 159 G3
Chadbournes
BWTH/CHD GL3 .... 113 K5 🔲
Chadleigh Gv
BRSG/KWL/STAPK BS4........ 345 L4
Chad Rd CHELTW GL51 .... 115 H2
Chadwick Cl GLE GL4 .... 159 M1
Chaffinch Cl VGL2 .... 112 F4 🔲
Chaffinch St STNHO GL10 .... 207 H3 🔲
Chaingate La YATE/CS BS37 . 309 H5

Chakeshill Cl
HNBRY/STHM BS10 .... 315 L8
Chakeshill Dr
HNBRY/STHM BS10 .... 315 L8
Chalcombe Cl
BRSTK/PCHW BS34............ 316 E3
Chalcroft Wk
BMSTRD/HC/WWD BS13 ..... 345 G7
Chalford Av CHELTW GL51 .... 114 D4
Chalford Cl YATE/CS BS37 .... 319 M4
Chalford Rd GLE GL4 .... 160 A2
Chalks Rd EVILLE/WHL BS5 .. 336 F3
Challen Cl LED HR8 .... 19 M1 🔲
Challender Av
HNBRY/STHM BS10 .... 315 H8 🔲
Challoner Ct CBRIS/FH BS1 .... 6 E7
Chamberlayne Cl COTS GL54 . 102 A4
Champion Rd
KGWD/HNM BS15 .... 338 C1
Champneys Av
HNBRY/STHM BS10 .... 315 H8 🔲
Chamwells Av VGL2 .... 5 M1
Chamwells Wk VGL2 .... 112 D7
Chancel Cl GLE GL4 .... 5 M7
HNLZ/SM/SNYPK/WT BS9.... 324 F8
Chancel Pk CHELTS GL53 .... 116 B5
Chancel Wy CHELTS GL53 ... 116 C5
CIR GL7 .... 244 E7 🔲
Chancery St EVILLE/WHL BS5 . 336 D4
Chandag Rd KEYN BS31 ...... 348 C2
Chandler Rd CHELTE/BC GL52 . 94 B1
Chandos Dr BWTH/CHD GL3 . 138 A6
Chandos Rd KEYN BS31 ...... 348 A4
RDLND/MONT BS6 .... 335 K2
STROUD GL5 .... 208 C7
Chandos St COTS GL54 .... 74 C6
Channell's Hl
HNLZ/SM/SNYPK/WT BS9.... 325 J3
Channel Vw CHEP NP16 ...... 270 A5
Channon's Hl MANG/FISH BS16 . 327 H7
Chantry Cl LYD GL15 .... 225 J2 🔲
Chantry Ct TET GL8 .... 282 A4 🔲
Chantry Gdns MIM GL56 .... 57 J6 🔲
Chantry Ga CHELTE/BC GL52 . 94 A1 🔲
Chantry Gv AVONM BS11 ..... 324 E1 🔲
Chantry La MANG/FISH BS16 . 328 B2 🔲
Chantry Rd CFTN/FAIL BS8 .. 335 K2 🔲
THNB/SVB BS35 .... 293 K1
Chapel Cl CIR GL7 .... 236 B8
CIR GL7 .... 266 F4
Chapel Gdns
HNBRY/STHM BS10 .... 325 J2
MIM GL56 .... 37 G2
VGL2 .... 159 H4
Chapel Green La
RDLND/MONT BS6 .... 335 K1
Chapel Hay Cl BWTH/CHD GL3 . 113 L7 🔲
Chapel Hay La BWTH/CHD GL3.. 113 M7
Chapel Hl BRKLY GL13 .... 251 K4
CLFD GL16 .... 151 K1
LYD GL15 .... 224 D2
Chapel La AVONM BS11 .... 324 D1
BAD GL9 .... 323 J5
BDWAY WR12 .... 32 B1
CHCAM GL55 .... 11 L5
CHELT GL50 .... 2 C9
CHELTE/BC GL52 .... 72 D8
CHNTN OX7 .... 83 H6
CHNTN OX7 .... 104 C6
CHPMW/MSHF SN14 .... 330 E6
CIR GL7 .... 190 C6
COR/BOX SN13 .... 353 M6 🔲
COTS GL54 .... 121 M7
EVILLE/WHL BS5 .... 337 G5
KGWD/HNM BS15 .... 338 D3
MALM SN16 .... 285 G3
MANG/FISH BS16 .... 327 L4
MIM GL56 .... 57 G1
MTCHDN GL17 .... 131 L2
RSTROUD/NAIL GL6 .... 233 J6
RTEWK/TIB GL19 .... 65 J2
RWYE HR9 .... 84 E3
STROUD GL5 .... 207 M5
TEWK GL20 .... 27 K3
TEWK GL20 .... 27 J7
VGL2 .... 133 G2
WUE GL12 .... 294 C2
WUE GL12 .... 297 M3
YATE/CS BS37 .... 321 J5
Chapel Pth
CHPMW/MSHF SN14 .... 343 K8
Chapel Pitch NWNT GL18...... 85 K8
Chapel Rd
BMSTRD/HC/WWD BS13 ..... 345 J5
CIR GL7 .... 266 F5
CLFD GL16 .... 151 K6
EVILLE/WHL BS5 .... 336 D2 🔲
KGWD/HNM BS15 .... 337 L6
LYD GL15 .... 202 B1
STRAT CV37 .... 8 A1
THNB/SVB BS35 .... 272 E6
Chapel St CBRISNE BS2 .... 7 L6
CHELT GL50 .... 2 C4
CHNTN OX7 .... 125 L1
COTS GL54 .... 102 A3
DSLY GL11 .... 229 H6
MIM GL56 .... 80 D8
STROUD GL5 .... 208 F4
THNB/SVB BS35 .... 293 K4
Chapel Wk BAD GL9 .... 299 K8
CHELT GL50 .... 2 C6
CLFD GL16 .... 152 M1
Chapel Wy
BRSG/KWL/STAPK BS4........ 337 G5
Chaplin Rd EVILLE/WHL BS5 . 336 D2
Chapman Wy CHELTW GL51 . 115 H4 🔲
Chapter St CBRISNE BS2 ...... 336 A3 🔲
Charbon Ga
BRSTK/PCHW BS34............ 317 G6 🔲
Charborough Rd
BRSTK/PCHW BS34............ 326 B1
Chardstock Av
HNLZ/SM/SNYPK/WT BS9.... 324 E3
Chardwar Gdns COTS GL54 .. 123 H6 🔲
Charfield Cl KGWD/HNM BS15. 338 C3 🔲

Charfield Rd
HNBRY/STHM BS10 .... 325 L2
WUE GL12 .... 276 F5
Chargrove
OLD/WMLY/WICK BS30 ...... 338 E5 🔲
YATE/CS BS37 .... 319 M4
Chargrove La CHELTW GL51 . 114 F5
Charis Av HNBRY/STHM BS10 . 325 L4
Charlcombe La
CBATH/BATHN BA1 .... 351 H8
Charlcombe Rd
HNLZ/SM/SNYPK/WT BS9.... 325 H5
Charlecote Av GL GL1 .... 159 L3
Charlecote Cnr
CHELTE/BC GL52 .... 72 A8 🔲
Charles Av
BRSTK/PCHW BS34............ 317 C7 🔲
Charles Cl THNB/SVB BS35 ... 273 L8 🔲
Charles Pl CFTN/FAIL BS8..... 335 J5
Charles Rd BRSTK/PCHW BS34 . 316 D8
Charles St CBRISNE BS2 .... 6 F1
CHELTW GL51 .... 2 A2
GL GL1 .... 5 G7
Charlesway MIM GL56 .... 79 L3
Charleswood Rd LYD GL15 ... 201 G1
Charlham La CIR GL7 .... 264 F4 🔲
Charlock Cl GLE GL4 .... 136 C2 🔲
Charlotte Cl CBRIS/FH BS1 .... 6 C4
CBRISNE BS2 .... 7 J1 🔲
Charlotte St South CBRIS/FH BS1.. 6 C4
Chariton Av BRSTK/PCHW BS34.. 326 B1
Chariton Cl CHELTS GL53 .... 116 C6
Chariton Dr CHELTS GL53 ...... 3 H9
Chariton Gdns
HNBRY/STHM BS10 .... 315 M7
Chariton La HNBRY/STHM BS10 . 315 M6
HNBRY/STHM BS10 .... 315 J8
Chariton Mead Dr
HNBRY/STHM BS10 .... 315 M7 🔲
Chariton Pk KEYN BS31 .... 347 M6
Chariton Park Dr CHELTS GL53 . 116 A4
Chariton Park Ga CHELTS GL53.. 116 A5
Chariton Pl
HNBRY/STHM BS10 .... 315 M7 🔲
Chariton Rd
HNBRY/STHM BS10 .... 325 K2
KGWD/HNM BS15 .... 337 K2
MALM SN16 .... 303 M6
TET GL8 .... 281 L4
Chariton St EVILLE/WHL BS5 . 336 D4 🔲
Chariton Wy VGL2 .... 112 E6
Charminster Rd
MANG/FISH BS16 .... 327 K8
Charnell Rd MANG/FISH BS16 . 328 A7
Charnhill Brow
MANG/FISH BS16 .... 328 C7
Charnhill Crs MANG/FISH BS16 . 328 B7
Charnhill Dr MANG/FISH BS16 . 328 B8
Charnhill Rdg MANG/FISH BS16 . 328 C7
Charnhill V MANG/FISH BS16 . 328 B7
Charnwood CHELTS GL53 ..... 115 M6 🔲
Charnwood Ct LYD GL15 ..... 201 K6 🔲
Charnwood Rd CHELTS GL53 . 115 M6 🔲
HGRV/WHIT BS14 .... 346 D8
Charterhouse Rd
EVILLE/WHL BS5 .... 336 F3 🔲
Chartist La RTEWK/TIB GL19 .. 44 A7
Chartist Piece RTEWK/TIB GL19 . 66 E4
Chartists Wy CHEP NP16....... 270 A6
Chartist Wy RTEWK/TIB GL19 . 66 E4
Chartwell Cl VGL2 .... 135 J5
Chase Av CHELTE/BC GL52 ... 116 E5
Chasefield La
MANG/FISH BS16 .... 327 K7 🔲
Chase La GLE GL4 .... 5 L9
GLE GL4 .... 136 D4
WUE GL12 .... 296 E5
Chasely Crs CHELTW GL51 ... 115 G6 🔲
Chase Rd KGWD/HNM BS15 . 337 M1
The Chase BWTH/CHD GL3 .. 113 M7
GLE GL4 .... 136 F6
MANG/FISH BS16 .... 327 L8 🔲
STROUD GL5 .... 207 M4
Chasewood Cnr
RSTROUD/NAIL GL6 .... 209 M7 🔲
Chatcombe Cl CHELTS GL53 . 116 D7 🔲
Chatcombe Rd GLE GL4 ...... 136 D6 🔲
Chatsworth Av GL GL1 .... 159 L2
Chatsworth Dr CHELTS GL53 . 115 M3
Chatsworth Pk THNB/SVB BS35.. 293 L1
Chatsworth Rd
BRSG/KWL/STAPK BS4........ 336 E7
MANG/FISH BS16 .... 327 K8
Chatterton Gn
HGRV/WHIT BS14 .... 346 B8 🔲
Chatterton Rd YATE/CS BS37 . 319 M2
Chatterton Sq CBRIS/FH BS1 .... 7 H7
Chaucer Cl GL GL1 .... 135 M6
Chaucer Rd DSLY GL11 .... 253 L4
Chaundey Gv
BMSTRD/HC/WWD BS13 ..... 345 K6
Chavenage La TET GL8 .... 281 L3
Cheapside CBRISNE BS2 ...... 336 B3 🔲
STROUD GL5 .... 208 D4
Cheapside St BMSTR BS3 .... 7 K9
Cheap St COTS GL54 .... 167 J7
Cheddar Gv
BMSTRD/HC/WWD BS13 ..... 345 J3
Chedworth KGWD/HNM BS15 . 328 A8 🔲
YATE/CS BS37 .... 319 K4
Chedworth Rd GLE GL4 ...... 135 M8
HORF/LLZ BS7 .... 326 C5
Chedworth Wy
CHELTW GL51 .... 115 G3 🔲
Cheese La CBRISNE BS2 .... 7 H4
Chelford Gv
BRSTK/PCHW BS34............ 316 D3 🔲
Chelmer Gv KEYN BS31 .... 348 B7
Chelmsford Av CHELTW GL51 . 115 J6
Chelmsford Wk
BRSG/KWL/STAPK BS4........ 337 H6 🔲
Chelsea Cl CHELTS GL53 ...... 115 J3 🔲
KEYN BS31 .... 348 C6 🔲
Chelsea Pk EVILLE/WHL BS5 . 336 E3
Chelsea Rd EVILLE/WHL BS5 . 336 D2

Chelston Rd
BRSG/KWL/STAPK BS4........ 345 M4
Cheltenham La
RDLND/MONT BS6 .... 336 A1 🔲
Cheltenham Rd BDWAY WR12 . 32 C4
CHELTE/BC GL52 .... 94 B2 🔲
CIR GL7 .... 214 B8
COTS GL54 .... 74 A8
EVE WR11 .... 30 D1
GL GL1 .... 5 K4
RDLND/MONT BS6 .... 335 M2
RSTROUD/NAIL GL6 .... 185 H3
RSTROUD/NAIL GL6 .... 210 C2
TEWK GL20 .... 27 J6
VGL2 .... 112 E8
Cheltenham Rd East BWTH/CHD GL3 .. 113 H6
Chelt Rd CHELTE/BC GL52 ...... 3 L2
Chelvy Cl BMSTRD/HC/WWD BS13 . 345 M8
Chelwood Rd KEYN BS31 ..... 349 G7
Chelworth Rd HGHW SN6 .... 288 D5
Chepstow Pk
MANG/FISH BS16 .... 328 B2 🔲
Chepstow Rd
BRSG/KWL/STAPK BS4........ 345 M3
Chequers Cl
OLD/WMLY/WICK BS30 ...... 338 E8 🔲
Chequers Rd GLE GL4 .... 136 C4
Cherington KGWD/HNM BS15 . 337 K6
YATE/CS BS37 .... 319 M5
Cherington Rd
HNBRY/STHM BS10 .... 325 L4
CHELTW GL51 .... 115 H6 🔲
Cheriton Pl
HNLZ/SM/SNYPK/WT BS9.... 325 K4
OLD/WMLY/WICK BS30 ...... 338 E5
Cherrington Dr GLE GL4 ...... 137 G6
Cherry Av CHELTS GL53 ...... 116 E7
Cherry Bank NWNT GL18 ...... 86 C4 🔲
Cherry Cl VGL2 .... 159 G4
Cherry Garden La
OLD/WMLY/WICK BS30 ...... 348 D1
Cherry Garden Rd
OLD/WMLY/WICK BS30 ...... 348 E2
Cherry Gdns
OLD/WMLY/WICK BS30 ...... 348 E2
Cherry Gv MANG/FISH BS16 . 328 C5
Cherry La CBRIS/FH BS1 .... 6 F1
Cherry Orch TEWK GL20 ...... 27 G5
WUE GL12 .... 277 L3
Cherry Orchard Cl CHCAM GL55 . 34 E1
Cherry Orchard La
CHPMW/MSHF SN14 .... 313 K6
TEWK GL20 .... 25 M5
The Cherry Orch CHELTW GL51.. 92 A7
Cherry Rd
CHPMW/MSHF SN14 .... 343 J6 🔲
LGASH BS41 .... 344 B1
YATE/CS BS37 .... 320 C2 🔲
Cherry Tree Cl KEYN BS31 .... 347 L7 🔲
RSTROUD/NAIL GL6 .... 232 C7
Cherrytree Ct
MANG/FISH BS16 .... 329 L6 🔲
Cherrytree Crs
MANG/FISH BS16 .... 337 L1
Cherrytree La CIR GL7 .... 238 F1
Cherry Tree La CLFD GL16 ... 152 A7 🔲
Cherry Tree Rd HGHW SN6 .. 288 E3
Cherrytree Rd
KGWD/HNM BS15 .... 337 L1
Cherry Wk LYD GL15 .... 201 J7
Cherry Wd
OLD/WMLY/WICK BS30 ...... 348 D1
Cherrywood Gdns GLE GL4 .. 136 A8 🔲
Cherston Ct GLE GL4 .... 137 G3
Chertsey Rd RDLND/MONT BS6.. 335 K2
Chervil Cl GLE GL4 .... 136 D7
Cherwell Cl THNB/SVB BS35 . 293 L4 🔲
Cherwell Rd KEYN BS31 ...... 348 C7
Chesham Wy KGWD/HNM BS15 . 337 M2 🔲
Cheshire Cl YATE/CS BS37 ... 310 A8
Cheshire Rd BWTH/CHD GL3 . 113 G5
The Chesils COTS GL54 .... 74 B3 🔲
Chesley Hl
OLD/WMLY/WICK BS30 ...... 339 H4
Chessel Cl ALMDB BS32 ...... 306 C6 🔲
Chessell Av THNB/SVB BS35 . 304 E4 🔲
Chessell St BMSTR BS3 .... 335 K8
Chessgrove La MTCHDN GL17 . 107 G8
Chessington Av
HGRV/WHIT BS14 .... 346 D6
Chestal DSLY GL11 .... 253 L6 🔲
Chester Cl RTEWK/TIB GL19 .. 69 G6 🔲
Chester Crs CIR GL7 .... 238 D3
Chesterfield Av
RDLND/MONT BS6 .... 336 A1 🔲
Chesterfield Rd
MANG/FISH BS16 .... 328 A6
RDLND/MONT BS6 .... 336 A1
Chestermaster Cl
ALMDB BS32 .... 306 C6 🔲
Chester Park Rd
MANG/FISH BS16 .... 337 K1
Chester Rd EVILLE/WHL BS5 . 337 G2 🔲
GLE GL4 .... 136 E3
Chesters
OLD/WMLY/WICK BS30 ...... 338 C7 🔲
Chester St CIR GL7 .... 238 C5
EVILLE/WHL BS5 .... 336 D1 🔲
Chesterton Gv CIR GL7 .... 238 C5
Chesterton La CIR GL7 .... 238 A4
Chester Wk CHELT GL50........ 2 C4
Chestnut Av STNHO GL10 .... 207 H5
Chestnut Cl CIR GL7 .... 264 F4
CLFD GL16 .... 151 M7
HGRV/WHIT BS14 .... 347 G6
LED HR8 .... 19 M4
RSTROUD/NAIL GL6 .... 232 D7
TET GL8 .... 281 M3 🔲
VGL2 .... 159 G4 🔲
Chestnut Dr THNB/SVB BS35 . 293 L2 🔲
YATE/CS BS37 .... 320 C2 🔲
Chestnut Hl RSTROUD/NAIL GL6.. 232 D7
Chestnut La STROUD GL5 ..... 208 C5

Chestnut Pl CHELTS GL53 .... 115 K7
Chestnut Rd GLE GL4 .... 137 C6
  KGWD/HNM BS15 .... 328 B8
  LGASH BS41 .... 344 D1
  MANG/FISH BS16 .... 327 M5
The Chestnuts GL GL1 .... 4 D8
Chestnut Wk
  BMSTRD/HC/WWD BS13 .... 345 J5
  KEYN BS31 .... 349 G8
Chestnut Wy KGWD/HNM BS15 .... 328 B8
Chetwode Cl
  HNBRY/STHM BS10 .... 315 M8
Chevening Cl
  BRSTK/PCHW BS34 .... 316 F7
Cheviot Cl VGL GL2 .... 159 C3
Cheviot Dr THNB/SVB BS35 .... 294 A3
Cheviot Rd CHELTE/BC GL52 .... 94 D7
Cheviot Wy
  OLD/WMLY/WICK BS30 .... 338 G6
Chewton Cl MANG/FISH BS16 .... 327 K8
Cheyne Rd
  HNLZ/SM/SNYPK/WT BS9 .... 324 F5
Cheyney Cl GLE GL4 .... 136 D5
Chichester Wy
  YATE/CS BS37 .... 309 M8
Chickadee Cl VGL GL15 .... 198 E7
Chicknalls La LYD GL15 .... 178 F6
Childswickham Rd
  BDWAY WR12 .... 32 D3
Chillington Ct
  BRSTK/PCHW BS34 .... 316 A2
Chillwood Cl YATE/CS BS37 .... 309 C8
Chiltern Av CHELTE/BC GL52 .... 72 A7
Chiltern Cl HGRV/WHIT BS14 .... 346 D7
  OLD/WMLY/WICK BS30 .... 338 E6
Chiltern Pk THNB/SVB BS35 .... 294 A3
Chiltern Rd CHELTE/BC GL52 .... 3 M1
  VGL GL2 .... 159 C3
Chilton Rd
  BRSG/KWL/STAPK BS4 .... 346 C7
The Chine MANG/FISH BS16 .... 326 F6
Chine Vw MANG/FISH BS16 .... 328 B3
Chiphouse Rd
  KGWD/HNM BS15 .... 338 A1
Chippenham Rd
  CHPMW/MSHF SN14 .... 342 C3
Chipperfield Dr
  KGWD/HNM BS15 .... 338 B2
Chipping Cl WUE GL12 .... 277 K4
Chipping Gdns WUE GL12 .... 277 J4
The Chippings
  MANG/FISH BS16 .... 326 F6
Chipping St TET GL8 .... 282 A4
Chisbury Cl EVILLE/WHL BS5 .... 326 E8
Chislet Wy GLE GL4 .... 159 M2
Chittening Rd AVONM BS11 .... 314 A4
Chock La
  HNLZ/SM/SNYPK/WT BS9 .... 325 J4
Choirs Cl GLE GL4 .... 137 C5
Chosen Dr BWTH/CHD GL3 .... 113 K6
Chosen View Rd CHELTW GL51 .... 93 K7
Chosen Wy GLE GL4 .... 137 H3
Christchurch Av
  MANG/FISH BS16 .... 327 M6
Christchurch La
  MANG/FISH BS16 .... 327 M6
Christchurch Rd CFTN/FAIL BS8 .... 335 J4
Christmas St CBRIS/FH BS1 .... 6 E5
Christowe La CHELTS GL53 .... 116 A4
Chubb Cl SN16 .... 303 J6
  OLD/WMLY/WICK BS30 .... 338 B6
Church Av CIR GL7 .... 238 E6
  EVILLE/WHL BS5 .... 336 D2
  HNLZ/SM/SNYPK/WT BS9 .... 325 G7
  OLD/WMLY/WICK BS30 .... 338 E4
  WUE GL12 .... 275 G4
Church Cl BDWAY WR12 .... 32 E4
  FRCTL/WBN BS36 .... 318 D3
Churchend VGL GL2 .... 204 F7
Churchend La WUE GL12 .... 276 B7
Churchfarm Cl YATE/CS BS37 .... 310 B8
Church Farm La MIM GL56 .... 36 C7
Church Farm Rd
  MANG/FISH BS16 .... 328 E5
Churchfield Rd GLE GL4 .... 161 G1
  STROUD GL5 .... 208 F5
Churchfields CHELTE/BC GL52 .... 72 C7
Church Gdns LYD GL15 .... 225 J1
Church HI
  BRSG/KWL/STAPK BS4 .... 347 G1
  MTCHDN GL17 .... 128 C7
  RSTROUD/NAIL GL6 .... 210 C3
  THNB/SVB BS35 .... 292 B8
Churchhill Rd CHNTN OX7 .... 105 M2
  RSTROUD/NAIL GL6 .... 233 K2
Churchill Cl
  OLD/WMLY/WICK BS30 .... 338 C6
  RSTROUD/NAIL GL6 .... 232 D7
Churchill Dr CHELTE/BC GL52 .... 3 J8
  HNLZ/SM/SNYPK/WT BS9 .... 324 F4
Churchill Gv TEWK GL20 .... 48 D5
Churchill Meadow LED HR8 .... 19 L4
Churchill Pl CIR GL7 .... 242 F4
Churchill Rd
  BRSG/KWL/STAPK BS4 .... 336 E7
  CHELTS GL53 .... 115 M6
  CHNTN OX7 .... 104 C6
  CIR GL7 .... 238 E2
  EVE WR11 .... 30 B2
  GL GL1 .... 136 A4
  RSTROUD/NAIL GL6 .... 232 D7
Churchill Wy MTCHDN GL17 .... 130 C1
  RSTROUD/NAIL GL6 .... 185 G3
Church La BAD GL9 .... 313 G6
  BDWAY WR12 .... 53 M2
  BMSTR BS3 .... 335 M8
  BRKLY GL13 .... 227 G2
  BRKLY GL13 .... 227 G8
  BUR/CRTN OX18 .... 172 A5
  CBATH/BATHN BA1 .... 352 B7
  CBRIS/FH BS1 .... 7 H5
  CFTN/FAIL BS8 .... 6 A5
  CHELTW GL51 .... 139 G1
  CHNTN OX7 .... 125 M1
  CHPMW/MSHF SN14 .... 313 M2
  CHPMW/MSHF SN14 .... 342 C3
  CIND GL14 .... 132 B7
  CIR GL7 .... 211 M8
  CIR GL7 .... 239 M6
  CIR GL7 .... 245 M1
  CIR GL7 .... 263 H4
  COR/BOX SN13 .... 353 L6
  COTS GL54 .... 52 F5
  COTS GL54 .... 118 E3
  FRCTL/WBN BS36 .... 318 F5
  FRCTL/WBN BS36 .... 318 E5
  GLE GL4 .... 136 F3
  GLE GL4 .... 160 A3
  HNBRY/STHM BS10 .... 325 G1
  LGASH BS41 .... 344 E1
  LYD GL15 .... 223 M8
  LYD GL15 .... 224 C6
  MALM SN16 .... 302 F4
  MANG/FISH BS16 .... 328 A1
  MIM GL56 .... 81 G5
  OLD/WMLY/WICK BS30 .... 349 G4
  RTEWK/TIB GL19 .... 46 F5
  RTEWK/TIB GL19 .... 91 H3
  STNHO GL10 .... 207 G4
  VGL GL2 .... 133 M1
  VGL GL2 .... 134 A4
  VGL GL2 .... 158 E5
  VGL GL2 .... 182 B3
  WUE GL12 .... 295 J2
  WUE GL12 .... 296 C5
  YATE/CS BS37 .... 309 H2
  YATE/CS BS37 .... 321 K4
Church Pde
  BRSG/KWL/STAPK BS4 .... 347 G1
Church Piece CHELTS GL53 .... 116 D6
Church Pl MIM GL56 .... 103 J3
Church Ri CIR GL7 .... 111 J4
Church Rd ALMDB BS32 .... 306 C6
  BDWAY WR12 .... 31 H2
  BMSTR BS3 .... 6 D9
  BMSTRD/HC/WWD BS13 .... 345 J6
  BRSTK/PCHW BS34 .... 316 C8
  BRSTK/PCHW BS34 .... 317 G8
  BWTH/CHD GL3 .... 113 L7
  CFTN/FAIL BS8 .... 334 F5
  CFTN/FAIL BS8 .... 334 C3
  CHELTE/BC GL52 .... 72 B7
  CHELTS GL53 .... 115 L7
  CHELTW GL51 .... 93 J5
  CHELTW GL51 .... 115 H3
  CHEP NP16 .... 270 B3
  CIND GL14 .... 154 A4
  CIND GL14 .... 155 J7
  CIND GL14 .... 178 B2
  CIR GL7 .... 217 K1
  CIR GL7 .... 218 D6
  CIR GL7 .... 261 H4
  COTS GL54 .... 98 E5
  DSLY GL11 .... 229 K8
  EVILLE/WHL BS5 .... 336 F3
  FRCTL/WBN BS36 .... 318 A7
  FRCTL/WBN BS36 .... 318 C2
  HGRV/WHIT BS14 .... 346 D8
  HNLZ/SM/SNYPK/WT BS9 .... 324 F8
  HNLZ/SM/SNYPK/WT BS9 .... 325 J4
  HORF/LLZ BS7 .... 326 A5
  KGWD/HNM BS15 .... 337 K6
  KGWD/HNM BS15 .... 338 A3
  LED HR8 .... 20 A3
  LYD GL15 .... 223 G2
  LYD GL15 .... 224 E2
  LYD GL15 .... 225 J2
  MANG/FISH BS16 .... 327 K4
  MANG/FISH BS16 .... 337 M1
  MIM GL56 .... 103 J5
  MTCHDN GL17 .... 107 H8
  MTCHDN GL17 .... 128 C7
  OLD/WMLY/WICK BS30 .... 339 L5
  OLD/WMLY/WICK BS30 .... 340 C2
  OLD/WMLY/WICK BS30 .... 349 G3
  RSTROUD/NAIL GL6 .... 232 C5
  STNHO GL10 .... 207 G8
  STROUD GL5 .... 208 A5
  STROUD GL5 .... 232 B1
  TEWK GL20 .... 51 L4
  THNB/SVB BS35 .... 272 D7
  THNB/SVB BS35 .... 293 K1
  THNB/SVB BS35 .... 304 C5
  THNB/SVB BS35 .... 307 J1
  THNB/SVB BS35 .... 315 J2
  VGL GL2 .... 111 J4
  VGL GL2 .... 112 E7
  VGL GL2 .... 179 M2
  YATE/CS BS37 .... 310 A8
  YATE/CS BS37 .... 320 A1
Churchside MANG/FISH BS16 .... 327 K4
Churchst TEWK GL20 .... 27 G5
Church St BDWAY WR12 .... 11 H7
  BDWAY WR12 .... 32 E3
  CBATH/BATHN BA1 .... 351 H5
  CBRIS/FH BS1 .... 7 H5
  CHCAM GL55 .... 12 E6
  CHELT GL50 .... 2 D5
  CHELTS GL53 .... 116 C6
  CHNTN OX7 .... 104 C7
  CHNTN OX7 .... 125 L1
  CHNTN OX7 .... 149 K1
  CIND GL14 .... 154 E4
  CIR GL7 .... 238 D4
  CIR GL7 .... 241 K7
  CLFD GL16 .... 151 M7
  COTS GL54 .... 102 A3
  EVILLE/WHL BS5 .... 336 D4
  EVILLE/WHL BS5 .... 336 D4
  GL GL1 .... 4 D8
  LED HR8 .... 20 A3
  LYD GL15 .... 198 F5
  MIM GL56 .... 58 C6
  NWNT GL18 .... 86 C3
  RSTROUD/NAIL GL6 .... 232 E7
  SHPSTR CV36 .... 16 B5
  STNHO GL10 .... 207 J7
  STNHO GL10 .... 231 G6
  STROUD GL5 .... 208 E4
  TET GL8 .... 257 L2
  TET GL8 .... 281 M5
  TEWK GL20 .... 48 A6
  WUE GL12 .... 277 K4
Church Vw ALMDB BS32 .... 306 B7
  BRKLY GL13 .... 251 L3
  COTS GL54 .... 78 E6
  HGHW SN6 .... 266 D7
  MIM GL56 .... 36 B7
Churchview Dr GLE GL4 .... 136 F3
Church Wk HGHW SN6 .... 287 C2
  LYD GL15 .... 176 F7
  LYD GL15 .... 202 A2
Churchward Cl
  KGWD/HNM BS15 .... 337 K6
Churchward Rd
  KGWD/HNM BS15 .... 337 M4
Church Wy GLE GL4 .... 136 E5
  LYD GL15 .... 178 E8
  NWNT GL18 .... 86 C3
Churchways HGRV/WHIT BS14 .... 346 E7
Churchways Av HORF/LLZ BS7 .... 326 A5
Churchways Crs HORF/LLZ BS7 .... 326 A5
Churclands Rd BMSTR BS3 .... 345 K1
Churn Av CHELTE/BC GL52 .... 3 K4
Churn Cl CIR GL7 .... 263 H4
Churn HI CIR GL7 .... 190 C6
Churston Ct
  HGRV/WHIT BS14 .... 346 C8
Cicely Wy GLE GL4 .... 137 H6
Cidermill Cl CHEP NP16 .... 270 B7
Cidermill La CHCAM GL55 .... 12 E8
Cidermill Orch CHCAM GL55 .... 11 M4
Cinderford Rd LYD GL15 .... 178 D8
Cinder HI CLFD GL16 .... 175 K1
  LYD GL15 .... 198 F5
Cinderhill MTCHDN GL17 .... 128 F3
Cinder La CIR GL7 .... 243 C5
The Circle STROUD GL5 .... 208 E3
Circular Rd
  HNLZ/SM/SNYPK/WT BS9 .... 335 C1
Cirencester Rd BWTH/CHD GL3 .... 138 C7
  CHELTS GL53 .... 116 C5
  CHELTS GL53 .... 116 C4
  CIR GL7 .... 239 J7
  CIR GL7 .... 242 D5
  CIR GL7 .... 263 L1
  CIR GL7 .... 264 A4
  RSTROUD/NAIL GL6 .... 234 C4
  STROUD GL5 .... 233 G4
  TET GL8 .... 282 A4
City Bank Rd CIR GL7 .... 238 D4
City Rd CBRISNE BS2 .... 336 A3
Claire's Cl STROUD GL5 .... 233 J2
The Clamp
  OLD/WMLY/WICK BS30 .... 338 E8
Clanage Rd BMSTR BS3 .... 335 G7
Clanna La LYD GL15 .... 224 B4
Clapton Rw COTS GL54 .... 123 H6
Clapton Wk
  MANG/FISH BS16 .... 324 D6
Clare Av HORF/LLZ BS7 .... 325 L6
Clare Ct STROUD GL5 .... 209 G4
Claremont Av HORF/LLZ BS7 .... 325 L8
Claremont Rd GL GL1 .... 5 H4
  HORF/LLZ BS7 .... 325 M8
Claremont St EVILLE/WHL BS5 .... 336 C2
Clarence Av MANG/FISH BS16 .... 328 A6
Clarence Gdns
  MANG/FISH BS16 .... 328 A6
Clarence Pde CHELT GL50 .... 2 C5
Clarence Pl CBRISNE BS2 .... 6 C1
  CBRISNE BS2 .... 335 L3
Clarence Rd CBRIS/FH BS1 .... 7 C8
  CBRISNE BS2 .... 7 L2
  CHELT GL50 .... 2 E3
  CHELTE/BC GL52 .... 2 E3
  KGWD/HNM BS15 .... 337 H4
  MANG/FISH BS16 .... 327 M6
  TEWK GL20 .... 48 A7
  WUE GL12 .... 277 K4
Clarence Sq CHELT GL50 .... 2 E2
Clarence St CHELT GL50 .... 2 C4
  GL GL1 .... 4 F6
Clarendon Rd COTS GL54 .... 74 B4
  RDLND/MONT BS6 .... 335 L1
Clare Pl CHELTS GL53 .... 115 M4
Clare Rd EVILLE/WHL BS5 .... 336 D1
  KGWD/HNM BS15 .... 337 L1
  RDLND/MONT BS6 .... 335 M2
Clare St CHELTS GL53 .... 2 C9
  CHELTS GL53 .... 115 M4
  EVILLE/WHL BS5 .... 336 B3
  GL GL1 .... 4 D4
Clare Wk THNB/SVB BS35 .... 293 K1
Claridge Cl GL GL4 .... 136 F7
Clark Cl SHPSTR CV36 .... 16 B6
Clark Rd BMSTR BS3 .... 335 J7
Clarken Coombe LGASH BS41 .... 334 C8
Clarke St BMSTR BS3 .... 6 F9
Clarkia Cl BWTH/CHD GL3 .... 113 H4
Clark's La CIR GL7 .... 238 D8
  LYD GL15 .... 202 D1
  SHPSTR CV36 .... 61 J6
Clark St EVILLE/WHL BS5 .... 336 C3
Clarrie Rd TET GL8 .... 282 A3
Clatworthy Dr
  HGRV/WHIT BS14 .... 346 C4
Claudians Cl GLE GL4 .... 137 G4
Claudius Wy LYD GL15 .... 201 K7
Clavell Rd HNBRY/STHM BS10 .... 325 H1
Claverham Rd
  MANG/FISH BS16 .... 327 J6
Claverton Rd West KEYN BS31 .... 348 F8
Clay Bottom EVILLE/WHL BS5 .... 336 F1
Clayburn Cl VGL GL2 .... 111 G6
Clayfield YATE/CS BS37 .... 310 A6
Clayfield Rd
  BRSG/KWL/STAPK BS4 .... 337 C8
Clay HI EVILLE/WHL BS5 .... 337 G1
Clay La BRSTK/PCHW BS34 .... 316 E4
  OLD/WMLY/WICK BS30 .... 348 A2
  THNB/SVB BS35 .... 294 A2
Claymore Cresent
  KGWD/HNM BS15 .... 337 K2
Claypiece Rd
  BMSTRD/HC/WWD BS13 .... 345 H7
Claypit HI YATE/CS BS37 .... 320 D4
Clay Pit Rd
  HNLZ/SM/SNYPK/WT BS9 .... 325 J8
Claypits HI STNHO GL10 .... 205 M2
Claypits La STROUD GL5 .... 209 G7
Claypool Rd KGWD/HNM BS15 .... 337 M4
Clay Rd CLFD GL16 .... 151 L4
Clays Rd CLFD GL16 .... 175 L7
Clayton St EVILLE/WHL BS5 .... 336 D3
Clearwater Dr VGL GL2 .... 159 G2
Cleaves Av
  CHPMW/MSHF SN14 .... 343 J8
Cleave St CBRISNE BS2 .... 336 C1
Cleeve Av MANG/FISH BS16 .... 328 A4
Cleeve Cloud La
  CHELTE/BC GL52 .... 94 F8
Cleeve Ct CHELTE/BC GL52 .... 72 B8
Cleevecroft Av CHELTE/BC GL52 .... 72 C8
Cleeve Gdns MANG/FISH BS16 .... 327 M4
Cleeve Gv KEYN BS31 .... 347 M6
Cleeve HI MANG/FISH BS16 .... 327 M4
Cleeve Hill Extension
  MANG/FISH BS16 .... 328 A5
Cleevelands Av CHELT GL50 .... 93 M7
Cleevelands Cl CHELT GL50 .... 94 A6
Cleevelands Dr CHELT GL50 .... 94 A6
Cleeveland St CHELTW GL51 .... 2 A2
Cleeve La
  OLD/WMLY/WICK BS30 .... 339 M2
Cleeve Lawns MANG/FISH BS16 .... 327 M4
Cleeve Lodge Rd
  MANG/FISH BS16 .... 328 A4
Cleeve Mill La NWNT GL18 .... 86 D2
Cleevemount Cl
  CHELTE/BC GL52 .... 3 G1
Cleevemount Rd
  CHELTE/BC GL52 .... 94 F7
Cleeve Park Rd
  MANG/FISH BS16 .... 327 M4
Cleeve Ri NWNT GL18 .... 86 D3
Cleeve Rd
  BRSG/KWL/STAPK BS4 .... 336 D8
  CHELTE/BC GL52 .... 72 C5
  GLE GL4 .... 136 D7
  MANG/FISH BS16 .... 327 L3
  MANG/FISH BS16 .... 328 A5
  YATE/CS BS37 .... 309 M2
Cleeve View Rd CHELTE/BC GL52 .... 3 J4
Cleeve Wood Rd
  MANG/FISH BS16 .... 327 M4
Clegram Rd GL GL1 .... 135 M4
Clematis Ct CHELTE/BC GL52 .... 72 A8
Clements End Rd CLFD GL16 .... 175 L7
Clement St CBRISNE BS2 .... 7 J1
  GL GL1 .... 5 J9
Clencher's Mill La LED HR8 .... 20 E6
Clevedale MANG/FISH BS16 .... 327 M4
Clevedon Rd GL GL1 .... 136 B5
  HORF/LLZ BS7 .... 325 M7
Clevedon Sq CHELTW GL51 .... 115 J1
Cleveland Ter
  RDLND/MONT BS6 .... 335 M3
Cleveland Cl THNB/SVB BS35 .... 294 A2
Cleve Rd BRSTK/PCHW BS34 .... 316 C7
Clewson Ri HGRV/WHIT BS14 .... 346 B8
Cliff Court Dr MANG/FISH BS16 .... 327 K4
Clifford Gdns AVONM BS11 .... 324 A5
Clifford Rd MANG/FISH BS16 .... 327 L7
Cliffords HGHW SN6 .... 288 E3
Cliff Vw CHEP NP16 .... 270 D4
Clift House Rd BMSTR BS3 .... 335 H4
Clifton Down
  CFTN/FAIL BS8 .... 335 H4
Clifton Down Rd
  CFTN/FAIL BS8 .... 335 H4
Clifton Gv
  HNLZ/SM/SNYPK/WT BS9 .... 325 G6
Clifton HI CFTN/FAIL BS8 .... 335 J5
Clifton Pk CFTN/FAIL BS8 .... 335 J5
Clifton Park Rd CFTN/FAIL BS8 .... 335 H3
Clifton Pl EVILLE/WHL BS5 .... 7 M1
Clifton Rd CFTN/FAIL BS8 .... 335 J5
  GL GL1 .... 4 D9
Clifton St BMSTR BS3 .... 335 L8
Clifton V CFTN/FAIL BS8 .... 335 J5
Clifton Vale Cl CFTN/FAIL BS8 .... 335 J5
Cliftonwood Crs CFTN/FAIL BS8 .... 6 A5
Clifton Wood Rd CFTN/FAIL BS8 .... 6 A4
Cliftonwood Ter
  CFTN/FAIL BS8 .... 335 J5
Clift Pl CBRIS/FH BS1 .... 6 F6
Clift Rd BMSTR BS3 .... 335 J7
Clingre Down DSLY GL11 .... 228 E7
Clingre La DSLY GL11 .... 228 D7
Clinton Rd BMSTR BS3 .... 345 L1
Clissard Wy BUR/CRTN OX18 .... 197 L5
Clive Rd HGRV/WHIT BS14 .... 346 E4
Cloisters Rd FRCTL/WBN BS36 .... 318 A5
The Cloisters CHELTE/BC GL52 .... 72 A7
Clomoney Wy VGL GL2 .... 112 F6
Clonmel Rd
  BRSG/KWL/STAPK BS4 .... 345 M2
Close Gdns COTS GL54 .... 78 E6
  TET GL8 .... 281 M4
The Close BRSTK/PCHW BS34 .... 316 E2
  CHELTE/BC GL52 .... 94 E3
  CHELTS GL53 .... 115 M7
  CIR GL7 .... 244 E6
  CIR GL7 .... 263 J4
  CLFD GL16 .... 151 M7
  DSLY GL11 .... 229 G3
  DSLY GL11 .... 230 A4
  FRCTL/WBN BS36 .... 318 E5
  HNBRY/STHM BS10 .... 315 H6
  MANG/FISH BS16 .... 327 M8
  VGL GL2 .... 182 B6
  VGL GL2 .... 205 G8
Clothier Rd
  BRSG/KWL/STAPK BS4 .... 347 H1
Clouds Hill Av EVILLE/WHL BS5 .... 337 G3
Clouds Hill Rd EVILLE/WHL BS5 .... 337 H3
The Cloud WUE GL12 .... 277 K4
Clovelly Cl EVILLE/WHL BS5 .... 337 H3
Clovelly Rd EVILLE/WHL BS5 .... 337 H3
Clover Cl CLFD GL16 .... 175 L4
Cloverdale Dr
  OLD/WMLY/WICK BS30 .... 338 C8
Clover Dr VGL GL2 .... 159 G5
Clover Gnd
  HNLZ/SM/SNYPK/WT BS9 .... 325 K3
Cloverlea Rd
  OLD/WMLY/WICK BS30 .... 338 E6
Clover Leaze
  BRSTK/PCHW BS34 316
Clyde Av KEYN BS31 348
Clyde Crs CHELTE/BC GL52 3
Clyde Gdns EVILLE/WHL BS5 337
Clyde Gv BRSTK/PCHW BS34 326
Clyde La RDLND/MONT BS6 336
Clyde Rd BRSG/KWL/STAPK BS4 336
  BWTH/CHD GL3 138
  FRCTL/WBN BS36 318
  RDLND/MONT BS6 335
Clydesdale Rd COR/BOX SN13 353
Clyde Ter BMSTR BS3 335
  BRSG/KWL/STAPK BS4 336
Coach Cl BRKLY GL13 227
Coach Rd RWYE HR9 106
Coalpit Rd CBATH/BATHN BA1 352
Coalsack La FRCTL/WBN BS36 318
Coalville Rd FRCTL/WBN BS36 318
Coalway Rd CLFD GL16 175
Coape Rd HGRV/WHIT BS14 347
Coates Gdns STNHO GL10 207
The Cobbler's Cl
  CHELTE/BC GL52 72
Cobblestone Ms CFTN/FAIL BS8 335
Cobden St EVILLE/WHL BS5 336
Coberley KGWD/HNM BS15 337
Coberley Rd CHELTW GL51 114
  GLE GL4 136
Cobham Ct CHELTW GL51 93
Cobham Rd CHELTW GL51 93
Cobhorn Dr
  BMSTRD/HC/WWD BS13 345
Cobourg Rd RDLND/MONT BS6 336
Cochran Cl BWTH/CHD GL3 113
Cockatoos La RWYE HR9 84
Cock La CHPMW/MSHF SN14 330
Cock Rd KGWD/HNM BS15 338
Codrington Pl CFTN/FAIL BS8 335
Codrington Rd HORF/LLZ BS7 325
Cogan Rd MANG/FISH BS16 328
Cogsall Rd HGRV/WHIT BS14 347
Colchester Cl CIND GL14 156
  MTCHDN GL17 130
Colchester Crs
  BRSG/KWL/STAPK BS4 345
Coldharbour La
  BRSTK/PCHW BS34 327
  MANG/FISH BS16 327
  NWNT GL18 64
Coldharbour Rd LYD GL15 198
  RDLND/MONT BS6 325
Coldicotts Cl CHCAM GL55 34
Coldpark Gdns
  BMSTRD/HC/WWD BS13 345
Coldpark Rd
  BMSTRD/HC/WWD BS13 345
Cold Pool La CHELTW GL51 114
Coldray Cl VGL GL2 5
Coldrick Cl HGRV/WHIT BS14 346
Coldwell STNHO GL10 207
Coldwell Cl STNHO GL10 207
Coldwell La STNHO GL10 207
Cole Av VGL GL2 135
Colebridge Av VGL GL2 112
Colebrook Rd
  KGWD/HNM BS15 337
Coleford Rd CHEP NP16 246
  HNBRY/STHM BS10 325
  LYD GL15 200
Colemead
  BMSTRD/HC/WWD BS13 345
Coleridge Rd
  EVILLE/WHL BS5 326
Colerne Dr BWTH/CHD GL3 137
Cole Rd CBRISNE BS2 7
Colesborne Cl YATE/CS BS37 320
Colesbourne Rd CHELTW GL51 114
Coleshill Dr
  BMSTRD/HC/WWD BS13 345
Colin Cl THNB/SVB BS35 293
Colin Rd GLE GL4 136
College Av MANG/FISH BS16 327
College Baths Rd CHELTS GL53 2
College Ct MANG/FISH BS16 327
College Flds CFTN/FAIL BS8 335
  VGL GL2 112
College Ga CHELTS GL53 2
College Gn CBRIS/FH BS1 6
College Lawn CHELTS GL53 116
College Park Dr
  HNBRY/STHM BS10 325
College Pl CHELT GL50 .... 2 C
College Rd CFTN/FAIL BS8 335
  CHELTS GL53 ....
  CIND GL14 154
  HNLZ/SM/SNYPK/WT BS9 325
  MANG/FISH BS16 327
  STROUD GL5 208
  TEWK GL20 26
College Sq CBRIS/FH BS1 6
College St CBRIS/FH BS1 6
  GL GL1 4
College Vw CIR GL7 238
Collett Cl KGWD/HNM BS15 .... 337 K
Colletts Dr CHELTW GL51 93
Colletts Flds BDWAY WR12 33
Colletts Gdns BDWAY WR12 33
Collett Wy YATE/CS BS37 309
Colliers Break MANG/FISH BS16 328
Colliers La CBATH/BATHN BA1 351
Colliers Pitch LYD GL15 224
Colliers Wd RSTROUD/NAIL GL6 232
Collin Cl BDWAY WR12 11
Collingbourne Rd GLE GL4 .... 136 C
Collingwood Av
  KGWD/HNM BS15 338
Collingwood Rd
  RDLND/MONT BS6 335
Collin La BDWAY WR12 10
Collin Rd BRSG/KWL/STAPK BS4 336
Collins Av BRSTK/PCHW BS34 66
Collins Cl RTEWK/TIB GL19 66
Collinson Rd
  BMSTRD/HC/WWD BS13 345
Colliter Crs BMSTR BS3 345
Collum End Ri CHELTS GL53 115
Colne Av CHELTE/BC GL52 3

oln Sq *THNB/SVB* BS35 .... **293** L3
olston Av *CBRIS/FH* BS1 .... 6 E4
olston Cl *FRCTL/WBN* BS36 .... **318** A7
  MANG/FISH BS16 .... **327** M8 🔢
olston Dl *MANG/FISH* BS16 .... **327** G7
olston Hl *MANG/FISH* BS16 .... **326** F7
olston Pde *CBRIS/FH* BS1 .... 7 G6
olston Rd *EVILLE/WHL* BS5 ...... **336** E2 🔢
olston St *CBRIS/FH* BS1 .... 6 E3
  MANG/FISH BS16 .... **327** M8
oltham Flds *CHELTE/BC* GL52 ... 3 H7
oltham Rd *CHELTE/BC* GL52 ..... 3 H9
olthurst Dr *KGWD/HNM* BS15 .. **337** M6
oltman Cl *VGL* GL2 .... 5 L6
olts Gn *YATE/CS* BS37 .... **321** G3
olumbia Cl *GL* GL1 .... 5 G4
olumbia St *CHELTE/BC* GL52 ... 2 F4
olwell Av *BWTH/CHD* GL3 .... **137** J2
olwyn Dr *CHELTW* GL51 .... **115** G5
olwyn Rd *EVILLE/WHL* BS5 ...... **336** E2 🔢
ombe Cross Wk
  BMSTRD/HC/WWD BS13 .... **345** K8 🔢
ombermere *THNB/SVB* BS35 ... **293**M3
ombfactory La
  EVILLE/WHL BS5 .... **336** D3 🔢
omb Paddock
  HNLZ/SM/SNYPK/WT BS9 .... **325** K4
ombrook Cl *GLE* GL4 .... **137** G7 🔢
ommercial Rd *CBRIS/FH* BS1 ... 6 E4
  GL GL1 .... 4 C6
  RSTROUD/NAIL GL6 .... **234** A1
ommercial St *CHELT* GL50 .... 2 C9
  CIND GL14 .... **154** B3
he Common (East)
  ALMDB BS32 .... **316** E2
ommonfield Rd *AVONM* BS11 .. **324** C2 🔢
ommon Hl *HGHW* SN6 .... **288** E3
ommon La *CHNTN* OX7 .... **105** L1
ommon Mead La
  MANG/FISH BS16 .... **327** J2
ommonmead La
  YATE/CS BS37 .... **321** H2
ommon Rd *FRCTL/WBN* BS36 . **318** B4 🔢
  KGWD/HNM BS15 .... **337** K8
  RSTROUD/NAIL GL6 .... **232** F5
he Common *BRKLY* GL13 .... **227** L8
  BRSTK/PCHW BS34 .... **316** D2
  CIR GL7 .... **238** F7
  MANG/FISH BS16 .... **327** K4
ompton Cl *BWTH/CHD* GL3 .... **113** J3 🔢
  RTEWK/TIB GL19 .... 66 D5
ompton Ct *SHPSRT* CV36 .... 61 G7
ompton Rd *CHELTW* GL51 ...... 93 K7 🔢
ompton's Aly *TEWK* GL20 .... 48 A5 🔢
ompton St *EVILLE/WHL* BS5 ... **336** E4 🔢
omyn Wk *MANG/FISH* BS16 .... **327** J6
oncorde Dr
  HNBRY/STHM BS10 .... **325** K1 🔢
oncorde Wy *GLE* GL4 .... **136** D2
ondicote La *COTS* GL54 .... 78 E6
  COTS GL54 .... **100** F4
ondover Rd
  BRSG/KWL/STAPK BS4 .... **337** H8
onduit Av *CHCAM* GL55 .... 34 D2
onduit Pl *CBRISNE* BS2 .... **336** C2 🔢
onduit Rd *CBRISNE* BS2 .... **336** C2
onduit St *GL* GL1 .... **136** A4
oneygar Rd *CIR* GL7 .... **218** C6
oneygree La *BDWAY* WR12 ..... 32 F6
oney Hill Pde *GLE* GL4 .... **136** E4 🔢
oney Hill Rd *GLE* GL4 .... **136** F4
ongleton Rd
  EVILLE/WHL BS5 .... **336** F3 🔢
onham Hl *KGWD/HNM* BS15 ... **337** J6
onham Rd *KGWD/HNM* BS15 .. **337** H6
onham V *KGWD/HNM* BS15 ..... **337** K6
  KGWD/HNM BS15 .... **337** H6
onifer Cl *FRCTL/WBN* BS36 .... **318** C2
  MANG/FISH BS16 .... **327** M5 🔢
he Conifers *GL* GL1 .... **136** C4 🔢
onigree La *TEWK* GL20 .... 48 A7
oniston Av
  HNLZ/SM/SNYPK/WT BS9 .... **325** G5
oniston Cl
  OLD/WMLY/WICK BS30 .... **338** F5 🔢
oniston Rd
  BRSTK/PCHW BS34 .... **316** A3
  CHELTW GL51 .... **115** G4
  VGL GL2 .... **112** E7
onnaught Rd
  BRSG/KWL/STAPK BS4 .... **346** A3 🔢
onnemara Cl *NWNT* GL18 .... 86 B4 🔢
onstable Cl *KEYN* BS31 .... **348** B5 🔢
onstable Rd *HORF/LLZ* BS7 .... **326** C5
onstance St *STROUD* GL5 .... **208** B6
onstantine Av
  BRSTK/PCHW BS34 .... **317** C6
onstitution Hl *CFTN/FAIL* BS8 .. 6 A4
  CFTN/FAIL BS8 .... **335** J3
onvent Cl *HNBRY/STHM* BS10 .. **314** F8 🔢
onvent La *STROUD* GL5 .... **232** B4
onway Gn *KEYN* BS31 .... **348** C8
onway Rd
  BRSG/KWL/STAPK BS4 .... **336** E7
  BWTH/CHD GL3 .... **137** J3
onyger Gv *TET* GL8 .... **282** A3
onygre Gv
  BRSTK/PCHW BS34 .... **316** E8 🔢
onygre Rd *BRSTK/PCHW* BS34 . **316** D8
ook Cl *OLD/WMLY/WICK* BS30 .. **338** F7
ooke's Dr *THNB/SVB* BS35 ..... **315** J2
ooks Cl *ALMDB* BS32 .... **306** E8
ook's Folly Rd
  HNLZ/SM/SNYPK/WT BS9 .... **324** F8 🔢
ooks La *CHNTN* OX7 .... 83 H7
  FRCTL/WBN BS36 .... **318** F8 🔢
  RTEWK/TIB GL19 .... 43 M4
ooksley Rd *EVILLE/WHL* BS5 .. **336** E3 🔢
ooks Orch *GL* GL1 .... 5 H1
ookspool *TET* GL8 .... **282** A3 🔢
ookworthy Cl
  EVILLE/WHL BS5 .... **336** D5 🔢
oomb Dr *CIND* GL14 .... **154** A6
oombe Av *THNB/SVB* BS35 .... **293** K1 🔢
oombe Bridge Av
  HNLZ/SM/SNYPK/WT BS9 ...... **324** F5

Coombe Cl
  HNBRY/STHM BS10 .... **314** F8 🔢
Coombe Dl
  HNLZ/SM/SNYPK/WT BS9 ..... **324** C3
Coombe Gdns
  HNLZ/SM/SNYPK/WT BS9 ..... **325** G5
Coombe Glen La *CHELTW* GL51 .. **114** F5
Coombe La
  HNLZ/SM/SNYPK/WT BS9 ..... **324** F5
  STNHO GL10 .... **231** K1
  WUE GL12 .... **277** M3
Coombe Meade
  CHELTE/BC GL52 .... 72 E3
Coombe Rd *EVILLE/WHL* BS5 ... **336** E1 🔢
  WUE GL12 .... **277** L3
Coombes Wy
  OLD/WMLY/WICK BS30 .... **338** F7
Coombe Wy
  HNBRY/STHM BS10 .... **325** H2
Coombs Rd *CLFD* GL16 .... **151** K8
Cooperage La *BMSTR* BS3 .... 6 A7
Cooperage Rd *EVILLE/WHL* BS5 . **336** E4
Co-operation Rd
  EVILLE/WHL BS5 .... **336** D1
Cooper Rd
  HNLZ/SM/SNYPK/WT BS9 ..... **325** H4
  THNB/SVB BS35 .... **293** K4
Coopers Cl *MALM* SN16 .... **303** J6
Coopers Dr *YATE/CS* BS37 ...... **310** B6
Coopers Elm *VGL* GL2 .... **159** H1
Coopers Rd *CLFD* GL16 .... **151** J4
Cooper's Vw *BWTH/CHD* GL3 .. **138** A2 🔢
Coopers Wy *NWNT* GL18 .... 86 D3
The Coots *HGRV/WHIT* BS14 ... **347** C5
Copeland Dr
  HGRV/WHIT BS14 .... **346** D6 🔢
Cope Pk *ALMDB* BS32 .... **306** E6
Copford La *LGASH* BS41 .... **344** D2
Copley Ct *KGWD/HNM* BS15 .... **338** A6 🔢
Copley Dr *CLFD* GL16 .... **175** K2 🔢
Copley Gdns *HORF/LLZ* BS7 .... **326** D5 🔢
Copper Beech Gv *VGL* GL2 ...... **159** G2
Coppice Daw Pitch
  RTEWK/TIB GL19 .... **132** C1
Coppice Ga *CHELTW* GL51 .... 93 H6
Coppice Hl *RSTROUD/NAIL* GL6 . **234** C1
Coppice Md *MTCHDN* GL17 ..... **128** C5
The Coppice *ALMDB* BS32 .... **317** G4
  BMSTRD/HC/WWD BS13 .... **345** G7
Copsehill Rd *COTS* GL54 .... **123** C1
Copse Rd
  BRSG/KWL/STAPK BS4 .... **336** D8
  KEYN BS31 .... **348** C1
The Copse *GLE* GL4 .... **137** G4 🔢
Copt Elm Cl *CHELTS* GL53 ...... **116** C5
Copt Elm Rd *CHELTS* GL53 ...... **116** C5
Copthorne Cl *HGRV/WHIT* BS14 . **346** D6
Coral Cl *GL* GL1 .... **135** K8
Corbet Cl *AVONM* BS11 .... **324** D1
Corder's La *HNBRY/STHM* BS10 . 58 C6
Cordingley Cl *BWTH/CHD* GL3 .. **113** L7
Cordwell Wk
  HNBRY/STHM BS10 .... **325** M4 🔢
Corey Cl *CBRISNE* BS2 .... **336** B2 🔢
Corfe Cl *CHELTE/BC* GL52 .... 94 E8 🔢
Corfe Crs *KEYN* BS31 .... **348** A6
Corfe Pl *OLD/WMLY/WICK* BS30 . **348** C2
Corfe Rd
  BRSG/KWL/STAPK BS4 .... **345** M4 🔢
Coriander Dr *ALMDB* BS32 .... **317** J4
  BWTH/CHD GL3 .... **113** H5
Coriander Wk
  EVILLE/WHL BS5 .... **336** E1 🔢
Corinium Ga *CIR* GL7 .... **238** D2
Cormorant Wk *TEWK* GL20 ..... 48 C7 🔢
Corncroft La *GLE* GL4 .... **160** E1
Corndean La *COTS* GL54 .... 96 C2
Corner Rd *LYD* GL15 .... **201** H2
Cornfield Cl *ALMDB* BS32 .... **316** E2
Cornfield Dr *CHELTE/BC* GL52 .. 72 A7 🔢
  VGL GL2 .... **159** G4
Cornfield Wy *EVE* WR11 .... 29 K1
Cornflower Rd *GLE* GL4 .... **137** C6
Corn Gastons *MALM* SN16 ...... **303** G7 🔢
Cornhill *STROUD* GL5 .... **208** E4
Cornhill Dr *HGRV/WHIT* BS14 .. **346** C4
Cornish Gv *HGRV/WHIT* BS14 .. **347** C5 🔢
Cornish Rd *CHNTN* OX7 .... **105** M2
  HGRV/WHIT BS14 .... **347** C5
Cornish Wk *HGRV/WHIT* BS14 .. **347** C5
Cornleaze
  BMSTRD/HC/WWD BS13 .... **345** J6 🔢
Cornmeadow Dr
  CHELTW GL51 .... 92 F6 🔢
Corn St *CBRIS/FH* BS1 .... 6 F4
Cornwall Av *CHELT* GL50 .... 2 C5
Cornwall Cl *KEYN* BS31 .... **115** J1
Cornwallis Av *CFTN/FAIL* BS8 .. **335** H5 🔢
Cornwallis Crs *CFTN/FAIL* BS8 . **335** H5 🔢
Cornwall Rd *HORF/LLZ* BS7 ..... **325**M7
Corolin Rd *VGL* GL2 .... **135** K7
Coronation Av *KEYN* BS31 .... **347**M7
  MANG/FISH BS16 .... **327** J7
Coronation Cl *CHCAM* GL55 .... **12** D8 🔢
  OLD/WMLY/WICK BS30 .... **338** C6 🔢
Coronation Gv *VGL* GL2 .... 5 M5
Coronation Pl *CBRIS/FH* BS1 ... 6 F4 🔢
Coronation Rd *BMSTR* BS3 .... 6 B7
  BMSTR BS3 .... **335** J7
  CHELTE/BC GL52 .... 94 C7
  CIND GL14 .... **154** B4
  KGWD/HNM BS15 .... **338** C2
  MANG/FISH BS16 .... **328** A6
  OLD/WMLY/WICK BS30 .... **338** C6
  STROUD GL5 .... **208** D5
  TET GL8 .... **281**M2
Coronation St *CIR* GL7 .... **242** D4
Corpus St *CHELTS* GL53 .... 2 F7
The Corriett *DSLY* GL11 .... **229** J6 🔢
Corsend Rd *RTEWK/TIB* GL19 .. 88 E4
Corsley Wk
  BRSG/KWL/STAPK BS4 .... **346** B3 🔢
Cossham Cl *THNB/SVB* BS35 .. **293** L1 🔢
Cossham Rd *EVILLE/WHL* BS5 . **336** F3
  MANG/FISH BS16 .... **329** L7
Cossham St *MANG/FISH* BS16 .. **328** D6
Cossham Wk *EVILLE/WHL* BS5 .. **337** J2

Cossington Rd
  BRSG/KWL/STAPK BS4 .... **346** B3
Cossins Rd *RDLND/MONT* BS6 . **325** K8
Costard Av *SHPSRT* CV36 .... 16 A6 🔢
Costers Cl *THNB/SVB* BS35 ..... **293** J5
Costiland Dr
  BMSTRD/HC/WWD BS13 .... **345** H5 🔢
Cote Dr
  HNLZ/SM/SNYPK/WT BS9 ..... **325** J7
Cote House La
  HNLZ/SM/SNYPK/WT BS9 ..... **325** J6
Cote La
  HNLZ/SM/SNYPK/WT BS9 ..... **325** J7
Cote Lea Pk
  HNLZ/SM/SNYPK/WT BS9 ..... **325** J4 🔢
Cote Paddock *HNLZ/SM/SNYPK/WT* BS9
  325 J7
Cote Pk *HNLZ/SM/SNYPK/WT* BS9 . **325** J6
Cotham Brow *RDLND/MONT* BS6 ... **335**
  M1 🔢
Cotham Gdns
  RDLND/MONT BS6 .... **335** K2 🔢
Cotham Gv *RDLND/MONT* BS6 .. **335**M2
Cotham Hl
  RDLND/MONT BS6 .... **335** K2 🔢
Cotham Lawn Rd
  RDLND/MONT BS6 .... **335** L3
Cotham Pk *RDLND/MONT* BS6 .. **335** L2
Cotham Pk North
  RDLND/MONT BS6 .... **335** L2
Cotham Rd *RDLND/MONT* BS6 .. **335** L3
Cotham Side
  RDLND/MONT BS6 .... **335**M2
Cotham V *RDLND/MONT* BS6 ... **335** L2
Cotman Wk *HGRV/WHIT* BS14 .. **346** D6
Cotrith Gv *HNBRY/STHM* BS10 . **315** C8
Cotsmore Rd *MIM* SL56 .... 58 E6
Cotswold Av *CIR* GL7 .... **238** B4
  STNHO GL10 .... **206** B4 🔢
Cotswold Cl *CIR* GL7 .... **238** B4
  RSTROUD/NAIL GL6 .... **233** K2 🔢
  TET GL8 .... **282** A3 🔢
Cotswold Edge *CHCAM* GL55 .... 8 F7
Cotswold Gn *STNHO* GL10 .... **207** B3
  TEWK GL20 .... 48 B4
  VGL GL2 .... **112** F6 🔢
  WUE GL12 .... **277** L4
Cotswold Md
  RSTROUD/NAIL GL6 .... **185** G4
Cotswold Rd *BMSTR* BS3 .... **335**M8
  CHELTE/BC GL52 .... 3 K1
  STROUD GL5 .... **208** A3
  YATE/CS BS37 .... **320** D3
Cotswold Vw *CHELTE/BC* GL52 . 72 D8
  KGWD/HNM BS15 .... **337**M1
  RTEWK/TIB GL19 .... 68 D3
  WUE GL12 .... **276** D6 🔢
  WUE GL12 .... **296** E5 🔢
Cotswold Wy *BDWAY* WR12 ..... 33 G4
  BDWAY WR12 .... 54 B3
  CBATH/BATHN BA1 .... **350** B3
  CHCAM GL55 .... 12 C7
  CHELTE/BC GL52 .... 95 J8
  CHELTW GL51 .... **139** H6
  COTS GL54 .... 75 K3
  COTS GL54 .... 96 B4
  COTS GL54 .... **117** J3
  DSLY GL11 .... **230** E6
  DSLY GL11 .... **253** G5
  RSTROUD/NAIL GL6 .... **161** H8
  STNHO GL10 .... **231** G3
  WUE GL12 .... **277** L4 🔢
  YATE/CS BS37 .... **321** J6
Cottage Rd *VGL* GL2 .... **110** F6 🔢
Cottage Pitch *NWNT* GL18 .... 86 C1
Cottage Pl *CBRISNE* BS2 .... 6 E1
Cottage Rake Av *CHELTW* GL51 . 93 L6
Cotteswold Ri *STROUD* GL5 ..... **208** F4
Cotteswold Rd *GLE* GL4 .... **136** C5
  TEWK GL20 .... 48 B4
Cottington Ct
  KGWD/HNM BS15 .... **338** A6 🔢
Cottisford Rd *EVILLE/WHL* BS5.. **326** D7
Cottle Gdns *HGRV/WHIT* BS14 .. **347** H5
Cottle Rd *HGRV/WHIT* BS14 ..... **347** H5
Cotton Cl *GLE* GL4 .... **137** H6
Cotton's La *EVE* WR11 .... 29 J2
Cottonwood Dr
  OLD/WMLY/WICK BS30 .... **338** C8
Cottrell Av *KGWD/HNM* BS15 .. **337** L1
Cottrell Rd *EVILLE/WHL* BS5 .... **326** E8
Coulson's Cl
  HGRV/WHIT BS14 .... **346** C8 🔢
Coulson's Rd *HGRV/WHIT* BS14 . **346** B8
Coulson Wk
  KGWD/HNM BS15 .... **337** L1 🔢
Counterpool Rd
  KGWD/HNM BS15 .... **337** L4
Counterslip *CBRIS/FH* BS1 .... 7 G4
Counterslip Gdns
  HGRV/WHIT BS14 .... **346** E1 🔢
Countess Lilias Rd *CIR* GL7 ..... **238** C5 🔢
Countess Wk
  MANG/FISH BS16 .... **326** F5 🔢
County Court Rd *CHELT* GL50 .. 2 D5 🔢
County St *BRSG/KWL/STAPK* BS4 . 7 K9
Court Av *BRSTK/PCHW* BS34 ... **317** H6 🔢
Courtbrook *CIR* GL7 .... **242** E5
Court Cl *HORF/LLZ* BS7 .... **326** A4
Court Dr *RTEWK/TIB* GL19 .... 68 F7
Courtenay St *CHELT* GL50 .... 2 D2
Courteney Crs
  BRSG/KWL/STAPK BS4 .... **345** M4 🔢
Court Farm *MALM* SN16 .... **285** J3
  RTEWK/TIB GL19 .... **109** K3
Court Farm La *MTCHDN* GL17 .. **130** C1
Court Farm Rd
  HGRV/WHIT BS14 .... **346** C8
  OLD/WMLY/WICK BS30 .... **347**M2
Courtfield Dr
  CHELTE/BC GL52 .... **116** D5 🔢
Courtfield Gv *MANG/FISH* BS16 . **327** J7

Courtfield Rd *VGL* GL2 .... **159** G3
Court Gdn *DSLY* GL11 .... **254** D3
Court Gdns *CBATH/BATHN* BA1 . **352** C8
  VGL GL2 .... **135** K5
The Court Gdns *VGL* GL2 .... **179**M1
Courthouse Gdns *DSLY* GL11 .. **229** H5
Courtiers Dr *CHELTE/BC* GL52 .. 72 C8
Courtlands *ALMDB* BS32 .... **316** A6
  KEYN BS31 .... **348** A6
Courtlands La *BMSTR* BS3 ...... **335** J8
Court La *LYD* GL15 .... **224** E5
  OLD/WMLY/WICK BS30 .... **339** K6
Court Md *BRKLY* GL13 .... **251** C8
Court Meadow *BRKLY* GL13 .... **251** C8
  WUE GL12 .... **277** L4
Courtney Cl *TEWK* GL20 .... 48 A8
Courtney Rd *KGWD/HNM* BS15 . **338** A4
Courtney Wy *KGWD/HNM* BS15 . **338** C4
Court Orch *WUE* GL12 .... **277** L4
Court Pl *GLE* GL4 .... **136** F5
Court Rd *BWTH/CHD* GL3 .... **138** A5
  CHELTE/BC GL52 .... 94 E7
  FRCTL/WBN BS36 .... **318** A3
  HORF/LLZ BS7 .... **326** B5
  KGWD/HNM BS15 .... **337**M4
  LYD GL15 .... **201** K5
  NWNT GL18 .... 86 D2
  OLD/WMLY/WICK BS30 .... **338** D8
  STNHO GL10 .... **206** D8
  WUE GL12 .... **275** K7
Courtside Ms
  RDLND/MONT BS6 .... **335** L2 🔢
Court View Cl *ALMDB* BS32 ..... **306** C6
Court Wy *STROUD* GL5 .... **208** C6
Courville Cl *THNB/SVB* BS35 ... **293** J7
Cousins Cl
  HNBRY/STHM BS10 .... **314** F8 🔢
Cousins Ms
  BRSG/KWL/STAPK BS4 .... **337** H5 🔢
Cousins Wy *MANG/FISH* BS16 . **328** C3
Cousley Cl *BWTH/CHD* GL3 ..... **137** J4
Couzens Cl *YATE/CS* BS37 ...... **320** D1
Couzens Pl
  BRSTK/PCHW BS34 .... **317** H6 🔢
Coventry Cl *TEWK* GL20 .... 48 B7 🔢
Coventry Wk
  BRSG/KWL/STAPK BS4 .... **337** H5 🔢
Coverham Cl *CLFD* GL16 .... **151** K5 🔢
Coverham Rd *CLFD* GL16 .... **151** J6
Cowcombe Hl
  RSTROUD/NAIL GL6 .... **234** C2
Cowdray Rd
  BRSG/KWL/STAPK BS4 .... **345** M4 🔢
Cowhorn Hl
  OLD/WMLY/WICK BS30 .... **338** E7
Cow La *STROUD* GL5 .... **232** C5
Cowler Wk
  BMSTRD/HC/WWD BS13 .... **345** H7 🔢
Cowley Cl *CHELTW* GL51 .... **114** F4
Cowley Rd *GLE* GL4 .... **136** A8
Cowling Dr *HGRV/WHIT* BS14 .. **346** E6
Cowling Rd *HGRV/WHIT* BS14 .. **346** E6
Cowl La *COTS* GL54 .... 74 C6
Cowlsmead *CHELTW* GL51 ...... **138** F1
Cowper Rd *CHELTW* GL51 ...... **115** C2 🔢
  RDLND/MONT BS6 .... **335** K2
Cowper St *EVILLE/WHL* BS5 .... **336** E4 🔢
Cowship La *WUE* GL12 .... **295** K4
Cowslip Meadow
  CHELTE/BC GL52 .... 72 D8
Cowswell La
  RSTROUD/NAIL GL6 .... **209** L8
Coxbury & Wyegate La
  CLFD GL16 .... **174** C8
Cox Ct *OLD/WMLY/WICK* BS30 . **338** B7
Cox La *CHNTN* OX7 .... **105** K1
Coxmoor Cl *CHNTN* OX7 .... **104** B7
Cox's Hl *HGHW* SN6 .... **287** C1
Cox's Wy *BWTH/CHD* GL3 ...... **137** J5
Coxwell St *CIR* GL7 .... **238** C5
Cozens La *CHNTN* OX7 .... **104** B7
Crabtree La *CIR* GL7 .... **212** C1
  CIR GL7 .... **238** F4 🔢
Crabtree Pk *CIR* GL7 .... **242** F5
Crab Tree Pl *CHELT* GL50 .... 2 B1
Crabtree Rd *CIND* GL14 .... **153**M2
Crabtree Wk
  EVILLE/WHL BS5 .... **336** F1 🔢
Craddock Rd *NWNT* GL18 .... 86 B3
Cradock Cl
  OLD/WMLY/WICK BS30 .... **338** D7 🔢
Crail Vw *COTS* GL54 .... **169** K2
Cranberry Wk
  HNLZ/SM/SNYPK/WT BS9 ..... **324** E3 🔢
Cranbourne Rd
  BRSTK/PCHW BS34 .... **316** B4
Cranbrook Rd
  RDLND/MONT BS6 .... **325** L8
Crandell Cl *HNBRY/STHM* BS10 . **315** H7
Crane Cl *KGWD/HNM* BS15 ..... **338** D3 🔢
Cranford Cl *CHELTE/BC* GL52 .. 72 E8
Cranham *YATE/CS* BS37 .... **319** L4 🔢
Cranham Cl *GLE* GL4 .... **137** G6 🔢
  KGWD/HNM BS15 .... **338** B1 🔢
Cranham Dr *BRSTK/PCHW* BS34.. **316** E2
Cranham La *BWTH/CHD* GL3 ... **113**M8
Cranham Rd *CHELTE/BC* GL52 .. 3 H7
  HNBRY/STHM BS10 .... **325** L3
Cranhams La *CIR* GL7 .... **238** B5
Cranleigh Court Rd
  YATE/CS BS37 .... **319** M1 🔢
Cranleigh Gdns
  HNLZ/SM/SNYPK/WT BS9 ..... **325** C7
Cranleigh Rd
  HGRV/WHIT BS14 .... **346** D6 🔢
Cranmoor Gn *THNB/SVB* BS35 . **304** A4
Cranmore Av *KEYN* BS31 .... **348** A5
Cranmore Crs
  HNBRY/STHM BS10 .... **325**M2
Cranside Av *RDLND/MONT* BS6 . **325** L8
Cransley Crs
  HNLZ/SM/SNYPK/WT BS9 ..... **325** L4
Crantock Av
  BMSTRD/HC/WWD BS13 .... **345** K3
Crantock Dr *ALMDB* BS32 .... **306** E6
Crantock Rd *YATE/CS* BS37 .... **319**M2

Cranwell Cl *GLE* GL4 .... **136** E7
Cranwell Gv *HGRV/WHIT* BS14 . **346** C6
The Crapen *DSLY* GL11 .... **229** G7
Crashmore La *TEWK* GL20 ...... 28 B6
Craven Cl
  OLD/WMLY/WICK BS30 .... **338** B6
Craven Dr *BWTH/CHD* GL3 ..... **113** J5
Craven Wy
  OLD/WMLY/WICK BS30 .... **338** B6
Crawley Hl *DSLY* GL11 .... **230** D8
Crawley La *DSLY* GL11 .... **230** D8
Crawshay Pl *CIND* GL14 .... **154** A3
Craydon Gv *HGRV/WHIT* BS14 . **346** F7
Craydon Rd *HGRV/WHIT* BS14 . **346** F6
Craydon Wk
  HGRV/WHIT BS14 .... **346** F6 🔢
The Crease *NWNT* GL18 .... 86 D3 🔢
Crediton Crs
  BRSG/KWL/STAPK BS4 .... **346** B2
Credon Rd *GLE* GL4 .... **137** C2
Crescent Cl *CLFD* GL16 .... **151** J8
  STNHO GL10 .... **207** G5
Crescentdale *VGL* GL2 .... **112** C5
Crescent Pl *CHELT* GL50 .... 2 C5
Crescent Rd *MANG/FISH* BS16 . **327** L5
  STNHO GL10 .... **207** G5
Crescent Ter *CHELT* GL50 .... 2 D5
The Crescent *BRKLY* GL13 ...... **226** F3
  BWTH/CHD GL3 .... **137**M5
  CLFD GL16 .... **151** J8
  CLFD GL16 .... **175** K1 🔢
  DSLY GL11 .... **229** H7
  HNLZ/SM/SNYPK/WT BS9 ..... **324** E5
  HNLZ/SM/SNYPK/WT BS9 ..... **325** L5
  MANG/FISH BS16 .... **327** H2
  MANG/FISH BS16 .... **327** M8
  MTCHDN GL17 .... **106** C8
  OLD/WMLY/WICK BS30 .... **339** K4
The Crest
  BRSG/KWL/STAPK BS4 .... **346** E1
Crest Wy *GLE* GL4 .... **137** H2
Creswicke Av
  KGWD/HNM BS15 .... **337** L6 🔢
Creswicke Rd
  BRSG/KWL/STAPK BS4 .... **346** A4
Crew's Hole Rd
  EVILLE/WHL BS5 .... **337** H5 🔢
Cribbs Cswy
  HNBRY/STHM BS10 .... **315** K4
Cricklade Rd *CIR* GL7 .... **238** E5
  HORF/LLZ BS7 .... **326** A4
Cricklade St *CIR* GL7 .... **238** C2
  CIR GL7 .... **240** F5
Criftycraft La *BWTH/CHD* GL3 .. **113** L8
Cripps Rd *BMSTR* BS3 .... **335** L8
  CIR GL7 .... **238** C3
Crispin Cl *COTS* GL54 .... 74 C5
  VGL GL2 .... **112** E6
Crispin La *THNB/SVB* BS35 ..... **293** K2 🔢
Crispin Rd *COTS* GL54 .... 74 C5
Crispin Wy *KGWD/HNM* BS15 .. **338** D5
Critchford La *COTS* GL54 .... 98 D3
Crockwell St *SHPSRT* CV36 ..... 61 H4
Croft Av *CHELTS* GL53 .... **116** C6
  MANG/FISH BS16 .... **326** E7 🔢
Croft Cl *BWTH/CHD* GL3 .... **113**M7
  NWNT GL18 .... 86 D2 🔢
  OLD/WMLY/WICK BS30 .... **348** F3
Crofters Wk *ALMDB* BS32 .... **316** F3
Croft Gdns *CHELTS* GL53 .... **116** D7
Croft Holm *MIM* SL56 .... 58 E6
The Croftlands *TEWK* GL20 ..... 27 H5 🔢
Croft La *CIR* GL7 .... **188** C4
  HGHW SN6 .... **264** D7
Crofton Av *HORF/LLZ* BS7 ...... **326** B5 🔢
Croft Rd *CHELTS* GL53 .... **116** C6
  NWNT GL18 .... 86 D2
Crofts End Rd *EVILLE/WHL* BS5 . **337** G2
Crofts Fld *TEWK* GL20 .... 47 J2 🔢
Croft St *CHELTS* GL53 .... **115** L5
The Croft *CIR* GL7 .... **242** E4
  DSLY GL11 .... **229** J7
  MANG/FISH BS16 .... **328** B6
  OLD/WMLY/WICK BS30 .... **338** E8 🔢
  RSTROUD/NAIL GL6 .... **185** H2
Croft Thorne Cl
  CHELTW GL51 .... **115** H6 🔢
Croft Vw
  HNLZ/SM/SNYPK/WT BS9 ..... **325** L5 🔢
Crokeswood Wk
  AVONM BS11 .... **324** C2 🔢
Crome Rd *HORF/LLZ* BS7 .... **326** D4
Cromer Rd *EVILLE/WHL* BS5 ... **336** E1
Cromers Cl *TEWK* GL20 .... 49 G2 🔢
Cromhall La *WUE* GL12 .... **295** G2
Cromwell Ct
  KGWD/HNM BS15 .... **338** A6 🔢
Cromwell Rd *CHELTE/BC* GL52 .. 3 J2
  CHEP NP16 .... **270** A6
  EVILLE/WHL BS5 .... **337** J3
  RDLND/MONT BS6 .... **335**M1
Cromwells Hide
  MANG/FISH BS16 .... **327** G6 🔢
Cromwell St *GL* GL1 .... 4 F7
Crooked End Pl
  MTCHDN GL17 .... **129** H3 🔢
Croomes Hl *MANG/FISH* BS16 . **327**M5
Cropthorne Rd
  HORF/LLZ BS7 .... **326** C2 🔢
Cropthorne Rd South
  HORF/LLZ BS7 .... **326** C3 🔢
Crosby Rw *CFTN/FAIL* BS8 ...... **335** J5
Crosscombe Dr
  BMSTRD/HC/WWD BS13 .... **345** K8
Cross Elms La
  HNLZ/SM/SNYPK/WT BS9 ..... **325** G6
Cross Farm Cl *LYD* GL15 .... **224** E5
Crossfield Rd *MANG/FISH* BS16 . **328** A8
Crossfields *COTS* GL54 .... **118** C8 🔢
Cross Hands Rd
  THNB/SVB BS35 .... **304** F4
Cross Hayes La *MALM* SN16 ... **303** J8 🔢
Cross Keys La *GL* GL1 .... 4 E5
Crossleaze Rd
  KGWD/HNM BS15 .... **337** L8
Crossley Cl *FRCTL/WBN* BS36 . **318** B4 🔢
Cross Leys *CHNTN* OX7 .... **105**M1
Crossman Av *FRCTL/WBN* BS36 . **318** A6

Cross St KEYN BS31 ..... 348 B4
KGWD/HNM BS15 ..... 337 L2
The Cross TEWK GL20 ..... 25 J3 1
Cross Tree Gv ALMDB BS32 ..... 316 F3
Cross Tree La CIR GL7 ..... 221 K5
Crossways Rd
BRSG/KWL/STAPK BS4 ..... 346 C2
THNB/SVB BS35 ..... 293 M2
Crow Ash CLFD GL16 ..... 151 K6
Crow Ash Rd CLFD GL16 ..... 151 J6
Crowfield La NWNT GL18 ..... 63 M1
Crowgate La CIND GL14 ..... 157 G3
Crow La CBRIS/FH BS1 ..... 6 F4
HNBRY/STHM BS10 ..... 325 H1
Crow Meadow WUE GL12 ..... 277 H7
Crown Cl CHELTE/BC GL52 ..... 72 B8
Crowndale Rd
BRSG/KWL/STAPK BS4 ..... 336 C8
Crown Dr CHELTE/BC GL52 ..... 94 B1
Crown Gdns
OLD/WMLY/WICK BS30 ..... 338 D4
Crown Hl EVILLE/WHL BS5 ..... 337 H3
Crown Hill Wk EVILLE/WHL BS5 .. 337 H3
Crown La LYD GL15 ..... 176 E7
Crownleaze MANG/FISH BS16 ..... 327 M8
Crown Meadow CLFD GL16 ..... 175 M2 1
Crown Rd KGWD/HNM BS15 ..... 337 M1
OLD/WMLY/WICK BS30 ..... 338 E5
Crows Gv ALMDB BS32 ..... 306 F8
Crowther Pk HORF/LLZ BS7 ..... 326 C7
Crowther Rd HORF/LLZ BS7 ..... 326 C7
Crowthers Av YATE/CS BS37 ..... 310 A8
Crowther St BMSTR BS3 ..... 335 K8 1
Croydon St EVILLE/WHL BS5 ..... 336 D3
Crucible Cl CLFD GL16 ..... 175 K2
Crudwell La TET GL8 ..... 282 F5
The Crunnis ALMDB BS32 ..... 317 G5
Crypt Ct GL GL1 ..... 135 L8
Crythan Wk CHELTW GL51 ..... 115 H6 5
Cuckoo La FRCTL/WBN BS36 ..... 318 B8
Cuckoo Rw RSTROUD/NAIL GL6 .. 233 H5
Cud La RSTROUD/NAIL GL6 ..... 184 D3
Cudnall St CHELTS GL53 ..... 116 C4
Cuffington Av
BRSG/KWL/STAPK BS4 ..... 336 F7
Culleysgate La
OLD/WMLY/WICK BS30 ..... 340 B5
Cullimore Vw CIND GL14 ..... 154 A6
Cullingham Cl RTEWK/TIB GL19 ..... 66 D4
Culross Cl CHELT GL50 ..... 94 A7
Culverhay WUE GL12 ..... 277 K4
Culver Hl STROUD GL5 ..... 232 C3
Culverhill Rd YATE/CS BS37 ..... 320 C2
Culvers Rd KEYN BS31 ..... 348 A5
Culver St CBRIS/FH BS1 ..... 6 C4
NWNT GL18 ..... 86 C4
The Culvert ALMDB BS32 ..... 316 F3 2
Culverwell Rd
BMSTRD/HC/WWD BS13 ..... 345 J7
Cumberland Basin Rd
CFTN/FAIL BS8 ..... 335 H6
Cumberland Cl CBRIS/FH BS1 ..... 335 J6
Cumberland Crs CHELTW GL51 ..... 115 J2
Cumberland Gv
RDLND/MONT BS6 ..... 336 B1 4
Cumberland Pl
CFTN/FAIL BS8 ..... 335 H5 3
Cumberland Rd
CBRIS/FH BS1 ..... 335 H6 3
Cumberland St CBRISNE BS2 ..... 7 G1
Cumbria Cl THNB/SVB BS35 ..... 294 A2
Cunningham Gdns
MANG/FISH BS16 ..... 327 K6 1
Cupola Cl CLFD GL16 ..... 175 K2
Curland Gv HGRV/WHIT BS14 ..... 346 D6 4
Curlew Cl MANG/FISH BS16 ..... 327 H5 1
TEWK GL20 ..... 48 F2 1
Curlew Rd GLE GL4 ..... 136 E5
Cursey La CHELTW GL51 ..... 70 D6
RTEWK/TIB GL19 ..... 70 A6
The Cursus CIR GL7 ..... 244 E6
Curtis Hayward Dr VGL GL2 ..... 159 G2
Curtis La BRSTK/PCHW BS34 ..... 317 J8
Custom Cl HGRV/WHIT BS14 ..... 346 C4
Cut & Fry Rd LYD GL15 ..... 201 L1
Cutham La CIR GL7 ..... 190 B8
Cuthwine Pl CIR GL7 ..... 244 E6
Cutler Rd
BMSTRD/HC/WWD BS13 ..... 345 H5
STROUD GL5 ..... 208 F3
Cutsdean Cl CHELTE/BC GL52 ..... 71 M7
Cut Throat La LED HR8 ..... 20 B1
RWYE HR9 ..... 84 B6
Cuttsheath Rd WUE GL12 ..... 294 E3
Cutwell TET GL8 ..... 281 M5
Cylde Pk RDLND/MONT BS6 ..... 335 K1
Cynder Wy MANG/FISH BS16 ..... 328 C2
Cypress Gdns CFTN/FAIL BS8 ..... 335 G5
Cypress Gv
HNLZ/SM/SNYPK/WT BS9 ..... 325 L5
Cypress Rd TEWK GL20 ..... 48 C7
Cypress Wk
CHPMW/MSHF SN14 ..... 343 H5
Cyrus Ct MANG/FISH BS16 ..... 328 D4 2

D

Daffodil Cl GLE GL4 ..... 137 G6
Daffodil Leaze STNHO GL10 ..... 207 K8
Daffodil Wy NWNT GL18 ..... 41 H8
NWNT GL18 ..... 62 C3
NWNT GL18 ..... 62 E5
NWNT GL18 ..... 63 L1
Daglingworth Pth CIR GL7 ..... 212 E7
Dainty St GL GL1 ..... 136 B4 2
Dairy Farm HGHW SN6 ..... 287 G3
Dairy La EVE WR11 ..... 30 B7
Daisy Bank STROUD GL5 ..... 209 G5
Daisybank Rd CHELTS GL53 ..... 140 A1
Daisy Green La WUE GL12 ..... 276 F1
Daisy Rd EVILLE/WHL BS5 ..... 336 E1
Dakota Dr HGRV/WHIT BS14 ..... 346 C7
Dalby Av BMSTR BS3 ..... 335 M8
Daldry Gdns THNB/SVB BS35 .. 292 C8 1
Dalebrook RWYE HR9 ..... 84 F3 1
Dale Cl GLE GL4 ..... 136 B6
Dale St CBRISNE BS2 ..... 7 J1
COTS GL54 ..... 99 J8
EVILLE/WHL BS5 ..... 337 H3
Dale Wk CHELTE/BC GL52 ..... 72 C8
Dalkeith Av
KGWD/HNM BS15 ..... 337 L2 1
Dallaway STROUD GL5 ..... 233 G1
Dalrymple Rd CBRISNE BS2 ..... 336 A2 4
Dalston Rd BMSTR BS3 ..... 6 B8 1
Dalton Sq CBRISNE BS2 ..... 336 A3 5
Damery La BRKLY GL13 ..... 251 H8
WUE GL12 ..... 251 L8
WUE GL12 ..... 275 L1
Dampier Rd BMSTR BS3 ..... 335 J8
The Damsels TET GL8 ..... 282 A4
Damson Cl GLE GL4 ..... 137 G7
Danbury Crs
HNBRY/STHM BS10 ..... 325 L2
Danbury Wk
HNBRY/STHM BS10 ..... 325 L2 1
Danby Cl CIND GL14 ..... 154 C3
Danby Rd LYD GL15 ..... 177 L8
Dancey Md
BMSTRD/HC/WWD BS13 ..... 345 G5
Dancey Rd BWTH/CHD GL3 ..... 113 H5
Dane Cl VGL GL2 ..... 112 E6 1
Dane La CIR GL7 ..... 211 L7
Danes Hl CHEP NP16 ..... 270 D4
Danford La RTEWK/TIB GL19 ..... 88 F5
Dangerfield Av
BMSTRD/HC/WWD BS13 ..... 345 G5
Daniels Rd STROUD GL5 ..... 209 H5
Dapps Hl KEYN BS31 ..... 348 B6
Darell Cl VGL GL2 ..... 159 H4
Dark La CHELTW GL51 ..... 93 J4
CIR GL7 ..... 190 C7
MALM SN16 ..... 303 H8
RSTROUD/NAIL GL6 ..... 232 C7
RSTROUD/NAIL GL6 ..... 234 A1
STROUD GL5 ..... 208 D6
Darks Rd NWNT GL18 ..... 85 G5
Darley Cl HNBRY/STHM BS10 ..... 314 F8
Darlingscote Rd SHPSTR CV36 ..... 15 L3
Darnell's La RWYE HR9 ..... 84 E5
Darnley Av HORF/LLZ BS7 ..... 326 B5
Darren Rd CLFD GL16 ..... 151 K6
Dart Cl THNB/SVB BS35 ..... 293 K3 1
VGL GL2 ..... 159 H1
Darters Cl LYD GL15 ..... 225 J1 1
Dartmoor St BMSTR BS3 ..... 6 B9
BMSTR BS3 ..... 335 K8 1
Dart Rd CHELTE/BC GL52 ..... 3 L2
Darwin Cl CHELTW GL51 ..... 114 E2
Darwin Rd GLE GL4 ..... 136 B6
Daston Cl BDWAY WR12 ..... 33 G3 2
Daubeny Cl MANG/FISH BS16 ..... 327 K6
Davallia Dr CHELTW GL51 ..... 115 H6
Daventry Rd
BRSG/KWL/STAPK BS4 ..... 346 B2
Daventry Ter GL GL1 ..... 5 G9 1
Davey St CBRISNE BS2 ..... 336 B2
David French Ct
CHELTW GL51 ..... 115 J6 2
Davids Cl THNB/SVB BS35 ..... 293 J7
David's La THNB/SVB BS35 ..... 293 J7
David's Rd HGRV/WHIT BS14 ..... 346 E5
David St CBRISNE BS2 ..... 7 J3
Davies Dr
BRSG/KWL/STAPK BS4 ..... 337 H6 3
Davies Rd MIM GL56 ..... 58 E5
Davis Cl
OLD/WMLY/WICK BS30 ..... 338 B6 1
Davis Ct THNB/SVB BS35 ..... 293 L1
Dawes Cl CIR GL7 ..... 220 B8
The Dawes VGL GL2 ..... 159 H3
Dawley Cl FRCTL/WBN BS36 ..... 318 A4 3
Dawlish Rd BMSTR BS3 ..... 345 M1
The Dawneys MALM SN16 ..... 284 A5
Dawn Ri KGWD/HNM BS15 ..... 338 C2
Daws Ct MANG/FISH BS16 ..... 327 K7 3
Day House La WUE GL12 ..... 297 L3
Daylesford Cl CHELTW GL51 ..... 114 F3
Days Ct MALM SN16 ..... 284 A5
Day's La MIM GL56 ..... 57 G1
Day's Rd CBRISNE BS2 ..... 7 M4
Deacon Cl CHELTW GL51 ..... 115 H4 2
FRCTL/WBN BS36 ..... 318 A6
Deacons Pl CHELTE/BC GL52 ..... 94 A1 2
Deadmill La CBATH/BATHN BA1 ..... 351 L8
Deakin Cl CHELTW GL51 ..... 93 K4 1
Dean Av THNB/SVB BS35 ..... 293 L1
Dean Cl KGWD/HNM BS15 ..... 337 J7
Dean Ct LYD GL15 ..... 201 K6
Dean Crs BMSTR BS3 ..... 6 E8 2
CIND GL14 ..... 154 E4
Deanery Rd CBRIS/FH BS1 ..... 6 C5
KGWD/HNM BS15 ..... 338 D3
Dean La BMSTR BS3 ..... 6 D9
CHELTE/BC GL52 ..... 71 G6
Dean Rd CIND GL14 ..... 154 E5
YATE/CS BS37 ..... 309 L8
Deans Ct CHELTW GL51 ..... 115 H4 5
Dean's Dr EVILLE/WHL BS5 ..... 337 J1 1
Deansfield HGHW SN6 ..... 288 F4
Deans Md AVONM BS11 ..... 324 C3
Dean's Quarry STROUD GL5 ..... 233 H3
Dean's Ter GL GL1 ..... 4 F2
Dean St BMSTR BS3 ..... 6 D9
CBRISNE BS2 ..... 336 A3
Dean's Wk GL GL1 ..... 4 E3
MTCHDN GL17 ..... 129 M4
Deans Wy CHELTE/BC GL52 ..... 72 B8
GL GL1 ..... 4 F2
Deansway Rd MTCHDN GL17 ..... 106 C8
Dean Vw CIND GL14 ..... 154 A6
De Clifford Rd AVONM BS11 ..... 324 E1
Deep Coombe Rd
BMSTR BS3 ..... 345 J1 1
Deep Pit Rd EVILLE/WHL BS5 ..... 337 H2
Deep St CHELTE/BC GL52 ..... 94 D7
Deerhurst KGWD/HNM BS15 ..... 338 A1 2
YATE/CS BS37 ..... 319 L3
Deerhurst Cl GLE GL4 ..... 137 G7 6
MIM GL56 ..... 82 B2
Deerhurst Pl VGL GL2 ..... 159 G2
Deering Cl AVONM BS11 ..... 324 D2
Deer Pk LYD GL15 ..... 201 J1
Deer Park Rd BWTH/CHD GL3 .. 137 J2 1
Deerswood KGWD/HNM BS15 ..... 338 C1
De Havilland Rd COTS GL54 ..... 124 D6
Delabere Av MANG/FISH BS16 ..... 327 K6
Delabere Rd CHELTE/BC GL52 ..... 94 C1
Delavale Rd COTS GL54 ..... 74 C5
Delius Gv
BRSG/KWL/STAPK BS4 ..... 345 M4 7
Delkin Rd DSLY GL11 ..... 229 H7
The Dell ALMDB BS32 ..... 317 G4
GLE GL4 ..... 137 G4
HNLZ/SM/SNYPK/WT BS9 ..... 325 H6
MIM GL56 ..... 35 H8 1
OLD/WMLY/WICK BS30 ..... 338 E6 1
TEWK GL20 ..... 27 G4
Dell Vw CHEP NP16 ..... 270 A3
Delmont Gv STROUD GL5 ..... 208 E3
Delphinium Dr
CHELTE/BC GL52 ..... 72 A8 3
Delta Dr TEWK GL20 ..... 48 E3
Delvin Rd HNBRY/STHM BS10 ..... 325 L3
Denbigh Dr CHEP NP16 ..... 270 C6
Denbigh Rd CHELTW GL51 ..... 115 G5
Denbigh St CBRISNE BS2 ..... 336 A2
Dene Cl KEYN BS31 ..... 348 B8
Denehurst MTCHDN GL17 ..... 129 H6
Dene Rd HGRV/WHIT BS14 ..... 346 E7
Denham Cl CHELTE/BC GL52 ..... 72 E8
GL GL1 ..... 159 L1
Denleigh Cl HGRV/WHIT BS14 ..... 346 C7
Denley Cl CHELTE/BC GL52 ..... 94 B1
Denmark Dr CHEP NP16 ..... 270 D4
Denmark Pl HORF/LLZ BS7 ..... 326 A8 1
Denmark Rd GL GL1 ..... 5 H2
Denmark St CBRIS/FH BS1 ..... 6 D4
Dennisworth
MANG/FISH BS16 ..... 329 K6 1
Dennor Pk HGRV/WHIT BS14 ..... 346 D4
Denny Isle Dr THNB/SVB BS35 ..... 304 C6
Dennyview Rd CFTN/FAIL BS8 ..... 334 B3
Denston Wk
BMSTRD/HC/WWD BS13 ..... 345 J4
Denton Patch
MANG/FISH BS16 ..... 328 D4 3
Dent's La RTEWK/TIB GL19 ..... 88 F8
Dentwood Gv
HNLZ/SM/SNYPK/WT BS9 ..... 324 D4
Denys Ct THNB/SVB BS35 ..... 292 B8
Derby Rd GL GL1 ..... 5 J8
HORF/LLZ BS7 ..... 326 A8
Derby St EVILLE/WHL BS5 ..... 336 F4
Derham Rd
BMSTRD/HC/WWD BS13 ..... 345 J6
Dermot St CBRISNE BS2 ..... 336 C2 3
Derricke Rd HGRV/WHIT BS14 ..... 347 H5
Derrick Rd KGWD/HNM BS15 ..... 337 M3
Derry Rd BMSTR BS3 ..... 345 K1 1
The Derry HGHW SN6 ..... 287 G3
Derwent Cl BRSTK/PCHW BS34 .. 316 C3
BWTH/CHD GL3 ..... 138 A6
Derwent Dr TEWK GL20 ..... 48 C3
Derwent Gv KEYN BS31 ..... 348 C6
Derwent Rd EVILLE/WHL BS5 ..... 337 H2
Desford Cl GLE GL4 ..... 137 H6 3
Despenser Rd TEWK GL20 ..... 48 A7
Detmore Cl CHELTE/BC GL52 ..... 116 E6
Devereaux Crs STROUD GL5 ..... 207 L4
Devereaux Rd STROUD GL5 ..... 207 L5
De Verose Ct KGWD/HNM BS15 .. 338 A7
The Devil's Elbow
RSTROUD/NAIL GL6 ..... 233 G7
Devil's La WUE GL12 ..... 296 B1
Devizes Rd COR/BOX SN13 ..... 353 M7
Devon Av CHELTW GL51 ..... 115 H2
Devon Gv EVILLE/WHL BS5 ..... 336 E3
Devon Rd EVILLE/WHL BS5 ..... 336 E2
Devonshire Pl TEWK GL20 ..... 48 B7 2
Devonshire Rd
RDLND/MONT BS6 ..... 325 K7
Devonshire St CHELT GL50 ..... 2 B4
Dewey Cl CHELTE/BC GL52 ..... 72 D8
Dewfalls Dr ALMDB BS32 ..... 316 F2
Dial La MANG/FISH BS16 ..... 327 M5
Diamond Rd EVILLE/WHL BS5 ..... 337 H4
Diamond St BMSTR BS3 ..... 335 L8 2
Diana Gdns ALMDB BS32 ..... 317 G3
Dianas Cl BWTH/CHD GL3 ..... 137 H5 2
Dibden Cl MANG/FISH BS16 ..... 328 C3
Dibden La MANG/FISH BS16 ..... 328 C4
TEWK GL20 ..... 51 M4
Dibden Rd MANG/FISH BS16 ..... 328 C3
Dickens Cl GLE GL4 ..... 136 B6
HORF/LLZ BS7 ..... 326 C3
Dickens Ms GLE GL4 ..... 136 B6 1
Didsbury Cl HNBRY/STHM BS10 ..... 325 H2
Digbeth St COTS GL54 ..... 102 A3 2
Digby Dr TEWK GL20 ..... 48 B3
Dighton Ga
BRSTK/PCHW BS34 ..... 317 G6 3
Dighton St CBRISNE BS2 ..... 6 F1
Dikler Cl COTS GL54 ..... 123 K7
Dill Av CHELTW GL51 ..... 93 G7
Dimore Cl VGL GL2 ..... 159 G4
Dinas Rd CHELTW GL51 ..... 115 H5
Dinely St GL GL1 ..... 5 G8
Dingle Cl
HNLZ/SM/SNYPK/WT BS9 ..... 324 E5
Dingle Rd
HNLZ/SM/SNYPK/WT BS9 ..... 324 E4
The Dingle FRCTL/WBN BS36 ..... 318 A8
HNLZ/SM/SNYPK/WT BS9 ..... 324 E4
YATE/CS BS37 ..... 310 B7
Dingle Vw
HNLZ/SM/SNYPK/WT BS9 ..... 324 E4
Dinglewell GLE GL4 ..... 137 H4
Dinglewood Cl
HNLZ/SM/SNYPK/WT BS9 ..... 324 F4 1
Dings Wk CBRISNE BS2 ..... 7 L4 2
Discovery Rd BWTH/CHD GL3 ..... 137 H5
Distel Cl CHELTW GL51 ..... 93 L6
Ditch La CIR GL7 ..... 192 E5
Dixon Rd BRSG/KWL/STAPK BS4 ..... 347 H1
Dobbie Rd STRAT CV37 ..... 9 K2
Dock Gate La CFTN/FAIL BS8 ..... 335 J6 2
Dockham Rd CIND GL14 ..... 154 C3
Dockins Hill Wy MTCHDN GL17 ..... 130 C4
Dock La TEWK GL20 ..... 27 G4
Dock Rd BRKLY GL13 ..... 226 D2
Doctors Hl COR/BOX SN13 ..... 353 J6
Dodd Dr COTS GL54 ..... 124 D7
Dodington Cl GLE GL4 ..... 136 F4 2
Dodington La YATE/CS BS37 ..... 320 D5
Dodington Rd YATE/CS BS37 ..... 320 D4
Dodisham Wk MANG/FISH BS16 ..... 327 K5
Dog La CHELTW GL51 ..... 138 F5
Dollar St CIR GL7 ..... 238 C2
Dolman Cl
HNBRY/STHM BS10 ..... 315 H8 2
Domby Cl CLFD GL16 ..... 175 K2
Dominion Rd MANG/FISH BS16 .. 327 H8
Donald Rd
BMSTRD/HC/WWD BS13 ..... 345 H4
Doncaster Rd
HNBRY/STHM BS10 ..... 325 K2
Doncombe Hl
CHPMW/MSHF SN14 ..... 343 G4
Doncombe La
CHPMW/MSHF SN14 ..... 343 H4
Donegal Rd
BRSG/KWL/STAPK BS4 ..... 345 M2
Dongola Av HORF/LLZ BS7 ..... 326 A7
Dongola Rd HORF/LLZ BS7 ..... 326 A7
The Donkey Fld CIR GL7 ..... 240 A2
Donkey La MIM GL56 ..... 57 G2
Donnington Rd SHPSTR CV36 ..... 16 B4
Donside CIR GL7 ..... 214 A8
Doone Rd HORF/LLZ BS7 ..... 326 B3
Dora Wk GL GL1 ..... 136 B4 3
Dorcas Av BRSTK/PCHW BS34 ..... 317 H6
Dorchester Rd HORF/LLZ BS7 ..... 326 C4
Dorester Cl HNBRY/STHM BS10 .. 315 L7
Dorian Cl HORF/LLZ BS7 ..... 326 A4
Dorian Rd HORF/LLZ BS7 ..... 326 A4
Dorian Wy HNBRY/STHM BS10 ..... 326 A3
Dorington Ct
RSTROUD/NAIL GL6 ..... 209 M7 2
Dormer Cl FRCTL/WBN BS36 ..... 318 F5
Dormer Rd CHELTW GL51 ..... 93 H7
EVILLE/WHL BS5 ..... 326 C8
Dorney Rd GL GL1 ..... 136 A4
Dorrit Cl GL GL1 ..... 136 B5
Dorset Av CHELTW GL51 ..... 115 J1
Dorset Gv CBRISNE BS2 ..... 336 C1 4
Dorset Rd
HNLZ/SM/SNYPK/WT BS9 ..... 325 K5
KGWD/HNM BS15 ..... 337 M2
Dorset St BMSTR BS3 ..... 335 K8 3
Dorset Wy YATE/CS BS37 ..... 310 C8
Doubledays HGHW SN6 ..... 288 F3
Double Vw CIND GL14 ..... 154 B4 1
Douglas Rd HORF/LLZ BS7 ..... 326 B4
KGWD/HNM BS15 ..... 337 M4
Doulton Wy HGRV/WHIT BS14 ..... 346 C6
Douro Rd CHELT GL50 ..... 115 K2
Dovecote YATE/CS BS37 ..... 320 A4
Dovedale THNB/SVB BS35 ..... 293 M4
Dove La CBRISNE BS2 ..... 336 B3
Dovercourt Rd HORF/LLZ BS7 ..... 326 C6
Doverdale Dr VGL GL2 ..... 112 F7
Dover Hay CHELTW GL51 ..... 115 H5 1
Dover's Vw CHCAM GL55 ..... 11 M4
Dove St CBRISNE BS2 ..... 335 M3
Dove St South CBRISNE BS2 ..... 6 F1
CBRISNE BS2 ..... 335 M3
Dovey Ct
OLD/WMLY/WICK BS30 ..... 338 E6
Dowdeswell Cl
HNBRY/STHM BS10 ..... 315 H8 3
Dowding Cl YATE/CS BS37 ..... 320 E1 1
Dowding Wy BWTH/CHD GL3 .. 113 L6 1
Dowers' La CIR GL7 ..... 213 J4
Dowling Rd
BMSTRD/HC/WWD BS13 ..... 345 M8
Down Ampney Rd CIR GL7 ..... 264 C5
Downend Pk HORF/LLZ BS7 ..... 326 B5
Downend Park Rd
MANG/FISH BS16 ..... 327 M6 3
Downend Rd HORF/LLZ BS7 ..... 326 B6
KGWD/HNM BS15 ..... 337 M2
MANG/FISH BS16 ..... 327 L6
Downfield STROUD GL5 ..... 208 B3
Downfield Cl THNB/SVB BS35 ..... 293 H6
Downfield Dr
FRCTL/WBN BS36 ..... 318 D3 2
Downfield La TEWK GL20 ..... 26 D4
Downfield Rd CFTN/FAIL BS8 ..... 335 J2
STROUD GL5 ..... 208 B4
Down Hatherley La VGL GL2 ..... 113 G1
Downleaze
HNLZ/SM/SNYPK/WT BS9 ..... 325 H8
MANG/FISH BS16 ..... 327 M3
Down Leaze THNB/SVB BS35 ..... 293 J6 3
Downman Rd HORF/LLZ BS7 ..... 326 C6
Down Rd CHPMW/MSHF SN14 ..... 342 F1
FRCTL/WBN BS36 ..... 318 A7
THNB/SVB BS35 ..... 293 J6
Downs Cl THNB/SVB BS35 ..... 293 J6 4
Downs Cote Av
HNLZ/SM/SNYPK/WT BS9 ..... 325 H5
Downs Cote Dr
HNLZ/SM/SNYPK/WT BS9 ..... 325 H5
Downs Cote Gdns
HNLZ/SM/SNYPK/WT BS9 ..... 325 H5
Downs Cote Pk
HNLZ/SM/SNYPK/WT BS9 ..... 325 J5
Downs Cote Vw
HNLZ/SM/SNYPK/WT BS9 ..... 325 J5
Downside Close
OLD/WMLY/WICK BS30 ..... 338 B6 2
Downside Rd CFTN/FAIL BS8 ..... 335 J2 2
Downs Pk East
RDLND/MONT BS6 ..... 325 J6
Downs Pk West
HNLZ/SM/SNYPK/WT BS9 ..... 325 J6
Downs Rd
HNLZ/SM/SNYPK/WT BS9 ..... 325 J5
The Downs WUE GL12 ..... 296 B4
Downs Wy CIR GL7 ..... 214 C5
The Down ALMDB BS32 ..... 292 F8
THNB/SVB BS35 ..... 293 H6
Downton Rd
BRSG/KWL/STAPK BS4 ..... 345 M3
STNHO GL10 ..... 207 G5
Down Vw RSTROUD/NAIL GL6 ..... 210 B7
Downy Cl VGL GL2 ..... 159 G1
Dowry Rd CFTN/FAIL BS8 ..... 335 J5 3
Dowry Sq CFTN/FAIL BS8 ..... 335 H5 1
Dowty Rd CHELTW GL51 115
Doynton La
CHPMW/MSHF SN14 330
Dozule Cl STNHO GL10 207
Dragon Rd FRCTL/WBN BS36 317
Dragons Hill Cl KEYN BS31 348
Dragons Hill Ct KEYN BS31 348
Dragons Hill Gdns
KEYN BS31 ..... 348 B
Dragonswell Rd
HNBRY/STHM BS10 325
Dragon Wk EVILLE/WHL BS5 ..... 337 H
Drag Rd RWYE HR9 126
Drake Cl BWTH/CHD GL3 ..... 113 H
Drake La DSLY GL11 253
Drake Rd BMSTR BS3 335
Drakes Pl CHELT GL50 115
Drapers Ct CHELTE/BC GL52 ..... 72 D8
Draper's La RTEWK/TIB GL19 67
Draycot Pl CBRIS/FH BS1 6
Draycott DSLY GL11 229
Draycott Crs DSLY GL11 229
Draycott Rd HORF/LLZ BS7 ..... 326 B6
Draydon Rd
BRSG/KWL/STAPK BS4 345
Drayton Cl CHELTW GL51 93
GLE GL4 ..... 136 E
HGRV/WHIT BS14 ..... 346 D
Drayton Rd CHELTW GL51 115
HNLZ/SM/SNYPK/WT BS9 ..... 324 E
Drayton Wy GLE GL4 136
Dr Brown's Cl
RSTROUD/NAIL GL6 233
Dr Browns Rd
RSTROUD/NAIL GL6 233
Dr Crawfords Wy
RSTROUD/NAIL GL6 ..... 233 H
Dr. Crouch's Rd
RSTROUD/NAIL GL6 209
Drews Cl BWTH/CHD GL3 ..... 113 L
Drews Ct BWTH/CHD GL3 113
Driffield Rd LYD GL15 201
Drifton Hl CHPMW/MSHF SN14 .. 333
The Driftway SHPSTR CV36 16
Drift Wy CIR GL7 238
Drinkwater Cl LED HR8 ..... 19 L
Drivemoor GLE GL4 136
Drivers La MIM GL56 82
The Drive DSLY GL11 229
HGRV/WHIT BS14 346
HNLZ/SM/SNYPK/WT BS9 325
Dr Newton's Wy STROUD GL5 208
Druetts Cl
HNBRY/STHM BS10 ..... 326 A5
Drugger's End La RGTMLV WR13 .. 22
Druid Cl
HNLZ/SM/SNYPK/WT BS9 325
Druid Hl
HNLZ/SM/SNYPK/WT BS9 325
Druid Rd
HNLZ/SM/SNYPK/WT BS9 324
Druids Cl GLE GL4 ..... 136 E
Druids Oak VGL GL2 159
Druid Stoke Av
HNLZ/SM/SNYPK/WT BS9 324
Druid Woods
HNLZ/SM/SNYPK/WT BS9 ..... 324 E6
Drummond Ct
OLD/WMLY/WICK BS30 ..... 338 B7
Drummond Rd CBRISNE BS2 ..... 336 A2
MANG/FISH BS16 ..... 327 H8
Drury La RTEWK/TIB GL19 43
Drybrook Rd MTCHDN GL17 129
Dryleaze KEYN BS31 348
WUE GL12 277
YATE/CS BS37 ..... 310 A6
Dryleaze Rd MANG/FISH BS16 327
Dry Meadow La VGL GL2 112
Dubbers La EVILLE/WHL BS5 337
Dublin Crs
HNLZ/SM/SNYPK/WT BS9 325
Duchess Rd CFTN/FAIL BS8 335
Duchess Wy MANG/FISH BS16 326
Ducie Rd EVILLE/WHL BS5 ..... 336 D
MANG/FISH BS16 328
Ducie St GL GL1 ..... 136 B4
Duckmoor Rd BMSTR BS3 335
Duck St WUE GL12 294
Duckworth Cl CHELTS GL53 ..... 115 M6
Dudbridge Hl STROUD GL5 208
Dudbridge Meadow
STROUD GL5 ..... 208 B6
Dudbridge Rd STROUD GL5 ..... 208 B
Duderstadt Cl STROUD GL5 ..... 208 B3
Dudley Cl KEYN BS31 348
Dudley Ct
OLD/WMLY/WICK BS30 ..... 338 B7
Dudley Gv HORF/LLZ BS7 ..... 326 E
Duffield's La MONM NP25 ..... 174 E
Dugar Wk RDLND/MONT BS6 325
Dugdale Rd CIR GL7 238
Duglynch La COTS GL54 ..... 73 M
Duke of York Rd CLFD GL16 150
Duke St CHELTE/BC GL52 3
Dukes Wy TEWK GL20 ..... 48 E
Dulverton Pl MIM GL56 58
Dulverton Rd HORF/LLZ BS7 .. 325 M7
Dumaine Av BRSTK/PCHW BS34 .. 317
Dumbleton Gv CHELTW GL51 .. 114 D5
Dunalley Pde CHELT GL50 ..... 2 D
Dunalley St CHELT GL50 ..... 2 D
Dunbar Cl CHELTW GL51 ..... 92 F
Duncan Gdns
CBATH/BATHN BA1 350
Duncombe La
KGWD/HNM BS15 337
Duncombe Rd
KGWD/HNM BS15 ..... 337 K2
Duncroft Rd GLE GL4 ..... 137 H
Dundas Cl
HNBRY/STHM BS10 ..... 325 G1
Dundonald Rd
RDLND/MONT BS6 325
Dundridge Gdns
EVILLE/WHL BS5 ..... 337 J5
Dundridge La EVILLE/WHL BS5 337
Dundry Cl KGWD/HNM BS15 ..... 337 M5
Dundry La LGASH BS41 ..... 344 D

undry Vw
  BRSG/KWL/STAPK BS4........ 346 C2
unford Rd BMSTR BS3........ 335 M8
unkeld Av BRSTK/PCHW BS34 .. 326 B1
unkerry Rd BMSTR BS3........ 335 M8
unlin Cl VGL GL2 .... 158 F1
unmail Rd HNBRY/STHM BS10.. 325 L1
unmore St BMSTR BS3 .... 7 K8
unns Copse LED HR8 .... 20 A5
unsdown La
  CHPMW/MSHF SN14 .... 331 J6
unsmore Gn RTEWK/TIB GL19 .. 46 E6
unstan Gln BWTH/CHD GL3.... 113 M7
unster Cl CHELTW GL51 ...... 92 F8
  GL GL1 .... 159 K2
unster Gdns CHELTW GL51 .... 92 F8
unster Gv BRSG/KWL/WICK BS30 .. 348 D1
unster La CHELTW GL51 ...... 92 F8
unster Rd BRSG/KWL/STAPK BS4 .. 346
  B3
  CHELTW GL51 .... 92 F8
  KEYN BS31 .... 348 A7
urand Cl VGL GL2 .... 112 E5
urban Rd BRSTK/PCHW BS34 .. 316 B3
urbin Wk EVILLE/WHL BS5 .... 7 M1
urbridge Rd RTEWK/TIB GL19 .. 65 G2
urdham Pk RDLND/MONT BS6.. 325
urham Cl CHELTW GL51 ...... 115 J6
urham Gv KEYN BS31 .... 347 M7
urham Cl CBRISNE BS2 ...... 336 C1
  GLE GL4 .... 136 E3
  WUE GL12 .... 276 B6
urleigh Cl
  BMSTRD/HC/WWD BS13...... 345 J5
urley Hl KEYN BS31 .... 347 K3
urley La KEYN BS31 .... 347 M4
urnford Av BMSTR BS3 ...... 335 J7
urnford St BMSTR BS3 ...... 335 J7
urn's Rd WUE GL12 .... 277 L4
ursley Cl YATE/CS BS37 ..... 320 A2
ursley Rd AVONM BS11 ...... 324 A4
  DSLY GL11 .... 229 G8
  VGL GL2 .... 229 H1
urville Rd
  BMSTRD/HC/WWD BS13...... 345 K5
urweston Wk
  HGRV/WHIT BS14 .... 346 F5
utton Cl HGRV/WHIT BS14 ... 346 F5
utton Leys COTS GL54 .... 169 K2
uttons La HGRV/WHIT BS14 .. 346 F6
uttons La MTCHDN GL17 ..... 129 H5
utton Wk HGRV/WHIT BS14 .. 346 F5
ve House Rd WUE GL12 ...... 277 H6
versbrook WUE GL12 .... 277 K4
vers Cl
  BMSTRD/HC/WWD BS13...... 345 M7
yer's La CHCAM GL55 .... 12 B8
  YATE/CS BS37 .... 309 J8
yer St CIR GL7 .... 238 D3
yke House La LED HR8 ...... 42 E4
ylan Thomas Ct
  OLD/WMLY/WICK BS30 ...... 338 C6
ynevor St GL GL1 .... 136 B4
yrham Cl
  HNLZ/SM/SNYPK/WT BS9..... 325 M5
  KGWD/HNM BS15 .... 338 B3
  THNB/SVB BS35 .... 273 L8
yrham Pde
  BRSTK/PCHW BS34 .... 316 E3
yrham Rd KGWD/HNM BS15 .. 338 B3

E

agle Crs MANG/FISH BS16 .... 329 L7
agle Dr BRSTK/PCHW BS34 ... 316 A3
agle Mill Cl STROUD GL5 ..... 208 F6
agle Pk CBATH/BATHN BA1 ... 352 B6
agle Rd BRSG/KWL/STAPK BS4 .. 346 F1
  CBATH/BATHN BA1 .... 352 B6
agle Wy GLE GL4 .... 136 E6
ardisland Rd GLE GL4 .... 160 A1
arl Russell Wy
  EVILLE/WHL BS5 .... 336 D4
arls Cnr MALM SN16 .... 285 C3
arlsmead MANG/FISH BS16... 326 F7
aristone Cl
  OLD/WMLY/WICK BS30 ...... 338 C7
aristone Crs
  OLD/WMLY/WICK BS30 ...... 338 C6
arl St CBRIS/FH BS1 .... 6 F1
arly Wy HNBRY/STHM BS10 .. 326 K3
arthcott Rd THNB/SVB BS35 .. 308 A3
asedale Cl
  HNLZ/SM/SNYPK/WT BS10 .... 325 M1
ast Approach Dr
  CHELTE/BC GL52 .... 94 A7
astbourne Rd
  EVILLE/WHL BS5 .... 336 D3
astbrook Rd GLE GL4 .... 136 E3
astbury Cl THNB/SVB BS35 ... 293 L2
astbury Rd MANG/FISH BS16 .. 327 C4
astcote Pk HGRV/WHIT BS14 .. 346 D6
astcott Wy BWTH/CHD GL3 ... 113 J5
ast Cft
  HNLZ/SM/SNYPK/WT BS9..... 325 L4
ast Dr STROUD GL5 .... 207 L4
ast End COTS GL54 .... 169 K2
ast End Rd CHELTS GL53 ..... 116 E6
astern Av GLE GL4 .... 136 E3
  MTCHDN GL17 .... 130 C7
astern Wy CIND GL14 .... 154 A7
astfield HGHW SN6 .... 287 H2
  HNLZ/SM/SNYPK/WT BS9..... 325 K4
astfield Dr YATE/CS BS37 ... 310 A3
astfield Rd
  HNLZ/SM/SNYPK/WT BS9..... 325 J4
  RDLND/MONT BS6 .... 335 M1
  RSTROUD/NAIL GL6 .... 233 K5
astfield Ter
  HNLZ/SM/SNYPK/WT BS9..... 325 K4
ast Gable CHELTE/BC GL52 ... 72 D8
astgate St GL GL1 .... 4 F6
ast Gv RDLND/MONT BS6 .... 336 B2
ast Hill Eastfield Rd
  HNLZ/SM/SNYPK/WT BS9 .... 325 J4

Eastington Rd COTS GL54 ..... 169 K2
Eastlake Cl HORF/LLZ BS7 .... 326 D4
Eastland Av THNB/SVB BS35 .. 293 L1
Eastland Rd THNB/SVB BS35 .. 293 L1
Eastleigh Cl
  MANG/FISH BS16 .... 328 A7
Eastleigh Rd
  HNBRY/STHM BS10 .... 325 M8
  MANG/FISH BS16 .... 328 A7
Eastley Cl WUE GL12 .... 275 G4
Eastlyn Rd
  BMSTRD/HC/WWD BS13 ..... 345 K3
Eastmead La
  HNLZ/SM/SNYPK/WT BS9 .... 325 Q7
Eastnor Rd HGRV/WHIT BS14 .. 346 C8
Easton Hill Rd THNB/SVB BS35.. 293 M1
Easton Rd CBRISNE BS2....... 7 L2
  EVILLE/WHL BS5............. 336 D3
Easton Wy EVILLE/WHL BS5 .. 336 C2
Eastover Cl
  HNLZ/SM/SNYPK/WT BS9 .... 325 J3
East Pde
  HNLZ/SM/SNYPK/WT BS9 .... 324 E5
East Pk EVILLE/WHL BS5 ..... 336 E1
East Park Dr
  EVILLE/WHL BS5 .... 336 E1
East Priory Cl
  HNLZ/SM/SNYPK/WT BS9 .... 325 J4
East Ridge Dr
  BMSTRD/HC/WWD BS13...... 345 H6
Eastrip La CHPMW/MSHF SN14.. 343 L8
East Shrubbery
  RDLND/MONT BS6 .... 335 K1
East St BMSTR BS3 .... 6 E9
  BMSTR BS3 .... 335 L8
  CBRISNE BS2 .... 7 J1
  LYD GL15 .... 198 F5
  MIM GL56 .... 58 D6
  SHPSTR CV36 .... 61 H5
  TEWK GL20 .... 48 A3
East Vw MANG/FISH BS16 .... 328 B5
Eastville GLE GL4 .... 5 L8
Eastwood Crs
  BRSG/KWL/STAPK BS4........ 337 H7
Eastwood Rd
  BRSG/KWL/STAPK BS4........ 337 H7
  MTCHDN GL17 .... 129 M5
Eaton Cl HGRV/WHIT BS14 ... 347 C6
  MANG/FISH BS16 .... 327 K7
Eaton Crs CFTN/FAIL BS8 .... 335 J3
Eaton Pl CHELT GL50 .... 2 D7
Eaton St BMSTR BS3 .... 335 L8
Ebenezer La
  HNLZ/SM/SNYPK/WT BS9 .... 324 F5
  HNLZ/SM/SNYPK/WT BS9 .... 325 G6
Ebenezer St EVILLE/WHL BS5 .. 336 F4
Ebley Rd STNHO GL10 .... 207 H5
Ebor Rd VGL GL2 .... 136 E2
Ebrington Cl GLE GL4 .... 136 F3
Eddys La MTCHDN GL17 ..... 128 E5
Edendale Approach Rd
  CHELTW GL51 .... 114 E3
Eden Gv HORF/LLZ BS7 ...... 326 C2
Eden Park Cl
  CBATH/BATHN BA1 .... 352 L7
Eden Park Dr
  CBATH/BATHN BA1 .... 352 L7
Eden's HI NWNT GL18........ 65 J8
Edenwall Rd CLFD GL16 ..... 175 L4
Edgecorner La
  CHPMW/MSHF SN14 .... 323 J8
Edgecumbe Rd
  RDLND/MONT BS6 .... 335 M1
Edge End Rd CLFD GL16 ..... 151 M7
Edgefield Cl HGRV/WHIT BS14 .. 346 B8
Edgefield Rd HGRV/WHIT BS14 .. 346 B8
Edge Hills Cl CIND GL14 ..... 154 B2
Edge Hills Rd CIND GL14 .... 154 B2
Edge La RSTROUD/NAIL GL6 .. 184 E3
Edge Rd RSTROUD/NAIL GL6 .. 185 G3
Edgeware Rd BMSTR BS3 .... 6 C8
  MANG/FISH BS16 .... 327 L7
Edgewood Cl
  HGRV/WHIT BS14 .... 346 D3
  OLD/WMLY/WICK BS30 ...... 338 C8
Edgeworth YATE/CS BS37 .... 319 L5
Edgeworth Cl GLE GL4 ...... 137 G6
Edinburgh Pl CHELTW GL51 .. 115 C1
  CLFD GL16 .... 175 M1
Edinburgh Rd KEYN BS31 .... 348 A7
Edington Gv
  HNBRY/STHM BS10 .... 325 J1
Edmond Rd CHEP NP16 ...... 270 C3
Edmonds Cl STRAT CV37 ..... 9 K1
Edmund La MANG/FISH BS16 .. 327 M5
Edmund Ct MANG/FISH BS16 .. 329 K5
Edna Av BRSG/KWL/STAPK BS4 .. 337 C8
Edward Pl TEWK GL20 .... 48 B8
Edward Rd
  BRSG/KWL/STAPK BS4........ 336 D7
  KGWD/HNM BS15 .... 338 A3
Edwards Cl CIR GL7 .... 240 F5
  MTCHDN GL17 .... 128 C6
Edward St CHELT GL50....... 115 L4
  EVILLE/WHL BS5 .... 336 F1
  EVILLE/WHL BS5 .... 336 E3
Edwin Short Cl
  OLD/WMLY/WICK BS30 ...... 349 C3
Edwy Pde GL GL1 .... 4 F2
Effingham Rd
  RDLND/MONT BS6 .... 336 A1
Egerton Brow
  HORF/LLZ BS7 .... 325 M7
Egerton Rd HORF/LLZ BS7 ... 325 M7
Eggshill La YATE/CS BS37 ... 319 M2
Eighth Av HORF/LLZ BS7 .... 326 B3
Elberton Rd KGWD/HNM BS15 .. 338 C3
Elberton Rd
  HNLZ/SM/SNYPK/WT BS9 .... 324 D4
  THNB/SVB BS35 .... 292 B5
Elbury Rd KGWD/HNM BS15 .. 337 L1
Elderberry Wk
  HNBRY/STHM BS10 .... 325 L1
Eldersfield Cl COTS GL54 .... 74 C4
  VGL GL2 .... 159 G1
Elderwood Dr
  OLD/WMLY/WICK BS30 ...... 338 C8

Elderwood Rd
  HGRV/WHIT BS14 .... 346 D4
Elderwood Wy GL GL1 ...... 135 L8
Eldon Av CHELTE/BC GL52 .... 3 J5
Eldon Rd CHELTE/BC GL52..... 3 J5
Eldon Ter BMSTR BS3 .... 335 M8
Eldon Wy
  BRSG/KWL/STAPK BS4........ 336 E6
Eldorado Crs CHELT GL50 .... 115 J2
Eldorado Rd CHELT GL50 .... 115 J2
Eldred Cl
  HNLZ/SM/SNYPK/WT BS9..... 324 E6
Eleventh Av HORF/LLZ BS7 ... 326 D2
Elfin Rd MANG/FISH BS16 .... 327 J6
Elf Meadow CIR GL7 .... 241 G4
Elgar Cl
  BRSG/KWL/STAPK BS4........ 345 M5
  LED HR8 .... 19 L4
Elgin Av HORF/LLZ BS7 ...... 326 B2
Elgin Pk RDLND/MONT BS6 ... 335 K1
Elgin Rd MANG/FISH BS16.... 327 K1
Eliot Cl HORF/LLZ BS7....... 326 C3
  VGL GL2 .... 135 L7
Elizabeth Cl THNB/SVB BS35 .. 293 M3
Elizabeth Crs
  BRSTK/PCHW BS34 .... 317 C2
Elizabeth Gdns CIR GL7 ..... 241 L6
  TET GL8 .... 281 M3
Elizabeths Ms
  BRSG/KWL/STAPK BS4........ 337 H5
Elizabeth Wy CIR GL7 .... 238 E7
Ellacombe Rd
  OLD/WMLY/WICK BS30 ...... 348 A1
Ellan Hay Rd ALMDB BS32.... 317 J3
Ellbridge Cl
  HNLZ/SM/SNYPK/WT BS9..... 324 F6
Ellenborough Rd
  CHELTE/BC GL52 .... 94 C1
Ellendene Dr TEWK GL20 .... 49 C4
Ellenor Dr TEWK GL20 ...... 51 L4
Ellencroft Wy WUE GL12 .... 277 H3
Ellesmere THNB/SVB BS35 ... 293 L3
Ellesmere Gv CHELT GL50 ... 115 K5
Ellesmere Rd
  BRSG/KWL/STAPK BS4 ...... 346 F2
  KGWD/HNM BS15 .... 337 M3
Ellfield Cl
  BMSTRD/HC/WWD BS13...... 345 H5
Ellicks Cl ALMDB BS32 ...... 317 C1
Ellicott Rd HORF/LLZ BS7 .... 326 B5
Ellinghurst Cl
  HNBRY/STHM BS10 .... 325 J1
Elliott Av MANG/FISH BS16 ... 327 L2
Elliott Pl CHELTW GL51 ..... 115 H4
Elliott Rd CIR GL7 .... 238 D5
Ellis Av BMSTRD/HC/WWD BS13.. 345 J3
Ellison Cl BWTH/CHD GL3 ... 137 J5
Elliston La CHELTW GL51 .... 115 L1
Elliston La RDLND/MONT BS6 .. 335 L1
Ellisbridge Cl KEYN BS31 .... 348 D6
Ellsworth Rd
  HNBRY/STHM BS10 .... 325 H1
Ellwood Rd CLFD GL16 ...... 175 L5
Elmbridge Rd VGL GL2....... 136 E1
Elmbury Dr TEWK GL20 ..... 48 D5
Elm Cl BRSTK/PCHW BS34 ... 316 F4
  CHELTE/BC GL52 .... 94 C6
  CHELTW GL51 .... 93 K8
  CHEP NP16 .... 270 C1
  STNHO GL10 .... 207 J7
  STRAT CV37 .... 8 A1
  YATE/CS BS37 .... 320 C2
Elmcroft Crs HORF/LLZ BS7 .. 326 C7
Elmdale CHEP NP16 .... 270 A2
Elmdale Crs THNB/SVB BS35 .. 293 L2
Elmdale Rd BMSTR BS35 ..... 345 K1
  CFTN/FAIL BS8 .... 6 B1
Elm Dr BWTH/CHD GL3 ...... 137 M5
Elmer Cl MALM SN16 .... 303 J4
Elmfield KGWD/HNM BS15 ... 338 A5
Elmfield Av CHELTW GL51 ... 93 L7
Elmfield Cl KGWD/HNM BS15 .. 338 A5
Elmfield Rd CHELTW GL51 ... 2 A1
  CHELTW GL51 .... 93 L7
  HNLZ/SM/SNYPK/WT BS9..... 325 J3
Elm Garden Dr CHELTW GL51 .. 114 C4
Elm Gv CHCAM GL55 .... 13 M6
  RTEWK/TIB GL19 .... 108 C7
Elmgrove Av
  EVILLE/WHL BS5 .... 336 D3
Elmgrove Dr YATE/CS BS37 .. 320 B1
Elmgrove Pk
  RDLND/MONT BS6 .... 335 M2
Elmgrove Rd BWTH/CHD GL3 .. 137 H4
  MANG/FISH BS16 .... 327 C6
  RDLND/MONT BS6 .... 335 M2
Elmgrove Rd East VGL GL2 .. 159 C4
Elmgrove Rd West VGL GL2 .. 158 F4
Elm Hayes
  BMSTRD/HC/WWD BS13...... 345 H5
Elmhirst Gdns YATE/CS BS37 .. 320 C1
Elmhurst Av EVILLE/WHL BS5.. 326 E8
Elming Down Cl ALMDB BS32 .. 316 F5
Elmira Rd GLE GL4 .... 136 B7
Elm La RDLND/MONT BS6 .... 335 K1
Elmlea Av
  HNLZ/SM/SNYPK/WT BS9..... 324 F6
Elmlea Rd STNHO GL10 ..... 207 J7
Elmleaze VGL GL2 .... 112 F8
Elmleigh Av MANG/FISH BS16 .. 328 D6
Elmleigh Cl MANG/FISH BS16 .. 328 C6
Elmleigh Rd MANG/FISH BS16 .. 328 C6
Elmley Rd EVE WR11 .... 29 K2
Elmore KGWD/HNM BS15 .... 338 B1
  YATE/CS BS37 .... 319 M3
Elmore La VGL GL2 .... 158 L1
Elmore Rd BRSTK/PCHW BS34 .. 316 B2
  HORF/LLZ BS7 .... 326 C5
Elm Pk BRSTK/PCHW BS34 ... 326 C1
Elm Rd CHEP NP16 .... 270 C1
  CHPMW/MSHF SN14 .... 343 J6
  HORF/LLZ BS7 .... 326 A6
  KGWD/HNM BS15 .... 338 A4
  SHPSTR CV36 .... 16 B7
  STROUD GL5 .... 208 A3

TEWK GL20 .... 49 G3
Elmsdale Rd LED HR8 .... 19 M4
Elms Gv BRSTK/PCHW BS34 .. 316 D2
Elm Side VGL GL2 .... 90 F6
Elms Rd STNHO GL10 .... 207 G3
Elm St CHELTW GL51 .... 93 K7
Elm Tree Av MANG/FISH BS16 .. 328 C4
Elmtree Cl KGWD/HNM BS15 .. 337 M2
Elmtree Dr
  BMSTRD/HC/WWD BS13...... 345 H6
Elm Vw CIR GL7 .... 262 B7
Elmvil Rd TEWK GL20 .... 48 D4
Elm Wd YATE/CS BS37 ...... 320 A3
Elphick Rd CIR GL7 .... 214 B7
Elsbert Dr
  BMSTRD/HC/WWD BS13...... 345 C5
Elstree Rd EVILLE/WHL BS5... 337 C2
Elstub La HORF/LLZ BS7 ..... 229 C6
Elton La HORF/LLZ BS7 ...... 335 M1
Elton Rd CFTN/FAIL BS8 ..... 6 B2
  CIND GL14 .... 154 F3
  CIND GL14 .... 155 L3
  HORF/LLZ BS7 .... 325 M8
  KGWD/HNM BS15 .... 337 K2
Elton St CBRISNE BS2 .... 7 K1
Elvard Cl
  BMSTRD/HC/WWD BS13...... 345 J7
Elvard Rd
  BMSTRD/HC/WWD BS13...... 345 J6
Elvaston Rd BMSTR BS3 ..... 336 A8
Ely Cl
  HNLZ/SM/SNYPK/WT BS9..... 324 D4
Embassy Rd EVILLE/WHL BS5.. 337 G2
Embassy Wk EVILLE/WHL BS5 .. 337 G2
Embleton Rd
  HNBRY/STHM BS10 .... 325 J1
Embrook MIM GL56 .... 103 G3
Emerald Cl GL GL1 .... 135 L8
Emersons Green La
  MANG/FISH BS16 .... 328 D5
Emerson Sq HORF/LLZ BS7 .. 326 C3
Emersons Wy
  MANG/FISH BS16 .... 328 E4
Emery Rd
  BRSG/KWL/STAPK BS4........ 347 H2
Emet Gv MANG/FISH BS16.... 328 D5
Emet La MANG/FISH BS16 .... 328 D5
Emlyn Rd EVILLE/WHL BS5 ... 336 E1
Emma-chris Wy
  BRSTK/PCHW BS34 .... 326 E1
Emmerson La CIR GL7 ...... 235 H5
Emmett Wd HGRV/WHIT BS14 .. 346 D8
Emperor Cl CHELTW GL51 ... 114 F1
Empire Wy VGL GL2 .... 135 K6
Emra Cl EVILLE/WHL BS5 .... 337 H2
Enborne Cl GLE GL4 .... 159 M2
Enfield Rd MANG/FISH BS16 .. 327 J8
Engine Common La
  YATE/CS BS37 .... 309 L5
England's Crs FRCTL/WBN BS36.. 318 A4
Englishcombe Rd
  BMSTRD/HC/WWD BS13...... 345 L8
Ennerdale Av VGL GL2 ...... 112 E6
Ennerdale Rd
  HNBRY/STHM BS10 .... 325 M1
Enterprise Wy CHELTW GL51 .. 93 K8
Epney Cl BRSTK/PCHW BS34 .. 316 B1
Epney Rd GL GL1 .... 135 L8
Epsom Cl MANG/FISH BS16 .. 328 B2
Epworth Rd
  HNBRY/STHM BS10 .... 325 J1
Erin Pk STROUD GL5 .... 208 C6
Erin Wk BRSG/KWL/STAPK BS4 .. 345 M3
Ermin Pk BWTH/CHD GL3 .... 137 M5
Ermin Pl CIR GL7 .... 238 E5
Erminster Dr BWTH/CHD GL3 .. 137 J4
Ermin St BWTH/CHD GL3 .... 137 M5
Ermin Wy BWTH/CHD GL3 ... 138 D7
Ermleet Rd
  RDLND/MONT BS6 .... 335 L1
Ernest Barker Cl
  EVILLE/WHL BS5 .... 336 D4
Ernestville Rd MANG/FISH BS16.. 327 H8
Eros Cl STROUD GL5 .... 208 C6
Errington Cl CIR GL7 .... 238 D5
Eskdale THNB/SVB BS35 .... 293 M4
Esland Pl CIR GL7 .... 238 D5
Essery Rd EVILLE/WHL BS5 ... 336 E1
Essex Av CHELTW GL51 ..... 115 J1
Essex Cl BWTH/CHD GL3 .... 113 J3
Essex Pl COTS GL54 .... 123 C4
Esson Rd KGWD/HNM BS15 .. 337 K2
Estate Rd CIND GL14 .... 153 M1
Estcote Rd CIR GL7 .... 238 C2
Estcourt Cl GL GL1 .... 5 J1
  VGL GL2 .... 5 L3
Estcourt Rd GL GL1 .... 5 J1
  VGL GL2 .... 5 L3
Estoril YATE/CS BS37 ...... 320 B2
Estune Wk LGASH BS41 ..... 344 C2
Ethelbene Rd STROUD GL5 .. 207 M3
Etheridge Pl VGL GL2 ...... 5 L6
Etloe Rd RDLND/MONT BS6 .. 335 J2
Eton Rd BRSG/KWL/STAPK BS4 .. 336 F8
Ettington Cl CHELTW GL51 .. 92 E8
Ettrick Dr MANG/FISH BS16 .. 327 K5
Eugene St CBRISNE BS2 ..... 6 E1
  EVILLE/WHL BS5 .... 7 K1
Evans Cl BRSG/KWL/STAPK BS4 .. 337 H5
Evans Rd RDLND/MONT BS6 .. 335 K1
Evans Wk GLE GL4 .... 136 D7
Evelyn Cl CHELTS GL53 ..... 116 A6
Evelyn Rd
  HNBRY/STHM BS10 .... 325 L4
Evenlode Av STROUD GL5 ... 208 A3
Evenlode Gdns AVONM BS11 .. 324 D6
  MIM GL56 .... 58 E6
Evenlode Rd GLE GL4 ...... 159 M2
  MIM GL56 .... 58 E6
Evenlode Wy KEYN BS31 .... 348 C3
Evercreech Rd
  HGRV/WHIT BS14 .... 346 C7
Everest Av MANG/FISH BS16 .. 327 G7
Everest Cl RSTROUD/NAIL GL6.. 233 G5
Everest Rd CHELTS GL53 .... 116 A7
  MANG/FISH BS16 .... 327 G7
Everlands DSLY GL11 .... 229 J6

Eve Rd EVILLE/WHL BS5...... 336 D2
Everside Cl DSLY GL11 ...... 229 H5
Everside La DSLY GL11 ...... 229 H5
Evesham Rd BDWAY WR12 ... 10 B7
  CHELT GL50 .... 94 A4
  CHELTE/BC GL52 .... 2 E3
  CHELTE/BC GL52 .... 2 F2
  CHELTE/BC GL52 .... 72 B7
  COTS GL54 .... 74 C2
  COTS GL54 .... 101 M2
Evington Rd CHELTW GL51 .. 115 G1
Ewelme Cl DSLY GL11 ...... 253 L3
Ewens Rd CHELTE/BC GL52 .. 3 J8
Ewlyn Rd CHELTS GL53 ..... 115 M5
Exeter Buildings
  RDLND/MONT BS6 .... 335 K1
Exeter Rd BMSTR BS3 ...... 6 A9
Exley Cl OLD/WMLY/WICK BS30 .. 338 E6
Exmoor St BMSTR BS3 ...... 6 B9
Exmouth Ct CHELTS GL53 .. 115 M4
Exmouth Rd
  BRSG/KWL/STAPK BS4........ 346 B2
Exmouth St CHELTS GL53 ... 115 M4
Eyer's La CBRISNE BS2 ...... 7 J2
Eynon Cl CHELTS GL53 ..... 115 L6

F

Faber Gv
  BMSTRD/HC/WWD BS13 ..... 345 L7
Fabian Dr BRSTK/PCHW BS34... 317 G6
Factory Rd FRCTL/WBN BS36 .. 318 B4
Failand Cresent
  HNLZ/SM/SNYPK/WT BS9..... 324 E6
Failand Wk
  HNLZ/SM/SNYPK/WT BS9 .... 324 E5
Fairacre Cl HORF/LLZ BS7 ... 326 D6
Fairacres Cl KEYN BS31 ..... 348 A7
Fairfax Cl CIR GL7 .... 238 D4
Fairfax Rd CIR GL7 .... 238 D4
Fairfax St CBRIS/FH BS1 .... 7 G3
Fairfield Av CHELTS GL53 ... 115 M6
Fairfield Cl
  CHPMW/MSHF SN14 .... 342 B5
  CLFD GL16 .... 175 K2
Fairfield Pde CHELTS GL53 .. 115 M6
Fairfield Park Rd
  CHELTS GL53 .... 115 M5
Fairfield Pl BMSTR BS3 ..... 6 B9
Fairfield Rd BMSTR BS3..... 6 B9
  CHELTS GL53 .... 115 M5
  CHEP NP16 .... 270 A5
  LYD GL15 .... 201 J8
  RDLND/MONT BS6 .... 336 B1
Fairfields CIND GL14 .... 154 A3
Fairfields Rd LED HR8 ...... 19 M4
Fairfields St CHELTS GL53 .. 115 M5
Fairfield Wk CHELTS GL53 .. 115 M5
Fairfoot Rd
  BRSG/KWL/STAPK BS4........ 336 C8
Fairford Cl KGWD/HNM BS15 .. 338 B1
Fairford Crs BRSTK/PCHW BS34.. 316 D3
Fairford Rd CIR GL7 .... 218 C7
  KGWD/HNM BS15 .... 338 B1
Fair Furlong
  BMSTRD/HC/WWD BS13...... 345 J7
Fairhaven YATE/CS BS37 .... 320 B2
Fairhaven Av BWTH/CHD GL3 .. 138 A5
Fairhaven Rd CHELTS GL53 .. 115 M5
  RDLND/MONT BS6 .... 325 L7
Fairhaven St CHELTS GL53 .. 115 M5
Fair Lawn
  OLD/WMLY/WICK BS30 ...... 338 D7
Fairlawn Rd
  RDLND/MONT BS6 .... 336 B1
Fairlyn Dr KGWD/HNM BS15 .. 338 B8
Fairmile Gdns VGL GL2 ..... 112 B6
Fairmount Rd CHELTW GL51 .. 115 H2
Fairoaks
  OLD/WMLY/WICK BS30 ...... 338 C8
Fairview CHPMW/MSHF SN14 .. 343 L5
Fair View Cl
  RSTROUD/NAIL GL6 .... 232 D6
Fair View Dr RDLND/MONT BS6 .. 335 L1
Fairview Rd CHELTE/BC GL52 .. 2 E4
  KGWD/HNM BS15 .... 338 B3
Fairview Wy CHELTE/BC GL52 .. 2 F4
Fairwater Pk GLE GL4 ...... 136 F2
Fairway BRSG/KWL/STAPK BS4 .. 346 F2
  TEWK GL20 .... 49 G3
Fairway Cl
  OLD/WMLY/WICK BS30 ...... 338 D7
Fairways Av CLFD GL16 ..... 175 K2
Falcon Cl BRSTK/PCHW BS34 .. 316 A3
  HNLZ/SM/SNYPK/WT BS9..... 325 H3
  VGL GL2 .... 112 E5
Falcondale Rd
  HNLZ/SM/SNYPK/WT BS9..... 325 H3
Falcondale Wk
  HNLZ/SM/SNYPK/WT BS9..... 325 J3
Falcon Dr BRSTK/PCHW BS34 .. 316 A3
Falconer Rd CBATH/BATHN BA1.. 350 C8
Falcon La LED HR8 .... 19 H3
Falcon Wy BRSTK/PCHW BS34 .. 316 A3
Faldo Cl GLE GL4 .... 137 H6
Falfield Rd
  BRSG/KWL/STAPK BS4........ 336 E8
  GL GL1 .... 135 L8
Falfield Wk
  HNBRY/STHM BS10 .... 325 L3
Falkland Pl CHELTW GL51 ... 92 F8
Falkland Rd
  RDLND/MONT BS6 .... 336 B1
Falkner St GL GL1 .... 5 G9
Fallodon Ct
  HNLZ/SM/SNYPK/WT BS9..... 325 K6
Fallodon Wy
  HNLZ/SM/SNYPK/WT BS9..... 325 K6
Fallowfield
  OLD/WMLY/WICK BS30 ...... 338 E7
Fallows Rd COTS GL54 ..... 169 K2
Falmouth Rd HORF/LLZ BS7 .. 325 M1
Fancy Rd LYD GL15......... 177 G5

Fane Cl *HNBRY/STHM* BS10 .... 315 J8 🗓
Fanshawe Rd *HGRV/WHIT* BS14.. 346 C4
Fant Hl *RBANSW* OX15 .... 17 L6
Faraday Cl *GL* GL1 .... 136 B4 🗓
Farfield La *HGHW* SN6 .... 289 G7
Far Handstones
  OLD/WMLY/WICK BS30 .... 338 C7
Faringdon Rd *CHELTW* GL51 ...... 114 F4 🗓
Farington Rd
  HNLZ/SM/SNYPK/WT BS9 .... 325 M4
Farleigh Cl *CHELTE/BC* GL52 .... 116 E5 🗓
Farleigh La *WUE* GL12 .... 295 L1
Farleigh Rd *KEYN* BS31 .... 347 M7
Farleigh Wk
  BMSTRD/HC/WWD BS13 .... 345 J3
Farley Cl *BRSTK/PCHW* BS34 ...... 316 E4
Farman Crs *COTS* GL54 .... 124 C7
Farm Cl *MANG/FISH* BS16 .... 328 D5 🗓
  SHPSTR CV36 .... 16 A5 🗓
Farmcote *WUE* GL12 .... 297 M3
Farmcote Cl
  RSTROUD/NAIL GL6 .... 209 M7
Farmcote Gdns *COTS* GL54 .... 74 B6
Farm Ct *MANG/FISH* BS16 .... 328 A4
Farmer Rd
  BMSTRD/HC/WWD BS13 .... 345 C7
Farmers La *BDWAY* WR12 .... 32 A1
Farmfield Rd *CHELTW* GL51 ...... 115 H6
Farm Hl *TET* GL8 .... 257 K3
Farmhill Crs *STROUD* GL5 .... 208 B3
Farmhill La *STROUD* GL5 .... 208 B3
Farmington Ri *COTS* GL54 ...... 169 K1 🗓
Farmington Rd *CHELTW* GL51 ...... 115 G3
  COTS GL54 .... 169 K1
Farm La *CHELTS* GL53 .... 115 K7
  CHELTW GL51 .... 138 F2
  TET GL8 .... 279 L8
  TEWK GL20 .... 27 C5
  TEWK GL20 .... 27 L3
  THNB/SVB BS35 .... 304 F8
Farm Lees *WUE* GL12 .... 276 C5
Farm Rd *MANG/FISH* BS16 .... 328 A4
  MTCHDN GL17 .... 129 H5
  RSTROUD/NAIL GL6 .... 211 L2
Farm St *GL* GL1 .... 4 F9
Farmwell Cl
  BMSTRD/HC/WWD BS13 .... 345 K6 🗓
Farndale *EVILLE/WHL* BS5 .... 337 J5
Farne Cl
  HNLZ/SM/SNYPK/WT BS9 .... 325 K6
Farrant Av *BWTH/CHD* BS3 ...... 113 J5
Farrant Cl
  BRSG/KWL/STAPK BS4 .... 345 M5
Farriers Cft
  RSTROUD/NAIL GL6 .... 209 M7 🗓
Farriers End *VGL* GL2 .... 159 H1
Farriers Reach
  CHELTE GL52 .... 71 M7 🗓
The Farriers Clf *TET* GL8 .... 220 B7
  STROUD GL5 .... 208 E4
Farr's La *CBRIS/FH* BS1 .... 6 E5
Far Sandfield *BWTH/CHD* BS3 .... 113 L6
Farthing Cft *VGL* GL2 .... 110 F7
The Farthings *COTS* GL54 .... 142 F8
Far Wells Rd
  RSTROUD/NAIL GL6 .... 210 C3
Far Westrip *STNHO* GL10 .... 207 K3
Fauconberg Rd *CHELT* GL50 ...... 2 B6
Faulkner's Cl *CIR* GL7 .... 242 E6
Fawkes Cl *KGWD/HNM* BS15 ...... 338 D3
Fawkes Pl *STROUD* GL5 .... 208 E4 🗓
Fawley Dr *CHELTE/BC* GL52 ...... 94 E7
Featherbed La *SHPSTR* CV36 ...... 39 J1 🗓
  THNB/SVB BS35 .... 272 D5
Featherstone Rd
  MANG/FISH BS16 .... 327 H7 🗓
Feeder Rd *CBRISNE* BS2 .... 7 L6
  CBRISNE BS2............ 336 E5
Felix Rd *EVILLE/WHL* BS5 .... 336 D3
Fell Mill La *SHPSTR* CV36 .... 16 C5
Felstead Rd
  HNBRY/STHM BS10 .... 326 A2
Feltham Rd *MANG/FISH* BS16...... 329 L6
Felton Gv
  BMSTRD/HC/WWD BS13 .... 345 K3
Fenhill La *MIM* GL56 .... 57 K6
Fennel Cl *GLE* GL4 .... 136 E7
Fennel Dr *ALMDB* BS32 .... 317 J4
Fennell Gv
  HNBRY/STHM BS10 .... 325 J1 🗓
Fennell's Vw *STROUD* GL5 .... 209 G2
Fenshurst Gdns *LGASH* BS41 .... 344 B3
Fenswood Md *LGASH* BS41 .... 344 A3
Fenswood Rd *LGASH* BS41 .... 344 A2
Fenton Cl *KEYN* BS31 .... 348 F8
Fenton Rd *HORF/LLZ* BS7 .... 325 M7
Fermaine Av
  BRSG/KWL/STAPK BS4............ 337 H4
Fernbank Rd
  RDLND/MONT BS6 .... 335 L1
Fernbrook Cl *MANG/FISH* BS16 .. 327 K2
Fern Cl *HNBRY/STHM* BS10 ...... 315 K8
Ferndale Av
  OLD/WMLY/WICK BS30 .... 338 B8
Ferndale Cl *CIND* GL14 .... 154 B2 🗓
  VGL GL2 .... 112 D6 🗓
Ferndale Rd *CBATH/BATHN* BA1.. 351 L8
  HORF/LLZ BS7 .... 326 C1
  RSTROUD/NAIL GL6 .... 184 C8 🗓
Ferndales Cl *CHELTW* GL51 ...... 115 H6 🗓
Ferndene *ALMDB* BS32 .... 316 E1
Ferndown *YATE/CS* BS37 .... 320 A2
Ferndown Rd *AVONM* BS11 .... 324 C4 🗓
Ferndown Rd *LED* HR8 .... 19 M5
Ferney *DSLY* GL11 .... 253 L3
Fern Gv *BRSTK/PCHW* BS34 ...... 316 F4
Fernhill *ALMDB* BS32 .... 306 D3
Fernhill La *AVONM* BS11 .... 324 D2
Fernhurst Rd
  EVILLE/WHL BS5 .... 337 H2 🗓
Fern Lawn *GLE* GL4 .... 160 F1
Fernleaze *FRCTL/WBN* BS36 ...... 318 C6
Fernleigh Crs *CHELTW* GL51 ...... 115 G5
Fern Rd *CLFD* GL16 .... 176 A4
  MANG/FISH BS16 .... 327 M6
Fernsteed Rd
  BMSTRD/HC/WWD BS13 .... 345 H5
The Ferns *TET* GL8 .... 281 M4

Fern St *CBRISNE* BS2 .... 336 B2
Ferris Court Vw
  RSTROUD/NAIL GL6 .... 209 M7
Ferry Gdns *VGL* GL2 .... 158 F2 🗓
Ferry La *TEWK* GL20 .... 25 G3
Ferry Rd *KGWD/HNM* BS15 .... 347 M2
Ferry St *CBRIS/FH* BS1 .... 7 G5
Ferry Wy *CHEP* NP16 .... 270 D7 🗓
Festival Rd *STNHO* GL10 .... 207 G4
Fewster Rd *RSTROUD/NAIL* GL6 .. 232 D7
Fewster Sq
  RSTROUD/NAIL GL6 .... 232 D7 🗓
Fiddes Rd *RDLND/MONT* BS6 .... 325 L7
Fiddler's Green La
  CHELTW GL51 .... 114 E2
The Fiddle *HGHW* SN6 .... 288 E4
Fidges La *RSTROUD/NAIL* GL6.... 210 A5
Field Badgers *CHCAM* GL55...... 34 E1
Field Cl *CIR* GL7 .... 263 J4
  COTS GL54 .... 73 M2
Fieldcote Dr *BWTH/CHD* GL3 .... 137 H4
Field Ct *TET* GL8 .... 281 M3
Field Court Dr *VGL* GL2 .... 159 G3
Field Court Gdns *VGL* GL2 ...... 159 G3
Fielden *GLE* GL4 .... 136 F8
Field End *BWTH/CHD* GL3 .... 113 J4
Fieldfare *GLE* GL4 .... 136 F6
Field Farm Cl
  BRSTK/PCHW BS34 .... 317 H7
Fieldgate Rd *CHELTE/BC* GL52 .. 72 C7
Field La *CHPMW/MSHF* SN14 .... 331 H5
  DSLY GL11 .... 228 F5
  DSLY GL11 .... 228 F7
  DSLY GL11 .... 229 M4
  OLD/WMLY/WICK BS30 .... 338 A8
  THNB/SVB BS35 .... 292 B3
  THNB/SVB BS35 .... 294 A8
Field Rd *CHNTN* OX7 .... 104 B8
  KGWD/HNM BS15 .... 337 L2
  RSTROUD/NAIL GL6 .... 184 C8 🗓
  STROUD GL5 .... 208 E5 🗓
Fields La *BDWAY* WR12 .... 11 L8
Fields Rd *COTS* GL54 .... 167 K8
Field View Dr *MANG/FISH* BS16 .. 327 L5
Fieldways *RSTROUD/NAIL* GL6 .... 232 C7
Fiennes Cl *MANG/FISH* BS16 .... 328 A7 🗓
Fiery La *DSLY* GL11 .... 254 E1
Fifth Av *HORF/LLZ* BS7 .... 326 A5
Filbert Cl *GLE* GL4 .... 136 F8 🗓
Filby Dr *BRSTK/PCHW* BS34 ...... 316 E3 🗓
Filkins Rd *CIR* GL7 .... 221 L8
Filton Av *BRSTK/PCHW* BS34 .... 316 D8
  HORF/LLZ BS7 .... 326 A5
Filton Gv *HORF/LLZ* BS7 .... 326 B5
Filton La *BRSTK/PCHW* BS34 .... 326 F1
Filton Rd *BRSTK/PCHW* BS34 .... 326 F1
  HORF/LLZ BS7 .... 326 B4
  MANG/FISH BS16 .... 327 H2
Filton Wy *GLE* GL4 .... 136 D4
Filwood Broadway
  BRSG/KWL/STAPK BS4............ 346 A3
Filwood Ct *MANG/FISH* BS16 .... 327 K8 🗓
Filwood Dr *KGWD/HNM* BS15...... 338 B3
Filwood Rd *MANG/FISH* BS16 .... 327 J8
Finch Cl *THNB/SVB* BS35 .... 293 L1
Finchcroft La *CHELTE/BC* GL52.. 94 E8
Finch Rd *VGL* GL2 .... 112 F5
  YATE/CS BS37 .... 320 B3
Finlay Pl *GLE* GL4 .... 136 B6 🗓
Finlay Rd *GLE* GL4 .... 136 B6
Finstock Cl *CHELTW* GL51 ...... 115 H3 🗓
Fircroft Cl *GLE* GL4 .... 137 H3
Fircroft Rd *VGL* GL2 .... 112 B6 🗓
Fire Engine La
  FRCTL/WBN BS36 .... 318 F4 🗓
Firethorne Cl *VGL* GL2 .... 112 D6 🗓
Firework Cl *KGWD/HNM* BS15 .... 338 D3
Firfield St *BRSG/KWL/STAPK* BS4 .. 7 J1 🗓
Fir Grove Crs *YATE/CS* BS37 .... 320 C1
Fir Rd *CHPMW/MSHF* SN14 ...... 343 H5
Firs Cl *CHNTN* OX7 .... 125 M1
Firs Rd *RSTROUD/NAIL* GL6 ...... 232 E6
First Av *BRSG/KWL/STAPK* BS4 .. 337 G6
  DSLY GL11 .... 253 L3
The Firs *CHELTW* GL51 .... 93 K4
  STRAT CV37 .... 9 M1
Fir Tree Cl *BRSTK/PCHW* BS34.... 316 A4
  CHELTE/BC GL52 .... 94 C7
Fir Tree La *EVILLE/WHL* BS5 .... 337 J5
Fir View Rd *CIND* GL14 .... 154 A7
Firwood Dr *GLE* GL4 .... 136 A8
Fisher Av *KGWD/HNM* BS15 ...... 338 C2
Fisher Cl *COTS* GL54 .... 102 A4 🗓
Fisherman's Wk *CHEP* NP16 .... 270 B6 🗓
Fishers Rd *BRKLY* GL13 .... 227 C7
Fishers Wy *STROUD* GL5 .... 208 C7
Fish Hl *BDWAY* WR12 .... 33 J4
Fishponds Rd *EVILLE/WHL* BS5 .. 336 E1 🗓
Fishpool Hl *HNBRY/STHM* BS10 .. 315 K7
Fitchett Wk
  HNBRY/STHM BS10 .... 315 H8
Fitzgerald Rd *BMSTR* BS3 .... 336 B8
Fitzhamon Pl *TEWK* GL20 .... 49 H4
Fitzroy Rd *MANG/FISH* BS16 .... 337 K1
Fitzroy St *BRSG/KWL/STAPK* BS4 .. 7 M9
Five Acre Dr *MANG/FISH* BS16 .. 327 H4
Five Acres *DSLY* GL11 .... 253 J3
Five Mile Dr *MIM* GL56 .... 58 A8
Five Trees Ct *TET* GL8 .... 281 M3 🗓
Flaxley Rd *GLE* GL4 .... 135 M8
Flaxley St *CIND* GL14 .... 154 B3
Flaxman Cl *HORF/LLZ* BS7 ...... 326 D5
Flaxpits La *FRCTL/WBN* BS36 .... 317 M5
Flecker's Dr *CHELTW* GL51 ...... 115 H4
Fleece Rd *BDWAY* WR12 .... 32 F2
Fleet La *TEWK* GL20 .... 26 C5
Fleet Rd *TEWK* GL20 .... 26 C5
Fleming Cl *GLE* GL4 .... 112 E5
Flint Rd *CHELTW* GL51 .... 115 C5
Flisteridge Rd *MALM* SN16 ...... 285 K8
Florence Pk *ALMDB* BS32 .... 306 M4
  RDLND/MONT BS6 .... 325 K7
Florence Rd *MANG/FISH* BS16 .. 328 A8
Florida Bvd *CIR* GL7 .... 242 F6
Florida Dr *CHELTE/BC* GL52...... 94 E7

Flowers Hl
  BRSG/KWL/STAPK BS4............ 347 G2
Flowers Hill Cl
  BRSG/KWL/STAPK BS4 .... 347 G2 🗓
Flower Wy *VGL* GL2 .... 112 D7
Flowerwell Rd
  BMSTRD/HC/WWD BS13 .... 345 K6 🗓
The Folders *LYD* GL15 .... 201 K8 🗓
Foley Cl *GLE* GL4 .... 135 M8 🗓
Foley Ri *RTEWK/TIB* GL19 .... 89 G5
Foley Rd *WUE* GL18 .... 86 C3
Folland Av *BWTH/CHD* GL3 ...... 137 K5
Folliard Dr *COTS* GL54 .... 124 C6
Folleigh Cl *LGASH* BS41 .... 344 D1
Folleigh Dr *LGASH* BS41 .... 344 D1
Folleigh La *LGASH* BS41 .... 344 D1
Folliot Cl *MANG/FISH* BS16 ...... 327 J3
Folly Bridge Cl
  YATE/CS BS37 .... 319 M1 🗓
Folly Brook Rd
  MANG/FISH BS16 .... 328 C1
Folly Fld *COTS* GL54 .... 123 J4 🗓
Folly La *MANG/FISH* BS16 ...... 328 C1
  CHELT GL50 .... 2 C1
  CLFD GL16 .... 151 J2
  MTCHDN GL17 .... 107 L5
  STROUD GL5 .... 208 B3
Folly Ri *STROUD* GL5 .... 208 F2
Folly Rd *YATE/CS* BS37 .... 308 B7
The Folly *MANG/FISH* BS16 ...... 328 B4
Fontana Cl
  OLD/WMLY/WICK BS30 .... 338 D8
Fonthill Rd *HNBRY/STHM* BS10 .. 325 M1
Fontmell Cl
  HGRV/WHIT BS14 .... 346 F4 🗓
Fontwell Dr *MANG/FISH* BS16 .. 328 B2
Footes La *FRCTL/WBN* BS36 .... 318 D4
Footshill Cl *KGWD/HNM* BS15 .. 337 L5
Footshill Dr *KGWD/HNM* BS15 .. 337 L4
Footshill Rd *KGWD/HNM* BS15 .. 337 L5
Fop St *DSLY* GL11 .... 254 C2
Forbes Cl *GLE* GL4 .... 137 H5
Forde Cl
  OLD/WMLY/WICK BS30 .... 338 B6 🗓
Fordell Pl
  BRSG/KWL/STAPK BS4............ 336 C8 🗓
Ford House Rd *NWNT* GL18...... 64 E8
Ford La *MANG/FISH* BS16 .... 328 D5
  NWNT GL18 .... 85 J4
Ford St *EVILLE/WHL* BS5 .... 336 E5 🗓
Forest Av *MANG/FISH* BS16...... 327 K8
Forest Cl *CLFD* GL16 .... 150 E5
Forest Dr *HNBRY/STHM* BS10.... 315 L8
Forest Edge *KGWD/HNM* BS15 .. 337 L7
Foresters Rd *TEWK* GL20 .... 48 A7
Forest Hills *ALMDB* BS32 .... 306 D6
Forest Patch *CLFD* GL16 .... 151 J6
Fore Rd *CIND* GL14 .... 154 C2
  MTCHDN GL17 .... 128 C7
Forest Rd *CIND* GL14 .... 154 B3
  CLFD GL16 .... 151 M6
  CLFD GL16 .... 175 L4
  KGWD/HNM BS15 .... 337 M4
  LYD GL15 .... 200 D2
  LYD GL15 .... 201 J7
  MANG/FISH BS16 .... 327 K8
  MTCHDN GL17 .... 129 H5
  WUE GL12 .... 275 K7
Forest Vale Rd *CIND* GL14 ...... 129 M8
  CIND GL14 .... 154 A8
Forest Vw *CIND* GL14 .... 154 A6
Forest View Rd *BRKLY* GL13 .... 227 G7
  GLE GL4 .... 160 A2
Forest Wk *KGWD/HNM* BS15 .... 337 K1 🗓
  MANG/FISH BS16 .... 337 K1 🗓
Forge Hl *MTCHDN* GL17 .... 128 B5
Forge La *NWNT* GL18 .... 65 L8
Forrester Gn
  CHPMW/MSHF SN14 .... 343 K8
Forsdene Wk *CLFD* GL16 .... 175 M1
Forsyte Wy *BWTH/CHD* GL3 ...... 136 D4
Forsythia Cl *BWTH/CHD* GL3 .... 113 J5 🗓
Fortey Rd *COTS* GL54 .... 169 J1
Fortfield Rd *HGRV/WHIT* BS14 .. 346 D6
Fortfields *DSLY* GL11 .... 253 K3 🗓
Fortina Cl *CHELT* GL50 .... 93 L6 🗓
Fort La *DSLY* GL11 .... 253 L5
Fort View Ter *STROUD* GL5 ...... 208 A5
Forty Acre La *STROUD* GL5 ...... 209 J4
  THNB/SVB BS35 .... 293 J8
Forty's Pitch *RWYE* HR9 .... 84 F2
The Forty *HGHW* SN6 .... 288 F4
Foscombe La *RTEWK/TIB* GL19.. 89 H2
Fosscross La *COTS* GL54 .... 192 A5
Fosse Cl *CIR* GL7 .... 238 E2
  GLE GL4 .... 137 C5
Fossedale Av *HGRV/WHIT* BS14 .. 346 D5
Fosse Folly *COTS* GL54 .... 102 A2 🗓
Fosse La *CBATH/BATHN* BA1...... 352 C7
  COTS GL54 .... 102 A2 🗓
Fosseway Av *MIM* GL56 .... 58 C7
Fosseway Cl
  CHPMW/MSHF SN14 .... 343 K8
  MIM GL56 .... 58 D7
Fosseway Dr *MIM* GL56 .... 58 D7
The Fosseway *CFTN/FAIL* BS8.... 335 J5
Foss Fld *THNB/SVB* BS35 .... 273 C4
Foss La *THNB/SVB* BS35 .... 273 G4
Foster Cl *CHELTE/BC* GL52 ...... 72 C6
Foster St *EVILLE/WHL* BS5 ...... 336 D1
Foundry La *EVILLE/WHL* BS5 .... 337 H1
Foundry Rd *CIND* GL14 .... 154 A2
  MALM SN16 .... 303 H7
Fountain Crs *WUE* GL12 .... 277 L5
Fountaine Cl
  EVILLE/WHL BS5 .... 336 E1 🗓🗓
Fountains Dr
  OLD/WMLY/WICK BS30 .... 338 B5
Fountain St *RSTROUD/NAIL* GL6.. 232 D8
Fountain Wy *CHEP* NP16 .... 270 B7 🗓
Four Acre La *MANG/FISH* BS16.. 328 A3
Four Acre Rd *HGHW* SN6 .... 287 H3
Four Acre Crs *MANG/FISH* BS16 .. 328 A2
Four Acre Rd *MANG/FISH* BS16 .. 328 A2
Four Acres
  BMSTRD/HC/WWD BS13............ 345 G7

Four Acres Cl
  BMSTRD/HC/WWD BS13 .... 345 H7
Fourth Av *DSLY* GL11 .... 253 L3
  HORF/LLZ BS7 .... 326 C1
Fowler's Hl *CIR* GL7 .... 218 D5
Fowler's Rd *CHNTN* OX7 .... 104 C7
Fox And Hounds La
  KEYN BS31 .... 348 B6 🗓
Fox Av *YATE/CS* BS37 .... 319 M1
Foxborough Gdns
  ALMDB BS32 .... 316 F1 🗓
Fox Cl *BWTH/CHD* GL3 .... 137 H6
  STROUD GL5 .... 207 L4
Foxcombe Rd
  HGRV/WHIT BS14 .... 346 D7 🗓
Foxcote *KGWD/HNM* BS15 .... 338 B4
  VGL GL2 .... 112 D6 🗓
Foxcote Hl *SHPSTR* CV36 .... 14 D2
Foxcote Rd *BMSTR* BS3 .... 335 J8
Foxcott *HGHW* SN6 .... 264 D7
Fox Cl *OLD/WMLY/WICK* BS30 .. 338 B8
Foxcroft Cl *ALMDB* BS32 .... 317 H5
Foxcroft Rd *EVILLE/WHL* BS5 .. 336 F3
Fox Den Rd *BRSTK/PCHW* BS34 .. 316 F8
  BRSTK/PCHW BS35 .... 326 F1
Fox Elms Rd *GLE* GL4 .... 160 A1
Foxe Rd *FRCTL/WBN* BS36 .... 318 C3
Foxes Bank Dr *CIR* GL7 .... 238 B5 🗓
Foxes Bridge Rd *CIND* GL14 .... 153 M2
Foxes Cl *COTS* GL54 .... 123 H5 🗓
  RSTROUD/NAIL GL6 .... 210 A7
Foxes Dell *RSTROUD/NAIL* GL6 .. 232 C6
Foxes Rw *MIM* GL56 .... 80 C7
Foxfield Av *ALMDB* BS32 .... 306 F8
Foxglove Cl *GLE* GL4 .... 137 C6
  MANG/FISH BS16 .... 327 C7 🗓
  THNB/SVB BS35 .... 293 M1 🗓
Foxglove Wy *CLFD* GL16 .... 175 L4
Foxgrove Dr *CHELTE/BC* GL52 .. 3 K5
Fox Hl *TET* GL8 .... 282 A4
Foxholes La *ALMDB* BS32 .... 292 E8
Foxleaze *HGHW* SN6 .... 288 F2
Foxleigh Crs *VGL* GL2 .... 113 C6 🗓
Foxmoor *CHELTE/BC* GL52 ...... 72 A7
Foxmoor La *STROUD* GL5 .... 207 L3
Fox's La *CLFD* GL16 .... 175 M1
Foxtail Cl *GLE* GL4 .... 136 C7
Foxwell Dr *BWTH/CHD* GL3 .... 137 J3
Fraley Rd
  HNLZ/SM/SNYPK/WT BS9...... 325 J4
Frampton Ct
  OLD/WMLY/WICK BS30 .... 338 B7 🗓
Frampton Crs *MANG/FISH* BS16.. 327 L2 🗓
Frampton Dr *BDWAY* WR12 ...... 11 C7 🗓
Frampton End Rd
  FRCTL/WBN BS36 .... 318 E2
Frampton Ms *CHELTW* GL51 .... 114 D4 🗓
Frampton Rd *GL* GL1 .... 135 M4
France La *BAD* GL9 .... 312 C1
Francis Pl
  OLD/WMLY/WICK BS30 .... 338 B7
Francis Rd *BMSTR* BS3 .... 345 L1 🗓
  HNBRY/STHM BS10 .... 325 L3 🗓
Francis St *CHELTS* GL53 .... 115 M4 🗓
Francis Wy
  OLD/WMLY/WICK BS30 .... 338 F5
Francombe Gv
  HNBRY/STHM BS10 .... 326 A5
Frank Brookes Rd
  CHELTW GL51 .... 93 J7 🗓
Franklyn La *CBRISNE* BS2 ...... 336 B2 🗓
Franklyn St *CBRISNE* BS2 ...... 336 B2
Fraser St *BMSTR* BS3 .... 335 M8
Frayne Rd *BMSTR* BS3 .... 335 J7
Frazier's Folly *CIR* GL7 .... 238 F7
Freame Rd *RSTROUD/NAIL* GL6.. 209 M7
Frederick Pl *CFTN/FAIL* BS8...... 6 A1
Frederick Thomas Rd
  DSLY GL11 .... 229 C7
Fredrick St
  BRSG/KWL/STAPK BS4 .... 7 L9 🗓
Freeland Buildings
  EVILLE/WHL BS5 .... 336 E1 🗓
Freeland Pl *CFTN/FAIL* BS8 .... 335 H5 🗓
Freemans Cl *TEWK* GL20 .... 26 B4 🗓
Freemantle Gdns
  EVILLE/WHL BS5 .... 326 E8 🗓
Freemantle Rd
  EVILLE/WHL BS5 .... 326 E8 🗓
Freestone Rd *CBRISNE* BS2...... 7 K5
Free Tank *CBRISNE* BS2 .... 7 L5
Freezinghill La
  OLD/WMLY/WICK BS30 .... 340 C8
Fremantle La
  RDLND/MONT BS6 .... 335 M2 🗓
Fremantle Rd
  RDLND/MONT BS6 .... 335 M2 🗓
Frenchay Cl *MANG/FISH* BS16 .. 327 K4
Frenchay Park Rd
  MANG/FISH BS16 .... 327 H5
Frenchay Rd *MANG/FISH* BS16.. 327 L4
French La *CLFD* GL16 .... 174 E4
  MONN NP25 .... 174 B3
Freshland Wy
  KGWD/HNM BS15 .... 337 L5
Fretherne Rd *GL* GL1 .... 135 M8
Frewin Cl *CHELTW* GL51 .... 114 F3
Frewins La *CLFD* GL16 .... 174 E4
Friars Cl *CHELT* GL50 .... 115 K6 🗓
Friar's Wk *NWNT* GL18 .... 86 C2 🗓
Friary Grange Pk
  FRCTL/WBN BS36 .... 318 A5
Friary Rd *GLE* GL4 .... 137 C5
  HORF/LLZ BS7 .... 325 M8
Fridays Ham La *HGHW* SN6...... 263 H8
Friday St *RSTROUD/NAIL* GL6 .. 185 H3 🗓
  RSTROUD/NAIL GL6 .... 233 J5
  STRAT CV37 .... 8 A1
  VGL GL2 .... 156 A3 🗓
Friendship Rd
  BRSG/KWL/STAPK BS4............ 346 B1
Friezewood Rd *BMSTR* BS3 ...... 335 J7
Fripp Cl *EVILLE/WHL* BS5 .... 336 D5 🗓
Frith La *WUE* GL12 .... 296 C8
The Frith *RSTROUD/NAIL* GL6 .. 209 M8
Frithwood Cl
  RSTROUD/NAIL GL6 .... 209 M8 🗓

Frithwood Pk
  RSTROUD/NAIL GL6 .... 209 M8
Frobisher Rd *BMSTR* BS3 335
Frocester Hl *STNHO* GL10 230
Frog Furlong La *VGL* GL2 112
Frog La *CBRIS/FH* BS1 6
  DSLY GL11 252
  FRCTL/WBN BS36 319
  RTEWK/TIB GL19 108
  STNHO GL10 230
Frogmarsh La *STROUD* GL5 232
Frogmore Rd *RTEWK/TIB* GL19 .. 108
Frogmore St *CBRIS/FH* BS1 ...... 6 D
Frome Av *STROUD* GL5 208
Frome Brook Rd *LED* HR8 19
Frome Ct *THNB/SVB* BS35 293
Frome Gdns *STROUD* GL5 208
Frome Gln *FRCTL/WBN* BS36 318
Frome Park Rd *STROUD* GL5 208
Frome Pl *MANG/FISH* BS16 ...... 327 G
Frome Rd *YATE/CS* BS37 320
Fromeside *STROUD* GL5 208
Frome St *CBRISNE* BS2 .... 7 J
Frome Valley Rd
  MANG/FISH BS16 327
Frome Valley Walkway
  FRCTL/WBN BS36 318
  FRCTL/WBN BS36 319
  MANG/FISH BS16 319
  YATE/CS BS37 309
Frome Valley Wy *YATE/CS* BS37.. 321
Frome Vw *FRCTL/WBN* BS36 318
Frome Wy *FRCTL/WBN* BS36...... 318
Front St *STNHO* GL10 231
Froomshaw Rd
  MANG/FISH BS16 327
Frost Rd *LED* HR8 19
Frowens La *RWYE* HR9 84
Fry's Cl *MANG/FISH* BS16 .... 326 F
Frys Hl *KGWD/HNM* BS15 .... 338 A
  KGWD/HNM BS15 .... 338 A
Fulbrook Cl *CHELTW* GL51 ...... 92 F
Fulford Rd
  BMSTRD/HC/WWD BS13 345
Fulford Wk
  BMSTRD/HC/WWD BS13 .... 345 K
Fullers Av *HGHW* SN6 337
Fuller's La *RTEWK/TIB* GL19 88
Fulmar Cl *THNB/SVB* BS35 ...... 293 M
Fulton Rd *COTS* GL54 124
Furber Cl *EVILLE/WHL* BS5 337
Furber Rdg *EVILLE/WHL* BS5 337
Furber Rd *EVILLE/WHL* BS5 337
Furber V *EVILLE/WHL* BS5 337
Furlong Cl *LED* HR8 .... 19 M
Furlong La *CHELTE/BC* GL52 72
Furlong Meadow *SHPSTR* CV36.. 16
Furlong Rd *GL* GL1 136
The Furlong
  HNLZ/SM/SNYPK/WT BS9 325
Furnace Cl *CIND* GL14 .... 154 A
Furnace La *NWNT* GL18 86
Furnace Va *LYD* GL15 202
Furnwood *EVILLE/WHL* BS5 337
Furze Cft *VGL* GL2 159
Furze Hill Rd *SHPSTR* CV36 16
Furze La *CHCAM* GL55 13
Furze Rd *MANG/FISH* BS16 327
The Furze *GLE* GL4 136
Furzewood Rd
  KGWD/HNM BS15 338
Fylton Cft *HGRV/WHIT* BS14 346

G

Gabb La *RTEWK/TIB* GL19 68
Gable Cl *THNB/SVB* BS35 315
Gable Point *CHELTE/BC* GL52 .. 72
Gable Rd *EVILLE/WHL* BS5 ...... 336 C
Gadshill Dr *BRSTK/PCHW* BS34.. 317
Gadshill Rd *CHELTS* GL53 116
  EVILLE/WHL BS5............ 326
Gadwell Rd *TEWK* GL20 48
Gages Cl *KGWD/HNM* BS15 338
Gages Rd *KGWD/HNM* BS15 338
Gainsborough Dr *GL* GL1 159
Gainsborough Rd *KEYN* BS31.... 348
Gallivan Cl *BRSTK/PCHW* BS34 .. 316
Gallops La *CHELTE/BC* GL52 94
Galway Rd
  BRSG/KWL/STAPK BS4............ 346
Gambier Parry Gdns *VGL* GL2 .. 112
Gambles La *CHELTE/BC* GL52 .. 112
Gambril La *WUE* GL12 275
Ganborough Rd *MIM* GL56 58
Gander Cl
  BMSTRD/HC/WWD BS13 .... 345 K
Gander La *TEWK* GL20 48
  TEWK GL20 50
Gannaway La *TEWK* GL20 48
Gannet Cl *BWTH/CHD* GL3 ...... 138 A
Gannicox Rd *STROUD* GL5 208
Ganzell La *DSLY* GL11 253
Garden City Wy *CHEP* NP16 .... 270 A
Garden Cl *CHCAM* GL55 34
  CIR GL7 .... 238 C
  EVE WR11 10
  HNLZ/SM/SNYPK/WT BS9 325
Gardeners Wk *LGASH* BS41 .... 344 D
Gardeners Wy *NWNT* GL18 ...... 86 B
  STNHO GL10 207
Gardenia Gv *CHELTW* GL51 115
Garden Rd *CHELTS* GL53 115
The Gardens *CHELTE/BC* GL52 .. 94 A
  MANG/FISH BS16 327
The Garden *STROUD* GL5 .... 232 C
Garden Wy *VGL* GL2 112
Gardiner Cl *RSTROUD/NAIL* GL6.. 210
Gardiners Cl *BWTH/CHD* GL3 .. 113 J
Gardner Av
  BMSTRD/HC/WWD BS13............ 345
Gardner's La *CHELTW* GL51 93
Garfield Rd *EVILLE/WHL* BS5.... 337
Garlands Rd *LYD* GL15 224
Garnalls Rd *GLE* GL4 137
Garnet St *BMSTR* BS3............ 345

arnett Pl *MANG/FISH* BS16 .... 328 B4
arrett Dr *ALMDB* BS32 .... 316 F4 🛾
arth Rd
  BMSTRD/HC/WWD BS13 .... 345 J3
he Garth *LED* HR8 .... 19 M1 🛾
arvey Cl *CHEP* NP16 .... 270 B7
asferry Rd *CBRIS/FH* BS1 .... 6 B7
he Gaskins *HORF/LLZ* BS7 .... 326 C6
ias La *CBRISNE* BS2 .... 7 L5
  HGHW SN6 .... 288 D7
assons Rd *CIR* GL7 .... 244 E6
aston Av *KEYN* BS31 .... 348 B6
astord Rd *MALM* SN16 .... 303 H8
he Gastons *AVONM* BS11 .... 324 C3
asworks La *COTS* GL54 .... 123 H6
atcombe Cl *CHELTE/BC* GL52 ... 72 A8 🛾
atcombe Dr
  BRSTK/PCHW BS34 .... 317 G7
atcombe Rd
  BMSTRD/HC/WWD BS13 .... 345 K6
atehouse Av
  BMSTRD/HC/WWD BS13 .... 345 J6
atehouse Cl
  BMSTRD/HC/WWD BS13 .... 345 J6 🛾
atehouse Ct
  BMSTRD/HC/WWD BS13 .... 345 K6 🛾
atehouse Wy
  BMSTRD/HC/WWD BS13 .... 345 J6
atesby Md *BRSTK/PCHW* BS34 .. 317 G6
athorne Rd *BMSTR* BS3 .... 6 A9
atmeres Rd *GLE* GL4 .... 136 E8 🛾
atton Rd *CBRISNE* BS2 .... 336 C2
atton Wy *GLE* GL4 .... 137 H2
aunt's Earthcott La
  ALMDB BS32 .... 307 K6
aunt's La *CBRIS/FH* BS1 .... 6 D3 🛾
aunts Rd *YATE/CS* BS37 .... 320 D3
ay Elms Rd
  BMSTRD/HC/WWD BS13 .... 345 J7
ayner Rd *HORF/LLZ* BS7 .... 326 C2
ays Rd *KGWD/HNM* BS15 .... 337 K7
aythorne Crs *YATE/CS* BS37 ... 319 M1
azelle Cl *VGL* GL2 .... 159 H1
azzard Cl *FRCTL/WBN* BS36 ... 318 A4
ee Moors *KGWD/HNM* BS15 ... 338 B4 🛾
efle Cl *CBRIS/FH* BS1 .... 6 A7
enista Wy *CHELTW* GL51 .... 115 H6 🛾
eoffrey Cl
  BMSTRD/HC/WWD BS13 .... 345 G5
eorge Ct
  RSTROUD/NAIL GL6 .... 185 H3 🛾
eorge Dowty Dr *TEWK* GL20 ... 49 G2 🛾
eorge La *CHCAM* GL55 .... 34 C1
  CHPMW/MSHF SN14 .... 342 A2
  CIND GL14 .... 154 E1
eorge Readings Wy
  CHELTW GL51 .... 93 H7
eorge Rd *LYD* GL15 .... 177 J8
eorge St *EVILLE/WHL* BS5 ..... 336 E3 🛾
  GL GL1 .... 5 C5
  RSTROUD/NAIL GL6 .... 210 C2
  RSTROUD/NAIL GL6 .... 232 E7
  STROUD GL5 .... 208 E4
eorge Whitefield Cl
  GLE GL4 .... 136 E7 🛾
eorge Whitefield Ct
  CBRIS/FH BS1 .... 7 H2 🛾
eorgian Cl *GLE* GL4 .... 137 C8
erald Rd *BMSTR* BS3 .... 345 J8
eralds Wy *RSTROUD/NAIL* GL6 .. 210 A8
ere Cl *GLE* GL4 .... 159 M2
errard Cl
  BRSG/KWL/STAPK BS4 .... 345 M4
errard Rd *COTS* GL54 .... 124 D8
errards Rd *SHPSTR* CV36 .... 16 B6
errish Av *EVILLE/WHL* BS5 ..... 336 E3
  MANG/FISH BS16 .... 328 B6
ervase Rd *COTS* GL54 .... 74 C4
ibbsfold Rd
  BMSTRD/HC/WWD BS13 .... 345 L8
ibraltar Wy *CHEP* NP16 .... 270 D7
ibson Rd *STROUD* GL5 .... 209 H4
ibson Rd *BWTH/CHD* GL3 ...... 113 G4
  LED HR8 .... 19 L2
  RDLND/MONT BS6 .... 335 M2
iddynap La *STROUD* GL5 .... 232 C4
iffard Wy *CHELTS* GL53 .... 115 M7
ifford Cl *VGL* GL2 .... 112 E6 🛾
  YATE/CS BS37 .... 309 J3
ifford Rd *HNBRY/STHM* BS10 .. 315 H7
iffords Pl
  BMSTRD/HC/WWD BS13 .... 345 J4
ilbert Hl *BRKLY* BS13 .... 227 G7 🛾
ilbert Rd *EVILLE/WHL* BS5 ..... 336 E3
  KGWD/HNM BS15 .... 337 M2
  VGL GL2 .... 112 E6 🛾
ilberts La *GLE* GL4 .... 160 B4
ilda Cl *HGRV/WHIT* BS14 .... 346 D6
ilda Crs *HGRV/WHIT* BS14 ..... 346 D5
ilda Sq West *HGRV/WHIT* BS14.. 346 D6
ilder Rd *CHELTE/BC* GL52 .... 94 B1
ilders Paddock
  CHELTE/BC GL52 .... 72 B7 🛾
iles Av *HGHW* SN6 .... 288 F4
iles Cox *VGL* GL2 .... 159 H3
illard Cl *KGWD/HNM* BS15 ..... 337 K3
illard Rd *KGWD/HNM* BS15 ... 337 K3
ill Av *MANG/FISH* BS16 .... 327 K5
illebank Cl
  HGRV/WHIT BS14 .... 346 F6 🛾
illett Cl *COTS* GL54 .... 74 C6 🛾
illett's La *RBANSW* OX15 .... 17 L7
illingham Hl
  EVILLE/WHL BS5 .... 337 K6 🛾
illingstool *THNB/SVB* BS35 ..... 293 L3
illray Cl *HORF/LLZ* BS7 .... 326 C5
ilpin Av *GLE* GL4 .... 137 H2
ilpin Cl *KGWD/HNM* BS15 ...... 338 B2 🛾
ilroy Cl *OLD/WMLY/WICK* BS30.. 338 D8
ilslake Av *HNBRY/STHM* BS10 .. 315 K8
imson Cl *GLE* GL4 .... 159 M1
ipsy La *RSTROUD/NAIL* GL6 ... 234 D2
  STNHO GL10 .... 231 C2
ipsy Patch La
  BRSTK/PCHW BS34 .... 316 E5
he Glades *EVILLE/WHL* BS5 .... 337 L6 🛾
ladiator Cl *BWTH/CHD* GL3 ... 138 A6 🛾

Gladstone Dr
  MANG/FISH BS16 .... 328 A8 🛾
Gladstone La
  FRCTL/WBN BS36 .... 318 E4 🛾
Gladstone Rd *CHELTS* GL53 .... 116 C6
  GL GL1 .... 135 L5
  HGRV/WHIT BS14 .... 346 D5
  KGWD/HNM BS15 .... 337 M2 🛾
Gladstone St *BMSTR* BS3 ...... 335 J8
  EVILLE/WHL BS5 .... 336 F4 🛾
  MANG/FISH BS16 .... 327 M8
Glaisdale Rd *MANG/FISH* BS16 .. 327 J4
Glamorgan Rd *CHELTW* GL51 .. 115 G5 🛾
Glanville Gdns
  KGWD/HNM BS15 .... 338 A4
Glass House La *CBRISNE* BS2 .. 336 D6 🛾
Glastonbury Cl
  OLD/WMLY/WICK BS30 .... 338 B6 🛾
Glebe Cl *CIR* GL7 .... 214 B7 🛾
  COTS GL54 .... 102 A3 🛾
  LGASH BS41 .... 344 D1
  MTCHDN GL17 .... 106 C8
  NWNT GL18 .... 86 B2
  VGL GL2 .... 205 H1
Glebe Ct *NWNT* GL18 .... 86 B2
Glebe Farm Ct *CHELTW* GL51 .. 115 H6 🛾
Glebe Fld *ALMDB* BS32 .... 306 C6
Glebeland Dr *TEWK* GL20 ...... 27 H5 🛾
Glebelands Rd
  BRSTK/PCHW BS34 .... 316 C8 🛾
Glebe La *GLE* GL4 .... 261 H4
Glebe Orch *LED* HR8 .... 40 C5
Glebe Rd *BDWAY* WR12 .... 31 H2
  CHELTE/BC GL52 .... 94 D7
  EVILLE/WHL BS5 .... 337 G3 🛾
  LGASH BS41 .... 344 E2
  NWNT GL18 .... 86 B3
  RSTROUD/NAIL GL6 .... 233 K5 🛾
The Glebe *CIR* GL7 .... 211 M8
  THNB/SVB BS35 .... 304 E4
Glebe Wy *NWNT* GL18 .... 86 B2
Gledemoor Dr
  FRCTL/WBN BS36 .... 318 E4
Glena Av *BRSG/KWL/STAPK* BS4.. 346 D1
Glenarm Rd
  BRSG/KWL/STAPK BS4............ 347 G1
Glenarm Wk
  BRSG/KWL/STAPK BS4............ 347 G1
Glen Av *CFTN/FAIL* BS8 .... 334 B3
Glenavon Pk
  HNLZ/SM/SNYPK/WT BS9 .... 324 E7 🛾
Glen Brook
  HNLZ/SM/SNYPK/WT BS9 .... 324 F7
Glenburn Rd *KGWD/HNM* BS15 .. 337 K2
Glencairn Av *GL* GL1 .... 159 L2
Glencairn Crt *CHELTW* GL51 ... 115 J3 🛾
Glencairn Park Rd
  CHELTW GL51 .... 115 J3
Glen Cl *SHPSTR* CV36 .... 16 B5
Glencoe La *MTCHDN* GL17 ..... 130 C4
Glen Ct *STNHO* GL10 .... 207 H3 🛾
Glencoyne Sq
  HNBRY/STHM BS10 .... 325 L1
Glendale *CFTN/FAIL* BS8 .... 335 H5 🛾
  MANG/FISH BS16 .... 327 L8 🛾
Glendare St *EVILLE/WHL* BS5 .. 336 E5 🛾
Glendevon Rd
  HGRV/WHIT BS14 .... 346 C8 🛾
Glendower Cl
  BWTH/CHD GL3 .... 113 H3 🛾
Glen Dr
  HNLZ/SM/SNYPK/WT BS9 .... 324 F6
Gleneagles *YATE/CS* BS37 ..... 320 A2
Gleneagles Dr
  HNBRY/STHM BS10 .... 314 F8 🛾
Gleneagles Rd
  OLD/WMLY/WICK BS30 .... 338 D5 🛾
Glenfall *YATE/CS* BS37 .... 319 M4
Glenfall St *CHELTE/BC* GL52 .... 2 F4
Glenfall Wy *CHELTE/BC* GL52 .. 116 D5 🛾
Glenfrome Rd *CBRISNE* BS2 .... 336 C1
  EVILLE/WHL BS5 .... 326 B8
Glen La *BRSG/KWL/STAPK* BS4 .. 346 F1
Glenlea Gv *CHELTW* GL51 ..... 115 H6 🛾
Glen Pk *EVILLE/WHL* BS5 .... 336 E1
Glen Park Crs *STROUD* GL5 .... 208 C3
Glen Park Gdns
  EVILLE/WHL BS5 .... 337 J3
Glenroy Av *KGWD/HNM* BS15 .. 337 K2
Glensanda Ct *CHELT* GL50 .... 2 C7
Glenside Cl *MANG/FISH* BS16 .. 327 L4
Glenside Pk
  MANG/FISH BS16 .... 327 G6 🛾
The Glen *KGWD/HNM* BS15 ..... 337 K7
  RDLND/MONT BS6 .... 325 K8
  YATE/CS BS37 .... 320 A1
Glenthorne Cl *STNHO* GL10 ... 207 H2 🛾
Glentworth Rd *CFTN/FAIL* BS8 .. 6 A4 🛾
  RDLND/MONT BS6 .... 335 L1 🛾
Glenwood *MANG/FISH* BS16 ... 327 L8 🛾
Glenwood Dr
  OLD/WMLY/WICK BS30 .... 338 B7 🛾
Glenwood Rd
  HNBRY/STHM BS10 .... 325 L4
Glevum Cl *VGL* GL2 .... 5 L1
Glevum Wy *GLE* GL4 .... 137 G2
Gloster Av *EVILLE/WHL* BS5 ... 326 F8 🛾
Gloucester
  BRSTK/PCHW BS34 .... 316 F6
Gloucester La *CBRISNE* BS2 ..... 7 K2 🛾
  CHCAM GL55 .... 8 F8
Gloucester Pl *CHELTE/BC* GL52 .. 2 E5
Gloucester Rd *ALMDB* BS32 .... 306 E6
  BRKLY GL13 .... 226 E3
  BRSTK/PCHW BS34 .... 316 D2
  CBATH/BATHN BA1 .... 351 A6
  CBATH/BATHN BA1 .... 351 K6
  CHELTW GL51 .... 114 C4
  CHEP NP16 .... 270 C1
  CIR GL7 .... 214 A7
  CLFD GL16 .... 175 K1
  COTS GL54 .... 118 B8
  HORF/LLZ BS7 .... 335 M1
  MALM SN16 .... 303 J7 🛾
  MANG/FISH BS16 .... 328 A8 🛾
  MTCHDN GL17 .... 130 D2
  NWNT GL18 .... 87 J1

  RSTROUD/NAIL GL6 .... 185 H1
  RTEWK/TIB GL19 .... 66 E5
  RTEWK/TIB GL19 .... 70 A4
  STNHO GL10 .... 207 H3
  TEWK GL20 .... 48 A7
  THNB/SVB BS35 .... 293 L1
  THNB/SVB BS35 .... 307 H1
Gloucester Rd North
  BRSTK/PCHW BS34 .... 316 C8
  BRSTK/PCHW BS34 .... 326 C1
  HORF/LLZ BS7 .... 326 B2
Gloucestershire Wy
  BWTH/CHD GL3 .... 114 B7
  CHELTE/BC GL52 .... 73 J3
  CHEP NP16 .... 270 A3
  CLFD GL16 .... 176 D2
  COTS GL54 .... 75 K6
  COTS GL54 .... 77 H2
  COTS GL54 .... 101 K1
  COTS GL54 .... 121 J7
  COTS GL54 .... 141 G6
  LYD GL15 .... 200 C2
  LYD GL15 .... 223 J6
  MTCHDN GL17 .... 107 H5
  RTEWK/TIB GL19 .... 108 A7
Gloucester St *CBRISNE* BS2 ...... 7 H1 🛾
  CFTN/FAIL BS8 .... 335 H4 🛾
  CIR GL7 .... 238 B1
  COTS GL54 .... 74 B7
  EVILLE/WHL BS5 .... 326 F8
  NWNT GL18 .... 86 D3
  STROUD GL5 .... 208 E4 🛾
  WUE GL12 .... 277 J3
Glynbridge Gdns *CHELTW* GL51 .. 93 H6
  CHELTW GL51 .... 115 G7
Glyndthorpe Gv
  CHELTW GL51 .... 115 G6 🛾
Glynfield Ri *STROUD* GL5 .... 207 L4
Glynrosa Rd *CHELTS* GL53 .... 116 D6 🛾
Glyn V *BMSTR* BS3 .... 345 M2
Goddard Wy *GLE* GL4 .... 159 M1
Godfrey Cl *CHELTW* GL51 ..... 115 J4
Godfrey Ct
  OLD/WMLY/WICK BS30 .... 338 B7 🛾
Godwin Rd *COTS* GL54 .... 74 C4
Goffenton Dr *MANG/FISH* BS16 .. 327 K5
Goldcrest Cl *STNHO* GL10 ..... 207 H3 🛾
Goldcrest Rd *YATE/CS* BS37 ... 320 B4
Golden Cl *GL* GL1 .... 159 L1
Golden Farm Rd *CIR* GL7 ...... 238 E3 🛾
Golden La *CHNTN* OX7 .... 83 J6
  WUE GL12 .... 277 H7
Golden Miller Rd *CHELT* GL50 .. 93 L6
Goldney Av *CFTN/FAIL* BS8 .... 335 J5
  OLD/WMLY/WICK BS30 .... 338 E4
Goldney Rd *CFTN/FAIL* BS8 .... 335 J5
Goldsborough Cl *GLE* GL4 .... 136 D4
Goldsbury Wk *AVONM* BS11 ... 324 C2
Goldsmith Rd *CHELTW* GL51 .. 115 G1
Golf Club La *BWTH/CHD* GL3.. 137 J3
Golf Course La
  BRSTK/PCHW BS34 .... 316 B8
Golf Course Rd
  RSTROUD/NAIL GL6 .... 185 H2
Gooch Ct
  OLD/WMLY/WICK BS30 .... 338 E8
Goodeve Rd
  HNLZ/SM/SNYPK/WT BS9 .... 334 F1
Goodhind St *EVILLE/WHL* BS5.. 336 C3
Goodier's La *TEWK* GL20 .... 26 C5
Goodmoor Crs *BWTH/CHD* GL3 .. 113 J5
Goodneston Rd
  MANG/FISH BS16 .... 327 J8
Goodrich Hl *RTEWK/TIB* GL19 .. 89 J3
Goodridge Av *GL* GL1 .... 135 J8
Goodring Hl *AVONM* BS11 .... 324 C2
Good Shepherd Cl
  HORF/LLZ BS7 .... 325 L7 🛾
Goodwin Cl *GL* GL1 .... 136 A4 🛾
Goodwin Dr *HGRV/WHIT* BS14 .. 346 B7
Goodwood Gdns
  MANG/FISH BS16 .... 328 B2 🛾
Goodyere St *GL* GL1 .... 4 F8
Goolden St
  BRSG/KWL/STAPK BS4 .... 336 C6 🛾
Goose Acre *ALMDB* BS32 ...... 317 H5 🛾
  ALMDB BS32 .... 317 J5 🛾
Gooseacre La *CIR* GL7 .... 238 C1 🛾
Goose Green
  OLD/WMLY/WICK BS30 .... 338 E2
  YATE/CS BS37 .... 310 A8
Goose Green Wy *YATE/CS* BS37 .. 309 L7
Gooseland Cl
  HGRV/WHIT BS14 .... 346 B8 🛾
Gooselands *MALM* SN16 .... 283 M6
Goose La *CIND* GL14 .... 157 H3
  STRAT CV37 .... 9 L1
Gopshill La *COTS* GL54 .... 73 M2
Gordon Av *EVILLE/WHL* BS5 ... 337 G2
Gordon Rd *EVILLE/WHL* BS5 ... 337 G2
  VGL GL2 .... 111 C6 🛾
Gordon Rd *CBRISNE* BS2 .... 336 B2
  CHELTS GL53 .... 115 L6
  EVILLE/WHL BS5 .... 336 F1
Gore Rd *BMSTR* BS3 .... 335 J8
Gore's Marsh Rd *BMSTR* BS3 .. 345 J1
Gorham Cl *AVONM* BS11 ...... 324 E1 🛾
Gorlands Rd *YATE/CS* BS37 ... 320 E2
Gorlangton Cl
  HGRV/WHIT BS14 .... 346 C4
Gorse Cl *COTS* GL54 .... 123 K6
  GLE GL4 .... 137 H7
Gorse Cover Rd
  THNB/SVB BS35 .... 304 C4
Gorse Hl *EVE* WR11 .... 29 K1
  MANG/FISH BS16 .... 327 L8
Gorse La *CFTN/FAIL* BS8 .... 6 A4
  CHPMW/MSHF SN14 .... 341 G3
  CLFD GL16 .... 175 L6 🛾
Gorse Meadow *COTS* GL54 ... 123 K7
The Gorse *COTS* GL54 .... 123 J6

Gorsley Gdns *RWYE* HR9 .... 84 E3 🛾
Gosditch *HGHW* SN6 .... 264 E7
  HGHW SN6 .... 287 C3
Gosditch St *CIR* GL7 .... 238 C2 🛾
Gosforth Rd
  HNBRY/STHM BS10 .... 325 K2
Goshawk Rd *VGL* GL2 .... 135 H8
Goslet Rd *HGRV/WHIT* BS14 ... 347 G6
Gossington Br *VGL* GL2 .... 228 F3
Goss Wood Cnr *VGL* GL2 ...... 159 G3 🛾
Gotherington Flds
  CHELTE/BC GL52 .... 72 A3
Gotherington La
  CHELTE/BC GL52 .... 72 C6
Gotley Rd
  BRSG/KWL/STAPK BS4 .... 346 F1
Gott Dr *BRSG/KWL/STAPK* BS4 .. 336 F6
Gouda Wy *GL* GL1 .... 4 E3
Gould Dr *TEWK* GL20 .... 49 G2
Goulston Rd
  BMSTRD/HC/WWD BS13 .... 345 J6
Goulston Wk
  BMSTRD/HC/WWD BS13 .... 345 J6 🛾
Goulter St *EVILLE/WHL* BS5 ... 336 D5 🛾
Gourney La *AVONM* BS11 ...... 324 D1
Cover Rd *KGWD/HNM* BS15 ... 337 L8
Gowle Rd *STROUD* GL5 .... 208 F5
Grace Cl *YATE/CS* BS37 .... 320 E2
Grace Ct *MANG/FISH* BS16 .... 327M5
Grace Dr *COTS* GL54 .... 169 J1
  KGWD/HNM BS15 .... 338 C2
Grace Park Rd
  BRSG/KWL/STAPK BS4 .... 346 F2
Grace Mead *MANG/FISH* BS16 .. 327 L6
Graces Pitch *NWNT* GL18 .... 86 C3
Grafton La *RTEWK/TIB* GL19 ... 44 D5
Grafton Rd *CHELT* GL50 .... 115 L4
  VGL GL2 .... 5 M3
Graham Pl *CHELTW* GL51 .... 92 F8
Graham Rd *BMSTR* BS3 .... 335 L8 🛾
  EVILLE/WHL BS5 .... 336 D2 🛾
  MANG/FISH BS16 .... 328 A5
Grahamstown Gv *CHEP* NP16 .. 270 D3 🛾
Grahamstown Rd *CHEP* NP16 .. 270 C4
Grainger Ct *AVONM* BS11 ...... 324 A4 🛾
Grampian Cl
  OLD/WMLY/WICK BS30 .... 338 E7 🛾
Granbrook La *CHCAM* GL55 ..... 9 G7
Granby Hl *CFTN/FAIL* BS8 ...... 335 H5
Granby Rd *SHPSTR* CV36 .... 16 D1
Grandmother's Rock La
  OLD/WMLY/WICK BS30 .... 349M1
Grange Av *BRSTK/PCHW* BS34 .. 316 E5
  KGWD/HNM BS15 .... 337M6
Grange Cl *ALMDB* BS32 .... 316 E1
  RSTROUD/NAIL GL6 .... 233 H5
Grange Cl North
  HNLZ/SM/SNYPK/WT BS9 .... 325 K5 🛾
Grange Ct *CIR* GL7 .... 214 B7
  KGWD/HNM BS15 .... 337 M6 🛾
  TEWK GL20 .... 49 H2
Grange Court La
  RTEWK/TIB GL19 .... 108 C8
Grange Court Rd *CIND* GL14 ... 132 D7
  HNLZ/SM/SNYPK/WT BS9 .... 325 J5
Grange Dr *CHELTE/BC* GL52 .... 72 B8
  MANG/FISH BS16 .... 327 L5
Grange Pk
  HNLZ/SM/SNYPK/WT BS9 .... 325 K5
  MANG/FISH BS16 .... 327 L3
  RWYE HR9 .... 126 D4
Grange Rd
  BMSTRD/HC/WWD BS13 .... 345 J6
  CFTN/FAIL BS8 .... 335 J4
  GL GL1 .... 159 L1
  GLE GL4 .... 159M2
  KEYN BS31 .... 348 B3
  TEWK GL20 .... 49 H2
The Grange *CHNTN* OX7 .... 104 B7
  HNLZ/SM/SNYPK/WT BS9 .... 324 F4
Grange Vw *STROUD* GL5 .... 208 E3
Grangeville Cl
  OLD/WMLY/WICK BS30 .... 338 D8
Grange Wk *CHELTS* GL53 ...... 116 D6
Grangewood Cl
  MANG/FISH BS16 .... 327 L5 🛾
Granley Cl *CHELTW* GL51 ...... 115 H3 🛾
Granley Dr *CHELTW* GL51 ..... 115 H3 🛾
Granley Gdns *CHELTW* GL51 .. 115 H3
Granley Rd *CHELTW* GL51 ..... 115 H3
Granna La *CHELTE/BC* GL52 .... 72 F3
Granny's La
  KGWD/HNM BS15 .... 338 A5 🛾
Gransmoor Gra *BWTH/CHD* GL3.. 137 K4
Grantham La
  KGWD/HNM BS15 .... 337 L3 🛾
Grantham Rd *KGWD/HNM* BS15.. 337 L2
Grantley Crs *CIR* GL7 .... 238 C4 🛾
Grantson Cl
  BRSG/KWL/STAPK BS4 .... 347 G1
Granville Cl *KGWD/HNM* BS15 .. 337 K8
Granville Rd *CBATH/BATHN* BA1.. 351 J4
Granville St *CHELT* GL50 .... 2 B3
  EVILLE/WHL BS5 .... 336 E5
  GL GL1 .... 135 L5
Grasby Cl *GLE* GL4 .... 137 G4 🛾
Grasington Dr *YATE/CS* BS37 .. 320 C2
Grasmere Cl
  HNBRY/STHM BS10 .... 325 J3
Grasmere Rd *CHELTW* GL51 ... 115 H4 🛾
  VGL GL2 .... 112 E7
Grass Meers Dr
  HGRV/WHIT BS14 .... 346 C7
Grassmere Gdns
  OLD/WMLY/WICK BS30 .... 338 F5
Gratitude Rd *EVILLE/WHL* BS5 .. 336 C2
Gratton Rd *CHELT* GL50 .... 115 L5
Gratton St *CHELT* GL50 .... 2 C9
Gravel Hill Rd *YATE/CS* BS37 ... 310 B3
Gravel Pit La *CHELTE/BC* GL52.. 94 E6
Gravel Pits Cl *TEWK* GL20 ...... 27 H5 🛾
Gravel Wk *CHELTE/BC* GL52 ... 94 E3
Graveney Cl
  BRSG/KWL/STAPK BS4 .... 346 F2 🛾
Graveney Rd *COTS* GL54 .... 169 J1
Gravney Ct *CHELTW* GL51 ...... 93 G7
Gray Cl *VGL* GL2 .... 112 F4

Grayle Rd *HNBRY/STHM* BS10 .. 315 H8
Grayling Cl *GLE* GL4 .... 137 G7 🛾
Gray Rd *CIR* GL7 .... 239 H7
Gray's Cl *HNBRY/STHM* BS10 .. 325 G9 🛾
Gray's La *MIM* GL56 .... 58 D6
Grayston Cl *TEWK* GL20 .... 48 C3
Great Ann St *CBRISNE* BS2 ...... 7 K2
Great Brockeridge
  HNLZ/SM/SNYPK/WT BS9 .... 325 H5
Great Dowles
  OLD/WMLY/WICK BS30 .... 338 C7
Greatfield Dr *CHELTS* GL53 ... 116 B6
Greatfield La *CHELTW* GL51 ... 115 H6 🛾
Great George St *CBRIS/FH* BS1 .. 6 B4
  CBRISNE BS2 .... 7 J2
Great Gv *GLE* GL4 .... 136 F4
Great Hayles Rd
  HGRV/WHIT BS14 .... 346 C4
Great Leaze
  OLD/WMLY/WICK BS30 .... 338 C7
Great Meadow Rd *ALMDB* BS32.. 317 H4
Great Norwood St *CHELT* GL50... 2 B9
Great Park Rd *ALMDB* BS32 ... 306 E8
Great Stoke Wy
  BRSTK/PCHW BS34 .... 316 F8
  BRSTK/PCHW BS34 .... 326 F1
Great Western Ct *GL* GL1 .... 5 J7
Great Western La
  EVILLE/WHL BS5 .... 336 E5 🛾
Great Western Rd
  BRKLY GL13 .... 226 D2 🛾
  CHELT GL50 .... 2 A4
  GL GL1 .... 5 C5
Great Western Ter *CHELT* GL50.... 2 A4
Grebe Cl *GLE* GL4 .... 136 E6
Grebe Sq *COTS* GL54 .... 124 C7
Green Acre *BWTH/CHD* GL3 ... 138 A6
  LYD GL15 .... 200 D4
Greenacre Rd *HGRV/WHIT* BS14.. 346 C6
Greenacres *CBATH/BATHN* BA1 .. 350 D8
  TEWK GL20 .... 26 B4
Greenaways *NWNT* GL18 .... 86 B2 🛾
Green Bank *BWTH/CHD* GL3 ... 138 A7
Greenbank Av *EVILLE/WHL* BS5.. 336 C2
Greenbank Av West
  EVILLE/WHL BS5 .... 336 D2 🛾
Greenbank Cl *MTCHDN* GL17 .. 129M5
Greenbank Rd *BMSTR* BS3 ..... 335 J7
  EVILLE/WHL BS5 .... 336 C2
  KGWD/HNM BS15 .... 337M6
Greenbank Vw
  EVILLE/WHL BS5 .... 336 E1
Green Cl *BDWAY* WR12 .... 32 A1
  BWTH/CHD GL3 .... 138 A7
  DSLY GL11 .... 254 E1
Green Cft *EVILLE/WHL* BS5 .... 337 J2
Greendale Rd *BMSTR* BS3 ..... 336 A8
  RDLND/MONT BS6 .... 325 K7
Green Dell Cl
  HNBRY/STHM BS10 .... 314 F8 🛾
Greenditch Av
  BMSTRD/HC/WWD BS13 .... 345 L6
Greenditch St *THNB/SVB* BS35 .. 305 L2
Greendown *EVILLE/WHL* BS5 ... 337 J4
Green Dragon Rd
  FRCTL/WBN BS36 .... 317M6
Greenfield Av
  HNBRY/STHM BS10 .... 325 M3 🛾
Greenfield Rd *CLFD* GL16 ...... 151 K8
  HNBRY/STHM BS10 .... 325 M3 🛾
  MTCHDN GL17 .... 128 C6
Greenfields Cl *SHPSTR* CV36 ... 16 B6
Green Gdns *BWTH/CHD* GL3 ... 138 A7
Green Hayes *YATE/CS* BS37 ... 320 E3
Greenhill *THNB/SVB* BS35 ..... 293 J7
Greenhill Cl *CIND* GL14 .... 154 C2
Greenhill Ct *GL* GL1 .... 159 J1
Greenhill Down
  THNB/SVB BS35 .... 293 J7
Greenhill Gdns *THNB/SVB* BS35 .. 293 J7
Greenhill Gv *BMSTR* BS3 ...... 345 J1
Greenhill La *AVONM* BS11 ..... 324 C2
  THNB/SVB BS35 .... 293 H8
Greenhill Rd *THNB/SVB* BS35 .. 293 J7
Greenhills Cl *CHELTS* GL53 ... 116 A6
Greenhills Rd *CHELTS* GL53 ... 116 A6
Greenhouse La
  RSTROUD/NAIL GL6 .... 185 J4
The Greenings
  CHELTW GL51 .... 115 H6 🛾🛾
Greenlands Wy
  HNBRY/STHM BS10 .... 315 G9
Green La *BWTH/CHD* GL3 ...... 113 L8
  BWTH/CHD GL3 .... 137 J5
  BWTH/CHD GL3 .... 138 E8
  CHPMW/MSHF SN14 .... 342 A3
  CHPMW/MSHF SN14 .... 343 J8 🛾
  COTS GL54 .... 167 L7
  FRCTL/WBN BS36 .... 317 L4
  HNBRY/STHM BS10 .... 314 E2
  MIM GL56 .... 81 G4
  RWYE HR9 .... 106 B2
  SHPSTR CV36 .... 16 B6
  TEWK GL20 .... 48 E4
  THNB/SVB BS35 .... 304 D3
  VGL GL2 .... 159 G5
  VGL GL2 .... 182 C4
  WUE GL12 .... 294 D2
Green Lane Cl *COTS* GL54 ..... 123 C4
  SHPSTR CV36 .... 16 B6 🛾
Greenleaze
  BRSG/KWL/STAPK BS4 .... 346 D2
Greenleaze Av
  MANG/FISH BS16 .... 327M2
Green Meadow Bank
  CHELTE/BC GL52 .... 72 A7
Greenmore Rd
  BRSG/KWL/STAPK BS4 .... 346 D1
Greenore *KGWD/HNM* BS15 ... 337 L4
Greenpark Rd
  HNBRY/STHM BS10 .... 326 A2 🛾
Greenridge Cl
  BMSTRD/HC/WWD BS13 .... 345 G7 🛾
Green's Cl *COTS* GL54 .... 148 B4
Green Side *MANG/FISH* BS16 .. 328 C5
Greenside Cl
  HNBRY/STHM BS10 .... 314 F8 🛾
Green St *BMSTR* BS3 .... 7 J9

BWTH/CHD GL3 .... 138 A7
CHEP NP16 .... 270 A4
DSLY GL11 .... 229 L6
Greenstreet STNHO GL10 .... 207 H3 ▣
Green St TEWK GL20 .... 46 F5
The Green BRSTK/PCHW BS34 .... 317 G7
CHCAM GL55 .... 34 L1
CHNTN OX7 .... 83 J6
CHNTN OX7 .... 104 C6
CIND GL14 .... 155 H7
CIR GL7 .... 238 E3
CIR GL7 .... 242 D4
DSLY GL11 .... 254 E1 ▣
KGWD/HNM BS15 .... 338 A1
MALM SN16 .... 285 C3
MIM GL56 .... 58 D5 ▣
SHPSTR CV36 .... 59 M1
TET GL8 .... 282 A4
THNB/SVB BS35 .... 306 C1
WUE GL12 .... 295 K3
Greenview
OLD/WMLY/WICK BS30 .... 348 C1 ▣
Green Wk
BRSG/KWL/STAPK BS4 .... 346 C2 ▣
Green Wy BWTH/CHD GL3 .... 138 A6
Greenway CHELTE/BC GL52 .... 72 D8
Greenway Bush La BMSTR BS3 .. 335 J7
Greenway CI CHELTW GL51 .... 138 F2 ▣
Greenway Dr
HNBRY/STHM BS10 .... 325 M3 ▣
Greenway La CHELTE/BC GL52 .. 116 C4
CHELTS GL53 .... 139 K4
CHELTW GL51 .... 138 F2
CHPMW/MSHF SN14 .... 340 F7
COTS GL54 .... 74 A2
Greenway Pk
HNBRY/STHM BS10 .... 325 M3 ▣
Greenway Rd CIND GL14 .... 154 A4
MIM GL56 .... 35 C8
RDLND/MONT BS6 .... 335 K1
SHPSTR CV36 .... 16 A5
Greenways COTS GL54 .... 74 D4 ▣
KGWD/HNM BS15 .... 338 C2 ▣
LYD GL15 .... 201 H8
Greenways Dr CLFD GL16 .... 175 L3
Greenways Rd YATE/CS BS37 .... 310 B7
The Greenway
MANG/FISH BS16 .... 327 L8 ▣
Greenwood CI BWTH/CHD GL3 .. 137 H5
HORF/LLZ BS7 .... 326 A4 ▣
Greenwood Dr THNB/SVB BS35 .. 293 H7
Greenwood Rd
BRSG/KWL/STAPK BS4 .... 346 C2 ▣
Greet Rd COTS GL54 .... 74 D5
Gregory Ct
OLD/WMLY/WICK BS30 .... 338 C5 ▣
Grenadier CI BWTH/CHD GL3 .. 137 H5
Grenadier Rd CHELTW GL51 .... 93 G7 ▣
Grenville CI BWTH/CHD GL3 .... 113 H5
EVILLE/WHL BS5 .... 337 H3
Grenville PI CBRIS/FH BS1 .... 335 H6 ▣
Grenville Rd RDLND/MONT BS6 .. 326 A4
COTS GL54 .... 74 C4
Greve Ct
OLD/WMLY/WICK BS30 .... 338 B7 ▣
Grevel La CHCAM GL55 .... 12 E7
Greville CI GL1 .... 112 A7
Greville Ct CHELTW GL51 .... 115 H3 ▣
Greville Rd BMSTR BS3 .... 6 A9
Greville St BMSTR BS3 .... 6 C9
Grevil Rd CHELTW GL51 .... 93 H7
Greyfriars Wk CIR GL7 .... 238 E5 ▣
Greygoose La MIM GL56 .... 82 D5
Greyhound Gdns VGL GL2 .... 112 F6
Greylag Crs TEWK GL20 .... 48 C6
Greylands Rd
BMSTRD/HC/WWD BS13 .... 345 H4
Greys CI RSTROUD/NAIL GL6 .. 209 M7 ▣
Greystoke Av
HNBRY/STHM BS10 .... 325 J3
Greystoke Gdns
HNLZ/SM/SNYPK/WT BS9 .... 325 J3 ▣
Greystones MANG/FISH BS16 .. 328 A2 ▣
Greystones La COTS GL54 .... 123 J5
Grierson CI BWTH/CHD GL3 .... 137 K5 ▣
Griffin CI COTS GL54 .... 102 B3
Griffiths Av CHELTW GL51 .... 115 H3
Griffon CI VGL GL2 .... 135 K7
Griggfield Wk
HGRV/WHIT BS14 .... 346 B4 ▣
Griggs CI CHCAM GL55 .... 12 E8
Grimsbury Rd
KGWD/HNM BS15 .... 338 C3
Grimwade CI CHELTW GL51 .... 115 H2
Grindell Rd EVILLE/WHL BS5 .. 336 F4
Grinfield Av
BMSTRD/HC/WWD BS13 .... 345 L7
Grinfield CI
BMSTRD/HC/WWD BS13 .... 345 L7 ▣
Grinfield Ct
BMSTRD/HC/WWD BS13 .... 345 L7 ▣
Grisedale CI VGL GL2 .... 112 C6
Grist Mill CI CHELTW GL51 .... 92 F6
Grittleton Rd HORF/LLZ BS7 .. 326 A3
Grocyn CI
CHPMW/MSHF SN14 .... 343 K8 ▣
Grosvenor PI South
CHELTE/BC GL52 .... 2 E5
Grosvenor Rd CBRISNE BS2 .. 336 A3 ▣
STNHO GL10 .... 207 H2
VGL GL2 .... 5 M5
Grosvenor St CHELTE/BC GL52 .. 2 E6
Grosvenor Ter CHELTE/BC GL52 .. 2 E6
Ground CHNTN OX7 .... 149 L1 ▣
Grove CI CBRIS/FH BS1 .... 6 F6
HNLZ/SM/SNYPK/WT BS9 .... 324 A4
Grove Bank MANG/FISH BS16.. 327 L2
Grove Crs CLFD GL16 .... 151 K8
GLE GL4 .... 136 F2
Grovefield CI CHELTS GL53 .... 116 C5 ▣
Grovefield Wy CHELTW GL51 .. 114 D4
Grovelands GLE GL4 .... 137 G2
Grove La CHPMW/MSHF SN14 .. 330 E4
CIR GL7 .... 238 D2
LYD GL15 .... 201 K5

VGL GL2 .... 182 B7
Grove Pk
BRSG/KWL/STAPK BS4 .... 346 F1 ▣
RDLND/MONT BS6 .... 335 L1
Grove Park Av
BRSG/KWL/STAPK BS4 .... 346 F1
Grove Park Rd
BRSG/KWL/STAPK BS4 .... 346 F1
STROUD GL5 .... 208 E3
Grove Rd BWTH/CHD GL3 .... 113 H5
CLFD GL16 .... 151 J5
HNLZ/SM/SNYPK/WT BS9 .... 324 F3
LYD GL15 .... 201 G2
LYD GL15 .... 201 H8
MANG/FISH BS16 .... 327 G7
RDLND/MONT BS6 .... 335 K1
Grovesend Rd THNB/SVB BS35 .. 293 K3
THNB/SVB BS35 .... 294 A4
Grove St CHELT GL50 .... 2 B4
GL1 .... 5 H9
The Grove CBRIS/FH BS1 .... 5 H9
CHELT GL50 .... 115 K3
CHELTE/BC GL52 .... 3 J6
MALM SN16 .... 284 E2
OLD/WMLY/WICK BS30 .... 338 C7
STROUD GL5 .... 207 M7
TET GL8 .... 257 L3
YATE/CS BS37 .... 309 J3
Grove Vw MANG/FISH BS16 .... 327 G5 ▣
Guernsey Av
BRSG/KWL/STAPK BS4 .... 337 H7
Guest Av MANG/FISH BS16 .... 328 D5
Guggle La COTS GL54 .... 169 J1
Guildford Rd BRSG/KWL/STAPK BS4 .. 337 G6
Guildings Wy STNHO GL10 .... 207 J6
Guinea La MANG/FISH BS16 .... 327 J6 ▣
Guinea St CBRIS/FH BS1 .... 6 F7
GL1 .... 5 G3
Guise Av BWTH/CHD GL3 .... 138 B7
Guise CI VGL GL2 .... 159 H3
Gullimores Gdns
BMSTRD/HC/WWD BS13 .... 345 K7 ▣
Gullivers PI YATE/CS BS37 .... 320 C3
Gullons CI
BMSTRD/HC/WWD BS13 .... 345 J5 ▣
Gullon Wk
BMSTRD/HC/WWD BS13.... 345 H6
Gully La BRKLY GL13 .... 274 A4
The Gully FRCTL/WBN BS36.... 318 B4
Gumstool Hi TET GL8 .... 282 A4 ▣
Gunhouse La STROUD GL5 .... 208 F6
Gunning CI KGWD/HNM BS15.. 337 M5
Gunter's Hl EVILLE/WHL BS5 .. 337 J3 ▣
Gupshill CI TEWK GL20 .... 48 A8 ▣
Gurney CI GLE GL4 .... 159 M1
Guthrie Rd CFTN/FAIL BS8.... 335 J3
Gwentlands CI CHEP NP16 .... 270 A4
Gwernant Rd CHELTW GL51 .. 115 H5
Gwilliam St BMSTR BS3 .... 335 M8
Gwinnette Ct CHELTW GL51 .. 139 G1
Gwy Ct CHEP NP16 .... 270 B2 ▣
Gwyn St CBRISNE BS2 .... 336 A2
Gyde Rd RSTROUD/NAIL GL6 .. 185 H2
Gypsy La NWNT GL18 .... 85 G5

H

Hackers La CHNTN OX7 .... 105 G7
Hacket Hi THNB/SVB BS35 .... 294 B3
Hacket La THNB/SVB BS35 .... 294 A3
Hack La BWTH/CHD GL3 .... 61 G2
Hadfield CI RTEWK/TIB GL19 .. 66 D4
Hadley Ct
OLD/WMLY/WICK BS30 .... 338 D5 ▣
Hadley Rd DSLY GL11 .... 229 G7
Hadow Wy VGL GL2 .... 159 H3
Hadrian CI
HNLZ/SM/SNYPK/WT BS9 .... 324 E7 ▣
LYD GL15 .... 201 K7
Hadrians Wy GLE GL4 .... 137 H4
Hague Av DSLY GL11 .... 229 H7 ▣
Hailes Rd GLE GL4 .... 136 F4
Hailes St COTS GL54 .... 74 D6
Hailey Av CHNTN OX7 .... 105 M2
Hailey Rd CHNTN OX7 .... 105 M2
Hakeburn Rd CIR GL7 .... 238 C2 ▣
Halbrow Crs MANG/FISH BS16.. 327 L6
Haldon CI BMSTR BS3 .... 345 M2
Hale CI KGWD/HNM BS15 .... 337 M7 ▣
Hale La RSTROUD/NAIL GL6 .. 185 H3
Hales CI CHELTE/BC GL52 .... 3 K5
Hales Horn CI ALMDB BS32 .. 316 F5
Hale's Rd CHELTE/BC GL52 .... 3 H7
Halfacre CI HGRV/WHIT BS14 .. 346 C8
Halfacre La HGRV/WHIT BS14.. 346 D8
Halfway Br VGL GL2 .... 133 J1
Halfway Pitch
RSTROUD/NAIL GL6 .... 184 D7
Halifax Rd YATE/CS BS37 .... 309 M7
Halland Rd CHELTS GL53 .... 115 M6
Hallards CI AVONM BS11 .... 324 B3
Hallen CI HNBRY/STHM BS10 .. 314 F8
Hall End La YATE/CS BS37 .... 309 L1
Hallen Dr
HNLZ/SM/SNYPK/WT BS9 .... 324 E4
Hallen Rd HNBRY/STHM BS10.. 314 E7
HNBRY/STHM BS10 .... 315 G8
Hall La CBATH/BATHN BA1 .... 350 D1
CBATH/BATHN BA1 .... 351 G1
CHPMW/MSHF SN14 .... 341 G8
YATE/CS BS37 .... 311 M6
Hallmead CI CHELTW GL51 .... 92 F6 ▣
Hall Rd CHELTS GL53 .... 115 M7
Hallsfield HGHW SN6 .... 288 F3
Halls Rd KGWD/HNM BS15 .... 337 M3 ▣
Hall St BMSTR BS3 .... 345 K1
Halmore La BRKLY GL13 .... 227 J3
Halsbury Rd RDLND/MONT BS6 .. 325 K7
Halstock Av
MANG/FISH BS16 .... 327 H8 ▣
Halston Dr CBRISNE BS2 .... 336 B3
Halswell Gdns
BMSTRD/HC/WWD BS13.... 345 K7
Halt End HGRV/WHIT BS14 .. 346 E8

Halwyn CI
HNLZ/SM/SNYPK/WT BS9 .... 324 F6 ▣
Hamble CI THNB/SVB BS35 .... 293 L3
Hambledon CI CIR GL7 .... 239 G8 ▣
Hambridge La CIR GL7 .... 244 E6
Hambrook La
BRSTK/PCHW BS34 .... 317 H7
Hambrook St CHELTE/BC GL52.. 116 D4
Hambutts Dr
RSTROUD/NAIL GL6 .... 185 G3
Hambutts Md
RSTROUD/NAIL GL6 .... 185 G3
Ham CI CHELTE/BC GL52 .... 116 E4
Hamer St VGL GL2 .... 5 K6
Ham Farm La MANG/FISH BS16 .. 328 D5
Hamfield La BRKLY GL13 .... 226 E8
Hamilton Cft CIR GL7 .... 241 K7
Hamilton Rd BMSTR BS3 .... 6 B8
EVILLE/WHL BS5 .... 336 C3
Ham La CIR GL7 .... 263 H5
CIR GL7 .... 267 G5
LGASH BS41 .... 344 F8
MANG/FISH BS16 .... 327 G5
OLD/WMLY/WICK BS30 .... 340 A2
THNB/SVB BS35 .... 272 E5
Hamlen CI RTEWK/TIB GL19 .. 108 C7
Hammersmith Bottom CIR GL7 .. 219 L6
Hammersmith Rd
EVILLE/WHL BS5 .... 336 F3 ▣
Ham Mill La STROUD GL5 .... 208 F8
Hammond CI
BRSG/KWL/STAPK BS4 .... 346 F2 ▣
Hammond Dr COTS GL54 .... 169 J1 ▣
Hammonds HGHW SN6 .... 289 G3 ▣
Hammond Wy CIR GL7 .... 238 B3 ▣
GLE GL4 .... 136 F2 ▣
Hampden CI YATE/CS BS37 .. 309 M7
Hampden Rd
BRSG/KWL/STAPK BS4 .... 336 D8 ▣
Hampden Wy GL GL1 .... 4 F6
Hampshire Gdns CLFD GL16 .. 175 J2
Hampshire Wy YATE/CS BS37 .. 310 B7 ▣
Hampstead Rd
BRSG/KWL/STAPK BS4 .... 336 E8
Hampton CI BWTH/CHD GL3 .. 137 K4 ▣
CHELT GL50 .... 115 J6 ▣
OLD/WMLY/WICK BS30 .... 338 C6
Hampton Gv CIR GL7 .... 241 K6
Hampton Hi TET GL8 .... 257 L1
Hampton La RDLND/MONT BS6 .. 335 K2
Hampton Pk
RDLND/MONT BS6 .... 335 K2 ▣
Hampton Rd
RDLND/MONT BS6 .... 335 K1
Hampton St
KGWD/HNM BS15 .... 337 M2 ▣
TET GL8 .... 281 M3
Ham Rd CHELTE/BC GL52 .... 116 E4
RTEWK/TIB GL19 .... 89 K2
Hams Rd KEYN BS31 .... 348 B4
LYD GL15 .... 201 K8
The Ham DSLY GL11 .... 230 C6
Hanbury CI KGWD/HNM BS15.. 337 M6
Hanbury Rd CFTN/FAIL BS8.... 335 J3
Handel Av EVILLE/WHL BS5 .. 336 F4 ▣
Handel Rd KEYN BS31 .... 347 M6
Handford Wy
OLD/WMLY/WICK BS30 .... 338 D8 ▣
Hanford Ct HGRV/WHIT BS14 .. 346 F4 ▣
Hang Hill Rd LYD GL15 .... 200 C2
Hanham Rd KGWD/HNM BS15.. 337 M5
Hanks CI MALM SN16 .... 303 J6
Hanley La CHEP NP16 .... 246 F4
Hanman Rd GL GL1 .... 136 A4
Hannah Rd CIR GL7 .... 239 H7
Hannah PI VGL GL2 .... 113 C4
Hannam CI CHELTS GL53 .... 115 M7
Hannington Br HGHW SN6 .... 267 K6
Hannis Rd CHNTN OX7 .... 105 M2
Hanover Ct CBRIS/FH BS1 .... 7 H2 ▣
Hanover PI CBRIS/FH BS1 .... 6 B7
EVILLE/WHL BS5 .... 336 C4 ▣
Hanover St CHELT GL50 .... 2 D2
Hanover Wy BWTH/CHD GL3 .. 113 H4
Hanson Av SHPSTR CV36 .... 16 A6 ▣
Hanstone CI CIR GL7 .... 238 E5
Harbour La LYD GL15 .... 225 K3
Harbourside TEWK GL20 .... 48 B4
Harbour Vw TEWK GL20 .... 48 B4 ▣
Harbour Wall
HNLZ/SM/SNYPK/WT BS9 .... 324 E7 ▣
Harbour Wy CBRIS/FH BS1 .... 6 C6
Harbury Ms GL GL1 .... 5 K9
Harbury Rd
HNLZ/SM/SNYPK/WT BS9 .... 325 L4
Harcombe HI FRCTL/WBN BS36 .. 318 A7
Harcombe Rd
FRCTL/WBN BS36 .... 317 M6
Harcourt Av EVILLE/WHL BS5 .. 337 J5 ▣
Harcourt HI RDLND/MONT BS6 .. 325 J8
Harcourt Rd RDLND/MONT BS6 .. 325 K7
Hardenhuish Rd
BRSG/KWL/STAPK BS4 .... 336 F6 ▣
Harden Rd HGRV/WHIT BS14 .. 347 G6
Harding's Dr DSLY GL11 .... 253 J2
Hardwick Av CHEP NP16 .... 270 A3 ▣
Hardwick Bank Rd TEWK GL20.. 26 C8
Hardwick CI
BRSG/KWL/STAPK BS4 .... 337 G8 ▣
OLD/WMLY/WICK BS30 .... 338 F6 ▣
Hardwicke YATE/CS BS37 .... 319 L4
Hardy Av BMSTR BS3 .... 335 J8
Hardy Ct
OLD/WMLY/WICK BS30 .... 338 B6
Hardy La ALMDB BS32 .... 306 B3
Hardy Rd BMSTR BS3 .... 345 K1 ▣
CHELTE/BC GL52 .... 72 C7
Harebell PI GLE GL4 .... 136 F6
Hareclive Rd
BMSTRD/HC/WWD BS13.... 345 K6
Harefield CI
KGWD/HNM BS15 .... 347 L1 ▣
Hare La GL GL1 .... 4 F5

Harescombe YATE/CS BS37 .... 320 A4
Haresdown Hl CIR GL7 .... 260 B4
Haresfield CIR GL7 .... 214 B7
Haresfield La VGL GL2 .... 159 H6
Harewood CI GL GL1 .... 159 L2
Harewood Rd EVILLE/WHL BS5 .. 337 J2
Harford Br COTS GL54 .... 121 M1
Harford CI
HNLZ/SM/SNYPK/WT BS9 .... 324 E4 ▣
Harford Dr MANG/FISH BS16 .. 327 L2
Harlech Wy
OLD/WMLY/WICK BS30 .... 348 D1
Harleston St EVILLE/WHL BS5.... 7 K1
Harleys Fld GLE GL4 .... 136 F4
Harmer CI HNBRY/STHM BS10 .. 315 H8
Harnham CI COTS GL54 .... 142 F7
Harnhill CI
BMSTRD/HC/WWD BS13 .... 345 K7 ▣
Harold Rd LYD GL15 .... 177 L8
Harolds Wy KGWD/HNM BS15 .. 337 L5
Harper Rd STROUD GL5 .... 208 A3 ▣
Harper's La MALM SN16 .... 303 H8
Harpfield Rd CHELTE/BC GL52 .. 94 B1
Harp HI CHELTE/BC GL52 .... 3 L5
Harptree Ct
OLD/WMLY/WICK BS30 .... 338 C7 ▣
Harptree Gv BMSTR BS3 .... 345 K1 ▣
Harrington Av
HGRV/WHIT BS14 .... 347 G5
Harrington CI
OLD/WMLY/WICK BS30 .... 349 G3
Harrington Dr CHELTW GL51 .. 115 G4 ▣
Harrington Gv
HGRV/WHIT BS14 .... 347 G5 ▣
Harrington Rd
HGRV/WHIT BS14 .... 347 G5
Harrington Wk
HGRV/WHIT BS14 .... 347 G5 ▣
Harris Barton FRCTL/WBN BS36.. 318 C4
Harris CI BWTH/CHD GL3 .... 113 C6
Harris Ct
OLD/WMLY/WICK BS30 .... 338 B7 ▣
Harris Gdns COTS GL54 .... 124 C7 ▣
Harris La CFTN/FAIL BS8.......... 334 A3
Harrison CI CIND GL14 .... 155 H7 ▣
Harrison Rd CHELTW GL51.... 138 F1
Harrison Wy LYD GL15 .... 225 L1
Harris Rd HGHW SN6 .... 287 J2
Harrowdene Rd
BRSG/KWL/STAPK BS4 .... 336 D8
Harrow Rd
BRSG/KWL/STAPK BS4 .... 336 F8
Harry Stoke Rd
BRSTK/PCHW BS34 .... 317 G4
Harry Yates Wy CHELTW GL51 .. 92 F7
Hartbury CI CHELTW GL51 .... 92 E8
Hartcliffe Rd
BRSG/KWL/STAPK BS4 .... 346 A3
Hartcliffe Wk
BRSG/KWL/STAPK BS4 .... 346 B3 ▣
Hartcliffe Wy BMSTR BS3 .... 345 L2
BRSG/KWL/STAPK BS4 .... 345 L4
Hartfield Av RDLND/MONT BS6 .. 335 L3
Hartgill CI
BMSTRD/HC/WWD BS13 .... 345 K8
Hart Gn CIND GL14 .... 154 A5
Hartington Pk
RDLND/MONT BS6 .... 335 K1 ▣
Hartland GL GL1 .... 135 L3
Hartland Rd GLE GL4 .... 136 B5
Hart La MTCHDN GL17 .... 129 C3
Hartlebury Wy
CHELTE/BC GL52 .... 116 C3
Hartley Bridge Hl
RSTROUD/NAIL GL6 .... 256 B3
Hartley CI CHELTS GL53 .... 116 B7
YATE/CS BS37 .... 320 C2
Harts Cft YATE/CS BS37 .... 310 B7 ▣
Harvest Gv CHELTW GL51 .... 92 F6 ▣
Harvest Wy VGL GL2 .... 159 H4
Harvey CI VGL GL2 .... 135 L6
Harvey's La COTS GL54 .... 74 B6
Harwell CI GLE GL4 .... 159 M2 ▣
Hasfield CI VGL GL2 .... 159 G2
Hasfield Rd RTEWK/TIB GL19 .. 67 H7
Haskins Ct
OLD/WMLY/WICK BS30 .... 338 C7 ▣
Haslette Wy CHELTW GL51 .... 115 G6
Hassell Dr CBRISNE BS2 .... 7 L2
Hastings CI BMSTR BS3 .... 345 L2 ▣
Hastings HI CHNTN OX7 .... 105 C6
Hastings PI TEWK GL20 .... 48 A7 ▣
Hastings Rd BMSTR BS3 .... 345 L2
CIND GL14 .... 154 A3
Hatchet La BRSTK/PCHW BS34.. 317 G4
Hatchet Rd BRSTK/PCHW BS34 .. 317 G7
Hatchmere THNB/SVB BS35 .. 293 M3
Hatfield Rd GL GL1 .... 136 C4
Hathaway CI VGL GL2 .... 135 K7
Hatherley YATE/CS BS37 .... 320 A4
Hatherley Brake
CHELTW GL51 .... 115 G4 ▣
Hatherley Court Rd
CHELTW GL51 .... 115 K4
Hatherley Ga CHELTW GL51 .. 115 K3
Hatherley La CHELTW GL51 .. 114 E3
Hatherley Rd CHELTW GL51 .. 114 F4
GL GL1 .... 136 C4
HORF/LLZ BS7 .... 326 A1
Hatherley St CHELT GL50 .... 115 K4
Hatherop Rd CIR GL7 .... 242 F4
Hathway Wy EVILLE/WHL BS5 .. 336 C3
Hatters' La YATE/CS BS37 .... 320 E2
Hatton CI MTCHDN GL17 .... 152 C1
Havelock Rd BWTH/CHD GL3 .. 137 J3
Haven Av STNHO GL10 .... 207 G5
The Haven KGWD/HNM BS15 .. 338 A2
Haverstock Rd
BRSG/KWL/STAPK BS4 .... 346 F1
Haviland Gv CBATH/BATHN BA1 .. 350 C4
Haw Br RTEWK/TIB GL19 .... 68 D1
Hawburn CI
BRSG/KWL/STAPK BS4 .... 346 F1

Hawcombe Ms
CHELTW GL51 .... 115 H6 ▣
Haweswater CI
OLD/WMLY/WICK BS30 .... 338 F5
Haweswater Rd
CHELTW GL51 .... 115 G5
Hawk CI GLE GL4 .... 136 H ▣
Hawkers HI CIR GL7 217
Hawker Sq COTS GL54 .... 124 C
Hawkesbury Rd BAD GL9 .... 297 M
MANG/FISH BS16 .... 327 C
Hawkesley Dr
BRSTK/PCHW BS34 .... 316 F
Hawkfield CI
BMSTRD/HC/WWD BS13.... 345 L
Hawkfield Rd
BMSTRD/HC/WWD BS13.... 345 L
Hawkfield Wy
BMSTRD/HC/WWD BS13 .... 345 M6
Hawkins CI
OLD/WMLY/WICK BS30 .... 338 E7
Hawkins Crs ALMDB BS32 .... 316 F
Hawkins St CBRISNE BS2 7
Hawkley Dr ALMDB BS32 .... 306 M
Hawkridge Dr MANG/FISH BS16.. 329
Hawksmoor CI
HGRV/WHIT BS14 .... 346 C
Hawkswood Rd CHELT GL50 .. 115 K
Hawksworth Dr
KGWD/HNM BS15 .... 337 M
Haw La THNB/SVB BS35 .... 306 G
Haw Rd CLFD GL16 .... 152 A
Haw St DSLY GL11 .... 230 F
WUE GL12 277
Hawthorn Av
KGWD/HNM BS15 .... 337 M5
Hawthorn CI
BRSTK/PCHW BS34 .... 316 A
CHEP NP16 .... 270 A7
WUE GL12 .... 276 C7
Hawthorn Crs
THNB/SVB BS35 .... 293 L1
Hawthorn Dr BUR/CRTN OX18 .. 197
BWTH/CHD GL3 .... 113 H6
CHELTE/BC GL52 .... 72 C8
CLFD GL16 .... 175 J
Hawthorne Av GLE GL4 .... 136 E
Hawthorne CI MANG/FISH BS16.. 329 J
Hawthorne HI NWNT GL18 .... 85 J
The Hawthornes
CHELTW GL51 .... 114 F5
MANG/FISH BS16 .... 328 E
Hawthorne St
BRSG/KWL/STAPK BS4 .... 336 C
Hawthorn Ri STROUD GL5 .... 207 M3
Hawthorn Rd CHELTW GL51 .. 93 G8
Hawthorns La KEYN BS31 .... 348 A
Hawthorns Rd MTCHDN GL17 .. 129 L
The Hawthorns DSLY GL11 .. 229 C
LYD GL15 .... 201 K
RSTROUD/NAIL GL6 .... 209 H
Hawthorn Wy
BRSTK/PCHW BS34 .... 317 G
SHPSTR CV36 .... 16 B
Haycombe HGRV/WHIT BS14 .. 346 B5
Haycroft CI CHELTE/BC GL52 .. 72 A
Haycroft Dr GLE GL4 .... 136 F
Hayden La CHELTW GL51 .... 114 C
Hayden Rd CHELTW GL51 .... 93 G
Haydock CI MANG/FISH BS16 .. 328 B2
Haydon Gdns HORF/LLZ BS7 .. 326 D6
Haydons CI CHCAM GL55 .... 12 F7
Hayeley Dr BRSTK/PCHW BS34.. 317 G
Hayes CI CBRISNE BS2 .... 7 L
Hayes CI VGL GL2 .... 112 E5
Haye's La BAD GL9 .... 323 C
Hayes Rd CHELTE/BC GL52 .... 3 K
RSTROUD/NAIL GL6 .... 209 J
Hayfield CHPMW/MSHF SN14.... 342 C
Hayfield Wy CHELTE/BC GL52 .. 71 M
Hayhedge La
RSTROUD/NAIL GL6 .... 210 F
Hay La CIR GL7 .... 216 F
RSTROUD/NAIL GL6 .... 210 F
Hay Leaze YATE/CS BS37 .... 309 M7
The Haymarket CBRIS/FH BS1 .... 6 F
Haymead La TET GL8 .... 279 M
Hay Meadow SHPSTR CV36 .... 16 A
Haymes Dr CHELTE/BC GL52 .. 94 E
Haymes Rd CHELTE/BC GL52 .. 94 E
Haynes La MANG/FISH BS16 .. 327 M
Hays CI BDWAY WR12 .... 11 C
Hay St CHPMW/MSHF SN14 .... 342 J
Haysum's CI CHCAM GL55 .... 34 E
Haythorn Ct MANG/FISH BS16 .. 328 E
Haytor Pk
HNLZ/SM/SNYPK/WT BS9 .... 324 F
Hayward CI GLE GL4 .... 136 F
Hayward Rd EVILLE/WHL BS5 .. 336 E
MANG/FISH BS16 .... 327 M
Haywards La CHELTE/BC GL52 3
Hayward's Rd CHELTE/BC GL52 3
Haywood Pitch RWYE HR9 .... 85 C
Hazebrouck CI CHELTW GL51 .. 115 C
Hazel Av RDLND/MONT BS6 .. 335 K
Hazelbury Dr
OLD/WMLY/WICK BS30 .... 339 H
Hazelbury HI COR/BOX SN13.... 353 M
Hazelbury Rd HGRV/WHIT BS14.. 346 F
Hazel CI VGL GL2 .... 112 D
Hazel Cote Rd
HGRV/WHIT BS14 .... 346 E
Hazel Cresent THNB/SVB BS35.. 293 M
Hazelcroft BWTH/CHD GL3 .. 113 K5
Hazeldene Rd
BRSTK/PCHW BS34 .... 316 C
Hazelgrove
FRCTL/WBN BS36 .... 317 M6
Hazel Gv HORF/LLZ BS7 .... 326 C
Hazel La ALMDB BS32 .... 293 C
Hazells La CIR GL7 .... 221 K
Hazel Rd MTCHDN GL17 .... 129 M
The Hazels GL7 .... 242 J
Hazelton Rd HORF/LLZ BS7.... 325 M
Hazel Wy CHPMW/MSHF SN14.... 343 J

Hazelwood Rd
HNLZ/SM/SNYPK/WT BS9 ... 324 F8
Hazle Cl LED HR8 ... 19 M5
Hazlecote La TET GL8 ... 256 B5
Hazledean Rd CHELTW GL51 ... 92 F7 2
Hazlewood Cl CHELT GL50 ... 115 K6
Hazlitt Cft CHELTW GL51 ... 92 F7
Headford Av EVILLE/WHL BS5 ... 337 K4
Headford Rd
BRSG/KWL/STAPK BS4 ... 345 M2
Headington Cl
KGWD/HNM BS15 ... 337 M7 2
Headlam Cl GLE GL4 ... 159 M2 3
The Headlands STROUD GL5 ... 232 B1
The Headland CHEP NP16 ... 270 C7
Headley Ct
BMSTRD/HC/WWD BS13 ... 345 K5
Headley La
BMSTRD/HC/WWD BS13 ... 345 K5
Headley Park Av
BMSTRD/HC/WWD BS13 ... 345 K4
Headley Park Rd
BMSTRD/HC/WWD BS13 ... 345 J4
Headley Rd
BMSTRD/HC/WWD BS13 ... 345 J5
Headley Wk
BMSTRD/HC/WWD BS13 ... 345 K4
Healey Dr
CHPMW/MSHF SN14 ... 330 E5 1
Heapey Cl CHELTW GL51 ... 114 F1 3
Hearne Cl CHELTS GL53 ... 116 D5
Hearne Rd CHELTS GL53 ... 116 D5
Heart Meers
HGRV/WHIT BS14 ... 346 D6 5
Heart of England Wy
CHCAM GL55 ... 13 G2
Heath Cl FRCTL/WBN BS36 ... 318 A5
Heathcote Dr FRCTL/WBN BS36 .. 318 F4
Heathcote Rd
MANG/FISH BS16 ... 328 A6 2
MANG/FISH BS16 ... 337 K1
Heathcote Wk KGWD/HNM BS15 337 L1
Heath Ct MANG/FISH BS16 ... 327 M4 2
Heathdean Rd BWTH/CHD GL3 .. 113 H5 1
Heather Av FRCTL/WBN BS36 ... 318 D5
GLE GL4 ... 137 H7
Heather Cl KGWD/HNM BS15 ... 337 K3
STROUD GL5 ... 208 C7
Heatherdene HGRV/WHIT BS14 .. 346 B4
Heathfield Cl
CBATH/BATHN BA1 ... 350 C8
KEYN BS31 ... 347 L6
Heathfield Crs
HGRV/WHIT BS14 ... 346 C7
Heathfield Rd STROUD GL5 ... 208 B2
Heathfields MANG/FISH BS16 ... 327 M3
Heath Gdns FRCTL/WBN BS36 ... 318 E5
MANG/FISH BS16 ... 327 M3
Heath House La
MANG/FISH BS16 ... 326 E6 2
Heath Rdg LGASH BS41 ... 344 C1
Heath Ri
OLD/WMLY/WICK BS30 ... 338 D6 2
Heath Rd EVILLE/WHL BS5 ... 326 D8
KGWD/HNM BS15 ... 337 K7
MANG/FISH BS16 ... 327 M4
Heath St EVILLE/WHL BS5 ... 336 E1
Heathville Rd GL GL1 ... 5 H3
Heath Wk MANG/FISH BS16 ... 327 M4
Heazle Pl STROUD GL5 ... 208 E3
Hebden Cl BWTH/CHD GL3 ... 138 B6
Heber St EVILLE/WHL BS5 ... 336 E4
Hebron Rd BMSTR BS3 ... 335 L8 5
Hedgeditch La TET GL8 ... 301 M4
Hedgemead Vw
MANG/FISH BS16 ... 326 F6
The Hedgerow VGL GL2 ... 112 D7 1
Hedwick St EVILLE/WHL BS5 ... 337 G4
Heggard Cl
BMSTRD/HC/WWD BS13 ... 345 J6 3
Helens Cl CHELTW GL51 ... 92 F8
Hellier Wk
BMSTRD/HC/WWD BS13 ... 345 L8 1
Hembury Cl VGL GL2 ... 158 F4
Hemmingsdale Rd VGL GL2 ... 4 A7
Hemming Wy CHELTE/BC GL52 ... 72 B8
The Hemplands COTS GL54 ... 191 M1
Hemplow Cl HGRV/WHIT BS14 ... 346 F4
Hempsted La VGL GL2 ... 135 K5
Hempton La ALMDB BS32 ... 316 C1
Henacre Rd AVONM BS11 ... 324 B3
Henbrook La RBANSW OX15 ... 17 M8
Henbury Rd
HNBRY/STHM BS10 ... 325 G1 3
HNLZ/SM/SNYPK/WT BS9 ... 325 J3
KGWD/HNM BS15 ... 337 K6 5
Henbury Road Henbury Hl
HNLZ/SM/SNYPK/WT BS9 ... 325 H3
Hencliffe Rd HGRV/WHIT BS14 ... 346 F5
Hencliffe Wy KGWD/HNM BS15 .. 337 K8
Henderson Rd
KGWD/HNM BS15 ... 337 K6
Hendingham Cl GL GL1 ... 159 K1
Hendre Rd BMSTR BS3 ... 345 J1
Hendrick Dr CHEP NP16 ... 270 C3 2
Heneage La WUE GL12 ... 275 H3
Henfield Crs
OLD/WMLY/WICK BS30 ... 338 D7
Henfield Rd FRCTL/WBN BS36 ... 318 E7
Hengaston St BMSTR BS3 ... 345 K1 7
Hengrove Av HGRV/WHIT BS14 .. 346 D3
Hengrove La HGRV/WHIT BS14 .. 346 D3
Hengrove Rd
BRSG/KWL/STAPK BS4 ... 346 C1
Hengrove Wy
BMSTRD/HC/WWD BS13 ... 345 K6
BRSG/KWL/STAPK BS4 ... 346 A5
Henleaze Av
HNLZ/SM/SNYPK/WT BS9 ... 325 J6
Henleaze Gdns
HNLZ/SM/SNYPK/WT BS9 ... 325 J6
Henleaze Pk
HNLZ/SM/SNYPK/WT BS9 ... 325 L6
Henleaze Park Dr
HNLZ/SM/SNYPK/WT BS9 ... 325 L5
Henleaze Rd
HNLZ/SM/SNYPK/WT BS9 ... 325 J6
Henleaze Ter
HNLZ/SM/SNYPK/WT BS9 ... 325 K4
Henley Gv
HNLZ/SM/SNYPK/WT BS9 ... 325 K6
Henley La COR/BOX SN13 ... 353 K8
Henley Pl GL GL1 ... 135 M5
Henley Rd CHELTW GL51 ... 92 E8
LYD GL15 ... 200 D2
Henlow Dr DSLY GL11 ... 253 K3
Hennessy Cl HGRV/WHIT BS14 ... 346 A8
Henrietta St CBRISNE BS2 ... 335 M3 5
CHELT GL50 ... 2 D4
EVILLE/WHL BS5 ... 336 D2 5
Henry Rd GL GL1 ... 5 H3
Henry Ryder Cl GLE GL4 ... 137 H5 3
Henry St BMSTR BS3 ... 7 K9
GL GL1 ... 5 G4
Henry Williamson Ct
OLD/WMLY/WICK BS30 ... 338 C6 5
Henshaw Cl
KGWD/HNM BS15 ... 337 L1 2
Henshaw Rd KGWD/HNM BS15 ... 337 L1
Henshaw Wk KGWD/HNM BS15 .. 337 L1
Hensman's Hl CFTN/FAIL BS8 ... 335 J5
Hentley Tor WUE GL12 ... 277 L5
Hepburn Rd CBRIS/FH BS1 ... 336 A3
Herald Cl
HNLZ/SM/SNYPK/WT BS9 ... 324 F6
Herapath St EVILLE/WHL BS5 ... 336 E5
Herbert Crs EVILLE/WHL BS5 ... 326 F8 2
Herbert Howells Cl LYD GL15 ... 225 J1 2
Herbert St BMSTR BS3 ... 6 D9
EVILLE/WHL BS5 ... 336 E3
GL GL1 ... 5 J8
Herberts Wy LYD GL15 ... 201 L2
Hercules Cl BRSTK/PCHW BS34 ... 316 F5
Herd La TET GL8 ... 282 A4
Hereford Pl CHELT GL50 ... 2 B3
Hereford Rd CBRISNE BS2 ... 336 C1 6
LED HR8 ... 19 L1
Hereford St BMSTR BS3 ... 335 M8 5
Hereward Rd CIR GL7 ... 238 C2
Herkomer Cl HORF/LLZ BS7 ... 326 D4
Hermitage Cl AVONM BS11 ... 324 A4
Hermitage Dr DSLY GL11 ... 253 K3
Hermitage Rd MANG/FISH BS16 ... 327 M6
Hermitage St CHELTS GL53 ... 115 M4
Hern La NAIL BS48 ... 344 A6
Heron Cl CHELTW GL51 ... 115 G4
Heron Rd EVILLE/WHL BS5 ... 336 D2
Heron Wy GLE GL4 ... 136 E6
YATE/CS BS37 ... 320 B4
Herridge Cl
BMSTRD/HC/WWD BS13 ... 345 K7
Herridge Rd
BMSTRD/HC/WWD BS13 ... 345 K7
Hersey Gdns
BMSTRD/HC/WWD BS13 ... 345 G8
Hersta Cl CIR GL7 ... 238 E3 5
Hertford Rd CHELTE/BC GL52 ... 72 B7
Hesding Cl KGWD/HNM BS15 ... 337 L8 1
Hestercombe Rd
BMSTRD/HC/WWD BS13 ... 345 K5 1
Hester's Way La CHELTW GL51 ... 92 F7
Hester's Way Rd CHELTW GL51 ... 92 F8
Hethersett Rd GL GL1 ... 5 J8
Hetton Gdns CHELTS GL53 ... 116 C5
Hewelsfield La LYD GL15 ... 198 F6
Hewland Ct AVONM BS11 ... 324 E1 5
Hewlett Pl CHELTE/BC GL52 ... 2 F6
Hewlett Rd CHELTE/BC GL52 ... 2 F6
Hewlett Wy CIND GL14 ... 154 A7
Heyford Av EVILLE/WHL BS5 ... 326 D8
Heyron Wk
BMSTRD/HC/WWD BS13 ... 345 K7
Heywood Rd CIND GL14 ... 154 B2
Hiam's La VGL GL2 ... 89 G8
Hiatt Rd RSTROUD/NAIL GL6 ... 233 G4
Hibbs Cl CHPMW/MSHF SN14 ... 342 B3
Hickley Gdns BWTH/CHD GL3 ... 138 A5
Hicks Av DSLY GL11 ... 229 H7
MANG/FISH BS16 ... 328 D3
Hicks Beach Rd CHELTW GL51 ... 92 F8
Hicks Common Rd
FRCTL/WBN BS36 ... 318 A5
Hicks Ct
OLD/WMLY/WICK BS30 ... 338 B7 10
Hidcote Av CHELTW GL51 ... 115 J6 6
Hidcote Cl
RSTROUD/NAIL GL6 ... 209 M7 5
Hidcote Rd CHCAM GL55 ... 13 K4
Higham St
BRSG/KWL/STAPK BS4 ... 7 K8 2
Highbank Pk VGL GL2 ... 112 B6
High Bannerdown
CBATH/BATHN BA1 ... 352 D7
High Beech Av CLFD GL16 ... 151 M6
Highbeech Rd LYD GL15 ... 200 C3
MTCHDN GL17 ... 128 E6
Highbury La CHELTE/BC GL52 ... 2 E6
Highbury Rd BMSTR BS3 ... 345 L2
HORF/LLZ BS7 ... 326 B4
LYD GL15 ... 200 C3
MONM NP25 ... 174 B3
Highbury Vls CBRISNE BS2 ... 6 C1
Highclere Rd VGL GL2 ... 159 G1
Highcroft
OLD/WMLY/WICK BS30 ... 338 E5 4
Highdale Cl HGRV/WHIT BS14 ... 346 D7
High Delf Wy LYD GL15 ... 201 G2
High Elm KGWD/HNM BS15 ... 338 A5 5
Higher Newmarket Rd
RSTROUD/NAIL GL6 ... 232 B7
Highett Dr EVILLE/WHL BS5 .. 336 C2 10
Highfield LYD GL15 ... 202 D1
Highfield Av KGWD/HNM BS15 ... 337 M6
Highfield Cl LYD GL15 ... 200 C2
Highfield Gdns
OLD/WMLY/WICK BS30 ... 348 E1
Highfield Gv HORF/LLZ BS7 ... 325 M6
Highfield La LYD GL15 ... 201 L6
YATE/CS BS37 ... 311 M6
Highfield Pl GLE GL4 ... 136 D4
Highfield Rd GLE GL4 ... 136 D4
LYD GL15 ... 200 C2
LYD GL15 ... 201 L6
MTCHDN GL17 ... 129 G3
RSTROUD/NAIL GL6 ... 184 C8
STROUD GL5 ... 209 G5
TET GL8 ... 281 M2
YATE/CS BS37 ... 320 C2
Highfields BAD GL9 ... 312 B1
Highfields Ap DSLY GL11 ... 253 L3 1
Highfields Cl
BRSTK/PCHW BS34 ... 317 H8
Highfield Wy
RSTROUD/NAIL GL6 ... 210 C7
High Furlong DSLY GL11 ... 229 H6 2
High Gv
HNLZ/SM/SNYPK/WT BS9 ... 324 D4
Highgrove St
BRSG/KWL/STAPK BS4 ... 7 L9
Highgrove Wy BWTH/CHD GL3 ... 113 H4
Highland Crs CFTN/FAIL BS8 ... 335 J1 3
Highland Rd CHELTS GL53 ... 116 A7
Highlands Dr DSLY GL11 ... 253 G7
Highland Sq CFTN/FAIL BS8 ... 335 J1 4
Highlands Rd LGASH BS41 ... 344 C1
Highleaze Rd
OLD/WMLY/WICK BS30 ... 338 E7
Highliffe Dr VGL GL2 ... 159 J2
Highmead Gdns
BMSTRD/HC/WWD BS13 ... 345 G7
Highmore Gdns HORF/LLZ BS7 ... 326 E4
Highnam Cl BRSTK/PCHW BS34 .. 316 D2
High Nash CLFD GL16 ... 175 K2
High Orchard St GL GL1 ... 4 C8
High Pk HGRV/WHIT BS14 ... 346 D2
Highridge Crs
BMSTRD/HC/WWD BS13 ... 345 H6
Highridge Gn
BMSTRD/HC/WWD BS13 ... 345 G5
Highridge Pk
BMSTRD/HC/WWD BS13 ... 345 H6 3
Highridge Rd BMSTR BS3 ... 345 K1 3
LGASH BS41 ... 344 E8
Highridge Wk
BMSTRD/HC/WWD BS13 ... 345 G4
High Rd HGHW SN6 ... 287 H2
High St BAD GL9 ... 298 B8
BAD GL9 ... 323 G1
BDWAY WR12 ... 32 F3
BDWAY WR12 ... 33 G3 3
BDWAY WR12 ... 53 M2
BRKLY GL13 ... 251 G1
CBATH/BATHN BA1 ... 351 H6
CBATH/BATHN BA1 ... 352 B8
CBRIS/FH BS1 ... 6 F3
CFTN/FAIL BS8 ... 335 J1
CHCAM GL55 ... 9 G7
CHCAM GL55 ... 12 E8
CHELT GL50 ... 2 B3
CHELTE/BC GL52 ... 2 E5
CHELTE/BC GL52 ... 94 E7
CHEP NP16 ... 270 A3
CHNTN OX7 ... 149 K1
CHPMW/MSHF SN14 ... 330 F7
CHPMW/MSHF SN14 ... 342 A3
CHPMW/MSHF SN14 ... 343 K8
CIND GL14 ... 129 G8
CIND GL14 ... 154 D3
CIND GL14 ... 154 B2
CIND GL14 ... 155 J7
CIND GL14 ... 156 B2
CIR GL7 ... 241 L6
CIR GL7 ... 241 K7
CIR GL7 ... 242 E4
CIR GL7 ... 244 E8
CIR GL7 ... 263 H5
CIR GL7 ... 266 F5
CLFD GL16 ... 175 J6
CLFD GL16 ... 175 K1
COR/BOX SN13 ... 353 M5
COTS GL54 ... 102 A3
COTS GL54 ... 123 H5
COTS GL54 ... 142 D8
COTS GL54 ... 169 J1
DSLY GL11 ... 229 H5
EVILLE/WHL BS5 ... 336 D2
FRCTL/WBN BS36 ... 317 M5
GL GL1 ... 136 B4
GLE GL4 ... 161 G1
HGHW SN6 ... 288 F4
HNLZ/SM/SNYPK/WT BS9 ... 325 J3
KEYN BS31 ... 348 A5
KEYN BS31 ... 349 G8
KGWD/HNM BS15 ... 337 L6
KGWD/HNM BS15 ... 338 D3
KGWD/HNM BS15 ... 338 A3
LED HR8 ... 20 A3
LYD GL15 ... 198 F6
LYD GL15 ... 200 C3
LYD GL15 ... 202 D1
LYD GL15 ... 224 F3
LYD GL15 ... 225 H1
MALM SN16 ... 303 J8 2
MANG/FISH BS16 ... 327 L7
MIM GL56 ... 57 G1
MIM GL56 ... 58 C5 2
MIM GL56 ... 79 K4
MTCHDN GL17 ... 128 F6
MTCHDN GL17 ... 128 F3
MTCHDN GL17 ... 129 M3
MTCHDN GL17 ... 130 C1
NWNT GL18 ... 86 C2
OLD/WMLY/WICK BS30 ... 338 F7
OLD/WMLY/WICK BS30 ... 338 F4
OLD/WMLY/WICK BS30 ... 339 K5
OLD/WMLY/WICK BS30 ... 340 B2
OLD/WMLY/WICK BS30 ... 349 G3
RSTROUD/NAIL GL6 ... 210 C3
RSTROUD/NAIL GL6 ... 233 J5 2
RSTROUD/NAIL GL6 ... 234 B1
SHPSTR CV36 ... 16 B5 1
STNHO GL10 ... 207 J8
STNHO GL10 ... 207 H4
STROUD GL5 ... 208 E4
STROUD GL5 ... 232 B2
TET GL8 ... 257 K2
TEWK GL20 ... 27 G5
TEWK GL20 ... 48 A4
THNB/SVB BS35 ... 293 K2
VGL GL2 ... 155 M8
VGL GL2 ... 181 H4
WUE GL12 ... 277 H7
WUE GL12 ... 277 K4 3
WUE GL12 ... 296 C5
WUE GL12 ... 297 M4
YATE/CS BS37 ... 308 F7
YATE/CS BS37 ... 320 D2
High Vw CHEP NP16 ... 270 A3 2
VGL GL2 ... 135 J5
Highview Rd CIND GL14 ... 154 C3 1
KGWD/HNM BS15 ... 338 A1
LYD GL15 ... 177 K8
MTCHDN GL17 ... 129 K5
Highview Wy LYD GL15 ... 200 D3
Highway YATE/CS BS37 ... 320 B1
Highwood Av CHELTS GL53 ... 115 L5
Highwood La
BRSTK/PCHW BS34 ... 316 A4
HNBRY/STHM BS10 ... 315 M4
Highwood Rd
BRSTK/PCHW BS34 ... 316 A4
Highworth Crs YATE/CS BS37 ... 319 M3
Highworth Rd
BRSG/KWL/STAPK BS4 ... 336 F6
GL GL1 ... 136 B5
Hilirise LYD GL15 ... 200 D2
Hilcote Dr COTS GL54 ... 123 J7
Hildyard Cl VGL GL2 ... 159 G4
Hillands Dr CHELTS GL53 ... 115 M7
Hillary Rd CHELTS GL53 ... 116 A7
Hill Av BMSTR BS3 ... 336 A8
Hillborough Rd GLE GL4 ... 136 A8
Hillbrook Rd
THNB/SVB BS35 ... 293 M3 1
Hill Burn
HNLZ/SM/SNYPK/WT BS9 ... 325 L5
Hillburn Rd EVILLE/WHL BS5 ... 337 J3
Hill Cl DSLY GL11 ... 229 H7 2
TEWK GL20 ... 27 K4
Hillcot Cl VGL GL2 ... 159 G2
Hill Court Rd CHELTE/BC GL52 ... 94 A7
Hill Crest BRSG/KWL/STAPK BS4 .. 346 D2
VGL GL2 ... 111 G5
Hillcrest BRKLY GL13 ... 227 H8
CHPMW/MSHF SN14 ... 343 L5
THNB/SVB BS35 ... 293 K2
Hillcrest La CLFD GL16 ... 151 M8
Hillcrest Rd CLFD GL16 ... 151 K6
STROUD GL5 ... 208 A3
Hill End Dr HNBRY/STHM BS10 ... 314 F8
Hill End Rd TEWK GL20 ... 26 B5 1
Hillersland La CLFD GL16 ... 151 J4
Hillesley Rd WUE GL12 ... 277 H7
Hillfield CHELTW GL51 ... 115 H2
STROUD GL5 ... 208 B4 1
Hillfield Court Rd GL GL1 ... 5 J4
Hillfield Dr LED HR8 ... 20 A2
Hillfields Av MANG/FISH BS16 ... 327 L8
Hill Gv
HNLZ/SM/SNYPK/WT BS9 ... 325 L5
Hillgrove St CBRISNE BS2 ... 336 A3 6
Hillgrove St North
CBRISNE BS2 ... 335 M3 7
Hill Hay Rd GLE GL4 ... 136 E8
Hill House Rd MANG/FISH BS16 ... 328 B6
Hillier Cl STROUD GL5 ... 208 F2 1
Hillier Dr CHELTW GL51 ... 115 H6
Hill La RBANSW OX15 ... 17 L6
STRAT CV37 ... 9 K2
THNB/SVB BS35 ... 273 G3
YATE/CS BS37 ... 321 K4
Hill Lawn BRSG/KWL/STAPK BS4 .. 336 F8
Hillmill La WUE GL12 ... 277 M7
Hill Rd DSLY GL11 ... 253 J2
GLE GL4 ... 136 B7
WUE GL12 ... 277 L5
Hillsborough Rd
BRSG/KWL/STAPK BS4 ... 336 E7
Hills Cl KEYN BS31 ... 348 C6
Hillsdon Rd
HNLZ/SM/SNYPK/WT BS9 ... 325 H3
Hillside EVE WR11 ... 29 K2
HGHW SN6 ... 287 L6
MANG/FISH BS16 ... 328 B6
RSTROUD/NAIL GL6 ... 210 D7
Hillside Av KGWD/HNM BS15 ... 337 L3
Hillside Cl CHELTE/BC GL52 ... 72 E8 1
CHELTW GL51 ... 115 J4
FRCTL/WBN BS36 ... 318 E4
LYD GL15 ... 200 D2
Hillside Gdns CHELTE/BC GL52 ... 72 E8
Hillside La FRCTL/WBN BS36 ... 318 E4 2
Hillside Rd EVILLE/WHL BS5 ... 337 J4
LGASH BS41 ... 344 D1
MTCHDN GL17 ... 129 M2
Hillside St BRSG/KWL/STAPK BS4 ... 7 L9
Hillside Ter MTCHDN GL17 ... 128 C5 1
Hill St BMSTR BS3 ... 7 J9
CBRIS/FH BS1 ... 6 C4
EVILLE/WHL BS5 ... 337 H3
LYD GL15 ... 201 J8
The Hill ALMDB BS32 ... 306 D7
STROUD GL5 ... 208 D4
Hilltop LYD GL15 ... 200 C3
Hill Top Cl STROUD GL5 ... 209 G4
Hilltop Gdns EVILLE/WHL BS5 ... 337 J4
Hill Top La NWNT GL18 ... 86 D1
Hill Top Rd CHELT GL50 ... 93 M6
Hilltop Rd MANG/FISH BS16 ... 337 M1
Hilltop Vw DSLY GL11 ... 229 H7
EVILLE/WHL BS5 ... 337 J4
Hill Top Vw
RSTROUD/NAIL GL6 ... 209 M7 5
Hill Vw CFTN/FAIL BS8 ... 6 A4
HNLZ/SM/SNYPK/WT BS9 ... 325 L5
LYD GL15 ... 201 J8
MANG/FISH BS16 ... 337 M1
Hillview Av BWTH/CHD GL3 ... 137 M5
Hill View Cl
OLD/WMLY/WICK BS30 ... 338 E7
Hillview Dr BWTH/CHD GL3 ... 137 H3
Hillview La TEWK GL20 ... 26 B4
Hillview Ri CLFD GL16 ... 151 J5
Hill View Rd
BMSTRD/HC/WWD BS13 ... 345 J4
CHELTE/BC GL52 ... 3 L4
MANG/FISH BS16 ... 329 L6
Hillview Rd BWTH/CHD GL3 ... 137 H3
Hillyfield Rd
BMSTRD/HC/WWD BS13 ... 345 J5
Hilton Cl VGL GL2 ... 135 K5
Hinders La RTEWK/TIB GL19 ... 131 M1
Hinton Cl KEYN BS31 ... 349 G8
Hinton Dr
OLD/WMLY/WICK BS30 ... 338 E5
Hinton Rd EVILLE/WHL BS5 ... 336 E2
GL GL1 ... 5 H1
MANG/FISH BS16 ... 327 J7 2
Hisnams Fld CHELTE/BC GL52 ... 72 B8 1
Hitchen Cl CHPMW/MSHF SN14 .. 342 B3
Hitchen Hollow CHEP NP16 ... 270 D7
Hitchings LYD GL15 ... 178 D8
Hitchings Skilling
CHPMW/MSHF SN14 ... 343 K8 2
The Hithe STROUD GL5 ... 208 D8
Hobbes Cl MALM SN16 ... 303 H7
The Hobbins SHPSTR CV36 ... 16 A6
Hobb's La CBRIS/FH BS1 ... 6 D4 3
CIR GL7 ... 189 L4
KGWD/HNM BS15 ... 338 D2
MTCHDN GL17 ... 107 J8
NAIL BS48 ... 344 A7
Hobby Cl CHELTS GL53 ... 115 L6
Hobwell La LGASH BS41 ... 344 E1 2
Hockey's La MANG/FISH BS16 ... 327 J7 2
Hoddon La MANG/FISH BS16 ... 329 L6
Hodge La MALM SN16 ... 303 H7
Hodges Wy CIND GL14 ... 154 A4 1
Hogarth Wk HORF/LLZ BS7 ... 326 D4
Hogues Wk
BMSTRD/HC/WWD BS13 ... 345 K7 4
Holbeach Wy HGRV/WHIT BS14 .. 346 C8
Holbrook Wk MTCHDN GL17 ... 128 C8
Holbrook Crs
BMSTRD/HC/WWD BS13 ... 345 M7
Holbrook La
OLD/WMLY/WICK BS30 ... 339 J4
Holcombe Gv KEYN BS31 ... 347 M6
Holcot Cl CLFD GL16 ... 175 M1
Holcot Rd CLFD GL16 ... 175 M2
Holdenhurst Rd
KGWD/HNM BS15 ... 337 L2
Holder Cl TET GL8 ... 281 M4
Holder Rd CHELTE/BC GL52 ... 94 B1 2
Holders La NWNT GL18 ... 63 M7
Holders Wk LGASH BS41 ... 344 B2
Holford Ct HGRV/WHIT BS14 ... 346 D6
Holford Crs CIR GL7 ... 267 G5
Hollams Rd TEWK GL20 ... 48 B4
Holland Ct GL GL1 ... 5 K3
Hollies Hl RSTROUD/NAIL GL6 ... 232 E7
Hollies La CBATH/BATHN BA1 ... 352 C5
Hollingham La
RSTROUD/NAIL GL6 ... 256 A2
Hollins Cl CHEP NP16 ... 270 B2 2
Hollis Cl LGASH BS41 ... 344 B3
Hollis Gdns CHELTW GL51 ... 114 F5
Hollis Rd CHELTW GL51 ... 114 F5
Hollister's Dr
BMSTRD/HC/WWD BS13 ... 345 M8
Holloway MALM SN16 ... 303 J8
Holloway Hl
CHPMW/MSHF SN14 ... 333 G3
Holloway Rd
RSTROUD/NAIL GL6 ... 210 C3
Hollow La STROUD GL5 ... 208 F4
Hollow Rd ALMDB BS32 ... 306 C7
KGWD/HNM BS15 ... 338 A3
The Hollows EVE WR11 ... 30 D1
FRCTL/WBN BS36 ... 328 E1
The Hollow MTCHDN GL17 ... 129 K4
Hollway Cl HGRV/WHIT BS14 ... 347 G6 2
Hollway Rd HGRV/WHIT BS14 ... 347 G6
Hollybush Cl BAD GL9 ... 323 J5
Hollybush La
HNLZ/SM/SNYPK/WT BS9 ... 325 G7
Holly Cl CHEP NP16 ... 270 A6 2
EVILLE/WHL BS5 ... 337 J1
MANG/FISH BS16 ... 329 L6
THNB/SVB BS35 ... 293 H7
Holly Crs KGWD/HNM BS15 ... 338 A2 3
Holly Dr CHPMW/MSHF SN14 .. 343 H5 1
Holly End VGL GL2 ... 159 H3
Holly Gn KGWD/HNM BS15 ... 338 C2
Holly Gv MANG/FISH BS16 ... 327 L8
The Holly Gv VGL GL2 ... 159 H3
Hollyguest Rd
KGWD/HNM BS15 ... 338 A5
Holly Hl YATE/CS BS37 ... 309 G8
Hollyhill Rd CIND GL14 ... 153 M2
Holly Hill Rd KGWD/HNM BS15 ... 338 B3
Hollyhock La
RSTROUD/NAIL GL6 ... 185 H3 6
Holly La CLFD GL16 ... 176 A6
Hollyleigh Av
BRSTK/PCHW BS34 ... 326 B1
Holly Lodge Rd
EVILLE/WHL BS5 ... 337 H1
Hollymead La
HNLZ/SM/SNYPK/WT BS9 ... 325 G7
Hollyridge HGRV/WHIT BS14 ... 346 E5
Holly Rd SHPSTR CV36 ... 16 B7
Holly Tree Gdn STROUD GL5 ... 207 M5 1
Holly Tree Pl LYD GL15 ... 201 M2
Holly Wk KEYN BS31 ... 347 M8
Hollywell Rd MTCHDN GL17 ... 106 C8
Hollywood La THNB/SVB BS35 ... 315 J4
Hollywood Rd
BRSG/KWL/STAPK BS4 ... 336 F8
Holmdale Rd
BRSTK/PCHW BS34 ... 316 D8
Holmer Crs CHELTW GL51 ... 114 F5 3
Holme Rd TEWK GL20 ... 48 B8 2
Holmesdale Rd BMSTR BS3 ... 336 A8
Holmes Gv
HNLZ/SM/SNYPK/WT BS9 ... 325 K6
Holmes Hill Rd EVILLE/WHL BS5 .. 337 H3
Holmes St EVILLE/WHL BS5 ... 336 D5 7
Holm La THNB/SVB BS35 ... 305 J1
Holmleigh Rd GL GL1 ... 135 L8
Holmoak Rd KEYN BS31 ... 347 L7
Holmwood KGWD/HNM BS15 ... 337 L6
Holmwood Cl
FRCTL/WBN BS36 ... 317 M5 1
GL GL1 ... 159 M1 1
Holmwood Dr GL GL1 ... 159 M1
Holmwood Gdns
HNLZ/SM/SNYPK/WT BS9 ... 325 J3
Holsom Cl HGRV/WHIT BS14 ... 347 G5

Holsom Rd *HGRV/WHIT* BS14 ... 347 H5 🔢

Holst Gdns
  BRSG/KWL/STAPK BS4 ... 345 L4
Holst Wy *GLE* GL4 ... 159 M1
Holtham Av *BWTH/CHD* GL3 ... 113 K4
Holton Rd *HORF/LLZ* BS7 ... 326 C5
Holtsdown La
  CBATH/BATHN BA1 ... 352 A3
Holts Rd *NWNT* GL18 ... 86 B3
The Holt *GLE* GL4 ... 137 C4
Holyrood Cl
  BRSTK/PCHW BS34 ... 316 F7 🔢
Holy Well Cl
  BRSG/KWL/STAPK BS4 ... 337 C5 🔢
Holywell Rd *DSLY* GL11 ... 229 J7
  WUE GL12 ... 277 L3
Homeapple Hl
  OLD/WMLY/WICK BS30 ... 339 G4
Home Cl *HNBRY/STHM* BS10 ... 326 A1
  MIM GL56 ... 103 H2
Homecroft Dr *CHELTW* GL51 ... 93 C6
Home Farm La *CFTN/FAIL* BS8 ... 334 C4
Home Farm Wy
  THNB/SVB BS35 ... 315 J2
Homefield *RSTROUD/NAIL* GL6 ... 232 D3 🔢
  THNB/SVB BS35 ... 293 M3 🔢
  YATE/CS BS37 ... 310 A8
Homefield Cl *KEYN* BS31 ... 349 G8
Home Field Cl *MANG/FISH* BS16 ... 328 D5 🔢
Homefield Rd *KEYN* BS31 ... 349 G8
  MANG/FISH BS16 ... 329 K6
  HNLZ/SM/SNYPK/WT BS9 ... 325 K4
Homeground La *CIR* GL7 ... 243 C4
Homeleaze Rd
  HNBRY/STHM BS10 ... 315 M8
Home Md
  OLD/WMLY/WICK BS30 ... 338 C7
Homemead Dr
  BRSG/KWL/STAPK BS4 ... 346 F2 🔢
The Homend *LED* HR8 ... 20 A2
The Homend *LED* HR8 ... 19 M1
Home Orch *YATE/CS* BS37 ... 319 M1
Homestead Cl *TEWK* GL20 ... 27 H5 🔢
Homestead Gdns
  MANG/FISH BS16 ... 327 K2
Homestead Rd
  BRSTK/PCHW BS34 ... 316 D8
Honeyborne Wy *WUE* GL12 ... 296 D6 🔢
Honeybourne Rd *EVE* WR11 ... 11 L3
Honey Garston Cl
  BMSTRD/HC/WWD BS13 ... 345 K7 🔢
Honey Garston Rd
  BMSTRD/HC/WWD BS13 ... 345 K7
Honey Hill Rd *KGWD/HNM* BS15... 338 B3
Honeymead
  HGRV/WHIT BS14 ... 346 E5 🔢
Honeysuckle Cl *ALMDB* BS32 ... 317 G1 🔢
  CHELTE/BC GL52 ... 94 E8 🔢
Honeysuckle Dr *GLE* GL4 ... 137 G6
Honey Suckle La
  MANG/FISH BS16 ... 327 G7 🔢
Honeysuckle Wy
  CHELTE/BC GL52 ... 72 A6
Honeythorn Cl *VGL* GL2 ... 135 K4
Honiton Rd *MANG/FISH* BS16 ... 327 J8 🔢
Honyatt Rd *GL1* ... 5 H3
Hookshouse La *TET* GL8 ... 280 F8
  TET GL8 ... 281 J5
Hook's La *NWNT* GL18 ... 87 H2
Hoo La *CHCAM* GL55 ... 12 D8
  RTEWK/TIB GL19 ... 69 M3
Hooper Rd *HGRV/WHIT* BS14 ... 346 F6
Hopechapel Hl
  CFTN/FAIL BS8 ... 335 H5 🔢
Hope Mill La *STROUD* GL5 ... 233 G1
Hope Orch *CHELTW* GL51 ... 92 F7
  YATE/CS BS37 ... 319 J1
Hopes Cl *LYD* GL15 ... 225 L1
Hope Sq *CFTN/FAIL* BS8 ... 335 H5 🔢
Hope St *CHELT* GL51 ... 93 K8
Hopetoun Rd *CBRISNE* BS2 ... 326 B8 🔢
Hopewell Gdns *AVONM* BS11 ... 324 B4
Hopewell St *GL* GL1 ... 5 H9
Hopkin Cl *THNB/SVB* BS35... 293 M4
Hopland Cl
  OLD/WMLY/WICK BS30 ... 338 D8
Hopp's Rd *KGWD/HNM* BS15 ... 337 M4
Hopton Rd *DSLY* GL11 ... 229 J6
Hopyard La *NWNT* GL18 ... 86 C1
The Hopyard *TEWK* GL20 ... 48 F2
Horcott Rd *CIR* GL7 ... 242 D5
Horesham Gv
  BMSTRD/HC/WWD BS13 ... 345 L6 🔢
Horfield Rd *CBRISNE* BS2 ... 6 E2
Horley Rd *CBRISNE* BS2 ... 336 C2
Hornbeam Ms *VGL* GL2 ... 112 D6 🔢
Horn La *MIM* GL56 ... 81 H5
Horns Rd *STROUD* GL5 ... 208 F5
Horsbere Rd *BWTH/CHD* GL3 ... 137 J3
Horsecroft Gdns
  OLD/WMLY/WICK BS30 ... 338 C5 🔢
Horsefair *SHPSTR* CV36 ... 16 E5 🔢
Horsefair Cl *CHELTS* GL53 ... 116 C6 🔢
Horse Fair La *HGHW* SN6 ... 289 C3
Horsefair La *NWNT* GL18 ... 86 A2
Horsefair St *CHELTS* GL53 ... 116 C5 🔢
The Horsefair *CBRIS/FH* BS1 ... 7 G2
Horse La *THNB/SVB* BS35 ... 273 M6
Horse Lane Orch *LED* HR8 ... 20 A3
Horsepool La *LYD* GL15 ... 198 E7
  OLD/WMLY/WICK BS30 ... 340 B3
Horse Pool La *RWYE* HR9 ... 126 E6 🔢
Horsepool Rd
  BMSTRD/HC/WWD BS13 ... 345 G7 🔢
The Horsepool *CLFD* GL16 ... 151 J5 🔢
Horseshoe Dr
  HNLZ/SM/SNYPK/WT BS9 ... 324 F7
Horseshoe La *YATE/CS* BS37 ... 320 D2
Horse St *YATE/CS* BS37 ... 320 E3
Horsford Rd *WUE* GL12 ... 276 D6
Horslea *MTCHDN* GL17 ... 128 D6
Horsley Cl *GLE* GL4 ... 137 C6
Horsley Hl *RSTROUD/NAIL* GL6 ... 256 C1
Horsley Rd *RSTROUD/NAIL* GL6 ... 256 C1
Hortham La *ALMDB* BS32 ... 306 C3
Horton Hl *YATE/CS* BS37 ... 311 K6

Horton Rd *VGL* GL2 ... 5 K6
  YATE/CS BS37 ... 320 E1
Horton St *CBRISNE* BS2 ... 7 K4
Horwood Ct
  OLD/WMLY/WICK BS30 ... 338 C7 🔢
Horwood La *WUE* GL12 ... 296 D7
Hosey Wk
  BMSTRD/HC/WWD BS13 ... 345 J6
Hospital Rd *MIM* GL56 ... 58 C5
Host St *CBRIS/FH* BS1 ... 6 E3
Hottom Gdns *HORF/LLZ* BS7 ... 326 C4
Hot Water La *KGWD/HNM* BS15 ... 328 B8
Hotwell Rd *CFTN/FAIL* BS8 ... 335 H5 🔢
Houlton St *CBRISNE* BS2 ... 7 J1
Hounds Rd *YATE/CS* BS37 ... 320 D3
Howard Av *EVILLE/WHL* BS5 ... 337 C3
Howard Cl *KEYN* BS31 ... 348 E8
  TEWK GL20 ... 49 C3
Howard Rd *BMSTR* BS3 ... 345 L1
  CLFD GL16 ... 151 M8
  MANG/FISH BS16 ... 327 M7
  RDLND/MONT BS6 ... 325 K7
  TEWK GL20 ... 49 C3
  THNB/SVB BS35 ... 293 L1 🔢
Howard St *EVILLE/WHL* BS5 ... 337 C2
  GL GL1 ... 136 A4
Howcroft *BWTH/CHD* GL3 ... 113 L7
Howcroft Gdns
  HNLZ/SM/SNYPK/WT BS9 ... 325 G7 🔢
Howell Rd *CHELTW* GL51 ... 93 H7
Howell's La *LYD* GL15 ... 178 E5
Howells Md
  MANG/FISH BS16 ... 328 D4 🔢
Howells Rd *TEWK* GL20 ... 48 A5 🔢
Howes Cl
  OLD/WMLY/WICK BS30 ... 338 C5
Howett Rd *EVILLE/WHL* BS5 ... 336 E4 🔢
Howgate Cl *GLE* GL4 ... 137 H5
Howmead *BRKLY* GL13 ... 227 G7
Howsmoor La *MANG/FISH* BS16 ... 328 D3
Hoylake Dr *OLD/WMLY/WICK* BS30 338 D5
Hucclecote La *BWTH/CHD* GL3 ... 137 M1
Hucclecote Rd *BWTH/CHD* GL3 ... 137 H5
Huckford La *FRCTL/WBN* BS36 ... 318 C7
Huckford Rd *FRCTL/WBN* BS36 ... 318 A6
Huckley Wy *ALMDB* BS32 ... 317 H5
Huddleston Rd *COTS* GL54 ... 74 C4 🔢
Hudd's Hill Rd *EVILLE/WHL* BS5 ... 337 H5
Hudd's Vale Rd
  EVILLE/WHL BS5 ... 337 G3 🔢
Hudman's Cl *TEWK* GL20 ... 26 C5
Hudson La *YATE/CS* BS37 ... 320 B3
Hudson La *CIND* GL14 ... 154 A6
Hudson La *MALM* SN16 ... 303 H7
Hudsons Vw *CIND* GL14 ... 154 A6
Hughenden Rd
  CFTN/FAIL BS8 ... 335 J1 🔢
  HORF/LLZ BS7 ... 326 A6
Hughes Crs *CHEP* NP16 ... 270 A4
Hughes Ter *LYD* GL15 ... 176 E6
Hulbert Cl
  BRSG/KWL/STAPK BS4 ... 347 J1 🔢
  CHELTW GL51 ... 93 J4
Hulse Rd *BRSG/KWL/STAPK* BS4... 346 F2
Humber Pl *BWTH/CHD* GL3 ... 138 B6
Humber Rd *CHELTE/BC* GL52 ... 3 K4
  AVONM BS11 ... 324 A3 🔢
Humberstan Wk
Humphreys Cl
  RSTROUD/NAIL GL6 ... 208 A2
Humphrys Barton
  BRSG/KWL/STAPK BS4 ... 337 H6
Hungerford Cl
  BRSG/KWL/STAPK BS4 ... 347 G3
Hungerford Crs
  BRSG/KWL/STAPK BS4 ... 347 G3
Hungerford Gdns
  BRSG/KWL/STAPK BS4 ... 347 G3
Hungerford Rd
  BRSG/KWL/STAPK BS4 ... 347 G3
Hungerford St *CHELT* GL50 ... 2 C2
Hungerford Wk
  BRSG/KWL/STAPK BS4 ... 347 G2
Hunger Hl *DSLY* GL11 ... 253 J3
Hung Rd *AVONM* BS11 ... 324 A5
Hunters Cl *KGWD/HNM* BS15 ... 337 L6 🔢
Hunters Dr *KGWD/HNM* BS15 ... 338 B2
Hunters Ga *GLE* GL4 ... 136 F7
Hunters Md *BAD* GL9 ... 312 C1
Hunters Rd *CHELTE/BC* GL52 ... 72 A7
  KGWD/HNM BS15 ... 337 L6
Hunters Rd East
  KGWD/HNM BS15 ... 337 L6
Hunter's Wy
  BRSTK/PCHW BS34 ... 316 D8
  COTS GL54 ... 118 C7
  STROUD GL5 ... 207 M4
Hunthill *CIND* GL14 ... 156 E1
Huntingdon Cl *STROUD* GL5 ... 207 M5 🔢
Huntingham Rd
  BMSTRD/HC/WWD BS13 ... 345 G7
Huntley Cl *GLE* GL4 ... 137 C6
Hunts Cl *BUR/CRTN* OX18 ... 173 M7
Huntscote Rd *CHELTW* GL51 ... 93 K4
Huntsfield Cl *CHELT* GL50 ... 94 A7 🔢
Hunts Grove Vw *VGL* GL2 ... 159 K4
Huntsmans Cl
  CHELTE/BC GL52 ... 72 C7 🔢
Huntsmans Meet *COTS* GL54 ... 118 C7 🔢
Hurcombe Wy *BWTH/CHD* GL3... 138 A5
Hurle Crs *CFTN/FAIL* BS8 ... 335 J2
Hurle Rd *CFTN/FAIL* BS8 ... 335 K2
Hurlingham Rd
  RDLND/MONT BS6 ... 336 B1
Hurn La *KEYN* BS31 ... 348 B7
Hurst Cl *VGL* GL2 ... 112 F6
Hurston Rd
  BRSG/KWL/STAPK BS4 ... 345 M3
Hurst Rd *BRSG/KWL/STAPK* BS4... 346 B3
Hurst Wk
  BRSG/KWL/STAPK BS4 ... 346 A3
Hurstwood Rd
  MANG/FISH BS16 ... 327 M6
Husbandmans Cl
  SHPSTR CV36 ... 16 B5 🔢

Hutton Cl
  HNLZ/SM/SNYPK/WT BS9 ... 324 F4
Huxley Ct *CIR* GL7 ... 263 J4
Huxley Rd *GL* GL1 ... 136 B4
Huxley Wy *CHELTE/BC* GL52 ... 71 M7
Huyton Rd *EVILLE/WHL* BS5 ... 327 C8 🔢
Hyatts Wy *CHELTE/BC* GL52 ... 72 C8
Hyde Cl *GL* GL1 ... 5 J4
Hyde La *CHELT* GL50 ... 93 M4
  CIND GL14 ... 155 H6
  GL GL1 ... 5 J4
  GL GL1 ... 182 A6
Hyde Park Cnr *RTEWK/TIB* GL19... 43 J8
Hyde's La *CHPMW/MSHF* SN14 ... 341 J5
The Hyde *COTS* GL54 ... 74 B6
Hyett Rd *STROUD* GL5 ... 208 A4
Hygrove La *VGL* GL2 ... 134 D2
Hyland Gv
  HNLZ/SM/SNYPK/WT BS9 ... 325 H3

I

Icehouse La *MIM* GL56 ... 79 J1
Icombe Cl *CHELTE/BC* GL52 ... 72 B8 🔢
Ida Rd *EVILLE/WHL* BS5 ... 336 E3 🔢
Iddesleigh Rd
  RDLND/MONT BS6 ... 325 K8 🔢
Idsall Dr *CHELTE/BC* GL52 ... 94 E7
Idstone Rd *MANG/FISH* BS16 ... 327 K8
Iford Cl *KEYN* BS31 ... 349 G8
Ilchester Crs
  BMSTRD/HC/WWD BS13 ... 345 K2
Ilchester Rd
  BMSTRD/HC/WWD BS13 ... 345 K3
Iles Cl *KGWD/HNM* BS15 ... 337 M7
Ilex Cl *BMSTRD/HC/WWD* BS13 ... 345 H5
Ilminster Av
  BRSG/KWL/STAPK BS4 ... 346 B3
Ilsyn Gv *HGRV/WHIT* BS14 ... 346 F4
Imber Court Cl
  HGRV/WHIT BS14 ... 346 D3
Imjin Rd *CHELTE/BC* GL52 ... 3 M4
Imperial Circ *CHELT* GL50 ... 2 D5 🔢
Imperial La *CHELT* GL50 ... 2 C6
Imperial Rd *HGRV/WHIT* BS14... 346 E4
  RDLND/MONT BS6 ... 335 K2 🔢
Imperial Sq *CHELT* GL50 ... 2 C7
Imperial Wk *HGRV/WHIT* BS14 ... 346 E4
Inchbrook Hl
  RSTROUD/NAIL GL6 ... 232 C5
India Rd *GL* GL1 ... 5 J8
Ingleside Rd *KGWD/HNM* BS15... 337 L2
Inglestone Rd *WUE* GL12 ... 296 D6
Ingmire Rd *EVILLE/WHL* BS5 ... 326 D8
Ingst Rd *THNB/SVB* BS35 ... 291 L7
Inkerman Rd *HORF/LLZ* BS7 ... 326 A4
The Inner Down *ALMDB* BS32 ... 292 F8
Inner Loop Rd *CHEP* NP16 ... 270 A4
Innerstone La *RTEWK/TIB* GL19 ... 65 K3
Innox Gdns
  BMSTRD/HC/WWD BS13 ... 345 J6 🔢
Innox La *CBATH/BATHN* BA1 ... 351 K6
Inns Court Av
  BRSG/KWL/STAPK BS4 ... 345 M4
Inns Court Dr
  BRSG/KWL/STAPK BS4 ... 345 M5 🔢
Innsworth La *BWTH/CHD* GL3 ... 113 H4
  VGL GL2 ... 112 C6
Insley Gdns *GLE* GL4 ... 137 H3
Instow Rd
  BRSG/KWL/STAPK BS4 ... 346 A3
Instow Wk
  BRSG/KWL/STAPK BS4 ... 346 A3 🔢
Inverlea Ct *CHCAM* GL55 ... 8 F7
Ipswich Pl
  BRSG/KWL/STAPK BS4 ... 337 C5
Irby Rd *BMSTR* BS3 ... 335 J8
Irena Rd *MANG/FISH* BS16 ... 337 H1 🔢
Ireton Rd *BMSTR* BS3 ... 335 K8
Iron Acton Wy *YATE/CS* BS37 ... 309 J8
Iron Hogg La *WUE* GL12 ... 274 E8
Ironmonger's La *BRKLY* GL13 ... 227 K7
Ironmould La
  BRSG/KWL/STAPK BS4 ... 347 K3
Ironstone Cl *LYD* GL15 ... 200 C3 🔢
Irving Cl *MANG/FISH* BS16 ... 328 A7 🔢
Isbourne Rd *CHELTE/BC* GL52... 3 L3
Isbourne Wy *COTS* GL54 ... 74 D3
Isleys Ct
  OLD/WMLY/WICK BS30 ... 338 B8 🔢
Islington Rd *BMSTR* BS3 ... 6 B8
Ismay Rd *CHELTW* GL51 ... 93 G7
Ison Hill Rd
  HNBRY/STHM BS10 ... 314 F8 🔢
Itchington Rd *THNB/SVB* BS35 ... 294 C7
Ivor Rd *EVILLE/WHL* BS5 ... 336 E3
Ivory Cl *GL* GL1 ... 159 L1
Ivy Bank *CHELTE/BC* GL52 ... 94 E8 🔢
Ivy House La *RWYE* HR9 ... 84 E2 🔢
Ivy La *MANG/FISH* BS16 ... 327 J8 🔢
Ivywell Rd
  HNLZ/SM/SNYPK/WT BS9 ... 325 C8
Izod's Cl *CHCAM* GL55 ... 34 D1 🔢

J

Jackbarrow Rd *CIR* GL7 ... 188 C3
Jackson Cl *THNB/SVB* BS35 ... 304 F4 🔢
Jackson Crs *VGL* GL2 ... 113 C5
Jackson Rd *CHNTN* OX7 ... 125 M1
  CIR GL7 ... 239 H8
Jacobs Cl *TET* GL8 ... 282 A2 🔢
Jacob St *CBRISNE* BS2 ... 7 H3
Jacob's Wells Rd *CFTN/FAIL* BS8... 6 A4
Jamaica St *CBRISNE* BS2 ... 335 M3
James Cl *MANG/FISH* BS16 ... 328 A7 🔢
James Grieve Rd
  BWTH/CHD GL3 ... 137 H5
Jameson Cl *MIM* GL56 ... 58 C6 🔢
James Orch *BRKLY* GL13 ... 226 F8
James Rd *MANG/FISH* BS16 ... 328 A8
James St *CBRISNE* BS2 ... 336 C1
  EVILLE/WHL BS5 ... 7 K1

James Wk *LYD* GL15 ... 201 H2
James Wy *BWTH/CHD* GL3 ... 137 L5
Jane St *EVILLE/WHL* BS5 ... 336 D4
Japonica Cl *BWTH/CHD* GL3 ... 113 J4 🔢
Japonica Dr *CHELTW* GL51 ... 115 J6
Jardine St *CHELTE/BC* GL52 ... 72 A7
Jarvis St *EVILLE/WHL* BS5 ... 336 D5
Jasmine Cl *GLE* GL4 ... 136 F7
Jasmine Gv *AVONM* BS11 ... 324 E1 🔢
Jasmin Wy *CHELTW* GL51 ... 115 H6
Jasper St *BMSTR* BS3 ... 335 K8 🔢
Javelin Wy *BWTH/CHD* GL3 ... 138 B6
Jay's Md *WUE* GL12 ... 277 L4
Jaythorpe *GLE* GL4 ... 136 F8
Jean Rd *BRSG/KWL/STAPK* BS4... 347 G1
Jefferies Cl *CIR* GL7 ... 242 F4
Jefferies Hill Bottom
  KGWD/HNM BS15 ... 337 K6
Jeffery Ct
  OLD/WMLY/WICK BS30 ... 338 D5
Jena St *KEYN* BS31 ... 348 F8
Jenkin's La *RSTROUD/NAIL* GL6 ... 184 B4
Jenner Cl *GLE* GL4 ... 137 H3
  YATE/CS BS37 ... 320 F3
Jenner St *BRKLY* GL13 ... 227 G8 🔢
Jenner Wk *CHELT* GL50 ... 2 C1
Jersey Av
  BRSG/KWL/STAPK BS4 ... 337 H7
  CHELTE/BC GL52 ... 3 H5
Jersey Rd *GL* GL1 ... 5 H5
Jersey St *CHELTE/BC* GL52 ... 2 F4
Jesson Rd *CHELTE/BC* GL52 ... 72 C8
Jessop Av *CHELT* GL50 ... 2 B5
Jessop Dr *COTS* GL54 ... 145 J8
Jessop Under/Pass *BMSTR* BS3 ... 335 H7
Jewson Cl *GLE* GL4 ... 159 M1 🔢
Jeynes Rw *TEWK* GL20 ... 48 B4
Job's La *BUR/CRTN* OX18 ... 197 L2
  TEWK GL20 ... 27 M4
Jocelyn Rd *HORF/LLZ* BS7 ... 326 B4
Jockey La *EVILLE/WHL* BS5 ... 337 J4
John Betjeman Cl
  MALM SN16 ... 303 J6 🔢
John Bevan Cl *STROUD* GL5 ... 208 F3 🔢
John Carr's Ter *CFTN/FAIL* BS8... 6 A4
John Daniels Wy
  BWTH/CHD GL3 ... 113 K7
John Lee Rd *LED* HR8 ... 19 L3
John of Gaunt Rd *CIR* GL7 ... 266 F5
Johnson Dr
  OLD/WMLY/WICK BS30 ... 338 B6
Johnsons La *EVILLE/WHL* BS5 ... 336 F2
Johnsons Rd *EVILLE/WHL* BS5 ... 336 F3
Johnsons Wy *LYD* GL15 ... 201 L1
Johnstone Cl *RTEWK/TIB* GL19 ... 66 D5 🔢
Johnstone Rd *NWNT* GL18 ... 86 B3
John St *CBRIS/FH* BS1 ... 6 F3
  CBRISNE BS2 ... 336 C1
  KGWD/HNM BS15 ... 337 L3
  STROUD GL5 ... 208 E4 🔢
John Tame Cl *CIR* GL7 ... 242 F3
John Wesley Rd
  EVILLE/WHL BS5 ... 337 K5
John Woolfe Ct *MIM* GL56 ... 35 H5
Jordans Cl *BDWAY* WR12 ... 11 C8 🔢
Jordans Wy *VGL* GL2 ... 112 B6
Jordan Wk *ALMDB* BS32 ... 316 F3 🔢
Josend Crs *RTEWK/TIB* GL19 ... 68 A5
Joyford Hl *CLFD* GL16 ... 151 K5 🔢
Joy Hl *CFTN/FAIL* BS8 ... 335 H5 🔢 🔢
Joyner Rd *CHELTW* GL51 ... 93 J7
Joys Green Rd *MTCHDN* GL17 ... 128 C6
Jubilee Cl *DSLY* GL11 ... 229 C5
  LED HR8 ... 20 A5
Jubilee Dr *TEWK* GL20 ... 27 H5
  THNB/SVB BS35 ... 293 M3
Jubilee Gdns *CIR* GL7 ... 263 H5
  YATE/CS BS37 ... 320 C1 🔢
Jubilee La *WUE* GL12 ... 295 J4
Jubilee Pl *CBRIS/FH* BS1 ... 6 F6 🔢
  RTEWK/TIB GL19 ... 66 C5
Jubilee Rd
  BRSG/KWL/STAPK BS4 ... 346 E2
  CBRISNE BS2 ... 336 C2
  DSLY GL11 ... 253 J1
  EVILLE/WHL BS5 ... 337 H4
  KGWD/HNM BS15 ... 328 A8
  LYD GL15 ... 201 L8
  MTCHDN GL17 ... 130 C3
  RSTROUD/NAIL GL6 ... 232 C6
Jubilee St *CBRISNE* BS2 ... 7 K4
Jubilee Wy *BRKLY* GL13 ... 226 F3
  THNB/SVB BS35 ... 292 B3
Judge's La *NWNT* GL18 ... 107 L2
Julian Cl *GLE* GL4 ... 136 F7 🔢
  HNLZ/SM/SNYPK/WT BS9 ... 324 F7
Julian Rd
  HNLZ/SM/SNYPK/WT BS9 ... 325 G8
Julius Rd *HORF/LLZ* BS7 ... 325 M8
Julius Wy *LYD* GL15 ... 201 K7
Jumpers La *BRKLY* GL13 ... 227 G8
Junction Rd
  BRSG/KWL/STAPK BS4 ... 336 E7
  CHNTN OX7 ... 105 C7
Juniper Av *GLE* GL4 ... 136 D7
Juniper Cl *EVILLE/WHL* BS5 ... 336 E1 🔢
Juniper Wy *ALMDB* BS32 ... 317 H4
  STNHO GL10 ... 207 H5
Jupiter Rd *BRSTK/PCHW* BS34 ... 315 M4
Jupiter Wy *GLE* GL4 ... 137 H5
Justice Av *KEYN* BS31 ... 349 C8
Justice Rd *MANG/FISH* BS16 ... 327 J8 🔢
Justicia Wy *CHELTW* GL51 ... 115 H6

K

Kansas Dr *CIR* GL7 ... 242 F6
Kathdene Gdns *HORF/LLZ* BS7 ... 326 B8
Katherine St *WUE* GL12 ... 276 C6 🔢
Katherine's Wk *CIR* GL7 ... 244 F7
Katifer La *MALM* SN16 ... 303 J3 🔢
Kaybourne Crs *BWTH/CHD* GL3 ... 113 M6
Kayte Cl *CHELTE/BC* GL52 ... 94 B1
Kayte La *CHELTE/BC* GL52 ... 94 C2

Keats Av *VGL* GL2 ... 135 L2
Keats Gdns *STROUD* GL5 ... 208 C2 🔢
Keble Av
  HNBRY/STHM BS10 ... 345 H3
Keble Cl *CIR* GL7 ... 238 D7
  CIR GL7 ... 244 F6
Keble Lawns *CIR* GL7 ... 242 F4
Keble Rd *MIM* GL56 ... 58 D4
Keedwell Hl *LGASH* BS41 ... 344 B7
Keeds La *LGASH* BS41 ... 344 B7
Keedwell Hl *LGASH* BS41 ... 344 B7
The Keelings *CIND* GL14 ... 154 A6
Keels *HGHW* SN6 ... 288 D3
Keen's Gv *THNB/SVB* BS35 ... 304 E6
Keepers Ml *CHELTE/BC* GL52 ... 72 D5
The Keep
  OLD/WMLY/WICK BS30 ... 338 F7
Keetley Cl *SHPSTR* CV36 ... 16 E5
Keinton Wk *HNBRY/STHM* BS10... 326 A5
Kelbra Crs *FRCTL/WBN* BS36 ... 318 C2
Kellaway Av
  HNBRY/STHM BS10 ... 326 A5
  RDLND/MONT BS6 ... 325 M6
Kellaway Crs *HORF/LLZ* BS7 ... 325 M5
Kells Meend *CLFD* GL16 ... 151 J3
Kells Rd *CLFD* GL16 ... 151 J3
Kellys La *CHEP* NP16 ... 247 C2
Kelston Cl *KEYN* BS31 ... 348 F7
Kelston Gdns
  HNBRY/STHM BS10 ... 325 M4
Kelston Gv *KGWD/HNM* BS15 ... 338 A7
Kelston Rd *HNBRY/STHM* BS10 ... 325 M4
  KEYN BS31 ... 347 M8
Kelston Wk *MANG/FISH* BS16 ... 327 K8
Kemble Cl *KGWD/HNM* BS15 ... 338 A5 🔢
  CHELTW GL51 ... 114 C4
Kemble Dr *CIR* GL7 ... 238 D7
Kemble Gv *CHELTW* GL51 ... 114 C4
Kemble Rd *CIR* GL7 ... 159 M4
Kemerton Rd *CHELT* GL50 ... 115 H7
  TEWK GL20 ... 48 A3
Kemperleye Wy *ALMDB* BS32 ... 316 F4 🔢
Kempe's Cl *LGASH* BS41 ... 344 C2
Kempley Brook Dr *LED* HR8 ... 19 L2 🔢
Kempsford Acre
  CHELTE/BC GL52 ... 72 D8
Kemps La *RSTROUD/NAIL* GL6 ... 185 H4
Kempton Cl *THNB/SVB* BS35 ... 273 K8 🔢
Kempton Gv *CHELTW* GL51 ... 114 F7
Kencot Wk
  BMSTRD/HC/WWD BS13 ... 345 K8
Kencourt Cl *VGL* GL2 ... 5 L1
Kendall Gdns *MANG/FISH* BS16 ... 327 M4
Kendall Rd *MANG/FISH* BS16 ... 327 M4
Kendon Dr *HORF/LLZ* BS7 ... 326 C2
  VGL GL2 ... 112 E5
Kendon Dr *HNBRY/STHM* BS10... 325 M4
Kendon Wy *HNBRY/STHM* BS10... 325 M4
Kendrick St *STROUD* GL5 ... 208 E4 🔢
Kenelm Dr *CHELTS* GL53 ... 115 L5
Kenelm Gdns *CHELT* GL50 ... 115 K5
Kenelm Ri *COTS* GL54 ... 74 C1
Kenilworth *YATE/CS* BS37 ... 320 E1
Kenilworth Av *VGL* GL2 ... 5 L1
Kenilworth Cl *KEYN* BS31 ... 347 M8
Kenilworth Dr
  OLD/WMLY/WICK BS30 ... 348 D2
Kenilworth Rd
  RDLND/MONT BS6 ... 335 L2
Kenmare Rd
  BRSG/KWL/STAPK BS4 ... 346 A4
Kenmore Crs *HORF/LLZ* BS7 ... 326 A2
Kenmore Dr *HORF/LLZ* BS7 ... 326 A2
Kenmore Gv *HORF/LLZ* BS7 ... 326 A2
Kennard Ri *KGWD/HNM* BS15 ... 337 L3
Kennard Rd *KGWD/HNM* BS15 ... 337 L2
Kennedy Cl *GLE* GL4 ... 137 H4
Kennedy Wy *YATE/CS* BS37 ... 320 A4
Kennel Dr *BAD* GL9 ... 323 C4
Kennel La *BWTH/CHD* GL3 ... 138 A4
  CHNTN OX7 ... 105 K4
  MIM GL56 ... 80 C7
Kennel Lodge Rd *BMSTR* BS3 ... 335 C5
Kenneth Cl *CHELTS* GL53 ... 116 A4
Kenneth Rd
  BRSG/KWL/STAPK BS4 ... 346 E2
Kennet Rd *KEYN* BS31 ... 348 E3
Kennett Gdns *GLE* GL4 ... 137 C2
Kennet Wy *THNB/SVB* BS35 ... 293 M4 🔢
Kennington Av *HORF/LLZ* BS7 ... 326 A8
  KGWD/HNM BS15 ... 337 M2 🔢
Kennion Rd *EVILLE/WHL* BS5 ... 337 J4 🔢
Kennmoor Cl
  OLD/WMLY/WICK BS30 ... 338 C7
Kenn Rd *EVILLE/WHL* BS5 ... 337 J3
Kensal Av *BMSTR* BS3 ... 336 A4
Kensal Rd *BMSTR* BS3 ... 336 A4
Kensington Av *CHELTW* GL51 ... 115 J4
Kensington Cl
  THNB/SVB BS35 ... 293 K1 🔢
Kensington Pk
  EVILLE/WHL BS5 ... 336 C2 🔢
Kensington Park Rd
  BRSG/KWL/STAPK BS4 ... 346 E2
Kensington Pl *CFTN/FAIL* BS8 ... 335 J1
Kensington Rd
  EVILLE/WHL BS5 ... 337 J3
  MANG/FISH BS16 ... 327 M7 🔢
  RDLND/MONT BS6 ... 335 L1
Kent Av *YATE/CS* BS37 ... 310 B6
Kent Cl *BRSTK/PCHW* BS34 ... 316 F2
  BWTH/CHD GL3 ... 113 M4
Kent End *HGHW* SN6 ... 287 J2
Kentmere Cl *CHELTW* GL51 ... 115 C4
Kenton Dr *VGL* GL2 ... 112 E6
Kenton Ms
  HNLZ/SM/SNYPK/WT BS9... 325 L4
Kent Rd *HORF/LLZ* BS7 ... 326 A1
Kents Gn *KGWD/HNM* BS15 ... 338 A4
Kent St *BMSTR* BS3 ... 335 L8 🔢
Keriston Av *BWTH/CHD* GL3 ... 113 J4
Kerrin La *LYD* GL15 ... 224 B3
Kerry Rd *BRSG/KWL/STAPK* BS4... 346 C3
Kersteman Rd
  RDLND/MONT BS6 ... 325 M8 🔢
Kerstin Cl *CHELT* GL50 ... 93 L4
Kestrel Cl *BRSTK/PCHW* BS34 ... 316 A2
  CHELTS GL53 ... 115 J3
  THNB/SVB BS35 ... 293 M1 🔢

YATE/CS BS37......................320 B3
Kestrel Ct STNHO GL10........207 H4 ☑
Kestrel Dr MANG/FISH BS16..329 L7
Kestrel La VGL GL2..............135 H8
Keswick Rd CHELTS GL51.......115 C4
Keswick Wk
HNBRY/STHM BS10................325 L1 ☑
Ketch Rd BMSTR BS3.............336 B8
Kevin Cl GLE GL4.................136 F5
Kew Pl CHELTS GL53..............2 C9
Kew La NWNT GL18................85 K3
Kewstone Rd
HNLZ/SM/SNYPK/WT BS9........325 G7
Kew Wk BRSG/KWL/STAPK BS4...345 J7
Keynsham Bank CHELTE/BC GL52...3 F7
Keynshambury Rd CHELTS GL53...2 F7
Keynsham By-pass KEYN BS31...348 A4
Keynsham La LYD GL15............225 L7
Keynsham Rd CHELTS GL53.......2 F8
OLD/WMLY/WICK BS30............348 B4
Keynsham St CHELTE/BC GL52...3 C8
Keys Av HORF/LLZ BS7............326 D4
Kibble's La GLE GL14.............154 A6
Kidnalls Rd LYD GL15............201 H2
Kidnams Wk VGL GL2..............182 A6
Kidnappers La CHELTS GL53.....115 K7
CHELTS GL53.......................115 K6 ☑
Kilbirnie Rd HGRV/WHIT BS14...346 C8
Kildare Rd
BRSG/KWL/STAPK BS4............345 M3
Kildare La COTS GL54.............142 F7
Kilkenny St CBRISNE BS2.........7 K4
Killcott Rd WUE GL12............297 M3
Kilmersdon Rd
BMSTRD/HC/WWD BS13...........345 L8
Kilminster Ct BWTH/CHD GL3...113 J5 ☑
Kilmore La TEWK GL20............26 B5
Kiln Cl KGWD/HNM BS15..........337 K2
Kilnhurst Cl
OLD/WMLY/WICK BS30............348 B1
Kilvert Cl BRSG/KWL/STAPK BS4...336 F6
Kimberley Av MANG/FISH BS16...327 L6
Kimberley Cl LYD GL15............201 K8
MANG/FISH BS16...................328 B4 ☑
VGL GL2..............................112 F7
Kimberley Crs MANG/FISH BS16...327 L6
Kimberley Dr LYD GL15............201 K8
Kimberley Rd
KGWD/HNM BS15...................337 M2 ☑
MANG/FISH BS16...................327 L6
Kimberley Wk
CHELTE/BC GL52...................116 E1 ☑
Kimbrose Wy GL GL1..............4 D6
Kimmins Rd CHELTW GL10.......207 J3
Kinber Cl CBATH/BATHN BA1....350 C8
King Alfreds Av CHEP NP16......270 C4
King Alfred Wy CHELTE/BC GL52...3 H7
King Arthur Cl CHELTS GL53.....116 B4
Kingcombe La CHCAM GL55......12 B7
King Edward's Av GLE GL4.......136 A5
Kingfisher Cl ALMDB BS32.......317 G2 ☑
THNB/SVB BS35.....................293 M1 ☑
Kingfisher Dr
MANG/FISH BS16...................327 G5
Kingfisher Ri VGL GL2.............158 F2 ☑
Kingfisher Rd YATE/CS BS37.....320 C3
King George Cl CHELTS BS53....116 B5
King Georges Fld COTS GL54....102 B3
King George's Rd
BMSTRD/HC/WWD BS13...........345 H6
Kingham Rd CHNTN OX7..........104 F6
King Henry Cl CHELTS GL53.....116 B5
Kingham Rd CHELTS GL53........116 B5
Kings Av KGWD/HNM BS15.......337 K7
RDLND/MONT BS6..................325 L7
King's Barton St GL GL1...........4 F7
Kingley Rd STROUD GL5..........208 A4
King Rd BRSG/KWL/STAPK BS4...346 D2
Kingrove Crs YATE/CS BS37......320 E3
Kingrove La YATE/CS BS37.......320 L4
Kings Av KGWD/HNM BS15.......337 K7
RDLND/MONT BS6..................325 L7
King's Barton St GL GL1...........4 F7
Kingsclere Dr CHELTE/BC GL52...72 A8
Kingscote Av CHELTW GL51......114 F4
Kingscote Cl BWTH/CHD GL3....113 M7
CHELTW GL51.......................114 F4 ☑
Kingscote Dr GLE GL4.............137 G6
Kingscote Gv CHELTW GL51......114 F4 ☑
Kingscote Pk EVILLE/WHL BS5...337 K5
Kingscote Rd East
CHELTW GL51.......................114 F4
Kingscote Rd West
CHELTW GL51.......................114 F5
Kingscourt Cl HGRV/WHIT BS14...346 C8
Kingscourt La STROUD GL5.......208 C7
Kingscroft Rd BWTH/CHD GL3...137 J4
Kingsdale Rd BDWAY WR12......33 G3
Kingsdale CHELTW GL51..........93 J7
Kingsdown DSLY GL11............253 J1
Kingsditch La CHELTW GL51.....93 J7
Kingsdown Pde
RDLND/MONT BS6..................6 E1
RDLND/MONT BS6..................335 M3
Kings Dr DSLY GL11...............253 J1
HORF/LLZ BS7.......................326 D2
KGWD/HNM BS15...................337 K7
Kings Elm VGL GL2................90 F6
Kingsfield La KGWD/HNM BS15...338 A6
OLD/WMLY/WICK BS30............338 A7
Kings Ga TEWK GL20..............48 D5
King's Head La
BMSTRD/HC/WWD BS13...........345 G4
COTS GL54...........................142 F8
Kingshill CIR GL7..................238 F3
Kingshill La CIR GL7...............238 F5
DSLY GL11............................253 J1
Kingshill Pk DSLY GL11..........229 J8
Kingshill Rd
BRSG/KWL/STAPK BS4............346 D2
DSLY GL11............................253 J1
Kingsholme Ct GL GL1.............4 F1
Kingsholme Rd
KGWD/HNM BS15...................337M1
Kingsholm Rd GL GL1.............4 F3
HNBRY/STHM BS10................325M3

Kingsholm Sq GL GL1.............4 F1
Kingsland Cl CBRISNE BS2.......7 L4
Kingsland Rd CBRISNE BS2......7 L4
Kingsland Road Br CBRISNE BS2...7 L4
Kings La CIR GL7...................221 M6
Kingsleigh Ct
KGWD/HNM BS15...................338 B4 ☑
Kingsleigh Gdns
KGWD/HNM BS15...................338 B4 ☑
Kingsley Gdns CHELTS GL51.....115 G2
Kingsley Rd EVILLE/WHL BS5....336 E2
GLE GL4................................136 C6
RDLND/MONT BS6..................335M1
Kings Md CIND GL14..............155 H7
Kingsmead
CIR GL7................................258 E5 ☑
GLE GL4................................137 G7
RSTROUD/NAIL GL6................185 G3
Kingsmead Av CHELTW GL51....93 H7
Kingsmead Cl CHELTW GL51....93 H7
Kings Meade CLFD GL16..........175 K1 ☑
Kings Meadow COTS GL54.......123 H5 ☑
MALM SN16..........................284 A6
Kingsmead Rd CHELTW GL51....93 H7
EVILLE/WHL BS5...................337 J2
Kingsmead Wk
EVILLE/WHL BS5...................337 J2
Kingsmill
HNLZ/SM/SNYPK/WT BS9........324 F6
King's Mill La
RSTROUD/NAIL GL6................185 G5
King's Parade Av
CFTN/FAIL BS8......................335 K2 ☑
King's Parade Ms
CFTN/FAIL BS8......................335 J2 ☑
Kings Park Av CBRISNE BS2.....336 E5 ☑
King Sq CBRISNE BS2.............335 M3 ☑
King's Rd
BRSG/KWL/STAPK BS4............336 E8
CFTN/FAIL BS8......................335 J4 ☑
CHELTE/BC GL52...................3 H6
STNHO GL10.........................207 H2
STROUD GL5.........................208 D5
Kingsville Rd CHELTW GL51.....93 J6 ☑
Kings Wk
BMSTRD/HC/WWD BS13..........345 G4
King's Wall MALM SN16..........303 J8
Kingsway BRSTK/PCHW BS34...316 C5
CIR GL7................................239 G5
CLFD GL16............................151 M8
DSLY GL11............................229 J8
EVILLE/WHL BS5...................337 K4
Kingsway Av KGWD/HNM BS15...337 K3
Kingsway Crs
KGWD/HNM BS15...................337 K3
Kingsway La MTCHDN GL17.....129 G4
Kingswear Rd BMSTR BS3........345M2
Kings Well La COTS GL54........94 D6
Kings Weston Av AVONM BS11...324 B3
Kings Weston Rd
AVONM BS11.........................324 F1 ☑
Kingswood Cl CHELTE/BC GL52...72 B8
Kingswood WUE GL12............297M3
Kington La THNB/SVB BS35......293 H2
Kington Rd THNB/SVB BS35.....272 F6
King William Av CBRIS/FH BS1...6 F5 ☑
King William Dr CHELTS GL53...116 B5
King William St BMSTR BS3......6 B9
Kinmoor GLE GL4..................136 F8
Kinsale Rd HGRV/WHIT BS14....346 E4
Kinsale Wk
BRSG/KWL/STAPK BS4............346 A2 ☑
Kinsham La TEWK GL20...........27 K7
Kinvara Rd
BRSG/KWL/STAPK BS4............346 A3 ☑
Kipling Cl VGL GL2................135 L7
Kipling Rd CHELTW GL51.........115 G2
DSLY GL11............................253 L4
HORF/LLZ BS7.......................326 D2
Kirby Rd COTS GL54..............124 D8
Kirkby Rd AVONM BS11...........324 C2
Kirtlington Rd
EVILLE/WHL BS5...................326 D8 ☑
Kitchener Av GL GL1...............136 A6
Kitefield HGHW SN6..............288 F3 ☑
Kite Hay Cl MANG/FISH BS16...327 G6 ☑
Kites Cl ALMDB BS32..............316 E1 ☑
Kitesnest La STROUD GL5........208 D7
Klondyke Av VGL GL15...........201 K8
Knap La RSTROUD/NAIL GL6....185 H4
WUE GL12.............................275 K8
Knapp Cl LED HR8.................19M1
Knapp La CHELT GL50............2 B4
DSLY GL11............................229 H6
DSLY GL11............................230 C6
LED HR8..............................20 A2
LYD GL15.............................224 C5
RSTROUD/NAIL GL6................209 K1
RSTROUD/NAIL GL6................233 K3
Knapp Rdg LED HR8..............20 A1
Knapp Rd CHELT GL50............2 B4
THNB/SVB BS35.....................293M2
WUE GL12.............................277 L4
Knapps La EVILLE/WHL BS5.....337 G1
The Knapp DSLY GL11............253 J1
YATE/CS BS37.......................310 B6 ☑
Knightcott Rd CFTN/FAIL BS8...334 B3
Knighton Rd
HNBRY/STHM BS10................326 A2

Knightsbridge Crs
CHELTS GL53........................3 H9 ☑
Knights Crs NWNT GL18.........86 A3
Knights Wy NWNT GL18.........86 A3
TEWK GL20...........................48 C5
Knightwood Rd
BRSTK/PCHW BS34................317 H6
Knockley Patch LYD GL15.......200 D1
Knole Cl ALMDB BS32............306 D7
Knole La HNBRY/STHM BS10...315 J8
Knole Pk ALMDB BS32............306 B8
Knoll HI
HNLZ/SM/SNYPK/WT BS9........324 F8
The Knoll CIR GL7..................266 F4
STROUD GL5.........................208 F4 ☑
Knollys End VGL GL2..............159 H3
Knovill Cl AVONM BS11...........324 D2
Knowle
BRSG/KWL/STAPK BS4............336 C8 ☑
Knowles Rd GL GL1................136 B4
Knowsley Rd
MANG/FISH BS16...................327 G8 ☑
Knox Rd LYD GL15.................200 F4
Kyderminster Rd COTS GL54....74 C4
Kyght Cl KGWD/HNM BS15......338 C3
Kynges Mill Cl MANG/FISH BS16...327 J4

L

The Labbott KEYN BS31...........348 A6
Laburnum Ct CHELTW GL51......114 E1 ☑
Laburnum Gdns VGL GL2.........159 H2 ☑
Laburnum Gv MANG/FISH BS16...327 K7
Laburnum Rd GL GL1..............135M6
KGWD/HNM BS15...................337 L6 ☑
STNHO GL10.........................207 H4 ☑
Laburnum Wk STNHO GL10.....207 H4 ☑
Lacca Cl VGL GL2..................112 F6 ☑
Lacemakers Rd MALM SN16.....303 J6
Lacey Rd HGRV/WHIT BS14.....347 G5
Lacock Dr
OLD/WMLY/WICK BS30............338 B6
Lacy Cl VGL GL2....................112 C5
Ladd Cl KGWD/HNM BS15.......338 B4 ☑
Ladden Ct THNB/SVB BS35......293 L3 ☑
The Ladder RSTROUD/NAIL GL6...232 E7
Ladies Mile
HNLZ/SM/SNYPK/WT BS9........335 H2
Ladman Gv HGRV/WHIT BS14...347 G5
Ladman Rd HGRV/WHIT BS14...347 G5
Ladybellegate St GL GL1..........4 D6
Lady Chapel Rd GLE GL4.........137 G5
Lady Margaret Ct
CHEP NP16...........................270 B7 ☑
Lady Md HGHW SN6..............288 F3
Ladysmith Rd CHELTE/BC GL52...3 M3
GL GL1.................................136 A5
RDLND/MONT BS6..................325 K7 ☑
Ladywell Cl VGL GL2..............135 K4
Laggar La STROUD GL5...........232 J1
Lake La VGL GL2...................109 K8
VGL GL2...............................181 J5
Lakemead Gv
BMSTRD/HC/WWD BS13..........345 H5
Lake Rd HNBRY/STHM BS10....325 L4
Lakers Rd CLFD GL16.............151 K5
Lakeside CIR GL7...................242 D5
CIR GL7................................263 K4
MANG/FISH BS16...................327 G8
Lake Side NWNT GL18............86 C2
Lakeside Av LYD GL15............225 L1
Lakeside Dr LYD GL15............225 L1
Lake St CHELTE/BC GL52........94 D6
VGL GL2...............................133M6
Lake View Rd EVILLE/WHL BS5...336 F3
Lakewood Crs
HNBRY/STHM BS10................325 K3
Lakewood Rd
HNBRY/STHM BS10................325 K3
Lambert Av CHELTW GL51.......138 F2
Lambert Cl
BRSG/KWL/STAPK BS4............345M5
CHELTW GL51.......................138 F2
Lambert Dr CHELTW GL51.......138 F2
Lambert Gdns CHELTW GL51...138 F2
Lamberts Fld COTS GL54.........123 J6
Lamb La CIND GL14...............154 B3
Lambley Rd EVILLE/WHL BS5...337 G3
Lambourn Cl VGL GL2............113 C8
Lambourne Av
RTEWK/TIB GL19...................108 D8
Lambourne Cl LED HR8...........20 A5
Lambourn Rd KEYN BS31........348 C7
Lambrook Rd MANG/FISH BS16...327 J7
Lambs Barn Pitch NWNT GL18...64 B8
Lambsdowne DSLY GL11.........229 H8
Lambsquay Rd CLFD GL16.......175 L5
Lamb St CBRISNE BS2............7 K2
Lamord Ga BRSTK/PCHW BS34...317 G6
Lampern Vw DSLY GL11..........254 D2
Lampeter Rd
HNLZ/SM/SNYPK/WT BS9........325 H4
The Lampreys GLE GL4...........136 D5
Lampton Av
BMSTRD/HC/WWD BS13..........346 A8
Lampton Gv
BMSTRD/HC/WWD BS13..........346 A8
Lampton Rd LGASH BS41........344 B2
Lanaway Rd
MANG/FISH BS16...................327 K5 ☑
Lancashire Rd HORF/LLZ BS7...326 A8
Lancaster Cl
BRSTK/PCHW BS34................316 F7 ☑
Lancaster Ct LYD GL15...........201 K6
Lancaster Dr LYD GL15............201 K6
Lancaster Rd CBRISNE BS2......336 C1 ☑
CIR GL7................................267 G5
TEWK GL20...........................48 B7
YATE/CS BS37.......................310 A8
Lancaster St
EVILLE/WHL BS5...................336 E4 ☑
Lancaut La CHEP NP16...........246 B5
Lancelot Ct VGL GL2..............204 F7
Landseer Rd HORF/LLZ BS7.....326 D4
The Land FRCTL/WBN BS36.....318 E4

Lane End COTS GL54..............148 B3
Lanercost Rd
HNBRY/STHM BS10................325 L1
Lanesborough Ri
HGRV/WHIT BS14...................346 F4
Lanescourt TEWK GL20...........48 A5
The Lane BDWAY WR12..........32 B6
MIM.....................................81M4
RSTROUD/NAIL GL6................207M1
SHPSTR CV36.......................38 C3
SHPSTR CV36.......................38 C8
THNB/SVB BS35.....................315 H1
Langdale Gdns VGL GL2..........112 E6 ☑
Langdale Rd CHELTW GL51......115 H4
MANG/FISH BS16...................327 H7 ☑
Langdon Rd CHELTS GL53.......115M5
Langet CIR GL7.....................263 C4
Langetts Rd CLFD GL16..........175 K1
Langfield Cl
HNBRY/STHM BS10................315 H8 ☑
Langford Rd
BMSTRD/HC/WWD BS13..........345 H3
Langford Wy KGWD/HNM BS15...338 A4
Langham Rd
BRSG/KWL/STAPK BS4............346 D1 ☑
Langhill Av
BRSG/KWL/STAPK BS4............345 M4 ☑
The Langland LED HR8...........19M1
Langley Crs BMSTR BS3..........345 G2
Langley Mow
MANG/FISH BS16...................328 D4 ☑
Langley Rd COTS GL54...........73 K6
GLE GL4................................136 D6
Langridge La
CBATH/BATHN BA1................350 D4
Langston Cl CHNTN OX7........105 C6
Langthorn Cl FRCTL/WBN BS36...318 D4
Langtoft Rd STROUD GL5........209 G4
Langton Cl GLE GL4...............137 C2
Langton Court Rd
BRSG/KWL/STAPK BS4............336 F6
Langton Grove Rd
CHELTS GL53........................116 C4 ☑
Langton Pk BMSTR BS3..........6 C9
Langton Pl CHELTS GL53........116 C4 ☑
Langton Rd
BRSG/KWL/STAPK BS4............336 F6
Langton Wy
BRSG/KWL/STAPK BS4............337 C5
Lanham Gdns VGL GL2...........159 H4
Lannett Rd GL GL1.................136 A5
Lansdown STROUD GL5..........208 E4
YATE/CS BS37.......................320 A3 ☑
Lansdown Castle Dr
CHELTW GL51.......................115 H3 ☑
Lansdown Cl CHELTW GL51.....115 J3 ☑
KGWD/HNM BS15...................337M1
Lansdown Crs CHELT GL50......115 K3
Lansdown Crescent La
CHELT GL50..........................2 A7
Lansdown La
CBATH/BATHN BA1................350 C4
OLD/WMLY/WICK BS30............349 K3
Lansdown Lodge Dr
CHELTW GL51.......................115 J3 ☑
Lansdown Pde CHELT GL50......115 K3
Lansdown Pk
CBATH/BATHN BA1................351 C8
Lansdown Place La CHELT GL50...2 A7
Lansdown Rd
CBATH/BATHN BA1................350 C4
CFTN/FAIL BS8......................335 J4
CHELT GL50..........................2 A8
CHELT GL50..........................115 J3
GL GL1.................................5 J2
KEYN BS31...........................349 G8
KGWD/HNM BS15...................337M1
MANG/FISH BS16...................329 L5
RDLND/MONT BS6..................335 L2
Lansdown Ter
RDLND/MONT BS6..................325 M6 ☑
Lansdown Terrace La CHELT GL50...2 A6
Lansdown Vw
KGWD/HNM BS15...................338 A3
Lansdown Wk CHELT GL50......2 A7
LYD GL15.............................200 D3
Lantern Cl BRKLY GL13..........227 G8 ☑
CIND GL14............................154 A3
Lapdown La BAD GL9............331M2
Lapwing Cl ALMDB BS32........316 F1
TEWK GL20...........................48 F2 ☑
Lapwing Gdns
MANG/FISH BS16...................327 H5 ☑
Larch Cl CHELTS GL53............116 D6
The Larches GLE GL4.............137 G4
Larchmere Gv CHELTW GL51...115 G6 ☑
Larch Ri CLFD GL16...............151 J7
Larch Rd CHPMW/MSHF SN14...343 H5
KGWD/HNM BS15...................328 A8
Larch Wy BRSTK/PCHW BS34...316 A4
Larchwood Dr GLE GL4...........136 A8
Larkfield FRCTL/WBN BS36......318 F4 ☑
Larkham Cl GLE GL4...............136 D8
Larkhay Rd BWTH/CHD GL3.....137 J2
Larkhill Cl CHEP NP16............270 A4 ☑
Lark Ri CLFD GL16.................151 J7
Larkrise DSLY GL11................229 H6
Larksfield Rd MTCHDN GL17....129M5
STROUD GL5.........................208 D4
Lark's La YATE/CS BS37..........308 D4
Larksleaze Rd
OLD/WMLY/WICK BS30............348 A1
Larkspear Cl GLE GL4.............136 A6
Larkspur Cl THNB/SVB BS35....293M1
Larput Pl CHELT GL50............2 C1
Lasbury Gv
BMSTRD/HC/WWD BS13..........345 L6 ☑
Lasne Crs BWTH/CHD GL3......138 B7
Lassington Gv VGL GL2...........110 A5
Lassington La VGL GL2...........110 A5
Latchen Rd MTCHDN GL17......131 H1 ☑
Latchen Orch MTCHDN GL17...131 H1 ☑

Latimer Cl
BRSG/KWL/STAPK BS4............337 G5
Latimer Rd CIND GL14............154 C2
Latteridge La THNB/SVB BS35...308 C3
Latteridge Rd YATE/CS BS37....308 F3
Latton Rd HORF/LLZ BS7........326 B3
Launceston Av
KGWD/HNM BS15...................337 K6
Launceston Rd
KGWD/HNM BS15...................337 K2 ☑
Laundry Rd CLFD GL16..........174 E4
Laura Cl VGL GL2..................5 L1
Laurel Av TEWK GL20............48 C7
Laureldene CLFD GL16............175 L6
Laurel Dr CHELTE/BC GL52......94 D7
CHPMW/MSHF SN14..............343 H5
Laurel Ga GLE GL4................137 H7
The Laurels GL GL1................136 B4 ☑
HNBRY/STHM BS10................315 J5
MANG/FISH BS16...................328 C5
Laurel St KGWD/HNM BS15.....337M3
Laurence Cl CHELTS GL51.......138 F1
Laurie Crs
HNLZ/SM/SNYPK/WT BS9........325M5
Laurie Lee Ct
OLD/WMLY/WICK BS30............338 C6 ☑
Lavender Cl THNB/SVB BS35....293M2
Lavender La CIR GL7...............238 C4
Lavender Ms CHELTE/BC GL52...72 A8 ☑
Lavender Rd CHELTW GL51.....115 H6
Lavender Vw GLE GL4............137 H7
Lavender Wy ALMDB BS32......317 H4
Lavenham Rd YATE/CS BS37....319 K1
Lavers Cl KGWD/HNM BS15....338 A5
Lavington Dr VGL GL2............113 C7
Lavington Rd EVILLE/WHL BS5...337 K5
Lawford Av BRSTK/PCHW BS34...316 C5
Lawfords Ga CBRISNE BS2......7 K2
Lawn Av MANG/FISH BS16......327 K6
Lawn Crs CHELTW GL51..........139 G1
Lawn Rd MANG/FISH BS16......327 K6
RTEWK/TIB GL19...................89 J3
Lawnside RSTROUD/NAIL GL6...232 B7
Lawnside LED HR8.................19M3
Lawns Pk STROUD GL5...........232 B1
Lawns Rd YATE/CS BS37.........320 A1
The Lawns CHELTE/BC GL52....72 D4
GLE GL4................................136 F8
STNHO GL10.........................207 G3
Lawrence Av
EVILLE/WHL BS5...................336 D2 ☑
Lawrence Cl
CHELTE/BC GL52...................116 D5 ☑
KGWD/HNM BS15...................338 C1
Lawrence Dr YATE/CS BS37.....319 K1
Lawrence Gv DSLY GL11.........253 H1
HNLZ/SM/SNYPK/WT BS9........325 K6
Lawrence HI CBRISNE BS2......7 L2
EVILLE/WHL BS5...................336 D4
Lawrence Rd CIR GL7.............238 B4
TET GL8...............................257M2
Lawrence's Meadow
CHELTE/BC GL52...................72 C3 ☑
Lawrence Wy GL GL1.............4 E2
Lawrence Wy North GL GL1.....111M7
Lawrence Weston Rd
AVONM BS11.........................324 E2 ☑
Lawson Gld CHELTS GL53.......116 C7 ☑
Laxey Rd HORF/LLZ BS7.........326 B4
Laxton Cl THNB/SVB BS35......292 C8
Laxton Dr WUE GL12.............277 H7
Laxton Rd BWTH/CHD GL3......137 J5
CHELTW GL51.......................115 G1
Laymore Rd CIND GL14..........153M2
Laynes Rd BWTH/CHD GL3......137 J3
Lays Dr KEYN BS31................347 L7
Leacey Ct BWTH/CHD GL3......113 J4 ☑
Lea Crs VGL GL2...................112 E6 ☑
Leacy Ms BWTH/CHD GL3......113 J4
Leadon Cl BMSTRD/HC/WWD BS13...138 A6
Leadon Wy LED HR8..............19 L2
Leafield Rd CIR GL7...............242 F4
Leaholme Gdns
HGRV/WHIT BS14...................346 C8
Leaman Cl YATE/CS BS37........320 D2 ☑
Leamington Rd BDWAY WR12...32 F1
Leaping Stocks Rd
RWYE HR9............................126 E5 ☑
Leap V MANG/FISH BS16........328 C3
Leap Valley Crs
MANG/FISH BS16...................328 C3
Lea Rd BWTH/CHD GL3..........138 B6
Lears Dr CHELTE/BC GL52......72 C8
Leaside Cl DSLY GL11............229 J7
Leasow La COTS GL54...........123 L7
The Leasows CHCAM GL55.....34 D1
Leaze Cl BRKLY GL13.............227 G8
The Leaze CIR GL7.................263 H5
HGHW SN6...........................287M2
YATE/CS BS37.......................319M1
Lechlade Rd CIR GL7..............220 B8
CIR GL7................................245 L1
FGDN SN7...........................269 G2
HGHW SN6...........................268 C5
Lechmere Rd CHELTW GL51....93 C8 ☑
Leckhampton Farm Ct
CHELTS GL53........................115 K8 ☑
Leckhampton Ga
CHELTW GL51.......................115 J7 ☑
Leckhampton HI CHELTS GL53...139 J4
Leckhampton La CHELTW GL51...139 J1
Leckhampton Rd CHELTS GL53...115M7
Leda Av HGRV/WHIT BS14......346 C4
Ledbury Rd MANG/FISH BS16...327 L7
Ledbury Road Crs
RTEWK/TIB GL19...................66 C4
Ledmore Rd CHELTS GL53......116 D5
Leechpool Wy YATE/CS BS37...310 A3
Lee Cl BRSTK/PCHW BS34......316 B3
CHELTW GL51.......................93 H8
Lee Rd TEWK GL20................49 C3
Lees HI KGWD/HNM BS15.......338 A1
Lees La OLD/WMLY/WICK BS30...338 H6
Leicester Sq
MANG/FISH BS16...................327 M8 ☑
Leicester St BMSTR BS3..........6 E9

Leicester Wk
  BRSG/KWL/STAPK BS4 .... 337 H6
Leigh La CBATH/BATHN BA1 .. 341 J8
  YATE/CS BS37 .... 329 K2
Leigh Rd CFTN/FAIL BS8 .... 335 K3
Leigh St BMSTR BS3 .... 335 J7
Leighton Rd BMSTR BS3 .... 6 B8
  BRSG/KWL/STAPK BS4 .... 346 D1
  CBATH/BATHN BA1 ...... 350 E8
  CHELTE/BC GL52 .... 3 C5
Leinster Av
  BRSG/KWL/STAPK BS4 .... 345 M4
  BRSG/KWL/STAPK BS4 .... 346 A3
Leinster Cl CHELTW GL51 ... 92 E7
Leland Cl MALM SN16 ...... 303 J5
Lemon La CBRISNE BS2 .... 336 A3
Lena Av EVILLE/WHL BS5 .... 336 E2
Lena St EVILLE/WHL BS5 .... 336 D2
The Lennards Cl GL7 ...... 263 J4
Lenover Gdns
  BMSTRD/HC/WWD BS13 ... 345 K7
Lensbrook LYD GL15 .... 202 C4
Leonard La CBRIS/FH BS1 ..... 6 E3
Leonard Rd EVILLE/WHL BS5 . 336 E4
  GL GL1 .... 136 B5
Leonards Av EVILLE/WHL BS5 . 336 E2
Leopold Rd RDLND/MONT BS6 . 336 A1
Letch Hill Dr COTS GL54 .... 123 K4
Letch La COTS GL54 .... 123 H6
Leven Cl VGL GL2 .... 112 F7
Lever's HI DSLY GL11 ...... 230 E5
Lewington Rd
  MANG/FISH BS16 .... 327 L1
Lewins Md CBRIS/FH BS1 ..... 6 F2
Lewin St EVILLE/WHL BS5 ... 336 F4
Lewis Av VGL GL2 .... 112 B5
Lewis Cl OLD/WMLY/WICK BS30 . 348 F6
Lewisham Rd GL GL1 .... 136 A6
Lewis La CIR GL7 .... 238 D3
Lewis Rd
  BMSTRD/HC/WWD BS13 ... 345 J3
  CHELTE GL50 .... 114 F1
  CHNTN OX7 .... 105 M1
Lewis St CBRISNE BS2 .... 7 M6
  CBRISNE BS2 .... 336 D6
Lewiston Rd STROUD GL5 .... 233 J1
Lewis Wy CHEP NP16 .... 270 B7
Lewton La FRCTL/WBN BS36 . 318 A4
Leyland Wk
  BMSTRD/HC/WWD BS13 ... 345 H7
Ley La THNB/SVB BS35 ...... 292 B8
Ley Orch BDWAY WR12 ...... 11 H7
Ley Rd CIND GL14 .... 133 H5
Leysbourne CHCAM GL55 .... 12 E8
Leyson Rd CHELTW GL51 .... 114 E5
The Leys BRKLY GL13 .... 227 C7
  CHNTN OX7 .... 105 M1
The Ley COR/BOX SN13 ..... 353 M6
Leyton Vls RDLND/MONT BS6 . 335 K1
Libby's Dr STROUD GL5 ..... 208 F3
Libertus Ct CHELTW GL51 ... 115 J2
Libertus Rd CHELTW GL51 ... 115 H2
Lichfield Dr CHELT GL50 .... 115 J6
Lichfield Rd
  BRSG/KWL/STAPK BS4 .... 337 G5
  GLE GL4 .... 136 E3
Lidderdale Rd COTS GL54 ... 124 D8
Liddington Cl CHELTS GL53 . 115 M7
Liddington Rd VGL GL2 ..... 113 G8
Lifford Gdns BDWAY WR12 .... 32 E3
Lightenbrook La VGL GL2 ... 204 E8
Lightwood La
  RSTROUD/NAIL GL6 ...... 184 A8
Lilac Cl CHELTW GL51 ...... 115 J6
  HNBRY/STHM BS10 .... 325 L2
Lilac Wy GL GL1 .... 135 L8
  VGL GL2 .... 159 G2
Lillian St EVILLE/WHL BS5 .. 336 E3
Lilliesfield Av GLE GL4 .... 137 G3
Lilliput Av YATE/CS BS37 ... 320 C3
Lilliput Ct YATE/CS BS37 ... 320 C3
Lilly Hall La LED HR8 .... 19 H6
Lilstock Av HORF/LLZ BS7 .. 326 B7
Lilton Wk
  BMSTRD/HC/WWD BS13 ... 345 J2
Lilymead Av
  BRSG/KWL/STAPK BS4 .... 336 C8
Lime Av BAD GL9 .... 322 E2
Lime Cl CHELTE/BC GL52 .... 94 C6
  CHPMW/MSHF SN14 ...... 343 H6
  HNBRY/STHM BS10 .... 315 K8
Lime Crt YATE/CS BS37 ..... 310 C7
  THNB/SVB BS35 .... 293 H6
Lime Gv STROUD GL5 .... 208 E4
Lime Kiln Cl BRSTK/PCHW BS34 . 326 F1
Lime Kiln Gdns ALMDB BS32 . 306 F8
Limekiln Gv VGL GL2 .... 110 F6
Limekiln La RSTROUD/NAIL GL6 . 210 E4
Limekiln Rd WUE GL12 ...... 309 L1
Limerick Rd RDLND/MONT BS6 . 335 L1
Lime Rd BMSTR BS3 .... 6 A9
  KGWD/HNM BS15 .... 337 J6
  TEWK GL20 .... 48 C8
Limes Cl CIR GL7 .... 238 C4
Limes Pl HCHW SN6 .... 264 E7
Limes Rd CIR GL7 .... 261 H4
The Limes BAD GL9 .... 323 G1
  VGL GL2 .... 112 A6
Limestone Link
  CBATH/BATHN BA1 ...... 352 C5
  CHPMW/MSHF SN14 ...... 341 J6
Lime St RTEWK/TIB GL19 .... 67 J3
Lime Tree Av BDWAY WR12 ... 32 F2
Lime Wy LYD GL15 .... 201 K7
Linacre Crs CIR GL7 .... 238 B5
Lincoln Av CHELTW GL51 ... 115 J6
Lincoln Cl KEYN BS31 ...... 347 L7
  TEWK GL20 .... 47 M7
Lincoln Green La TEWK GL20 . 47 M8
Lincoln St EVILLE/WHL BS5 .. 336 D4
Lincombe Av MANG/FISH BS16 . 327 M5
Lincombe Rd MANG/FISH BS16 . 327 L6
Linden Av EVILLE/WHL BS5 .. 336 C4
Linden Cl CHELTE/BC GL52 .. 94 C6
  CHEP NP16 .... 270 A4
  CHPMW/MSHF SN14 ...... 343 H5
  FRCTL/WBN BS36 .... 318 A5

KGWD/HNM BS15 .... 337 K1
Linden Dr ALMDB BS32 ...... 316 F3
Linden Rd GL GL1 .... 135 M4
  RDLND/MONT BS6 .... 325 L2
Lindrea St BMSTR BS3 ...... 335 K8
Lindsay Rd HORF/LLZ BS7 ... 326 C7
Linegar Wood Rd CIND GL14 . 154 A6
Lines Wy HGRV/WHIT BS14 .. 346 E8
The Line RWYE HR9 .... 84 C5
Linfoot Rd TET GL8 .... 281 M4
Lingfield Pk FRCTL/WBN BS36 . 328 E2
Linkend Rd RTEWK/TIB GL19 .. 46 A8
Link Rd BRSTK/PCHW BS34 ... 316 B8
  LYD GL15 .... 201 H1
  TEWK GL20 .... 48 B5
  YATE/CS BS37 .... 320 B2
The Links CLFD GL16 ...... 175 J2
Links Vw CIR GL7 .... 214 B6
Linnell Cl HORF/LLZ BS7 .... 326 D5
Linnet Cl BRSTK/PCHW BS34 . 316 A3
  GLE GL4 .... 136 E6
Linsley Wy GLE GL4 .... 159 M2
Lintern Crs
  OLD/WMLY/WICK BS30 ... 338 C5
Lintham Dr KGWD/HNM BS15 . 338 B5
Linton Rd RWYE HR9 .... 84 F3
Linwell Cl CHELTW GL51 .... 93 K6
Linworth Rd CHELTE/BC GL52 . 72 C8
Lion Cl VGL GL2 .... 159 M1
Lipson Rd CHELTW GL51 .... 93 C7
Lisburn Rd
  BRSG/KWL/STAPK BS4 .... 346 A3
Lisle Pl WUE GL12 .... 277 J4
Litfield Rd CFTN/FAIL BS8 .. 335 H1
Lithgow Rd COTS GL54 ..... 124 D8
Little Acorns CHELTE/BC GL52 . 72 A6
Little Ann St CBRISNE BS2 .... 7 K2
Little Birch Cft
  HGRV/WHIT BS14 .... 346 C8
Little Bishop St CBRISNE BS2 . 336 A3
Little Bristol La WUE GL12 .. 276 C6
Little Caroline Pl
  CFTN/FAIL BS8 .... 335 H6
Little Cleevemount
  CHELTE/BC GL52 .... 3 G1
Littlecote Cl CHELTE/BC GL52 . 72 B8
Littledean YATE/CS BS37 ... 320 A5
Littledean Hill Rd CIND GL14 . 154 C3
Little Dowles
  OLD/WMLY/WICK BS30 ... 338 C7
Littledown Rd CHELTS GL53 . 116 A7
Little Elmbridge VGL GL2 ... 112 F7
Little Fld GLE GL4 .... 136 F4
Littlefield VGL GL2 .... 159 G1
Little George St CBRISNE BS2 .. 7 K1
Little Gn RTEWK/TIB GL19 ... 43 J7
Little Green La THNB/SVB BS35 . 304 C4
Little Hayes
  MANG/FISH BS16 .... 327 K5
Little Headley Cl
  BMSTRD/HC/WWD BS13 ... 345 K4
Little Herbert's Cl CHELTS GL53 . 116 D6
Little Herbert's Rd CHELTS GL53 . 116 D6
Little Holbury VGL GL2 ..... 182 A6
Little Horcott La CIR GL7 ... 242 E5
Little King St CBRIS/FH BS1 .. 6 F5
Little Lancarridge VGL GL2 . 110 F7
Little Marcle Rd LED HR8 ... 19 L4
Littlemead COR/BOX SN13 .. 353 K6
Little Meadow ALMDB BS32 . 317 H5
Little Normans VGL GL2 .... 112 E6
Little Orch CHELTE/BC GL52 . 72 A7
Little Paradise BMSTR BS3 ... 6 E9
Little Parr Cl
  MANG/FISH BS16 .... 326 E6
Little Paul St CBRISNE BS2 .. 335 L3
Little Stoke La
  BRSTK/PCHW BS34 .... 316 E4
Little Stoke Rd
  HNLZ/SM/SNYPK/WT BS9 . 325 G2
Littleton Rd BMSTR BS3 .... 345 M1
Little Trewen La RWYE HR9 .. 126 B2
Little Withey Md
  HNLZ/SM/SNYPK/WT BS9 . 325 H5
Littlewood Cl HGRV/WHIT BS14 . 346 D8
Littleworth CHCAM GL55 .... 12 D8
Livia Wy LYD GL15 .... 201 K7
Llandilo St GL GL1 .... 136 B4
Llanthony Rd VGL GL2 .... 4 A8
Lime Tree Cl GL GL1 .... 136 A6
Lobleys Dr GLE GL4 .... 137 H6
Lockemor Rd
  BMSTRD/HC/WWD BS13 ... 346 B7
Lockeridge La UUSV WR8 .... 23 K1
Lock Gdns
  BMSTRD/HC/WWD BS13 ... 345 G4
Locking HI STROUD GL5 .... 208 E4
Lockingwell Rd KEYN BS31 . 347 M6
Locklease Rd HORF/LLZ BS7 . 326 C5
Locombe HI CIR GL7 .... 220 D3
Locombe PI WUE GL12 ..... 277 L5
Loden Brook La LED HR8 ... 19 M2
Lodersfield CIR GL7 .... 244 E7
Lodge Cswy MANG/FISH BS16 . 327 H8
Lodge Dr LGASH BS41 ...... 344 D1
  OLD/WMLY/WICK BS30 ... 348 E1
Lodge Gdns LYD GL15 ...... 198 F5
Lodgemore Cl STROUD GL5 . 208 C4
Lodgemore La STROUD GL5 . 208 C4
Lodge Rd KGWD/HNM BS15 . 337 L1
  OLD/WMLY/WICK BS30 ... 339 J3
  YATE/CS BS37 .... 319 J1
Lodgeside Av
  KGWD/HNM BS15 .... 337 L2
Lodgeside Gdns
  KGWD/HNM BS15 .... 337 L2
Lodge St CBRIS/FH BS1 ...... 6 D3
Lodge Wk MANG/FISH BS16 . 327 H8
Lodore Rd MANG/FISH BS16 . 327 H8
Lodway Rd
  BRSG/KWL/STAPK BS4 .... 346 E1
Logan Rd HORF/LLZ BS7 .... 325 M8
Logus Ct
  OLD/WMLY/WICK BS30 ... 338 B7

Loiterpin LYD GL15 .... 178 D7
Lombard St BMSTR BS3 .... 6 E9
Lomond Rd HORF/LLZ BS7 .. 326 B2
London Rd CBRISNE BS2 .... 336 B2
  CHELTE/BC GL52 .... 2 F7
  CHELTE/BC GL52 .... 117 G7
  CHELTS GL53 .... 3 H9
  CIR GL7 .... 238 D3
  COR/BOX SN13 .... 353 M5
  GL GL1 .... 5 H4
  MIM GL56 .... 58 D5
  OLD/WMLY/WICK BS30 ... 338 E4
  OLD/WMLY/WICK BS30 ... 340 A5
  SHPSTR CV36 .... 16 B7
  STROUD GL5 .... 208 E5
  TET GL8 .... 281 M5
  TET GL8 .... 282 A3
London Rd East
  CBATH/BATHN BA1 ...... 352 C8
London St KGWD/HNM BS15 . 337 M3
Lone La MONM NP25 .... 174 A4
Longacre Rd HGRV/WHIT BS14 . 346 C8
Long Acres Cl
  HNLZ/SM/SNYPK/WT BS9 . 324 F4
Long Ashton Rd LGASH BS41 . 344 C4
Longaston Cl VGL GL2 ..... 204 F7
Longaston La VGL GL2 ..... 204 F6
Long Beach Rd
  OLD/WMLY/WICK BS30 ... 348 C1
Longborough Dr GLE GL4 .. 137 G6
Long Cl ALMDB BS32 .... 317 C5
  MANG/FISH BS16 .... 327 L5
Long Cft YATE/CS BS37 .... 309 M6
Long Cross AVONM BS11 .... 324 A2
Longden Rd MANG/FISH BS16 . 328 B5
Long Eaton Dr
  HGRV/WHIT BS14 .... 346 D3
Long Eights TEWK GL20 ..... 48 F2
Long Fld VGL GL2 .... 110 F5
Longfield VGL GL2 .... 159 G1
Longfield Rd HORF/LLZ BS7 . 326 A5
Longford YATE/CS BS37 .... 319 L3
Longford Av
  HNBRY/STHM BS10 .... 325 M3
Longford La VGL GL2 ...... 112 C5
Longford Ms VGL GL2 ...... 112 B5
Long Furlong CHELTE/BC GL52 . 72 B4
Long Furlong La TET GL8 ... 281 L6
Long Handstones
  OLD/WMLY/WICK BS30 ... 338 C7
Longhill Rd DSLY GL11 ..... 212 D2
Longhope Cl GLE GL4 ...... 137 G6
Longhope Rd RTEWK/TIB GL19 . 108 B8
Longland Ct VGL GL2 ...... 112 D6
  VGL GL2 .... 112 D6
Longland Gdns VGL GL2 .... 112 D7
Longlands Cl CHELTE/BC GL52 . 72 D7
Longlands Rd CHELTE/BC GL52 . 72 D7
Longleat Av VGL GL2 ...... 159 L2
Longleat Cl
  HNLZ/SM/SNYPK/WT BS9 . 325 L6
Longlength La
  RSTROUD/NAIL GL6 ...... 256 C5
Long Marston Rd STRAT CV37 .. 8 E3
Long Md YATE/CS BS37 ..... 310 A6
Longmead Av HORF/LLZ BS7 . 325 M6
Long Meadow
  MANG/FISH BS16 .... 326 F6
Longmeadow Rd KEYN BS31 . 347 L7
Longmoor Rd BMSTR BS3 ... 345 J1
Longmore Av COTS GL54 ... 124 D7
Long Mynd Av CHELTW GL51 . 115 C5
Longney Pl BRSTK/PCHW BS34 . 316 E2
Longney Rd GL GL1 .... 135 L8
Longreach Gv
  HGRV/WHIT BS14 .... 346 F4
Longridge La RTEWK/TIB GL19 . 89 H5
Long Rw MANG/FISH BS16 .. 328 C6
Long Rw CBRIS/FH BS1 .... 7 C5
  HGHW SN6 .... 266 D7
Longs Dr YATE/CS BS37 .... 309 L8
  YATE/CS BS37 .... 319 M1
Longsmith St GL GL1 .... 4 E5
Longsplatt COR/BOX SN13 .. 353 L8
Long St DSLY GL11 .... 253 K7
  TET GL8 .... 282 A4
  WUE GL12 .... 277 K4
Longs Vw WUE GL12 .... 276 C5
Longtree Cl TET GL8 .... 281 M2
Longville Cl GLE GL4 ...... 137 H6
Longway Av CHELTS GL53 .. 116 B7
  HGRV/WHIT BS14 .... 346 B7
Longwood
  BRSG/KWL/STAPK BS4 .... 347 J1
Longwood La CFTN/FAIL BS8 . 334 A7
The Lonk CLFD GL16 .... 151 K5
Lonsdale Rd VGL GL2 ...... 136 C1
Loop Rd CHEP NP16 .... 270 D5
Lorain Wk HNBRY/STHM BS10 . 325 H1
Lord Aston Dr CHEP NP16 .. 270 B7
Lords Gn CHELTE/BC GL52 ... 72 E8
Lord's HI CLFD GL16 .... 175 K1
Lords Piece Rd CHNTN OX7 . 105 M2
Loriners Cl VGL GL2 .... 159 H1
Lorton Rd HNBRY/STHM BS10 . 325 K2
Louisa St CBRISNE BS2 ...... 7 K4
Louise Av MANG/FISH BS16 . 328 C6
Lovedays Md STROUD GL5 .. 208 C3
Love La CIR GL7 .... 238 D5
  YATE/CS BS37 .... 310 C7
  YATE/CS BS37 .... 320 C3
Lovelinch Gdns LGASH BS41 . 344 B2
Lovell Av
  OLD/WMLY/WICK BS30 ... 338 F2
Lovell's HI KGWD/HNM BS15 . 337 K6
Loveringe Cl
  HNBRY/STHM BS10 .... 315 H7
Lover's La MALM SN16 ..... 303 J8
Lovers Wk RWYE HR9 .... 84 F3
Lovett Cl RTEWK/TIB GL19 .. 66 D4
Lowbourne HGRV/WHIT BS14 . 346 B5
Lowdilow La CHELTW GL51 .. 92 F2
Lower Ashley Rd
  EVILLE/WHL BS5 .... 336 C2
  RDLND/MONT BS6 .... 336 B2
Lower Berrycroft BRKLY GL13 . 227 C8

Lower Castle St CBRIS/FH BS1 .. 7 H2
Lower Chapel La
  FRCTL/WBN BS36 .... 318 E4
Lower Chapel Rd
  KGWD/HNM BS15 .... 337 L6
Lower Cheltenham Pl
  RDLND/MONT BS6 .... 336 B2
Lower Churchfield Rd
  STROUD GL5 .... 208 F5
Lower Church La CBRISNE BS2 .. 6 D3
Lower Church St CHEP NP16 . 270 D2
Lower Clifton HI CFTN/FAIL BS8 . 6 A4
  CFTN/FAIL BS8 .... 335 J5
Lower Cock Rd
  KGWD/HNM BS15 .... 338 B4
Lower College St CBRIS/FH BS1 . 6 C5
Lower Common LYD GL15 ... 224 C2
Lower Court Rd ALMDB BS32 . 306 C6
Lower Cft GL7 .... 242 F4
Lower End CHNTN OX7 ...... 83 H7
Lower Fallow Cl
  HGRV/WHIT BS14 .... 346 B8
Lower Gay St CBRISNE BS2 .. 335 M3
Lower Grove Rd
  MANG/FISH BS16 .... 327 C3
Lower Guinea St CBRIS/FH BS1 .. 6 F7
Lower Hanham Rd
  KGWD/HNM BS15 .... 337 L8
Lower High St CHCAM GL55 . 12 D8
Lower House Crs
  BRSTK/PCHW BS34 ...... 316 D7
Lower Kingsdown Rd
  CBATH/BATHN BA1 ...... 353 H8
  COR/BOX SN13 .... 353 J7
Lower Kitesnest La
  RSTROUD/NAIL GL6 ...... 184 B8
Lower Knole La
  HNBRY/STHM BS10 .... 315 J8
Lower Lamb St CBRIS/FH BS1 .. 6 C5
Lower Lode La TEWK GL20 ... 47 L7
Lower Maudlin St
  CBRIS/FH BS1 .... 6 F2
Lower Meadow VGL GL2 .... 159 H4
Lower Mill St CHELTW GL51 . 115 K1
Lower Moor Rd YATE/CS BS37 . 310 A7
Lower Newmarket Rd
  RSTROUD/NAIL GL6 ...... 232 B7
Lower Northend
  CBATH/BATHN BA1 ...... 352 B6
Lower Park Rw CBRIS/FH BS1 .. 6 E3
Lower Park St COTS GL54 .. 102 A3
Lower Poole Rd DSLY GL11 . 253 K3
Lower Quay St GL GL1 .... 4 D3
Lower Redland Rd
  RDLND/MONT BS6 .... 335 K1
Lower Rd CIND GL14 ...... 178 B2
  CLFD GL16 .... 151 K6
  LED HR8 .... 19 L4
  LYD GL15 .... 177 J3
  LYD GL15 .... 198 F6
Lower Sidney St BMSTR BS3 . 335 L4
Lower Station Approach Rd
  CBRIS/FH BS1 .... 7 J6
Lower Station Rd
  MANG/FISH BS16 .... 327 H7
Lower Stone Cl
  FRCTL/WBN BS36 .... 318 E3
Lower St MIM GL56 .... 57 H1
  RSTROUD/NAIL GL6 ...... 184 B8
  STROUD GL5 .... 208 E5
Lower Tockington Rd
  ALMDB BS32 .... 306 D3
Lower Tuffley La VGL GL2 ... 135 K7
Lower Washwell La
  RSTROUD/NAIL GL6 ...... 185 H3
Loweswater Cl CHELTW GL51 . 115 H4
Loweswater Rd CHELTW GL51 . 115 H4
Lowlis Cl HNBRY/STHM BS10 . 315 H8
Lowther Rd
  HNBRY/STHM BS10 .... 325 L1
Loxton Sq HGRV/WHIT BS14 . 346 C6
Lucas Ct BRSG/KWL/STAPK BS4 . 346 F3
Luccombe HI
  RDLND/MONT BS6 .... 335 K1
Luckington Rd HORF/LLZ BS7 . 326 A5
Luckley Av
  BMSTRD/HC/WWD BS13 ... 345 L6
Luckwell Rd BMSTR BS3 .... 335 K8
Lucky La BMSTR BS3 .... 6 E8
Ludgate HI WUE GL12 ...... 277 L4
Ludlow Cl CBRISNE BS2 .... 336 B2
  KEYN BS31 .... 347 M6
  OLD/WMLY/WICK BS30 ... 348 D1
Ludlow Rd HORF/LLZ BS7 ... 326 B4
Ludwell Cl FRCTL/WBN BS36 . 317 M6
The Luggs STNHO GL10 ..... 207 J8
Luke La BWTH/CHD GL3 .... 113 C5
Lullington Rd
  BRSG/KWL/STAPK BS4 .... 346 D1
Luisgate Rd
  BMSTRD/HC/WWD BS13 ... 345 J4
Lulworth Crs MANG/FISH BS16 . 328 B3
Lulworth Rd KEYN BS31 .... 348 A1
Lurgan Wk
  BRSG/KWL/STAPK BS4 .... 345 M2
Lurks La RSTROUD/NAIL GL6 . 184 D7
Lux Furlong
  HNLZ/SM/SNYPK/WT BS9 . 324 D4
Luxton St EVILLE/WHL BS5 .. 336 D3
Lych Gate Ms LYD GL15 .... 225 J1
Lyddington Rd HORF/LLZ BS7 . 326 A2
Lydfield Rd LYD GL15 ...... 201 J8
Lydford Wk BMSTR BS3 .... 345 L1
Lydiard Cft KGWD/HNM BS15 . 337 L2
Lydney Rd HNBRY/STHM BS10 . 325 M3
  LYD GL15 .... 200 C4
  MANG/FISH BS16 .... 328 A7
Lydstep Ter BMSTR BS3 .... 6 C9
Lyefield Rd East CHELTS GL53 . 116 C5
Lyefield Rd West CHELTS GL53 . 116 C5
Lye La CHELTE/BC GL52 .... 94 F2
Lygon Ct CIR GL7 .... 242 F5
Lynbrook LGASH BS41 ..... 344 B2
Lynch Ct
  OLD/WMLY/WICK BS30 ... 338 B7
Lynch Rd BRKLY GL13 ...... 226 F8

  RSTROUD/NAIL GL6 ...... 210 C2
Lyncombe Wk
  MANG/FISH BS16 .... 337 H5
Lyncroft VGL GL2 .... 134 F1
Lyndale Av
  HNLZ/SM/SNYPK/WT BS9 . 325 H3
Lyndale Rd EVILLE/WHL BS5 . 336 F4
  YATE/CS BS37 .... 319 M3
Lynde Cl
  BMSTRD/HC/WWD BS13 ... 345 H5
Lyndhurst Cl CHELTE/BC GL52 . 72 D8
Lyndhurst Rd
  HNLZ/SM/SNYPK/WT BS9 . 325 H2
  KEYN BS31 .... 348 B1
Lyndley Cha CHELTE/BC GL52 . 71 L7
Lyng Cl GLE GL4 .... 137 C2
Lynmouth Rd BWTH/CHD GL3 . 137 H6
  CBRISNE BS2 .... 336 C1
Lynmouth Rd MANG/FISH BS16 . 326 F6
  CBRISNE BS2 .... 336 C1
Lynton Pl EVILLE/WHL BS5 .. 336 E4
Lynton Rd BMSTR BS3 ..... 345 M3
  GLE GL4 .... 137 H4
Lynton Wy MANG/FISH BS16 . 327 G3
Lynt Rd HGHW SN6 .... 268 C2
Lynwood Rd LYD GL15 ..... 201 J7
Lynworth La TEWK GL20 ..... 26 E5
Lynworth Pl CHELTE/BC GL52 . 3 H1
Lyons Court Rd
  HGRV/WHIT BS14 .... 346 F4
Lypiatt Dr CHELT GL50 ...... 2 A5
Lypiatt La CHELT GL50 ...... 2 A6
Lypiatt Rd CHELT GL50 ...... 2 A6
Lypiatt St CHELT GL50 ...... 2 A5
Lypiatt Vw RSTROUD/NAIL GL6 . 209 M4
Lyppiatt Rd EVILLE/WHL BS5 . 336 F4
Lyppincourt Rd
  HNBRY/STHM BS10 .... 315 J8
Lysander Ct BWTH/CHD GL3 . 113 L6
Lysander Rd
  BRSTK/PCHW BS34 ...... 315 M7
  HNBRY/STHM BS10 .... 315 J8
Lysander Wk
  BRSTK/PCHW BS34 ...... 317 G6
Lysons Av GL GL1 .... 135 M4
Lytchet Dr MANG/FISH BS16 . 328 C3
Lysons Av GL GL1 .... 135 M4
Lytton Gv HORF/LLZ BS7 ... 326 C5
  KEYN BS31 .... 348 C1
Lyveden Gdns
  BMSTRD/HC/WWD BS13 ... 345 K6
Lyvedon Wy LGASH BS41 ... 344 D2

M

Mabel's Furlong LED HR8 .... 20 A4
Macarthur Rd COTS GL54 ... 169 J2
Macauley Rd HORF/LLZ BS7 . 326 C2
Macey's Rd
  BMSTRD/HC/WWD BS13 ... 345 M8
Machen Rd CLFD GL16 ..... 151 M7
Machin Cl HNBRY/STHM BS10 . 315 H6
Machin Gdns
  HNBRY/STHM BS10 .... 315 H6
Machin Rd HNBRY/STHM BS10 . 315 H6
The Macies CBATH/BATHN BA1 . 350 D4
Mackenzie Wy CHELTW GL51 . 93 M6
Mackie Av BRSTK/PCHW BS34 . 326 D2
Mackie Gv BRSTK/PCHW BS34 . 326 D2
Mackie Rd BRSTK/PCHW BS34 . 326 D2
Macmillan Wy CIR GL7 .... 189 M8
  CIR GL7 .... 213 H7
  CIR GL7 .... 235 M1
  COTS GL54 .... 121 M4
  COTS GL54 .... 122 F7
  COTS GL54 .... 168 C3
  MIM GL56 .... 103 K4
  SHPSTR CV36 .... 61 H7
  TET GL8 .... 258 F7
  TET GL8 .... 281 C2
  TET GL8 .... 300 C2
Macmillian Wy TET GL8 .... 281 H4
Macrae Ct KGWD/HNM BS15 . 338 A3
Madeline Rd
  MANG/FISH BS16 .... 337 H1
Madison Cl YATE/CS BS37 .. 319 M4
Madleaze Rd GL GL1 .... 4 B8
Madsbury Rd KGWD/HNM BS15 . 338 A4
Maesknoll Rd
  BRSG/KWL/STAPK BS4 .... 336 C5
Magdala Rd GL GL1 .... 5 H7
Magdalene Pl CBRISNE BS2 . 336 B2
Magdalen Rd TET GL8 ..... 281 M4
Maggs Cl HNBRY/STHM BS10 . 315 L8
Maggs La EVILLE/WHL BS5 . 337 C1
  HGRV/WHIT BS14 .... 346 D2
Magnolia Cl CHEP NP16 ... 270 B6
Magnolia Wk VGL GL2 ..... 159 G2
Magpie Bottom La
  KGWD/HNM BS15 .... 337 L5
Magpie Ct STNHO GL10 .... 207 H3
Maida Vale Rd CHELTS GL53 . 115 M5
Maidenhall VGL GL2 .... 110 F7
Maidenhead Rd
  BMSTRD/HC/WWD BS13 ... 345 M4
Maidstone St BMSTR BS3 .. 336 B8
Main Av CLFD GL16 .... 151 M4
  LYD GL15 .... 201 H4
  LYD GL15 .... 224 C2
  LYD GL15 .... 224 B8
  MANG/FISH BS16 .... 328 E6
  RSTROUD/NAIL GL6 ...... 184 B4
Main St BDWAY WR12 ...... 11 C5
  CHNTN OX7 .... 125 M5
  EVE WR11 .... 30 C2
  MIM GL56 .... 81 L1
  SHPSTR CV36 .... 38 C2
  TEWK GL20 .... 28 F7
Main Vw FRCTL/WBN BS36 .. 318 F4
Maisemore YATE/CS BS37 .. 319 M4
Maisemore Av
  BRSTK/PCHW BS34 ...... 316 D4
Maitlands GLE GL4 .... 160 B6
Makin Cl
  OLD/WMLY/WICK BS30 ... 338 E6
Malago Rd BMSTR BS3 ..... 335 L8

alago Wk
BMSTRD/HC/WWD BS13 345 G7
alden Rd CHELTE/BC GL52 2 F3
e Maldens SHPSTR CV36 16 A6
aldon Gdns GL GL1 136 B4
aldowers La EVILLE/WHL BS5 337 J2
alet Cl VGL GL2 112 E6
allard Cl ALMDB BS32 316 F1
EVILLE/WHL BS5 337 H2
VGL GL2 158 F2
YATE/CS BS37 320 C3
alleson Rd CHELTE/BC GL52 72 B3
allow Cl THNB/SVB BS35 293 M1
e Mall CFTN/FAIL BS8 335 H4
almains Dr MANG/FISH BS16 327 K2
almesbury Cl
OLD/WMLY/WICK BS30 338 B6
RDLND/MONT BS6 325 L7
almesbury Rd CHELTW GL51 93 J6
GLE GL4 136 D4
SWDNW SN5 287 H8
almsey Cl TEWK GL20 48 B8
althouse La CHELT GL50 2 D2
COTS GL54 74 C6
COTS GL54 123 G1
SHPSTR CV36 61 H5
althouse Wk TET GL8 281 M3
e Maltings MALM SN16 303 J8
alvern Ct EVILLE/WHL BS5 337 H4
alvern Dr
OLD/WMLY/WICK BS30 338 E6
THNB/SVB BS35 293 M3
alvern Pl CHELT GL50 115 K3
alvern Rd
BRSG/KWL/STAPK BS4 336 F8
CHELT GL50 115 K2
EVILLE/WHL BS5 337 H4
GL GL1 5 H1
RTEWK/TIB GL19 66 E4
e Malverns GLE GL4 136 F5
alvern St CHELTW GL51 93 K7
alvern Wy CLFD GL16 152 A4
ancroft Av AVONM BS11 324 B4
andalay Dr VGL GL2 90 F6
andara Gv GLE GL4 136 F7
andarin Wy CHELTW GL51 93 K6
angotsfield Rd
MANG/FISH BS16 328 B7
anilla Rd CFTN/FAIL BS8 335 J4
ankley Rd STNHO GL10 207 H7
anley Gdns VGL GL2 112 E6
annings Rd MTCHDN GL17 129 M2
anor Av DSLY GL11 229 H6
anor Cl ALMDB BS32 306 D2
CIR GL7 214 B6
CIR GL7 242 F4
DSLY GL11 229 G5
FRCTL/WBN BS36 318 E5
RSTROUD/NAIL GL6 233 H5
TEWK GL20 50 C5
e Manor Cl CFTN/FAIL BS8 334 C3
anor Ct CHELTW GL51 93 J5
anor Court Dr HORF/LLZ BS7 326 A4
anor Farm COTS GL54 124 A7
anor Farm Cl CHNTN OX7 104 B6
anor Farm Crs ALMDB BS32 316 F2
anor Gdns STROUD GL5 232 C1
anor Gv ALMDB BS32 316 D1
MANG/FISH BS16 328 C7
anor La CFTN/FAIL BS8 334 B3
CHELTE/BC GL52 72 D3
FRCTL/WBN BS36 318 B4
SHPSTR CV36 16 B5
WUE GL12 276 C7
WUE GL12 277 L4
anor Orch HGHW SN6 289 G3
anor Pk ALMDB BS32 306 E1
CHELTW GL51 114 F6
RDLND/MONT BS6 325 K8
TEWK GL20 48 C3
VGL GL2 113 G7
anor Pl MANG/FISH BS16 327 L2
TEWK GL20 48 B8
anor Rd
BMSTRD/HC/WWD BS13 345 H5
CFTN/FAIL BS8 334 B5
CHELTW GL51 93 J5
HORF/LLZ BS7 326 A7
KEYN BS31 348 C8
LYD GL15 201 L8
MANG/FISH BS16 327 H6
MANG/FISH BS16 328 C7
OLD/WMLY/WICK BS30 339 L6
YATE/CS BS37 309 J4
anor St RSTROUD/NAIL GL6 210 C2
anor Wk THNB/SVB BS35 273 K8
anor Wy YATE/CS BS37 320 E1
anse Gdns CHELTW GL51 115 H4
e Manse La RWYE HR9 84 E2
ansel Cl KEYN BS31 348 E8
ansell Cl VGL GL2 135 L6
anse Rd MTCHDN GL17 129 M3
anser St CHELT GL50 2 C1
ansfield Ms VGL GL2 159 H4
ansfield St BMSTR BS3 345 K1
anston Cl HGRV/WHIT BS14 346 E4
anworthy Rd
BRSG/KWL/STAPK BS4 336 F8
anx Rd HORF/LLZ BS7 326 B4
aple Av CHEP NP16 270 A7
MANG/FISH BS16 327 L8
THNB/SVB BS35 293 L2
aple Cl BRSTK/PCHW BS34 316 E4
DSLY GL11 229 J8
HGRV/WHIT BS14 346 F6
OLD/WMLY/WICK BS30 338 D7
VGL GL2 159 G3
aple Ct VGL GL2 113 G7
aple Dr BWTH/CHD GL3 137 M4
CHELTS GL53 116 D6
STROUD GL5 208 C2
apleleaze
BRSG/KWL/STAPK BS4 336 F8
aplemeade HORF/LLZ BS7 325 L7
apleridge La YATE/CS BS37 310 E4
aple Rd
BRSG/KWL/STAPK BS4 336 F6
HORF/LLZ BS7 325 M6
The Maples CIR GL7 238 B6
GLE GL4 137 G5
Maplestone Rd
HGRV/WHIT BS14 346 C8
Maple Wk KEYN BS31 347 M7
MANG/FISH BS16 329 L6
Marbeck Rd
HNBRY/STHM BS10 325 K2
Marchant Cl CHELTW GL51 93 H8
Mardale Cl
HNBRY/STHM BS10 325 L1
Marden Rd KEYN BS31 348 C7
Mardon Rd
BRSG/KWL/STAPK BS4 336 F5
Mardyke Ferry Rd
CBRIS/FH BS1 6 A6
Marefield Cl GLE GL4 137 G4
Margaret Rd LED HR8 19 M3
TEWK GL20 48 B7
Margate St BMSTR BS3 336 A8
Margery La CLFD GL16 175 G7
Margrett Rd CHELT GL50 2 C2
Marguerite Rd
BMSTRD/HC/WWD BS13 345 H3
Marians Wk CLFD GL16 151 J5
Marigold Wk BMSTR BS3 345 J1
Marina Gdns MANG/FISH BS16 327 G8
Mariners Dr
HNLZ/SM/SNYPK/WT BS9 324 F7
Mariners' Pth
HNLZ/SM/SNYPK/WT BS9 324 F7
Marion Rd KGWD/HNM BS15 337 K8
Marion Wk EVILLE/WHL BS5 337 J4
Marissal Cl HNBRY/STHM BS10 315 G8
Marissal Rd HNBRY/STHM BS10 315 G8
Mariston Wy
OLD/WMLY/WICK BS30 338 E5
Marjoram Cl GLE GL4 137 H6
Marjoram Pl ALMDB BS32 317 H4
Market La COTS GL54 74 D2
Market Pde GL GL1 4 F5
Market Pl CHPMW/MSHF SN14 342 C3
CHPMW/MSHF SN14 343 K8
CIR GL7 238 C2
CIR GL7 242 E4
CLFD GL16 175 K1
COR/BOX SN13 353 M5
SHPSTR CV36 16 B5
TET GL8 282 A4
Market Sq COTS GL54 102 A3
MANG/FISH BS16 327 L8
Market St CHELTW GL51 2 A3
CIND GL14 154 B2
LED HR8 19 M3
RSTROUD/NAIL GL6 232 D8
WUE GL12 277 K4
Mark La CBRIS/FH BS1 6 D4
Marksbury Rd BMSTR BS3 345 L1
Marlborough Av
EVILLE/WHL BS5 327 G8
Marlborough Cl
CHELTE/BC GL52 72 A8
CHELTS GL53 116 B5
Marlborough Crs GLE GL4 136 C5
Marlborough Dr
MANG/FISH BS16 327 K2
Marlborough Hl
RDLND/MONT BS6 6 E1
Marlborough Hill Pl
CBRISNE BS2 6 E1
Marlborough Rd GLE GL4 136 C4
Marlborough St CBRIS/FH BS1 6 F1
CBRISNE BS2 6 E2
EVILLE/WHL BS5 327 G8
Marle Hl RSTROUD/NAIL GL6 234 B1
Marle Hill Pde CHELT GL50 2 D2
Marle Hill Rd CHELT GL50 2 D1
Marlepit Gv
BMSTRD/HC/WWD BS13 345 H5
Marleyfield Cl
BWTH/CHD GL3 113 J4
Marleyfield Wy BWTH/CHD GL3 113 J4
Marley La RSTROUD/NAIL GL6 234 D2
Marlfield Wk
BMSTRD/HC/WWD BS13 345 G4
Marling Cl STROUD GL5 232 D3
Marling Crs STROUD GL5 208 A4
Marling Rd EVILLE/WHL BS5 337 J4
Marlstone Rd DSLY GL11 229 H7
Marlwood Dr
HNBRY/STHM BS10 315 J8
Marmaduke St BMSTR BS3 336 B8
Marment Rd DSLY GL11 229 G7
Marmion Crs
HNBRY/STHM BS10 315 H8
Marne Cl HGRV/WHIT BS14 346 F6
Marram Cl GLE GL4 137 H6
Marshacre La THNB/SVB BS35 292 B5
Marshall Av SHPSTR CV36 16 A6
Marshall's La CIND GL14 154 B2
Marsham Wy
OLD/WMLY/WICK BS30 338 A6
Marsh Cl CHELTW GL51 2 A1
FRCTL/WBN BS36 318 A7
Marsh Common
THNB/SVB BS35 304 F5
Marsh Dr CHELTW GL51 2 B1
Marshfield La
OLD/WMLY/WICK BS30 349 J2
Marshfield Rd BAD GL9 332 A2
MANG/FISH BS16 327 K7
Marsh Gdns CHELTW GL51 2 B1
Marsh La CHELTW GL51 2 B1
CHPMW/MSHF SN14 323 K7
EVILLE/WHL BS5 336 E4
STNHO GL10 207 H8
Marshmouth La COTS GL54 123 J6
Marsh Rd BMSTR BS3 335 H8
CHEP NP16 270 B6
STNHO GL10 207 G7
Marsh St CBRIS/FH BS1 6 E4
Marsh Ter CHELTW GL51 138 F1
Marshwall La ALMDB BS32 306 B5
Marsh Wy CLFD GL16 175 L7
Marsland Rd CHELTW GL51 114 F1
Marston Rd
BRSG/KWL/STAPK BS4 346 D1
CHELTE/BC GL52 94 B7
Marten Cl BWTH/CHD GL3 137 J6
Marten Rd CHEP NP16 270 A5
Martin Cl BRSTK/PCHW BS34 316 A3
CIR GL7 238 C4
Martindale Rd BWTH/CHD GL3 113 K5
Martingale Rd
BRSG/KWL/STAPK BS4 336 F7
Martins Cl KGWD/HNM BS15 337 L6
Martins Cft
CHPMW/MSHF SN14 343 L8
Martin's Rd KGWD/HNM BS15 337 L6
The Martins CHEP NP16 270 C2
STROUD GL5 207 M3
Martin St BMSTR BS3 335 K8
Martins Wy LED HR8 19 M5
Martlock Crs BMSTR BS3 345 L2
Martock Rd BMSTR BS3 345 L2
KEYN BS31 348 C8
Marwood Rd
BRSG/KWL/STAPK BS4 346 A3
Marybush La CBRISNE BS2 7 H3
Marygold Leaze
OLD/WMLY/WICK BS30 338 C7
Mary Gv VGL GL2 110 F6
Mary Rose Av BWTH/CHD GL3 113 H4
Mary St EVILLE/WHL BS5 336 F3
Mascot Rd BMSTR BS3 335 M8
Masefield Av VGL GL2 135 L7
Masefield Rd CIR GL7 238 B5
Masefield Wy HORF/LLZ BS7 326 C4
Maskelyne Av
HNBRY/STHM BS10 325 M4
Mason Rd STROUD GL5 209 H4
Masons Vw FRCTL/WBN BS36 318 A4
Massey Pde GL GL1 136 B4
Massey Rd GLE GL4 136 C4
LED HR8 19 L3
Materman Rd HGRV/WHIT BS14 347 G6
Matford Cl FRCTL/WBN BS36 318 A6
HNBRY/STHM BS10 315 M7
Matford La BRKLY GL13 251 H7
Mathern Wy CHEP NP16 270 A6
Mathews Wy STROUD GL5 208 B3
Matson Av GLE GL4 136 E8
Matson La GLE GL4 160 D1
Matson Pl GL GL1 136 C4
Matthews Cl HGRV/WHIT BS14 347 H5
Matthew's Rd
EVILLE/WHL BS5 336 E4
Maugersbury Pk COTS GL54 102 A4
Maules La MANG/FISH BS16 327 H1
Maunsell Rd AVONM BS11 324 D1
Maurice Rd RDLND/MONT BS6 336 A1
Mautravers Cl ALMDB BS32 316 F4
Mawley Rd CIR GL7 218 D6
Maxse Rd
BRSG/KWL/STAPK BS4 336 D8
Mayalls Cl RTEWK/TIB GL19 68 B5
The Mayalls TEWK GL20 26 C5
Maybec Gdns
EVILLE/WHL BS5 337 J5
Maybourne
BRSG/KWL/STAPK BS4 347 J1
Maybrook St BRKLY GL13 227 G8
May Bush La RWYE HR9 126 E6
Maycliffe Pk RDLND/MONT BS6 336 B1
Maycroft La BRKLY GL13 251 K5
DSLY GL11 251 M6
May Evans Cl DSLY GL11 229 H6
Mayfair Cl VGL GL2 135 K3
Mayfield Av MANG/FISH BS16 337 J1
Mayfield Cl CHELTE/BC GL52 94 B1
Mayfield Dr BWTH/CHD GL3 137 H2
GLE GL4 137 H3
Mayfield Pk MANG/FISH BS16 337 J1
Mayfield Pk North
MANG/FISH BS16 337 J1
Mayfield Pk South
MANG/FISH BS16 337 J1
Mayfields KEYN BS31 348 A6
May La CHCAM GL55 13 L7
DSLY GL11 253 J2
May Meadow La MTCHDN GL17 130 C2
Maynard Cl
BMSTRD/HC/WWD BS13 345 L6
Maynard Rd
BMSTRD/HC/WWD BS13 345 L6
Mayo Rd SHPSTR CV36 16 B4
Maypole Gn LYD GL15 200 C3
Maypole Rd LYD GL15 200 C3
May's Crs COTS GL54 169 J1
Mays La TET GL8 257 M3
May St KGWD/HNM BS15 337 L2
Maythorn Dr CHELTW GL51 92 F7
Maytree Av
BMSTRD/HC/WWD BS13 345 K4
Maytree Cl
BMSTRD/HC/WWD BS13 345 K4
May Tree Cl CIR GL7 236 F5
May Tree Sq GLE GL4 136 E4
Mayville Av BRSTK/PCHW BS34 316 C8
Maywood Crs MANG/FISH BS16 327 K7
Maywood Rd MANG/FISH BS16 327 L7
Maze St EVILLE/WHL BS5 336 D5
Maze Wk CLFD GL16 151 J5
Mead Cl AVONM BS11 324 A5
CHELTS GL53 116 A6
Meade-king Gv CHELTE/BC GL52 72 D8
Meadgate MANG/FISH BS16 328 D3
Mead La KEYN BS31 349 H7
LYD GL15 225 H2
THNB/SVB BS35 305 M1
Meadoway CHELTE/BC GL52 94 A1
Meadowbank LYD GL15 201 L8
Meadow Cl CHELTW GL51 114 E2
CIR GL7 238 C4
LYD GL15 202 B2
MANG/FISH BS16 328 B4
TEWK GL20 48 D3
Meadow Court Dr
OLD/WMLY/WICK BS30 338 E8
Meadowcroft GLE GL4 137 G6
MANG/FISH BS16 328 C3
Meadowland Rd
HNBRY/STHM BS10 315 G7
Meadow La CHELTW GL51 115 G6
Meadow La (West) STROUD GL5 208 A5
Meadowleaze VGL GL2 112 F8
Meadow Md FRCTL/WBN BS36 318 D3
YATE/CS BS37 310 A6
Meadow Pk CBATH/BATHN BA1 352 D7
Meadow Rd CIND GL14 154 C3
CIR GL7 238 C4
STNHO GL10 207 H3
WUE GL12 275 K7
YATE/CS BS37 320 C2
Meadows Dean MTCHDN GL17 130 D2
Meadowside
THNB/SVB BS35 293 M3
Meadowside Dr
HGRV/WHIT BS14 346 C8
The Meadows
KGWD/HNM BS15 337 M7
Meadow St CBRISNE BS2 7 H2
Meadowsweet Av
BRSTK/PCHW BS34 316 D8
Meadow V DSLY GL11 229 H7
EVILLE/WHL BS5 337 J2
Meadow Vw FRCTL/WBN BS36 318 E4
Meadow Wk CLFD GL16 175 L7
Meadow Wy ALMDB BS32 317 G4
BWTH/CHD GL3 113 K4
CHNTN OX7 104 B7
CIR GL7 263 G4
STROUD GL5 208 A5
Mead Ri BMSTR BS3 7 J8
Mead Rd BRSTK/PCHW BS34 317 H5
CHELTS GL53 116 A6
GLE GL4 137 G5
YATE/CS BS37 320 E3
Meads Cl CHELTE/BC GL52 72 C8
CLFD GL16 151 J8
The Meads
CHPMW/MSHF SN14 323 K8
MANG/FISH BS16 328 B4
TET GL8 279 L8
Mead St BMSTR BS3 7 J8
The Mead BRSTK/PCHW BS34 316 D7
CIR GL7 238 B2
HGHW SN6 287 H3
THNB/SVB BS35 293 J6
Meadvale Cl VGL GL2 112 B5
Meadway
HNLZ/SM/SNYPK/WT BS9 324 E5
Mead Wy THNB/SVB BS35 293 K4
Meadway Rd STNHO GL10 207 G5
Meardon Rd
HGRV/WHIT BS14 347 G5
Mede Cl CBRIS/FH BS1 7 G7
Medical Av CFTN/FAIL BS8 6 D3
Medina Cl THNB/SVB BS35 293 L4
Medoc Cl CHELTW GL51 93 K6
Medway Cl KEYN BS31 348 B8
Medway Ct THNB/SVB BS35 293 M3
Medway Crs BWTH/CHD GL3 138 B6
Medway Dr FRCTL/WBN BS36 318 D4
KEYN BS31 348 C8
Meeks Well La RWYE HR9 126 E5
Meendhurst Rd CIND GL14 154 A4
Meend La MTCHDN GL17 129 G4
Meerbrook Wy VGL GL2 159 H4
Meere Bank AVONM BS11 324 D2
Meerstone Wy GLE GL4 136 F8
Meg Thatchers Cl
EVILLE/WHL BS5 337 K4
Melbourne Cl CHELTS GL53 115 L5
STNHO GL10 207 G2
Melbourne Dr STNHO GL10 207 G3
YATE/CS BS37 320 D2
Melbourne Rd HORF/LLZ BS7 325 M7
Melbourne St GL GL1 136 C4
Melbourne St East GL GL1 136 B4
Melbourne St West GL GL1 136 B4
Melbury Rd
BRSG/KWL/STAPK BS4 346 C1
Melick Cl GLE GL4 136 C6
Melita Rd RDLND/MONT BS6 326 A8
Mellent Av
BMSTRD/HC/WWD BS13 345 L8
Melmore Gdns CIR GL7 238 E5
Melody Wy VGL GL2 113 G6
Melrose Av CFTN/FAIL BS8 335 K3
YATE/CS BS37 320 B1
Melrose Cl YATE/CS BS37 320 C1
Melrose Pl CFTN/FAIL BS8 335 K3
Melton Crs HORF/LLZ BS7 326 C4
Melville COTS GL54 123 H3
Melville Rd BWTH/CHD GL3 113 K6
RDLND/MONT BS6 335 K2
Melville Ter BMSTR BS3 335 L8
Melvin Sq
BRSG/KWL/STAPK BS4 346 A2
Memorial Cl KGWD/HNM BS15 337 K7
Memorial Rd KGWD/HNM BS15 337 K6
Mendip Cl CHELTE/BC GL52 3 J1
KEYN BS31 347 M6
VGL GL2 159 G3
Mendip Crs MANG/FISH BS16 328 C4
Mendip Rd BMSTR BS3 335 M8
CHELTE/BC GL52 3 J2
Mendip Vw
OLD/WMLY/WICK BS30 339 L4
Mendip View Av
MANG/FISH BS16 327 J8
Meon Cl STRAT CV37 9 K2
Meon Rd CHCAM GL55 9 G6
Merchants Md VGL GL2 158 F2
Merchants Rd CFTN/FAIL BS8 335 J4
GL GL1 4 C8
Merchant St CBRIS/FH BS1 7 G2
Mercia Dr CBRISNE BS2 336 C1
Mercian Cl CIR GL7 238 D4
Mercian Wy CHEP NP16 270 C4
Mercia Rd COTS GL54 74 C5
GL GL1 4 E3
Mercier Cl YATE/CS BS37 320 B1
Mercury Wy GLE GL4 137 H5
Merestones Cl CHELT GL50 115 K5
Merestones Dr CHELT GL50 115 K5
Merestones Rd CHELT GL50 115 K5
Merevale Rd VGL GL2 5 M3
Merfield Rd
BRSG/KWL/STAPK BS4 346 D1
Meridian Pl CFTN/FAIL BS8 6 A3
Meridian Rd RDLND/MONT BS6 335 L2
Meridian V CFTN/FAIL BS8 6 A3
Meriet Av
BMSTRD/HC/WWD BS13 345 K7
Merioneth St BMSTR BS3 336 B8
Meriton St CBRISNE BS2 336 D6
Merlin Cl CHELTS GL53 115 L6
HNLZ/SM/SNYPK/WT BS9 325 H3
Merlin Dr VGL GL2 159 G1
Merlin Hvn WUE GL12 277 J4
Merlin Rdg MANG/FISH BS16 329 L7
Merlin Rd BRSTK/PCHW BS34 315 L5
Merlin Wy CHELTS GL53 115 L6
YATE/CS BS37 320 B4
Merrett's Orch VGL GL2 204 F8
Merriville Gdns CHELTW GL51 93 J8
Merriville Rd CHELTW GL51 93 J8
Merrymouth Rd CHNTN OX7 149 J1
Merrywalks STROUD GL5 208 D4
Merryweather Cl ALMDB BS32 316 E3
Merrywood Rd BMSTR BS3 6 C8
Mersey Rd CHELTE/BC GL52 3 K4
Merstham Rd CBRISNE BS2 336 C1
Merton Rd HORF/LLZ BS7 326 A6
The Mertons CIND GL14 155 H7
Mervyn Rd HORF/LLZ BS7 326 A7
Meteor Wy BWTH/CHD GL3 138 A6
Metford Gv RDLND/MONT BS6 325 K8
Metford Pl
RDLND/MONT BS6 325 L8
Metford Rd RDLND/MONT BS6 325 K8
Metz Wy GL GL1 5 H6
GLE GL4 136 E3
VGL GL2 5 K7
The Mews LED HR8 19 M2
Meysey Cl CIR GL7 241 L6
Michaelmas Ct GL GL1 5 J3
Michael Pym's Rd
MALM SN16 303 J6
Michaels Md CIR GL7 238 B5
Michaels Wy CLFD GL16 175 L7
Mickle Md VGL GL2 110 F6
Middle Av CBRIS/FH BS1 6 E5
Middle Cft GLE GL4 136 F4
Middlecroft STNHO GL10 206 B4
Middledown Rd
CHPMW/MSHF SN14 341 J2
Middle Gnd HGHW SN6 288 E3
Middlehay Ct CHELTE/BC GL52 72 A8
Middle Hl RSTROUD/NAIL GL6 210 A7
STROUD GL5 208 F4
Middle Hill Crs
RSTROUD/NAIL GL6 210 B8
Middle Leazes STROUD GL5 208 F4
Middle Rd BUR/CRTN OX18 172 D5
KGWD/HNM BS15 328 A8
STROUD GL5 209 G8
Middle Spillman's STROUD GL5 208 C5
Middle St CHEP NP16 270 A3
STROUD GL5 208 E4
Middleton Lawn VGL GL2 113 G4
Middleton Rd AVONM BS11 324 B3
Middle Tynings
RSTROUD/NAIL GL6 232 C7
Middle Wy CHEP NP16 270 B6
Midland Rd CBRISNE BS2 7 K3
CIR GL7 238 D5
GL GL1 4 F9
MANG/FISH BS16 327 M7
STNHO GL10 207 G3
Midland St CBRISNE BS2 7 K4
Midland Ter
MANG/FISH BS16 327 H8
Midland Wy THNB/SVB BS35 293 K3
Midway RSTROUD/NAIL GL6 210 B8
Midwinter Av CHELTW GL51 2 A1
Midwinter Gdns CHELTW GL51 93 L7
Midwinter Rd COTS GL54 169 J1
Milbourne La MALM SN16 303 L7
Milbourne Pk MALM SN16 303 L7
Mildred St EVILLE/WHL BS5 336 E4
Mile End Rd CLFD GL16 151 L8
Miles Ct
OLD/WMLY/WICK BS30 338 B7
Miles Rd CFTN/FAIL BS8 335 J2
Milestone Wk CLFD GL16 175 L7
Milford Av
OLD/WMLY/WICK BS30 339 K4
Milford Cl VGL GL2 112 D6
Milford St BMSTR BS3 6 C9
Millard Cl HNBRY/STHM BS10 325 L1
Mill Av BDWAY WR12 32 D4
CBRIS/FH BS1 6 F5
Millbank DSLY GL11 229 J6
Millbank Cl
BRSG/KWL/STAPK BS4 337 G8
Millbridge Rd BWTH/CHD GL3 137 J4
Millbrook Av
BRSG/KWL/STAPK BS4 337 H8
Millbrook Cl GL GL1 5 J7
OLD/WMLY/WICK BS30 338 E5
Millbrook Gdns CHELTW GL51 115 K1
RWYE HR9 106 C3
Millbrook Gn LYD GL15 224 F2
Millbrook Ley MIM GL56 80 C7
Millbrook Rd YATE/CS BS37 319 K1
Millbrook St CHELTW GL51 115 K1
GL GL1 5 H7
Mill Cl CIR GL7 263 J4
FRCTL/WBN BS36 318 E4
WUE GL12 277 L5
Mill Crs YATE/CS BS37 319 K7
Millend LYD GL15 202 E1
Millend La STNHO GL10 206 B4
Miller Cl RTEWK/TIB GL19 89 J3
VGL GL2 112 F6
Miller Craddock Wy LED HR8 19 M5
Miller's Court Rd RGTMLV WR13 22 E5
RGTMLV WR13 23 G6
Millers Dr
OLD/WMLY/WICK BS30 338 E6
Millers Dyke VGL GL2 158 F2
Millers Gn MTCHDN GL17 129 K4
Mill Farm Dr STROUD GL5 208 A3
Millfield EVE WR11 30 D1
THNB/SVB BS35 293 L1
Millfield Dr
OLD/WMLY/WICK BS30 338 E5
Millfields BWTH/CHD GL3 137 J3

Millground Rd
  BMSTRD/HC/WWD BS13.... **345** G7
Mill Gv *VGL* GL2 .... **158** F2
Millham Rd *CHELTE/BC* GL52... **72** C7
Mill HI *CHEP* NP16................... **222** B4
  LYD GL15 .... **222** D3
Millhill La *CLFD* GL16............. **175** H5
Millhouse Dr *CHELT* GL50....... **93** L6
Milliman CI
  BMSTRD/HC/WWD BS13.... **345** L6
Millin Av *GLE* GL4.................. **135** M8
Milling CI *HGHW* SN6............ **287** H2 🔟
Milling Crs *LYD* GL15 .... **224** F3
Mill La *ALMDB* BS32 .... **306** C2
  BMSTR BS3 .... **6** E5
  BWTH/CHD GL3 .... **138** B5
  CHCAM GL55 .... **8** F7
  CHELTE/BC GL52 .... **71** G7
  CHELTE/BC GL52 .... **94** E7
  CIR GL7 .... **242** D4
  CIR GL7 .... **245** G8
  COR/BOX SN13............................ **353** L4
  COTS GL54 .... **74** C6 🔟
  COTS GL54 .... **101** J4
  COTS GL54 .... **123** G1
  FRCTL/WBN BS36 .... **318** D3
  MALM SN16 .... **303** J8
  MTCHDN GL17.............................. **131** J2
  NWNT GL18 .... **85** H5
  OLD/WMLY/WICK BS30 .... **338** E6
  OLD/WMLY/WICK BS30 .... **340** B2
  OLD/WMLY/WICK BS30 .... **349** H2
  RSTROUD/NAIL GL6 .... **161** L5
  RTEWK/TIB GL19 .... **44** A7
  RTEWK/TIB GL19 .... **66** A3
  TET GL8 .... **257** L2
  WUE GL12 .... **275** G4
  YATE/CS BS37 .... **321** H5
Mill Pitt Gdns *BWTH/CHD* GL3.. **137** J3
Millpond End *STROUD* GL5....... **232** C1 🔟
Mill Rd *FRCTL/WBN* BS36....... **317** M7
Mills CI *BDWAY* WR12 .... **32** F3
Mill St *CHELTE/BC* GL52 .... **94** D6
  TEWK GL20 .... **47** M5 🔟
Mill Vw *COTS* GL54 .... **169** J1
Millview *MIM* GL56 .... **57** H1
Millward Gv *MANG/FISH* BS16... **327** L7
Mill Wy *DSLY* GL11 .... **229** H7
Milne Pastures *TEWK* GL20 ...... **48** E4 🔟
Milner Gn
  OLD/WMLY/WICK BS30 .... **338** C6
Milner Rd *HORF/LLZ* BS7........ **326** B6
Milo PI *GL* GL1 .... **136** A5
Milsom St *CHELT* GL50 .... **2** C3
  EVILLE/WHL BS5.............................. **7** L1
Milton Av *CHELTW* GL51 .... **115** G2 🔟
  VGL GL2 .... **135** L6
Milton CI *YATE/CS* BS37 .... **319** M1
Milton Gv *STROUD* GL5........... **209** G4
Milton Pk *EVILLE/WHL* BS5 ..... **336** E4 🔟
Milton Rd *CHELTW* GL51......... **115** H2
  HORF/LLZ BS7............................. **326** A5
  YATE/CS BS37 .... **319** M1
Miltons CI
  BMSTRD/HC/WWD BS13.... **345** M7
Milton St *CIR* GL7 .... **242** D5
Milverton Gdns
  RDLND/MONT BS6 .... **336** B1 🔟
Milward Rd *KEYN* BS31 .... **348** A5
Mimosa Av *CHELTW* GL51 ...... **115** J7
Mina Rd *CBRISNE* BS2 .... **326** B8
Minehead Rd
  BRSG/KWL/STAPK BS4............. **346** B2
Mine Pitts La *RWYE* HR9 .... **126** E7
Minerva CI *GLE* GL4................ **137** H5
Minerva Wk *LYD* GL15 .... **201** K6
Minetts Av *CHELTE/BC* GL52 ..... **72** C5
Minety La *MALM* SN16............ **285** K5
Minnow La *BUR/CRTN* OX18 ... **172** D5
Minor's La *HNBRY/STHM* BS10 .. **314** C3
Minsmere Rd *KEYN* BS31........ **348** L3
Minster CI *CHELTE/BC* GL52 ..... **72** A7
Minster Gdns *GLE* GL4........... **137** H5 🔟
Minstrel Wy *BWTH/CHD* GL3... **113** H3
Minton CI *HGRV/WHIT* BS14.... **346** D6
Minto Rd *CBRISNE* BS2 .... **336** C1
Miserden Rd *CHELTW* GL51 ..... **114** F3
Miss Grace's La *CHEP* NP16 .... **222** E8
Mission Rd *YATE/CS* BS37 .... **309** J7
Mitchell La *CBRIS/FH* BS1 .... **7** G5
Mitchell Wk
  OLD/WMLY/WICK BS30 .... **338** F5 🔟
Mitford Br *SHPSTR* CV36 .... **38** C4
Mitre Pitch *WUE* GL12 .... **277** L4 🔟
Mitre St *CHELTS* GL53 .... **2** E7
Mitton Wy *TEWK* GL20 .... **48** C3
Mivart St *EVILLE/WHL* BS5....... **336** D1
Moat Bank *TEWK* GL20 .... **24** B6
Moat La *CHELTW* GL51 .... **92** E5
  RTEWK/TIB GL19 .... **66** D3
  RTEWK/TIB GL19 .... **108** E3
The Moat *CHNTN* OX7 .... **104** B6
  VGL GL2 .... **159** H2 🔟
Modecombe Gv
  HNBRY/STHM BS10 .... **315** H8 🔟
Moffat Rd *RSTROUD/NAIL* GL6.. **232** C6
Mogg St *CBRISNE* BS2............. **336** C1
Mogridge CI *BWTH/CHD* GL3... **137** J4 🔟
Molesworth CI
  BMSTRD/HC/WWD BS13......... **345** J7
Molesworth Dr
  BMSTRD/HC/WWD BS13......... **345** J7
Monarch CI *GLE* GL4 .... **137** G7 🔟
Monarch's Wy *BAD* GL9 .... **298** A8
  CHCAM GL55 .... **12** F6
  CHCAM GL55 .... **34** D4
  CIR GL7 .... **236** D6
  COTS GL54 .... **101** J9
  COTS GL54 .... **123** H6
  COTS GL54 .... **145** H8
  COTS GL54 .... **168** B5
  COTS GL54 .... **191** H1
  EVILLE/WHL BS5.......................... **336** F5
  KGWD/HNM BS15 .... **347** K1
  LGASH BS41 .... **344** A1
  MIM GL56 .... **79** M5
  MIM GL56 .... **102** B2

Monica Dr *CHELT* GL50 .... **94** A7
Monkey Meadow *TEWK* GL20 .... **49** G2 🔟
Monkey Puzzle CI
  STROUD GL5 .... **208** A5 🔟
Monk Rd *HORF/LLZ* BS7.......... **325** M7
Monks Av *KGWD/HNM* BS15 ... **337** K3 🔟
Monks Cft *CHELTW* GL51 .... **115** G2
Monks La *TEWK* GL20 .... **49** G8
Monks Meadow *LED* HR8 .... **40** B5 🔟
Monk's Park Av *HORF/LLZ* BS7.. **326** A2
Monks Park Wy
  HNBRY/STHM BS10 .... **326** A3
Monkton Rd *KGWD/HNM* BS15.. **337** K7
Monmouth HI *ALMDB* BS32 ..... **305** M7
Monmouth Rd *CLFD* GL16........ **151** M5
  HORF/LLZ BS7............................. **325** M7
  KEYN BS31 .... **347** M6
Monmouth St *BMSTR* BS3 .... **336** B8 🔟
Monsdale CI
  HNBRY/STHM BS10 .... **325** J1
Monsdale Dr
  HNBRY/STHM BS10 .... **315** J8
Monson Av *CHELT* GL50 .... **2** D3
Montague CI
  BRSTK/PCHW BS34 .... **317** G6 🔟
Montague HI *CBRISNE* BS2 ... **335** M3 🔟
Montague HI South
  CBRISNE BS2 .... **6** F1 🔟
Monterey CI *TEWK* GL20 .... **48** C8
Montfort Rd *VGL* GL2............... **112** D6
Montgomery CI
  BWTH/CHD GL3 .... **137** K5 🔟
Montgomery Rd
  CHELTW GL51 .... **114** F5 🔟
  BMSTR BS3 .... **336** B8 🔟
Montpellier *GL* GL1 .... **4** E7
Montpellier Dr *CHELT* GL50......... **2** D7
Montpellier Gv *CHELT* GL50......... **2** C9
Montpellier Pde *CHELT* GL50 ..... **2** C8
Montpellier Retreat *CHELT* GL50.. **2** C9
Montpellier Rd *LYD* GL15......... **200** E2
Montpellier Spa Rd *CHELT* GL50.. **2** C7
Montpellier St *CHELT* GL50......... **2** B7
Montpellier Ter *CHELT* GL50 .... **2** B8
Montpellier Vls *CHELT* GL50 .... **2** C9
Montpellier Wk *CHELT* GL50 .... **2** C8
Montreal Av *HORF/LLZ* BS7...... **326** B3
Montrose Av
  RDLND/MONT BS6 .... **335** L2
Montrose Dr
  OLD/WMLY/WICK BS30 .... **338** D5
Montrose Pk
  BRSG/KWL/STAPK BS4............. **346** F1
Montroy CI
  HNLZ/SM/SNYPK/WT BS9......... **325** L5
Montserrat *STROUD* GL5 .... **208** F8
Moon CI *CHPMW/MSHF* SN14... **353** K1 🔟
Moon's La *RSTROUD/NAIL* GL6.. **210** D6
Moon St *CBRISNE* BS2................ **7** G1
Moor Court Dr *CHELTE/BC* GL52... **3** H3
Moor Croft Dr
  OLD/WMLY/WICK BS30 .... **338** B7
Moordell CI *YATE/CS* BS37 ...... **319** M2
Moorend Crs *CHELTS* GL53 ...... **115** L5
Moorend Gdns *AVONM* BS11 ... **324** B4
Moorend Gld *CHELTS* GL53 ..... **116** B5
Moorend Gv *CHELTS* GL53 .... **115** L6
Moorend La *VGL* GL2 .... **204** F8
Moorend Park Rd *CHELTS* GL53 .. **115** L5
Moorend Rd *CHELTS* GL53 ...... **115** M6
  MANG/FISH BS16 .... **317** M8
  RTEWK/TIB GL19 .... **67** H2
Moorend St *CHELTS* GL53 .... **115** L5
Moore La *COTS* GL54 .... **123** H5
Moorfield Rd *BWTH/CHD* GL3... **138** B6
Moorgate *CIR* GL7 .... **244** D7
Moor Gv *AVONM* BS11 .... **324** B3
Moor Hall PI *STROUD* GL5 .... **208** A3 🔟
Moorhen Ct *VGL* GL2 .... **159** F7 🔟
Moorhill St *EVILLE/WHL* BS5.... **336** D2 🔟
Moorhouse La *AVONM* BS11 .... **314** B6
  HNBRY/STHM BS10 .... **314** D7
Moorland CI *CIND* GL14 .... **154** B2 🔟
Moorland Rd *YATE/CS* BS37 ..... **319** M2
Moorlands Rd *MANG/FISH* BS16.. **337** J1
Moor La *ALMDB* BS32 .... **306** B4
  CIR GL7 .... **242** F5
  COTS GL54 .... **123** J4
Moorpark Av *YATE/CS* BS37 .... **319** L2
Moors Av *CHELTW* GL51 .... **93** J7
Moorslade La *WUE* GL12......... **275** G3
Moor St *CHEP* NP16 .... **270** A3
  GL GL1 .... **136** B4
  VGL GL2 .... **181** J2
Mop Hale *MIM* GL56 .... **35** H8
Mopla Rd *CHEP* NP16............... **270** B1
Moravian Rd *KGWD/HNM* BS15.. **337** M3
Morcroft PI *LYD* GL15............. **201** G2 🔟
Morden Wk
  HGRV/WHIT BS14....................... **346** F4 🔟
Morestail Dr *CIR* GL7 .... **238** B5 🔟
Moreton CI *CHELTE/BC* GL52.... **94** C1
  HGRV/WHIT BS14....................... **346** C7
Moreton La *TEWK* GL20 .... **27** H4
Morgans La *MTCHDN* GL17...... **129** K5
Morgan St *CBRISNE* BS2 .... **336** B2
Mork La *LYD* GL15 .... **198** F4
Mork Rd *LYD* GL15 .... **198** E4
Morlands Dr *CHELTS* GL53....... **116** D7
Morley Av *BWTH/CHD* GL3 ...... **113** J5
  MANG/FISH BS16 .... **328** C2
Morley CI *BRSTK/PCHW* BS34 ... **316** D4 🔟
  MANG/FISH BS16 .... **327** M8
Morley Rd *BMSTR* BS3 .... **6** C8
  MANG/FISH BS16 .... **327** M8
Morley Sq *HORF/LLZ* BS7......... **326** A7 🔟
Morley St *CBRISNE* BS2 .... **336** B2
  EVILLE/WHL BS5............................ **336** D4
Morley Ter *KGWD/HNM* BS15 ... **337** M2 🔟
Morman CI *MTCHDN* GL17....... **129** M3

Morningside CI
  CHELTE/BC GL52........................... **94** E7 🔟
Mornington Dr *CHELTS* GL53 .. **115** M5 🔟
Mornington Rd
  CFTN/FAIL BS8 .... **335** J1 🔟
Morpeth Rd
  BRSG/KWL/STAPK BS4............. **345** M3
Morpeth St *GL* GL1 .... **136** B4 🔟
Morris CI *LYD* GL15 .... **177** L8
Morris Hill CI *CHELTW* GL51 ...... **93** K5
Morris La *CBATH/BATHN* BA1 ... **352** D8
Morris Orch *DSLY* GL11 .... **229** H5
Morris Rd *BDWAY* WR12............. **32** F3
  HORF/LLZ BS7............................. **326** C6
Morse La *MTCHDN* GL17.......... **129** J3
Morse Rd *EVILLE/WHL* BS5 ...... **336** E4 🔟
  MTCHDN GL17.............................. **129** J4
Mortimer Rd
  BRSTK/PCHW BS34 .... **326** D2
  CFTN/FAIL BS8 .... **335** J4
  VGL GL2 .... **112** E6 🔟
Morton St *EVILLE/WHL* BS5 ...... **336** D4 🔟
  GL GL1 .... **136** B4
  THNB/SVB BS35 .... **273** L7
Morton Wy *THNB/SVB* BS35 .... **294** A3
Morwent CI *GLE* GL4................ **137** C5
Mosedale *MIM* GL56 .... **58** E6
Moselle Dr *BWTH/CHD* GL3 ..... **113** J5
Mosley Crs *STROUD* GL5.......... **208** A4 🔟
Mosley Rd *STROUD* GL5 .... **208** A3
Mottershead Dr *VGL* GL2......... **113** C4
Mottershead Rd *CIR* GL7.......... **239** H8
Moulder Rd *VGL* GL2 .... **48** C5
Mountbatten CI *YATE/CS* BS37.. **309** M8
Mount CI *FRCTL/WBN* BS36 ..... **318** B3
  MTCHDN GL17.............................. **129** M5
Mount Crs *FRCTL/WBN* BS36.... **318** A6
Mounteney's La *WUE* GL12 ...... **296** F5
Mount Gdns *KGWD/HNM* BS15.. **337** M5
Mount Hill Rd
  KGWD/HNM BS15 .... **337** L5
Mountjoy's La *CIND* GL14 .... **154** B2 🔟
Mountjoy's Lane End
  CIND GL14 .... **154** B2 🔟
Mount Pleasant *CHEP* NP16 .... **270** A3
  CIR GL7 .... **244** E7
  LYD GL15 .... **225** L1
  WUE GL12 .... **277** L4
Mount Pleasant CI
  COTS GL54 .... **102** B3 🔟
Mount Pleasant Rd *CIND* GL14... **154** B4
Mount Pleasant Ter *BMSTR* BS3... **6** B8 🔟
Mount St *CIR* GL7 .... **238** C4
  GL GL1 .... **4** D4 🔟
Mousell La *CIND* GL14............. **154** B3
Mousetrap La *COTS* GL54 .... **123** G5
Mow Barton
  BMSTRD/HC/WWD BS13.... **345** G5
  YATE/CS BS37 .... **319** M1 🔟
Mowberry CI *VGL* GL2 .... **112** E6 🔟
Mowbray Av *TEWK* GL20 .... **48** B8
Mowbray Rd *HGRV/WHIT* BS14.. **346** E4
Mowcroft Rd
  BMSTRD/HC/WWD BS13.... **345** L7
Moxham Dr
  BMSTRD/HC/WWD BS13.... **345** J7
Moyle Old School La
  CHEP NP16 .... **246** C7 🔟
Muirfield
  OLD/WMLY/WICK BS30 .... **338** C5
Mulberry CI *KGWD/HNM* BS15... **338** A3
  VGL GL2 .... **159** G5
Mulberry Rd *KGWD/HNM* BS15.. **338** B2
Mulberry Wk
  HNLZ/SM/SNYPK/WT BS9......... **324** E3 🔟
Muller Av *HORF/LLZ* BS7 .... **326** B7
Muller Rd *EVILLE/WHL* BS5 ...... **326** C8 🔟
  HORF/LLZ BS7............................. **326** B5
Mulling CI
  CHPMW/MSHF SN14................... **343** K8 🔟
Mulready Cl *HORF/LLZ* BS7...... **326** E5
Mumbleys La *THNB/SVB* BS35... **293** G4
Munday CI
  RSTROUD/NAIL GL6 .... **209** M7 🔟
Munsley Gv *GLE* GL4................ **136** E8
Murford Av
  BMSTRD/HC/WWD BS13.... **345** K7
Murford Wk
  BMSTRD/HC/WWD BS13.... **345** K7
Murray CI *CHELTE/BC* GL52 ..... **72** B6 🔟
Murray St *BMSTR* BS3 .... **6** D9
Murrells Rd *CLFD* GL16........... **127** K8
Murvagh CI *CHELTS* GL53 .... **2** F9 🔟
Muscroft Rd *CHELTE/BC* GL52 ... **94** F7
Musgrove CI *AVONM* BS11 ...... **324** E1
Mushet PI *CLFD* GL16.............. **175** J2
Mutsilver Ms *VGL* GL2 .... **113** G6 🔟
Muzzle Patch *VGL* GL2 .... **109** M3
Myers Rd *VGL* GL2 .... **5** L6
Myrtle CI *GLE* GL4 .... **136** C6
Myrtle Dr *AVONM* BS11 .... **324** A6
Myrtle PI *CHEP* NP16 .... **270** B2 🔟
Myrtle Rd *CBRISNE* BS2............. **6** D1
The Myrtles *CHEP* NP16 .... **270** C1
Myrtle St *BMSTR* BS3 .... **6** B9
Mythe Rd *TEWK* GL20 .... **48** A3

N

Naas La *LYD* GL15 .... **225** M4
  VGL GL2 .... **159** J4
Nags Head HI *EVILLE/WHL* BS5... **337** J5
Nailsea CI
  BMSTRD/HC/WWD BS13.... **345** J4
Nailsworth Av *YATE/CS* BS37 ... **320** A2
Naishcombe HI
  OLD/WMLY/WICK BS30 .... **339** L4
The Naite *THNB/SVB* BS35........ **272** F5
Napier Miles Rd *AVONM* BS11... **324** C3
Napier Rd *CBATH/BATHN* BA1... **350** C8
  EVILLE/WHL BS5.......................... **336** D1
  RDLND/MONT BS6 .... **335** J4
Napier St *EVILLE/WHL* BS5 ...... **336** D5 🔟
  GL GL1 .... **5** H1 🔟
Napping La *MTCHDN* GL17 ...... **131** H1
The Napping *MTCHDN* GL17 .... **107** H8

Narles Rd *VGL* GL2................... **205** J8
Narroways Rd *CBRISNE* BS2..... **326** C8
Narrowcut La
  RSTROUD/NAIL GL6 .... **256** B2
Narrow La *MANG/FISH* BS16 ... **328** A7
Narrow Pln *CBRISNE* BS2............ **7** H4
Narrow Quay *CBRIS/FH* BS1 .... **6** E5
The Narrows *CHCAM* GL55 .... **34** A1
Naseby Wk *EVILLE/WHL* BS5 .... **337** H2
Nash CI *KEYN* BS31................. **348** C6 🔟
Nash Dr *HORF/LLZ* BS7............ **326** E4
Nash's La *CHCAM* GL55............. **13** M5
Nash Wy *CLFD* GL16 .... **175** K2 🔟
Nasse Ct *DSLY* GL11 .... **229** H6
Nastend La *STNHO* GL10 .... **206** D3
Nature CI *BWTH/CHD* GL3 .... **137** M6
Naunton Crs *CHELTS* GL53 ...... **115** M5
Naunton La *CHELTS* GL53 .... **115** M5
Naunton Pde *CHELTS* GL53 ..... **116** A5
Naunton Park CI *CHELTS* GL53 .. **116** A5
Naunton Park Rd *CHELTS* GL53.. **116** A5
Naunton Ter *CHELTS* GL53 ...... **116** A5
Naunton Wy *CHELTS* GL53........ **115** M5
Neads Dr
  OLD/WMLY/WICK BS30 .... **338** E6 🔟
Neath Rd *EVILLE/WHL* BS5 ...... **336** F3 🔟
Nebsworth La *SHPSTR* CV36...... **13** M2
Needham Av *VGL* GL2.............. **159** K5
Nelson Rd *MANG/FISH* BS16 ... **327** M6 🔟
  MANG/FISH BS16 .... **327** M7 🔟
Nelson St *BMSTR* BS3 .... **345** J1 🔟
  CBRIS/FH BS1 .... **6** F3
  CHEP NP16 .... **270** B3 🔟
  GL GL1 .... **136** B5
  STROUD GL5 .... **208** E4
  TEWK GL20 .... **48** A3 🔟
Nene CI *VGL* GL2...................... **159** G1
Neptune CI *GLE* GL4................ **137** H5 🔟
Neston Wk
  BRSG/KWL/STAPK BS4............. **346** B3 🔟
Netham Rd *EVILLE/WHL* BS5 .... **336** F5
Nethercote Dr *COTS* GL54 .... **123** J6 🔟
Nethercote Farm Dr *COTS* GL54.. **123** J7 🔟
Netherend Crs *LYD* GL15 .... **224** B6
Netherhope La *CHEP* NP16 .... **246** D6
Netheridge CI *VGL* GL2 .... **135** J7
Netherley La *RTEWK/TIB* GL19 .. **44** D3
Netherwood Gdns *CHELTW* GL51.. **93** J8
Nettlestone CI
  HNBRY/STHM BS10 .... **315** G7 🔟
Nettleton Rd *CHELTW* GL51...... **115** G4
  CHPMW/MSHF SN14................... **323** K8
  GL GL1 .... **5** G6
Nevalan Dr *EVILLE/WHL* BS5 .... **337** J5
Neville Rd *KGWD/HNM* BS15.... **338** A1
  TEWK GL20 .... **48** B6
Nevil Rd *HORF/LLZ* BS7............ **326** A7
Newark Rd *GL* GL1 .... **135** L5
New Barn Av *CHELTE/BC* GL52 ... **94** C7
New Barn CI *CHELTE/BC* GL52 ... **94** C7
New Barn La *CHELTE/BC* GL52 ... **94** A6
Newbrick Rd
  BRSTK/PCHW BS34 .... **317** J6
Newbridge Rd
  BRSG/KWL/STAPK BS4............. **336** F5
Newbridge Rd
  BRSG/KWL/STAPK BS4............. **336** F5
New Brunswick Av
  EVILLE/WHL BS5.......................... **337** K4
New Buildings
  MANG/FISH BS16 .... **327** H7
Newbury Pk *LED* HR8................. **19** L4
Newbury Rd *HORF/LLZ* BS7...... **326** C4
New Charlotte St *BMSTR* BS3....... **6** F8
New Cheltenham Rd
  KGWD/HNM BS15 .... **337** M2
New Church St *TET* GL8............ **281** M4
Newcombe Dr
  HNLZ/SM/SNYPK/WT BS9......... **324** E7 🔟
Newcombe Rd
  HNLZ/SM/SNYPK/WT BS9......... **325** H4
Newcourt Pk *CHELTS* GL53 ...... **116** C5
Newcourt Rd *CHELTS* GL53 ...... **116** C6
New Cut *DSLY* GL11 .... **254** D2
Newent Av *KGWD/HNM* BS15 ... **337** K4
Newent La *RTEWK/TIB* GL19 .... **108** B8
Newerne St *LYD* GL15 .... **201** J8
New Fosseway Rd
  HGRV/WHIT BS14....................... **346** D5
Newfoundland Rd *CBRISNE* BS2... **7** J1
  CBRISNE BS2 .... **336** C2 🔟🔟
Newfoundland St *CBRISNE* BS2.... **7** H1
Newfoundland Wy *CBRISNE* BS2... **7** K1
Newgate *CBRIS/FH* BS1 .... **7** G3
Newgrounds La *VGL* GL2.......... **204** C5
New Inn La *GL* GL1 .... **4** F5
  TET GL8 .... **257** L3
New John St *BMSTR* BS3 .... **335** L8 🔟
New Kingsley Rd *CBRISNE* BS2.... **7** J4 🔟
Newland Dr
  BMSTRD/HC/WWD BS13.... **345** J7 🔟
Newland Rd
  BMSTRD/HC/WWD BS13.... **345** J7
Newlands Av *FRCTL/WBN* BS36... **318** E4
Newlands Rd *KEYN* BS31.......... **347** M7
The Newlands
  MANG/FISH BS16 .... **327** K4
Newland St CLFD* GL16............... **175 J7
  GL GL1 .... **5** H4 🔟
Newland Wk
  BMSTRD/HC/WWD BS13.... **345** J8
New La *THNB/SVB* BS35............ **293** L6
New Leaze *ALMDB* BS32 .... **306** E8
Newleaze Gdns *TET* GL8 .... **281** L3 🔟
Newlyn Av
  HNLZ/SM/SNYPK/WT BS9......... **324** F6
Newlyn Wk
  BRSG/KWL/STAPK BS4............. **346** D2 🔟
Newlyn Wy *YATE/CS* BS37........ **320** B1
Newman CI *YATE/CS* BS37 .... **319** K7
Newmarket Rd
  RSTROUD/NAIL GL6 .... **232** C7
Newmills HI *RWYE* HR9............ **127** G1
New Mills La *WUE* GL12 .... **298** A2
New Mills Wy *LED* HR8.............. **19** L2
Newnham CI *HGRV/WHIT* BS14 .. **346** F4

Newnham PI
  BRSTK/PCHW BS34 .... **316** B**
Newton HI *TET* GL8 .... **282**
Newton Rd *TET* GL8 .... **282**
Newpit La
  OLD/WMLY/WICK BS30 .... **339**
Newport St *BMSTR* BS3 .... **336** A**
Newquay Rd
  BRSG/KWL/STAPK BS4............. **346**
New Queen St *BMSTR* BS3 .... **7**
  KGWD/HNM BS15 .... **337**
New Rd *BRSTK/PCHW* BS34 ...... **316**
  BRSTK/PCHW BS34 .... **316**
  BRSTK/PCHW BS34 .... **326**
  CHCAM GL55 .... **13**
  CHELTE/BC GL52........................... **94**
  CHNTN OX7 .... **125**
  CIND GL14 .... **152**
  CLFD GL16 .... **152**
  CLFD GL16 .... **176**
  DSLY GL11 .... **229**
  DSLY GL11 .... **253**
  LYD GL15 .... **176**
  LYD GL15 .... **200**
  LYD GL15 .... **201**
  LYD GL15 .... **202**
  LYD GL15 .... **224**
  MIM GL56 .... **58**
  MTCHDN GL17.............................. **130**
  MTCHDN GL17.............................. **152**
  RGTMLV WR13 .... **33**
  RSTROUD/NAIL GL6 .... **233**
  STRAT CV37 .... **8**
  STROUD GL5 .... **208**
  THNB/SVB BS35 .... **306**
  WUE GL12 .... **277**
  WUE GL12 .... **294**
  YATE/CS BS37 .... **309**
New Rutland Ct *CHELT* GL50....... **2**
Newry Wk
  BRSG/KWL/STAPK BS4............. **346**
New Stadium Rd
  EVILLE/WHL BS5.......................... **336**
New Station Rd
  MANG/FISH BS16 .... **327**
Newstead Rd *GLE* GL4.............. **137**
New St *BDWAY* WR12 .... **32**
  BRKLY GL13.................................. **287**
  CBRISNE BS2................................... **7**
  CHELT GL50 .... **2**
  CHELTS GL53 .... **116** C
  CHNTN OX7 .... **83**
  GL GL1 .... **4**
  LED HR8 .... **19**
  MTCHDN GL17.............................. **130**
  RSTROUD/NAIL GL6 .... **185**
  SHPSTR CV36 .... **16**
  STNHO GL10 .... **206**
  WUE GL12 .... **276**
New Thomas St *CBRISNE* BS2 ...... **7**
Newton Av *GLE* GL4 .... **136**
Newton CI *CHELTW* GL51 .... **115**
  KGWD/HNM BS15 .... **338**
  LED HR8 .... **20** A**
  RTEWK/TIB GL19 .... **106**
Newton Rd *CHELTW* GL51 .... **115**
  OLD/WMLY/WICK BS30 .... **338**
Newton St *EVILLE/WHL* BS5 .... **7**
Newtown *WUE* GL12 .... **276**
Newtown Rd *CIND* GL14 .... **129**
New Tyning La *YATE/CS* BS37 .... **311**
New Wk *KGWD/HNM* BS15........ **337**
New Walls *BRSG/KWL/STAPK* BS4... **6**
Niblett CI *KGWD/HNM* BS15 ..... **338** B**
Niblett's HI *EVILLE/WHL* BS5 .... **337**
Nibley La *YATE/CS* BS37........... **309**
Nibley Rd *AVONM* BS11 .... **324**
Nicholas La *EVILLE/WHL* BS5.... **337**
Nicholas Rd *EVILLE/WHL* BS5 ... **337**
Nicholas St *BMSTR* BS3 .... **7** H**
Nicholettes
  OLD/WMLY/WICK BS30 .... **338**
Nicholls La *FRCTL/WBN* BS36 ... **318**
Nicolson CI *BWTH/CHD* GL3...... **113**
Niebull CI *MALM* SN16............. **303**
Nigel Pk *AVONM* BS11 .... **324**
Nightingale CI
  FRCTL/WBN BS36......................... **318**
  THNB/SVB BS35 .... **293** M
Nightingale La
  FRCTL/WBN BS36......................... **318**
Nind La *WUE* GL12 .... **277**
Nine Elms Rd *VGL* GL2............. **113**
Nine Tree HI *CBRISNE* BS2 .... **335**
Nine Wells Rd *CLFD* GL16......... **175**
Ninth Av *HORF/LLZ* BS7............ **326**
Noake Rd *BWTH/CHD* GL3 .... **137**
Noble Av
  OLD/WMLY/WICK BS30 .... **338**
Nodens Wy *LYD* GL15 .... **201**
Norbury Av *GLE* GL4................. **136**
Norden Dr *RWYE* HR9............... **106** E
Nordown CI *DSLY* GL11 .... **229**
Nordown Rd *DSLY* GL11............ **229**
Norfolk Av *CBRISNE* BS2 .... **7**
  CHELTW GL51 .... **115**
  RDLND/MONT BS6 .... **336** A
Norfolk Gv *KEYN* BS31 .... **347**
Norfolk PI *BMSTR* BS3 .... **335**
Norfolk St *GL* GL1 .... **4**
Norland Rd *CFTN/FAIL* BS8 ...... **335** H
Norley Rd *HORF/LLZ* BS7.......... **326**
Norluck Ct *SHPSTR* CV36 .... **16** E
Normal Ter *CHELT* GL50 .... **2**
Norman Ball Wy *VGL* GL2 .... **136**
Normanby Rd
  EVILLE/WHL BS5.......................... **336**
Norman Gv *KGWD/HNM* BS15 ... **337** M
Norman HI *DSLY* GL11.............. **229**
Norman Rd *CBRISNE* BS2 .... **336** C
  KEYN BS31 .... **348**
  OLD/WMLY/WICK BS30 .... **338**
Normanton Rd
  CFTN/FAIL BS8 .... **335**
Norman Wy *MTCHDN* GL17....... **129**

rrisville Rd RDLND/MONT BS6 336
A2
rse Wy CHEP NP16 ... 270 D4
rtenham Cl
CHELTE/BC GL52 ... 71 M7
rth Av MTCHDN GL17 ... 129 M3
EWK GL20 ... 49 J3
rthbank Cl CHELTW GL51 .... 114 D4
rthbrook Rd GLE GL4 ... 136 E2
rthcote Rd CFTN/FAIL BS8 ... 335 H2
EVILLE/WHL BS5 ... 337 G3
MANG/FISH BS16 ... 328 B5
rthcote St
VILLE/WHL BS5 ... 336 D2
rthcot La MIM GL56 ... 35 K7
rth Cft
OLD/WMLY/WICK BS30 ... 338 F7
rth Devon Rd
MANG/FISH BS16 ... 327 J6
rthdown Cl LED HR8 ... 19 L2
rth East Rd
THNB/SVB BS35 ... 293 L1
rthen Cl CIR GL7 ... 267 G5
rthend Av KGWD/HNM BS15 .. 337 M1
rthend Rd KGWD/HNM BS15 .. 338 A1
rthfield YATE/CS BS37 ... 319 M3
rthfield Av KGWD/HNM BS15.. 337 M6
rthfield Rd EVILLE/WHL BS5 .. 337 K4
GLE GL4 ... 136 B6
TET GL8 ... 282 A3
rthfield Sq GLE GL4 ... 136 B6
rthfields Rd
RSTROUD/NAIL GL6 ... 232 D7
rthfield Ter CHELT GL50 ... 2 D3
rthgate St GL GL1 ... 4 E5
rth Green St
CFTN/FAIL BS8 ... 335 H5
rth Hall Ms CHELTE/BC GL52 ... 3 H4
rth Hill Rd CIR GL7 ... 238 E5
rth Home Rd CIR GL7 ... 238 E4
rthington La CIND GL14 ... 179 L5
rthlands Wy TET GL8 ... 282 A3
rthleach Wk AVONM BS11 .. 324 B6
rth Leaze LGASH BS41 ... 344 D1
rthleaze TET GL8 ... 282 A3
rthmead LED HR8 ... 19 M2
rthmead La YATE/CS BS37 ... 308 F5
rth Meadow Rd HGHW SN6 ... 288 E3
rthmoor La CIR GL7 ... 263 J2
rthover Rd
HNLZ/SM/SNYPK/WT BS9 ... 325 H2
rth Pk KGWD/HNM BS15 ... 338 A2
rth Pl CHELT GL50 ... 2 E4
CHELTE/BC GL52 ... 2 E4
rth Rd BMSTR BS3 ... 335 J7
BRSTK/PCHW BS34 ... 317 G7
CFTN/FAIL BS8 ... 334 F5
CLFD GL16 ... 151 M8
FRCTL/WBN BS36 ... 318 B4
GL GL1 ... 5 H1
RDLND/MONT BS6 ... 335 M1
RTEWK/TIB GL19 ... 108 C8
THNB/SVB BS35 ... 293 L1
YATE/CS BS37 ... 309 K5
YATE/CS BS37 ... 319 L1
rth Rd East CHELTW GL51 ... 114 D4
rth Rd West CHELTW GL51 ... 114 D4
rth Stoke La
OLD/WMLY/WICK BS30 ... 349 J3
rth St BMSTR BS3 ... 6 A9
BMSTR BS3 ... 335 J7
CBRIS/FH BS1 ... 7 G1
CHELT GL50 ... 2 D4
COTS GL54 ... 74 D3
MANG/FISH BS16 ... 327 M6
OLD/WMLY/WICK BS30 ... 338 E7
WUE GL12 ... 296 C5
rthumberland Rd RDLND/MONT BS6
335 L1
rthumbria Dr
HNLZ/SM/SNYPK/WT BS9 ... 325 K6
rth Upton La GLE GL4 ... 137 G4
rth Vw MANG/FISH BS16 ... 327 M7
RDLND/MONT BS6 ... 325 J7
rthville Rd HORF/LLZ BS7 ... 326 C2
rth Wall HGHW SN6 ... 288 F3
rthway BRSTK/PCHW BS34 ... 317 D6
rth Wy CIR GL7 ... 238 C3
rthway La TEWK GL20 ... 48 C4
rthwaylane TEWK GL20 ... 48 F3
rthway La TEWK GL20 ... 49 G2
rthwick Rd HORF/LLZ BS7 ... 326 B3
THNB/SVB BS35 ... 304 F3
rthwood Cl CIND GL14 ... 154 B2
rthwoods Wk
HNBRY/STHM BS10 ... 315 M8
rton Cl COTS GL54 ... 74 C3
KGWD/HNM BS15 ... 338 B4
RWYE HR9 ... 126 D4
rton Rdg
RSTROUD/NAIL GL6 ... 232 B6
rton Rd
BRSG/KWL/STAPK BS4 ... 346 C1
rton Vw CHCAM GL55 ... 8 F8
rtonwood
RSTROUD/NAIL GL6 ... 232 B6
rwich Dr
BRSG/KWL/STAPK BS4 ... 337 G5
CHELTW GL51 ... 115 J5
rwood Rd CHELT GL50 ... 115 L4
stle Rd COTS GL54 ... 169 K2
tch Rd CIR GL7 ... 188 C3
tgrove Cl CHELTW GL51 ... 115 G3
GL GL1 ... 159 L1
tley Pl BWTH/CHD GL3 ... 137 J4
ttingham Rd CHELTE/BC GL52.. 72 B6
HORF/LLZ BS7 ... 326 A8
ttingham St BMSTR BS3 ... 336 B8
urse Cl CHELTS GL53 ... 115 K7
va Scotia Pl CBRIS/FH BS1 ... 335 J6
vers Crs
BRSG/KWL/STAPK BS4 ... 345 L3
vers Hl
BRSG/KWL/STAPK BS4 ... 345 L3
vers La
BRSG/KWL/STAPK BS4 ... 345 L4
vers Park Dr
BRSG/KWL/STAPK BS4 ... 345 L3

Novers Park Rd
BRSG/KWL/STAPK BS4 ... 345 M3
Novers Rd
BRSG/KWL/STAPK BS4 ... 345 L3
Noverton Av CHELTE/BC GL52 ... 94 F7
Noverton La CHELTE/BC GL52 ... 94 E7
Nugent Hl RDLND/MONT BS6 ... 335 M2
Nunnery La DSLY GL11 ... 253 J4
Nunny Cl CHELTW GL51 ... 114 E2
Nupdown Rd THNB/SVB BS35 ... 249 G6
Nup End RTEWK/TIB GL19 ... 89 J3
Nupend Gdns MTCHDN GL17 ... 131 H1
Nupend La MTCHDN GL17 ... 131 G1
Nup End La RTEWK/TIB GL19 ... 89 J3
The Nurseries
CHELTE/BC GL52 ... 94 A1
WUE GL12 ... 294 D6
Nursery Cl CHCAM GL55 ... 9 H6
CIR GL7 ... 238 D5
MIM GL56 ... 58 D4
STROUD GL5 ... 208 F5
Nursery Gdns
HNBRY/STHM BS10 ... 315 J8
Nursery Rd
CHPMW/MSHF SN14 ... 343 J8
CIR GL7 ... 238 E5
The Nursery BMSTR BS3 ... 335 K8
STNHO GL10 ... 207 J7
Nursery Vw CIR GL7 ... 238 E8
Nut Cft GLE GL4 ... 136 D4
Nutfield Gv BRSTK/PCHW BS34 .. 326 D1
Nutgrove Av BMSTR BS3 ... 336 A8
Nuthatch Dr MANG/FISH BS16 ... 327 H5
Nuthatch Gdns
MANG/FISH BS16 ... 327 J5
Nuthill GLE GL4 ... 137 H8
Nutley Av GL GL1 ... 159 L1
Nutmeg Cl GLE GL4 ... 136 F7
Nut Orchard La TEWK GL20 ... 26 B5
Nympsfield KGWD/HNM BS15 ... 338 A1
Nympsfield Rd GL GL1 ... 135 L8
RSTROUD/NAIL GL6 ... 231 M6
RSTROUD/NAIL GL6 ... 232 C7

O

Oak Av CHELTE/BC GL52 ... 3 J9
Oakbank GLE GL4 ... 136 A7
Oakbrook Dr CHELTW GL51 ... 114 E4
Oak Cl BRSTK/PCHW BS34 ... 316 F4
CHEP NP16 ... 270 A6
YATE/CS BS37 ... 309 M8
Oak Crs LYD GL15 ... 224 D5
Oakcroft Cl GLE GL4 ... 136 F8
Oakdale Av MANG/FISH BS16 ... 327 M3
Oakdale Cl MANG/FISH BS16 ... 328 A3
Oakdale Ct MANG/FISH BS16 ... 328 A4
Oakdale Rd HGRV/WHIT BS14 ... 346 C3
MANG/FISH BS16 ... 328 A3
Oakdene Av EVILLE/WHL BS5 ... 326 F8
Oak Dr BWTH/CHD GL3 ... 137 M5
DSLY GL11 ... 229 J8
STROUD GL5 ... 208 D5
TEWK GL20 ... 48 F3
Oakenhill Rd
BRSG/KWL/STAPK BS4 ... 347 G1
Oakenhill Wk
BRSG/KWL/STAPK BS4 ... 347 G1
Oakes La BAD GL9 ... 322 D5
Oakfield Gv CFTN/FAIL BS8 ... 6 A1
Oakfield Pl CFTN/FAIL BS8 ... 6 A1
Oakfield Rd CFTN/FAIL BS8 ... 335 J3
CHELTE/BC GL52 ... 72 C8
KEYN BS31 ... 348 B8
KGWD/HNM BS15 ... 337 M4
Oakfields CLFD GL16 ... 175 J1
Oakfield St CHELT GL50 ... 115 K4
The Oak Fld CIND GL14 ... 154 C3
Oakfield Wy BRKLY GL13 ... 226 F2
Oakford La CBATH/BATHN BA1 ... 352 C3
CHPMW/MSHF SN14 ... 352 D1
Oakham Rd MIM GL56 ... 82 D2
Oakhanger Dr AVONM BS11 ... 324 D2
Oakhill HNBRY/STHM BS10 ... 314 E7
Oakhill Av
OLD/WMLY/WICK BS30 ... 348 E1
Oakhill Pitch LYD GL15 ... 223 G5
Oakhill Rd MTCHDN GL17 ... 130 C1
Oakhunger La BRKLY GL13 ... 226 E7
Oakhurst Cl BWTH/CHD GL3 ... 113 H6
Oakhurst Ri CHELTE/BC GL52 ... 3 K8
Oakhurst Rd
HNLZ/SM/SNYPK/WT BS9 ... 325 H6
Oakland Av CHELTE/BC GL52 ... 3 H1
Oakland Dr LED HR8 ... 19 M4
Oakland Rd EVILLE/WHL BS5 ... 337 G3
MTCHDN GL17 ... 129 M5
RDLND/MONT BS6 ... 335 K2
Oaklands CIR GL7 ... 238 C5
CLFD GL16 ... 175 L7
Oaklands Cl
MANG/FISH BS16 ... 328 D6
Oaklands Dr ALMDB BS32 ... 306 C7
MANG/FISH BS16 ... 327 J3
OLD/WMLY/WICK BS30 ... 348 E1
Oaklands Pk LYD GL15 ... 200 F2
Oaklands Rd
MANG/FISH BS16 ... 328 C6
Oakland St CHELTS GL53 ... 116 C4
Oak La EVILLE/WHL BS5 ... 337 H1
TEWK GL20 ... 27 G5
Oaklea Rd LYD GL15 ... 177 L8
Oakleaze FRCTL/WBN BS36 ... 318 F4
Oakleaze Rd THNB/SVB BS35 ... 293 L2
Oakleigh Av EVILLE/WHL BS5 .. 336 F3
Oakleigh Gdns
OLD/WMLY/WICK BS30 ... 348 E1
Oakley Flats CIR GL7 ... 266 F5
Oakley Rd CHELTE/BC GL52 ... 3 K6
CIR GL7 ... 238 B5
HORF/LLZ BS7 ... 326 B4
Oakley Wy LYD GL15 ... 200 C4
Oak Manor Dr CHELTE/BC GL52 ... 3 J5
Oakmeade Pk
BRSG/KWL/STAPK BS4 ... 346 D1
Oak Meadow LYD GL15 ... 201 K5

Oakridge VGL GL2 ... 110 F5
Oakridge Cl GLE GL4 ... 137 G6
KGWD/HNM BS15 ... 338 C4
Oak Rd CHPMW/MSHF SN14 ... 343 H6
CIR GL7 ... 265 G4
HGHW SN6 ... 265 J7
HORF/LLZ BS7 ... 326 A6
Oaksey Rd MALM SN16 ... 285 L7
Oaks La RWYE HR9 ... 85 J8
The Oaks CHELTW GL51 ... 114 F5
CIR GL7 ... 261 H4
GLE GL4 ... 137 G5
Oak St CIR GL7 ... 244 E7
Oak Tree Av MANG/FISH BS16 ... 329 K7
Oak Tree Cl KGWD/HNM BS15 .. 337 L8
VGL GL2 ... 159 G4
Oaktree Ct AVONM BS11 ... 324 A4
Oaktree Crs ALMDB BS32 ... 316 D1
Oaktree Gdn GLE GL4 ... 136 E8
Oaktree Gdns
BMSTRD/HC/WWD BS13 ... 345 G6
Oak Tree Wk KEYN BS31 ... 347 M8
Oak Wy CIND GL14 ... 154 E3
CIR GL7 ... 263 H5
RTEWK/TIB GL19 ... 108 C8
STNHO GL10 ... 207 H4
Oakwood Av
HNLZ/SM/SNYPK/WT BS9 ... 325 K5
Oakwood Cl CIND GL14 ... 154 B2
LYD GL15 ... 200 C2
Oakwood Dr BWTH/CHD GL3 ... 137 H5
Oakwood Rd CLFD GL16 ... 175 L6
HNLZ/SM/SNYPK/WT BS9 ... 325 K5
LYD GL15 ... 200 C2
Oatfield VGL GL2 ... 159 G1
Oatfield Rd VGL GL2 ... 181 J5
Oathill La CIR GL7 ... 259 J3
Oatlands Av HGRV/WHIT BS14 ... 346 C5
Oatleys Crs LED HR8 ... 19 L3
Oatleys Rd LED HR8 ... 19 M4
Oatleys Ter LED HR8 ... 19 M4
Oberon Av EVILLE/WHL BS5 ... 337 G1
O'brien Rd CHELTW GL51 ... 93 J7
Ocker Hl RSTROUD/NAIL GL6 ... 208 A1
Octavia Pl LYD GL15 ... 201 K7
Oddington Rd COTS GL54 ... 102 B3
Offas Cl CHEP NP16 ... 270 C4
Offa's Dyke Pth CHEP NP16 ... 222 C8
LYD GL15 ... 222 A1
Office Rd CIND GL14 ... 154 A4
Ogbourne CHPMW/MSHF SN14 .. 343 K8
Ogbourne Cl VGL GL2 ... 113 G8
Okebourne Cl
HNBRY/STHM BS10 ... 315 K7
Okebourne Rd
HNBRY/STHM BS10 ... 315 K8
Okus Rd CHELTS GL53 ... 116 C6
Oldacre Dr CHELTE/BC GL52 ... 72 C6
Old Alexander Rd MALM SN16 ... 303 G7
Old Ashley Hl
RDLND/MONT BS6 ... 336 B1
Old Aust Rd ALMDB BS32 ... 306 E5
Old Bath Rd CHELTS GL53 ... 2 F9
CHELTS GL53 ... 116 A6
Old Bread St CBRISNE BS2 ... 7 J4
Old Brewery La TET GL8 ... 281 M4
Oldbridge Rd HGRV/WHIT BS14 .. 346 E8
Old Bristol Rd
RSTROUD/NAIL GL6 ... 232 D8
Old Bulwark Rd CHEP NP16 ... 270 A4
Old Burford Rd CHNTN OX7 ... 125 M1
Oldbury Cha
OLD/WMLY/WICK BS30 ... 348 C1
Oldbury Cl CHELTW GL51 ... 92 F8
Oldbury Court Dr
MANG/FISH BS16 ... 327 K5
Oldbury Court Rd
MANG/FISH BS16 ... 327 J6
Oldbury La
OLD/WMLY/WICK BS30 ... 339 M6
THNB/SVB BS35 ... 273 K7
Oldbury Orch BWTH/CHD GL3 ... 113 M7
Oldbury Rd CHELTW GL51 ... 92 F8
TEWK GL20 ... 48 A5
Oldbutt Rd SHPSTR CV36 ... 16 A6
Old Cheltenham Rd VGL GL2 ... 112 F7
Old Coach Rd CHEP NP16 ... 270 E8
CHPMW/MSHF SN14 ... 343 L1
Old Common
RSTROUD/NAIL GL6 ... 233 K4
The Old Common
RSTROUD/NAIL GL6 ... 209 M7
Old Court Dr RTEWK/TIB GL19 ... 109 K2
Old Dam Rd LYD GL15 ... 201 L4
Old Dean Rd MTCHDN GL17 ... 106 C8
Old Down Hl ALMDB BS32 ... 306 E1
Old Down Rd BAD GL9 ... 322 E3
Oldends La STNHO GL10 ... 206 F3
Old Farm La EVILLE/WHL BS5 .. 337 K5
Oldfield TEWK GL20 ... 48 B5
Oldfield Crs CHELTW GL51 ... 115 H3
Oldfield Pl CFTN/FAIL BS8 ... 335 H6
Oldfield Rd CFTN/FAIL BS8 ... 335 J6
Oldfields La THNB/SVB BS35 ... 307 L4
Old Forge Cl CHNTN OX7 ... 125 M1
Old Gloucester Rd
CHELTW GL51 ... 114 A1
COTS GL54 ... 122 E5
FRCTL/WBN BS36 ... 317 K4
MANG/FISH BS16 ... 327 K3
THNB/SVB BS35 ... 293 K6
WUE GL12 ... 294 D1
Old Hall Cl BDWAY WR12 ... 31 G2
Old Hl MTCHDN GL17 ... 131 J1
TET GL8 ... 257 M2
Old Horsley Rd
RSTROUD/NAIL GL6 ... 232 D8
Old Hospital La TEWK GL20 ... 48 B4
Old King Street Ct
CBRIS/FH BS1 ... 7 G2
Oldlands Av FRCTL/WBN BS36 ... 318 E5
Old La (Simmonds La)
RWYE HR9 ... 85 G3
Old London Rd WUE GL12 ... 277 J3
Old Manor Cl WUE GL12 ... 276 C6
Old Manor Gdns CHCAM GL55 ... 9 G7
Old Manor La TEWK GL20 ... 48 C3
Old Market RSTROUD/NAIL GL6 .. 232 D7

Old Market St CBRISNE BS2 ... 7 J3
Oldmead Wk
BMSTRD/HC/WWD BS13 ... 345 G4
Old Millbrook Ter
CHELTW GL51 ... 115 K1
Old Mill Cl YATE/CS BS37 ... 319 K7
The Old Ml BDWAY WR12 ... 32 E3
Oldminster Rd BRKLY GL13 ... 226 E2
Old Moat VGL GL2 ... 112 A1
Old Monmouth Rd
MTCHDN GL17 ... 131 H1
Old Neighbourhood
RSTROUD/NAIL GL6 ... 234 A1
Old Orchard Ct CIR GL7 ... 218 C6
The Old Orch MALM SN16 ... 303 J6
Old Painswick Rd GLE GL4 ... 136 D5
Old Pk CBRISNE BS2 ... 6 D2
Old Park Hl CBRISNE BS2 ... 6 D3
Old Quarry Ri AVONM BS11 ... 324 A4
Old Railway Cl MALM SN16 ... 303 J7
Old Rectory Cl STROUD GL5 ... 208 C6
Old Rectory Gdns MIM GL56 ... 79 K4
Old Rectory Rd WUE GL12 ... 277 H7
Old Reddings Cl
CHELTW GL51 ... 114 E4
Old Reddings Rd CHELTW GL51 .. 114 E4
Old Rd CHELTE/BC GL52 ... 94 E3
CLFD GL16 ... 175 M2
SHPSTR CV36 ... 16 B6
VGL GL2 ... 111 J3
Old Rw GL GL1 ... 5 H8
Old Sneed Av
HNLZ/SM/SNYPK/WT BS9 ... 324 F7
Old Sneed Pk
HNLZ/SM/SNYPK/WT BS9 ... 324 F7
Old Sneed Rd
HNLZ/SM/SNYPK/WT BS9 ... 324 F7
Old Station Dr CHELTS GL53 ... 115 M5
Old Station Rd NWNT GL18 ... 86 B2
Old Station Wy CLFD GL16 ... 175 K2
Old Town WUE GL12 ... 277 K4
Old Town Ms LYD GL15 ... 225 H1
Old Tram Rd GL GL1 ... 4 D7
Old Vicarage La CIR GL7 ... 261 H4
Oldwood La YATE/CS BS37 ... 309 K3
Olio La CHELTS GL53 ... 2 E8
Olive Gdns THNB/SVB BS35 ... 293 H7
Olive Gv DSLY GL11 ... 253 J1
Oliver's La MALM SN16 ... 303 J8
Ollney Rd RSTROUD/NAIL GL6 ... 233 H5
Olveston Rd HORF/LLZ BS7 ... 326 A6
Olympus Cl
BRSTK/PCHW BS34 ... 316 F5
Olympus Pk VGL GL2 ... 159 J1
Olympus Rd BRSTK/PCHW BS34 .. 315 M4
Onslow Rd NWNT GL18 ... 86 D3
Oram Ct OLD/WMLY/WICK BS30 .. 338 B7
The Orangery GLE GL4 ... 137 G4
Orange St CBRISNE BS2 ... 7 J1
Orchard Av BDWAY WR12 ... 33 G3
CBRIS/FH BS1 ... 6 D4
CHELTW GL51 ... 115 H1
CHEP NP16 ... 270 A6
THNB/SVB BS35 ... 293 L2
Orchard Bank COTS GL54 ... 148 B4
Orchard Bvd
OLD/WMLY/WICK BS30 ... 338 D7
Orchard Cl CHCAM GL55 ... 9 G6
CHNTN OX7 ... 83 J6
CIR GL7 ... 244 D7
CLFD GL16 ... 127 K7
CLFD GL16 ... 175 H6
DSLY GL11 ... 229 H6
FRCTL/WBN BS36 ... 318 A5
HNLZ/SM/SNYPK/WT BS9 ... 325 H6
KEYN BS31 ... 347 M5
KGWD/HNM BS15 ... 338 A3
LYD GL15 ... 224 F3
MTCHDN GL17 ... 130 C1
RWYE HR9 ... 106 B4
SHPSTR CV36 ... 16 B6
STNHO GL10 ... 207 K8
TEWK GL20 ... 27 H5
VGL GL2 ... 112 A6
VGL GL2 ... 158 F4
WUE GL12 ... 276 C6
YATE/CS BS37 ... 320 B1
Orchard Ct COTS GL54 ... 73 M1
RSTROUD/NAIL GL6 ... 185 H3
STNHO GL10 ... 207 G4
TEWK GL20 ... 48 B5
Orchard Dr BWTH/CHD GL3 ... 113 M7
TEWK GL20 ... 26 B4
THNB/SVB BS35 ... 291 J4
Orchard End RTEWK/TIB GL19 .. 69 G6
Orchard Farm Cl CHEP NP16 ... 270 D4
Orchard Fld TET GL8 ... 257 L3
Orchard Gdns
KGWD/HNM BS15 ... 338 B3
Orchard Ga LYD GL15 ... 202 D1
Orchard Gra THNB/SVB BS35 ... 293 K1
The Orchard Gv
CHELTW GL51 ... 138 F2
Orchard La CBRIS/FH BS1 ... 6 D4
LED HR8 ... 19 M3
Orchard Lea THNB/SVB BS35 ... 293 J6
Orchard Leaze DSLY GL11 ... 228 F7
Orchard Md RSTROUD/NAIL GL6.. 185 H4
RSTROUD/NAIL GL6 ... 232 D7
Orchard Pl LED HR8 ... 20 A5
Orchard Rdg TEWK GL20 ... 24 B6
Orchard Ri CIND GL14 ... 155 H7
DSLY GL11 ... 229 H8
MIM GL56 ... 79 K3
RTEWK/TIB GL19 ... 109 L2
THNB/SVB BS35 ... 306 C1
Orchard Rd CHELTE/BC GL52 ... 72 B8
CLFD GL16 ... 175 K1
COTS GL54 ... 74 B6
EVILLE/WHL BS5 ... 337 H3
FRCTL/WBN BS36 ... 318 F4
HORF/LLZ BS7 ... 326 A7
KGWD/HNM BS15 ... 338 A3
LGASH BS41 ... 344 B1
LYD GL15 ... 225 K1
MANG/FISH BS16 ... 329 K6
MTCHDN GL17 ... 128 C6
NWNT GL18 ... 64 B6

STROUD GL5 ... 207 L5
TEWK GL20 ... 51 L4
VGL GL2 ... 113 G7
Orchard Sq EVILLE/WHL BS5 ... 336 F4
The Orchards KGWD/HNM BS15.. 338 B3
LYD GL15 ... 201 J8
Orchard St CBRIS/FH BS1 ... 6 D4
WUE GL12 ... 277 K4
The Orchard
BRSTK/PCHW BS34 ... 317 H6
CIR GL7 ... 242 E4
DSLY GL11 ... 254 D2
LYD GL15 ... 224 B6
WUE GL12 ... 294 D6
Orchard V KGWD/HNM BS15 ... 338 B4
Orchard Vw STROUD GL5 ... 208 C7
Orchard Wk WUE GL12 ... 277 H7
Orchard Wy BWTH/CHD GL3 ... 113 K4
CHELTW GL51 ... 93 H8
CHNTN OX7 ... 104 B7
CLFD GL16 ... 151 K5
RTEWK/TIB GL19 ... 108 D7
Oridge St RTEWK/TIB GL19 ... 66 C8
Oriel Gv MIM GL56 ... 58 D7
Oriel Rd CHELT GL50 ... 2 D6
Oriole Wy GLE GL4 ... 136 E5
Orion Dr BRSTK/PCHW BS34 ... 316 F5
Orland Wy
OLD/WMLY/WICK BS30 ... 338 C8
Orlebar Gdns AVONM BS11 ... 324 D1
Orlham La LED HR8 ... 19 K6
Ormerod Rd CHEP NP16 ... 270 D4
HNLZ/SM/SNYPK/WT BS9 ... 325 G7
Ormond Pl CHELT GL50 ... 2 D5
Ormonds Cl ALMDB BS32 ... 317 G1
Ormsley Cl BRSTK/PCHW BS34 ... 316 E3
Orpen Gdns HORF/LLZ BS7 ... 326 D6
Orpheus Av BRSTK/PCHW BS34 .. 316 F5
Orrisdale Ter CHELTS GL53 ... 2 E7
Orwell Cl MALM SN16 ... 303 J6
Orwell Dr KEYN BS31 ... 348 B7
Orwell St BMSTR BS3 ... 336 A8
Osborne Av HORF/LLZ BS7 ... 326 B8
Osborne Cl
BRSTK/PCHW BS34 ... 316 F7
Osborne Rd BMSTR BS3 ... 6 C8
CFTN/FAIL BS8 ... 335 J2
THNB/SVB BS35 ... 304 B4
Osborne Ter BMSTR BS3 ... 345 K1
Osborne Vls CBRISNE BS2 ... 6 D1
Osbourne Av GL GL1 ... 159 L2
Osier Cl GLE GL4 ... 136 C7
Osprey Cl GLE GL4 ... 136 F6
Osprey Dr STNHO GL10 ... 207 H3
Osprey Pk THNB/SVB BS35 ... 273 M8
Osprey Rd CHELTS GL53 ... 115 L6
EVILLE/WHL BS5 ... 336 E4
Osric Rd GL GL1 ... 136 B5
Othello Cl CHELTW GL51 ... 115 G1
Otterford Cl
HGRV/WHIT BS14 ... 346 D6
Otter Rd BWTH/CHD GL3 ... 137 H6
Otters Fld COTS GL54 ... 74 D3
Ottery Cl AVONM BS11 ... 324 C2
Ottrells Md ALMDB BS32 ... 306 E8
Oval Ap VGL GL2 ... 181 H6
The Oval GL GL1 ... 135 M5
VGL GL2 ... 181 H6
Overbrook Cl GLE GL4 ... 136 E2
Overbrook Dr CHELTE/BC GL52 ... 3 H1
Overbrook Rd VGL GL2 ... 159 G3
Overbury Rd GL GL1 ... 5 K9
Overbury St CHELTS GL53 ... 116 C4
Over Cswy GL GL1 ... 111 K8
Overhill Rd CIR GL7 ... 214 B7
Over La ALMDB BS32 ... 306 C7
ALMDB BS32 ... 315 L2
Overley Rd CIR GL7 ... 212 D6
Overndale Rd MANG/FISH BS16 .. 327 L6
Overnhill Ct MANG/FISH BS16 ... 327 L6
Overnhill Rd MANG/FISH BS16 ... 327 L6
Over Old Rd VGL GL2 ... 89 G6
Overton La VGL GL2 ... 180 E1
Overton Park Rd CHELT GL50 ... 2 A5
Overton Rd HORF/LLZ BS7 ... 335 M1
Owen Gv
HNLZ/SM/SNYPK/WT BS9 ... 325 K6
Owen St EVILLE/WHL BS5 ... 336 D3
Owl Cl GLE GL4 ... 136 F6
Owls End Rd CHELTE/BC GL52 ... 72 C7
Owls Eye Cl CLFD GL16 ... 151 M7
Owls Head Rd
KGWD/HNM BS15 ... 338 A5
Oxbarton BRSTK/PCHW BS34 ... 317 H6
The Oxebode GL GL1 ... 4 E5
Oxen Leaze ALMDB BS32 ... 317 G1
Oxford Cl CHELTE/BC GL52 ... 3 G7
Oxford Pas CHELT GL50 ... 2 D4
Oxford Pl CFTN/FAIL BS8 ... 335 H5
EVILLE/WHL BS5 ... 336 C2
Oxford Rd GL GL1 ... 5 H3
Oxfordshire Wy COTS GL54 ... 123 J4
Oxford St BMSTR BS3 ... 7 K9
CBRISNE BS2 ... 7 L5
CHELTE/BC GL52 ... 2 F7
CHEP NP16 ... 270 A3
EVILLE/WHL BS5 ... 336 E4
GL GL1 ... 5 G4
LYD GL15 ... 225 J1
MALM SN16 ... 303 J8
MIM GL56 ... 58 D6
RDLND/MONT BS6 ... 335 L3
Oxford Wy CHELTW GL51 ... 115 J6
Oxleaze
BMSTRD/HC/WWD BS13 ... 345 M7
Oxleaze Cl TET GL8 ... 281 M3
Oxleaze Rd TET GL8 ... 259 G6
Oxmead Cl CHELTE/BC GL52 ... 72 D7
Oxmoor GLE GL4 ... 136 F8
Oxstalls Dr VGL GL2 ... 112 D7
Oxstalls La VGL GL2 ... 5 M2
Oxstalls Wy VGL GL2 ... 5 M1
VGL GL2 ... 112 D6
Oxway Cl SHPSTR CV36 ... 16 B5
Ozleworth KGWD/HNM BS15 ... 338 C3

P

Packer's Rd CIND GL14 154 B3
Packhorse La CIR GL7 217 K1
Paddock Cl ALMDB BS32 316 F1
MANG/FISH BS16 328 E5 1
Paddock Gdns
HGRV/WHIT BS14 346 C7
THNB/SVB BS35 293 J6
VGL GL2 112 F6
Paddock Ri STNHO GL10 207 H4
Paddocks La CHELT GL50 93 M7
The Paddocks CIR GL7 214 C6
THNB/SVB BS35 293 M2
Padin Cl RSTROUD/NAIL GL6 210 A7
Padstow Rd
BRSG/KWL/STAPK BS4 346 A3
Paganhill Est STROUD GL5 208 B3
Paganhill La STROUD GL5 208 B4
Page Rd MANG/FISH BS16 327 M7
Page's La TEWK GL20 25 M6
Pagets Rd CHELTE/BC GL52 94 C1
Painswick Av
BRSTK/PCHW BS34 316 D3
Painswick Dr YATE/CS BS37 320 A2 1
Painswick Old Rd STROUD GL5 208 E1
Painswick Rd BWTH/CHD GL3 137 M8
CHELT GL50 115 L4
GLE GL4 136 E7
GLE GL4 161 L4
RSTROUD/NAIL GL6 208 D1
STROUD GL5 208 D3
Palmdale Cl
OLD/WMLY/WICK BS30 348 C1 2
Palmer Av GLE GL4 137 H6
Palmers Cl
OLD/WMLY/WICK BS30 338 C5
Palmers Leaze ALMDB BS32 317 J4
Palmerston Rd
RDLND/MONT BS6 325 K7 2
Palmerston St BMSTR BS3 335 K8
Palm Rd CHPMW/MSHF SN14 343 J6
TEWK GL20 48 C7
Palmyra Rd BMSTR BS3 345 K1
Pancake La RTEWK/TIB GL19 91 L2
Parabola Cl CHELT GL50 2 B6
Parabola La CHELT GL50 2 A6
Parabola Rd CHELT GL50 2 A6
The Parade AVONM BS11 324 A5 2
YATE/CS BS37 320 C2 4
Paragon Ter CHELT GL50 2 D8
The Paragon
CFTN/FAIL BS8 335 H5 13
Parawell La LYD GL15 200 A4
Park Av ALMDB BS32 316 C1
BMSTR BS3 336 A8
EVILLE/WHL BS5 337 G3
FRCTL/WBN BS36 318 A5
FRCTL/WBN BS36 318 D4
VGL GL2 112 E6
Park Brake VGL GL2 110 F7
Parkbury Cl CHELTW GL51 115 J1
Park Cl CIR GL7 242 F4
KEYN BS31 347 M6
KGWD/HNM BS15 338 A4
LYD GL15 199 G6
OLD/WMLY/WICK BS30 338 D6 5
TET GL8 282 A4
Park Crs EVILLE/WHL BS5 336 F3
MANG/FISH BS16 327 L2
OLD/WMLY/WICK BS30 338 D6
Park Dr VGL GL2 159 H2
Park End HGHW SN6 287 H2 2
Parkend Br VGL GL2 182 B1
Parkend Rd CLFD GL16 175 M2
Park End Rd GL GL1 136 A4
Parkend Rd LYD GL15 177 K8
LYD GL15 200 D2
Parkend Wk CLFD GL16 175 L7
CLFD GL16 175 M2
Parker Pl BDWAY WR12 32 F3
Parkers Av
OLD/WMLY/WICK BS30 339 L4
Parkers Barton
EVILLE/WHL BS5 336 D5 10
Parkers Cl HNBRY/STHM BS10 316 A7
Parkers La MIM GL56 58 C6
Parker St BMSTR BS3 335 K8 5
Park Farm COTS GL54 123 H4
Park Farm Ct
OLD/WMLY/WICK BS30 338 B7 15
Parkfield Av EVILLE/WHL BS5 336 F4 5
Parkfield Rd MANG/FISH BS16 329 J4
Park Gv LYD GL15 200 F2
RDLND/MONT BS6 325 L6
Park Hl AVONM BS11 324 A5
LYD GL15 200 F2
Park Hill Common LYD GL15 223 J7
Park Hill La LYD GL15 222 F7
Park Hill Rd LYD GL15 223 J7
Parkhurst Av
MANG/FISH BS16 327 K7 4
Parkland Rd CHELTS GL53 116 B7
DSLY GL11 229 H7
Parklands KGWD/HNM BS15 337 M3 4
MALM SN16 303 G7
VGL GL2 159 G2
WUE GL12 277 K3
Parklands Cl MALM SN16 303 G7
Parkland Sq CIR GL7 238 B5
Parklands Rd BMSTR BS3 335 G7
Parkland Wy THNB/SVB BS35 273 K8
Park La CHELTE/BC GL52 94 D5
CIR GL7 238 C3
COTS GL54 118 D2
DSLY GL11 252 F4
FRCTL/WBN BS36 318 C7
MALM SN16 302 F7
STROUD GL5 232 B5
WUE GL12 278 C3
Park Md MALM SN16 303 H7
Park Ms CHELT GL50 115 L5
Park Pl CBRISNE BS2 6 D2
CFTN/FAIL BS8 6 B2
CHELT GL50 115 L4
EVILLE/WHL BS5 327 G8
HGHW SN6 287 H3
Park Rd AVONM BS11 324 A5
BMSTR BS3 6 B7
CHCAM GL55 34 D1
CLFD GL16 151 K8
GL GL1 4 F7
HORF/LLZ BS7 326 B2
KEYN BS31 348 A6
KGWD/HNM BS15 337 M2
MALM SN16 303 G6
MANG/FISH BS16 326 F6
MANG/FISH BS16 328 A6
MIM GL56 35 G8
NWNT GL18 88 A7
OLD/WMLY/WICK BS30 338 D6
RSTROUD/NAIL GL6 232 E8
STNHO GL10 207 G3
STROUD GL5 208 F5
THNB/SVB BS35 293 K1
WUE GL12 275 K7
Park Road Crs
RSTROUD/NAIL GL6 232 E8 1
Park Rw CBRIS/FH BS1 6 C3
FRCTL/WBN BS36 318 C3
Parkside CLFD GL16 175 K1
Parkside Av FRCTL/WBN BS36 318 A5
Parkside Dr BWTH/CHD GL3 113 H5
Parkside Gdns EVILLE/WHL BS5 326 D7
Parks Rd MTCHDN GL17 130 D2
Parkstone Av HORF/LLZ BS7 326 B5
Park St BAD GL9 312 C1
BRSG/KWL/STAPK BS4 7 M9
CBRIS/FH BS1 6 C3
CHELT GL50 2 B4
CIR GL7 238 C2 1
CIR GL7 242 E4
COTS GL54 102 A3
EVILLE/WHL BS5 337 H3 4
GL GL1 4 F4
YATE/CS BS37 308 F7
Park Street Av CBRIS/FH BS1 6 C3 1
The Park ALMDB BS32 306 E8
CHELT GL50 115 K4
COTS GL54 102 A4
KEYN BS31 348 A5
KGWD/HNM BS15 338 A3
MANG/FISH BS16 327 K2
OLD/WMLY/WICK BS30 348 D2
TEWK GL20 48 F2
Park Vw CHEP NP16 270 D3
CIR GL7 214 B7
KGWD/HNM BS15 338 A4
MTCHDN GL17 129 G3
VGL GL2 181 H4
Park View Av THNB/SVB BS35 293 L1
Park View Dr STROUD GL5 208 A3 5
Park View Rd BRKLY GL13 226 F8
Parkwall Crs
OLD/WMLY/WICK BS30 338 B7
Parkwall Rd
OLD/WMLY/WICK BS30 338 C7
Parkway BRSTK/PCHW BS34 317 J7
Park Wy CIR GL7 238 D7
OLD/WMLY/WICK BS30 338 D6
Park Wood Cl HGRV/WHIT BS14 346 B7
Parkwood Crs BWTH/CHD GL3 137 H5
Parkwood Gv CHELTS GL53 116 C7
Parliament St
BRSG/KWL/STAPK BS4 7 L9 5
GL GL1 4 E7
STROUD GL5 208 E4
Parliment Cl STROUD GL5 208 E4 5
Parnall Crs YATE/CS BS37 319 L1
Parnall Rd MANG/FISH BS16 327 J8
Parragate Rd CIND GL14 154 A2
Parr Cl BWTH/CHD GL3 113 H4 4
Parry Rd GL GL1 136 B5
Parry's Cl
HNLZ/SM/SNYPK/WT BS9 325 G6
Parrys Gv
HNLZ/SM/SNYPK/WT BS9 325 G6
Parry's La
HNLZ/SM/SNYPK/WT BS9 325 H6
Parslow Barton
EVILLE/WHL BS5 337 J4 5
Parsonage Farm HGHW SN6 288 F4 1
Parsonage Rd LGASH BS41 344 E1
Parsonage St DSLY GL11 253 J2 1
Parsons Av BRSTK/PCHW BS34 317 H6
Parsons Cl SHPSTR CV36 16 B6
Parsons Ct
RSTROUD/NAIL GL6 233 J5 4
Parsons La CHCAM GL55 11 M5
RTEWK/TIB GL19 44 A8
Parsons Paddock
HGRV/WHIT BS14 346 C4 1
Parson St BMSTR BS3 345 L2
Parsons Wk
OLD/WMLY/WICK BS30 338 F4
Partition St CBRIS/FH BS1 6 C5 2
Parton Dr BWTH/CHD GL3 113 L6
Parton Rd BWTH/CHD GL3 113 K5
Partridge Cl STNHO GL10 207 H3 5
VGL GL2 135 L6
Partridge Rd MANG/FISH BS16 329 L7
Partridge Wy CIR GL7 238 E2
Passage Rd HNBRY/STHM BS10 315 H7
HNBRY/STHM BS10 315 J8 4
HNLZ/SM/SNYPK/WT BS9 325 J3
VGL GL2 155 L8
VGL GL2 181 G3
Passage Road Brentry Hl
HNBRY/STHM BS10 315 J8
Passage St CBRIS/FH BS1 7 H4
Pastor's Hl LYD GL15 200 D3
Pasture La MIM GL56 57 H1
Patch Elm La YATE/CS BS37 309 G4
The Patches MTCHDN GL17 129 H5
Patch La YATE/CS BS37 309 J3
Paterson Rd CIR GL7 238 E3
Pates Av CHELTW GL51 115 K1
Patseamur Ms VGL GL2 113 G6 5
Patterdale Cl CHELTW GL51 93 H6 5
Paulman Gdns LGASH BS41 344 B3 1
Paul Md RSTROUD/NAIL GL6 184 D2
Pauls Cft HGHW SN6 289 G4
Paul's Ri STROUD GL5 232 C1
Paul St CBRISNE BS2 6 D1
GL GL1 136 B4 11
Paulton Dr HORF/LLZ BS7 325 L7
Paultow Av BMSTR BS3 336 A8 4
Paultow Rd BMSTR BS3 336 A8
Pauntley Court Dr
RTEWK/TIB GL19 65 G4
Pavey Cl
BMSTRD/HC/WWD BS13 345 L7
Pavey Rd
BMSTRD/HC/WWD BS13 345 L7
Pavilion Rd CHEP NP16 290 D1
Pawlett Rd
BMSTRD/HC/WWD BS13 345 L8
Pawlett Wk
BMSTRD/HC/WWD BS13 345 L8 2
Paxhill La TEWK GL20 26 B4
Paybridge Rd
BMSTRD/HC/WWD BS13 345 H7
Payford Br RTEWK/TIB GL19 65 H3
Paygrove La VGL GL2 112 F7
Payne Dr EVILLE/WHL BS5 336 D4 5
Paynes Meadow VGL GL2 182 B6
Paynes Pitch BWTH/CHD GL3 113 M8
Peach Cl TEWK GL20 48 C7
Peache Rd MANG/FISH BS16 328 A5
Peacock Cl CHELTW GL51 114 F1 4
GLE GL4 137 G6 5
NWNT GL18 86 C3 2
Peacock Gdns NWNT GL18 86 C3 5
Peacock La CIND GL14 154 B4
Peacocks La KGWD/HNM BS15 337 L3
Peak La DSLY GL11 230 C4
Peakstile Piece
CHELTE/BC GL52 72 D8 5
Pearces Hl MANG/FISH BS16 327 K4
Pearce Wy VGL GL2 135 K7
Pearcroft Rd STNHO GL10 207 H5
Pearl St BMSTR BS3 335 K8
The Pear Orch TEWK GL20 49 G2 5
Pearsall Rd
OLD/WMLY/WICK BS30 348 A1
Peart Cl
BMSTRD/HC/WWD BS13 345 G6
VGL GL2 5 L6
Peart Dr
BMSTRD/HC/WWD BS13 345 G7
Pear Tree Cl CHCAM GL55 34 E1 1
CHELTE/BC GL52 72 E8 2
VGL GL2 159 G4
Pear Tree Hey YATE/CS BS37 310 A6 2
Peartree La EVILLE/WHL BS5 337 K5
KGWD/HNM BS15 338 B1 4
Pear Tree Rd ALMDB BS32 316 E1
Pearwood Wy GL GL1 159 L1 1
Pecked La CHELTE/BC GL52 72 C7
Peel Cl CHELTS GL53 116 E6 5
Peel St CBRISNE BS2 336 B3
Pegasus Gdns VGL GL2 159 H1
Pegasus Rd BRSTK/PCHW BS34 315 M4
Peghouse Cl STROUD GL5 208 F3
Peghouse Ri STROUD GL5 208 F3
Pelham Crs BWTH/CHD GL3 113 J5
Pemberton Ct
MANG/FISH BS16 327 L6 1
Pembery Rd BMSTR BS3 335 K8 5
Pembridge Cl CHELTE/BC GL52 116 E5
Pembroke Av AVONM BS11 324 A5 5
Pembroke Gv CFTN/FAIL BS8 335 J4
Pembroke Pl CFTN/FAIL BS8 335 J6 5
Pembroke Rd AVONM BS11 324 A5 4
BMSTR BS3 6 C8
CFTN/FAIL BS8 335 J2
CHELTW GL51 115 G5
CHEP NP16 270 A6
KGWD/HNM BS15 338 A1 4
Pembroke St CBRISNE BS2 7 H1
CIND GL14 154 B3
GL GL1 5 G8
Pembroke V CFTN/FAIL BS8 335 J3
Pembury Rd GLE GL4 136 A7
Penard Wy KGWD/HNM BS15 338 B4 5
Penda Pl CHEP NP16 270 C3
Pendennis Av
MANG/FISH BS16 327 M7 5
Pendennis Pk
BRSG/KWL/STAPK BS4 346 F1
Pendennis Rd MANG/FISH BS16 327 M6
Pendil Cl CHELTW GL51 93 K5
Pendock Cl
OLD/WMLY/WICK BS30 348 E2 2
VGL GL2 159 G2 4
Pendock Ct
MANG/FISH BS16 328 D4 5
Pendock Rd FRCTL/WBN BS36 318 A6
MANG/FISH BS16 327 K5
Penfield Rd CBRISNE BS2 336 C1
Penharva Cl CHELTW GL51 93 J8 2
Penhill Rd GLE GL4 136 D6
Penmoel La CHEP NP16 246 C8
Penmoyle Gdns CHEP NP16 246 C7 2
Pennard Ct HGRV/WHIT BS14 346 D6
Penn Dr MANG/FISH BS16 327 L2
Penngrove
OLD/WMLY/WICK BS30 338 C8 4
Pennine Cl VGL GL2 159 G3
Pennine Rd CHELTE/BC GL52 94 D7
OLD/WMLY/WICK BS30 338 E7
Penn La STNHO GL10 207 K8
Pennlea
BMSTRD/HC/WWD BS13 345 K4
Penn St CBRIS/FH BS1 7 H2
Pennsylvania Av CHELTW GL51 93 H8
Penny Cl VGL GL2 112 F7
Pennylands Bank BDWAY WR12 32 C1
Penny La VGL GL2 228 C1
Pennyroyal Gv
MANG/FISH BS16 327 G6 7
Pennywell Rd EVILLE/WHL BS5 7 K1
EVILLE/WHL BS5 336 C2 15
Pen Park Rd
HNBRY/STHM BS10 315 L8
Penpole Av AVONM BS11 324 A5
Penpole La AVONM BS11 324 A4
Penpole Pk AVONM BS11 324 A4 5
Penpole Pl AVONM BS11 324 A5
Penrith Rd CHELTW GL51 115 H5
Penrose HGRV/WHIT BS14 346 B5
Penrose Cl RSTROUD/NAIL GL6 184 A8
Penrose Dr
BRSTK/PCHW BS34 316 F4 4
Penrose Rd VGL GL2 112 F5
Pensfield Pk
HNBRY/STHM BS10 315 M7
Pensford Ct
HGRV/WHIT BS14 346 F6 5
Pensile Rd RSTROUD/NAIL GL6 232 F7
Pentathlon Wy CHELT GL50 93 M6 1
Pentire Av
BMSTRD/HC/WWD BS13 345 J4
Pentland Av THNB/SVB BS35 294 A3
Perch Cl CLFD GL16 152 A7
Perch Dr CLFD GL16 152 A7
Percival Rd CFTN/FAIL BS8 335 H4
Percy St GL GL1 136 B4 12
Peregrine Cl VGL GL2 135 H8
Peregrine Rd CHELTS GL53 115 L6
Perricks Cl CIND GL14 132 C6
Perrinpit Rd FRCTL/WBN BS36 307 M8
Perrinsfield CIR GL7 244 F5
Perrott Rd KGWD/HNM BS15 338 C2 2
Perry Cl FRCTL/WBN BS36 317 M7
NWNT GL18 86 D3
Perrycroft Av
BMSTRD/HC/WWD BS13 345 J5
Perrycroft Rd
BMSTRD/HC/WWD BS13 345 J5
Perrygrove Rd CLFD GL16 175 K3
Perrymans Cl MANG/FISH BS16 327 J5
Perry Orch GLE GL4 161 G1
STROUD GL5 207 M3 2
Perry Rd CBRIS/FH BS1 6 D3
Perrys Lea ALMDB BS32 316 F1 4
Perry St EVILLE/WHL BS5 336 C3 11
Perry Wy VGL GL2 181 K7
Persh La VGL GL2 111 H4
Perth STNHO GL10 207 G2
Perwell Cl TEWK GL20 27 G4
Pesley Cl
BMSTRD/HC/WWD BS13 345 H7
Petercole Dr
BMSTRD/HC/WWD BS13 345 J5
Peter Pennell Cl CHELTW GL51 93 G7
Peters Fld VGL GL2 111 G6 5
Peterson Sq
BMSTRD/HC/WWD BS13 345 L8 5
Peter's St STNHO GL10 206 B8
Peter's Ter EVILLE/WHL BS5 336 D4
Petersway Gdns
EVILLE/WHL BS5 337 J5 5
Petherton Cl KGWD/HNM BS15 338 A4
Petherton Gdns
HGRV/WHIT BS14 346 D4
Petherton Rd
HGRV/WHIT BS14 346 D3
Pettigrove Gdns
KGWD/HNM BS15 338 A4
Pettigrove Rd
KGWD/HNM BS15 338 A5
Pettycroft MTCHDN GL17 129 G4
Petty La CHELTE/BC GL52 73 H8
Petty Marsh LYD GL15 198 F7
Petworth Cl GL GL1 159 L3
Pevelands DSLY GL11 229 H6
Pevensey Wk
BRSG/KWL/STAPK BS4 345 M4 5
Peverell Cl HNBRY/STHM BS10 315 H8
Peverell Dr HNBRY/STHM BS10 315 H8
Pheasant La CHELTW GL51 114 C2
Pheasant Md STNHO GL10 207 H3 10
The Pheasantry CIR GL7 265 G4
Pheasant Wy CIR GL7 238 F2
Phelps Wy RTEWK/TIB GL19 109 L3
Philadelphia Ct CBRIS/FH BS1 7 H2 4
Philippa Cl HGRV/WHIT BS14 346 C4
Philip's Cl LYD GL15 201 M2
Philip St BMSTR BS3 6 F9
CBRISNE BS2 336 D6
GL GL1 135 M4 1
Phillimore Gdns VGL GL2 181 J6
Phillimore Rd DSLY GL11 229 G7
Phillips La RTEWK/TIB GL19 44 B7
Phillips Rd BDWAY WR12 32 F2
Phippen St CBRIS/FH BS1 7 G6 1
Phipps St BMSTR BS3 6 A8
Phoenix Dr CHEP NP16 270 C7 1
Phoenix Gv RDLND/MONT BS6 325 L6
Phoenix Wy CIR GL7 238 C3 5
Piccadilly COTS GL54 98 E5
STROUD GL5 208 F4
Piccadilly Wy CHELTE/BC GL52 94 F7 1
Pickedmoor La THNB/SVB BS35 272 F6
Pickering Cl CHELTS GL53 115 L5 5
Pickering Rd CHELTS GL53 115 L5 4
Picton La RDLND/MONT BS6 336 A2
Picton St RDLND/MONT BS6 336 A2
The Piece BWTH/CHD GL3 113 L7
Pigeon House Dr
BMSTRD/HC/WWD BS13 345 M7 1
Pigeon La TEWK GL20 28 C3
Pigott Av
BMSTRD/HC/WWD BS13 345 J7
Pike Cnr BDWAY WR12 11 G7
Pike House Cl HGHW SN6 288 E3
Pike La RSTROUD/NAIL GL6 232 D8
Pike Rd CIR GL7 188 C3
CLFD GL16 151 K8
Pile Marsh EVILLE/WHL BS5 336 F4
Pilford Av CHELTS GL53 116 A7
Pilford Cl CHELTS GL53 116 A6
Pilford Ct CHELTS GL53 116 A8
Pilford Rd CHELTS GL53 116 A8
Pilgrim Cl GLE GL4 137 G5 5
Pilgrims Wy
MANG/FISH BS16 327 M3 2
Pilgrims Whf
BRSG/KWL/STAPK BS4 337 G4 5
Pilgrove Cl CHELTW GL51 92 F6
Pilgrove Wy CHELTW GL51 92 F6
Pilkington Cl
BRSTK/PCHW BS34 326 E1
Pillcroft Cl CHELTW GL51 138 C7
Pillcroft Rd CHELTW GL51 138 C6
Pilley Crs CHELTS GL53 115 M7
Pilley La CHELTS GL53 115 M7
Pillingers Rd KGWD/HNM BS15 337 L4
Pill La MIM GL56 82 B2
Pillowell Rd LYD GL15 201
Pillows Green Rd
RTEWK/TIB GL19 66
Pill Rd CFTN/FAIL BS8 334
Pilning St THNB/SVB BS35 305
Pimpernel Md ALMDB BS32 317 C
Pincoate VGL GL2 110
Pincot La RSTROUD/NAIL GL6 184
Pincots La WUE GL12 296
Pine Bank CHELTE/BC GL52 72
Pine Cl CHELTE/BC GL52 3
THNB/SVB BS35 293
Pine Crest Wy LYD GL15 200 C
Pinecroft HGRV/WHIT BS14 346 E
Pinedale LYD GL15 223
Pine Gv HORF/LLZ BS7 326
Pine Grove Pl HORF/LLZ BS7 325 M
Pinemount Rd BWTH/CHD GL3 137
Pine Ridge Cl
HNLZ/SM/SNYPK/WT BS9 324 E
Pine Rd HNBRY/STHM BS10 315
Pinery Rd GLE GL4 137 C
Pines Rd
OLD/WMLY/WICK BS30 348
The Pines COTS GL54 74 D
Pine Tree Dr GLE GL4 137
Pinetrees CHELTS GL53 116
Pine Tree Wy LYD GL15 202
Pinetum Dr VGL GL2 110
Pineway GLE GL4 136
Pinewood KGWD/HNM BS15 338 E
Pinewood Cl CIND GL14 154
HNLZ/SM/SNYPK/WT BS9 325
Pinewood Rd VGL GL2 159
Pinewood Wy
CHPMW/MSHF SN14 343
Pinford La RWYE HR9 84
Pingry La CLFD GL16 175
Pinhay Rd
BMSTRD/HC/WWD BS13 345 K
Pinkers Md MANG/FISH BS16 328
Pinlocks GLE GL4 137
Pinnells End La DSLY GL11 229
Pintail Cl VGL GL2 158
Pioneer Pk
BRSG/KWL/STAPK BS4 336
Pipe La CBRIS/FH BS1 6
Piper Rd YATE/CS BS37 310 A
Pipers Gv VGL GL2 110 F
Pippin Cl BWTH/CHD GL3 137
NWNT GL18 86 C
Pippin Ct
OLD/WMLY/WICK BS30 338 B7
Pippins Rd TEWK GL20 27
Pirton Crs BWTH/CHD GL3 113
Pirton La BWTH/CHD GL3 113
Pitch And Pay La
HNLZ/SM/SNYPK/WT BS9 325
Pitchcombe YATE/CS BS37 319 L
Pitchcombe Gdns
HNLZ/SM/SNYPK/WT BS9 324
Pitch La RDLND/MONT BS6 335
The Pitch RSTROUD/NAIL GL6 233
Pithay Ct CBRIS/FH BS1 6 F
Pitman Pl WUE GL12 277
Pitt Rd CHELTW GL51 115
Pitt Rd HORF/LLZ BS7 326
Pittsfield HGHW SN6 288
Pitt St GL GL1 4 E
Pittville Circ CHELTE/BC GL52 3
Pittville Circus Rd
CHELTE/BC GL52 3
Pittville Cl THNB/SVB BS35 273 L
Pittville Crs CHELTE/BC GL52 3
Pittville Crescent La
CHELTE/BC GL52 3
Pittville Lawn CHELTE/BC GL52 2
Pittville Ms CHELTE/BC GL52 2
Pittville St CHELTE/BC GL52 2
Pittway Av SHPSTR CV36 16
Pixash La KEYN BS31 348
Place Hl NWNT GL18 85
The Plain RSTROUD/NAIL GL6 208
Plaister's End LED HR8 19 M
Plantation Crs TEWK GL20 27 H
Players Cl MANG/FISH BS16 317
Playford Gdns AVONM BS11 324
Pleasant Rd MANG/FISH BS16 327
Pleasant Stile CIND GL14 154
Pleydells HGHW SN6 288 F
The Pleydells CIR GL7 239 M
The Plies CIR GL7 242
Plock Ct VGL GL2 112
Ploughmans Wy VGL GL2 159 C
Plover Cl YATE/CS BS37 319
Plummer's Hl EVILLE/WHL BS5 337
Plumpton Ct
MANG/FISH BS16 328 E
Plum Tree Cl GLE GL4 137 C
Pochard Cl VGL GL2 158
Pockhill La COTS GL54 123
Podsmead Pl GL GL1 135
Podsmead Rd GL GL1 135
Poets' Cl EVILLE/WHL BS5 336 F
Poets Pth LED HR8 41
NWNT GL18 41
Poets' Path No 1 NWNT GL18 41
NWNT GL18 64
Poets' Path No 2 NWNT GL18 42
Point Rd TET GL8 257
Polefield Gdns CHELTW GL51 115
Pollards La LYD GL15 202
Polly Barnes Cl
KGWD/HNM BS15 337 K
Polly Barnes Hl
KGWD/HNM BS15 337
Polygon Rd CFTN/FAIL BS8 335 J
Pomfrett Gdns
HGRV/WHIT BS14 347 G
Pomphrey Hl MANG/FISH BS16 328
Ponsford Rd
BRSG/KWL/STAPK BS4 346
Ponting Cl EVILLE/WHL BS5 337 J
Pool Cl MIM GL56 82
Pool Cnr ALMDB BS32 306
Poole Court Dr YATE/CS BS37 320
Poole Gnd VGL GL2 110 F
Pooles La STROUD GL5 208 A

oles Whf *CFTN/FAIL* BS8 .... 335 J6
oles Wharf Ct
  CFTN/FAIL BS8 .... 335 J6 ▣
ole Wy *CHELT* GL50 .... 2 B3
ol Gastons Rd *MALM* SN16 ..... 303 H7
olhay Ct *RTEWK/TIB* GL19 ..... 67 M1 ▣
ol Rd *KGWD/HNM* BS15 .... 328 A8
olway Cl *CLFD* GL16 .... 175 K1 ▣
olway Pl *CLFD* GL16 .... 175 K1
olway Rd *CLFD* GL16 .... 151 K8
olway Rd *CLFD* GL16 .... 151 L8
pes Cl *CHELT* GL50 .... 2 C2
pe's Ct *CIR* GL7 .... 214 A7
pes Meade *VGL* GL2 .... 111 G6 ▣
plar Av
  HNLZ/SM/SNYPK/WT BS9 .... 324 F5 ▣
plar Cl *GL* GL1 .... 135 M7
plar La *WUE* GL12 .... 296 D7
plar Pl *MANG/FISH* BS16 ...... 327 J8 ▣
plar Rd
  BMSTRD/HC/WWD BS13 .... 345 H4
  EVILLE/WHL BS5 .... 337 H4
  KGWD/HNM BS15 .... 337 J6
  OLD/WMLY/WICK BS30 .... 338 E5
plars Cl *CHCAM* GL55 .... 34 D1
The Poplars *CHELTW* GL51 ..... 115 G6
plar Ter *KGWD/HNM* BS15 ..... 338 B1
plar Wy *CHPMW/MSHF* SN14... 343 H6
ppy Fld *VGL* GL2 .... 111 G5 ▣
ppy Md *ALMDB* BS32 .... 317 G4
rchester Rd *BWTH/CHD* GL3 .. 137 H4
rlock Rd *BMSTR* BS3 .... 335 M8 ▣
rtland Pl *CBRISNE* BS2 .... 2 F3 ▣
  MANG/FISH BS16 .... 327 M8 ▣
  CHELTE/BC GL52 .... 2 F3
rtland Sq *CBRISNE* BS2 .... 7 H1
  CHELTE/BC GL52 .... 2 F3
rtland St *CBRISNE* BS2 .... 335 L3
  CFTN/FAIL BS8 .... 335 H4
  CHELTE/BC GL52 .... 2 E4
  MANG/FISH BS16 .... 327 M8 ▣
rt La *STROUD* GL5 .... 233 J2
rtmeirion Cl
  HGRV/WHIT BS14 .... 346 C6 ▣
rturet Wy *CHELTS* GL53 ...... 116 D5 ▣
rtwall La *CBRIS/FH* BS1 ...... 7 G6
rtwall La East *CBRIS/FH* BS1 .. 7 H6 ▣
rtwall Rd *CHEP* NP16 .... 270 A3
rtway *GLE* GL4 .... 161 H2
  HNLZ/SM/SNYPK/WT BS9 ..... 324 E8
rtway La *YATE/CS* BS37 ...... 320 C1
rtwell *HGHW* SN6 .... 288 F4 ▣
stlip Wy *CHELTW* GL51 .... 114 F3 ▣
st Office La *CHELT* GL50 ...... 2 D5
  CHELTE/BC GL52 .... 73 G8
  MIM GL56 .... 35 K7
  TEWK GL20 .... 48 A5 ▣
st Office Sq *CIR* GL7 .... 238 E7
he Post Paddocks *LYD* GL15 .. 224 A6
ticker's La *CIR* GL7 .... 193 L7 ▣
tters Croft *CHEP* NP16 ...... 270 D7
tters Field Rd
  CHELTE/BC GL52 .... 72 E8
tters La *SHPSTR* CV36 .... 15 J2
tters Pond *WUE* GL12 .... 277 K4
ttery Ct
  KGWD/HNM BS15 .... 337 K2 ▣
und Cl *BWTH/CHD* GL3 ...... 138 A7
  CIR GL7 .... 238 E7
  LED HR8 .... 19 M4
  SHPSTR CV36 .... 16 B5 ▣
  TEWK GL20 .... 26 B5
und Dr *MANG/FISH* BS16 .... 327 H6
und Farm La *RWYE* HR9 ...... 84 C2
und Hl *GL8* .... 257 L3 ▣
und La *CHCAM* GL55 .... 8 F8
  COTS GL54 .... 124 A7
  MANG/FISH BS16 .... 327 H7 ▣
  VGL GL2 .... 158 E6
und Meadow *LED* HR8 ...... 19 M4
und Rd *KGWD/HNM* BS15 .... 338 B1
he Pound *ALMDB* BS32 ...... 306 C6
  COTS GL54 .... 124 A7
untney Dr
  EVILLE/WHL BS5 .... 336 D3 ▣▣
untney Rd
  BRSG/KWL/STAPK BS4 .... 346 B3
eddy's La *EVILLE/WHL* BS5 ... 337 J5
escott *YATE/CS* BS37 .... 319 M3 ▣
escott Av *GLE* GL4 .... 136 D7
escott Wk *CHELTE/BC* GL52 .. 94 D7
ess Moor Dr
  OLD/WMLY/WICK BS30 ...... 338 B7 ▣▣
estbury *YATE/CS* BS37 .... 319 M3 ▣
estbury Rd *CHELTE/BC* GL52 .. 2 F3
eston Brook Cl *LED* HR8 ..... 19 M2
eston Wk
  BRSG/KWL/STAPK BS4 .... 346 C2 ▣
estwick Cl
  BRSG/KWL/STAPK BS4 .... 346 F2 ▣
etoria Rd
  BRSTK/PCHW BS34 .... 316 B3
ice St *GL* GL1 .... 135 M4
iddy Ct *HGRV/WHIT* BS14 .... 346 D6
iddy Dr *HGRV/WHIT* BS14 .... 346 D6
iestwood Cl I
  HNBRY/STHM BS10 .... 315 J8 ▣
imrose Cl *ALMDB* BS32 ...... 316 F1 ▣
  GLE GL4 .... 136 C7
  KGWD/HNM BS15 .... 337 K2
imrose Dr *CLFD* GL16 .... 175 L4
  MIM GL56 .... 58 D6
imrose Gdns
  THNB/SVB BS35 .... 293 M1
imrose Hill Rd *LYD* GL15... 201 J7
imrose Wy *LYD* GL15 .... 201 J6
ince Albert Ct
  BWTH/CHD GL3 .... 137 L5
ince Charles Rd *CIR* GL7...... 242 F4

Prince Crs *RTEWK/TIB* GL19 ..... 66 D5
Prince Rupert Rd *LED* HR8 ..... 19 L2
Princes Ct
  OLD/WMLY/WICK BS30 .... 338 D7
Princes' La *CFTN/FAIL* BS8 .... 335 H5
Princes' Pl *HORF/LLZ* BS7 .... 326 A8 ▣
Prince's Rd *CHELT* GL50 ...... 115 K4
  STROUD GL5 .... 208 A3 ▣
Princess Cl *KEYN* BS31 ...... 348 A6
Princess Elizabeth Wy
  CHELTW GL51 .... 114 F2
Princess Gdns
  MANG/FISH BS16 .... 326 F5 ▣
Princess Rw *CBRISNE* BS2 ..... 6 F1
Princess Royal Rd *GL15* 200 D2
Princess St *BMSTR* BS3 ...... 7 G1
  CBRISNE BS2 .... 7 L4
Prince's St *CBRISNE* BS2 ..... 336 B3 ▣
  CHELTE/BC GL52 .... 3 G6
Princess Victoria St
  CFTN/FAIL BS8 .... 335 H5
Prince St *CBRIS/FH* BS1 ...... 6 E6
  GL GL1 .... 5 G6 ▣
Prinknash Cl *GLE* GL4 .... 136 E7 ▣
Prinknash Rd *GLE* GL4 ...... 136 E7 ▣
Priors Lea *YATE/CS* BS37 .... 320 A2
Priory Av
  HNLZ/SM/SNYPK/WT BS9 ..... 325 J4
Priory Court Rd
  HNLZ/SM/SNYPK/WT BS9 ..... 325 J4
Priory Dene
  HNLZ/SM/SNYPK/WT BS9 ..... 325 J4 ▣
Priory Flds *RSTROUD/NAIL* GL6 .. 256 B3
Priory Gdns *HORF/LLZ* BS7 ... 326 B3
Priory La *CHELTE/BC* GL52 .... 72 C7
Priory Pl *CHELTS* GL53 ...... 2 F7
Priory Rd
  BRSG/KWL/STAPK BS4 .... 346 D1
  CFTN/FAIL BS8 .... 6 B1
  GL GL1 .... 4 E8 ▣
  KEYN BS31 .... 348 A4
Priory St *CHELTE/BC* GL52 .... 2 F7
Priory Ter *CHELTE/BC* GL52 .. 3 G6
Priory Wk *CHELTE/BC* GL52 .. 3 G6
Priory Wy *TET* GL8 .... 282 A3
Pritchard St *CBRISNE* BS2 .... 7 H1
Private Rd *STROUD* GL5 ...... 208 D8
Probertsbarn La *CLFD* GL16 .. 128 A5
Probyn Cl *MANG/FISH* BS16 .. 327 J4 ▣
Progress Cl *LED* HR8 .... 19 L1
Promenade *CHELT* GL50 ...... 2 C5
Prospect *COR/BOX* SN13 ..... 353 K7
Prospect Av
  KGWD/HNM BS15 .... 337 K2 ▣
Prospect Cl
  FRCTL/WBN BS36 .... 318 A7 ▣
  THNB/SVB BS35 .... 315 H1
Prospect Crs *KGWD/HNM* BS15 .. 338 B1
Prospect Gdns
  CBATH/BATHN BA1 .... 352 B6
Prospect La
  FRCTL/WBN BS36 .... 318 B3 ▣
Prospect Pl *CIR* GL7 .... 238 D4
  CLFD GL16 .... 175 K1 ▣
  EVILLE/WHL BS5 .... 336 B3
Prospect Rd *CIND* GL14 ...... 154 A3
  THNB/SVB BS35 .... 304 C5
Prospect Rw *HR9* 84 F3
Prosper Cl *CLFD* GL16 .... 175 M2
Providence La *LGASH* BS41 ... 344 B1
Providence Pl *CBRISNE* BS2 .. 7 J4 ▣
Providence Vw *LGASH* BS41 .. 344 C2 ▣
Prudham St *EVILLE/WHL* BS5 .. 336 E2 ▣
Pry La *BDWAY* WR12 .... 32 C3
Puck Pit La *COTS* GL54 ...... 74 D5
Puckrup La *TEWK* GL20 ...... 25 L6
Pudlicott La *COTS* GL54 ..... 35 L1
Pullar Cl *CHELTE/BC* GL52 .... 72 B7 ▣
Pullen Ct *CHELTE/BC* GL52 ... 72 C5
Pullens Rd *RSTROUD/NAIL* GL6 .. 185 L4
Pullin Ct *OLD/WMLY/WICK* BS30 .. 338 F7
Pullnoggin Pool La *RWYE* HR9 .. 126 D5
Pumphreys Rd *CHELTS* GL53... 116 C6
Pump La *ALMDB* BS32 .... 292 F7
  CBRIS/FH BS1 .... 7 G7
  TET GL8 .... 282 E7
Purbeck Wy *CHELTE/BC* GL52 .. 94 E8
Purcell Cl *BWTH/CHD* GL3 .... 113 H3
Purcell Wk
  BRSG/KWL/STAPK BS4 .... 345 M4 ▣▣
Purdown Rd *HORF/LLZ* BS7 ... 326 B6
Purley Av *CIR* GL7 .... 238 D3 ▣
Purley Rd *CIR* GL7 .... 238 D3
Pursey Dr *ALMDB* BS32 ...... 317 G5
Purslane Cl *GLE* GL4 .... 136 D7
Purton Cl *KGWD/HNM* BS15 .. 338 A5
Purton Pl *LYD* GL15 .... 225 L1
Purton Rd *HORF/LLZ* BS7 .... 335 M1 ▣
Puxley Cl *HGRV/WHIT* BS14 .. 347 G5 ▣
Puzzle Cl *LYD* GL15 .... 200 D3 ▣
Pye Cft *ALMDB* BS32 .... 307 G8
Pyecroft Av
  HNLZ/SM/SNYPK/WT BS9 ..... 325 K4
Pyke Rd *TEWK* GL20 .... 48 D5 ▣
Pylers Wy *LYD* GL15 .... 225 K1
Pylle Hill Crs *BMSTR* BS3 .... 7 J9
Pynne Rd *HGRV/WHIT* BS14 .. 347 G5 ▣
Pynne Rd *HGRV/WHIT* BS14 .. 347 M6
Pyrton Ms *CHELTW* GL51 .... 115 G6 ▣
Pystol La *LYD* GL15 .... 198 F6

Q

Quabbs La *MTCHDN* GL17 .... 129 L3
The Quadrangle *YATE/CS* BS37... 319 L2
Quadrant East
  MANG/FISH BS16 .... 327 L8 ▣
The Quadrant
  RDLND/MONT BS6 .... 325 K8 ▣
Quadrant West
  MANG/FISH BS16 .... 327 L8 ▣
Quail Cl *GLE* GL4 .... 137 G4
Quail Mdw *TET* GL8 .... 281 M3
Quaker La *THNB/SVB* BS35 ... 293 K2 ▣
Quaker's Cl
  MANG/FISH BS16 .... 327 M3 ▣

Quakers' Friars *CBRIS/FH* BS1 .. 7 G2 ▣
Quaker's Rd *MANG/FISH* BS16 .. 327 M3
Quantock Cl
  OLD/WMLY/WICK BS30 .... 338 E6
Quantock Rd *BMSTR* BS3 .... 335 M4
  VGL GL2 .... 159 G3
Quarhouse La *STROUD* GL5 ... 233 J1
The Quarries *ALMDB* BS32 ... 306 D6
Quarrington Rd *HORF/LLZ* BS7 .. 326 A6
Quarry Barton
  MANG/FISH BS16 .... 317 L7
Quarry Cl *CIR* GL7 .... 214 B7
Quarry Gdns *DSLY* GL11 ..... 228 F7
Quarry Hl *COR/BOX* SN13 .... 353 M5
Quarry La *AVONM* BS11 ...... 324 E2
  CHPMW/MSHF SN14 .... 343 K8
  FRCTL/WBN BS36 .... 318 A7
  RWYE HR9 .... 84 F3
Quarry Md *THNB/SVB* BS35... 293 H6
Quarry Rd *KGWD/HNM* BS15 .. 337 H5
  MANG/FISH BS16 .... 327 L4 ▣
  THNB/SVB BS35 .... 293 H6
  YATE/CS BS37 .... 320 C2
Quarry Steps *CFTN/FAIL* BS8 .. 335 J1 ▣
The Quarry *CIR* GL7 .... 217 H1
  CIR GL7 .... 242 F4
  DSLY GL11 .... 228 F7
Quarry Vw *CIR* GL7 .... 220 B8
  MANG/FISH BS16 .... 328 C2
Quarry Wy *MANG/FISH* BS16.. 327 G6
Quat Goose La *CLFD* GL16 ... 93 J4
Quayside La *EVILLE/WHL* BS5 .. 337 H5 ▣
Quay St *CBRIS/FH* BS1 .... 6 F3 ▣
  GL GL1 .... 4 D5 ▣
  TEWK GL20 .... 48 A5 ▣
The Quay *GL* GL1 .... 4 C5
Quedgeley *YATE/CS* BS37 .... 319 L3
Queen Anne's Rd *CIR* GL7 .... 238 E3 ▣
Queen Ann Rd *EVILLE/WHL* BS5 .. 336 D4
Queen Charlotte St
  CBRIS/FH BS1 .... 6 F4 ▣
Queen Charlton La
  HGRV/WHIT BS14 .... 346 F8
Queen Elizabeth Rd *CIR* GL7 .. 238 E3
Queens Acre *CIND* GL14 ..... 155 H7
Queen's Av *CFTN/FAIL* BS8 ... 6 B2
  SHPSTR CV36 .... 16 A5
Queen's Cl *BWTH/CHD* GL3 ... 137 J2
Queen's Ct *LED* HR8 .... 19 M3
Queensdale Crs
  BRSG/KWL/STAPK BS4 .... 346 C2
Queens Down Gdns
  BRSG/KWL/STAPK BS4 .... 336 D8
Queen's Dr *HORF/LLZ* BS7 .... 325 L7
  KGWD/HNM BS15 .... 337 K7
  STROUD GL5 .... 208 A4
Queens Fld *CIR* GL7 .... 242 F4
Queens Ga
  HNLZ/SM/SNYPK/WT BS9 ..... 324 F6
Queenshill Rd
  BRSG/KWL/STAPK BS4 .... 346 C2
Queensholm Av
  MANG/FISH BS16 .... 328 A2 ▣
Queensholm Cl
  MANG/FISH BS16 .... 328 A2
Queensholm Crs
  MANG/FISH BS16 .... 327 M2
Queensholm Dr
  MANG/FISH BS16 .... 328 A3
Queens La *CHELT* GL50 ...... 2 B7
Queensmead
  RSTROUD/NAIL GL6 .... 185 G4
  TEWK GL20 .... 27 J5
Queens Pde *CBRIS/FH* BS1 ... 6 B5
Queen Sq *CBRIS/FH* BS1 ..... 6 E5
  KEYN BS31 .... 349 H8 ▣
Queen Square Av
  CBRIS/FH BS1 .... 6 F5 ▣
Queen's Retreat
  CHELTW GL51 .... 115 K1 ▣
Queen's Rd
  BMSTRD/HC/WWD BS13 ...... 345 H7
  BRSG/KWL/STAPK BS4 .... 346 E2
  CFTN/FAIL BS8 .... 6 A2
  CFTN/FAIL BS8 .... 335 J4
  CFTN/FAIL BS8 .... 335 J4
  CHELTW GL51 .... 115 J3
  CHEP NP16 .... 270 A5
  EVILLE/WHL BS5 .... 337 H4
  HORF/LLZ BS7 .... 326 B7
  KEYN BS31 .... 347 M7
  LGASH BS41 .... 345 H8
  MANG/FISH BS16 .... 329 K6
  OLD/WMLY/WICK BS30 ...... 338 C5
  STNHO GL10 .... 207 H4
  STROUD GL5 .... 208 D5
  TEWK GL20 .... 48 C6
Queens Sq *COTS* GL54 .... 74 C6
Queen St *CBRISNE* BS2 ...... 7 H5
  CHELTW GL51 .... 2 A1
  CIR GL7 .... 238 D4
  COTS GL54 .... 167 J6
  EVILLE/WHL BS5 .... 326 F8 ▣
  KGWD/HNM BS15 .... 337 K4
  LYD GL15 .... 201 K7
Queens Wk *THNB/SVB* BS35 .. 273 K8
  CLFD GL16 .... 175 M1
Queen's Wy *LED* HR8 .... 19 M3
  WUE GL12 .... 277 K5
Queen Victoria Rd
  RDLND/MONT BS6 .... 338 D7
Queen Victoria St *CBRISNE* BS2.. 7 M4
Queenwood Gv *CHELTE/BC* GL52.. 94 F6
Quenneys Cl *GLE* GL4 .... 136 E8
Querns La *CIR* GL7 .... 238 C3 ▣
Querns Rd *CIR* GL7 .... 238 C3
Quickthorn Cl *HGRV/WHIT* BS14.. 346 C5
Quietways *STNHO* GL10 ..... 207 H3
Quinton Cl *BWTH/CHD* GL3 .. 113 K5 ▣

R

Rackham Cl *HORF/LLZ* BS7 .... 326 D5

Rackhay *CBRIS/FH* BS1 .... 6 F4 ▣
Radburn Rd *MIM* GL56 .... 58 E6 ▣
Radley Rd *MANG/FISH* BS16 .. 327 K7
Radnor Cl *CHELTW* GL51 ..... 115 G5
  HNLZ/SM/SNYPK/WT BS9 ..... 325 K6
  HORF/LLZ BS7 .... 325 M6
Raeburn Rd *EVILLE/WHL* BS5 .. 337 K4
Rag La *WUE* GL12 .... 295 M6
Raglan Pl *HORF/LLZ* BS7 ..... 325 M8 ▣
  THNB/SVB BS35 .... 293 K3
Raglan Rd *HORF/LLZ* BS7 .... 325 M8
Raglan St *GL* GL1 .... 5 H7
Raglan Wy *CHEP* NP16 ...... 270 B6
  DSLY GL11 .... 254 D2
Raikes Rd *GL* GL1 .... 135 M5
Railton Jones Cl
  BRSTK/PCHW BS34 .... 317 G8
Railway Dr *CLFD* GL16 ...... 175 K1
Railway Rd *CLFD* GL16 ...... 154 A6
Railway Ter *MANG/FISH* BS16 .. 327 L6
Raleigh Rd *BMSTR* BS3 ...... 6 A9
  BMSTR BS3 .... 335 J7
Ralph Rd *HORF/LLZ* BS7 ..... 326 B7
Ram Hl *FRCTL/WBN* BS36 .... 318 F7
Ramscombe La
  CBATH/BATHN BA1 .... 352 B5
Ramsdale Rd *VGL* GL2 .... 135 K8
Ramsey Rd *HORF/LLZ* BS7 ... 326 B4
Rance Pitch *GLE* GL4 .... 161 G1
Randall Cl *KGWD/HNM* BS15 .. 338 B1
Randall Rd *CFTN/FAIL* BS8 ... 335 J5
  COTS GL54 .... 124 D8
Randalls Cl
  RSTROUD/NAIL GL6 .... 185 H4 ▣
Randalls Gn *RSTROUD/NAIL* GL6.. 210 B8
Randolph Av
  BMSTRD/HC/WWD BS13 ...... 345 K6
  YATE/CS BS37 .... 309 M7
Randolph Cl
  BMSTRD/HC/WWD BS13 ...... 345 K6
  CHELTS GL53 .... 116 B5 ▣
Randwick Rd *GL* GL1 .... 159 M1
Rangers Cl *DSLY* GL11 .... 253 K4
Rangers Wk *KGWD/HNM* BS15 .. 337 L7
The Range *VGL* GL2 .... 110 F6
Ranmoor *GLE* GL4 .... 136 F8
Rannoch Rd
  BRSTK/PCHW BS34 .... 326 B1
Ratcliffe Dr *BRSTK/PCHW* BS34 . 317 G6
Ratcliff Lawns *CHELTE/BC* GL52 . 94 D3
Rathbone Cl *FRCTL/WBN* BS36 . 318 C6
Rathmore Cl *COTS* GL54 .... 74 C5
Ravendale Dr
  OLD/WMLY/WICK BS30 ...... 338 D8
Ravenglass Crs
  HNBRY/STHM BS10 .... 325 L1
Ravenhead Dr
  HGRV/WHIT BS14 .... 346 D3
Ravenhill Av *BMSTR* BS3 .... 346 B8
Ravenhill Rd *BMSTR* BS3 .... 336 B8
Ravensgate Rd *CHELTS* GL53 . 116 D3
Ravenswood Rd
  RDLND/MONT BS6 .... 335 L2
Rawens Wd
  OLD/WMLY/WICK BS30 ...... 338 D8 ▣
Rayens Cross Rd *LGASH* BS41 . 344 B2
Rayleigh Rd
  HNLZ/SM/SNYPK/WT BS9 ..... 324 F4
Raymend Rd *BMSTR* BS3 .... 336 A8
Raymend Wk *BMSTR* BS3 ... 346 A1
Raymill
  BRSG/KWL/STAPK BS4 .... 347 J1 ▣
Raymore Ri *LGASH* BS41 .... 344 B3
Raynes Rd *BMSTR* BS3 .... 335 J7
Reaburn Cl *CHELTE/BC* GL52 .. 116 D5 ▣
Read Wy *CHELTE/BC* GL52 ... 94 B1
Rea La *VGL* GL2 .... 135 H6
Rectory Cl *COTS* GL54 ...... 101 J4
  GLE GL4 .... 161 G1
  YATE/CS BS37 .... 310 B8 ▣
Rectory La *BRSTK/PCHW* BS34 . 316 C8
  HGHW SN6 .... 289 G3
  TET GL8 .... 257 L2
  VGL GL2 .... 135 J5
  WUE GL12 .... 295 J2
Rectory Meadow
  MTCHDN GL17 .... 107 G7
Rectory Rd *FRCTL/WBN* BS36 . 318 D3
  GLE GL4 .... 136 E7
Red Admiral Dr *GLE* GL4 .... 137 G4
Redbrook Rd *MONM* NP25 ... 178 B3
Redcar Ct *FRCTL/WBN* BS36 .. 328 B2 ▣
Redcatch Rd *BMSTR* BS3 .... 346 B1
  BRSG/KWL/STAPK BS4 .... 346 C1
Redcliff Backs *CBRIS/FH* BS1 .. 7 G5
Redcliffe Pde East *CBRIS/FH* BS1.. 6 F6
Redcliffe Pde West *CBRIS/FH* BS1.. 6 F6
Redcliffe Wy *CBRIS/FH* BS1 .. 7 G6
Redcliff Hl *CBRIS/FH* BS1 .... 7 G7
Redcliff Mead La *CBRIS/FH* BS1.. 7 H6
Redcliff St *CBRIS/FH* BS1 .... 7 G5
Redcross St *CBRISNE* BS2 .... 7 J3
Redding Cl *VGL* GL2 .... 159 G2
Reddings Cl *LYD* GL15 ...... 224 A5
Reddings La *CIND* GL14 ..... 154 C3
Reddings Pk *CHELTW* GL51 .. 114 F3 ▣
Reddings Rd *CHELTW* GL51 .. 114 E4
The Reddings *CHELTW* GL51 .. 114 F4
  CHEP NP16 .... 270 B6 ▣
  KGWD/HNM BS15 .... 338 B1
Red Ditch La *RTEWK/TIB* GL19 . 65 J7
Redesdale Pl *MIM* GL56 ..... 58 C7
Redfield Hl
  OLD/WMLY/WICK BS30 ...... 338 F7
Redfield Rd *BRSTK/PCHW* BS34 . 316 D4
Redford Crs
  BMSTRD/HC/WWD BS13 ...... 345 G5
Redford La *MANG/FISH* BS16 . 329 M7
Redford Wk
  BMSTRD/HC/WWD BS13 ...... 345 H8 ▣
Redgrove Pk *CHELTW* GL51 .. 114 F4
Redgrove Rd *CHELTW* GL51 .. 93 H7
Redham La *THNB/SVB* BS35 .. 305 K2
Redhill Cl *MANG/FISH* BS16 .. 327 G8
Redhill La *THNB/SVB* BS35 ... 292 A5
Red House La *ALMDB* BS32 .. 306 C7
Redhouse La *CLFD* GL16 .... 127 K8 ▣

Red House La
  RDLND/MONT BS6 .... 325 G5
Redhouse La *STROUD* GL5 ... 207 M3
Redland Cl *VGL* GL2 .... 112 D7
Redland Court Rd
  RDLND/MONT BS6 .... 325 L8
Redland Green Rd
  RDLND/MONT BS6 .... 335 K1
Redland Gv *RDLND/MONT* BS6 .. 335 L1
Redland Hl *RDLND/MONT* BS6 .. 335 K2
Redland Pk *RDLND/MONT* BS6 .. 335 K2
Redland Rd
  RDLND/MONT BS6 .... 325 K8 ▣
  RDLND/MONT BS6 .... 335 M1
Redland Ter
  RDLND/MONT BS6 .... 335 J1 ▣
Red La *TEWK* GL20 .... 48 A4
Red Lion La *HGHW* SN6 ..... 289 G4
Rednock Dr *DSLY* GL11 ...... 253 J1
Redpoll Wy *GLE* GL4 .... 136 G5
Red Rover Cl *CHELT* GL50 ... 93 L6
Redshelf Wk
  HNBRY/STHM BS10 .... 315 L8
Redstart Wy *GLE* GL4 .... 136 G5
Redthorne Wy *CHELTW* GL51.. 115 G6
Red Well Rd *GLE* GL4 .... 160 L1
Redwick Cl *AVONM* BS11 .... 324 E1
Redwick Gdns *THNB/SVB* BS35 . 304 E4
Redwick Rd *THNB/SVB* BS35 . 304 D2
Redwind Wy *VGL* GL2 .... 112 F6
Redwing Gdns
  MANG/FISH BS16 .... 327 G5 ▣
Redwood Cl *GL* GL1 .... 135 M7
  OLD/WMLY/WICK BS30 ...... 338 C8 ▣
Redwood Ct *TEWK* GL20 .... 49 G2 ▣
Redwood Wy
  CHPMW/MSHF SN14 .... 343 J6
Reed Cl *HNBRY/STHM* BS10 .. 325 M4 ▣
Reed Ct
  OLD/WMLY/WICK BS30 ...... 338 B8 ▣
Reedley Rd
  HNLZ/SM/SNYPK/WT BS9 ..... 325 G6
Reedling Cl *MANG/FISH* BS16 . 327 G5 ▣
Reeds *HGHW* SN6 .... 288 E3
Reeds Farm Rd *MALM* SN16 . 303 J7
Reevers Rd *NWNT* GL18 .... 86 D3
Reeves Cl *CIR* GL7 .... 238 A5 ▣
Regency Dr
  BRSG/KWL/STAPK BS4 .... 347 J1 ▣
Regent Rd *BMSTR* BS3 ...... 6 F8 ▣
Regents Cl *THNB/SVB* BS35... 273 K8
Regent St *CFTN/FAIL* BS8 .... 335 J5
  CHELT GL50 .... 2 D5
  GL GL1 .... 4 F9
  KGWD/HNM BS15 .... 337 L3
  LYD GL15 .... 201 J8
  STNHO GL10 .... 207 H5
Regent Wy *CHEP* NP16 ...... 270 A3 ▣
Regis Cl *CHELTS* GL53 ...... 116 C6
Reine Barnes Cl *DSLY* GL11 .. 253 K3
Remenham Dr
  HNLZ/SM/SNYPK/WT BS9 ..... 325 K6 ▣
Remenham Pk
  HNLZ/SM/SNYPK/WT BS9 ..... 325 K6
Remus Cl *GLE* GL4 .... 137 H5 ▣
Rendcomb Cl *GLE* GL4 ...... 137 G7 ▣
Rendcomb Dr *CIR* GL7 ...... 238 A4
Repton Dr
  BRSG/KWL/STAPK BS4 .... 336 E8
Reservoir Rd *GLE* GL4 ...... 136 B7
  STROUD GL5 .... 209 G4
Reynolds Cl *KEYN* BS31 ..... 348 C6
Reynold's Wk *HORF/LLZ* BS7 . 326 C4
Ribble Cl *BWTH/CHD* GL3 .... 138 B6
Ribblesdale *THNB/SVB* BS35 .. 293 L3
Ricardo Rd *RSTROUD/NAIL* GL6. 233 H5
Richard Pl *TEWK* GL20 ...... 48 B8
Richards Rd *CHELTW* GL51 .. 93 K7 ▣
Richeson Cl *HNBRY/STHM* BS10. 325 H1
Richeson Wk
  HNBRY/STHM BS10 .... 325 H1
Richmond Av
  BRSTK/PCHW BS34 .... 317 G6
  GLE GL4 .... 136 E5
  RDLND/MONT BS6 .... 336 B1 ▣
Richmond Cl *KEYN* BS31 .... 347 M7
Richmond Dl *HGHW* SN6 .... 287 H2
Richmond Dl *CFTN/FAIL* BS8 . 335 J1 ▣
Richmond Dr *CHELTE/BC* GL52 . 3 K5
Richmond Gdns *VGL* GL2 .... 112 G6
Richmond Hl *CFTN/FAIL* BS8 . 6 A2
Richmond Hill Av *CFTN/FAIL* BS8. 6 A3
Richmond Park Rd *CFTN/FAIL* BS8 335 J4
Richmond Rd *EVILLE/WHL* BS5. 337 G3
  MANG/FISH BS16 .... 328 C6
  RDLND/MONT BS6 .... 336 B1 ▣
The Richmonds *GLE* GL4 .... 136 F7
Richmond St *BMSTR* BS3 .... 7 J9
Richmond Ter *CFTN/FAIL* BS8 . 335 J4
Rickyard Wy *VGL* GL2 .... 182 A6
The Ride *KGWD/HNM* BS15 .. 338 C1
Ridgehill
  HNLZ/SM/SNYPK/WT BS9 ..... 325 J1
Ridgemont Rd *STROUD* GL5 .. 209 G4
Ridgemount Cl *BWTH/CHD* GL3. 137 M5
Ridge Pl *MTCHDN* GL17 ..... 152 C1
Ridgeview *LGASH* BS41 ...... 344 D1 ▣
Ridgeway *FRCTL/WBN* BS36 . 318 E4
  LED HR8 .... 20 E4
  LYD GL15 .... 177 L8
  YATE/CS BS37 .... 320 C1
Ridgeway Ct
  HNBRY/STHM BS10 .... 325 H2
Ridgeway Crs *RWYE* HR9 .... 126 D5 ▣
Ridgeway Gdns
  HGRV/WHIT BS14 .... 346 E6
  HGRV/WHIT BS14 .... 346 D7
Ridgeway Pde
  EVILLE/WHL BS5 .... 327 G8 ▣
Ridgeway Rd *LGASH* BS41 ... 344 C2
  .... 327 G8
The Ridgeway
  HNBRY/STHM BS10 .... 325 J2

MALM SN16 .... 284 A5
RSTROUD/NAIL GL6 .... 209 M7
Riding Barn Hl
  OLD/WMLY/WICK BS30 ... 339 H5
Ridingleaze AVONM BS11 .... 324 C2
Ridings Cl YATE/CS BS37 .... 320 E2
Ridings Rd FRCTL/WBN BS36 .. 318 E5
The Ridings
  BMSTRD/HC/WWD BS13 ... 345 G7
  FRCTL/WBN BS36 .... 318 A5
  RSTROUD/NAIL GL6 .... 232 E8
  VGL GL2 .... 111 J4
Ridler Rd LYD GL15 .... 225 L1
Rigsby's La MALM SN16 ...... 286 B6
Ringer's Cl RTEWK/TIB GL19 .. 69 G6
Ring Fence LYD GL15 .... 223 M5
Ringfield Cl
  RSTROUD/NAIL GL6 .... 232 E8
Ringwood Crs
  HNBRY/STHM BS10 .... 325 M2
Ripley Rd EVILLE/WHL BS5 ... 337 J2
Ripon Ct MANG/FISH BS16 .... 328 B2
Ripon Rd BRSG/KWL/STAPK BS4 .. 337 G5
Rippledale Cl CHELTW GL51 .. 115 G4
Risdale Rd BMSTR BS3 .... 345 G2
Rising Sun La CHELTE GL52 .... 95 G1
Rissington Cl CHELTW GL51 ... 115 G3
Rissington Rd COTS GL54 ...... 123 J6
  GLE GL4 .... 160 A1
Rivelands Rd CHELTW GL51 .... 93 K4
Riverland Dr
  BMSTRD/HC/WWD BS13 ... 345 H7
Riverleaze
  HNLZ/SM/SNYPK/WT BS9 .. 324 D6
River Leys CHELTW GL51 .... 93 H6
Rivermead Cl VGL GL2 .... 112 A6
River Rd YATE/CS BS37 .... 320 C2
Riverside COTS GL54 .... 74 D5
Riverside Cl AVONM BS11 ..... 324 B6
  CHELTE/BC GL52 .... 116 D5
Riverside Ct
  BRSG/KWL/STAPK BS4 ...... 337 H5
Riverside Pk THNB/SVB BS35 .. 304 B5
Riverside Wk
  EVILLE/WHL BS5 .... 337 H5 [10]
Riverside Wy KGWD/HNM BS15 .. 337 L8
Riversley Rd VGL GL2 .... 136 E1
River St CBRISNE BS2 .... 7 J2
River Vw CHEP NP16 .... 270 A3
  MANG/FISH BS16 .... 327 G6
Riverview Wy CHELTW GL51 ... 93 J7
River Wy CIR GL7 .... 263 G4
  SHPSTR CV36 .... 16 C4
Riverwood Rd
  MANG/FISH BS16 .... 327 L2
Riviera Crs MANG/FISH BS16 .. 328 A7
Roach's La BAD GL9 .... 322 E2
Road Hl CHPMW/MSHF SN14 .. 352 F2
  COR/BOX SN13 .... 353 C3
Robbers Rd STNHO GL10 ...... 207 L1
Robbins Cl ALMDB BS32 .... 317 H5
  CHPMW/MSHF SN14 .... 342 B3
  STROUD GL5 .... 207 L5
Robbins Ct MANG/FISH BS16 .. 328 D5
Robel Av FRCTL/WBN BS36 .... 318 C3
Robert Burns Av CHELTW GL51 .. 114 F4
Robert Ct MANG/FISH BS16 ... 328 D4
Robert Franklin Wy CIR GL7 ... 263 K4
Robert Raikes Av GLE GL4 ..... 159 M1
Roberts Cl CHELTE/BC GL52 .... 72 B7
  CIR GL7 .... 214 B8
Robertson Dr
  BRSG/KWL/STAPK BS4 ...... 337 H5
Robertson Rd CHELTW GL51 ... 138 F1
  EVILLE/WHL BS5 .... 336 E1
Roberts Rd BWTH/CHD GL3 .. 113 H4
  CHELTE/BC GL52 .... 94 F7
Robert St EVILLE/WHL BS5 .... 336 D1
  EVILLE/WHL BS5 .... 336 D4 [10]
Robin Cl HNBRY/STHM BS10 .. 325 K1
  RSTROUD/NAIL GL6 .... 210 A8
  TEWK GL20 .... 48 F2
Robin Ct STNHO GL10 .... 207 H3
Robinhood St GL GL1 .... 135 M4
Robins Cl CHELTE/BC GL52 ..... 3 J3
Robins End VGL GL2 .... 112 F4
Robinson Cl NWNT GL18 ...... 86 C2
Robinson Dr
  EVILLE/WHL BS5 .... 336 C3 [12]
Robinson La CIR GL7 .... 189 L4
Robinson Rd GL GL1 .... 135 M4
Robinson's Meadow LED HR8 .. 19 M2
Robinswood Gdns GLE GL4 ..... 136 B6
Robin Wy YATE/CS BS37 .... 320 B4
Rochester Rd
  BRSG/KWL/STAPK BS4 ...... 337 G6
  CHELT GL50 .... 115 J6
Rock And Fountain La
  CIND GL14 .... 156 F2
Rock Cl
  BRSG/KWL/STAPK BS4 ...... 347 G1
Rockfield CHPMW/MSHF SN14.. 343 K8
Rockingham Gdns
  AVONM BS11 .... 324 C3
Rockland Gv
  MANG/FISH BS16 .... 326 F6
Rockland Rd MANG/FISH BS16 . 327 L4
Rock La BRSTK/PCHW BS34 ... 317 H7
  CIND GL14 .... 156 F2
  CLFD GL16 .... 175 K3
Rockleaze
  RSTROUD/NAIL GL6 .... 256 D1
Rockleaze Av
  HNLZ/SM/SNYPK/WT BS9 .. 325 G1
Rockleaze Rd
  HNLZ/SM/SNYPK/WT BS9 .. 335 G1
Rockness Hl
  RSTROUD/NAIL GL6 .... 256 D1
Rock Rd DSLY GL11 .... 228 F7
  KEYN BS31 .... 348 A6
  OLD/WMLY/WICK BS30 ..... 339 M3
Rockside Av MANG/FISH BS16 . 328 B3
Rockside Dr
  HNLZ/SM/SNYPK/WT BS9 .. 325 K5
Rockside Gdns
  FRCTL/WBN BS36 .... 318 E3
  MANG/FISH BS16 .... 328 B3
Rocks Rd MTCHDN GL17 ...... 128 C5

The Rocks CLFD GL16 .... 175 K6
Rockstowes Wy
  HNBRY/STHM BS10 .... 315 M8
Rock St RTEWK/TIB GL19 ...... 68 F1
  THNB/SVB BS35 .... 293 K3
The Rock
  BRSG/KWL/STAPK BS4 ...... 337 G8
Rock Villa La CHEP NP16 ...... 270 B2
Rockwell Av AVONM BS11 ..... 324 D2
Rockwood Rd CHEP NP16 ..... 270 A4
Rodborough YATE/CS BS37 ... 319 L4
Rodborough Av STROUD GL5 . 208 D5
Rodborough Hl STROUD GL5 . 208 D5
Rodborough La STROUD GL5 . 208 E6
Rodbourne Rd
  HNBRY/STHM BS10 .... 325 M4
Rodfords Md BMSTRD/HC/WWD BS14 .. 346 C4
Rodford Wy YATE/CS BS37 .... 319 L4
Rodley Rd LYD GL15 .... 201 L8
Rodley Sq LYD GL15 .... 201 L8
Rodmead Wk
  BMSTRD/HC/WWD BS13 ... 345 J7
Rodney Av KGWD/HNM BS15 .. 337 J3
Rodney Cl VGL GL2 .... 112 D7
Rodney Crs BRSTK/PCHW BS34 . 316 C7
Rodney Rd CHELT GL50 .... 2 D6
  KGWD/HNM BS15 .... 337 J2
Rodney Wk KGWD/HNM BS15 . 337 J2
Rodway Hl MANG/FISH BS16 .. 328 C7
Rodway La VGL GL2 .... 89 L5
Rodway Rd BRSTK/PCHW BS34 . 316 A7
  MANG/FISH BS16 .... 328 C6
Rodway Vw KGWD/HNM BS15 . 328 B8
Roebuck Mdw
  MTCHDN GL17 .... 129 H5
Roegate Dr
  BRSG/KWL/STAPK BS4 ...... 337 G5
Rogers Cl
  OLD/WMLY/WICK BS30 ..... 338 D6
Rokeby Av RDLND/MONT BS6 . 336 C2
The Rollers RSTROUD/NAIL GL6 . 232 D7
Rolleston Wy CHELTW GL51 ... 115 H4
Rolling Stones CHCAM GL55 ... 12 E8
Roman Farm Ct
  AVONM BS11 .... 324 E1
Roman Hackle Av CHELT GL50 .. 93 L6
Roman Rd CHELTW GL51 ...... 115 J2
  GLE GL4 .... 137 G5
Roman Wk
  BRSG/KWL/STAPK BS4 ...... 336 E8
  BRSTK/PCHW BS34 .... 317 G6
Roman Wy CIND GL14 .... 154 D3
  CIR GL7 .... 244 F6
  CLFD GL16 .... 175 K2
  COTS GL54 .... 123 J4
  HNLZ/SM/SNYPK/WT BS9 .. 324 E7
Romney Av HORF/LLZ BS7 ... 326 D6
Romney Cl GL GL1 .... 136 A8
Romney Rd TET GL8 .... 281 L3
Ronald Rd MANG/FISH BS16 .. 327 H5
Ronayne Wk MANG/FISH BS16 . 327 L5
Ron Golding Cl MALM SN16 ... 303 J6
Rookery La BRKLY GL13 .... 227 C4
  CLFD GL16 .... 175 C7
  OLD/WMLY/WICK BS30 ..... 330 B8
  THNB/SVB BS35 .... 305 J5
Rookery Rd
  BRSG/KWL/STAPK BS4 ...... 336 C8
  VGL GL2 .... 112 F5
Rookery Wy HGRV/WHIT BS14 . 346 B7
Rooksmoor Hl STROUD GL5 .. 208 C8
Roosevelt Av CHELTE/BC GL52 .. 3 J9
Ropewalk TEWK GL20 .... 48 E5
The Rope Wk STROUD GL5 .... 209 C8
Rose Acre HNBRY/STHM BS10 . 315 J8
Rose & Crown Pas CHELT GL50 . 2 D4
Rosebay Md
  MANG/FISH BS16 .... 327 G7
Roseberry Pk EVILLE/WHL BS5 . 336 F5
Roseberry Rd EVILLE/WHL BS5 . 336 E4
Rosebery Av CBRISNE BS2 .... 336 C2
  GL GL1 .... 136 A6
Rosebery Mt DSLY GL11 .... 253 L3
Rosebery Pk DSLY GL11 .... 253 L3
Rosebery Rd DSLY GL11 .... 253 L3
Rose Cl FRCTL/WBN BS36 .... 318 A7
Rosedale Av STNHO GL10 ..... 207 H4
Rosedale Rd MANG/FISH BS16 . 327 K8
Rosefield Crs TEWK GL20 ...... 48 C5
Rose Green Rd EVILLE/WHL BS5 . 336 F1
Rosehill Ct GLE GL4 .... 214 C8
Rosehill St CHELTE/BC GL52 .... 3 H8
Rosehip Wy CHELTE/BC GL52 .. 72 A7
Rose La FRCTL/WBN BS36 .... 318 F4
Roselarge Gdns HNBRY/STHM BS10 ..... 325 J1
Rosemary Cl ALMDB BS32 .... 317 H4
  GLE GL4 .... 136 E7
Rosemary La CHEP NP16 ...... 246 F1
  EVILLE/WHL BS5 .... 336 E1
Rosemary Ter WUE GL12 ...... 277 K5
Rose Md HORF/LLZ BS7 .... 326 C4
Rose Oak Dr
  FRCTL/WBN BS36 .... 318 F4
Rose Oak Gdns
  FRCTL/WBN BS36 .... 318 F4
Rose Oak La FRCTL/WBN BS36 . 318 F4
Rose Rd EVILLE/WHL BS5 ..... 337 G4
Rosery Cl
  HNLZ/SM/SNYPK/WT BS9 .. 325 J3
The Rosery MANG/FISH BS16 .. 327 L8
Roses La CHNTN OX7 .... 83 H7
Rose St CBRIS/FH BS1 .... 7 H6
Roseville Av
  OLD/WMLY/WICK BS30 ..... 348 C1
Rose Wk MANG/FISH BS16 .... 327 L8
Rose Wy CIR GL7 .... 238 E5
Rosewood Av THNB/SVB BS35 . 293 H6
Rosling Rd HORF/LLZ BS7 .... 326 A5
Roslyn Rd RDLND/MONT BS6 . 335 L1
Rossall Av BRSTK/PCHW BS34 . 316 E5
Rossall Rd
  BRSG/KWL/STAPK BS4 ...... 336 F8
Ross Cl YATE/CS BS37 .... 320 D1
Rossiter's La EVILLE/WHL BS5 . 337 J5
Rosslyn Wy THNB/SVB BS35 .. 273 L8
Ross Rd CLFD GL16 .... 151 J4
  MTCHDN GL17 .... 106 C8

NWNT GL18 .... 86 B2
Rothermere Cl
  CHELTW GL51 .... 115 H6
Rothleigh CHELTW GL51 ...... 115 G6
Rougemont Gv CHEP NP16 ... 270 B7
The Roundabouts
  STROUD GL5 .... 233 H2
Round Barrow Cl
  CHPMW/MSHF SN14 .... 343 J8
Roundmoor Cl KEYN BS31 .... 348 F8
Roundmoor Gdns
  HGRV/WHIT BS14 .... 346 F4
Roundways FRCTL/WBN BS36 . 318 E5
Rouses La CIR GL7 .... 221 K6
Rousham Rd EVILLE/WHL BS5 . 326 C8
Rowacres HGRV/WHIT BS14 .. 346 B5
Rowan Cl
  CHPMW/MSHF SN14 .... 343 J6
  MANG/FISH BS16 .... 337 J1
Rowanfield Rd CHELTW GL51 .. 115 J2
Rowan Gdns BWTH/CHD GL3 . 137 M4
Rowan Gv DSLY GL11 .... 229 J8
The Rowans CHELTE/BC GL52 .. 72 D8
  MALM SN16 .... 303 H7
Rowan Wy CHELTW GL51 ..... 115 G6 [10]
  KGWD/HNM BS15 .... 337 K8
Rowberrow HGRV/WHIT BS14 . 346 B4
Rowcroft STROUD GL5 .... 208 D4
Rowcroft Retreat
  STROUD GL5 .... 208 D4
Rowland Av
  MANG/FISH BS16 .... 326 E7
Rowlandson Gdns
  HORF/LLZ BS7 .... 326 D5
Rowley DSLY GL11 .... 229 J6
Rowley St BMSTR BS3 .... 335 L8
Rownham Cl BMSTR BS3 ...... 335 G7
Rownham Hl CFTN/FAIL BS8 .. 335 G5
Rownham Md CFTN/FAIL BS8 . 335 J6
The Row THNB/SVB BS35 ..... 291 J4
Roxton Dr CHELTW GL51 ..... 114 E4
Royal Albert Rd
  RDLND/MONT BS6 .... 325 J7
Royal Cl HNBRY/STHM BS10 .. 314 F8
Royal Crs CHELT GL50 .... 2 C5
Royal Fort Rd CFTN/FAIL BS8 .. 6 D2
Royal Oak Ms CHELT GL50 ..... 2 C3
Royal Oak Rd GL GL1 .... 4 C4
  MTCHDN GL17 .... 128 F6
Royal Parade Ms CHELT GL50 .. 2 B7
Royal Pk CFTN/FAIL BS8 ...... 335 J4
Royal Rd MANG/FISH BS16 ... 328 C5
Royal Spring MTCHDN GL17 .. 131 K2
Royal Well La CHELT GL50 ..... 2 B5
Royal Well Pl CHELT GL50 ..... 2 C5
Royal Well Rd CHELT GL50 .... 2 D5
Royal York Crs
  CFTN/FAIL BS8 .... 335 H5 [11]
Royal York Vls
  CFTN/FAIL BS8 .... 335 J5 [10]
Royate Hl EVILLE/WHL BS5 ... 336 F1
Roycroft Rd
  BRSTK/PCHW BS34 .... 326 D1
Roy Kings Gdns
  OLD/WMLY/WICK BS30 ..... 338 E6
Royston Wk
  HNBRY/STHM BS10 .... 325 M1
Rozel Rd HORF/LLZ BS7 ...... 326 A5
Ruardean Rd MTCHDN GL17 .. 129 C5
Rubens Cl KEYN BS31 .... 348 C6
Ruby St BMSTR BS3 .... 335 K8
Rudford Cl BRSTK/PCHW BS34 . 316 D2
Rudge Cl KGWD/HNM BS15 .. 338 B1
The Rudge VGL GL2 .... 111 K3
Rudgeway Pk THNB/SVB BS35 . 307 C2
Rudgewood Cl
  BMSTRD/HC/WWD BS13 ... 345 M7
Rudhall Gv HNBRY/STHM BS10 . 326 A4
Rudhall Vw RWYE HR9 .... 106 D3
Rudthorpe Rd HORF/LLZ BS7 . 326 A6
Ruffet Cl CLFD GL16 .... 175 K3
Ruffet Rd FRCTL/WBN BS36 .. 318 D7
The Ruffitt CIND GL14 .... 154 D2
Rugby Rd
  BRSG/KWL/STAPK BS4 ...... 336 F8
Rumsey Cl GLE GL4 .... 137 G7
Runnings Rd CHELTW GL51 ... 93 J6
The Runnings CHELTW GL51 .. 93 J5
Runnymead Av
  BRSG/KWL/STAPK BS4 ...... 346 F2
Runnymede CHELTW GL51 .... 115 G6
  KGWD/HNM BS15 .... 338 A2
Runswick Rd
  BRSG/KWL/STAPK BS4 ...... 336 E8
Rupert St CBRIS/FH BS1 ...... 6 F3
  EVILLE/WHL BS5 .... 336 E4
Ruscombe Rd
  RSTROUD/NAIL GL6 .... 208 A2
Rush Cl ALMDB BS32 .... 316 F1
Rushley La COTS GL54 .... 74 D6
Rushmead La
  CHPMW/MSHF SN14 .... 342 A1
Rushton Dr FRCTL/WBN BS36.. 318 F4
Rushworth Cl CHELTW GL51 .. 114 F1
Rushy OLD/WMLY/WICK BS30.. 338 C7
Rushyleaze LYD GL15 .... 225 K1
Rushy Wy MANG/FISH BS16 .. 328 C2
Ruskin Gv HORF/LLZ BS7 ..... 326 C3
Ruspidge Cl GLE GL4 .... 137 G6
Ruspidge Rd CIND GL14 ...... 154 A7
Russell Av KGWD/HNM BS15 . 337 M4
Russell Gv RDLND/MONT BS6 . 325 L6
Russell Pl CHELTW GL51 ...... 2 A2
Russell Rd MANG/FISH BS16 .. 337 K1
  RDLND/MONT BS6 .... 325 K7
Russell St CHELTW GL51 .... 4 F6
  STROUD GL5 .... 208 E4 [10]
Russell Town Av
  EVILLE/WHL BS5 .... 336 D3
Russet Cl GL GL1 .... 135 K8
  LED HR8 .... 19 M5
  TEWK GL20 .... 27 H5
  THNB/SVB BS35 .... 292 C8
Russet Ct WUE GL12 .... 277 H7
Russet Rd CHELTW GL51 ...... 93 H8
Russett Wy NWNT GL18 ...... 86 D3
Russ St CBRISNE BS2 .... 7 J4

Rustic Cl GLE GL4 .... 136 E7
Rutherford Cl
  OLD/WMLY/WICK BS30 ..... 338 C8
Rutherford Wy CHELTW GL51.. 93 J6
Ruthven Rd
  BRSG/KWL/STAPK BS4 ...... 346 A3
Rutland Av
  OLD/WMLY/WICK BS30 ..... 348 C1
Rutland Rd HORF/LLZ BS7 ... 326 A8
Ryalls La VGL GL2 .... 205 G6
Rydal Rd VGL GL2 .... 5 M1
Ryder Cl DSLY GL11 .... 229 J7
Ryde Rd
  BRSG/KWL/STAPK BS4 ...... 346 D1
Rye Av CHELTW GL51 .... 92 F6
Rye Cl BMSTRD/HC/WWD BS13 . 345 G5
Ryeclose COTS GL54 .... 123 J6
Rye Crs COTS GL54 .... 123 K6
Ryecroft Ri LGASH BS41 ...... 344 D2
Ryecroft St GL GL1 .... 5 G9
Ryedown La
  BRSG/KWL/STAPK BS4 ...... 348 E2
Ryelands GL GL1 .... 135 L8
Ryelands Cl STNHO GL10 ..... 207 G3
Ryelands Rd LYD GL15 .... 200 D3
  STNHO GL10 .... 207 G3
The Ryelands
  RSTROUD/NAIL GL6 .... 207 M2
Ryeleaze Cl STROUD GL5 ..... 208 E4
Ryeleaze Rd STROUD GL5 .... 208 E4
Ryeworth Dr CHELTE/BC GL52 . 116 D4
Ryeworth Rd CHELTE/BC GL52 . 116 D4
Ryland Cl TET GL8 .... 282 A2
Ryland Pl CBRISNE BS2 .... 336 C1
Rylestone Cl FRCTL/WBN BS36 . 318 B3
Rylestone Gv
  HNLZ/SM/SNYPK/WT BS9 .. 325 H6
Rysdale Rd
  HNLZ/SM/SNYPK/WT BS9 .. 325 H5

S

Sabre Cl VGL GL2 .... 135 J8
Sabrina Wy
  HNLZ/SM/SNYPK/WT BS9 .. 324 E7
  LYD GL15 .... 201 K7
Saddlers La CHELT GL50 .... 2 A9
Saddlers Rd VGL GL2 .... 159 H1
Sadlers Av SHPSTR CV36 ..... 16 A5
Sadlier Cl AVONM BS11 ...... 324 B3
Saffron Cl GLE GL4 .... 136 C6
Saffron Rd TEWK GL20 .... 48 A5
Sages Md ALMDB BS32 .... 317 G3
St Agnes Av
  BRSG/KWL/STAPK BS4 ...... 346 B1
St Agnes Cl
  BRSG/KWL/STAPK BS4 ...... 346 B1
St Agnes Wk
  BRSG/KWL/STAPK BS4 ...... 346 B1
St Aidans Cl CHELTW GL51 ... 115 G1
  EVILLE/WHL BS5 .... 337 K5
St Aidan's Rd EVILLE/WHL BS5 . 337 J5
St Albans Ct CHELT GL50 ..... 115 J6
St Alban's Rd
  RDLND/MONT BS6 .... 325 K7
  VGL GL2 .... 135 L6
St Aldams Dr MANG/FISH BS16.. 329 K6
St Aldate St GL GL1 .... 4 F5
St Aldhelms Rd MALM SN16 .. 303 H7
St Aldwyn Rd GL GL1 .... 136 D5
St Aldwyn's Cl HORF/LLZ BS7 . 326 B5
St Andrews
  OLD/WMLY/WICK BS30 ..... 338 D5
  RTEWK/TIB GL19 .... 89 J3
  YATE/CS BS37 .... 320 B2
St Andrew's Av CHEP NP16 ... 270 A4
St Andrews Ct TEWK GL20 .... 49 H4
St Andrew's Rd
  RDLND/MONT BS6 .... 336 B1 [11]
  RDLND/MONT BS6 .... 336 A1
St Annal's Rd CIND GL14 ..... 154 B3
St Anne's Av KEYN BS31 ...... 347 M5
St Annes Cl BWTH/CHD GL3 .. 137 M5
  CHELTE/BC GL52 .... 3 G4
  OLD/WMLY/WICK BS30 ..... 338 D7
St Anne's Dr FRCTL/WBN BS36 . 318 E6
  OLD/WMLY/WICK BS30 ..... 339 K4
  OLD/WMLY/WICK BS30 ..... 348 E1
St Anne's Park Rd
  BRSG/KWL/STAPK BS4 ...... 337 G6
St Anne's Rd
  BRSG/KWL/STAPK BS4 ...... 337 G6
  CHELTE/BC GL52 .... 2 F5
  EVILLE/WHL BS5 .... 337 K5
St Anne's Ter
  BRSG/KWL/STAPK BS4 ...... 337 G6
  CHELTE/BC GL52 .... 2 F5
St Annes Wy LYD GL15 .... 198 F6
St Ann St CHEP NP16 .... 270 B2
St Ann Wy GL GL1 .... 4 C8
St Arild's Rd BAD GL9 .... 299 K7
St Aubin's Av
  BRSG/KWL/STAPK BS4 ...... 347 H5
St Augustine's Pde CBRIS/FH BS1 . 6 E4
St Augustine's Pl CBRIS/FH BS1 .. 6 E4
St Barbara's Cl TEWK GL20 ... 49 J4
St Barnabas Cl GLE GL4 ...... 136 A7
  OLD/WMLY/WICK BS30 ..... 338 E4
St Bartholomews NWNT GL18 . 86 C3
St Bartholomews Cl
  DSLY GL11 .... 229 H6
St Bartholomew's Rd
  HORF/LLZ BS7 .... 326 C5
St Bede's Rd KGWD/HNM BS15 . 337 L1
St Bernard's Rd AVONM BS11 . 324 A5
St Brelades Gv
  BRSG/KWL/STAPK BS4 ...... 337 G6
St Brendan's Rd STROUD GL5 . 209 G4
St Briavels Dr YATE/CS BS37 .. 319 M3
St Briavels Rd LYD GL15 ...... 223 K8
Saintbridge Cl GLE GL4 .... 136 E6
Saintbridge Pl GLE GL4 .... 136 E6
St Bruel's Cl LYD GL15 .... 199 G6
St Catherine St GL GL1 .... 4 E3
St Clements Ct KEYN BS31 ... 348 A7

St Clements Rd KEYN BS31 ... 348
St Cloes Pitch STROUD GL5 ... 232
St Cyril's Rd STNHO GL10 207
St David's Av
  OLD/WMLY/WICK BS30 338
St Davids Cl CHELTW GL51 ... 115
  CHEP NP16 270
  GL GL1 135
St David's Crs
  BRSG/KWL/STAPK BS4 337
  DSLY GL11 253
St Davids Rd TEWK GL20 49
  THNB/SVB BS35 293
St Dennis La MALM SN16 303
St Dunstan's Rd BMSTR BS3 .. 345
St Edwards Ct MIM GL56 58
St Edwards Dr COTS GL54 102
St Edward's Rd CFTN/FAIL BS8 . 6 A
  EVILLE/WHL BS5 ....
St Edwards Wk CHELTS GL53 . 116
St Edyth's Rd
  HNLZ/SM/SNYPK/WT BS9 .. 324
St Ewens Rd CHEP NP16 270
St Fagans Ct
  OLD/WMLY/WICK BS30 348
St Francis Dr FRCTL/WBN BS36 . 318
St Francis Rd BMSTR BS3 335
  KEYN BS31 347
St Gabriel's Rd
  EVILLE/WHL BS5 336
St George St CHEP NP16 270
St Georges Av
  EVILLE/WHL BS5 .... 337 H5
  STNHO GL10 207
St George's Cl CHELTW GL51 .. 115 K
  DSLY GL11 229
  GL GL1 135
  MIM GL56 58
  STNHO GL10 207
St George's Dr CHELTW GL51 . 115
St Georges Rd BWTH/CHD GL3 . 137
  CBRIS/FH BS1 6
  CHELT GL50 115
  CHELTW GL51 115
  DSLY GL11 229
  KEYN BS31 347
  TEWK GL20 49
St George's St CHELT GL50 2
St Georges Wy CHEP NP16 ... 270
St Giles Barton WUE GL12 .... 297 M
St Gregory's Rd HORF/LLZ BS7 . 326
St Gregory's Wk
  HORF/LLZ BS7 326
St Helena Rd
  RDLND/MONT BS6 325
St Helens Dr
  OLD/WMLY/WICK BS30 339
  OLD/WMLY/WICK BS30 348
St Helen's Wk EVILLE/WHL BS5 . 337
St Helier Av
  BRSG/KWL/STAPK BS4 337
St Hilary Cl
  HNLZ/SM/SNYPK/WT BS9 .. 324
St Ivel Wy
  OLD/WMLY/WICK BS30 338
St James' VGL GL2 159
St James Cl VGL GL2 159
St James Ct MIM GL56 .... 58 C
St James Pk CLFD GL16 175
St James' Pl CHELT GL50 2
St James' Sq CHELT GL50 2
St James St MANG/FISH BS16 . 328
St James St CHELTE/BC GL52 .. 2
  GL GL1 4
St Johns Av BWTH/CHD GL3 .. 113
  CHELTE/BC GL52 2
St John's Br CBRIS/FH BS1 6
St John's Cl CHELTE/BC GL52 .. 72 B
  CIR GL7 214
  SHPSTR CV36 16
St Johns Ct KEYN BS31 348
St John's Crs BMSTR BS3 335
St John's La BMSTR BS3 335
  BMSTR BS3 345
  GL GL1 4
St John's Rd BMSTR BS3 6
  BMSTR BS3 .... 335 L
  CFTN/FAIL BS8 335
  CIR GL7 238
  MTCHDN GL17 129
  SHPSTR CV36 39
  VGL GL2 135
St Johns Sq CIND GL14 154
St John's St BMSTR BS3 .... 335 L8
  CIR GL7 244
  CLFD GL16 .... 175 J
  MALM SN16 303
St John St BAD GL9 299
  THNB/SVB BS35 293
St Johns Wy YATE/CS BS37 ... 320
St Joseph's Rd
  HNBRY/STHM BS10 315
St Judes Wk CHELTS GL53 116
St Keyna Rd KEYN BS31 348
St Kilda Pde GL GL1 5
St Ladoc Rd KEYN BS31 347
St Laud Cl
  HNLZ/SM/SNYPK/WT BS9 .. 324
St Lawrence Cl CIR GL7 238
  VGL GL2 90
St Lawrence Rd CIR GL7 244
  GLE GL4 136
St Leonard's MALM SN16 285
St Leonards Cl GLE GL4 161
St Leonard's Rd
  EVILLE/WHL BS5 .... 336 E1
  HORF/LLZ BS7 326
St Lucia Cl HORF/LLZ BS7 326
St Lucia Crs HORF/LLZ BS7 ... 326
St Luke's Crs BMSTR BS3 336
St Luke's Gdns
  BRSG/KWL/STAPK BS4 347
St Luke's Pl CHELTS GL53 2
St Luke's Rd BMSTR BS3 7
  CHELT GL50 2
St Lukes St GL GL1 4
St Luke's Vw EVILLE/WHL BS5 . 336 D4
St Margaret's Cl KEYN BS31 .. 347 M5

Margaret's Dr
HNLZ/SM/SNYPK/WT BS9 ... **325** L6 🟦
TEWK GL20 ... **51** K4
Margaret's Rd *CHELT* GL50 ... **2** D3
GLE GL7 ... **137** H3 🟦
MTCHDN GL17 ... **129** C3
TEWK GL20 ... **51** L4
Marks Cl *KEYN* BS31 ... **348** A5 🟦
Mark's Rd *EVILLE/WHL* BS5 ... **336** D2 🟦
Mark's Ter
EVILLE/WHL BS5 ... **336** D2 🔟
Mark St *GL* GL1 ... **4** F2
Martin's Gdns
BRSG/KWL/STAPK BS4 ... **346** D2 🟦
Martin's La
CHPMW/MSHF SN14 ... **342** B3
Martin's Pk
CHPMW/MSHF SN14 ... **342** B3 🟦
Martin's Rd
BRSG/KWL/STAPK BS4 ... **346** D1
Martin's Wk
BRSG/KWL/STAPK BS4 ... **346** D2 🟦
Marys Cl *CIR* GL7 ... **267** C5
COTS GL54 ... **101** J3
Marys Dr *CIR* GL7 ... **242** F4
Mary's HI *STROUD* GL5 ... **232** C5
Marys La *MALM* SN16 ... **303** J7 🟦
TEWK GL20 ... **48** A5
Mary's Rd *CFTN/FAIL* BS8 ... **334** F5 🟦
CIR GL7 ... **238** C3
TET GL8 ... **281** M3
TEWK GL20 ... **47** M5
Mary's Sq *GL* GL1 ... **4** D4
LYD GL15 ... **201** L8
Mary's St *GL* GL1 ... **4** E4
MALM SN16 ... **303** J8 🟦
RSTROUD/NAIL GL6 ... **185** H3 🟦
Mary St *CHEP* NP16 ... **270** A3
THNB/SVB BS35 ... **293** K3 🟦
Mary's Wy *YATE/CS* BS37 ... **320** B1
Matthew's Av
RDLND/MONT BS6 ... **335** M2 🟦
Matthew's Rd
RDLND/MONT BS6 ... **335** M3
Matthias Pk *CBRISNE* BS2 ... **7** J2
Michael's Cl
FRCTL/WBN BS36 ... **318** A4
MTCHDN GL17 ... **130** C1
Michaels Ct
KGWD/HNM BS15 ... **337** K3 🟦
Michael's HI *CBRISNE* BS2 ... **335** L3
Michael's Pk *CFTN/FAIL* BS8 ... **6** C1
Michael's PI *STROUD* GL5 ... **207** M3 🟦
Michael's Rd *CHELT* GL50 ... **115** K6
CIR GL7 ... **238** C4 🟦
Michael's Sq *GL* GL1 ... **4** E7
Nicholas Cl *TEWK* GL20 ... **50** C5
Nicholas Dr *CHELT* GL50 ... **93** M6
Nicholas Pk
EVILLE/WHL BS5 ... **336** D2 🟦
Nicholas' Rd *CBRISNE* BS2 ... **336** B2
HGRV/WHIT BS14 ... **346** E7
Nicholas St *CBRIS/FH* BS1 ... **6** F4 🟦
Oswald's Rd *GL* GL1 ... **4** E1
RDLND/MONT BS6 ... **325** K8
Patricks Rd *TEWK* GL20 ... **49** H4
Pauls Ct *MIM* GL56 ... **58** C7 🟦
Paul's La *CHELT* GL50 ... **2** C3
Paul's Pde *CHELT* GL50 ... **2** D3
Paul's Rd *BMSTR* BS3 ... **6** E8
CFTN/FAIL BS8 ... **6** A2
CHELT GL50 ... **2** C3
GL GL1 ... **4** E9
Paul's St North *CHELT* GL50 ... **2** C3
Paul's St South *CHELT* GL50 ... **2** C3
Paul St *CBRISNE* BS2 ... **7** H1
Peters Cl *CHELTW* GL51 ... **93** J8
CIND GL14 ... **155** J7 🟦
CIR GL7 ... **259** L2
Peters Ct *MIM* GL56 ... **58** C7 🟦
Peter's Crs *FRCTL/WBN* BS36 ... **318** D4
Peter's Ri
BMSTRD/HC/WWD BS13 ... **345** J4
Peters Rd *CIR* GL7 ... **238** C3
GLE GL7 ... **136** E8
Peter's Sq *CHELTW* GL51 ... **93** J7 🟦
Peter's Wk
HNLZ/SM/SNYPK/WT BS9 ... **325** K6
Peters Wy *COTS* GL54 ... **74** C5
Philips Cswy
BRSG/KWL/STAPK BS4 ... **336** E7
CBRISNE BS2 ... **336** D5
Philip's Cl *BWTH/CHD* GL3 ... **137** J3 🟦
Philips Rd *CBRISNE* BS2 ... **7** K3
Phillips Rd *CBRISNE* BS2 ... **7** L3
Phillip's St *CHELT* GL50 ... **115** L4
Pierre Dr
OLD/WMLY/WICK BS30 ... **338** D5 🟦
Ronan's Av
RDLND/MONT BS6 ... **335** L2
Saviours Ri *FRCTL/WBN* BS36 ... **318** D5
Silas St *CBRISNE* BS2 ... **7** M6
Stephen's Av *CBRIS/FH* BS1 ... **6** E4 🟦
Stephens Cl *CHELT* GL50 ... **115** K4
KGWD/HNM BS15 ... **328** A8 🟦
Stephen's Rd *CHELT* GL50 ... **115** K4
MANG/FISH BS16 ... **327** M8
Stephen's St *CBRIS/FH* BS1 ... **6** E4
Swithins Rd *LYD* GL15 ... **201** L1
Swithuns Rd *GL* GL1 ... **135** J5
Tecla Rd *CHEP* NP16 ... **270** A5
Tewdric Rd *CHEP* NP16 ... **270** A4
Thomas St *CBRIS/FH* BS1 ... **7** G5
Vincent's HI
RDLND/MONT BS6 ... **335** J1 🟦
Vincent's Rd
CFTN/FAIL BS8 ... **335** J5 🟦
Vincent Wy
BWTH/CHD GL3 ... **113** J3 🟦
Werburgh's Pk
CBRISNE BS2 ... **336** C1
Werburgh's Rd
CBRISNE BS2 ... **336** B1 🟦
Whites Rd *CIND* GL14 ... **154** A5
Whytes Rd
BRSG/KWL/STAPK BS4 ... **345** M3

Salamanca Rd *CHELTE/BC* GL52 ... **3** M3
Salcombe Rd
BRSG/KWL/STAPK BS4 ... **346** C3
Salem Rd *FRCTL/WBN* BS36 ... **318** B4
Salisbury Av *CHELTW* GL51 ... **115** J6
KGWD/HNM BS15 ... **337** K3
Salisbury Gdns
MANG/FISH BS16 ... **328** A6
Salisbury Rd
BRSG/KWL/STAPK BS4 ... **336** F6
MANG/FISH BS16 ... **328** A5
RDLND/MONT BS6 ... **335** M1
Salisbury St *EVILLE/WHL* BS5 ... **336** D5
Salix Ct *CHELTW* GL51 ... **115** H7
Sallis Cl *TEWK* GL20 ... **48** F1
Sallybarn Cl
OLD/WMLY/WICK BS30 ... **348** A1
Sallysmead Cl
BMSTRD/HC/WWD BS13 ... **345** K7 🟦
Sallys Wy *FRCTL/WBN* BS36 ... **318** B4
Salmons Wy *MANG/FISH* BS16 ... **328** C3
Salter's La *COTS* GL54 ... **75** H5
Salter St *BRKLY* GL13 ... **227** G8
Salthrop Rd *HORF/LLZ* BS7 ... **326** A1
Saltmarsh Dr *AVONM* BS11 ... **324** C2
Salt Wy *CIR* GL7 ... **218** B2
Saltwell Av *HGRV/WHIT* BS14 ... **346** E6
Samian Wy *BRSTK/PCHW* BS34 ... **317** G6
Sampsons Rd
BMSTRD/HC/WWD BS13 ... **345** L7
Samuel St *EVILLE/WHL* BS5 ... **336** E3 🟦
Samuel White Rd
KGWD/HNM BS15 ... **337** L8
Samuel Wright Cl
OLD/WMLY/WICK BS30 ... **348** F8
Sanatorium Rd *GLE* GL4 ... **161** L4 🟦
Sandalwood Dr *VGL* GL2 ... **135** K4
Sandbach Rd
BRSG/KWL/STAPK BS4 ... **336** F5
Sandbed Rd *CBRISNE* BS2 ... **336** C1
Sandburrows Rd
BMSTRD/HC/WWD BS13 ... **345** G5
Sandburrows Wk
BMSTRD/HC/WWD BS13 ... **345** H5 🟦
Sandcroft *HGRV/WHIT* BS14 ... **346** B5
Sandfield *EVE* WR11 ... **30** A1
Sandfield La *EVE* WR11 ... **30** A1
Sandfield Rd *BWTH/CHD* GL3 ... **113** M6
The Sandfield *TEWK* GL20 ... **49** G2
Sandford Leaze *TET* GL8 ... **257** L2
Sandford Mill Cl *CHELTS* GL53 ... **3** G9 🟦
Sandford Mill Rd *CHELTS* GL53 ... **3** G9 🟦
Sandford St *CFTN/FAIL* BS8 ... **335** J6 🟦
CHELTS GL53 ... **2** E9
LYD GL15 ... **224** D3
Sandford St *CHELT* GL50 ... **2** D7
Sandford Wy *GL* GL1 ... **159** K1
Sandgate Rd
BRSG/KWL/STAPK BS4 ... **336** F6
Sand HI *BRSG/KWL/STAPK* BS4 ... **336** E7
Sandholme Cl
MANG/FISH BS16 ... **328** A3 🟦
Sandholme Rd
BRSG/KWL/STAPK BS4 ... **336** E7
Sandhurst Cl
BRSTK/PCHW BS34 ... **316** D2
Sandhurst La *VGL* GL2 ... **90** B8
VGL GL2 ... **111** M5
Sandhurst Rd
BRSG/KWL/STAPK BS4 ... **336** F7 🟦
CHELTE/BC GL52 ... **116** D5
GL GL1 ... **4** F1
Sandling Av *HORF/LLZ* BS7 ... **326** C4
Sandown Cl *MANG/FISH* BS16 ... **328** B2
Sandown Rd
BRSG/KWL/STAPK BS4 ... **336** F7
BRSTK/PCHW BS34 ... **316** E8 🟦
CHELTE/BC GL52 ... **72** B7
Sandpiper Cl *VGL* GL2 ... **158** F2 🟦
Sandpits La *BAD* GL9 ... **312** B2
RSTROUD/NAIL GL6 ... **207** L3
Sandpool La *CIR* GL7 ... **236** A8
Sandringham Av *GL* GL1 ... **159** L2
MANG/FISH BS16 ... **328** A3
Sandringham Pk
MANG/FISH BS16 ... **328** A3 🟦
Sandringham Rd
BRSG/KWL/STAPK BS4 ... **336** F8
BRSTK/PCHW BS34 ... **316** F7
Sands Cl *BDWAY* WR12 ... **32** F2
Sands Croft *BDWAY* WR12 ... **33** G2
Sands HI *CHPMW/MSHF* SN14 ... **331** G8
Sands La *EVE* WR11 ... **10** A1
Sandstar Cl *VGL* GL2 ... **112** F6 🟦
Sandstone Ri *FRCTL/WBN* BS36 ... **317** M7
Sandtumps *LYD* GL15 ... **223** L5
Sandwich Rd
BRSG/KWL/STAPK BS4 ... **336** F7 🟦
Sandy Cl *ALMDB* BS32 ... **317** G5
Sandycroft *BWTH/CHD* GL3 ... **113** J4
Sandy La *CHELTS* GL53 ... **116** B7
COTS GL54 ... **124** B7
EVILLE/WHL BS5 ... **326** E6
LYD GL15 ... **198** B8
THNB/SVB BS35 ... **291** J4
Sandy Lane Rd *CHELTS* GL53 ... **116** B6 🟦
Sandyleaze
HNLZ/SM/SNYPK/WT BS9 ... **325** G4
VGL GL2 ... **112** F8
Sandy Ldg *YATE/CS* BS37 ... **320** A3
Sandy Park Rd
BRSG/KWL/STAPK BS4 ... **336** F2
Sandy Pluck La *CHELTW* GL51 ... **138** D3
Sandyway La *RWYE* HR9 ... **126** C5
Saniger La *BRKLY* GL13 ... **226** E4
Sankey Gv *MIM* GL56 ... **58** D7
Sapperton La *CHELTS* GL53 ... **116** C8
Sapperton Rd *GLE* GL4 ... **136** B6
Sapphire Cl *GL* GL1 ... **159** K1
Sarah St *EVILLE/WHL* BS5 ... **336** D4
Sargent's La *RWYE* HR9 ... **84** F1
Sargent St *BMSTR* BS3 ... **7** G8
Sarnedy Rd *CLFD* GL16 ... **175** K1
Sarum Crs *HNBRY/STHM* BS10 ... **325** L2
Sassoon Ct
OLD/WMLY/WICK BS30 ... **338** B6 🟦

Satchfield Cl
HNBRY/STHM BS10 ... **325** H1
Satchfield Crs
HNBRY/STHM BS10 ... **325** H1
Sates Wy
HNLZ/SM/SNYPK/WT BS9 ... **325** L5
Saturn Cl *GLE* GL4 ... **137** H5
Saunders Cl *MTCHDN* GL17 ... **107** K6
RWYE HR9 ... **106** C3 🟦
Saunders Rd *MANG/FISH* BS16 ... **328** A7 🟦
Saunton Rd
BRSG/KWL/STAPK BS4 ... **346** A3 🟦
Savage HI *CLFD* GL16 ... **174** E4
Savages Wood Rd *ALMDB* BS32 ... **316** F3
Savernake Rd *GLE* GL4 ... **136** C4
Saville Cl *CHELT* GL50 ... **94** A7
Saville Gate Cl
HNLZ/SM/SNYPK/WT BS9 ... **325** H7 🟦
Saville PI *CFTN/FAIL* BS8 ... **335** J5 🟦🟦
Saville Rd
HNLZ/SM/SNYPK/WT BS9 ... **325** H8
Savoy Rd
BRSG/KWL/STAPK BS4 ... **336** F7
Saw Mill La *THNB/SVB* BS35 ... **293** K2 🟦
Sawpit La *RTEWK/TIB* GL19 ... **69** G6
Sawpits La *MIM* GL56 ... **103** J2
Sawpitts La *RWYE* HR9 ... **126** D5
Sawyers Ri *RTEWK/TIB* GL19 ... **89** J3 🟦
Saxon Cl *HGHW* SN6 ... **188** F4
VGL GL2 ... **112** E6 🔟
Saxon PI *CHEP* NP16 ... **270** C4
Saxon Rd *CBRISNE* BS2 ... **336** C1
CIR GL7 ... **238** E2
Saxon Wy *ALMDB* BS32 ... **316** E2
CHELTE/BC GL52 ... **3** J7
LED HR8 ... **19** L1
Sayers Crs *BWTH/CHD* GL3 ... **138** A6 🟦
Saylittle Ms *VGL* GL2 ... **113** G6 🟦
Say Wk *OLD/WMLY/WICK* BS30 ... **338** F4
Scandrett Cl
HNBRY/STHM BS10 ... **315** G8 🟦
Scantleberry Cl
MANG/FISH BS16 ... **327** M3 🟦
Scar HI *RSTROUD/NAIL* GL6 ... **232** F6
Scarr Rd *NWNT* GL18 ... **64** C5
School Cl *BRSTK/PCHW* BS34 ... **316** E3
CLFD GL16 ... **175** M1
DSLY GL11 ... **229** G7
EVILLE/WHL BS5 ... **336** F1
HGRV/WHIT BS14 ... **346** B7
SHPSTR CV36 ... **61** H5
School Crs *LYD* GL15 ... **201** K6
School HI *CHEP* NP16 ... **270** A3
RTEWK/TIB GL19 ... **66** E5
Schooler's La *MIM* GL56 ... **81** L8
School La *BAD* GL9 ... **323** G1
CBATH/BATHN BA1 ... **352** B2
CHELTE/BC GL52 ... **94** E3
CHELTW GL51 ... **139** G1
CIR GL7 ... **238** D4
CIR GL7 ... **240** A3
CIR GL7 ... **241** K7
CIR GL7 ... **263** L4
COTS GL54 ... **142** F1
HGHW SN6 ... **266** D7
MIM GL56 ... **57** G1
MTCHDN GL17 ... **107** G7
MTCHDN GL17 ... **128** F4
MTCHDN GL17 ... **128** C8
RSTROUD/NAIL GL6 ... **211** M2
TEWK GL20 ... **28** B4
VGL GL2 ... **158** F3
VGL GL2 ... **159** G3
VGL GL2 ... **182** A6
School Md *CHELTW* GL51 ... **115** J1
School Ms *GLE* GL4 ... **136** D7 🟦
School Rd *BDWAY* WR12 ... **31** G2
BRSG/KWL/STAPK BS4 ... **336** C8
BRSG/KWL/STAPK BS4 ... **347** G1
CHELTE/BC GL52 ... **72** C7
CHELTS GL53 ... **116** D5
CIR GL7 ... **261** H4
DSLY GL11 ... **253** L3
FRCTL/WBN BS36 ... **318** B3
KGWD/HNM BS15 ... **337** L3
LYD GL15 ... **201** H2
MTCHDN GL17 ... **128** C5 🟦
MTCHDN GL17 ... **129** C3
OLD/WMLY/WICK BS30 ... **338** F4
RSTROUD/NAIL GL6 ... **233** J5
RTEWK/TIB GL19 ... **68** F7
STRAT CV37 ... **8** A1
TEWK GL20 ... **51** L4
WUE GL12 ... **277** K4
School Wk *YATE/CS* BS37 ... **320** A1
School Wy *THNB/SVB* BS35 ... **304** C5 🟦
The Scop *ALMDB* BS32 ... **306** C6
Scott Av *VGL* GL2 ... **135** L7
Scott Ct
OLD/WMLY/WICK BS30 ... **338** B6 🟦
Scott Lawrence Cl
MANG/FISH BS16 ... **327** J4 🟦
Scott Wk
OLD/WMLY/WICK BS30 ... **338** F4
Scott Wy *YATE/CS* BS37 ... **320** B3
Scowles Rd *CLFD* GL16 ... **175** G1
Scrubbett's La *TET* GL8 ... **279** H2
Seabright Cl *CHELTW* GL51 ... **93** G6 🟦
Seabroke Rd *GL* GL1 ... **5** H2
Seabrook Rd *BWTH/CHD* GL3 ... **137** M6
Seacome Rd *CHELTW* GL51 ... **115** G1 🟦
Seagry Cl *HNBRY/STHM* BS10 ... **326** A2
Sea Mills La
HNLZ/SM/SNYPK/WT BS9 ... **324** E7
Searle Court Av
BRSG/KWL/STAPK BS4 ... **337** G6
Seaton Rd *EVILLE/WHL* BS5 ... **336** E2 🟦
Seawalls Rd
HNLZ/SM/SNYPK/WT BS9 ... **334** F1 🟦
Sebert St *GL* GL1 ... **5** G2
Second Av *DSLY* GL11 ... **253** L3
Secret La *GL* GL1 ... **4** F3 🟦
Sedbury La *CHEP* NP16 ... **270** C2
Seddon Rd *CBRISNE* BS2 ... **336** C1 🟦🟦
Sedgefield Gdns
MANG/FISH BS16 ... **328** B2 🟦

Sedgewick Gdns *CHELTW* GL51 ... **114** F5
Sedgley Cl *GL* GL1 ... **159** L1
Sedgley Rd *CHELTE/BC* GL52 ... **72** B7
Sefton Park Rd *HORF/LLZ* BS7 ... **326** B8
Sefton Wk *CHELTW* GL51 ... **114** F5
Selborne Rd *CHELTE/BC* GL52 ... **72** B7
HORF/LLZ BS7 ... **326** B6
Selbrooke Crs *MANG/FISH* BS16 ... **327** L5
Selby Rd *EVILLE/WHL* BS5 ... **337** H2
Selden Rd *HGRV/WHIT* BS14 ... **347** G6
Selkirk Cl *KGWD/HNM* BS15 ... **337** L1
Selkirk Gdns *CHELTE/BC* GL52 ... **3** G3
Selkirk St *CHELTE/BC* GL52 ... **2** F3
Sellars Rd *GLE* GL4 ... **158** F4
Selley Wk
BMSTRD/HC/WWD BS13 ... **345** L4
Selsey Rd *STROUD* GL5 ... **232** A1
Selsley HI *STROUD* GL5 ... **208** A6
Selworthy *CHELTW* GL50 ... **115** G6 🟦
KGWD/HNM BS15 ... **338** A4
Selworthy Cl *KEYN* BS31 ... **347** M6
Selworthy Rd
BRSG/KWL/STAPK BS4 ... **346** D1
Selwyn Cl *STNHO* GL10 ... **207** J6
Selwyn Rd *GLE* GL4 ... **136** B6
Seneca PI *EVILLE/WHL* BS5 ... **336** F4 🟦
Seneca St *EVILLE/WHL* BS5 ... **336** F4
Seneca Wy *CHELTW* GL51 ... **93** K6
Serlo Rd *GL* GL1 ... **4** E3
Sevelm *CHELTW* GL51 ... **115** G6 🟦
Seven Acres *GLE* GL4 ... **136** F4
Seven Acres La
CBATH/BATHN BA1 ... **352** B6
Sevenacres Rd
RSTROUD/NAIL GL6 ... **232** C7
Sevenleaze La
RSTROUD/NAIL GL6 ... **160** F5
RSTROUD/NAIL GL6 ... **184** D1
Seven Stars Rd *CIND* GL14 ... **154** A1
Seventh Av *GLE* GL4 ... **159** M1
HORF/LLZ BS7 ... **326** D2 🟦
Seven View Rd *THNB/SVB* BS35 ... **293** L1
Severn Av *CHEP* NP16 ... **270** C2
Severnbank Av *LYD* GL15 ... **201** L8
Severn Br *THNB/SVB* BS35 ... **291** G3
Severn Cl *WUE* GL12 ... **276** C7 🟦
Severn Crs *CHEP* NP16 ... **270** A4
Severn Dr *BRKLY* GL13 ... **227** G7
THNB/SVB BS35 ... **293** K1
Severn La *BRKLY* GL13 ... **250** A2
Severn Oaks *GLE* GL4 ... **159** H4
Severn St *CIND* GL14 ... **155** J7
Severnvale Dr *VGL* GL2 ... **159** G2
Severn Vw *CIND* GL14 ... **154** C2
Severn View Rd *LYD* GL15 ... **177** L8
LYD GL15 ... **223** M5
Severn Wy *BRKLY* GL13 ... **203** L6
BRKLY GL13 ... **226** C6
BRSTK/PCHW BS34 ... **316** B2
GL GL1 ... **4** B3
KEYN BS31 ... **348** C3
RTEWK/TIB GL19 ... **69** G4
THNB/SVB BS35 ... **291** G4
THNB/SVB BS35 ... **304** B5
VGL GL2 ... **135** H4
VGL GL2 ... **179** K2
Severnwood Gdns
THNB/SVB BS35 ... **304** C6
Sevier St *CBRISNE* BS2 ... **336** C1
Seymour Av *HORF/LLZ* BS7 ... **326** A7 🟦
Seymour Ga *CHCAM* GL55 ... **12** E8 🟦
Seymour PI *COTS* GL54 ... **74** C6
TEWK GL20 ... **48** A6
Seymour Rd *EVILLE/WHL* BS5 ... **336** C2
GL GL1 ... **135** M5
HORF/LLZ BS7 ... **326** A7 🟦
KGWD/HNM BS15 ... **337** L2 🟦
MANG/FISH BS16 ... **327** M7
Seyton Wk *BRSTK/PCHW* BS34 ... **317** G6
Sezincote Cl
RSTROUD/NAIL GL6 ... **209** M6 🟦
Shackel Hendy Ms
MANG/FISH BS16 ... **328** D6 🟦
Shackleton Av *YATE/CS* BS37 ... **320** B3
Shackleton Cl *BWTH/CHD* GL3 ... **113** M4
Shadwell Rd *HORF/LLZ* BS7 ... **325** M8
Shaftesbury Av
RDLND/MONT BS6 ... **336** A2
Shaft Rd *THNB/SVB* BS35 ... **304** C3
Shakespeare Av *HORF/LLZ* BS7 ... **326** C3
VGL GL2 ... **135** L7
Shakespeare Ct *TEWK* GL20 ... **48** A5 🟦
Shakespeare Rd *CHELTW* GL51 ... **115** G2
DSLY GL11 ... **253** L4
Shaldon Rd *HORF/LLZ* BS7 ... **326** C1
Shalford Cl *CIR* GL7 ... **238** B4 🟦
The Shallows *KEYN* BS31 ... **349** H8
The Shambles *STROUD* GL5 ... **208** E4 🟦
Shamrock Cl *BWTH/CHD* GL3 ... **113** M5
Shamrock Rd
EVILLE/WHL BS5 ... **326** F8 🟦
Shanklin Dr
BRSTK/PCHW BS34 ... **316** D8 🟦
Shannon Ct *THNB/SVB* BS35 ... **293** M3 🟦
Shannon Wy *TEWK* GL20 ... **48** E4
Shapcott Cl
BRSG/KWL/STAPK BS4 ... **346** D2 🟦
Shaplands
HNLZ/SM/SNYPK/WT BS9 ... **325** H7
Sharps Wy *CHEP* NP16 ... **270** B6 🟦
Sharry La *STRAT* CV37 ... **9** G1
Shaw Green La *CHELTE/BC* GL52 ... **94** D6
Shaymoor La *THNB/SVB* BS35 ... **305** H7
Shearmore Cl *HORF/LLZ* BS7 ... **326** C4 🟦
Shearwater Gv *VGL* GL2 ... **112** F5 🟦
Sheene La *BMSTR* BS3 ... **335** L8
Sheep Fair La
CHPMW/MSHF SN14 ... **342** B4

Sheepscombe Cl
CHELTW GL51 ... **115** G3 🟦
Sheeps Cft
BMSTRD/HC/WWD BS13 ... **345** J2 🟦
Sheep St *BUR/CRTN* OX18 ... **173** M6
CHCAM GL55 ... **34** D1
CIR GL7 ... **258** C3
COTS GL54 ... **102** A3
SHPSTR CV36 ... **16** B5
Sheepwood Rd
HNBRY/STHM BS10 ... **325** J2
Sheepwood Rd
HNBRY/STHM BS10 ... **325** J1
Sheevaun Cl *VGL* GL2 ... **112** F6 🟦
Shelburne Rd *CHELTW* GL51 ... **115** H4
Sheldare Barton
EVILLE/WHL BS5 ... **337** K4 🟦
Sheldrake Dr *MANG/FISH* BS16 ... **327** H5 🟦
Shelduck Rd *GL* GL2 ... **158** E2
Shellard Rd *BRSTK/PCHW* BS34 ... **316** C6
Shellards La *THNB/SVB* BS35 ... **293** L2
THNB/SVB BS35 ... **308** B1
Shellards Rd
OLD/WMLY/WICK BS30 ... **338** B8
Shelley Av *CHELTW* GL51 ... **115** G2
VGL GL2 ... **135** L7
Shelley Cl *EVILLE/WHL* BS5 ... **337** H3
Shelley Rd *CHELTW* GL51 ... **115** G2
Shelley Wy *HORF/LLZ* BS7 ... **326** C3
Shellmor Av *BRSTK/PCHW* BS34 ... **316** D2
Shellmor Cl *ALMDB* BS32 ... **316** F2 🟦
BRSTK/PCHW BS34 ... **316** E2
Shelly Rd *DSLY* GL11 ... **253** L4
Shephard Md *TEWK* GL20 ... **47** M6
Shepherdine Cl *LYD* GL15 ... **201** L8
Shepherd Rd *GL* GL1 ... **135** K8
Shepherd's Cl *CHCAM* GL55 ... **34** D1
LED HR8 ... **19** M5
MANG/FISH BS16 ... **328** A6
STROUD GL5 ... **208** F3 🟦
Shepherds Cft *STROUD* GL5 ... **208** F3
Shepherd's Leaze *WUE* GL12 ... **277** L5 🟦
Shepherds Md *TET* GL8 ... **282** A2
Shepherds Wk *WUE* GL12 ... **277** L5 🟦
Shepherds Wy *BWTH/CHD* GL3 ... **113** H4
CIR GL7 ... **258** C1
COTS GL54 ... **102** B3
COTS GL54 ... **169** H1
Shepherds Well *STROUD* GL5 ... **232** F2 🟦
Sheppard Rd *MANG/FISH* BS16 ... **327** L5
Sheppard Wy
RSTROUD/NAIL GL6 ... **233** G4
Shepperdine Rd
THNB/SVB BS35 ... **248** F7
Shepton Wk *BMSTR* BS3 ... **345** L1
Sherborne Cl *STNHO* GL10 ... **207** H3
Sherborne La *COTS* GL54 ... **148** B5
Sherborne PI *CHELTE/BC* GL52 ... **2** F5
Sherborne St *CHELTE/BC* GL52 ... **2** F4
CIR GL7 ... **244** E7
COTS GL54 ... **123** H5
GL GL1 ... **5** G4
Sherbourne Av *ALMDB* BS32 ... **317** G5
Sherbourne Cl
KGWD/HNM BS15 ... **338** B1
Sherbourne Ct *STNHO* GL10 ... **207** H3 🟦🟦
Sherbourne La *EVILLE/WHL* BS5 ... **337** G3
Shergar Cl *GLE* GL4 ... **136** F7
Sheridan Rd *HORF/LLZ* BS7 ... **326** C2
Sheridan Wy
OLD/WMLY/WICK BS30 ... **348** C3
Sherrin Wy
BMSTRD/HC/WWD BS13 ... **345** G8
The Sherry *COTS* GL54 ... **76** E6
Sherston Cl *MANG/FISH* BS16 ... **327** K6
Sherston Rd *HORF/LLZ* BS7 ... **326** A3 🟦
MALM SN16 ... **303** G7
Sherwell Rd
BRSG/KWL/STAPK BS4 ... **337** G3
Sherwood Cl *KEYN* BS31 ... **348** A6
Sherwood Gn *VGL* GL2 ... **112** B5
Sherwood Rd *KEYN* BS31 ... **348** A6
KGWD/HNM BS15 ... **337** J2
TET GL8 ... **281** M4
Shetland Rd
HNBRY/STHM BS10 ... **325** M2
Shiels Av *HORF/LLZ* BS7 ... **326** C1
Shiels Dr *ALMDB* BS32 ... **316** F4 🟦
Shilton Cl *KGWD/HNM* BS15 ... **338** A4 🟦
Shimsey Cl *MANG/FISH* BS16 ... **327** L5 🟦
Shilton Rd *HGRV/WHIT* BS14 ... **346** D6
Ship La *CBRIS/FH* BS1 ... **7** G7
Shipley Mow *MANG/FISH* BS16 ... **328** D3
Shipley Rd
HNLZ/SM/SNYPK/WT BS9 ... **325** J3
Shipnran Ct
MANG/FISH BS16 ... **328** A7 🟦
Shipston Rd *SHPSTR* CV36 ... **61** H7
Shipton HI *MALM* SN16 ... **303** J7 🟦
Shipton's Grave La
RSTROUD/NAIL GL6 ... **256** E2
Shipway Ct *CHELTE/BC* GL52 ... **72** B7 🟦
Shirehampton Rd *AVONM* BS11 ... **324** B4
HNLZ/SM/SNYPK/WT BS9 ... **324** E5 🟦
Shire Wy *YATE/CS* BS37 ... **319** L5
Shockerwick La
CBATH/BATHN BA1 ... **352** D7
Shophouse Rd *LYD* GL15 ... **175** K8
Shop La *BAD* GL9 ... **323** G1
Short Hedges Cl *COTS* GL54 ... **169** K2 🟦
Shorthill Rd *YATE/CS* BS37 ... **319** L7
Shortlands Rd *AVONM* BS11 ... **324** C2 🟦
Short La *LGASH* BS41 ... **344** B1
Short St *CBRISNE* BS2 ... **7** M6
CHELTS GL53 ... **115** L5
Short Wy *THNB/SVB* BS35 ... **293** K4
Shortwood HI *MANG/FISH* BS16 ... **328** F6
Shortwood Rd
BMSTRD/HC/WWD BS13 ... **346** A8
MANG/FISH BS16 ... **329** G2
RSTROUD/NAIL GL6 ... **232** B8
Shortwood Vw
KGWD/HNM BS15 ... **338** B3 🟦
Shortwood Wk
BMSTRD/HC/WWD BS13 ... **346** A8 🟦
Shotts La *NWNT* GL18 ... **85** G5
Shoulderway La *SHPSTR* CV36 ... **38** B2

Showering Cl
HGRV/WHIT BS14 ...... 346 F6
Showering Rd
HGRV/WHIT BS14 ...... 346 F6
Shrubbery Cottages
RDLND/MONT BS6 ...... 335 K1
Shrubbery Rd *BMSTR* BS16.. 327 M6
Shrublands *CHELTS* GL53 .... 116 B6
Shurdington Rd
BWTH/CHD GL3 .... 138 B6
CHELTS GL51 .... 115 K6
CHELTW GL51 .... 138 E3
Shutehay Dr *DSLY* GL11 ...... 229 H6
Shuter Rd
BMSTRD/HC/WWD BS13 .. 345 H6
Shute St *STNHO* GL10 .... 207 J8
Shutter La *CHELTE/BC* GL52 .. 72 F2
Sibland Cl *THNB/SVB* BS35 ... 293 M3
Sibland Ct *THNB/SVB* BS35 ... 293 M3
Sibland Rd *THNB/SVB* BS35... 293 M2
Sibland Wy *THNB/SVB* BS35 .. 293 L3
Sibree Cl *RSTROUD/NAIL* GL6 .. 209 L8
Sidcot *BRSG/KWL/STAPK* BS4 .. 347 C1
Siddington Rd *CIR* GL7........ 238 E5
Sideland Ct *HGRV/WHIT* BS14 .. 347 C5
Sidelands Rd *MANG/FISH* BS16.. 327 L5
Sidings Rd *CHNTN* OX7........ 104 F6
The Sidings *WUE* GL12 .... 276 D6
Sidmouth Gdns *BMSTR* BS3 .. 345 M1
Sidmouth Rd *BMSTR* BS3...... 345 M1
Sidney St *CHELTE/BC* GL52 2
GL GL1 .... 5 J7
Signal Rd *MANG/FISH* BS16 ... 328 A7
Silbury Rd *BMSTR* BS3........ 345 G1
Silcock Cl *BWTH/CHD* GL3.... 113 H4
Silcox Rd
BMSTRD/HC/WWD BS13 .. 345 L7
Silklands Gv
HNLZ/SM/SNYPK/WT BS9 .. 324 E5
Silk Mill La *COTS* GL54 .... 74 D6
Silley's Cl *CHEP* NP16 .... 270 B1
Silverbirch Cl
BRSTK/PCHW BS34 .... 316 F4
Silver Birch La *VGL* GL2 ...... 159 C2
Silverhill Rd *HNBRY/STHM* BS10.. 315 C8
Silver St *CBRIS/FH* BS1 .... 6 F2
CHPMW/MSHF SN14 ...... 343 K8
CIND GL14 .... 154 E4
CIR GL7 .... 238 C2
DSLY GL11 .... 230 C4
DSLY GL11 .... 253 K2
MALM SN16 .... 303 J8
MTCHDN GL17 .... 130 C2
TET GL8 .... 282 A4
VGL GL2 .... 156 A8
Silverthorn Cl *CHELT* GL50 ... 115 K6
Silverthorne La *CBRISNE* BS2 .. 7 L6
Silverton Ct
BRSG/KWL/STAPK BS4 .. 346 B2
Silvertree Gdns *STROUD* GL5 .. 209 G8
Silverwood Wy
CHELTW GL51 .... 115 G6
Simmonds Rd *GLE* GL4 ...... 137 H4
Simmonds Vw
BRSTK/PCHW BS34 .... 317 H7
Simon Rd *VGL* GL2 .... 112 E6
Simpson Rd *SHPSRT* CV36.... 16 B6
Sims La *VGL* GL2 .... 135 H7
Sinclair Rd *CHELTW* GL51 .... 138 F2
Sinderberry Dr *TEWK* GL20 .... 49 G2
Sinope St *GL* GL1.............. 5 H7
Sion Hl *CFTN/FAIL* BS8 .... 335 H5
Sion La *CFTN/FAIL* BS8 .... 335 H4
Sion Pl *CFTN/FAIL* BS8 .... 335 H4
Sion Rd *BMSTR* BS3 .... 335 L8
Sir John's La *EVILLE/WHL* BS5 .. 326 C7
HORF/LLZ BS7 .... 326 D7
Siskin Rd *COTS* GL54 .... 124 C6
Sissinghurst Gv *CHELTW* GL51 . 115 J6
Sisson End *VGL* GL2 .... 136 F1
Sisson Rd *VGL* GL2 .... 136 E1
Siston Cl *KGWD/HNM* BS15 .. 338 C1
Siston La
OLD/WMLY/WICK BS30 ... 339 G2
Sivell Cl *KGWD/HNM* BS15 ... 338 C1
Sivell Cl *VGL* GL2.............. 112 C5
Six Acres *GLE* GL4 .... 137 H8
Sixth Av *HORF/LLZ* BS7 ...... 326 C1
Skillicorne Ms *CHELTW* GL51 .. 115 J3
Skinner St *GL* GL1 .... 4 F3
Skippon Ct *KGWD/HNM* BS15 .. 338 A6
Skylark Wy *GLE* GL4 .... 136 D6
Slade Brook *STROUD* GL5 .... 209 G3
Slade Rd *LYD* GL15 .... 177 K8
The Slade *DSLY* GL11 .... 253 K3
Slad La *RSTROUD/NAIL* GL6 .. 209 J1
STROUD GL5 .... 209 H3
Slad Rd *RSTROUD/NAIL* GL6.. 185 K5
STROUD GL5 .... 208 F3
The Slad *CIND* GL14 .... 154 F3
Slaney St *GL* GL1 .... 136 B4
Sleep La *HGRV/WHIT* BS14.... 346 F6
Slimbridge La *YATE/CS* BS37 .. 320 B4
Slimbridge La *BRKLY* GL13.... 227 K2
Slimbridge Rd *GL* GL1 .... 135 M8
Sloan St *EVILLE/WHL* BS5 .... 336 D6
Slough La *CHPMW/MSHF* SN14 .. 341 H7
Slymbridge Av
HNBRY/STHM BS10 .... 315 J7
Smallbrook Rd *BDWAY* WR12 .. 32 F1
Small La *MANG/FISH* BS16 .... 327 G6
Small St *CBRIS/FH* BS1 .... 6 F5
CBRISNE BS2.................. 7 M6
Smarts Gn *YATE/CS* BS37 ...... 320 E3
Smeaton Rd *CBRIS/FH* BS1 ... 335 H6
Smith Barry Crs *COTS* GL54 .. 124 D7
Smith Barry Rd *COTS* GL54 ... 124 D7
Smithmead
BMSTRD/HC/WWD BS13 .. 345 K6
Smiths Ct *TEWK* GL20 .... 238 A4
Smith's Fld *CIR* GL7 .... 238 A4
Smiths Hl *CLFD* GL16 .... 176 A5
Smith's La *TEWK* GL20 .... 48 A5
Smith St *CHPMW/MSHF* SN14 .. 333 J4
Smithville Cl *LYD* GL15 ...... 199 G6
Smithville Pl *LYD* GL15 ...... 199 G6

Smithy Cl *CLFD* GL16 .... 127 K8
Smithy La *COTS* GL54 .... 74 C2
Smithyman Ct *CIND* GL14 .... 155 J7
The Smithy *CIR* GL7 .... 238 E4
LYD GL15 .... 178 E8
Smythe Cft *HGRV/WHIT* BS14.. 346 C8
Smythe Meadow
RSTROUD/NAIL GL6 .... 233 M1
Smythe Rd *CHELTW* GL51 .... 93 K5
Smyth Rd *BMSTR* BS3 .... 335 J8
Snake Dr *CIR* GL7 .... 218 C6
Snead Pk *GLE* GL4 .... 137 H6
Sneedhams Rd *GLE* GL4...... 160 D1
Snipehill Br *CHEP* NP16 ...... 270 E1
Snipe Rd *COTS* GL54 .... 124 C7
Snowberry Wk
EVILLE/WHL BS5 .... 337 G3
Snowdon Cl *MANG/FISH* BS16 .. 327 H7
Snowdon Gdns *BWTH/CHD* GL3.. 113 J4
Snowdonia Rd *TEWK* GL20 .... 48 C7
Snowdon Rd *MANG/FISH* BS16.. 327 H6
Snowdrop Cl *GLE* GL4 ...... 137 G6
Snowshill Cl *GLE* GL4 .... 136 F4
Snowshill Dr *CHELTE/BC* GL52 .. 72 A8
Snowshill Rd *BDWAY* WR12 .. 32 F4
GLE GL4 .... 137 G4
Snowswick La *FGDN* SN7 .... 269 G4
Sodbury Rd *WUE* GL12........ 296 C8
Solent Wy *THNB/SVB* BS35 .. 293 M4
Solsbury La *CBATH/BATHN* BA1 .. 352 A7
Solway Rd *COTS* GL54 ...... 92 F8
Somerby Cl *ALMDB* BS32 .... 316 F4
Somerdale Av
BRSG/KWL/STAPK BS4.... 346 B3
Somerdale Rd *KEYN* BS31 .... 348 B4
Somerdale Rd North
KEYN BS31 .... 348 B4
Somerford Rd *CIR* GL7........ 238 C4
Somergate Rd *CHELTW* GL51 .. 92 F7
Somermead *BMSTR* BS3 ...... 345 L2
Somerset Av *CHELTW* GL51 .. 115 J1
DSLY GL11 .... 253 K3
YATE/CS BS37 .... 310 B8
Somerset Cl *WUE* GL12 ...... 277 G7
Somerset Crs
BRSTK/PCHW BS34 .... 317 H6
Somerset Pl *GL* GL1 .... 4 D8
TEWK GL20 .... 48 B8
Somerset Rd
BRSG/KWL/STAPK BS4.... 336 C8
CIND GL14 .... 154 A3
Somerset Sq *CBRIS/FH* BS1 .. 7 G7
Somerset St *CBRIS/FH* BS1 .. 7 H7
CBRISNE BS2................ 335 M3
Somerset Ter *BMSTR* BS3 .... 336 A8
Somerset Wy *CHEP* NP16 .... 270 B6
Somerton Cl *KGWD/HNM* BS15.. 338 A4
Somerton Rd *HORF/LLZ* BS7 .. 326 A5
Somme Rd *CHELTE/BC* GL52 .. 3 M3
Sommerville Rd
RDLND/MONT BS6 .... 326 A8
Sommerville Rd South
RDLND/MONT BS6 .... 336 B1
Sopwith Rd *COTS* GL54 ...... 124 C6
Sorrel Cl *GLE* GL4 .... 136 C2
THNB/SVB BS35 .... 293 M1
Soundwell Rd
KGWD/HNM BS15 .... 337 L2
Southall Ter *NWNT* GL18 .... 107 L1
Southam La *CHELTE/BC* GL52 .. 94 B3
South Av *TEWK* GL20 .... 49 J4
YATE/CS BS37 .... 319 K2
Southbank *STROUD* GL5 .... 232 B1
Southbrook Rd *GLE* GL4 .... 136 C2
South Cerney Rd *CIR* GL7 .... 238 E7
South Cl *VGL* GL2 .... 5 M1
Southcourt Cl *CHELTS* GL53 .. 115 M6
Southcourt Dr *CHELTS* GL53 .. 115 M6
South Cft
HNLZ/SM/SNYPK/WT BS9 .. 325 L4
South Dene
HNLZ/SM/SNYPK/WT BS9 .. 325 G5
Southdown Rd
HNLZ/SM/SNYPK/WT BS9 .. 325 H3
Southend La *NWNT* GL18 .... 86 C4
The Southend *LED* HR8 ...... 20 A4
Southern Av *GL* GL1 .... 135 M7
Southernhay *CFTN/FAIL* BS8 .. 6 A5
MANG/FISH BS16 .... 327 L7
Southernhay Av *CFTN/FAIL* BS8.. 6 A6
Southey Av *KGWD/HNM* BS15 .. 337 M2
Southey St *CBRISNE* BS2 .... 336 B2
Southfield
RSTROUD/NAIL GL6 .... 233 H5
TET GL8 .... 281 M5
Southfield Ap *CHELTS* GL53.. 116 A7
Southfield Av
KGWD/HNM BS15 .... 338 A2
Southfield Cl *CHELTS* GL53 .. 116 A7
Southfield Ct
HNLZ/SM/SNYPK/WT BS9 .. 325 J4
Southfield Ri *CHELTS* GL53 .. 116 A7
Southfield Rd *CLFD* GL16 .... 151 M5
GLE GL4 .... 136 B7
HNLZ/SM/SNYPK/WT BS9 .. 325 J4
RDLND/MONT BS6 .... 335 M2
STROUD GL5 .... 232 C1
Southgate Crs *STROUD* GL5 .. 208 C6
Southgate Dr *CHELTS* GL53 .. 3 C7
Southgate Gdns
STROUD GL5 .... 208 C6
Southgate St *GL* GL1.......... 4 E6
South Green St
CFTN/FAIL BS8 .... 335 H5
South Gv *RDLND/MONT* BS6.. 325 L6
South Hayes *EVILLE/WHL* BS5.. 326 D7
Southleigh Rd *CFTN/FAIL* BS8.. 6 A1
South Liberty La *BMSTR* BS3 .. 345 G2
BMSTRD/HC/WWD BS13 .. 345 K1
South Lynn Gdns
SHPSRT CV36 .... 16 B6
Southmead Cfr *CIR* GL7...... 238 E5
Southmead La
RSTROUD/NAIL GL6 .... 186 C5
Southmead Rd
BRSTK/PCHW BS34 .... 326 A2

HNBRY/STHM BS10 .... 325 L3
HNLZ/SM/SNYPK/WT BS9 .. 325 K4
Southmead Wy
HNBRY/STHM BS10 .... 325 M3
Southover Cl
HNLZ/SM/SNYPK/WT BS9 .. 325 J3
South Pde *LED* HR8 .... 20 A4
South Rd *ALMDB* BS32 ...... 306 F5
BMSTR BS3 .... 335 L8
CLFD GL16 .... 151 L8
CLFD GL16 .... 175 M1
KGWD/HNM BS15 .... 337 M3
LYD GL15 .... 201 J7
RDLND/MONT BS6 .... 335 L1
Southsea Rd
BRSTK/PCHW BS34 .... 316 C4
Southside *TET* GL8 .... 302 A3
Southside Cl *AVONM* BS11.... 324 D4
Southside Rd *BMSTR* BS3 .... 335 K8
South Vw *FRCTL/WBN* BS36 .. 318 D4
MANG/FISH BS16 .... 328 A6
South View Crs
FRCTL/WBN BS36 .... 318 F5
South View Ri
FRCTL/WBN BS36 .... 318 F5
South View Wy *CHELTE/BC* GL52.. 94 E7
Southville Pl *BMSTR* BS3 ...... 6 E8
Southville Rd *BMSTR* BS3 .... 6 D8
South Wy *CIR* GL7 .... 238 C3
Southway Dr
OLD/WMLY/WICK BS30 ... 338 F6
Southwell St *CBRISNE* BS2 .... 6 D1
Southwood Av
HNLZ/SM/SNYPK/WT BS9 .. 324 E5
Southwood Cl *CIND* GL14 .... 154 B2
Southwood Dr
HNLZ/SM/SNYPK/WT BS9 .. 324 D3
Southwood Dr East
HNLZ/SM/SNYPK/WT BS9 .. 324 E3
Southwood La *CHELT* GL50 .. 2 B8
Sovereign Cha *RTEWK/TIB* GL19 .. 66 E4
Spa Gdns *TEWK* GL20 .... 48 D4
Spalding Cl *CBRISNE* BS2 .... 326 C8
Spaniorum Vw *THNB/SVB* BS35.. 315 H1
Spark Hl *DSLY* GL11 .... 229 H5
Spa Rd *GL* GL1................ 4 D8
Spar Rd *YATE/CS* BS37 ...... 319 M1
Sparrow Hl *CLFD* GL16 ...... 151 J8
Sparrows La *RWYE* HR9 ...... 84 F4
Spartan Cl *GLE* GL4 .... 137 G5
Spartley Dr
BMSTRD/HC/WWD BS13 .. 345 H5
Spartley Wk
BMSTRD/HC/WWD BS13 .. 345 H5
Speculation Rd *CIND* GL14 .. 129 M8
Speech House Rd *CIND* GL14 .. 153 L1
CLFD GL16 .... 152 A8
CLFD GL16 .... 152 E7
Speedwell *CLFD* GL16 .... 151 M7
Speedwell Av
EVILLE/WHL BS5 .... 336 F4
THNB/SVB BS35 .... 293 M1
Speedwell Cl *GLE* GL4 ...... 137 G6
Speedwell Rd *EVILLE/WHL* BS5.. 337 H2
KGWD/HNM BS15 .... 337 K2
Spencer Cl *BWTH/CHD* GL3 .. 137 H4
Spencer's Ct *THNB/SVB* BS35.. 293 K5
Spenser Av *CHELTW* GL51 .... 115 C2
Spenser Rd *CHELTW* GL51 .... 115 G2
Spey Cl *THNB/SVB* BS35 .... 293 L3
Spey La *VGL* GL2.............. 159 H1
Spider La *STROUD* GL5 ...... 208 F5
Spillman's Pitch *STROUD* GL5 .. 208 C5
Spillman's Rd *STROUD* GL5 .. 208 C5
The Spindles *CHELTS* GL51 .. 115 J7
Spine Rd East *HGHW* SN6 .... 263 J8
Spine Rd West *GL7*............ 286 C1
Spinnaker Rd *VGL* GL2 ...... 135 K3
Spinney Ct *STROUD* GL5 .... 233 H2
Spinney Rd *GLE* GL4 .... 136 F4
The Spinney *ALMDB* BS32.... 317 G4
CHELTE/BC GL52 .... 94 A7
CIR GL7 .... 244 E7
FRCTL/WBN BS36 .... 318 D4
Spires Vw *MANG/FISH* BS16 .. 327 C6
Spire Wy *GLE* GL4 .... 136 F3
Spitalgate La *CIR* GL7 .... 238 C2
Spitale Leys *COTS* GL54 ...... 74 C5
Splatt Br *VGL* GL2 .... 205 L1
Spout Hl *LYD* GL15............ 224 A4
Spouthouse La *DSLY* GL11.... 229 H6
Spout La *MTCHDN* GL17 ...... 129 K4
Spratsgate La *CIR* GL7 ...... 238 C7
CIR GL7 .... 262 C6
Spread Eagle Rd *GL* GL1 .... 4 F5
Springbank Cl *CHELTW* GL51 .. 92 F7
Springbank Dr *CHELTW* GL51 .. 92 E8
Springbank Gv *CHELTW* GL51.. 92 E8
Springbank Rd *CHELTW* GL51.. 92 E8
Springbank Wy *CHELTW* GL51.. 92 F7
Spring Di *RTEWK/TIB* GL19 .. 133 G1
Springdale *RWYE* HR9 ...... 84 F3
Springdale Cl *VGL* GL2 ...... 158 F3
Springfield *COTS* GL54 ...... 123 G6
DSLY GL11 .... 229 G7
MIM GL56 .... 35 H8
TEWK GL20 .... 48 D4
THNB/SVB BS35 .... 293 L3
VGL GL2 .... 159 G4
Springfield Av *HORF/LLZ* BS7 .. 326 B6
MANG/FISH BS16 .... 328 C5
Springfield Cl *CHELTW* GL51 .. 114 D4
CLFD GL16 .... 175 K1
MANG/FISH BS16 .... 328 C4
SHPSTR CV36 .... 16 B7
Springfield Dr *CIND* GL14 .... 154 A1
Springfield Gv
HNLZ/SM/SNYPK/WT BS9 .. 325 K6
Springfield La *BDWAY* WR12 .. 32 F2
Springfield Rd *CIR* GL7........ 218 C6
CIR GL7 .... 238 B5
LYD GL15 .... 201 J7
MANG/FISH BS16 .... 328 C5
RDLND/MONT BS6 .... 335 M2
SHPSTR CV36 .... 16 B7

STROUD GL5 .... 207 M3
STROUD GL5 .... 208 B3
Springfields *DSLY* GL11 .. 229 G7
TET GL8 .... 282 B3
Springfields Ct *DSLY* GL11 .. 229 C7
Spring Gdns
BRSG/KWL/STAPK BS4.... 346 C2
CIR GL7 .... 218 C6
CIR GL7 .... 244 E7
Spring Gv *LED* HR8 .... 20 A5
Spring Hl *CBRISNE* BS2 ...... 335 M3
Springhill *DSLY* GL11 .... 229 M7
Spring Hl *KGWD/HNM* BS15 .. 338 A1
RSTROUD/NAIL GL6 .... 232 D7
STNHO GL10 .... 206 C3
Springhill Cl *RSTROUD/NAIL* GL6.. 232 D7
Springhill Crs
RSTROUD/NAIL GL6 .... 232 D7
Springhill (Old Court)
DSLY GL11 .... 229 K8
Spring La *CHELTE/BC* GL52 .. 94 D6
CHELTE/BC GL52 .... 95 G1
CHNTN OX7 .... 125 K7
STROUD GL5 .... 208 E5
STROUD GL5 .... 209 G8
Springleaze
BRSG/KWL/STAPK BS4.... 346 C2
MANG/FISH BS16 .... 328 C4
Spring Meadow Rd *LYD* GL15 .. 201 J7
The Springs *LYD* GL15 ...... 201 J8
Spring St *BMSTR* BS3 .... 7 H8
Spring Street Pl *BMSTR* BS3 .. 7 H8
Springvale *COTS* GL54 ...... 123 H3
Springville Cl
OLD/WMLY/WICK BS30 ... 338 C8
Springwell Gdns
BWTH/CHD GL3 .... 113 K4
Springwood Dr
HNBRY/STHM BS10 .... 314 F8
Spruce Ride *CLFD* GL16 ...... 153 C7
Spruce Rd *CLFD* GL16 .... 151 M7
Spruce Wy
BRSTK/PCHW BS34 .... 316 A4
The Square
BRSG/KWL/STAPK BS4.... 346 C2
COTS GL54 .... 98 E5
LYD GL15 .... 198 F6
MTCHDN GL17 .... 128 E3
STROUD GL5 .... 208 E3
Squires Cl *RSTROUD/NAIL* GL6 .. 209 L8
Squires Ct
OLD/WMLY/WICK BS30 ... 338 B8
Squires Leaze *THNB/SVB* BS35.. 293 M1
The Squires *BDWAY* WR12 .. 32 B1
Squirrel Cl *VGL* GL2 .... 159 G4
Stackpool Rd *BMSTR* BS3 .... 6 C8
Stadium Rd *RDLND/MONT* BS6.. 325 L6
Stafford Cl *CLFD* GL16 ...... 151 M8
Stafford Crs *THNB/SVB* BS35 .. 293 K2
Stafford Rd *CBRISNE* BS2 .... 336 C1
Staffords Ct
OLD/WMLY/WICK BS30 ... 338 C5
Stafford St *BMSTR* BS3 ...... 6 E9
BMSTR BS3 .... 335 M8
Stag Hl *LYD* GL15 .... 177 J8
Stainer Cl
BRSG/KWL/STAPK BS4.... 345 M5
Staites Orch *GLE* GL4 .... 137 G8
Stamage's La
RSTROUD/NAIL GL6 .... 185 G4
Stambourne La *BRKLY* GL13 .. 227 G3
Stamp's Meadow *VGL* GL2 .. 112 B6
Stanborough La *COTS* GL54 .. 120 F4
Stanbridge Cl
MANG/FISH BS16 .... 328 B5
Stanbridge Rd
MANG/FISH BS16 .... 328 B5
Stanbury Av *MANG/FISH* BS16.. 327 K6
Stanbury Ms *BWTH/CHD* GL3 .. 137 K5
Stanbury Rd *BMSTR* BS3 .... 336 A8
Stancombe La *COTS* GL54 .... 74 D5
Stancombe Vw *COTS* GL54 .. 74 D5
Standfast Rd
HNBRY/STHM BS10 .... 315 H8
Standish Av *BRSTK/PCHW* BS34.. 316 D2
Standish Cl
HNBRY/STHM BS10 .... 325 H2
Standish La *VGL* GL2 .... 182 E5
Standle La *DSLY* GL11 .... 252 C1
Standon Wy
HNBRY/STHM BS10 .... 325 L1
Stanfield Cl *HORF/LLZ* BS7 .. 326 D5
Stanford Cl *FRCTL/WBN* BS36.. 318 B3
Stanford Rd *LYD* GL15 ...... 201 H8
TEWK GL20 .... 49 G3
Stanhope Rd
OLD/WMLY/WICK BS30 ... 348 B1
Stanhope St *CBRISNE* BS2.... 7 L7
Stank La *VGL* GL2 .... 158 E5
Stanks La *UUSV* WR8 .... 24 B1
Stanleigh Ter *VGL* GL2 ...... 111 J4
Stanley Av *BRSTK/PCHW* BS34.. 326 D1
HORF/LLZ BS7 .... 326 A8
Stanley Cha *EVILLE/WHL* BS5.. 336 F1
Stanley Crs *BRSTK/PCHW* BS34.. 326 D1
Stanley Gdns
OLD/WMLY/WICK BS30 ... 338 D7
Stanley Hl *BRSG/KWL/STAPK* BS4.. 7 L9
Stanley Md *ALMDB* BS32 .... 317 G2
Stanley Pk *EVILLE/WHL* BS5 .. 336 D2
Stanley Park Rd
MANG/FISH BS16 .... 328 A8
Stanley Pl *CHELTW* GL51 .... 92 F8
Stanley Rd *CHELTE/BC* GL52 .. 3 L7
GL GL1 .... 136 A5
KGWD/HNM BS15 .... 338 D2
RDLND/MONT BS6 .... 335 L1
Stanley St *BMSTR* BS3 .... 335 L8
Stanley St North
BMSTR BS3 .... 335 K8
Stanley St South *BMSTR* BS3 .. 335 L8
Stanley Ter *BMSTR* BS3 ...... 345 L1
GL GL1 .... 136 A4
The Stanley *GLE* GL4 .... 161 H1
Stanley Vw *STROUD* GL5 .... 208 B6
Stanley Wk *GLE* GL4 .... 161 H2
Stanmoor *GLE* GL4 .... 136 F8
Stansby Crs *BWTH/CHD* GL3 .. 113 J5

Stanshawe Crs *YATE/CS* BS37 .. 320
Stanshawes Dr *YATE/CS* BS37 .. 319
Stanshaw Rd *MANG/FISH* BS16.. 327
Stanshaws Cl
BRSTK/PCHW BS34 316
Stanthill Dr *DSLY* GL11 253
Stanton Cl *KGWD/HNM* BS15 .. 338
Stanton Dr *CHELTW* GL51 93
Stanton Rd *HNBRY/STHM* BS10.. 326
STROUD GL5 208
TEWK GL20 48
Stanton Wy *CHELTW* GL51 .. 115
Stantway La *CIND* GL14 156
Stanway
OLD/WMLY/WICK BS30 ... 348
Stanway Rd *BDWAY* WR12 .. 53
CHELTW GL51 114
GLE GL4 136
Stanway Wood Dr
CHELTE/BC GL52 72
Stanwick Crs *CHELTW* GL51 .. 93
Stanwick Dr *CHELTW* GL51 .. 93
Stanwick Gdns *CHELTW* GL51.. 93
Staple Gv *KEYN* BS31 347
Staple Grove Crs
EVILLE/WHL BS5 337
Staplehill Rd *MANG/FISH* BS16.. 327
Staples Rd *YATE/CS* BS37 319
Stapleton Cl
MANG/FISH BS16 326
Stapleton Rd *EVILLE/WHL* BS5.. 7
EVILLE/WHL BS5 326
EVILLE/WHL BS5 336
Star Barn Rd *FRCTL/WBN* BS36.. 318
Star Hl *RSTROUD/NAIL* GL6 .. 232
Star La *MANG/FISH* BS16 327
TET GL8 257
Starling Ct *STNHO* GL10 207
Station Av *MANG/FISH* BS16.. 327
Station Cl *BWTH/CHD* GL3 .. 113
OLD/WMLY/WICK BS30 ... 338
YATE/CS BS37 320
Station Dr *TEWK* GL20 27
Station La *HORF/LLZ* BS7 326
MTCHDN GL17 131
TEWK GL20 48
Station Rd *AVONM* BS11 324
BAD GL9 323
BDWAY WR12 31
BRKLY GL13 227
BRSG/KWL/STAPK BS4.... 346
BRSTK/PCHW BS34 316
BRSTK/PCHW BS34 316
BWTH/CHD GL3 113
CHCAM GL55 12
CHELTE/BC GL52 72
CHEP NP16 270
CHNTN OX7 104
CHNTN OX7 155
CIND GL14 155
CIR GL7 244
CIR GL7 261
CIR GL7 263
CLFD GL16 175
COTS GL54 118
COTS GL54 123
DSLY GL11 229
EVE WR11 29
FRCTL/WBN BS36 318
FRCTL/WBN BS36 318
GL GL1 5
HNBRY/STHM BS10 315
HORF/LLZ BS7 326
KEYN BS31 328
KGWD/HNM BS15 328
LYD GL15 225
LYD GL15 225
MANG/FISH BS16 328
MIM GL56 35
MIM GL56 35
OLD/WMLY/WICK BS30 ... 338
RDLND/MONT BS6.......... 335
RSTROUD/NAIL GL6 232
SHPSRT CV36 36
STROUD GL5 232
TEWK GL20 28
TEWK GL20 48
TEWK GL20 48
THNB/SVB BS35 304
THNB/SVB BS35 305
WUE GL12 276
WUE GL12 296
YATE/CS BS37 308
YATE/CS BS37 320
Station Ter *CHELT* GL50 2
CIND GL14 154
TEWK GL20 48
Station Ter *CIND* GL14 154
Station Wy *MANG/FISH* BS16 .. 328
Staunton Cl *GLE* GL4 137
Staunton Flds
HGRV/WHIT BS14 346
Staunton La *HGRV/WHIT* BS14 .. 346
Staunton Rd *CLFD* GL16 150
CLFD GL16 151
Staunton Wy
HGRV/WHIT BS14 346
Staveley Crs
HNBRY/STHM BS10 325
Staverton Connection
CHELTW GL51 114
Stavordale Gv
HGRV/WHIT BS14 346
Staynes Crs
KGWD/HNM BS15 338
Steam Mills Rd *CIND* GL14 .. 129
Stean Bridge Rd *ALMDB* BS32.. 317
Steel Av *LYD* GL15 201
Steel Ct *OLD/WMLY/WICK* BS30.. 338
Steel Mills *KEYN* BS31........ 348
Steels La *SHPSTR* CV36 16
Steeple Cl *GLE* GL4 136
Steeple Vw *LYD* GL15 225
Steep St *CHEP* NP16.......... 270
Stella Gv *BMSTR* BS3 345
Stella Wy *CHELTE/BC* GL52 .. 71
Stenders Rd *MTCHDN* GL17 .. 130
The Stenders *MTCHDN* GL17 .. 130

tephens Dr
OLD/WMLY/WICK BS30 ... 338 B6
tephens Pl CLFD GL16 ... 175 M1
tephen St EVILLE/WHL BS5 ... 336 E3
tepney Rd EVILLE/WHL BS5 ... 336 E2
tepney Wk EVILLE/WHL BS5 ... 336 E2
tepping Stone La
RSTROUD/NAIL GL6 ... 185 G5
teps Cl DSLY GL11 ... 229 H5 1
tep's La TET GL8 ... 233 L8
tepstairs La CIR GL7 ... 238 D4
terling Cl COTS GL54 ... 102 B3
terling Ct CHELTW GL51 ... 115 K1 5
terncourt Rd
MANG/FISH BS16 ... 327 J4
terrys Rd RWYE HR9 ... 85 G3
tevans Cl VGL GL2 ... 112 C6 1
tevens Crs BMSTR BS3 ... 7 J9
tevens Wk ALMDB BS32 ... 316 F3
tevens Wy RSTROUD/NAIL GL6 .. 256 B2
teward Rd TEWK GL20 ... 49 G3
tewarts Mill La GLE GL4 ... 137 G7
teway La CBATH/BATHN BA1 ... 352 C6
tgiles'sroad TEWK GL20 ... 27 G5
tibbs Ct
OLD/WMLY/WICK BS30 ... 338 B7 18
tibbs Hl EVILLE/WHL BS5 ... 337 J4
ticky La VGL GL2 ... 159 G5
tidcote La WUE GL12 ... 295 H6
tidcot La WUE GL12 ... 294 E6
tile Acres AVONM BS11 ... 324 C2
tillhouse La BMSTR BS3 ... 6 F8
tillingfleet Rd
BMSTRD/HC/WWD BS13 ... 345 L6
tillman Cl
BMSTRD/HC/WWD BS13 ... 345 G7
tinchcombe YATE/CS BS37 ... 320 A2 2
tirling Cl YATE/CS BS37 ... 309 M7 2
tirling Rd
BRSG/KWL/STAPK BS4 ... 336 E8 3
tirling Wy GL GL1 ... 159 K1
KEYN BS31 ... 348 A7 1
he Stirrup STROUD GL5 ... 207 M4
tocken Cl BWTH/CHD GL3 ... 137 K5
tock Hl THNB/SVB BS35 ... 292 D2
tock La BRKLY GL13 ... 227 G8
tockley Wy GLE GL4 ... 160 F5
he Stocks RSTROUD/NAIL GL6 .. 207 M1
tockton Cl
HGRV/WHIT BS14 ... 346 B7 1
OLD/WMLY/WICK BS30 ... 338 D8 3
tockwell Av MANG/FISH BS16 ... 328 C5
tockwell Cl MANG/FISH BS16 ... 328 B4
tockwell Dr MANG/FISH BS16 ... 328 C5
tockwell Gn CIND GL14 ... 154 A4
tockwell La CHELTE/BC GL52 ... 72 F8
LYD GL15 ... 224 F3
tockwells MIM GL56 ... 58 D6
tockwood Crs
BRSG/KWL/STAPK BS4 ... 346 B1
tockwood Hl KEYN BS31 ... 347 L4
tockwood La
HGRV/WHIT BS14 ... 347 G6
tockwood Ms
BRSG/KWL/STAPK BS4 ... 337 H6 5
tockwood Rd
BRSG/KWL/STAPK BS4 ... 347 H2
HGRV/WHIT BS14 ... 347 G6
toke Bridge Av
BRSTK/PCHW BS34 ... 316 F5
tokefield Cl THNB/SVB BS35 ... 293 K2
toke Gv
HNLZ/SM/SNYPK/WT BS9 ... 325 G5
toke Hamlet
HNLZ/SM/SNYPK/WT BS9 ... 325 H5 1
toke Hl
HNLZ/SM/SNYPK/WT BS9 ... 325 G7
toke La BRSTK/PCHW BS34 ... 316 E3
HNLZ/SM/SNYPK/WT BS9 ... 325 H5 2
MANG/FISH BS16 ... 327 G4
tokeleigh Wk
HNLZ/SM/SNYPK/WT BS9 ... 324 E6 4
tokemead
BRSTK/PCHW BS34 ... 316 E3 2
toke Mdw ALMDB BS32 ... 316 F2
toke Paddock Rd
HNLZ/SM/SNYPK/WT BS9 ... 324 F5
toke Park Cl
CHELTE/BC GL52 ... 72 B7 7
toke Park Ct CHELTE/BC GL52 ... 72 A7
toke Park Rd
HNLZ/SM/SNYPK/WT BS9 ... 325 G7
toke Park Rd South
HNLZ/SM/SNYPK/WT BS9 ... 325 G8
toke Rd CHELTE/BC GL52 ... 71 H6
HNLZ/SM/SNYPK/WT BS9 ... 325 H8
tokes Ct
OLD/WMLY/WICK BS30 ... 338 C7 7
tokes Cft CBRIS/FH BS1 ... 336 A3
tokes Rd TEWK GL20 ... 47 J3
toke View Rd
MANG/FISH BS16 ... 327 H8 6
toneberry Rd
HGRV/WHIT BS14 ... 346 C8
tone Br MIM GL56 ... 37 K6
tonebridge Pk
EVILLE/WHL BS5 ... 336 F1
tonechat Av GLE GL4 ... 136 E6
tonechat Gdns
MANG/FISH BS16 ... 327 G5
tone Cl GLE GL4 ... 137 G4
tonecote Rdg
RSTROUD/NAIL GL6 ... 209 M7
tonecroft Cl
CHELTE/BC GL52 ... 72 A7 3
toneford La EVE WR11 ... 10 F1
tonehenge Rd GLE GL4 ... 136 D4 2
tonehill
OLD/WMLY/WICK BS30 ... 338 A7
tonehouse Ct COTS GL54 ... 101 J4 1
tone La FRCTL/WBN BS36 ... 318 A7
tonelea DSLY GL11 ... 228 F7
toneleigh Cl CHELTS GL53 ... 115 M8 1
toneleigh Crs
BRSG/KWL/STAPK BS4 ... 346 C1
toneleigh Dr
OLD/WMLY/WICK BS30 ... 338 B6
Stoneleigh Rd
BRSG/KWL/STAPK BS4 ... 346 C1
Stoneleigh Wk
BRSG/KWL/STAPK BS4 ... 346 C1 1
The Stone Rd RTEWK/TIB GL19 ... 66 D5
Stones La HGHW SN6 ... 288 D2
Stoneville St CHELTW GL51 ... 2 A3
Stoney Fld VGL GL2 ... 111 G6 5
Stoney Pool CIR GL7 ... 240 F5
Stoney Rd RWYE HR9 ... 85 G4
Stoney Stile Rd
THNB/SVB BS35 ... 293 J6
Stony Riding
RSTROUD/NAIL GL6 ... 234 B1
Storrington Rd STNHO GL10 ... 207 H4
Stothard Rd HORF/LLZ BS7 ... 326 D4
Stottbury Rd HORF/LLZ BS7 ... 326 C8
Stoulgrove La CHEP NP16 ... 246 C7
Stoulton Gv
HNBRY/STHM BS10 ... 315 J8 5
Stour Ct SHPSTR CV36 ... 16 B6 3
Stourden Cl MANG/FISH BS16 ... 327 J4 4
Stourton Dr
OLD/WMLY/WICK BS30 ... 338 B7
Stover Rd YATE/CS BS37 ... 319 J1
Stow Br COTS GL54 ... 101 K8
Stow Ct CHELTW GL51 ... 115 J2 2
Stowe La LYD GL15 ... 198 E1
Stowell Hill Rd WUE GL12 ... 294 D5
Stowell Ms GLE GL4 ... 136 F4
Stowe Rd LYD GL15 ... 198 D4
Stow Hill Rd WUE GL12 ... 294 C5
Stowick Crs AVONM BS11 ... 324 E2
Stow Rd CHNTN OX7 ... 103 L8
CHNTN OX7 ... 125 L1
CIR GL7 ... 214 F7
MIM GL56 ... 58 C7
Strachans Cl STROUD GL5 ... 208 C4
Stradbrook Av EVILLE/WHL BS5 .. 337 K4
Stradling Rd AVONM BS11 ... 324 E1
Straight La RTEWK/TIB GL19 ... 66 E4
Straight St CBRISNE BS2 ... 7 J4
Strand La CIND GL14 ... 156 B4
Stratford Cl
HGRV/WHIT BS14 ... 346 B8 6
VGL GL2 ... 135 L7 1
Stratford Rd SHPSTR CV36 ... 16 B5
STRAT CV37 ... 8 F5
STROUD GL5 ... 208 B3
Strathmore Rd HORF/LLZ BS7 ... 326 A5
Stratton Hts CIR GL7 ... 214 B6
Stratton Rd GL GL1 ... 5 H9
KEYN BS31 ... 349 G8
Stratton St CBRISNE BS2 ... 7 H1
Strawberry La CIR GL7 ... 238 B2
Strawbridge Rd
EVILLE/WHL BS5 ... 336 D4 12
Stream Cl HNBRY/STHM BS10 ... 315 M8
Stream La NWNT GL18 ... 86 F1
Streamleaze THNB/SVB BS35 ... 293 L3
Streamside CHELTE/BC GL52 ... 72 B7 8
Stream Side MANG/FISH BS16 ... 328 B5
Streamside STROUD GL5 ... 208 E4 14
Streamside Rd YATE/CS BS37 .. 320 C2 6
The Stream MANG/FISH BS16 ... 327 K1
The Street BAD GL9 ... 299 L8
DSLY GL11 ... 230 A3
DSLY GL11 ... 252 F7
DSLY GL11 ... 254 D2
HGHW SN6 ... 264 D7
HGHW SN6 ... 265 M5
HGHW SN6 ... 266 C7
MALM SN16 ... 284 A6
MALM SN16 ... 285 H3
RSTROUD/NAIL GL6 ... 256 B2
STNHO GL10 ... 207 G8
STROUD GL5 ... 208 C8
TET GL8 ... 299 L1
TET GL8 ... 301 M3
THNB/SVB BS35 ... 292 C8
THNB/SVB BS35 ... 293 K6
VGL GL2 ... 181 H8
Stretford Av
EVILLE/WHL BS5 ... 336 F3 10
Stretford Rd EVILLE/WHL BS5 ... 336 F3
Strickland Rd CHELTE/BC GL52 ... 3 H8
Stride Cl THNB/SVB BS35 ... 304 C5 2
Striguil Rd CHEP NP16 ... 270 A5
Stringer's Cl STROUD GL5 ... 208 C7
Stringer's Dr STROUD GL5 ... 208 C6
Strode Common
THNB/SVB BS35 ... 293 H6
Strode Gdns THNB/SVB BS35 ... 293 H6
Strongbow Rd CHEP NP16 ... 270 A5
Stroud Rd AVONM BS11 ... 324 A6
BRSTK/PCHW BS34 ... 316 A3
CIR GL7 ... 237 J3
GL GL1 ... 136 A4
GLE GL4 ... 160 A1
RSTROUD/NAIL GL6 ... 184 F5
RSTROUD/NAIL GL6 ... 210 C2
RSTROUD/NAIL GL6 ... 232 D7
Stuart St EVILLE/WHL BS5 ... 336 E4
Studland Dr CHELTE/BC GL52 ... 94 E7
Stump La BWTH/CHD GL3 ... 137 K3
Stumpwell La WUE GL12 ... 276 F1
Sturden La MANG/FISH BS16 ... 317 L8
Sturdon Rd BMSTR BS3 ... 335 J8
Sturmer Cl YATE/CS BS37 ... 310 A7
Sturminster Cl
HGRV/WHIT BS14 ... 346 F5
Sturminster Rd
HGRV/WHIT BS14 ... 346 E6
Sturmyes Rd
RSTROUD/NAIL GL6 ... 210 C8
Sudbrook Wy GLE GL4 ... 136 D6
Sudeley Dr CIR GL7 ... 263 H5
Sudgrove Pk GLE GL4 ... 137 G6 11
Sudmeadow Rd VGL GL2 ... 135 K2
Suffolk Cl TET GL8 ... 282 A2 2
Suffolk Pde CHELT GL50 ... 2 C9
Suffolk Pl CIR GL7 ... 264 F4
Suffolk Rd CHELT GL50 ... 2 B8
Suffolk Sq CHELT GL50 ... 2 B8
Sugar Tump RWYE HR9 ... 84 F3 2
Sugley La RSTROUD/NAIL GL6 ... 256 A1
Sulgrave Cl GL GL1 ... 159 L2
Summer Cl STROUD GL5 ... 209 G4
Summer Crs STROUD GL5 ... 209 G4
Summerfield Cl CHELTW GL51 ... 93 H6 3
MIM GL56 ... 35 H8
Summerhayes
OLD/WMLY/WICK BS30 ... 338 F6 3
Summer Hl BRSG/KWL/STAPK BS4 .. 7 L9
Summerhill Rd
EVILLE/WHL BS5 ... 337 H3
Summerhill Ter
EVILLE/WHL BS5 ... 337 H4 1
Summerhouse La
CHEP NP16 ... 270 B7 2
Summerland Dr
BWTH/CHD GL3 ... 113 L6
Summerleaze KEYN BS31 ... 348 A4 1
LYD GL15 ... 225 K1
MANG/FISH BS16 ... 327 L8
Summerleaze Rd LYD GL15 ... 225 K1
Summers Dr
OLD/WMLY/WICK BS30 ... 340 C2
Summersfield Cl
RSTROUD/NAIL GL6 ... 233 K5
Summersfield Rd
RSTROUD/NAIL GL6 ... 233 K4
Summers Md YATE/CS BS37 ... 310 A6
Summers Rd CBRISNE BS2 ... 336 C2 17
COTS GL54 ... 74 C5
Summer St BMSTR BS3 ... 6 C9
STROUD GL5 ... 209 G4
Sundale RWYE HR9 ... 84 E3 2
Sundays Hl ALMDB BS32 ... 306 C7
Sundayshill La BRKLY GL13 ... 274 B3
Sunderland Ct
BWTH/CHD GL3 ... 113 L6 3
Sunderland Pl CFTN/FAIL BS8 ... 6 A1
Sundridge Pk YATE/CS BS37 ... 320 A3
Sun Green Cl LYD GL15 ... 200 C2 1
Sun Green Rd LYD GL15 ... 200 C2
The Sunground TET GL8 ... 257 L2
Sunningdale YATE/CS BS37 ... 320 A3
Sunningdale Dr
OLD/WMLY/WICK BS30 ... 338 D5
Sunny Bank CLFD GL16 ... 151 J8 2
KGWD/HNM BS15 ... 337 K2
Sunnybank Rd CLFD GL16 ... 151 J8 3
Sunnycroft Cl CHELTE/BC GL52 ... 94 C1
Sunnycroft Ms GL GL1 ... 136 A6 2
Sunnydene
BRSG/KWL/STAPK BS4 ... 336 F7
Sunnyfield La CHELTW GL51 ... 114 E6
Sunnyfield Rd VGL GL2 ... 158 F3
Sunny Hl
HNLZ/SM/SNYPK/WT BS9 ... 324 E4
Sunnyhill Dr AVONM BS11 ... 324 A5 5
Sunnymead KEYN BS31 ... 348 B8
Sunnymead Cl MTCHDN GL17 129 M3 1
Sunnyside FRCTL/WBN BS36 ... 318 D4
HNLZ/SM/SNYPK/WT BS9 ... 325 G6 3
Sunnyside La MANG/FISH BS16 .. 327 K1
YATE/CS BS37 ... 319 L2
Sunnyvale Dr
OLD/WMLY/WICK BS30 ... 338 D8
Sunny Wk KGWD/HNM BS15 ... 337 K2
Sunridge MANG/FISH BS16 ... 327 M5
Sunrise Gv
BRSG/KWL/STAPK BS4 ... 336 F7
Sun Rise Rd LYD GL15 ... 200 C2
Sunset La CHELTE/BC GL52 ... 94 E3
Sunset Pl RTEWK/TIB GL19 ... 108 C8
Sunshine Cl LED HR8 ... 19 L2 3
Sun St CHELTW GL51 ... 2 A1
TEWK GL20 ... 48 A4
Sun Tump LYD GL15 ... 200 C3
Surrey Av CHELTW GL51 ... 115 H1
Surrey Rd HORF/LLZ BS7 ... 326 A8 4
Surrey St CBRISNE BS2 ... 7 H1
Suspension Br CFTN/FAIL BS8 ... 335 G4
Sussex Av CHELTW GL51 ... 115 J1
Sussex Gdns BWTH/CHD GL3 ... 137 K4
Sussex St CBRISNE BS2 ... 7 L4
Sutherland Av
MANG/FISH BS16 ... 328 A4
YATE/CS BS37 ... 309 M7 3
Sutherland Pl CFTN/FAIL BS8 ... 335 J1
Sutton Av
BRSG/KWL/STAPK BS4 ... 336 F7
Sutton Cl DSLY GL11 ... 253 K3 3
Sutton La RBANSW OX15 ... 39 L3
Sutton Rd CIND GL14 ... 154 D5
CIND GL14 ... 178 B1
Swagwater La RWYE HR9 ... 84 F1
Swainswick HGRV/WHIT BS14 ... 346 B5
Swainswick La
CBATH/BATHN BA1 ... 351 M8
Swaish Dr
OLD/WMLY/WICK BS30 ... 338 B7
Swallow Crs VGL GL2 ... 112 F5
Swallow Cft STNHO GL10 ... 206 B4
Swallow Dr BRSTK/PCHW BS34 .. 316 A3
Swallow Pk THNB/SVB BS35 ... 273 L8
Swallows Ct
BRSTK/PCHW BS34 ... 317 G7
Swallowtail Cl CHELTW GL51 ... 114 F1 5
Swan Cl CIR GL7 ... 244 E7
MIM GL56 ... 58 C6
Swane Rd HGRV/WHIT BS14 ... 347 H5 3
Swan La FRCTL/WBN BS36 ... 317 L3
HGHW SN6 ... 287 K6
LYD GL15 ... 178 E8
Swanley La BRKLY GL13 ... 251 L6
Swanmoor Crs
HNBRY/STHM BS10 ... 315 J7
Swan Rd GL GL1 ... 5 G3
LYD GL15 ... 201 J8
Swanscombe Pl
CHELTW GL51 ... 115 G6 15
Swansfield CIR GL7 ... 244 F5 1
Swan St STROUD GL5 ... 208 E4 15
Swanswell Dr CHELTW GL51 ... 115 G3
Sweden La TEWK GL20 ... 50 F1
Sweetbriar Cl CHELTE/BC GL52 ... 72 A7
Sweetbriar St GL GL1 ... 4 F3
Sweets Cl KGWD/HNM BS15 ... 338 A1
Sweets Rd KGWD/HNM BS15 ... 337 M1
Swells Hl STROUD GL5 ... 233 G2
Swift Rd GLE GL4 ... 136 F6
Swifts Hill Vw STROUD GL5 ... 209 G2 1
Swilgate Rd TEWK GL20 ... 48 A6
Swindon Cl CHELTW GL51 ... 2 A1
Swindon La CHELTW GL51 ... 93 K5
Swindon Rd CHELT GL50 ... 2 C3
CHELTW GL51 ... 93 K6
CIR GL7 ... 238 F5
HGHW SN6 ... 289 G4
Swindon St CHELT GL50 ... 2 B3
Swinhay La WUE GL12 ... 276 C4
Swish La MTCHDN GL17 ... 129 K4
Swiss Rd BMSTR BS3 ... 345 H1
Swordfish Cl BWTH/CHD GL3 ... 113 L6 7
Swynford Cl CIR GL7 ... 266 F5 1
Sybil Rd GLE GL4 ... 136 B5
Sycamore Av CHEP NP16 ... 270 A6
Sycamore Cl EVILLE/WHL BS5 ... 337 G2
GL GL1 ... 135 M7
KGWD/HNM BS15 ... 337 K8 2
Sycamore Dr
BRSTK/PCHW BS34 ... 316 A4
STROUD GL5 ... 208 F3 3
THNB/SVB BS35 ... 293 L2 2
Sycamore Rd MTCHDN GL17 ... 129 M5
TEWK GL20 ... 49 G3
Sydenham Hl
RDLND/MONT BS6 ... 335 M2
Sydenham La
RDLND/MONT BS6 ... 335 M2
Sydenham Rd
BRSG/KWL/STAPK BS4 ... 336 C8
CHELTE/BC GL52 ... 3 G6
RDLND/MONT BS6 ... 335 M2
Sydenham Rd South
CHELTE/BC GL52 ... 3 G7
Sydenham Ter GL GL1 ... 136 A4 3
Sydenham Villas Rd
CHELTE/BC GL52 ... 3 G7
Sydenham Wy
KGWD/HNM BS15 ... 337 L8
Sydney STNHO GL10 ... 207 G2
Sydney Rw CBRIS/FH BS1 ... 6 A7
Sylvan Cl CLFD GL16 ... 175 K2
Sylvan Wy
HNLZ/SM/SNYPK/WT BS9 ... 324 D5
Sylvia Av BMSTR BS3 ... 336 B8
Symes Av
BMSTRD/HC/WWD BS13 ... 345 L8
Symington Rd
MANG/FISH BS16 ... 327 K6
Symn La WUE GL12 ... 277 K4
Synwell La WUE GL12 ... 277 L4
Syon Rd RSTROUD/NAIL GL6 ... 233 K5 3
Syston Wy KGWD/HNM BS15 ... 337 M2

T

Tabernacle Pitch WUE GL12 ... 277 K4 4
Tabernacle Rd
KGWD/HNM BS15 ... 337 L5
WUE GL12 ... 277 J3
Tabernacle Wk STROUD GL5 ... 208 D6
Tabrams Pitch
RSTROUD/NAIL GL6 ... 232 E7 2
Tackley Rd EVILLE/WHL BS5 ... 326 D8 3
Tadwick La CBATH/BATHN BA1 ... 351 K6
CBATH/BATHN BA1 ... 351 G2
Tailor's La STRAT CV37 ... 9 J2
Tainmor Cl VGL GL2 ... 113 G6
Tait's Hl DSLY GL11 ... 228 E7
Tait's Hill Rd DSLY GL11 ... 228 F8
Talbot Av KGWD/HNM BS15 ... 337 K2
Talbot Ms GL GL1 ... 135 M5 1
Talbot Rd
BRSG/KWL/STAPK BS4 ... 346 D1
CHELTW GL51 ... 115 J3
Talbot Sq COTS GL54 ... 101 M3
Talboys Wk TET GL8 ... 282 A3
Talgarth Rd HORF/LLZ BS7 ... 326 B7
Tallard's Pl CHEP NP16 ... 270 C3
Tall Elms Cl BWTH/CHD GL3 ... 113 K6 1
Tallis Gv BRSG/KWL/STAPK BS4 ... 345 M5
Tallis Rd BWTH/CHD GL3 ... 113 H3
Tally Ho La COTS GL54 ... 98 E6
Tamar Cl THNB/SVB BS35 ... 293 M4 5
Tamar Dr KEYN BS31 ... 348 C7
Tamarisk Cl CHELTW GL51 ... 115 J7
Tamar Rd BWTH/CHD GL3 ... 138 B5
CBRISNE BS2 ... 336 E5
CHELTE/BC GL52 ... 3 K3
Tamesis Dr CIR GL7 ... 261 H4 2
Tamworth Rd KEYN BS31 ... 348 A7 2
Tanglewood Wy
RSTROUD/NAIL GL6 ... 209 M7
Tanhouse La YATE/CS BS37 ... 309 L4
Tankard's Cl CFTN/FAIL BS8 ... 6 D2
Tankards Hl MIM GL56 ... 36 E1
Tanner Cl
OLD/WMLY/WICK BS30 ... 338 B6
Tanners Cl BWTH/CHD GL3 ... 138 A5
Tanner's La BUR/CRTN OX18 ... 173 M7
CHELTW GL51 ... 93 H8 3
CHPMW/MSHF SN14 ... 342 A3
Tanner's Rd CHELTW GL51 ... 93 H8
Tanorth Cl HGRV/WHIT BS14 ... 346 C8
Tanorth Rd HGRV/WHIT BS14 ... 346 B8
The Tanyard
OLD/WMLY/WICK BS30 ... 348 D1 3
Tapscott Ct WUE GL12 ... 277 J4 2
Tapsters
OLD/WMLY/WICK BS30 ... 338 C7 5
Target Cl LED HR8 ... 19 L2
STROUD GL5 ... 209 H4
Tarlton Cl GLE GL4 ... 137 G7 12
Tarnock Av HGRV/WHIT BS14 ... 346 C4
Tarragon Pl ALMDB BS32 ... 317 H4
Tarrington Rd GL GL1 ... 136 B4
Tatchley La CHELTE/BC GL52 ... 94 D7
Taunton Wk HORF/LLZ BS7 ... 326 C4 3
Taurus Cl VGL GL2 ... 112 B6 3
Taverner Cl
BRSG/KWL/STAPK BS4 ... 345 M4 11
Tavistock Rd
BRSG/KWL/STAPK BS4 ... 346 B2
Tavistock Wk
BRSG/KWL/STAPK BS4 ... 346 B2 2
Tayberry Gv CHELTW GL51 ... 115 H7 1
Tayler Rd COTS GL54 ... 169 J1
Taylor Cl KGWD/HNM BS15 ... 338 B3 5
Taylor Gdns
BMSTRD/HC/WWD BS13 ... 345 H7 3
Taylors Gnd VGL GL2 ... 159 H1 2
Tayman Cl
HNBRY/STHM BS10 ... 326 A5 4
Tayman Rdg
OLD/WMLY/WICK BS30 ... 348 F3
Taynton Cl
OLD/WMLY/WICK BS30 ... 348 D1
Teal Cl ALMDB BS32 ... 316 F1 3
VGL GL2 ... 158 F2
Teasel Cl VGL GL2 ... 112 B6 4
Teasel Md ALMDB BS32 ... 317 G4 3
Teddington Gdns GLE GL4 ... 136 C5
Ted Preston Cl TEWK GL20 ... 48 B7 3
Teewell Av MANG/FISH BS16 ... 328 A7
Teewell Cl MANG/FISH BS16 ... 328 A7 3
Teewell Hl MANG/FISH BS16 ... 328 A7
Teignmouth Rd
BRSG/KWL/STAPK BS4 ... 346 C2 5
Telegraph St SHPSTR CV36 ... 16 B5
Telephone Av CBRIS/FH BS1 ... 6 E4
Telford's Br VGL GL2 ... 111 K7
Telford Wk EVILLE/WHL BS5 ... 337 J2
Teme Rd CHELTE/BC GL52 ... 3 J5
Templar Rd YATE/CS BS37 ... 310 A8
Temple Back CBRIS/FH BS1 ... 7 H4
Temple Cl GLE GL4 ... 137 G3
LYD GL15 ... 201 H8
Templefields COTS GL54 ... 118 B8
Temple Ga CBRIS/FH BS1 ... 7 H6
Templeland Rd
BMSTRD/HC/WWD BS13 ... 345 H6 3
Temple Rose St CBRIS/FH BS1 ... 7 H5
Temple St BMSTR BS3 ... 345 K1 11
CBRIS/FH BS1 ... 7 G4
KEYN BS31 ... 348 A6
Temple Wy CBRIS/FH BS1 ... 7 H5
Templeway LYD GL15 ... 225 H1
Temple Way U/P CBRISNE BS2 ... 7 J3 1
Templeway West LYD GL15 ... 201 H8
Tenby Rd KEYN BS31 ... 347 M7
Tenby St EVILLE/WHL BS5 ... 336 D4
Tennessee Gv
RDLND/MONT BS6 ... 325 L6 3
Tenniscourt Rd
KGWD/HNM BS15 ... 338 C2
Tennis Rd
BRSG/KWL/STAPK BS4 ... 346 B1
Tennyson Av VGL GL2 ... 135 L7
Tennyson Cl KEYN BS31 ... 348 B5
Tennyson Rd CHELTW GL51 ... 115 H2
DSLY GL11 ... 253 L4
HORF/LLZ BS7 ... 326 A6 1
Tensing Rd CHELTS GL53 ... 116 A7
Tenth Av HORF/LLZ BS7 ... 326 D2
Tereslake Gn
HNBRY/STHM BS10 ... 315 M7
Tern Cl GLE GL4 ... 136 E5
Terrell Gdns
EVILLE/WHL BS5 ... 336 F4 11
Terrell St CBRISNE BS2 ... 6 E2
Terry Ruck Cl CHELTW GL51 ... 114 F1
Tetbury Cl BRSTK/PCHW BS34 ... 316 E3
Tetbury Hl MALM SN16 ... 303 J6
TET GL8 ... 257 L3
Tetbury La MALM SN16 ... 283 M5
RSTROUD/NAIL GL6 ... 233 G7
RSTROUD/NAIL GL6 ... 256 E1
TET GL8 ... 279 L8
Tetbury Rd CIR GL7 ... 237 M5
GLE GL4 ... 160 A2 1
KGWD/HNM BS15 ... 337 K3
Tetbury St RSTROUD/NAIL GL6 ... 233 J5
Teviot Rd KEYN BS31 ... 348 C7
Tewkesbury Rd
CBRISNE BS2 ... 336 C1 15
CHELTW GL51 ... 92 F5
COTS GL54 ... 101 L2
NWNT GL18 ... 86 C2
TEWK GL20 ... 48 D2
VGL GL2 ... 112 B6 5
Tewther Rd
BMSTRD/HC/WWD BS13 ... 345 L8
Teyfant Rd
BMSTRD/HC/WWD BS13 ... 346 A8
Teyfant Wk
BMSTRD/HC/WWD BS13 ... 346 A7 1
Thackeray Cl STRAT CV37 ... 9 J1
Thackeray Wk HORF/LLZ BS7 .. 326 C3 4
Thames Cl WUE GL12 ... 276 C7 3
Thames La HGHW SN6 ... 289 G3
Thames Pth CIR GL7 ... 237 G8
CIR GL7 ... 244 D8
HGHW SN6 ... 289 H3
Thames Rd CHELTE/BC GL52 ... 3 J3
Thames St CIR GL7 ... 244 E8
Thames Vw HGHW SN6 ... 287 H3
Thanet Rd BMSTR BS3 ... 345 K1
Thatchers Cl
EVILLE/WHL BS5 ... 337 K4 4
Thatchers End
CHELTE/BC GL52 ... 72 D8 3
Theescombe Hl STROUD GL5 ... 232 D5
The High Gv CHELTE/BC GL52 ... 72 A8
Theocs Cl TEWK GL20 ... 47 M7 1
There-and-back-again La
CFTN/FAIL BS8 ... 6 C3 2
Theresa Av HORF/LLZ BS7 ... 326 A7
Theresa St GL GL1 ... 135 M4 2
Thessaly Rd CIR GL7 ... 214 A7
Theyer Cl BWTH/CHD GL3 ... 138 A6
Theynes Cft LGASH BS41 ... 344 D2
Thicket Av MANG/FISH BS16 ... 327 L8
Thicket Rd MANG/FISH BS16 ... 327 L7
Thicket Wk THNB/SVB BS35 ... 293 L2 3
Thickwood La
CHPMW/MSHF SN14 ... 343 L5
Thiery Rd
BRSG/KWL/STAPK BS4 ... 346 E1
Thingwall Pk MANG/FISH BS16 ... 327 G8
Third Av DSLY GL11 ... 253 L3
HORF/LLZ BS7 ... 326 C2
Thirlestaine Rd CHELTS GL53 ... 2 D9
Thirlmere Ct
OLD/WMLY/WICK BS30 ... 338 F5

Thirlmere Rd
BRSTK/PCHW BS34 ... 316 C3
CHELTW GL51 ... 115 G4
Thistledown Cl CHELTW GL51 ... 92 F7
Thistle Downs TEWK GL20 ... 48 F2
Thistle St BMSTR BS3 ... 335 K8
Thomas Av MANG/FISH BS16 ... 328 D3
Thomas Cl LED HR8 ... 19 L2
Thomas Moore Cl
BWTH/CHD GL3 ... 113 J3
Thomas Pring Wk
EVILLE/WHL BS5 ... 337 J2
Thomas Stock Gdns GLE GL4 ... 137 G5
Thomas St CBRISNE BS2 ... 336 A3
CHEP NP16 ... 270 A3
CIR GL7 ... 238 C2
GL GL1 ... 5 G8
Thomas St North
RDLND/MONT BS6 ... 335 M2
Thomond Cl CHELTW GL51 ... 93 L7
Thompson Dr CHELTS GL53 ... 115 M7
Thompson Rd CIR GL7 ... 239 H7
HGRV/WHIT BS14 ... 347 G5
STROUD GL5 ... 208 F3
Thompson Wy VGL GL2 ... 112 F5
Thomson Rd
EVILLE/WHL BS5 ... 336 D3
Thoresby CHELT GL50 ... 94 A6
Thoresby Av GL GL1 ... 159 L2
Thornbury Cl CHELTW GL51 ... 115 K1
Thornbury Rd THNB/SVB BS35 ... 293 J6
Thorncliffe Dr CHELTW GL51 ... 115 K3
Thorn Cl YATE/CS BS37 ... 319 M2
Thorndale CFTN/FAIL BS8 ... 335 J3
Thornhaugh Ms
CHELTW GL51 ... 115 G6
Thornhayes Cl
FRCTL/WBN BS36 ... 318 C3
Thornhill Cl GL GL1 ... 135 M6
The Thornhills
MANG/FISH BS16 ... 327 K5
Thornleigh Rd HORF/LLZ BS7 ... 326 A6
Thornmead Gv
HNBRY/STHM BS10 ... 325 J1
Thorns Farm YATE/CS BS37 ... 320 A2
Thorn Tree Dr CHEP NP16 ... 270 B7
Thornwell Rd CHEP NP16 ... 270 B6
Thornycroft Cl HORF/LLZ BS7 ... 326 D4
Threadneedle St
STROUD GL5 ... 208 E4
Three Ashes La NWNT GL18 ... 64 C8
Three Queens' La CBRIS/FH BS1 ... 7 G5
Three Sisters La
CHELTE/BC GL52 ... 94 F8
Three Wells Rd
BMSTRD/HC/WWD BS13 ... 345 H7
Thrissell St EVILLE/WHL BS5 ... 7 L1
Throgmorton Rd
BRSG/KWL/STAPK BS4 ... 346 B4
Thrupp La STROUD GL5 ... 233 H1
Thrush Cl GLE GL4 ... 136 E5
Thurlestone HGRV/WHIT BS14 ... 346 B6
Thurlow Rd EVILLE/WHL BS5 ... 336 E1
Thurstons Barton
EVILLE/WHL BS5 ... 337 G2
Tibberton KGWD/HNM BS15 ... 338 C3
Tibberton Gv CHELTW GL51 ... 114 D4
Tibberton La RTEWK/TIB GL19 ... 108 D7
Tibbiwell La RSTROUD/NAIL GL6 .. 185 H3
Tibbott Rd HGRV/WHIT BS14 ... 346 E6
Tibbott Wk HGRV/WHIT BS14 ... 346 E6
Tiberius Av LYD GL15 ... 201 K7
Tichborne Rd EVILLE/WHL BS5 ... 336 E4
Tide Gv AVONM BS11 ... 324 C3
Tidenham Wy
BRSTK/PCHW BS34 ... 316 B2
Tidswell Cl VGL GL2 ... 159 H3
Tilemans La SHPSTR CV36 ... 16 A4
Tilling Rd HNBRY/STHM BS10 ... 326 A4
Tilling Wk HNBRY/STHM BS10 ... 326 A4
Tillis Vw CLFD GL16 ... 150 D6
Tilney Rd CHELT GL50 ... 93 M7
Tilnor Crs DSLY GL11 ... 229 H7
Tilsdown DSLY GL11 ... 229 H7
Tilsdown Cl DSLY GL11 ... 229 G7
Tilsley Rd CHNTN OX7 ... 105 M2
Tilting Rd THNB/SVB BS35 ... 293 K1
Timbercombe La CHELTS GL53 ... 116 D8
Timber Dene MANG/FISH BS16 ... 326 F7
Timberscombe Wk
HGRV/WHIT BS14 ... 346 E6
Timbrells Cl CIR GL7 ... 263 H4
Timmis Cl GLE GL4 ... 136 E7
Timms Gn BDWAY WR12 ... 11 G7
Timperley Wy CHELTW GL51 ... 114 F6
Timsbury Rd BMSTR BS3 ... 346 A1
Tindell Ct
OLD/WMLY/WICK BS30 ... 338 B7
Tinglesfield CIR GL7 ... 214 B7
Tinker's Cl MIM GL56 ... 58 D6
Tinkley La STNHO GL10 ... 231 G5
Tinmans Gn MONM NP25 ... 174 B3
Tintern Av EVILLE/WHL BS5 ... 336 F3
Tintern Cl
OLD/WMLY/WICK BS30 ... 338 B5
Tintern Rd GLE GL4 ... 135 M8
Tippetts Rd KGWD/HNM BS15 ... 337 M5
Tirle Bank Wy TEWK GL20 ... 48 D5
Tirlebrookgra TEWK GL20 ... 49 J4
Tirley Cl VGL GL2 ... 159 G2
Tirley St RTEWK/TIB GL19 ... 68 B5
Tiverton Cl CHELTW GL51 ... 92 F8
Tiverton Wk MANG/FISH BS16 ... 337 J1
Tivoli La CHELT GL50 ... 2 A9
Tivoli Ms CHELT GL50 ... 2 A8
Tivoli Rd CHELT GL50 ... 2 A9
Tivoli St CHELT GL50 ... 2 A9
Tivoli Wk CHELT GL50 ... 115 K3
Toadsmoor Rd
RSTROUD/NAIL GL6 ... 233 K2
Tobacco Cl COTS GL54 ... 74 B7
Tobacconist Rd
RSTROUD/NAIL GL6 ... 233 J5
Tobyfield Cl CHELTE/BC GL52 ... 72 C8
Tobyfield La CHELTE/BC GL52 ... 72 B8
Tobyfield Rd CHELTE/BC GL52 ... 72 C8
Tockington La ALMDB BS32 ... 306 C5
Tockington Park La
THNB/SVB BS35 ... 307 G3
Toghill La
OLD/WMLY/WICK BS30 ... 340 C2
Toll CFTN/FAIL BS8 ... 335 H4
Toll Bridge Rd
CBATH/BATHN BA1 ... 352 A8
Toll Down Wy
CHPMW/MSHF SN14 ... 323 J8
Tolsey La TEWK GL20 ... 48 A5
Tommy's Turn La RBANSW OX15 .. 39 M1
Tommy Taylor's La CHELT GL50 ... 93 M7
Tom Price Cl CHELTE/BC GL52 ... 2 F5
Tone Dr BWTH/CHD GL3 ... 138 B6
Tooke Rd RSTROUD/NAIL GL6 ... 233 G4
Top Rd CIND GL14 ... 178 B2
CIR GL7 ... 266 E4
Torchacre Ri DSLY GL11 ... 253 J2
Tormarton Crs
HNBRY/STHM BS10 ... 315 H7
Tormarton Rd BAD GL9 ... 323 G6
CHPMW/MSHF SN14 ... 332 C6
Toronto Rd HORF/LLZ BS7 ... 326 C3
Torpoint Rd BMSTR BS3 ... 345 M2
Torrance Cl
OLD/WMLY/WICK BS30 ... 338 F5
Torridge Rd KEYN BS31 ... 348 C7
Torrington Av
BRSG/KWL/STAPK BS4 ... 346 B3
Tortworth Rd HORF/LLZ BS7 ... 326 A6
Totshill Dr
BMSTRD/HC/WWD BS13 ... 346 A7
Totshill Gv
BMSTRD/HC/WWD BS13 ... 346 A7
Totterdown La CIR GL7 ... 242 E6
Totts La CHPMW/MSHF SN14 ... 343 K8
Touching End La
CHPMW/MSHF SN14 ... 342 B3
Touchstone Av
BRSTK/PCHW BS34 ... 317 G6
Tower Cl GLE GL4 ... 136 F3
Tower Hl CBRISNE BS2 ... 7 H4
Tower House Dr
RTEWK/TIB GL19 ... 44 A8
Tower La CBRIS/FH BS1 ... 6 F3
OLD/WMLY/WICK BS30 ... 338 C5
Tower Rd KGWD/HNM BS15 ... 337 L2
LYD GL15 ... 177 K8
Tower Rd North
KGWD/HNM BS15 ... 338 D3
Tower Rd South
OLD/WMLY/WICK BS30 ... 338 D5
Tower St CBRIS/FH BS1 ... 7 H5
CIR GL7 ... 238 D3
Townsend ALMDB BS32 ... 306 B7
MTCHDN GL17 ... 128 F4
MTCHDN GL17 ... 130 C1
Townsend Cl HGRV/WHIT BS14 ... 347 H6
LYD GL15 ... 199 G6
Townsend Rd HGRV/WHIT BS14 .. 347 H6
Townsend St CHELTW GL51 ... 2 B2
Toy La CHNTN OX7 ... 105 L1
Tozers Hl
BRSG/KWL/STAPK BS4 ... 346 E1
T Parkside Cl BWTH/CHD GL3 ... 113 H5
Trafalgar Dr BWTH/CHD GL3 ... 113 H3
Trafalgar Rd CIR GL7 ... 238 C1
Trafalgar St CHELT GL50 ... 2 C7
Trafalgar Ter BMSTR BS3 ... 345 K1
Traherne Cl LED HR8 ... 20 A3
Trajan Cl GLE GL4 ... 137 H5
Tralee Wk
BRSG/KWL/STAPK BS4 ... 345 M2
The Tram Rd CLFD GL16 ... 175 J1
Tramway Rd
BRSG/KWL/STAPK BS4 ... 336 E8
CIND GL14 ... 154 A7
Tranmere Av
HNBRY/STHM BS10 ... 315 J7
Tranmere Gv
HNBRY/STHM BS10 ... 315 J8
Tranton La THNB/SVB BS35 ... 249 L7
Tratman Wk
HNBRY/STHM BS10 ... 315 H8
Travers Cl
BRSG/KWL/STAPK BS4 ... 345 M5
Travers Wk BRSTK/PCHW BS34 ... 317 G6
Tredegar Rd MANG/FISH BS16 ... 327 K8
Tredworth Rd GL GL1 ... 136 B4
Treefield Pl CBRISNE BS2 ... 336 C1
Treelands Cl CHELTS GL53 ... 115 M6
Treelands Dr CHELTS GL53 ... 115 M6
Tree Leaze YATE/CS BS37 ... 320 B1
Tregarth Rd BMSTR BS3 ... 345 H2
Trelawney Av
EVILLE/WHL BS5 ... 336 F3
Trelawney Pk
BRSG/KWL/STAPK BS4 ... 336 F8
Trelawney Rd
RDLND/MONT BS6 ... 335 L2
Trenchard Gdns CIR GL7 ... 239 H8
Trenchard St CBRIS/FH BS1 ... 6 D4
Trench La ALMDB BS32 ... 306 F8
FRCTL/WBN BS36 ... 317 H1
Trendlewood Pk
MANG/FISH BS16 ... 327 G7
Trenley Rd DSLY GL11 ... 230 B4
Trent Dr THNB/SVB BS35 ... 293 M4
Trent Gv KEYN BS31 ... 348 C7
Trentham Cl CBRISNE BS2 ... 336 C1
Trent Rd BWTH/CHD GL3 ... 138 B6
Tresham Cl ALMDB BS32 ... 316 F1
Tretawn Gdns TEWK GL20 ... 48 D5
Trevanna Rd BMSTR BS3 ... 345 H2
Trevelyan Wk
HNBRY/STHM BS10 ... 315 H8
Treverdowe Wk
HNBRY/STHM BS10 ... 314 F8
Trevethin Cl
KGWD/HNM BS15 ... 337 L4
Trevisa Crs BRKLY GL13 ... 227 G8
Trevisa Gv HNBRY/STHM BS10 ... 315 L7
Trevor Rd BWTH/CHD GL3 ... 137 H5
Trewsbury Rd CIR GL7 ... 236 F5
Triangle South CFTN/FAIL BS8 ... 6 B3
The Triangle VGL GL2 ... 112 E8
Triangle West CFTN/FAIL BS8 ... 6 B3
Tribune Pl GLE GL4 ... 137 G5
Trident Cl MANG/FISH BS16 ... 328 C2
Trier Wy GL GL1 ... 4 E9
Trimnells CHPMW/MSHF SN14 ... 343 K8
Trinity Dr RSTROUD/NAIL GL6 ... 233 K5
Trinity La CHELTE/BC GL52 ... 2 E4
Trinity Rd CBRISNE BS2 ... 7 L2
CIR GL7 ... 238 C4
GLE GL4 ... 137 H5
MTCHDN GL17 ... 129 M5
STROUD GL5 ... 208 F5
Trinity St CBRISNE BS2 ... 7 L2
TEWK GL20 ... 48 A5
Trinity Wk CBRISNE BS2 ... 7 K2
Trinity Wy CIND GL14 ... 154 B2
Troon YATE/CS BS37 ... 320 A3
Troon Dr
OLD/WMLY/WICK BS30 ... 338 D5
Troopers' Hill Rd
EVILLE/WHL BS5 ... 337 H5
Trotman Av DSLY GL11 ... 229 H6
Troughton Pl TEWK GL20 ... 48 C5
Trowbridge Rd
HNBRY/STHM BS10 ... 325 L2
Trowbridge Wk
HNBRY/STHM BS10 ... 325 L2
Trubshaw Ct BWTH/CHD GL3 ... 113 L6
Truro Rd BMSTR BS3 ... 335 K8
Tryes Rd CHELT GL50 ... 115 L5
Trygrove GLE GL4 ... 136 F5
Trym Cross Rd
HNLZ/SM/SNYPK/WT BS9 ... 324 E6
Trymleaze
HNLZ/SM/SNYPK/WT BS9 ... 324 E6
Trym Rd
HNLZ/SM/SNYPK/WT BS9 ... 325 J4
Trym Side
HNLZ/SM/SNYPK/WT BS9 ... 324 E6
Trymwood Cl
HNBRY/STHM BS10 ... 325 H1
Tucker St CBRISNE BS2 ... 7 J1
Tuckett La MANG/FISH BS16 ... 327 L4
Tuckwell Rd CIR GL7 ... 267 G5
Tudor Cl OLD/WMLY/WICK BS30 .. 338 E8
Tudor Lodge Dr CHELT GL50 ... 115 L4
Tudor Pl TEWK GL20 ... 48 B7
Tudor Rd CBRISNE BS2 ... 336 B2
CIR GL7 ... 238 E2
EVILLE/WHL BS5 ... 336 E2
KGWD/HNM BS15 ... 337 L6
Tudor St GL GL1 ... 135 L5
Tudor Wk CLFD GL16 ... 151 J5
Tuffley Av GL GL1 ... 135 L5
Tuffley Crs GL GL1 ... 135 M6
Tuffley La GL GL1 ... 135 L8
Tuffley Rd HNBRY/STHM BS10 ... 325 L3
Tufthorn Av CLFD GL16 ... 175 K2
Tufthorn Cl CLFD GL16 ... 175 L3
Tufthorn Rd CLFD GL16 ... 175 L4
Tufton Av AVONM BS11 ... 324 C3
Tugela Rd
BMSTRD/HC/WWD BS13 ... 345 H4
Tug Wilson Closel TEWK GL20 ... 49 G1
The Tulworths VGL GL2 ... 112 D6
Tunacre VGL GL2 ... 110 F5
Tuners La MALM SN16 ... 284 A5
Tunstall Cl
HNLZ/SM/SNYPK/WT BS9 ... 325 G7
Turkdean Rd CHELTW GL51 ... 115 G3
Turley Rd EVILLE/WHL BS5 ... 336 F2
Turnberry
OLD/WMLY/WICK BS30 ... 338 D5
Turnbridge Rd
HNBRY/STHM BS10 ... 315 L7
Turnbury YATE/CS BS37 ... 320 A3
Turner Cl KEYN BS31 ... 348 C6
Turner Gdns HORF/LLZ BS7 ... 326 D5
Turner Rd DSLY GL11 ... 229 G7
Turners Cl VGL GL2 ... 110 F7
Turners Ct
OLD/WMLY/WICK BS30 ... 338 B7
Turnpike Av WUE GL12 ... 277 L5
Turnpike Cl YATE/CS BS37 ... 320 A1
Turnpike End CHEP NP16 ... 270 D7
Turnpike Ga WUE GL12 ... 296 C5
Turnstone Dr VGL GL2 ... 158 F2
Turtlegate Av
BMSTRD/HC/WWD BS13 ... 345 G7
Turtlegate Wk
BMSTRD/HC/WWD BS13 ... 345 G7
Turville Dr HORF/LLZ BS7 ... 326 C5
Tusculum Wy MTCHDN GL17 ... 130 C1
Tutnalls St LYD GL15 ... 201 K8
Tutton Hl CHPMW/MSHF SN14 ... 343 K8
Tweed Cl THNB/SVB BS35 ... 293 L3
Tweenbrook Av GL GL1 ... 136 A5
Tweeny La
OLD/WMLY/WICK BS30 ... 338 F5
The Twenties CIR GL7 ... 238 E7
Twenty Acres Rd
HNBRY/STHM BS10 ... 325 L1
Twickenham Rd
RDLND/MONT BS6 ... 325 L6
Twinberrow La DSLY GL11 ... 253 K4
Twixtbears TEWK GL20 ... 48 A4
Two Acres Rd HGRV/WHIT BS14 .. 346 C4
Two Hedges Rd CHELTE/BC GL52 .. 72 C8
Two Mile Ct
KGWD/HNM BS15 ... 337 K3
Twomile Hill Rd
KGWD/HNM BS15 ... 337 K3
Two Mile La VGL GL2 ... 110 D7
The Twynings
KGWD/HNM BS15 ... 338 A1
Twyver Bank GLE GL4 ... 137 H8
Twyver Cl GLE GL4 ... 137 H8
Tybalt Wy BRSTK/PCHW BS34 ... 317 G6
Tylea Cl CHELTW GL51 ... 114 E4
Tyler Cl KGWD/HNM BS15 ... 338 A5
Tyler's La MANG/FISH BS16 ... 327 M6
Tyler St CBRISNE BS2 ... 7 L5
Tylers Wy CHEP NP16 ... 270 D3
LYD GL15 ... 177 L8
RSTROUD/NAIL GL6 ... 210 B8
YATE/CS BS37 ... 310 B6
Tyndale Av MANG/FISH BS16 ... 327 J7
YATE/CS BS37 ... 309 M8
Tyndale Cl DSLY GL11 ... 253 G7
Tyndale Rd BWTH/CHD GL3 ... 137 J3
DSLY GL11 ... 228 F7
KGWD/HNM BS15 ... 338 A1
VGL GL2 ... 228 E2
Tyndale Vw THNB/SVB BS35 ... 293 K3
Tyndall Av CFTN/FAIL BS8 ... 6 C2
Tyndall Rd EVILLE/WHL BS5 ... 336 D3
Tyndalls Park Ms CFTN/FAIL BS8 ... 6 C1
Tyndall's Park Rd CFTN/FAIL BS8 ... 6 B1
Tyndalls Wy
HNBRY/STHM BS10 ... 326 A3
Tyne Rd HORF/LLZ BS7 ... 325 M8
Tyne St CBRISNE BS2 ... 336 C1
Tyning Cl HGRV/WHIT BS14 ... 346 C4
YATE/CS BS37 ... 320 A1
Tyning Crs VGL GL2 ... 204 F8
Tyning Rd BMSTR BS3 ... 336 B8
Tynings Ct BWTH/CHD GL3 ... 113 M6
Tynings Rd RSTROUD/NAIL GL6 .. 232 C7
The Tynings
RSTROUD/NAIL GL6 ... 233 K4
Tynte Av
BMSTRD/HC/WWD BS13 ... 345 M8
Tyntesfield Rd
BMSTRD/HC/WWD BS13 ... 345 J4
Tyrone Wk
BRSG/KWL/STAPK BS4 ... 346 A3
Tyrrel Wy BRSTK/PCHW BS34 ... 317 G5
Tythe Ct DSLY GL11 ... 229 H6
Tytherington Rd
THNB/SVB BS35 ... 294 B5
Tythe Rd BDWAY WR12 ... 32 F2
Tythings Crs NWNT GL18 ... 86 B3
The Tythings NWNT GL18 ... 86 B3

U

Uley Rd DSLY GL11 ... 253 L3
Ullenwood Rd GLE GL4 ... 136 F4
Ullswater Cl
OLD/WMLY/WICK BS30 ... 338 F5
YATE/CS BS37 ... 310 A8
Ullswater Rd CHELTW GL51 ... 115 G4
HNBRY/STHM BS10 ... 325 K2
Undercliff Av CHELTS GL53 ... 115 M8
Undercliff Ter CHELTS GL53 ... 115 M8
Underhill CHEP NP16 ... 222 B4
Underhill Rd GLE GL4 ... 136 E7
WUE GL12 ... 276 C6
Underwood Cl THNB/SVB BS35 ... 293 J7
Union Rd CBRISNE BS2 ... 7 L4
CLFD GL16 ... 151 L8
Union St CBRIS/FH BS1 ... 6 F2
CHELTE/BC GL52 ... 2 F4
COTS GL54 ... 102 A3
DSLY GL11 ... 253 K3
GL GL1 ... 5 G3
STROUD GL5 ... 208 E4
Unity Rd KEYN BS31 ... 348 C6
Unity St CBRIS/FH BS1 ... 6 D4
CBRISNE BS2 ... 7 J3
KGWD/HNM BS15 ... 337 L3
University Farm MIM GL56 ... 58 C6
University Rd CFTN/FAIL BS8 ... 6 B3
University Wk CFTN/FAIL BS8 ... 6 C2
Unlawater La CIND GL14 ... 155 J6
Unwin Cl CHELTW GL51 ... 114 E4
Unwin Rd CHELTW GL51 ... 114 E4
Upcott HGHW SN6 ... 264 E7
Up Hatherley Wy CHELTW GL51 .. 114 F6
Uphill Rd HORF/LLZ BS7 ... 326 B6
MTCHDN GL17 ... 128 C7
Upjohn Crs
BMSTRD/HC/WWD BS13 ... 345 M8
Uplands Cl CIND GL14 ... 154 C2
Uplands Rd MANG/FISH BS16 ... 327 L8
STROUD GL5 ... 208 E3
Upper Bath Rd
THNB/SVB BS35 ... 293 K3
Upper Bath St CHELT GL50 ... 2 B9
Upper Belgrave Rd
CFTN/FAIL BS8 ... 335 J1
Upper Belmont Rd
HORF/LLZ BS7 ... 326 A8
Upper Bilson Rd CIND GL14 ... 154 A2
Upper Byron Pl CFTN/FAIL BS8 ... 6 B3
Upper Chapel La
FRCTL/WBN BS36 ... 318 E4
Upper Cheltenham Pl
RDLND/MONT BS6 ... 336 A2
Upper Church Rd STROUD GL5 ... 207 M4
Upper Church St CHEP NP16 ... 270 A2
Upper Churnside CIR GL7 ... 238 E3
Upper Cranbrook Rd
RDLND/MONT BS6 ... 325 K7
Upperfield Rd CHELTW GL51 ... 93 J6
Upperfields LED HR8 ... 20 A2
Upper Hall Cl LED HR8 ... 20 A3
Upper Hayes Rd
RSTROUD/NAIL GL6 ... 232 C6
Upper Kitesnest La
RSTROUD/NAIL GL6 ... 184 B8
Upper Leazes STROUD GL5 ... 208 F4
Upper Ley COR/BOX SN13 ... 353 M6
Upper Lynch Rd
RSTROUD/NAIL GL6 ... 210 C8
Upper Maudlin St CBRISNE BS2 ... 6 E2
Upper Mill La CHELTE/BC GL52 ... 94 F6
Upper Nelson St
CHEP NP16 ... 270 A3
Upper Norwood St
CHELTS GL53 ... 115 L5
Upper Park St CHELTE/BC GL52 ... 3 G8
Upper Perry Hl BMSTR BS3 ... 6 C8
Upper Poole Rd DSLY GL11 ... 253 K3
Upper Quay St GL GL1 ... 4 D5
Upper Queen's Rd
STNHO GL10 ... 207 H4
Upper Rd LED HR8 ... 20 E4
LYD GL15 ... 201 H2
Upper Rodley Rd CIND GL14 ... 156 F3
Upper Sandhurst Rd
BRSG/KWL/STAPK BS4 ... 336 F7
Upper Springfield Rd
STROUD GL5 ... 208 E3
Upper Station Rd
MANG/FISH BS16 ... 327 L7
Upper Stone Cl
FRCTL/WBN BS36 ... 318
Upper Stowfield Rd
MTCHDN GL17 ... 128
Upper St BRSG/KWL/STAPK BS4 ... 7
CHPMW/MSHF SN14 ... 330
Upper Sydney St
BMSTR BS3 ... 335 K8
Upper Tockington Rd
THNB/SVB BS35 ... 306
Upper Tynings
RSTROUD/NAIL GL6 ... 232 C7
The Upper Tynings
RSTROUD/NAIL GL6 ... 207
Upper Washwell
RSTROUD/NAIL GL6 ... 185
Upper Wells St CBRIS/FH BS1 ... 6 D4
Upthorpe DSLY GL11 ... 229
Upthorpe La DSLY GL11 ... 229
Upton Cl GLE GL4 ... 137
Upton Gdns TET GL8 ... 281
Upton Hl GLE GL4 ... 160
Upton La GLE GL4 ... 137
GLE GL4 ... 160
Upton Rd BMSTR BS3 ... 6
Upton St GL GL1 ... 5
Urfords Dr MANG/FISH BS16 ... 327 L5
Usk Wy BWTH/CHD GL3 ... 138

V

Vaisey Fld VGL GL2 ... 182
Vaisey Rd CIR GL7 ... 214
Vale Bank VGL GL2 ... 155
Vale La BMSTRD/HC/WWD BS13 .. 345
Valens Ter COR/BOX SN13 ... 353
Valentine Cl CHEP NP16 ... 270
HGRV/WHIT BS14 ... 346
Valerian Cl AVONM BS11 ... 324
GLE GL4 ... 137
Vale Rd CIR GL7 ... 214
Vale St
BRSG/KWL/STAPK BS4 ... 336 C8
The Vale MANG/FISH BS16 ... 329
Vale View Ter
CBATH/BATHN BA1 ... 352
Vallenders Rd TEWK GL20 ... 27
Valley Cl RSTROUD/NAIL GL6 ... 233
Valley Gdns MANG/FISH BS16 ... 328
Valley La GLE GL4 ... 161
Valley Rd
BMSTRD/HC/WWD BS13 ... 345
CFTN/FAIL BS8 ... 334
CIND GL14 ... 154
LYD GL15 ... 225
MANG/FISH BS16 ... 328
MTCHDN GL17 ... 152
OLD/WMLY/WICK BS30 ... 338
WUE GL12 ... 277
Valley Vw DSLY GL11 ... 229
Valley View Rd
CBATH/BATHN BA1 ... 351
STROUD GL5 ... 209
Valley Wy CHPMW/MSHF SN14 .. 343
The Valls ALMDB BS32 ... 317
Valma Rocks
EVILLE/WHL BS5 ... 337 J5
Van Der Breen St
RSTROUD/NAIL GL6 ... 210
Vandyck Av KEYN BS31 ... 348
Varley Av BWTH/CHD GL3 ... 137 K5
Varnister La MTCHDN GL17 ... 129
Varnister Rd MTCHDN GL17 ... 129
Vassall Ct MANG/FISH BS16 ... 327
Vassall Rd MANG/FISH BS16 ... 327
Vatch La RSTROUD/NAIL GL6 ... 209
Vatch Vw STROUD GL5 ... 209
Vattingstone La
THNB/SVB BS35 ... 293
Vaughan Cl HNBRY/STHM BS10 .. 315
Vauxhall NWNT GL18 ... 86
Vauxhall Rd GL GL1 ... 5
Vauxhall Ter GL GL1 ... 5
Vayre Cl YATE/CS BS37 ... 320
Velhurst Dr RSTROUD/NAIL GL6 .. 209
Velthouse La MTCHDN GL17 ... 131
The Vennings DSLY GL11 ... 229
Venns Acre WUE GL12 ... 277
Vensfield Rd VGL GL2 ... 159
Vention La MTCHDN GL17 ... 128
Ventnor Rd BRSTK/PCHW BS34 .. 316
EVILLE/WHL BS5 ... 337
Vera Rd MANG/FISH BS16 ... 337
Verbena Cl GLE GL4 ... 137 G6
Vernal Cl GLE GL4 ... 137
Vernals La WUE GL12 ... 276
Verney Cl CHELTS GL53 ... 116 A5
Verney Rd STNHO GL10 ... 207
The Verneys CHELTS GL53 ... 116 A5
Vernon Cl KEYN BS31 ... 348
Vernon St
BRSG/KWL/STAPK BS4 ... 7 K8
Verrier Rd EVILLE/WHL BS5 ... 336 E4
Vertican Rd VGL GL2 ... 112
Vervain Cl BWTH/CHD GL3 ... 113
Verwood Dr
OLD/WMLY/WICK BS30 ... 348
Vetch Cl GLE GL4 ... 136
Viburnum Vw GLE GL4 ... 137 H6
Vicarage Cl BWTH/CHD GL3 ... 113
CHELTW GL51 ... 139
LYD GL15 ... 225 J2
Vicarage Ct CLFD GL16 ... 175 K1
KGWD/HNM BS15 ... 337 K6
Vicarage La BDWAY WR12 ... 32
BWTH/CHD GL3 ... 138
CHPMW/MSHF SN14 ... 343
SHPSTR CV36 ... 61
THNB/SVB BS35 ... 292
VGL GL2 ... 179
VGL GL2 ... 181
WUE GL12 ... 297 M3
Vicarage Rd BMSTR BS3 ... 6
BMSTRD/HC/WWD BS13 ... 345
CFTN/FAIL BS8 ... 334
EVILLE/WHL BS5 ... 336

FRCTL/WBN BS36............ 318 E6
GL GL1 .... 136 C4
KGWD/HNM BS15 .... 337 K6
THNB/SVB BS35 .... 304 E4
icarage St RSTROUD/NAIL GL6.. 185 H3
icars Cl MANG/FISH BS16 .... 327 K7 🗐
ickers Rd COTS GL54 .... 124 D6
ictoria Av EVILLE/WHL BS5 ... 336 E4
ictoria Cl THNB/SVB BS35 .... 273 K8
ictoria Crs THNB/SVB BS35 ... 304 C5
ictoria Dr DSTNHO GL10........ 206 B4
ictoria Gdns
  CBATH/BATHN BA1 .... 352 B8
  RDLND/MONT BS6 .... 335 M2 🗐
ictoria Pde EVILLE/WHL BS5... 336 E3
ictoria Pk KGWD/HNM BS15 ... 337 M3
  MANG/FISH BS16 .... 327 J6
ictoria Pl BMSTR BS3 ..... 335 L8 🗐
ctoria Retreat CHELT GL50 ...... 2 C9
ictoria Rd CBRISNE BS2 .... 7 L7
  CHEP NP16 .... 270 B6
  CIR GL7 .... 218 D6
  CIR GL7 .... 238 D3
  CLFD GL16 .... 175 J1
  KEYN BS31 .... 348 F8
  KGWD/HNM BS15 .... 337 L6
  LED HR8 .... 19 L4
  LYD GL15 .... 201 J8
  OLD/WMLY/WICK BS30 .... 338 F6
  STROUD GL5 .... 233 H2
  VGL GL2 .... 112 B5
ictoria Sq CFTN/FAIL BS8...... 335 J4
ictoria St CBRIS/FH BS1......... 7 G4
  CHELT GL50 .... 2 C2
  CIND GL14 .... 154 A3
  COTS GL54 .... 123 H6
  GL GL1 .... 5 G8
  MANG/FISH BS16 .... 327 M7
  RSTROUD/NAIL GL6 .... 185 H3 🗐
ictoria Ter CBRISNE BS2 .... 7 M6
  CFTN/FAIL BS8 .... 335 H5 🗐
  CHELTE/BC GL52 .... 3 H6
ictory Cl BWTH/CHD CL3 ...... 113 J3 🗐
ictory Rd GL GL1.................. 136 B4
  RSTROUD/NAIL GL6 .... 184 B8
iew Ct OLD/WMLY/WICK BS30 .. 339 L5
igor Rd
  BMSTRD/HC/WWD BS13 ...... 345 K6 🗐
iking Wy LED HR8................. 19 L2
illage Cl COTS GL54.............. 99 K7
illage Cl YATE/CS BS37 .... 319 M2
illage Rd CHELTW GL51 .... 93 H7
illa Wy LED HR8 .... 19 M5
illiers Rd EVILLE/WHL BS5 .... 336 D4
ilner La THNB/SVB BS35 .... 293 K4
ilverie Md CHELTE/BC GL52 ... 71 M7 🗐
impany Cl HNBRY/STHM BS10 .. 315 H8
impennys La THNB/SVB BS34 .. 314 F2
incent Av GL GL1................. 159 L2
incent Cl AVONM BS11 .... 324 E1
ine Ct CHELTW GL51 .... 2 B2
ine Ter GL GL1 .... 5 L7
ineyard La WUE GL12 .... 277 H6
ineyards Cl CHELTS GL53 ...... 116 D7
ineyard St COTS GL54........... 74 C6
ining Wk EVILLE/WHL BS5 .. 336 D3 🗐
inney La YATE/CS BS37 .... 311 G3
inny Av MANG/FISH BS16 ..... 328 C4
intery Leys
  HNLZ/SM/SNYPK/WT BS9... 325 K4
irginia Cl YATE/CS BS37 .... 320 C2
irginia Rd TEWK GL20 .... 49 G3
ittoria Wk CHELT GL50 .... 2 D7
vian St BMSTR BS3............ 335 M8
zard Cl DSLY GL11 .... 253 K3
owell Cl
  BMSTRD/HC/WWD BS13 .... 345 K7
oxwell La CHELTE/BC GL52 .... 72 A8
oyce Cl GLE GL4 .... 159 M1 🗐
ulcan Wy GLE GL4 .... 137 H5
yners Cl CIR GL7 .... 238 C5
yvyan Rd CFTN/FAIL BS8 ..... 335 J4
yvyan Ter CFTN/FAIL BS8 ..... 335 J4

W

Vade Rd YATE/CS BS37 .... 309 J8
Vades La RSTROUD/NAIL GL6... 184 D3
Vades Rd BRSTK/PCHW BS34... 316 D8
Vade St CBRISNE BS2 .... 7 J1
Vadham Cl CIR GL7 .... 220 B8 🗐
Vadham Dr MANG/FISH BS16 ... 327 K2
Vadham Gv MANG/FISH BS16 ... 328 D6
Vagtail Dr TEWK GL20 .... 48 F2 🗐
Vainbridge Crs
  THNB/SVB BS35 .... 304 E4
Vainbrook Dr EVILLE/WHL BS5 .. 336 F1
Vainlode La RTEWK/TIB GL19..... 90 D1
Vakefield Cl CIR GL7 .... 266 F5 🗐
Vakeford Rd
  MANG/FISH BS16 .... 328 C4 🗐
Valden Rd KEYN BS31 .... 348 C7
Valdrist Cl CHELTW GL51 .... 93 H6
Valham La VGL GL2 .... 112 A7
Valker Cl EVILLE/WHL BS5 .... 336 D4
Valker Rd MANG/FISH BS16 ... 328 C4
Valkers Gdn COTS GL54 .... 169 K2
Valker's La MTCHDN GL17 .... 129 H4
Valker St CBRISNE BS2 .... 6 D1
Valker Wy THNB/SVB BS35 .... 293 K4
Valkey Hl STROUD GL5 .... 208 C6
Valk Rd TEWK GL20 .... 48 B4 🗐
Valk Mill La WUE GL12........ 277 H7
he Walk WUE GL12 .... 277 H7
Vallbridge Rd STROUD GL5 ... 208 D4 🗐

Wallingford Rd
  BRSG/KWL/STAPK BS4....... 345 M4
Walliscote Av
  HNLZ/SM/SNYPK/WT BS9... 325 L5
Walliscote Rd
  HNLZ/SM/SNYPK/WT BS9... 325 L5
Wallscourt Rd
  BRSTK/PCHW BS34 .... 326 D1
Wallscourt Rd South
  BRSTK/PCHW BS34 .... 326 D2
Wallsend La
  CHPMW/MSHF SN14 .... 331 K6
Walnut Av YATE/CS BS37 .... 320 C1
Walnut Bank Dr TEWK GL20 .... 50 D4
Walnut Cl BDWAY WR12......... 32 E3
  CHELTE/BC GL52 .... 94 A7
  CLFD GL16 .... 175 M2
  GLE GL4 .... 136 F8 🗐
  KEYN BS31 .... 347 L7
  THNB/SVB BS35 .... 293 M2
Walnut Crs KGWD/HNM BS15... 338 B8
Walnut Dr CHPMW/MSHF SN14.. 343 H5
Walnut La KGWD/HNM BS15 ... 338 C3 🗐
Walnut Tree Cl ALMDB BS32 ... 306 C6 🗐
Walnut Wk
  BMSTRD/HC/WWD BS13 ...... 345 J5
Walsh Av BHGRV/WHIT BS14 ... 346 C4
Walshe Av YATE/CS BS37 .... 320 E2
Walsingham Rd
  RDLND/MONT BS6 .... 336 A1
Walterbush Rd CHNTN OX7 .... 105 M2
Walter St BMSTR BS3 .... 335 J7
Walton Av
  BRSG/KWL/STAPK BS4....... 336 F6
Walton Cl GLE GL4 .... 137 G8
  KEYN BS31 .... 347 M7
  OLD/WMLY/WICK BS30 .... 348 E2 🗐
Walton Heath YATE/CS BS37 ... 320 B2
Walton Ri
  HNLZ/SM/SNYPK/WT BS9... 325 J3
Walton St EVILLE/WHL BS5 .... 336 D2
Walwyn Cl MTCHDN GL17 ...... 130 C2
Wansbeck Rd KEYN BS31 ...... 348 C7 🗐
Wanscow Wk
  HNLZ/SM/SNYPK/WT BS9... 325 K5
Wapley Hl YATE/CS BS37 .... 320 A7
Wapley Rd YATE/CS BS37 ...... 320 C8
Wapping Rd CBRIS/FH BS1 .... 6 E6
Ward Av VGL GL2 .... 113 G5
Ward Cl CHELTE/BC GL52 ..... 72 C7 🗐
Warden Hill Cl CHELTW GL51 ... 115 H5 🗐
Warden Hill Rd CHELTW GL51 .. 115 H5
Warden Rd BMSTR BS3 .... 6 D9
Wardens' Wy COTS GL54 .... 97 J2
  COTS GL54 .... 99 H5
Wardour Rd
  BRSG/KWL/STAPK BS4....... 345 M3
Ward Rd COTS GL54 .... 169 J1
Wards Rd CHELTW GL51 .... 114 F5
Warend Hl DSLY GL11 .... 253 J5
Warleigh Dr CBATH/BATHN BA1.. 352 B7
Warman Cl HGRV/WHIT BS14 .. 347 H5
Warman Rd HGRV/WHIT BS14 .. 347 H5
Warmer's Inn La MALM SN16... 302 F3
Warmington Rd
  HGRV/WHIT BS14 .... 346 C4
Warminster Rd
  CBRISNE BS2 .... 336 C1 🗐
Warneford Pl MIM GL56 .... 58 D6
Warner Cl KGWD/HNM BS15 ... 338 B5 🗐
The Warns
  OLD/WMLY/WICK BS30 .... 338 C7 🗐
Warren Cl ALMDB BS32 .... 306 F8 🗐
  BWTH/CHD GL3 .... 113 J4
  CHELTW GL51 .... 115 H5
Warren Cft DSLY GL11 .... 252 F7
Warren Dr LED HR8 .... 20 A4
Warren Gdns
  HGRV/WHIT BS14 .... 347 H6 🗐
Warren La LGASH BS41 .... 344 A3
  RWYE HR9 .... 106 C1
Warren Rd BRSTK/PCHW BS34.. 316 D8
  TEWK GL20 .... 48 F3
Warren Slade CHEP NP16 ...... 270 B6 🗐
Warren Wy YATE/CS BS37 ..... 310 A8 🗐
Warrington Rd
  BRSG/KWL/STAPK BS4....... 346 F1
Warth La THNB/SVB BS35 ..... 290 E8
  VGL GL2 .... 156 A7
Warwick Av
  EVILLE/WHL BS5 .... 336 D2 🗐
  GL GL1 .... 159 L2
Warwick Cl
  OLD/WMLY/WICK BS30 .... 348 D1 🗐
  STROUD GL5 .... 208 C7
  THNB/SVB BS35 .... 293 J2
Warwick Crs CHELTE/BC GL52.. 116 D5
Warwick Pl CHELTE/BC GL52..... 2 E4
  SHPSTR CV36 .... 16 A5
  TEWK GL20 .... 48 B7
Warwick Rd
  EVILLE/WHL BS5 .... 336 D2 🗐
  KEYN BS31 .... 347 M7
  RDLND/MONT BS6 .... 335 K2 🗐
Washingpool Hill Rd
  ALMDB BS32 .... 306 E1
Washing Pound La
  HGRV/WHIT BS14 .... 346 D7
Washington Av
  EVILLE/WHL BS5 .... 336 E2
Washmeres
  CHPMW/MSHF SN14 .... 353 K1
Wasley Rd CHELTW GL51 ...... 115 G2
Watch Elm Cl ALMDB BS32 .... 317 G5
Watchill Av
  BMSTRD/HC/WWD BS13 ...... 345 H5
Watchill Cl
  BMSTRD/HC/WWD BS13 ...... 345 H5
Waterbridge Rd
  BMSTRD/HC/WWD BS13 ...... 345 H6
Watercress Rd CBRISNE BS2 ... 326 B8
Waterdale Cl
  HNBRY/STHM BS10 .... 325 L4
  VGL GL2 .... 158 F3 🗐
Waterdale Gdns
  HNLZ/SM/SNYPK/WT BS9... 325 L4
Waterford Cl THNB/SVB BS35... 293 M3

Waterford Rd
  HNLZ/SM/SNYPK/WT BS9... 325 K5 🗐
Watergates
  CHPMW/MSHF SN14 .... 343 L8
Watergripla TEWK GL20.......... 28 C4
Water La BMSTR BS3 .... 336 B8
  BRSG/KWL/STAPK BS4....... 346 F2
  CBRIS/FH BS1 .... 7 H4
  CHELTE/BC GL52 .... 116 D5 🗐
  KGWD/HNM BS15 .... 347 L3
  STROUD GL5 .... 208 A7
  STROUD GL5 .... 233 G3
  WUE GL12 .... 277 K5
Waterloo La CIR GL7 .... 242 D5
Waterloo Pl CBRISNE BS2 .... 7 K3
Waterloo Rd CBRISNE BS2 .... 7 K3
  ST CBRISNE BS2 .... 7 K2
  CFTN/FAIL BS8 .... 335 H4
  CHELTW GL51 .... 93 K8
Waterloo Wy YATE/CS BS37 .... 27 H5
Water Meadow VGL GL2 .... 159 G4
Watermill Cl WUE GL12 .... 275 G4 🗐
Watermoor Ct
  BWTH/CHD GL3 .... 113 K6 🗐
Watermoor Rd CIR GL7 .... 238 D3
Watermoor Wy CIR GL7 .... 238 D4 🗐
Watermore Cl
  FRCTL/WBN BS36.............. 318 E4
Watershoot Cl
  CHELTE/BC GL52 .... 94 C6 🗐
Waterside Cl COTS GL54 ...... 118 C7
  VGL GL2 .... 158 F2 🗐
Waterside Dr ALMDB BS32 .... 316 C2
Water's La
  HNLZ/SM/SNYPK/WT BS9... 325 J4
Waters Reach VGL GL2 .... 135 K5 🗐
Waters Rd KGWD/HNM BS15 ... 337 L3
Water St CHEP NP16 .... 270 A4 🗐
Waterton Cl BWTH/CHD GL3 ... 137 K5 🗐
Waterwheel Cl VGL GL2 .... 158 F2 🗐
Watery La GLE GL4 .... 161 H5
  LED HR8 .... 40 A4
  LYD GL15 .... 201 G8
  NWNT GL18........................ 86 A4
  OLD/WMLY/WICK BS30 .... 340 C3
  RWYE HR9 .... 106 B5
  SHPSTR CV36 .... 16 B5
  VGL GL2 .... 159 G3
  VGL GL2 .... 181 H8
Wathen Rd RDLND/MONT BS6.. 326 B8
Watkins Yd
  HNLZ/SM/SNYPK/WT BS9... 325 J3 🗐
Watledge Bank
  RSTROUD/NAIL GL6 .... 232 D6 🗐
Watledge Cl TEWK GL20 .... 48 B5 🗐
Watledge Rd STROUD GL5..... 232 D5
Watley's End Rd
  FRCTL/WBN BS36.............. 318 A4
Watson Av
  BRSG/KWL/STAPK BS4....... 336 F7
Watson Gv GLE GL4 .... 137 H6 🗐
Watson's Rd
  OLD/WMLY/WICK BS30 .... 338 D6
Watters Cl FRCTL/WBN BS36.... 318 F5
Watts Cl BWTH/CHD GL3 .... 137 J4
Wavell Cl YATE/CS BS37 .... 309 M7
Waveney Rd KEYN BS31 ...... 348 C8
Waverley Rd RDLND/MONT BS6.. 335 L2
  VGL GL2 .... 136 E1
  YATE/CS BS37 .... 319 K1
Waverley St
  EVILLE/WHL BS5 .... 336 C2 🗐
Wayfield Gdns
  CBATH/BATHN BA1 .... 352 B7
Wayford Cl KEYN BS31 ...... 348 C8 🗐
Waylands HGHW SN6 .... 289 G4
Wayleaze FRCTL/WBN BS36 ... 318 F4
Wayside Cl FRCTL/WBN BS36 .. 318 D4
Weald Cl GLE GL4 .... 136 E6
Weavers Cl DSLY GL11 .... 253 K3
  WUE GL12 .... 277 H8 🗐
Weavers Rd CIR GL7 .... 238 E3
  VGL GL2 .... 159 H1 🗐
Webb Crs CHNTN OX7 .... 105 M1
Webb Rd TET GL8 .... 281 L2 🗐
Webbs Heath
  OLD/WMLY/WICK BS30 .... 338 F4
Webbs Wy MALM SN16 .... 303 J6
Webbs Wood Rd ALMDB BS32... 317 H5
Webley Rd MTCHDN GL17 ..... 129 H5
Wedgewood Rd
  MANG/FISH BS16 .... 327 M2
Wedgwood Cl
  HGRV/WHIT BS14 .... 346 D6 🗐
Wedgwood Dr VGL GL2 ..... 112 E6 🗐
Wedmore Cl KGWD/HNM BS15.. 338 B4
Wedmore Rd KEYN BS31 ...... 348 F7
Wedmore V BMSTR BS3 ...... 346 A1 🗐
Weedon Cl CBRISNE BS2 ... 336 C1 🗐
Weigh Bridge Ct CHCAM GL55.. 12 E7 🗐
Weight Rd EVILLE/WHL BS5 .. 336 E4 🗐
Weir Bridge Cl GLE GL4 .... 137 G3
Weir La CFTN/FAIL BS8 .... 334 A4
  CHPMW/MSHF SN14 .... 342 B3
Welch Rd CHELTW GL51 .... 93 G7
Welland Cl CHELTE/BC GL52 .. 94 C7
Welland Dr CHELTE/BC GL52 .. 94 C7
Welland Lodge Rd
  CHELTE/BC GL52 .... 94 B7
Welland Rd KEYN BS31 ...... 348 B7 🗐
  VGL GL2 .... 159 H1
Wellbrook Rd CHELTE/BC GL52.. 72 B6
Well Cl CHEP NP16 .... 270 B7 🗐
  LGASH BS41 .... 344 D2
  TEWK GL20 .... 49 G2
Well Cross Rd GLE GL4 .... 136 B7
Well End STROUD GL5 .... 209 G3
Wellesley Rd CHELT GL50 .... 2 C1
Wellesley St GL GL1 .... 136 B5
Wellfield THNB/SVB GL20 ..... 48 D4 🗐
Wellgarth Rd BRSG/KWL/STAPK BS4 346 C1
Wellgarth Wk
  BRSG/KWL/STAPK BS4........ 346 C2

Well Hl RSTROUD/NAIL GL6 ... 233 J5
Well House Cl
  HNLZ/SM/SNYPK/WT BS9... 335 G1
Welling Cl DSLY GL11 .... 253 K4
Wellington Av
  RDLND/MONT BS6 .... 336 A2
Wellington Crs HORF/LLZ BS7 .. 326 A5
Wellington Dr
  HNLZ/SM/SNYPK/WT BS9... 325 M5
  YATE/CS BS37 .... 319 K1
Wellington Hl HORF/LLZ BS7 .. 326 A5
Wellington Hl West
  HNLZ/SM/SNYPK/WT BS9... 325 L4
Wellington La CHELT GL50....... 2 E1
  CHELTE/BC GL52 .... 2 E3
  RDLND/MONT BS6 .... 336 A2
Wellington Pk CFTN/FAIL BS8.. 335 J2
Wellington Rd CBRISNE BS2 ..... 7 H2 🗐
  COTS GL54 .... 124 C8
  KGWD/HNM BS15 .... 337 M1
  MIM GL56 .... 58 E6
  YATE/CS BS37 .... 310 A7
Wellington Sq CHELT GL50 .... 2 E2
Wellington St CHELT GL50 .... 2 E2
  GL GL1 .... 4 F7
Wellington Wk
  HNBRY/STHM BS10 .... 325 L4
Well La BAD GL9 .... 313 G6
  COTS GL54 .... 98 E5
  COTS GL54 .... 102 A3
  MTCHDN GL17 .... 129 K4
Wellmeadow CLFD GL16 ...... 150 D5
Wellmeadow La CLFD GL16... 151 K4
Well Pl CHELT GL50 .... 115 H5
Wells Cl CHELTW GL51 .... 115 H6
  HGRV/WHIT BS14 .... 346 E6
Wells Gdns BDWAY WR12 ...... 33 G3
Wellsprings Rd VGL GL2 .... 112 E8
Wells Rd BRSG/KWL/STAPK BS4 ... 7 K8
  BRSG/KWL/STAPK BS4....... 346 D1
  GLE GL4 .... 136 E2
  HGRV/WHIT BS14 .... 346 D3
  RSTROUD/NAIL GL6 .... 210 C3
Wells St BMSTR BS3 .... 335 J7 🗐
Wellstead Av YATE/CS BS37 ... 319 M2
Wellsway KEYN BS31 .... 348 B5
Welsford Av KGWD/HNM BS15.. 337 M6
Welsford Rd KGWD/HNM BS15.. 337 M6
Welsh Back CBRIS/FH BS1 .... 6 F6
Welsh House La NWNT GL18.... 64 D3
Welsh Wy CIR GL7 .... 213 G1
  CIR GL7 .... 217 H5
Welton Rd KGWD/HNM BS15 .. 337 L1 🗐
Welveland La GLE GL4 .... 137 G2
Welwyn Ms CHELTW GL51 ... 115 G6 🗐
Wendover Gdns CHELT GL50 .. 115 K2 🗐
The Wend MTCHDN GL17 ...... 131 H1
Wenlock Rd TEWK GL20........ 48 B6
Wenmore Cl MANG/FISH BS16.. 327 M2
Wentforth Dr
  KGWD/HNM BS15 .... 337 L1 🗐
Wentworth
  OLD/WMLY/WICK BS30 .... 338 C5 🗐
  YATE/CS BS37 .... 320 A7
Wentworth Cl CHELTW GL51 ... 92 F8 🗐
  VGL GL2 .... 112 D6 🗐
Wentworth Rd HORF/LLZ BS7.. 325 M8
Werth La RTEWK/TIB GL19 ..... 46 F8
Wesley Av KGWD/HNM BS15 .. 337 M6
Wesley Cl LYD GL15.............. 224 F3
  MANG/FISH BS16 .... 327 M8 🗐
Wesley Hl KGWD/HNM BS15 ... 337 M2 🗐
Wesley La
  OLD/WMLY/WICK BS30 .... 338 D6
Wesley Pl CFTN/FAIL BS8...... 335 J1
Wesley Rd CIND GL14 .... 154 B2
  HORF/LLZ BS7 .... 326 A7
  LYD GL15 .... 201 G2
  STNHO GL10 .... 207 G8
Wesley St BMSTR BS3 ..... 335 L8 🗐
Wessex Av HORF/LLZ BS7 ..... 326 A7
Wessex Dr CHELTE/BC GL52 .... 3 L5
Westacre Cl HNBRY/STHM BS10.. 325 J1
Westal Pk CHELTW GL51 ...... 115 K4
West Approach Dr
  CHELTE/BC GL52 .... 94 A7
West Av MTCHDN GL17 .... 129 M3
Westbourne Av KEYN BS31 ... 348 A6 🗐
Westbourne Cl
  MANG/FISH BS16 .... 328 B4 🗐
Westbourne Dr CHELTE/BC GL52.. 3 H4
  VGL GL2 .... 159 G4
Westbourne Pl CFTN/FAIL BS8... 6 A1
Westbourne Rd
  EVILLE/WHL BS5 .... 336 D3 🗐
  MANG/FISH BS16 .... 328 B3
West Broadway
  HNLZ/SM/SNYPK/WT BS9... 325 M5
Westbrook Rd
  BRSG/KWL/STAPK BS4....... 346 F3
Westbury Court Rd
  HNLZ/SM/SNYPK/WT BS9... 325 H4
Westbury Hl
  HNLZ/SM/SNYPK/WT BS9... 325 J4
Westbury La
  HNLZ/SM/SNYPK/WT BS9... 324 E4
Westbury Pk
  RDLND/MONT BS6 .... 325 J7
Westbury Rd CFTN/FAIL BS8 .. 335 J1 🗐
  CHELTS GL53 .... 116 A7
  GL GL1 .... 135 M8
  HNLZ/SM/SNYPK/WT BS9... 325 J5
West Coombe
  HNLZ/SM/SNYPK/WT BS9... 324 F5
Westcote Rd GLE GL4 ...... 159 M2 🗐
Westcourt Dr
  OLD/WMLY/WICK BS30 .... 338 D7
West Cft
  HNLZ/SM/SNYPK/WT BS9... 325 L4
West Dene
  HNLZ/SM/SNYPK/WT BS9... 325 G5
Westdown Gdns CHELTE/BC GL52.. 3 G5
West Dr CHELT GL50 .... 2 E2
Westend DSLY GL11 .... 228 F7
West End BMSTR BS3 .... 6 D8
  CBRISNE BS2 .... 6 E1
  CBRISNE BS2 .... 335 M3

CHNTN OX7 .... 104 B7
COTS GL54 .... 169 J1
RSTROUD/NAIL GL6 .... 233 H5
THNB/SVB BS35 .... 272 E5
West End La BDWAY WR12 ...... 32 D4
  BWTH/CHD GL3 .... 137 K5
Westend La THNB/SVB BS35 ... 272 D5
Westend Pde GL GL1 .... 4 A3
Westend Rd WUE GL12 .... 296 A4
Westend Ter GL GL1 .... 4 B3
Westering Cl
  MANG/FISH BS16 .... 328 C6 🗐
Westerleigh Cl
  MANG/FISH BS16 .... 328 B4 🗐
Westerleigh Rd
  MANG/FISH BS16 .... 328 C4
  MANG/FISH BS16 .... 328 A5
  MANG/FISH BS16 .... 329 K5
  YATE/CS BS37 .... 319 K7
Westerley Cl CIND GL14 .... 154 B4
Western Av CHEP NP16 .... 270 A6
  FRCTL/WBN BS36.............. 318 C3
Western Dr HGRV/WHIT BS14 .. 346 A4
Western Hlrd TEWK GL20 .... 50 F1
Western Rd CHELT GL50 .... 115 K2
  HORF/LLZ BS7 .... 326 A5
Western Wy NWNT GL18 .... 41 K8
Westfield DSLY GL11 .... 253 J1
West Fld VGL GL2 .... 110 F6
Westfield Av BWTH/CHD GL3 .. 137 M5
  TEWK GL20 .... 49 G3
Westfield Cl KEYN BS31 .... 347 L6
  KGWD/HNM BS15 .... 337 M6
Westfield Ct CIND GL14 .... 154 B2
Westfield La
  BRSTK/PCHW BS34 .... 317 G3
Westfield Pk RDLND/MONT BS6.. 335 K2
Westfield Pl CFTN/FAIL BS8 ... 335 H4 🗐
Westfield Rd BWTH/CHD GL3 .. 137 M5
  CIND GL14 .... 154 B2
  HNLZ/SM/SNYPK/WT BS9... 325 J3
Westfields WUE GL12 .... 277 J4
Westfield Ter VGL GL2 .... 112 A6
Westfield Wy ALMDB BS32 .... 316 F1
Westgate St GL GL1 .... 4 B3
West Gv RDLND/MONT BS6 ... 336 B2
West Hay Gv CIR GL7 .... 261 H4
Westland Av
  OLD/WMLY/WICK BS30 .... 338 E7
Westland Rd VGL GL2 .... 158 F4
West La CIR GL7 .... 261 H4
West Leaze Pl ALMDB BS32.... 317 G5
Westleigh Cl
  HNBRY/STHM BS10 .... 325 M2 🗐
  YATE/CS BS37 .... 319 L2
Westleigh Pk HGRV/WHIT BS14.. 346 C3
Westleigh Rd
  HNBRY/STHM BS10 .... 325 L2
West Littleton Rd
  CHPMW/MSHF SN14 .... 341 M1
West Ml CFTN/FAIL BS8 .... 335 H4
West Market Pl CIR GL7 ..... 238 C2 🗐
Westmarsh La THNB/SVB BS35.. 272 D6
Westmead Rd EVILLE/WHL BS5.. 337 K4
  VGL GL2 .... 112 F6
West Mill La HGHW SN6........ 288 E3
Westminster Cl CHELTS GL53 .... 3 H9
  HNLZ/SM/SNYPK/WT BS9... 325 J4 🗐
Westminster Rd
  EVILLE/WHL BS5 .... 336 F3 🗐
Westmoreland Rd
  RDLND/MONT BS6 .... 325 K8 🗐
Weston Av EVILLE/WHL BS5 .. 336 F4 🗐
Weston Cl
  HNLZ/SM/SNYPK/WT BS9... 324 E4
Weston Ct SHPSTR CV36 .... 61 J5
Weston Crs HORF/LLZ BS7 .... 326 A5
Weston Rd GL GL1 .... 4 E9
  LGASH BS41 .... 344 B2
Westons Brake
  MANG/FISH BS16 .... 328 C2
Westons Hill Dr
  MANG/FISH BS16 .... 328 C3
Westons Wy KGWD/HNM BS15.. 338 B4
Westover Cl
  HNLZ/SM/SNYPK/WT BS9... 325 H2
Westover Ct BWTH/CHD GL3 .. 113 K4
Westover Dr
  HNLZ/SM/SNYPK/WT BS9... 325 J3
Westover Gdns
  HNLZ/SM/SNYPK/WT BS9... 325 H3 🗐
Westover Ri
  HNLZ/SM/SNYPK/WT BS9... 325 J2
Westover Rd
  HNLZ/SM/SNYPK/WT BS9... 325 J3
West Pde
  HNLZ/SM/SNYPK/WT BS9... 324 E4
West Pk CFTN/FAIL BS8 .... 335 K3
West Park Rd MANG/FISH BS16.. 328 A6
West Priory Cl
  HNLZ/SM/SNYPK/WT BS9... 325 J4 🗐
West Rdg FRCTL/WBN BS36 ... 318 D4
Westridge Rd WUE GL12 ...... 277 J3 🗐
Westrip Pl RSTROUD/NAIL GL6.. 207 M3
West Rocke Av
  HNLZ/SM/SNYPK/WT BS9... 324 F4
West Shrubbery
  RDLND/MONT BS6 .... 335 K1 🗐
West St BMSTR BS3 .... 345 K1
  CBRISNE BS2 .... 7 K3
  CHNTN OX7 .... 104 B6
  KGWD/HNM BS15 .... 337 M3 🗐
  MALM SN16 .... 303 H8
  OLD/WMLY/WICK BS30 .... 338 E7
  SHPSTR CV36 .... 16 B6
  TET GL8 .... 281 M4
  WUE GL12 .... 294 C6
West Town Dr
  BRSG/KWL/STAPK BS4 ...... 346 F2 🗐
West Town Gv
  BRSG/KWL/STAPK BS4....... 346 F3
West Town La
  BRSG/KWL/STAPK BS4....... 346 F2
  HGRV/WHIT BS14 .... 346 D3
West Town Pk
  BRSG/KWL/STAPK BS4....... 346 F3
West Tynings
  RSTROUD/NAIL GL6 .... 232 C7 🗐

West Vw CIND GL14 .... 154 B4
  NWNT GL18 .... 86 B3
  THNB/SVB BS35 .... 293 H7
Westview RTEWK/TIB GL19 .... 69 G6
West View Rd BMSTR BS3 .... 335 K8
  CBATH/BATHN BA1 ...... 352 A8
  KEYN BS31 .... 348 A6
Westward Gdns LGASH BS41 .. 344 D1
Westward Rd
  BMSTRD/HC/WWD BS13 .... 345 H4
  STROUD GL5 .... 207 M5
West Wy CIR GL7 .... 238 C3
  CIR GL7 .... 244 E6
Westwick Rd RTEWK/TIB GL19 .. 108 C7
Westwood Crs
  BRSG/KWL/STAPK BS4 ..... 336 F6
Westwood La
  CHELTE/BC GL52 .... 94 F8
Westwood Rd
  BRSG/KWL/STAPK BS4 ..... 346 F3
Westwoods CBATH/BATHN BA1 .. 352 D8
Wetherby Ct
  FRCTL/WBN BS36 .... 328 B2
Wetherell Pl CFTN/FAIL BS8 ... 6 A3
Wetherleigh Dr VGL GL2 ...... 110 F6
Wexford Rd
  BRSG/KWL/STAPK BS4 ..... 345 M3
Weyhouse La STROUD GL5 .... 208 F6
Weymouth Rd BMSTR BS3 .... 345 M1
Whaddon Cl CHELTE/BC GL52 ... 3 J3
Whaddon Dr CHELTE/BC GL52 ... 3 H3
Whaddon Rd CHELTE/BC GL52 ... 3 L3
Whaddon Wy GLE GL4 .... 159 M2
Wharfdale Wy STNHO GL10 ... 207 G5
  VGL GL2 .... 158 F3
Wharfedale THNB/SVB BS35 ... 293 M3
The Wharfings HGHW SN6 .... 266 F5
Wharf La CIR GL7 .... 244 F7
  CIR GL7 .... 266 F5
Wharf Rd MANG/FISH BS16 .... 327 H7
The Wharf COR/BOX SN13 ..... 353 M4
Wharnecliffe Cl
  HGRV/WHIT BS14 .... 346 D6
Wharnecliffe Gdns
  HGRV/WHIT BS14 .... 346 D6
Whatley Rd CFTN/FAIL BS8 .... 335 J2
Wheatfield Ct CHCAM GL55 .... 8 F7
Wheatfield Dr ALMDB BS32 .... 316 F2
Wheat HI TET GL8 .... 281 L3
Wheathill Ct KEYN BS31 ...... 347 L6
Wheatland Dr CHELTW GL51 ... 92 F7
The Wheatridge (East) GLE GL4 .. 136 F7
The Wheatridge GLE GL4 ...... 136 F7
Wheatsheaf Dr CHELTE/BC GL52 .. 71 M7
Wheatstone Ct TEWK GL20 .... 49 G2
Wheatstone Rd GL GL1 ...... 136 A4
Wheatway GLE GL4 .... 136 F8
Wheelers Wk STROUD GL5 .... 208 B2
Whelford Rd CIR GL7 .... 266 F4
Whimbrel Rd VGL GL2 .... 158 E2
Whimsey Rd CIND GL14 ...... 129 M8
  CIND GL14 .... 153 M1
Whinchat Gdns
  MANG/FISH BS16 .... 327 H5
Whip La RSTROUD/NAIL GL6 ... 232 D6
Whippington Ct CBRIS/FH BS1 .. 7 G2
Whitby Rd
  BRSG/KWL/STAPK BS4 ..... 336 E7
Whitchurch La
  BMSTRD/HC/WWD BS13 ... 345 J6
  HGRV/WHIT BS14 .... 346 A6
Whitebeam Cl VGL GL2 ...... 112 D6
Whitechapel Rd LYD GL15 .... 200 D2
Whitecourt DSLY GL11 .... 254 D4
Whitecroft RSTROUD/NAIL GL6 .. 232 D7
Whitecroft Rd LYD GL15 ..... 200 D4
Whitecross Av
  HGRV/WHIT BS14 .... 346 E5
White Cross Rd LYD GL15 .... 225 J1
Whitecross Sq CHELTS GL53 ... 116 A4
Whitefield Av EVILLE/WHL BS5 .. 337 J2
  KGWD/HNM BS15 .... 337 M6
Whitefield Cl
  CBATH/BATHN BA1 .... 352 D7
  STNHO GL10 .... 207 G5
Whitefield Rd EVILLE/WHL BS5 .. 337 J1
Whitefields CHELTE/BC GL52 ... 71 M7
  YATE/CS BS37 .... 320 E2
Whitefriars La HGHW SN6 .... 263 G8
Whitehall Av EVILLE/WHL BS5 .. 337 G8
Whitehall Gdns
  EVILLE/WHL BS5 .... 336 F3
Whitehall La VGL GL2 .... 109 M4
Whitehall Rd EVILLE/WHL BS5 .. 336 E3
White Hart La COTS GL54 .... 102 A3
White Hart St CHELTW GL51 ... 2 B2
Whitehill La MTCHDN GL17 ... 129 L3
White Horse La
  RSTROUD/NAIL GL6 ...... 185 H3
White Horse Rd HGHW SN6 ... 288 Y3
  NWNT GL18 .... 85 H2
  TET GL8 .... 301 L3
Whitehouse Pk STROUD GL5 ... 208 A4
Whitehouse Pl BMSTR BS3 .... 7 G8
Whitehouse Rd
  THNB/SVB BS35 .... 304 E4
Whitehouse St BMSTR BS3 .... 7 G9
Whitehouse Wy
  CHELTE/BC GL52 .... 72 D8
Whiteladies Rd CFTN/FAIL BS8 .. 6 B2
  CFTN/FAIL BS8 .... 335 J1
Whitelands Rd CIR GL7 ...... 238 E2
Whiteleaze
  HNBRY/STHM BS10 .... 325 L4
White Lion Pk MALM SN16 .... 303 G7
White Lodge Rd
  MANG/FISH BS16 .... 328 B7
Whitemarsh Cl CHELTW GL51 .. 92 F7
Whites HI EVILLE/WHL BS5 .... 337 J5
Whiteshill MANG/FISH BS16 ... 317 M8
White St EVILLE/WHL BS5 .... 7 K1
White Tree Rd
  HNLZ/SM/SNYPK/WT BS9 ... 325 K7
Whitewall La THNB/SVB BS35 .. 294 B1
Whitewater Rd TET GL8 ...... 279 L7
White Wy CIR GL7 .... 190 E2
  CIR GL7 .... 214 D5

Whiteway DSLY GL11 .... 253 L4
Whiteway Cl
  BRSG/KWL/STAPK BS4 ..... 337 G5
  DSLY GL11 .... 253 L4
  EVILLE/WHL BS5 .... 337 J3
Whiteway Ms EVILLE/WHL BS5 .. 337 J3
Whiteway Rd EVILLE/WHL BS5 .. 337 J2
  GLE GL4 .... 136 D6
The Whiteway CIR GL7 ...... 214 D6
Whiteway Vw CIR GL7 .... 214 B8
Whitewell Cl GLE GL4 .... 137 G4
Whitewood Rd
  EVILLE/WHL BS5 .... 337 H2
Whitfield Cl
  KGWD/HNM BS15 .... 337 M1
Whitfield Rd THNB/SVB BS35 .. 293 L1
Whitfield St GL GL1 .... 4 F6
Whiting Rd
  BMSTRD/HC/WWD BS13 ... 345 J7
Whitland Av
  BMSTRD/HC/WWD BS13 ... 345 K6
Whitland Rd
  BMSTRD/HC/WWD BS13 ... 345 K6
Whitley Cl YATE/CS BS37 ..... 309 L8
Whitley Md BRSTK/PCHW BS34 .. 317 G8
Whitlow La CIND GL14 .... 132 E2
Whitmead Gdns
  BMSTRD/HC/WWD BS13 ... 345 L7
Whitmore Av
  BRSG/KWL/STAPK BS4 ..... 337 J8
Whitmore Rd COTS GL54 ..... 74 B4
The Whitmores COTS GL54 ... 123 H1
Whitson St CBRIS/FH BS1 .... 6 F1
Whittington Rd CHELTW GL51 .. 114 F3
  MANG/FISH BS16 .... 327 L5
Whittington Wy LYD GL15 ... 200 D4
Whittle Av GLE GL4 .... 159 M2
Whittle Cl CHELTW GL51 ..... 114 E2
Whittles La VGL GL2 .... 181 J6
Whittlestone Cl COTS GL54 ... 101 J3
Whittlestone Hollow
  COTS GL54 .... 101 J3
Whittock Rd HGRV/WHIT BS14 .. 346 F6
Whittock Sq HGRV/WHIT BS14 .. 346 F4
Whittucks Cl KGWD/HNM BS15 .. 337 M7
Whittucks Rd
  KGWD/HNM BS15 .... 337 M6
Whitwell Rd HGRV/WHIT BS14 .. 346 D6
Whitworth Ms
  BWTH/CHD GL3 .... 137 L5
Whitworth Rd GL GL1 .... 238 C4
Whornes Orch GLE GL4 ...... 137 H8
Whytes Cl
  HNLZ/SM/SNYPK/WT BS9 ... 325 J5
Wick Crs BRSG/KWL/STAPK BS4 .. 336 F8
The Wickets HORF/LLZ BS7 ... 326 B2
  KGWD/HNM BS15 .... 337 M1
Wickfield La CHELTE/BC GL52 .. 73 H7
Wickham Ct LYD GL15 .... 200 D2
Wickham Gln MANG/FISH BS16 .. 326 F6
Wickham HI MANG/FISH BS16 .. 326 F6
Wickham Vw
  MANG/FISH BS16 .... 326 F7
Wick La OLD/WMLY/WICK BS30 .. 349 J2
  RTEWK/TIB GL19 .... 69 H7
Wicklow Rd
  BRSG/KWL/STAPK BS4 ..... 346 A3
Wickridge Cl STROUD GL5 .... 208 E3
Wick Rd BRSG/KWL/STAPK BS4 .. 336 F8
  MALM SN16 .... 285 J3
  THNB/SVB BS35 .... 304 E4
Wick St RSTROUD/NAIL GL6 ... 185 G7
Wickwar Rd WUE GL12 ...... 277 G7
  YATE/CS BS37 .... 309 J3
Wickwater La CIR GL7 ...... 263 L7
Widcombe HGRV/WHIT BS14 .. 346 C6
Widcombe Cl
  EVILLE/WHL BS5 .... 337 J4
Widden St GL GL1 .... 5 H7
Wigmore Cl GLE GL4 .... 137 G5
Wigton Crs HNBRY/STHM BS10 .. 325 L1
Wilbye Gv
  BRSG/KWL/STAPK BS4 ..... 345 M5
Wilcox Cl KGWD/HNM BS15 .... 337 L1
Wildcountry La LGASH BS41 ... 344 A4
  NAIL BS48 .... 344 A6
Wildcroft Rd
  HNLZ/SM/SNYPK/WT BS9 ... 325 K6
Wildlife Wk BWTH/CHD GL3 ... 138 A7
Wildmoorway La GL GL1 ..... 263 K4
Wilkes Av BWTH/CHD GL3 .... 137 J3
Wilkes Meadow CLFD GL16 ... 151 M8
Wilkinson Rd CIR GL7 .... 238 C6
Willada Cl BMSTR BS3 .... 345 K1
Willcox Dr CHELTE/BC GL52 ... 72 D8
Willersey Rd CHELTW GL51 ... 115 G3
  EVE WR11 .... 10 A1
William Gough Cl
  CHELTW GL51 .... 92 F6
William Mason Cl
  EVILLE/WHL BS5 .... 336 D4
Williams Cl
  OLD/WMLY/WICK BS30 ... 348 B1
William Smith Cl CHNTN OX7 .. 105 G7
Williamson Rd HORF/LLZ BS7 .. 326 B8
Williams Orch VGL GL2 ...... 110 F6
William St BMSTR BS3 ...... 7 G8
  BMSTR BS3 .... 7 J9
  CBRISNE BS2 .... 7 L4
  CBRISNE BS2 .... 336 B2
  EVILLE/WHL BS5 .... 336 E3
  MANG/FISH BS16 .... 327 K8
Willinton Rd
  BRSG/KWL/STAPK BS4 ..... 346 A4
Willis Rd KGWD/HNM BS15 .... 338 B1
Willis Wk TEWK GL20 .... 49 G2
Willmott Cl HGRV/WHIT BS14 .. 346 B4
Willoughby Cl BMSTRD/HC/WWD BS13
  345 J4
  THNB/SVB BS35 .... 293 J7
Willoughby Rd
  HORF/LLZ BS7 .... 326 A6
Willow Av GLE GL4 .... 136 D4
Willow Bank Rd TEWK GL20 .. 51 K5
Willow Bed Cl MANG/FISH BS16 .. 327 K5
Willowbrook Dr CHELTW GL51 .. 92 F7

Willow Cl BRSTK/PCHW BS34 .. 316 A4
  CHELTE/BC GL52 .... 72 D8
  DSLY GL11 .... 229 J8
  EVE WR11 .... 29 K4
  LGASH BS41 .... 344 B2
  OLD/WMLY/WICK BS30 ... 338 F5
  STNHO GL10 .... 207 G4
  WUE GL12 .... 276 C7
Willowcroft Cl GLE GL4 ...... 136 F8
Willow End MIM GL56 .... 82 C2
The Willowfalls
  CBATH/BATHN BA1 ...... 352 A8
Willow Gv GLE GL4 .... 263 J5
  MANG/FISH BS16 .... 337 L1
Willow Hts LYD GL15 .... 201 K6
Willowherb Cl CHELTE/BC GL52 .. 3 M2
  CHELTE/BC GL52 .... 94 E8
Willowleaze VGL GL2 .... 112 F8
Willow Park Dr
  CHELTE/BC GL52 .... 72 B7
Willow Rd BDWAY WR12 ..... 11 G8
  CHELTS GL53 .... 116 E7
  CHELTS GL53 .... 116 D6
  KGWD/HNM BS15 .... 337 L8
  STNHO GL10 .... 207 G4
  STNHO GL10 .... 207 J7
The Willows ALMDB BS32 .... 316 F3
  MTCHDN GL17 .... 131 H1
  VGL GL2 .... 159 C2
  YATE/CS BS37 .... 319 M1
Willow View Cl MALM SN16 ... 303 F7
Willow Wk HNBRY/STHM BS10 .. 315 K8
  KEYN BS31 .... 347 M7
Willow Wy FRCTL/WBN BS36 .. 318 E1
  GLE GL4 .... 136 D4
Willsbridge HI
  OLD/WMLY/WICK BS30 ... 348 C1
Wills Dr EVILLE/WHL BS5 ..... 336 C3
Willway St BMSTR BS3 .... 7 G9
  CBRISNE BS2 .... 7 K3
Wilmot Ct
  OLD/WMLY/WICK BS30 ... 338 C5
Wilshire Av KGWD/HNM BS15 .. 337 M6
Wilson Pl CBRISNE BS2 ...... 336 B3
Wilson Rd CHELTW GL51 ..... 138 F2
Wilson St CBRISNE BS2 ...... 7 H1
Wilton Cl HNBRY/STHM BS10 .. 325 L3
Wilton Rd GL GL1 .... 135 M5
Wiltshire Av YATE/CS BS37 ... 310 C8
Wiltshire Pl
  KGWD/HNM BS15 .... 328 A8
Wimbledon Rd
  RDLND/MONT BS6 .... 325 L6
Wimborne Cl CHELTW GL51 ... 115 G5
Wimborne Rd BMSTR BS3 .... 345 L2
Winash Cl HGRV/WHIT BS14 ... 346 F4
Wincanton Cl
  FRCTL/WBN BS36 .... 328 B2
Wincel Rd COTS GL54 .... 74 D5
Winchcombe Rd EVE WR11 ... 10 D2
  FRCTL/WBN BS36 .... 318 D3
  GLE GL4 .... 160 A1
Winchcombe St CHELTE/BC GL52 .. 2 E5
Winchester Av
  BRSG/KWL/STAPK BS4 ..... 336 F8
Winchester Dr GLE GL4 ..... 136 A8
Winchester Rd
  BRSG/KWL/STAPK BS4 ..... 336 F8
Winchester Wy CHELTW GL51 .. 115 H5
Wincroft
  OLD/WMLY/WICK BS30 ... 338 C5
Windcliff Crs AVONM BS11 .... 324 A3
Windermere Rd
  BRSTK/PCHW BS34 .... 316 C3
  CHELTW GL51 .... 115 C4
  GLE GL4 .... 112 E7
Windermere Wy
  OLD/WMLY/WICK BS30 ... 338 B6
Windmill Cl BMSTR BS3 ...... 7 G9
Windmill Fld GLE GL4 .... 136 F4
Windmill HI BMSTR BS3 ...... 335 M8
Windmill La CIR GL7 .... 261 H3
  STROUD GL5 .... 232 F4
Windmill Rd CIR GL7 .... 261 H3
Windrush Ct THNB/SVB BS35 .. 293 L4
Windrush Rd CHELTE/BC GL52 .. 3 K3
  GLE GL4 .... 160 A1
  KEYN BS31 .... 348 C7
Windrush Wy COTS GL54 .... 120 D2
Windsor Av EVILLE/WHL BS5 .. 337 K5
  KEYN BS31 .... 348 A7
Windsor Cl
  BRSTK/PCHW BS34 .... 317 G7
  MANG/FISH BS16 .... 328 A4
Windsor Crs
  HNBRY/STHM BS10 .... 314 E7
Windsor Dr GL GL1 .... 159 L1
  LYD GL15 .... 201 K5
  YATE/CS BS37 .... 309 M8
  YATE/CS BS37 .... 319 M1
Windsor Pl CFTN/FAIL BS8 .... 335 H5
  MANG/FISH BS16 .... 328 C6
Windsor Rd DSLY GL11 ...... 253 K2
  OLD/WMLY/WICK BS30 ... 348 B1
  RDLND/MONT BS6 .... 336 A1
Windsor St CHELTE/BC GL52 ... 3 G2
Windsor Ter BMSTR BS3 ..... 7 J9
  CFTN/FAIL BS8 .... 335 H5
Windyridge Gdns CHELTW GL51 .. 93 L6
Windyridge Rd CHELTW GL51 .. 93 K6
Wineberry Cl EVILLE/WHL BS5 .. 337 K5
Wine St CBRIS/FH BS1 ...... 6 F3
Winfield NWNT GL18 .... 86 B3
Winfield Rd
  BMSTRD/HC/WWD BS13 ... 345 J3
Wingfield Rd BMSTR BS3 .... 346 A1
Wing La TEWK GL20 .... 27 M3
Winkworth Pl CBRISNE BS2 .. 336 B2
Winnycroft La GLE GL4 ..... 160 E2

Winsbury Wy ALMDB BS32 ... 316 E3
Winscombe Cl KEYN BS31 .... 347 M5
Winsford St EVILLE/WHL BS5 .. 7 L4
Winsham Cl
  HGRV/WHIT BS14 .... 346 D6
Winsley Rd GLE GL4 .... 136 E7
  RDLND/MONT BS6 .... 335 M2
Winston Cl LED HR8 .... 20 A5
Winstonian Rd CHELTE/BC GL52 .. 3 G4
Winston Rd BWTH/CHD GL3 .. 113 K6
Winterbotham Rd CHELTW GL51 .. 92 F8
  DSLY GL11 .... 229 H6
Winterbourne HI
  FRCTL/WBN BS36 .... 317 M6
Winterbourne Rd
  BRSTK/PCHW BS34 .... 317 G5
Winterspring La WUE GL12 ... 278 B8
Winterstoke Cl BMSTR BS3 ... 345 K1
Winterstoke Rd BMSTR BS3 .. 335 H8
Winterway MIM GL56 .... 35 H8
Wintles Cl MTCHDN GL17 .... 130 C2
Wintle's HI CIND GL14 ...... 156 C3
Wintles La CIND GL14 ...... 132 A5
Winton Cl CHELTW GL51 ..... 115 H4
Winton Rd CHELTW GL51 .... 115 J4
Winton St BRSG/KWL/STAPK BS4 .. 7 K9
Wirewood Cl CHEP NP16 .... 270 B1
Wirewood Crs CHEP NP16 ... 270 C1
Wishford Cl VGL GL2 .... 113 G7
Wisloe Rd VGL GL2 .... 229 G1
Wistaria Av YATE/CS BS37 ... 320 C2
Wistaria Rd TET GL8 .... 281 M3
Wisteria Wy BWTH/CHD GL3 .. 113 H5
Wistley Rd CHELTS GL53 ..... 116 D7
Witchell Rd
  EVILLE/WHL BS5 .... 336 E4
Witch Hazel Rd
  BMSTRD/HC/WWD BS13 ... 346 A8
Witcombe YATE/CS BS37 ..... 319 L4
Witcombe Cl KGWD/HNM BS15 .. 338 A2
Witcombe Pl CHELTE/BC GL52 .. 2 F6
Witham Rd KEYN BS31 ...... 348 C8
Witherlies Rd
  MANG/FISH BS16 .... 327 H5
The Withers CHELTE/BC GL52 .. 72 B7
Withey Cl West
  HNLZ/SM/SNYPK/WT BS9 ... 325 G6
The Witheys HGRV/WHIT BS14 .. 346 E7
Withington Cl
  OLD/WMLY/WICK BS30 ... 348 E1
Withleigh Rd
  BRSG/KWL/STAPK BS4 ..... 346 D1
Withy Br CHELTW GL51 ...... 92 C3
Withybridge Gdns CHELTW GL51 .. 92 C3
Withybridge La CHELTW GL51 .. 92 C6
Withy Cl East
  HNLZ/SM/SNYPK/WT BS9 ... 325 H6
Withyfield Rd CHELTE/BC GL52 .. 72 C7
Withyholt Pk CHELTS GL53 ... 116 B6
Withymead Rd
  CHPMW/MSHF SN14 ...... 342 D3
Withy Ms GLE GL4 .... 136 D8
Withypool CHELTW GL51 .... 115 G6
Withypool Gdns
  HGRV/WHIT BS14 .... 346 D6
Withy Wy DSLY GL11 .... 229 H6
Withywood Rd
  BMSTRD/HC/WWD BS13 ... 345 H7
Witley Lodge Cl
  CHELTW GL51 .... 114 F5
Witney Cl KEYN BS31 .... 348 F8
Witpit La CIR GL7 .... 239 H4
Woburn Av GL GL1 .... 159 L2
Woburn Cl
  OLD/WMLY/WICK BS30 ... 338 B6
Woburn Rd EVILLE/WHL BS5 .. 326 D8
Woefuldane Bottom
  RSTROUD/NAIL GL6 ...... 233 K6
Wolds End GL CHCAM GL55 .. 12 E7
Wolferton Rd
  RDLND/MONT BS6 .... 336 B1
Wolford Rd MIM GL56 ...... 37 L8
Wolfridge Gdns
  HNBRY/STHM BS10 .... 315 J7
Wolfridge La THNB/SVB BS35 .. 293 H7
Wolfridge Ride THNB/SVB BS35 .. 293 H7
Wolseley Rd HORF/LLZ BS7 ... 325 M8
  VGL GL2 .... 136 E1
Woodbine Cl GLE GL4 .... 137 G6
Woodbine Rd
  EVILLE/WHL BS5 .... 336 F3
Woodborough Cl
  RSTROUD/NAIL GL6 ...... 185 H4
Woodborough St
  EVILLE/WHL BS5 .... 336 D2
Woodbridge La COTS GL54 ... 166 E1
Woodbridge Rd
  BRSG/KWL/STAPK BS4 ..... 346 C1
Woodchester
  KGWD/HNM BS15 .... 328 A8
  YATE/CS BS37 .... 320 A5
Woodchester Rd
  HNBRY/STHM BS10 .... 325 L4
Woodcock Cl GLE GL4 ...... 136 E6
  STNHO GL10 .... 207 H2
Woodcock La STNHO GL10 ... 207 H3
Woodcote KGWD/HNM BS15 .. 337 M5
  VGL GL2 .... 112 D6
Woodcote Rd MANG/FISH BS16 .. 337 K1
Woodcote Wk
  MANG/FISH BS16 .... 337 K1
Woodcroft Av
  EVILLE/WHL BS5 .... 336 F2
Woodcroft Cl
  BRSG/KWL/STAPK BS4 ..... 337 G7
  CHEP NP16 .... 246 C7
Woodcroft La CHEP NP16 .... 246 C7
Woodcroft Rd
  BRSG/KWL/STAPK BS4 ..... 337 G7
Wood Edge Rd CLFD GL16 ... 175 L5
Woodend KGWD/HNM BS15 .. 337 M5
Woodend Cl GLE GL4 .... 137 G3
Woodend La BRKLY GL13 .... 273 M1
  CIND GL14 .... 179 M7
  DSLY GL11 .... 228 F4
  DSLY GL11 .... 229 H5
  RWYE HR9 .... 84 C4

MTCHDN GL17 129
Wood End St LED HR8 42
Wood End Wk
  HNLZ/SM/SNYPK/WT BS9 ... 324
Woodfield Rd DSLY GL11 229
  LED HR8 19
  RDLND/MONT BS6 335
Woodgate Cl CHELTS GL53 ... 116 E6
  GLE GL4 .... 137 G5
Woodgate Rd CIND GL14 154
  CLFD GL16 151
Woodgrove Rd
  HNBRY/STHM BS10 324
Woodhall Cl
  MANG/FISH BS16 .... 328 B5
Woodhouse Av ALMDB BS32 .. 306
Woodhouse Cl ALMDB BS32 .. 306
  CIR GL7 238
Woodhouse Dr STROUD GL5 .. 208
Woodhouse Gv HORF/LLZ BS7 .. 326
Woodington Ct
  OLD/WMLY/WICK BS30 ... 338 B7
Woodland Av DSLY GL11 .... 253 J1
  KGWD/HNM BS15 .... 337 M1
Woodland Cl BDWAY WR12 .. 31 HJ2
  MANG/FISH BS16 .... 337 L1
Woodland Dr DSLY GL11 .... 253 J1
Woodland Gn GLE GL4 137
Woodland Gv
  HNLZ/SM/SNYPK/WT BS9 ... 324
Woodland Pl LYD GL15 177
Woodland Ri LYD GL15 176
  LYD GL15 201
Woodland Rd CFTN/FAIL BS8 .. 6
  CFTN/FAIL BS8 335
  CLFD GL16 151
  LYD GL15 176
  LYD GL15 200
  MTCHDN GL17 129
  WUE GL12 275
Woodlands ALMDB BS32 306
  MANG/FISH BS16 .... 328 A5
  STNHO GL10 207
Woodlands Cl LYD GL15 200
Woodlands Dr STROUD GL5 .. 209 G8
Woodlands La ALMDB BS32 .. 316
  BRKLY GL13 251
Woodlands MI STROUD GL5 .. 209 G8
Woodlands Reach CIND GL14 .. 154
Woodlands Ri MANG/FISH BS16 .. 327 L4
Woodlands Rd CHELT GL50 .. 115
  CIR GL7 238
  WUE GL12 276
The Woodlands STROUD GL5 .. 208 F3
Woodland Ter
  KGWD/HNM BS15 337
  RDLND/MONT BS6 .... 335 K1
Woodland Vw CIR GL7 ...... 189 L4
Woodland Wy
  EVILLE/WHL BS5 337
Wood La CHPMW/MSHF SN14 .. 343
  EVE WR11 29
  NWNT GL18 85
  RSTROUD/NAIL GL6 232
  SHPSTR CV36 47
  VGL GL2 113
  YATE/CS BS37 311
Woodlea CHPMW/MSHF SN14 .. 343
Woodleaze
  HNLZ/SM/SNYPK/WT BS9 ... 324
Woodleigh THNB/SVB BS35 ... 293
Woodleigh Cl LED HR8 19
Woodleigh Fld VGL GL2 ..... 111 G5
Woodleigh Gdns
  HNBRY/STHM BS10 346
Woodleigh Rd LED HR8 19
Woodmancote DSLY GL11 ... 253
  YATE/CS BS37 .... 319 L7
Woodmancote Rd
  RDLND/MONT BS6 .... 336 A2
Woodmancote V
  CHELTE/BC GL52 .... 72 D8
Woodmans Cl YATE/CS BS37 .. 320
Woodmans Rd YATE/CS BS37 .. 320
Woodmans V YATE/CS BS37 .. 320 E2
Woodmans Wy CHELTE/BC GL52 .. 72 D8
Woodmarsh Cl
  HGRV/WHIT BS14 346
Woodmead Gdns
  BMSTRD/HC/WWD BS13 ... 345
Woodmead La
  OLD/WMLY/WICK BS30 ... 340
Woodpecker Crs
  MANG/FISH BS16 .... 329 L7
Woodpecker Rd VGL GL2 135
Woodpeckers
  RTEWK/TIB GL19 .... 89 J2
Woodrew Rd CLFD GL16 151
  KGWD/HNM BS15 337
Woodrow Wy VGL GL2 135
Woodruff Cl GLE GL4 136
Woodside LYD GL15 223
Woodside Av CIND GL14 154
Woodside Dr BUR/CRTN OX18 .. 197
Woodside Gv
  HNBRY/STHM BS10 314
Woodside La STNHO GL10 .... 231 H5
Woodside Rd
  BRSG/KWL/STAPK BS4 337
  FRCTL/WBN BS36 318
  KGWD/HNM BS15 337
  LYD GL15 225
  MANG/FISH BS16 327
  St CIND GL14 154
Woods Orch GLE GL4 160
Woods Orchard Rd GLE GL4 .. 160
Woodstock Av
  RDLND/MONT BS6 .... 335 L2
Woodstock Cl
  KGWD/HNM BS15 .... 338 B3
  TET GL8 .... 257 K2
Woodstock La TET GL8 257
Woodstock Rd
  KGWD/HNM BS15 .... 338 B4
  RDLND/MONT BS6 335
Woodstock Ter DSLY GL11 ... 253
Wood St EVILLE/WHL BS5 .... 336 D7
  STROUD GL5 .... 208 F4

Woodview Cl *AVONM* BS11 ...... **324** A4
Woodview Rd *DSLY* GL11 ...... **229** J7 🔢
Woodville Av *CLFD* GL16 ...... **151** M7
Woodville Rd *CIND* GL14 ...... **154** C3
  TEWK GL20 ...... **48** B8 🔢
Woodville Rd West *CIND* GL14 .... **154** B3
Woodward Cl *TET* GL8 ...... **281** M2 🔢
Woodward Dr
  OLD/WMLY/WICK BS30 ...... **338** B7
Woodwell Rd *AVONM* BS11 ...... **324** A5
Woodyleaze Dr
  KGWD/HNM BS15 ...... **337** L5
Woolaston Common *LYD* GL15 ... **223** M4
Woolcot St *RDLND/MONT* BS6 .... **335** K1
Woolley La *CBATH/BATHN* BA1 ... **351** J6
Woolley Rd *HGRV/WHIT* BS14 .... **347** G6 🔢
Woolridge Hl *RTEWK/TIB* GL19 ... **89** C7
Woolstone La *CHELTE/BC* GL52 ... **72** B2
Woolstrop Wy *VGL* GL2 ...... **135** J8
Woolthorpe La *VGL* GL2 ...... **156** A8
Wootton Crs
  BRSG/KWL/STAPK BS4 ...... **337** G5
Wootton Pk *HGRV/WHIT* BS14 .... **346** D2
Wootton Rd
  BRSG/KWL/STAPK BS4 ...... **337** G5
Worcester Cl *MANG/FISH* BS16 ... **337** K1
Worcester Crs *CFTN/FAIL* BS8 ... **335** J3 🔢
Worcester Pde *GL* GL1 ...... **4** F5
Worcester Rd *CFTN/FAIL* BS8 ..... **335** J3
  CHNTN OX7 ...... **83** M8
  CHNTN OX7 ...... **105** K1
  CIND GL14 ...... **154** C2
  KGWD/HNM BS15 ...... **337** M2 🔢
  LED HR8 ...... **20** A3
  RTEWK/TIB GL19 ...... **66** F8
Worcestershire Wy
  RGTMLV WR13 ...... **21** K3
Worcester St *GL* GL1 ...... **4** F4
Worcester Ter *CFTN/FAIL* BS8 ..... **335** J3
Worcester Wk *CLFD* GL16 ...... **151** M8
Vorchester Road
  RTEWK/TIB GL19 ...... **67** H5

Worcestershire Way Link
  TEWK GL20 ...... **24** F8
The Wordens *STROUD* GL5 ...... **207** M3 🔢
Wordsworth Av *CHELTW* GL51 ... **115** G2 🔢
Wordsworth Rd *DSLY* GL11 ...... **253** L4 🔢
  HORF/LLZ BS7 ...... **326** C4
Working La *CLSW* GL54 ...... **73** M2
Worldsend La *BRKLY* GL13 ...... **250** A3
World's End La *KEYN* BS31 ...... **52** A2
Worley Rdg *RSTROUD/NAIL* GL6 .. **232** C7
Wormcliff La *COR/BOX* SN13 ...... **353** J7
Wormwood Hl
  RSTROUD/NAIL GL6 ...... **256** B2
Worrall Rd *CFTN/FAIL* BS8 ...... **335** J1
Worrel's La *MANG/FISH* BS16 ...... **317** M8
Worsley St *EVILLE/WHL* BS5 ...... **336** F4 🔢
Worth Cl *KGWD/HNM* BS15 ...... **338** B5 🔢
Wortheys Cl *MALM* SN16 ...... **303** C3
Worthing Rd
  BRSTK/PCHW BS34 ...... **316** B3
The Worthys *ALMDB* BS32 ...... **317** J5
Wortley Rd *WUE* GL12 ...... **277** L5
Wotton Cl *GLE* GL4 ...... **136** F2 🔢
Wotton Crs *WUE* GL12 ...... **277** L5
Wotton Rd *WUE* GL12 ...... **276** C6
  YATE/CS BS37 ...... **309** G7
Wragg Castle La
  RSTROUD/NAIL GL6 ...... **184** E5
Wraxall Gv
  BMSTRD/HC/WWD BS13 ...... **345** H3
Wraxall Rd *KGWD/HNM* BS15 ...... **338** C5
  OLD/WMLY/WICK BS30 ...... **338** C5
Wrenbert Rd *MANG/FISH* BS16... **327** M6
Wren Cl *GLE* GL4 ...... **136** D5
Wren Dr *MANG/FISH* BS16 ...... **327** H5
Wren Ter *VGL* GL2 ...... **112** F5
Wright Cl *COTS* GL54 ...... **124** C5
Wright Rd *COTS* GL54 ...... **124** C5
Wrington Cl *BRSTK/PCHW* BS34... **316** E4
Wrington Crs
  BMSTRD/HC/WWD BS13 ...... **345** J4
Wroughton Dr
  BMSTRD/HC/WWD BS13...... **345** M7

Wroughton Gdns
  BMSTRD/HC/WWD BS13 ...... **345** M7 🔢
Wroxham Dr
  BRSTK/PCHW BS34 ...... **316** E3 🔢
Wyatt Av
  BMSTRD/HC/WWD BS13 ...... **345** H6
Wyatt Cl
  BMSTRD/HC/WWD BS13 ...... **345** H6
Wychavon Wy *TEWK* GL20 ...... **52** A2
Wychbury Cl *CHELTS* GL53 ...... **115** M6 🔢
Wychovon Wy *EVE* WR11 ...... **29** L6
Wychwood *KGWD/HNM* BS15 .... **337** M5
Wyck Beck Rd
  HNBRY/STHM BS10 ...... **315** J7
Wycliffe Rd
  HNLZ/SM/SNYPK/WT BS9 ...... **325** K4
Wycombe Gv
  BRSG/KWL/STAPK BS4 ...... **346** F1 🔢
Wydelands *MIM* GL56 ...... **35** K7
Wyebank Av *NP16* ...... **270** C3 🔢
Wyebank Cl *CHEP* NP16 ...... **270** C3 🔢
Wyebank Crs *CHEP* NP16 ...... **270** C3
Wyebank Pl *CHEP* NP16 ...... **270** C3 🔢
Wyebank Ri *CHEP* NP16 ...... **270** C3
Wyebank Rd *CHEP* NP16 ...... **270** C3
Wyebank Vw *CHEP* NP16 ...... **270** C3 🔢
Wyebank Wy *CHEP* NP16 ...... **270** C3
Wye Ct *THNB/SVB* BS35 ...... **293** L3
Wye Crs *CHEP* NP16 ...... **270** A4
Wye Croft Cl
  HNBRY/STHM BS10 ...... **315** M8
Wyedale Av
  HNLZ/SM/SNYPK/WT BS9 ...... **324** D4
Wye Rd *BWTH/CHD* GL3...... **138** B6
Wye Valley Wk *CHEP* NP16 ...... **222** A3
  CHEP NP16 ...... **246** A8
  RWYE HR9 ...... **128** C4
Wye View La *RWYE* HR9 ...... **126** E5
Wykis Ct *KGWD/HNM* BS15 ...... **338** A6 🔢
Wyman's La *CHELTW* GL51 ...... **93** K5
Wyman's Rd *CHELTE/BC* GL52 ... **3** J2

Wymbush Crs
  BMSTRD/HC/WWD BS13 ...... **345** L6
Wymbush Gdns
  BMSTRD/HC/WWD BS13 ...... **345** L6 🔢
Wyndbrook La *RTEWK/TIB* GL19 .. **44** B4
Wyndham Crs
  BRSG/KWL/STAPK BS4 ...... **337** H8
Wynols Cl *CLFD* GL16 ...... **175** M1
Wynols Hill La *CLFD* GL16 ...... **151** K8 🔢
Wynols Rd *CLFD* GL16 ...... **175** M1 🔢
The Wynstones
  KGWD/HNM BS15 ...... **337** L4
Wynyards Cl *STROUD* GL5 ...... **48** B5 🔢
Wyvern Rd *CHEP* NP16 ...... **290** D1

Y

Yanleigh Cl
  BMSTRD/HC/WWD BS13 ...... **344** E5
Yanley La *LGASH* BS41 ...... **344** D3
The Yard *EVE* WR11 ...... **30** D1
Yarlington Cl *CHELTE/BC* GL52 .. **72** A7 🔢
Yarnolds *CHELTW* GL51 ...... **138** F2
Yarrow Cl *GLE* GL4 ...... **136** C7
Yartleton La *MTCHDN* GL17 ...... **107** H4
Yate Rd *YATE/CS* BS37 ...... **308** F7
Yate Rocks *YATE/CS* BS37 ...... **310** B4
Yellow Hundred Cl *DSLY* GL11 ... **253** K2
Yeoman Cl *LED* HR8 ...... **19** L1
Yeomans Cl
  HNLZ/SM/SNYPK/WT BS9 ...... **324** F6 🔢
Yeomanside Cl
  HGRV/WHIT BS14 ...... **346** E6
Yeomeads *LGASH* BS41 ...... **344** B2
The Yetts *CHEP* NP16 ...... **270** D4
Yewcroft Cl *HGRV/WHIT* BS14 ... **346** C7
Yew Tree Cl *CHELTW* GL51 ...... **93** L6
Yewtree Cl *DSLY* GL11 ...... **228** F8
Yew Tree Dr *CHELTE/BC* GL52 ... **72** C3 🔢

  KGWD/HNM BS15 ...... **328** B8
Yew Tree Wy *BWTH/CHD* GL3 ... **113** J6
  STROUD GL5 ...... **209** G8
Yokehouse La
  RSTROUD/NAIL GL6 ...... **185** H5
York Av *HORF/LLZ* BS7 ...... **326** B7
York Cl *BRSTK/PCHW* BS34 ...... **316** F7
  FRCTL/WBN BS36 ...... **328** B2
  YATE/CS BS37 ...... **310** A7
York Gdns *CFTN/FAIL* BS8 ...... **335** H5
  FRCTL/WBN BS36 ...... **318** B3
Yorkley La *LYD* GL15 ...... **201** K2
Yorkley Wood Rd *LYD* GL15 ...... **201** J2
York Pl *CBRIS/FH* BS1 ...... **6** C5
  CFTN/FAIL BS8 ...... **6** A3
York Rd *BMSTR* BS3 ...... **7** G8
  CIND GL14 ...... **154** C2
  EVILLE/WHL BS5 ...... **336** E2
  GLE GL4 ...... **136** E3
  MANG/FISH BS16 ...... **328** A7
  RDLND/MONT BS6 ...... **336** A2
  TEWK GL20 ...... **48** A7
York Rw *CHELTE/BC* GL52 ...... **94** C7
York St *CBRISNE* BS2 ...... **7** G1
  CBRISNE BS2 ...... **336** B1 🔢
  CBRISNE BS2 ...... **336** C1 🔢
  CFTN/FAIL BS8 ...... **335** J1 🔢
  CHELTE/BC GL52 ...... **2** F4
  EVILLE/WHL BS5 ...... **336** E4 🔢
Youngs Ct *MANG/FISH* BS16 ..... **328** D3 🔢
Youngs Orch *STROUD* GL5 ...... **233** J2

Z

Zetland Rd *RDLND/MONT* BS6 ... **335** M1
Zinnia Cl *BWTH/CHD* GL3 ...... **113** H4
Zion Hl *RSTROUD/NAIL* GL6 ...... **184** B8
Zoons Rd *BWTH/CHD* GL3 ...... **137** J3

3-D Gallery
  CBRISNE BS2 ...... **6** E2
Abbey House Studio & Gallery
  CHEP NP16 ...... **222** A6
Abbeymead Primary School
  GLE GL4 ...... **137** H6
Abbotswood Infant School
  YATE/CS BS37 ...... **319** M5
Abbotswood Surgery
  YATE/CS BS37 ...... **319** M4
ABC Cinema
  CFTN/FAIL BS8 ...... **335** K3
Air Balloon Hill Junior &
  Infant School
  EVILLE/WHL BS5 ...... **337** J4
Airthrie School
  CHELT GL50 ...... **115** K2
Alderman Knight School
  TEWK GL20 ...... **48** E4
Allen School House
  OLD/WMLY/WICK BS30 ...... **338** C6
All Saints Exhibition Centre
  CBRIS/FH BS1 ...... **6** F3
Almondsbury Business Centre
  ALMDB BS32 ...... **306** F8
Almondsbury
  C of E VC Primary School
  ALMDB BS32 ...... **306** C7
Almondsbury Surgery
  ALMDB BS32 ...... **306** C6
Almondsbury Town
  Football Club
  ALMDB BS32 ...... **306** C7
Alstone Trading Estate
  CHELTW GL51 ...... **115** J2
Amberley House School
  CFTN/FAIL BS8 ...... **335** J2
Amberley Parochial School
  STROUD GL5 ...... **232** E4
Amberley Ridge
  Special School
  STROUD GL5 ...... **232** E2
Amelia Nutt Clinic
  BMSTRD/HC/WWD BS13 ...... **345** H7
Amphitheatre
  CBRIS/FH BS1 ...... **6** D6
Anchor Business Centre
  RDLND/MONT BS6 ...... **335** K2
Anderson Gallery
  BDWAY WR12 ...... **33** G3
Andoversford
  Industrial Estate
  COTS GL54 ...... **118** D8
Andoversford Primary School
  COTS GL54 ...... **118** C8
Andoversford Sports Club
  COTS GL54 ...... **118** C8
Ann Edwards School
  CIR GL7 ...... **263** H5
The Archway School
  STROUD GL5 ...... **208** B3
Aretians RFC Clubhouse
  BRSTK/PCHW BS34 ...... **316** D4
Army Apprentices College
  NP16 ...... **270** D8
Arnoldsfield Trading Estate
  WUE GL12 ...... **296** C6
Arnolfini Gallery
  CBRIS/FH BS1 ...... **6** E6
Art Gallery
  CHELT GL50 ...... **2** C8
Arthur Dye CP School
  CHELTW GL51 ...... **92** F7

Ashchurch Business Centre
  TEWK GL20 ...... **48** F3
Ashchurch County
  Primary School
  TEWK GL20 ...... **49** H4
Ashleworth C of E
  Primary School
  RTEWK/TIB GL19 ...... **89** J3
Ashley Down Junior School
  HORF/LLZ BS7 ...... **326** A7
Ashley Down OB Rugby Club
  HORF/LLZ BS7 ...... **326** D3
Ashley Trading Estate
  RDLND/MONT BS6 ...... **336** B1
Ashmead Business Park
  KEYN BS31 ...... **348** D6
Ashton Gate Primary School
  BMSTR BS3 ...... **335** J7
Ashton Keynes C of E School
  HGHW SN6 ...... **287** J2
Ashton Park School
  BMSTR BS3 ...... **335** G8
Ashton under Hill
  Primary School
  EVE WR11 ...... **29** K3
Ashton Vale Primary School
  BMSTR BS3 ...... **345** H1
Ashville Industrial Estate
  VGL GL2 ...... **135** L6
Ashville Trading Estate
  CHELTW GL51 ...... **93** K5
Ashville Trading Estate
  VGL GL2 ...... **135** L6
Ashwicke Hall (School)
  CHPMW/MSHF SN14 ...... **342** H1
Avening School
  TET GL8 ...... **257** K2
Avlon Works
  HNBRY/STHM BS10 ...... **304** D8
Avon Business Park
  MANG/FISH BS16 ...... **327** L4
Avon County Council
  BMSTR BS3 ...... **346** A1
Avondale Business Centre
  MANG/FISH BS16 ...... **337** L1
Avon & Somerset
  Constabulary
  CBRIS/FH BS1 ...... **6** F2
Avon Trading Estate
  CBRISNE BS2 ...... **7** L6
Axiom Arts Centre
  CHELTE/BC GL52 ...... **2** E4
Aylburton C of E School
  LYD GL15 ...... **224** F2
Azure School
  HNLZ/SM/SNYPK/WT BS9 ... **325** H4
Badminton Road Trading Estate
  YATE/CS BS37 ...... **319** L4
Badminton School
  HNLZ/SM/SNYPK/WT BS9 ... **325** H4
Badocks Wood Primary School
  HNBRY/STHM BS10 ...... **325** L3
Badsey First School
  EVE WR11 ...... **10** A1
Baileys Court Primary School
  ALMDB BS32 ...... **317** H5
Balaclava Industrial Estate
  MANG/FISH BS16 ...... **327** H8
Balcarras School
  CHELTS GL53 ...... **116** E6
Bank Leaze Primary School
  AVONM BS11 ...... **324** D1

Bankside Industrial Estate
  LED HR8 ...... **19** L4
Bank Yard Industrial Estate
  WUE GL12 ...... **277** J4
Bannerman Road
  Primary School
  EVILLE/WHL BS5 ...... **336** D2
Barley Close Primary School
  MANG/FISH BS16 ...... **328** C5
Barnack Trading Centre
  BMSTR BS3 ...... **345** L2
Barn Close Surgery
  BDWAY WR12 ...... **32** F3
Barnwood Business Centre
  GLE GL4 ...... **136** F2
Barnwood Business Centre
  GLE GL4 ...... **137** H2
Barnwood C of E
  Primary School
  GLE GL4 ...... **136** F2
Barrett Industrial Estate
  GL GL1 ...... **4** D1
Barrow Hospital
  NAIL BS48 ...... **344** C5
Barrs Court Primary School
  OLD/WMLY/WICK BS30 ...... **338** B6
Bartongate Surgery
  GL GL1 ...... **5** G7
Barton Hill Primary School
  EVILLE/WHL BS5 ...... **336** D5
Barton Hill Trading Estate
  EVILLE/WHL BS5 ...... **336** D5
Batheaston Medical Centre
  CBATH/BATHN BA1 ...... **352** C8
Batheaston Primary School
  CBATH/BATHN BA1 ...... **352** B7
Battledown Industrial Estate
  CHELTE/BC GL52 ...... **3** J7
Beachley Road
  Doctors Surgery
  CHEP NP16 ...... **270** C3
The Beacon Medical Practice
  RSTROUD/NAIL GL6 ...... **185** G4
Beacon Rise Junior School
  KGWD/HNM BS15 ...... **337** M5
Beaufort Community School
  GL GL1 ...... **159** K1
Bedminster Down School
  BMSTRD/HC/WWD BS13 ...... **345** H4
Beeches Trading Estate
  YATE/CS BS37 ...... **319** J1
Beech Green CP School
  VGL GL2 ...... **159** H2
Beechwood Shopping Centre
  CHELTE/BC GL52 ...... **2** E5
Beehive Trading Estate
  EVILLE/WHL BS5 ...... **337** G4
Begbrook Primary School
  MANG/FISH BS16 ...... **327** H5
Bells Hotel & the Royal
  Forest of Dean Golf Club
  CLFD GL16 ...... **175** K1
Benhall Infant School
  CHELTW GL51 ...... **114** F4
Berkeley Association
  Football Club
  BRKLY GL13 ...... **227** H7
Berkeley Castle
  BRKLY GL13 ...... **251** H1
Berkeley Hospital
  BRKLY GL13 ...... **227** G8

Berkeley Leisure Centre
  BRKLY GL13 ...... **227** G4
Berkeley Primary School
  BRKLY GL13 ...... **227** G8
Berkeley Vale
  Community School
  BRKLY GL13 ...... **227** G4
Berkhampstead School
  CHELTE/BC GL52 ...... **3** H4
Berry Hill R F C
  CLFD GL16 ...... **151** K5
Bettridge School
  CHELTW GL51 ...... **115** J5
Bibury C of E Primary School
  CIR GL7 ...... **217** K1
Birdlip School
  BWTH/CHD GL3 ...... **163** H2
Birdwell Primary School
  LGASH BS41 ...... **344** C3
Bishop Road Primary School
  HORF/LLZ BS7 ...... **325** M7
Bishops Cleeve Primary School
  CHELTE/BC GL52 ...... **72** B8
Bishops Cleeve Sports Centre
  CHELTE/BC GL52 ...... **94** C1
Bishopston House Clinic
  HORF/LLZ BS7 ...... **326** A7
Bishopsworth C of E School
  BMSTRD/HC/WWD BS13 ...... **345** H5
Bishopsworth Swimming Pool
  BMSTRD/HC/WWD BS13 ...... **345** J5
Bisley Blue Coat School
  RSTROUD/NAIL GL6 ...... **210** C3
Blackberry Hill Hospital
  MANG/FISH BS16 ...... **327** H6
Blackhorse CP School
  MANG/FISH BS16 ...... **328** C3
Blaise Hamlet (NT)
  HNBRY/STHM BS10 ...... **324** F1
Blakeney CP School
  LYD GL15 ...... **202** D1
Bledington County
  Primary School
  CHNTN OX7 ...... **125** M1
Blockley C of E School
  MIM GL56 ...... **35** G8
Blue Coat Church of
  England Primary School
  WUE GL12 ...... **277** K4
Bond Industrial Estate
  EVE WR11 ...... **10** A5
Bonds Mill Trading Estate
  STNHO GL10 ...... **206** E4
Bonville Business Centre
  BRSG/KWL/STAPK BS4 ...... **347** H1
Bourton Industrial Estate
  COTS GL54 ...... **123** H4
Bourton on the Water County
  Primary School
  COTS GL54 ...... **123** H4
Bowden Hall (Hotel)
  GLE GL4 ...... **137** J8
Bowling Club
  CHELT GL50 ...... **2** B8
Bowling Hill Business Park
  YATE/CS BS37 ...... **320** C2
Bownham Park School
  STROUD GL5 ...... **232** F1
Box C of E School
  COR/BOX SN13 ...... **353** M5
Box Surgery
  COR/BOX SN13 ...... **353** M5

Bradgate Surgery
  HNBRY/STHM BS10 ...... **315** J8
Brailes C of E Primary School
  RBANSW OX15 ...... **17** M8
Brailes Golf Club
  RBANSW OX15 ...... **39** M2
Bream Sports Club
  LYD GL15 ...... **200** C3
Bredon Hancocks
  Endowed First School
  TEWK GL20 ...... **27** G8
Bredon School
  TEWK GL20 ...... **47** G2
Brentry Hospital
  HNBRY/STHM BS10 ...... **325** K1
Brentry Primary School
  HNBRY/STHM BS10 ...... **315** K1
Briarwood School
  MANG/FISH BS16 ...... **327** K8
Brickhampton Court Golf Club
  BWTH/CHD GL3 ...... **113** K3
Brickwell Swimming Pools
  RSTROUD/NAIL GL6 ...... **233** M4
Bridge Farm Junior &
  Infant School
  HGRV/WHIT BS14 ...... **346** C6
Bridge House Gallery
  CIR GL7 ...... **244** D7
Brimscombe C of E
  Primary School
  STROUD GL5 ...... **233** H2
Brimscombe Mills Estate
  STROUD GL5 ...... **233** H2
Brimscombe Port
  Business Park
  STROUD GL5 ...... **233** H2
Brimsham Green School
  YATE/CS BS37 ...... **309** M7
Brislington Retail Park
  BRSG/KWL/STAPK BS4 ...... **347** G2
Brislington School
  BRSG/KWL/STAPK BS4 ...... **347** H3
Brislington Trading Estate
  BRSG/KWL/STAPK BS4 ...... **347** H1
Bristol Baptist College
  CFTN/FAIL BS8 ...... **335** H3
Bristol Business Park
  MANG/FISH BS16 ...... **327** H2
Bristol Cathedral
  CBRIS/FH BS1 ...... **6** D5
Bristol Cathedral School
  CBRIS/FH BS1 ...... **6** D5
Bristol City Council
  AVONM BS11 ...... **324** C4
Bristol City Council
  BMSTR BS3 ...... **7** G9
Bristol City Council
  BMSTRD/HC/WWD BS13 ... **345** K7
Bristol City Council
  BRSG/KWL/STAPK BS4 ...... **336** E7
Bristol City Council
  BRSG/KWL/STAPK BS4 ...... **337** H8
Bristol City Council
  BRSG/KWL/STAPK BS4 ...... **345** M4
Bristol City Council
  BRSG/KWL/STAPK BS4 ...... **346** C1
Bristol City Council
  CBRIS/FH BS1 ...... **6** C4
Bristol City Council
  CBRIS/FH BS1 ...... **7** G3
Bristol City Council
  CBRIS/FH BS1 ...... **7** K6

Bristol City Council *CBRIS/FH* BS1 ... 7 G1
Bristol City Council *CBRISNE* BS2 ... 336 B2
Bristol City Council *CFTN/FAIL* BS8 ... 6 A3
Bristol City Council *CFTN/FAIL* BS8 ... 6 C2
Bristol City Council *CFTN/FAIL* BS8 ... 335 J6
Bristol City Council *EVILLE/WHL* BS5 ... 336 F4
Bristol City Council *EVILLE/WHL* BS5 ... 336 D1
Bristol City Council *HGRV/WHIT* BS14 ... 346 B6
Bristol City Council *HGRV/WHIT* BS14 ... 346 E3
Bristol City Council *HNBRY/STHM* BS10 ... 315 K8
Bristol City Council *HNBRY/STHM* BS10 ... 325 M1
Bristol City Council *HNBRY/STHM* BS10 ... 325 K3
Bristol City Council *HNBRY/STHM* BS10 ... 326 A5
Bristol City Council *HNLZ/SM/SNYPK/WT* BS9 ... 335 J1
Bristol City Council *HORF/LLZ* BS7 ... 326 B2
Bristol City Football Club *BMSTR* BS3 ... 335 H8
Bristol Civil Service Sports Club *HORF/LLZ* BS7 ... 326 B5
Bristol Clifton & West of England Zoological Society *CFTN/FAIL* BS8 ... 335 H3
Bristol County Court *CBRISNE* BS2 ... 6 E2
Bristol County Sports Club *CBRIS/FH* BS1 ... 6 D3
Bristol Crown Court *CBRIS/FH* BS1 ... 6 E3
Bristol Dental Hospital *CBRIS/FH* BS1 ... 6 E2
Bristol General Hospital *CBRIS/FH* BS1 ... 6 F7
Bristol Grammar School *CFTN/FAIL* BS8 ... 6 B2
Bristol Grammar School *CFTN/FAIL* BS8 ... 334 A8
Bristol Harlequins RFC *BRSG/KWL/STAPK* BS4 ... 347 J1
Bristol Ice Rink *CBRIS/FH* BS1 ... 6 D3
Bristol Industrial Museum *CBRIS/FH* BS1 ... 6 D7
Bristol North Baths *HORF/LLZ* BS7 ... 325 M8
Bristol Old Vic (New Vic Theatre & Theatre Royal) *CBRIS/FH* BS1 ... 6 E4
Bristol Old Vic Theatre School *CFTN/FAIL* BS8 ... 335 J2
Bristol Old Vic Theatre School *HNLZ/SM/SNYPK/WT* BS9 ... 335 H2
Bristol Rovers Football Club *BRSG/KWL/STAPK* BS4 ... 347 H2
Bristol Royal Hospital for Sick Children *CFTN/FAIL* BS8 ... 6 D2
Bristol Royal Infirmary *CBRISNE* BS2 ... 6 E1
Bristol South Swimming Pool *BMSTR* BS3 ... 6 D9
Bristol Steiner Waldorf School *CFTN/FAIL* BS8 ... 6 A3
Bristol University *CFTN/FAIL* BS8 ... 6 D3
Bristol Vale Trading Estate *BMSTR* BS3 ... 345 J4
British Empire & Commonwealth Museum *CBRIS/FH* BS1 ... 7 J6
The British School *WUE* GL12 ... 277 L5
Broadfield House Glass Museum *CIR* GL7 ... 238 C3
Broadlands School *KEYN* BS31 ... 347 M5
Broadmead Lane Industrial Estate *KEYN* BS31 ... 348 C4
Broadwalk Shopping Centre *BRSG/KWL/STAPK* BS4 ... 346 D1
Broadway County Infant School *YATE/CS* BS37 ... 320 L2
Broadway Dental Health Centre *BDWAY* WR12 ... 32 F3
Broadway Primary School *BDWAY* WR12 ... 33 G2
Broadway Trading Estate *CIR* GL7 ... 263 J6
Broadway United Football Club *BDWAY* WR12 ... 32 D3
Brockeridge Infant School *FRCTL/WBN* BS36 ... 318 E4
Brockworth Comprehensive School *BWTH/CHD* GL3 ... 138 B5
Brockworth County Primary Infant School *BWTH/CHD* GL3 ... 138 A5
Bromesberrow C of E School *LED* HR8 ... 43 H2
Bromley Heath Infant School *MANG/FISH* BS16 ... 328 A3
Bromley Heath Junior School *MANG/FISH* BS16 ... 328 A3
Bromsberrow Heath Business Park *LED* HR8 ... 42 E5

Brookfield School *CHELTW* GL51 ... 115 J4
Brooklea Clinic *BRSG/KWL/STAPK* BS4 ... 337 G6
Brookside Business Centre *TEWK* GL20 ... 48 D4
Broomhill Infant School *BRSG/KWL/STAPK* BS4 ... 337 H8
Broomhill Jm School *BRSG/KWL/STAPK* BS4 ... 337 H8
Brunston Surgery *CLFD* GL16 ... 175 J2
B Tech Business Park *CIR* GL7 ... 238 D5
Burford Cottage Hospital *BUR/CRTN* OX18 ... 173 M6
Burford Golf Club *BUR/CRTN* OX18 ... 173 M8
Burford School *BUR/CRTN* OX18 ... 173 M7
Burford Surgery *BUR/CRTN* OX18 ... 173 M6
Burnbush Primary School *HGRV/WHIT* BS14 ... 346 F6
Burnbush School *HGRV/WHIT* BS14 ... 346 F5
Bush Industrial Estate *EVILLE/WHL* BS5 ... 336 F3
Business Park *VGL* GL2 ... 4 B7
The Business Park *BMSTRD/HC/WWD* BS13 ... 346 A8
Bussage C of E Primary School *RSTROUD/NAIL* GL6 ... 209 M7
Butcher Row Folk Museum *LED* HR8 ... 20 A3
Cab & Guildhall *CBRIS/FH* BS1 ... 6 F3
Cabot Primary School *CBRISNE* BS2 ... 336 B3
Cabot Tower *CFTN/FAIL* BS8 ... 6 B4
Cadbury Heath CP School *OLD/WMLY/WICK* BS30 ... 338 C6
Cadbury Heath Health Centre *OLD/WMLY/WICK* BS30 ... 338 C6
Cainscross Parish Council *STROUD* GL5 ... 207 M5
Callicroft Infant School *BRSTK/PCHW* BS34 ... 316 B3
Callicroft Junior School *BRSTK/PCHW* BS34 ... 316 A3
Callowell CP School *STROUD* GL5 ... 208 C2
Calton Junior School *GL* GL1 ... 136 A5
Cam Everlands CP School *DSLY* GL11 ... 229 J7
Cam Hopton School *DSLY* GL11 ... 229 J7
Cam House School *DSLY* GL11 ... 253 L1
Cam Sports Club *DSLY* GL11 ... 229 J7
Canons House *CBRIS/FH* BS1 ... 6 D6
The Card Gallery *YATE/CS* BS37 ... 320 D2
Carla Trading Estate *BMSTR* BS3 ... 335 H8
Carlyle Business Centre *CBRISNE* BS2 ... 7 M4
Carrant Brook Junior School *TEWK* GL20 ... 49 G2
Carrick Business Park *BRSG/KWL/STAPK* BS4 ... 347 H2
Cascade Swimming Pool *TEWK* GL20 ... 48 A5
Cashes Green CP School *RSTROUD/NAIL* GL6 ... 207 M3
Castle Business Centre *THNB/SVB* BS35 ... 293 K2
Castle CP School *KEYN* BS31 ... 347 M8
Castle Hill CP School *BWTH/CHD* GL3 ... 138 A7
Castlemorton School *RGTMLV* WR13 ... 22 E4
The Castle School *THNB/SVB* BS35 ... 293 K1
Cattle Market Industrial Estate *GL* GL1 ... 4 E1
Cedars Health Clinic *GL* GL1 ... 4 F6
Central Technology College *GLE* GL4 ... 136 D6
Central Trading Estate *BRSG/KWL/STAPK* BS4 ... 336 D7
Central Trading Estate *VGL* GL2 ... 135 J8
Centurion Industrial Estate *VGL* GL2 ... 135 K6
Chalford Hill County Primary School *RSTROUD/NAIL* GL6 ... 234 B1
Chandag County & Infant School *KEYN* BS31 ... 348 C6
Charborough Road CP School *BRSTK/PCHW* BS34 ... 326 B1
Charfield CP School *WUE* GL12 ... 276 B6
Charles Street Industrial Estate *GL* GL1 ... 5 G7
Charlotte Keel Health Clinic *EVILLE/WHL* BS5 ... 336 C2
The Charlton Kings Clinic *CHELTE/BC* GL52 ... 116 C4
Charlton Kings County Infants School *CHELTS* GL53 ... 116 D5
Charlton Kings Junior School *CHELTS* GL53 ... 116 D6
Chatterton House *CBRIS/FH* BS1 ... 7 G6

Cheddar Grove Primary School *BMSTRD/HC/WWD* BS13 ... 345 J3
Cheltenham Borough Council *CHELTW* GL51 ... 93 J7
Cheltenham Bournside School & Sixth Form Centre *CHELTW* GL51 ... 115 J5
Cheltenham College *CHELTS* GL53 ... 2 D9
Cheltenham College *CHELTS* GL53 ... 2 F9
Cheltenham College Junior School *CHELTS* GL53 ... 2 D9
Cheltenham Cricket Club *CHELTE/BC* GL52 ... 3 H5
Cheltenham General Hospital *CHELTS* GL53 ... 2 E8
Cheltenham & Gloucester College of Higher Education *CHELT* GL50 ... 115 L5
Cheltenham & Gloucester College of Higher Education *CHELTE/BC* GL52 ... 94 B7
Cheltenham & Gloucester College of Higher Education *CHELTW* GL51 ... 2 B1
Cheltenham Kingsmead School *CHELTW* GL51 ... 93 H7
Cheltenham Ladies College *CHELT* GL50 ... 2 A6
Cheltenham Ladies College *CHELT* GL50 ... 2 C6
Cheltenham Ladies College *CHELT* GL50 ... 115 K3
Cheltenham North Rugby Club *CHELTE/BC* GL52 ... 71 L7
Cheltenham Race Course *CHELTE/BC* GL52 ... 94 C5
Cheltenham Retail Park *CHELTW* GL51 ... 93 H6
Cheltenham Road Surgery *VGL* GL2 ... 5 L3
Cheltenham Saracens Sports Club *CHELT* GL50 ... 2 D3
Cheltenham Saracens Sports Club *CHELTW* GL51 ... 93 J8
Cheltenham Synagogue *CHELT* GL50 ... 2 B5
Cheltenham Theatre & Arts Club *CHELT* GL50 ... 2 E6
Cheltenham Town Association Football Club *CHELTE/BC* GL52 ... 3 H2
Cheltenham Tutorial College *CHELT* GL50 ... 2 C4
Chelworth Industrial Estate *HGHW* SN6 ... 288 C6
Chepstow Castle *CHEP* NP16 ... 270 A2
Chepstow County Court *CHEP* NP16 ... 270 B3
Chepstow Museum *CHEP* NP16 ... 270 A2
Cherry Garden Primary School *OLD/WMLY/WICK* BS30 ... 348 D1
Chesterfield Hospital *CFTN/FAIL* BS8 ... 335 J5
Chester Park Primary School *MANG/FISH* BS16 ... 327 J8
Chesterton County Primary School *CIR* GL7 ... 238 C5
Childswickham School *BDWAY* WR12 ... 32 B1
Chipping Campden School *CHCAM* GL55 ... 12 E7
Chipping Edge Estate *YATE/CS* BS37 ... 320 D2
Chipping Sodbury Library *YATE/CS* BS37 ... 320 D2
Chipping Sodbury School *YATE/CS* BS37 ... 320 D3
The Chipping Surgery *WUE* GL12 ... 277 J4
Chosen Hill Former Pupils Rugby Football Club *BWTH/CHD* GL3 ... 113 M6
Chosen Hill School *BWTH/CHD* GL3 ... 114 A6
Christchurch C of E Primary School *CFTN/FAIL* BS8 ... 335 J4
Christ Church C of E School *RSTROUD/NAIL* GL6 ... 234 A1
Christ Church C of E Vc Infant School *MANG/FISH* BS16 ... 327 M6
Christchurch Junior School *MANG/FISH* BS16 ... 327 M6
Christchurch School *CHELTW* GL51 ... 115 K2
Christ the King RC School *THNB/SVB* BS35 ... 293 L2
Churcham School *VGL* GL2 ... 133 K1
Churchdown School *BWTH/CHD* GL3 ... 113 K6
Churchdown Village County Junior School *BWTH/CHD* GL3 ... 113 L7
Churchdown Village Infant School *BWTH/CHD* GL3 ... 113 L6
Churchill Industrial Estate *CHELTS* GL53 ... 115 M5
Church of England School *CLFD* GL16 ... 175 J7
Church Street Gallery *COTS* GL54 ... 101 M3
Cirencester Business Estate *CIR* GL7 ... 238 E5
Cirencester College *CIR* GL7 ... 238 A3

Cirencester Comprehensive School *CIR* GL7 ... 237 M3
Cirencester County Junior School *CIR* GL7 ... 238 D3
Cirencester Golf Club *CIR* GL7 ... 214 B5
Cirencester Hospital *CIR* GL7 ... 238 B4
Cirencester Kingshill School *CIR* GL7 ... 238 F2
Cirencester Polo Club *CIR* GL7 ... 238 A3
Cirencester Rugby Union Club *CIR* GL7 ... 238 C1
Cirencester Town Council *CIR* GL7 ... 238 C2
Cirencester Town Football Club *CIR* GL7 ... 238 A4
City Business Park *CBRIS/FH* BS1 ... 6 F3
City Business Park *EVILLE/WHL* BS5 ... 7 L2
City Council Offices *GL* GL1 ... 4 C6
City of Bristol College *BMSTR* BS3 ... 346 A1
City of Bristol College *CBRIS/FH* BS1 ... 6 B5
City of Bristol College *HORF/LLZ* BS7 ... 326 B7
City & Port of Bristol Social & Sports Club *AVONM* BS11 ... 324 A6
Civil Service Sports Club *CHELTW* GL51 ... 93 H6
Civil Sports Club *GL* GL1 ... 5 G1
Claremont Special School *RDLND/MONT* BS6 ... 325 L6
Cleeve School *CHELTE/BC* GL52 ... 94 C1
Cleeve View Infant School *CHELTW* GL51 ... 93 L7
Clifton Cathedral Church *CFTN/FAIL* BS8 ... 335 J3
Clifton Clinic *CFTN/FAIL* BS8 ... 335 J4
Clifton College *CFTN/FAIL* BS8 ... 335 H3
Clifton College Preparatory School *CFTN/FAIL* BS8 ... 335 H2
Clifton College Sports Club *CFTN/FAIL* BS8 ... 334 D4
Clifton Down Shopping Centre *CFTN/FAIL* BS8 ... 335 K2
The Clifton Gallery *CFTN/FAIL* BS8 ... 335 H4
Clifton High Junior School *CFTN/FAIL* BS8 ... 335 J4
Clifton High School *CFTN/FAIL* BS8 ... 335 H3
Clifton Rugby Club *HNBRY/STHM* BS10 ... 315 H6
Close Farm Surgery *OLD/WMLY/WICK* BS30 ... 338 F6
Club House *LED* HR8 ... 18 A3
Club House *TEWK* GL20 ... 47 L8
Clyde House Surgery *RDLND/MONT* BS6 ... 335 K1
Coalway County Junior & Infant School *CLFD* GL16 ... 175 M2
Coberley School *CHELTS* GL53 ... 140 C6
Cold Aston C of E Primary School *COTS* GL54 ... 121 M7
Coleford County Primary School *CLFD* GL16 ... 151 K5
Coleford Health Centre *CLFD* GL16 ... 175 K2
Coleford Road Surgery *CHEP* NP16 ... 270 B1
Colerne C of E Primary School *CHPMW/MSHF* SN14 ... 343 K8
Colerne Rugby Football Club *CHPMW/MSHF* SN14 ... 343 H8
College House *MANG/FISH* BS16 ... 327 J6
College of Art & Technology *GL* GL1 ... 4 E6
College of St Mathias C of E (A) Infant School *MANG/FISH* BS16 ... 327 J6
College Pharmacy *CHELT* GL50 ... 2 C9
The College Yard Surgery *GL* GL1 ... 4 D4
Coln Gallery *CIR* GL7 ... 238 C2
Coln Gallery *CIR* GL7 ... 242 E4
Coln House Special School *CIR* GL7 ... 242 D5
Colston Hall *CBRIS/FH* BS1 ... 6 E3
Colston House Tennis Club *CIR* GL7 ... 221 M8
Colstons Collegiate Lower School *MANG/FISH* BS16 ... 326 F6
Colstons Girls School *RDLND/MONT* BS6 ... 336 A1
Colstons Primary School *RDLND/MONT* BS6 ... 335 L8
Colstons School *MANG/FISH* BS16 ... 326 F7
Commercial House Station Road Business Parkt *TEWK* GL20 ... 48 B5

Community Health Authority *KEYN* BS31 ... 348
Community Services Clinic *TEWK* GL20 ... 48
The Compton Clinic *RDLND/MONT* BS6 ... 325
Coney Hill Infant School *GLE* GL4 ... 136
Coniston Primary School *BRSTK/PCHW* BS34 ... 316
Connaught Infant & Primary School *BRSG/KWL/STAPK* BS4 ... 346
Connoisseur Gallery *TET* GL8 ... 282
Conygre Medical Centre *BRSTK/PCHW* BS34 ... 316
Copse Surgery *RTEWK/TIB* GL19 ... 66
Corbett House Clinic *EVILLE/WHL* BS5 ... 336
Corinium Business Park *CIND* GL14 ... 129
Corinium Museum *CIR* GL7 ... 238
Coroners Court *CBRISNE* BS2 ... 336
Cossham Memorial Hospital *KGWD/HNM* BS15 ... 337
Cotham Galleries *RDLND/MONT* BS6 ... 335
Cotham Grammar School *RDLND/MONT* BS6 ... 335
Cotham Park Rugby Club *CFTN/FAIL* BS8 ... 334
Cotham Road Surgery *RDLND/MONT* BS6 ... 335
Cotswold Bowl (Cheltenham) *CHELTW* GL51 ... 93
Cotswold Chine Home School *RSTROUD/NAIL* GL6 ... 232
Cotswold District Council *CIR* GL7 ... 238
Cotswold Edge Golf Club *WUE* GL12 ... 254
Cotswold Motor Museum & Toy Collection *COTS* GL54 ... 123
Cotswold Nuffield Hospital *CHELTW* GL51 ... 115
Cotswold School *COTS* GL54 ... 123
Cotswold Sports Centre *CIR* GL7 ... 238
The Cotswold Teddy Bear Museum *BDWAY* WR12 ... 33
Council Offices *GLE* GL4 ... 136
Council Offices *MIM* GL56 ... 58
Council Offices *TEWK* GL20 ... 47
County Library *GL* GL1 ... 4
County Police Court *CHCAM* GL55 ... 12
Courtney Primary School *KGWD/HNM* BS15 ... 338
Courtside Surgery *YATE/CS* BS37 ... 320
Courtyard Shopping Centre *CHELT* GL50 ... 2
Cowdy Gallery *NWNT* GL18 ... 86
The Craft Gallery *HORF/LLZ* BS7 ... 326
Cribbs Causeway Shopping Centre *BRSTK/PCHW* BS34 ... 315
Cricklade Hotel & Country Club *HGHW* SN6 ... 288
Cricklade Leisure Centre *HGHW* SN6 ... 288
Cricklade Town Council *HGHW* SN6 ... 288
Croft Primary School *RSTROUD/NAIL* GL6 ... 185
Crofts End Industrial Estate *EVILLE/WHL* BS5 ... 337
Crofts End Trading Estate *EVILLE/WHL* BS5 ... 337
Crooks Industrial Estate *CHELTS* GL53 ... 115
Crossways Junior & Infant School *THNB/SVB* BS35 ... 293
Crown Court *CBRIS/FH* BS1 ... 6
Crudwell C of E Primary School *MALM* SN16 ... 284
The Crypt School *GL* GL1 ... 135
Culverhay Surgery *WUE* GL12 ... 277
Culverhill School *YATE/CS* BS37 ... 319
Custom House *CBRIS/FH* BS1 ... 6
Cutlers Brook Junior School *CBRISNE* BS2 ... 336
Daniels Industrial Estate *STROUD* GL5 ... 208
Darcy Galleries *CHELT* GL50 ... 2
David Hamiltons Practice *RDLND/MONT* BS6 ... 335
Dean Close Junior School *CHELTW* GL51 ... 115
Dean Close School *CHELTW* GL51 ... 115
Dean Heritage Museum *CIND* GL14 ... 178
Dean Lane Family Practice *BMSTR* BS3 ...
Deerhurst C of E Primary School *RTEWK/TIB* GL19 ... 69

Deers Wood Primary School
KGWD/HNM BS15 .... 338 C1
The Dell Primary School
CHEP NP16 .... 270 A2
Dene Magna
Community School
MTCHDN GL17 .... 130 D3
Denmark Road High
School for Girls
GL GL1 .... 5 H2
The Diane Breen Gallery
CIR GL7 .... 217 K1
Didbrook CP School
COTS GL54 .... 53 K8
Dilke Memorial Hospital
CIND GL14 .... 153 L5
Dinglewell Primary School
GLE GL4 .... 137 H4
Dixon Business Centre
BRSG/KWL/STAPK BS4 .... 347 H1
Docks Industrial Estate
AVONM BS11 .... 314 A3
The Doctors Surgery
EVILLE/WHL BS5 .... 336 D2
Dodington Parish Council
YATE/CS BS37 .... 320 C3
Dodington Park
YATE/CS BS37 .... 321 J7
Dormer House PNEU School
MIM GL56 .... 58 D5
Down Ampney C of E
Primary School
CIR GL7 .... 265 G4
Downend Cricket Club
MANG/FISH BS16 .... 327 M5
Downend School
MANG/FISH BS16 .... 328 A6
Downend Surgery
MANG/FISH BS16 .... 327 M6
Downs Fitness &
Health Centre
RDLND/MONT BS6 .... 335 J1
Dr Bells C of E School
MANG/FISH BS16 .... 327 J7
Drybrook Primary School
MTCHDN GL17 .... 129 L4
Drybrook Rugby Football Club
MTCHDN GL17 .... 129 M3
Drybrook Surgery
MTCHDN GL17 .... 129 L4
Duckmoor Road Industrial
Estate
BMSTR BS3 .... 335 H8
Dunalley County Primary
School
CHELT GL50 .... 2 E1
Dunalley Street School
CHELT GL50 .... 2 D3
Dunmail Primary School
HNBRY/STHM BS10 .... 325 L1
Dursley C of E Primary School
DSLY GL11 .... 253 L3
Dursley Day Hospital
DSLY GL11 .... 252 F2
Dursley Magistrates Court
DSLY GL11 .... 229 H8
Dursley Town Council
DSLY GL11 .... 253 K2
Eagles Wood Business Park
ALMDB BS32 .... 306 E8
Eastbrook Road
Trading Estate
GLE GL4 .... 136 E3
Eastcombe CP School
RSTROUD/NAIL GL6 .... 209 M6
Eastern Avenue Retail Park
GLE GL4 .... 5 M9
East Gloucestershire NHS Trust
CHELTW GL51 .... 115 G1
Eastington CP School
STNHO GL10 .... 206 C3
Eastington Trading Estate
STNHO GL10 .... 206 B2
Eastnor Castle
LED HR8 .... 20 F5
Eastnor C of E Primary School
LED HR8 .... 20 E4
Easton Business Centre
EVILLE/WHL BS5 .... 336 D3
Easton CEVA Primary School
EVILLE/WHL BS5 .... 7 M1
Easton Leisure Centre
EVILLE/WHL BS5 .... 7 M1
Eastpark Trading Estate
EVILLE/WHL BS5 .... 336 F2
Eastville Health Centre
EVILLE/WHL BS5 .... 336 D1
Ebley Industrial Estate
STROUD GL5 .... 207 M5
Eight Bells Gallery
TET GL8 .... 282 A4
Eldersfield Lawn School
RTEWK/TIB GL19 .... 68 A1
The Ellen Badger Hospital
SHPSTR CV36 .... 16 C5
Ellwood County Primary
School
CLFD GL16 .... 175 M6
Ellwood Football Club
CLFD GL16 .... 176 A6
Elmbridge Junior School
VGL GL2 .... 136 E1
Elmbridge Rugby Club
VGL GL2 .... 112 F8
Elmfield Junior School
CHELTW GL51 .... 93 L7
Elmlea Infant School
HNLZ/SM/SNYPK/WT BS9 ..... 325 H6
Elmlea Junior School
HNLZ/SM/SNYPK/WT BS9 ..... 325 H6
Elm Park School
FRCTL/WBN BS36 .... 318 A5
The Elms Day Hospital
THNB/SVB BS35 .... 293 K2
Embleton Junior School
HNBRY/STHM BS10 .... 325 K2
English Bicknor C of E Primary
CLFD GL16 .... 127 L7

English Estates Workshops
CIND GL14 .... 153 M2
Evergreen Industrial Estate
CIR GL7 .... 263 H6
Everyman Theatre
CHELT GL50 .... 2 D5
Exhibition Centre
CBRIS/FH BS1 .... 6 D5
Explore @ Bristol
CBRIS/FH BS1 .... 6 D5
The Eye Clinic
CBRIS/FH BS1 .... 7 G2
Fairfield Grammar School
RDLND/MONT BS6 .... 336 B1
Fairford C of E Primary School
CIR GL7 .... 242 E3
Fairford Football Club
CIR GL7 .... 243 G4
Fairford Hospital
CIR GL7 .... 242 E4
Fair Furlong Primary School
BMSTRD/HC/WWD BS13 ...... 345 J7
Fairway Industrial Centre
BRSTK/PCHW BS34 .... 316 B8
Falconride Primary School
KGWD/HNM BS15 .... 338 A2
The Family Practice
RDLND/MONT BS6 .... 335 L3
Family & Youth Court
CBRIS/FH BS1 .... 6 F3
Farmors School
CIR GL7 .... 242 E3
Feathers Gallery
BDWAY WR12 .... 32 F4
Federated Primary Schools of
Ebrington & St James
CHCAM GL55 .... 34 E1
Ferry Steps Trading Estate
CBRISNE BS2 .... 7 L8
Field Court C of E
Junior & Infant School
VGL GL2 .... 159 H3
Filand School
MALM SN16 .... 303 H5
Filton Avenue Junior School
HORF/LLZ BS7 .... 326 C4
Filton Clinic
HORF/LLZ BS7 .... 326 C1
Filton College
BRSTK/PCHW BS34 .... 316 C7
Filton High School
BRSTK/PCHW BS34 .... 316 F8
Filton Hill CP School
BRSTK/PCHW BS34 .... 316 D7
Filton Park School
BRSTK/PCHW BS34 .... 326 B1
Filton Recreation Centre
BRSTK/PCHW BS34 .... 326 C1
Filton Shield Road School
HORF/LLZ BS7 .... 326 C2
Filton Town Council
BRSTK/PCHW BS34 .... 326 C1
Filwood Swimming Baths
BRSG/KWL/STAPK BS4 .... 346 A3
Finlay Primary School
GLE GL4 .... 136 C5
Fire Service Technical College
MIM GL56 .... 59 G5
Fire Station
CBRIS/FH BS1 .... 7 H4
The Firs Surgery
CHPMW/MSHF SN14 .... 343 J8
Fishponds Health Centre
MANG/FISH BS16 .... 327 K7
The Florence Brown School
BRSG/KWL/STAPK BS4 .... 345 M3
The Florence Brown School
CBRISNE BS2 .... 7 J2
Flower Gallery
FRCTL/WBN BS36 .... 317 M5
Folk House
CBRIS/FH BS1 .... 6 D3
Fonthill Junior School
HNBRY/STHM BS10 .... 326 A1
Forest Health Care
CIND GL14 .... 154 B3
Forest Hills Golf Club
CLFD GL16 .... 151 L7
Forest of Dean District Council
CIND GL14 .... 154 B2
Forest of Dean District Council
CLFD GL16 .... 175 J1
Forest View Primary School
CIND GL14 .... 154 C2
Forest View Upper School
CIND GL14 .... 154 C2
Fosse Cross Industrial Estate
CIR GL7 .... 191 K4
Fosse Way Business Centre
MIM GL56 .... 58 D5
Foster Almshouses
CBRIS/FH BS1 .... 6 E3
Fouracres Primary School
BMSTRD/HC/WWD BS13 ...... 345 G7
Foxmoor CP School
STROUD GL5 .... 207 M4
Frampton Cotterell
C of E School
FRCTL/WBN BS36 .... 318 C3
Frampton on Severn
C of E School
VGL GL2 .... 181 H5
Francis Woodcock
Trading Estate
GL GL1 .... 5 J9
Frenchay C of E School
MANG/FISH BS16 .... 327 K4
Frenchay Health Authority
MANG/FISH BS16 .... 327 L6
Frenchay Hospital
MANG/FISH BS16 .... 327 K3
Frenchay Village Museum
MANG/FISH BS16 .... 327 H4
The Friends of
Gloucester Cathedral
GL GL1 .... 4 E4
Frithwood Surgery
RSTROUD/NAIL GL6 .... 209 M7

Frome Bank Junior School
YATE/CS BS37 .... 309 M8
Fromeside Clinic
MANG/FISH BS16 .... 327 H6
Fulford Special School
BMSTRD/HC/WWD BS13 ...... 345 L7
Gable House Surgery
MALM SN16 .... 303 J8
The Galleries Shopping Centre
CBRIS/FH BS1 .... 7 G2
The Gallery
CIR GL7 .... 238 C3
Gastrells CP School
STROUD GL5 .... 208 C7
Gas Works
HNBRY/STHM BS10 .... 314 D3
Gay Elms Junior & Infant School
BMSTRD/HC/WWD BS13 ...... 345 J7
Georgian House
CBRIS/FH BS1 .... 6 C4
Glebe Infant School
NWNT GL18 .... 86 D2
Glenfall CP School
CHELTE/BC GL52 .... 116 E5
Glenfrome Primary School
EVILLE/WHL BS5 .... 326 E7
Glevum Industrial Estate
GLE GL4 .... 136 C4
Glevum Shopping Centre
GLE GL4 .... 136 F7
Gloucester City
Association Football Club
VGL GL2 .... 135 K3
Gloucester City Council
GL GL1 .... 4 C6
Gloucester City Council
GL GL1 .... 4 F8
Gloucester City Council
GL GL1 .... 4 E1
Gloucester
County Constabulary
GL GL1 .... 5 J8
Gloucester
County Constabulary
STNHO GL10 .... 207 H4
Gloucester County Council
CHELT GL50 .... 2 AB
Gloucester County Council
CHELT GL50 .... 115 K3
Gloucester County Council
GLE GL4 .... 136 C4
Gloucester County Council
VGL GL2 .... 206 B1
Gloucester Crown &
County Court
GL GL1 .... 4 D6
Gloucester Folk Museum
GL GL1 .... 4 C5
Gloucester Retail Park
GLE GL4 .... 136 E2
Gloucester Road
Industrial Estate
MALM SN16 .... 303 J7
Gloucester Road
Primary School
CHELTW GL51 .... 115 K1
Gloucester Royal Hospital
GL GL1 .... 5 K5
Gloucester Rugby Football Club
GL GL1 .... 4 F2
Gloucestershire
Aviation Museum
BWTH/CHD GL3 .... 113 L3
Gloucestershire
College of Arts & Technology
GL GL1 .... 4 F7
Gloucestershire
Community Health Centre
GL GL1 .... 5 H5
Gloucestershire County Council
CHELTS GL53 .... 2 F7
Gloucestershire County Council
CHELTW GL51 .... 114 B4
Gloucestershire County Council
CIR GL7 .... 238 D5
Gloucestershire County Council
CLFD GL16 .... 175 J1
Gloucestershire County Council
COTS GL54 .... 123 J4
Gloucestershire County Council
GL GL1 .... 4 F6
Gloucestershire County Council
GL GL1 .... 4 D4
Gloucestershire County Council
GL GL1 .... 5 K3
Gloucestershire County Council
GL GL1 .... 5 K8
Gloucestershire County Council
KGWD/HNM BS15 .... 338 A3
Gloucestershire County Council
STROUD GL5 .... 208 C7
Gloucestershire County
Cricket Club
HORF/LLZ BS7 .... 326 A8
Gloucestershire County
Library Arts &
Museums Service
CHELT GL50 .... 2 B1
Gloucestershire Health
Authority
GL GL1 .... 4 D6
Gloucestershire Islamic
Secondary School for Girls
GL GL1 .... 5 H7
Gloucestershire Royal Hospital
GL GL1 .... 5 J4
Gloucester Sports Club
GL GL1 .... 4 D8
Glynne Wickham
Studio Theatre
CFTN/FAIL BS8 .... 6 C3
Golf Course
HGHW SN6 .... 288 D3
Goodridge Industrial Estate
VGL GL2 .... 135 J7
Goodridge Trading Estate
VGL GL2 .... 135 J8

Gordon League Rugby
Football Club
VGL GL2 .... 135 K4
Gorsley Goffs C of E
Primary School
RWYE HR9 .... 84 E2
Granby House Clinic
BMSTR BS3 .... 335 L8
Grange Infant School
GL GL1 .... 159 L1
Grange Junior School
GL GL1 .... 135 L8
Grange Road Surgery
BMSTRD/HC/WWD BS13 ...... 345 H6
Greatfield Park Primary School
CHELTW GL51 .... 115 H6
Great Rissington CP School
COTS GL54 .... 148 C4
Great Western Business Park
YATE/CS BS37 .... 309 K8
The Great Western
Railway Museum
CLFD GL16 .... 175 K1
Gretton School
COTS GL54 .... 73 M2
Greyholme Surgery
CHELTE/BC GL52 .... 72 B7
Greystones Gallery
CIR GL7 .... 244 E7
Grimsbury Park School
OLD/WMLY/WICK BS30 .... 338 D4
Grove Industrial Estate
BRSTK/PCHW BS34 .... 316 D4
Grove Road Day Hospital
RDLND/MONT BS6 .... 335 J1
Hadwen Practice
GLE GL4 .... 137 G7
Hambrook CP School
MANG/FISH BS16 .... 317 M8
Hambrook Sports Club
MANG/FISH BS16 .... 317 M8
Hampton Street
Industrial Estate
TET GL8 .... 281 L2
Hanham Abbots Junior School
KGWD/HNM BS15 .... 337 L7
Hanham Business Park
KGWD/HNM BS15 .... 337 K6
Hanham C of E Primary School
KGWD/HNM BS15 .... 337 K7
Hanham High School
KGWD/HNM BS15 .... 337 L7
Hanham Surgery
KGWD/HNM BS15 .... 337 M7
Hannah More Primary School
CBRISNE BS2 .... 7 K4
The Happening Art Gallery
RDLND/MONT BS6 .... 335 K2
Hardwicke Parochial
Primary School
VGL GL2 .... 159 G5
Harclive Primary School
BMSTRD/HC/WWD BS13 ...... 345 L7
Haresfield C of E Primary
School
STNHO GL10 .... 183 K2
Harewood Junior &
Infant School
GL GL1 .... 159 L2
Harlequin Gallery
CHELTE/BC GL52 .... 2 E5
Hartcliffe Health Centre
BMSTRD/HC/WWD BS13 ...... 345 L7
Hartcliffe School
BMSTRD/HC/WWD BS13 ...... 346 A7
Hartpury College
RTEWK/TIB GL19 .... 110 D1
Harveys Wine Museum
CBRIS/FH BS1 .... 6 D4
Hatherley Infant School
GL GL1 .... 136 C4
Hatherop Castle School
CIR GL7 .... 218 E4
Hatherop C of E School
CIR GL7 .... 218 F4
Hawkesbury Upton
Primary School
BAD GL9 .... 298 B8
Hayward Road
Industrial Estate
MANG/FISH BS16 .... 327 M8
Headley Park Primary School
BMSTRD/HC/WWD BS13 ...... 345 K4
Heath House Priory Hospital
HORF/LLZ BS7 .... 326 D7
Heathville Road Surgery
GL GL1 .... 5 H4
Hempsted School
VGL GL2 .... 135 J4
Henbury Court Junior &
Primary School
HNBRY/STHM BS10 .... 315 H8
Henbury Manor School
HNBRY/STHM BS10 .... 325 G1
Henbury Old Boys A F C
HNBRY/STHM BS10 .... 325 H1
Henbury School
HNBRY/STHM BS10 .... 315 G8
The Henbury Surgery
HNBRY/STHM BS10 .... 315 H8
Henbury Swimming Pool
HNBRY/STHM BS10 .... 325 H1
Henfield Business Park
FRCTL/WBN BS36 .... 328 F1
Hengrove School
HGRV/WHIT BS14 .... 346 D4
Henleaze Infant School
RDLND/MONT BS6 .... 325 L6
The Herd AFC Club House
CIR GL7 .... 238 B4
The Heron Primary School
GLE GL4 .... 136 F6
The Heywood School
CIND GL14 .... 154 C1
Heywood Sports Centre
CIND GL14 .... 154 C1
Highbridge Health Centre
BMSTRD/HC/WWD BS13 ...... 345 H5

Highcroft Junior School
FRCTL/WBN BS36 .... 318 E3
Highnam Business Centre
VGL GL2 .... 110 F6
Highnam School
VGL GL2 .... 110 F6
The High Street Medical Centre
STNHO GL10 .... 207 G3
Hillesley C of E Va
Primary School
WUE GL12 .... 298 A3
Hillfields Park Primary School
MANG/FISH BS16 .... 327 L8
Hillview County
Primary School
BWTH/CHD GL3 .... 137 H3
The Hindu Temple
EVILLE/WHL BS5 .... 336 E3
Hippodrome Theatre
CBRIS/FH BS1 .... 6 E4
H & L Estate
STROUD GL5 .... 208 A5
H & L Trading Estate
STROUD GL5 .... 208 A5
HM Young Offender Institute
WUE GL12 .... 274 F1
Holloway Dental
Health Centre
HGRV/WHIT BS14 .... 347 G6
Hollywood Bowl
CBRISNE BS2 .... 336 E6
Holst Birthplace Museum
CHELTE/BC GL52 .... 2 E3
Holts Health Centre
NWNT GL18 .... 86 C3
Holy Apostles C of E School
CHELTE/BC GL52 .... 3 K6
Holy Family RC Primary School
BRSTK/PCHW BS34 .... 316 D3
Holymead Infant School
BRSG/KWL/STAPK BS4 .... 346 F1
Holymead School
BRSG/KWL/STAPK BS4 .... 336 F8
Holy Trinity Primary School
ALMDB BS32 .... 316 E1
Holy Trinity School
CHELTE/BC GL52 .... 2 F4
Homedowns Business Park
TEWK GL20 .... 49 G6
Homeopathic Hospital
CFTN/FAIL BS8 .... 335 L3
Honeybourne
Airfield Industrial Estate
EVE WR11 .... 11 K2
Hopelands School
STNHO GL10 .... 207 H4
Hopes Hill Primary School
MTCHDN GL17 .... 131 K2
Horcott Industrial Estate
CIR GL7 .... 242 D6
Horcott Road Industrial Estate
CIR GL7 .... 242 E5
Horfield C of E School
HNBRY/STHM BS10 .... 325 M4
Horfield Health Centre
HORF/LLZ BS7 .... 326 C5
Horfield Sports Centre
HORF/LLZ BS7 .... 326 B4
Horsley School
RSTROUD/NAIL GL6 .... 256 B2
Horton Primary School
YATE/CS BS37 .... 311 L6
Hospital
PTSHD/EG BS20 .... 324 A7
Hotspots Indoor Sports Centre
BRSG/KWL/STAPK BS4 .... 347 H1
Hotwells Primary School
CFTN/FAIL BS8 .... 335 H5
Ilminster Avenue
Junior School
BRSG/KWL/STAPK BS4 .... 346 C3
Inchbrook Trading Estate
STROUD GL5 .... 232 C1
Innsworth County
Primary School
VGL GL2 .... 112 F5
Innsworth Technology Park
VGL GL2 .... 112 E4
The Institute of
Cosmetic Surgery
CFTN/FAIL BS8 .... 335 J2
Iron Acton C of E School
YATE/CS BS37 .... 309 G7
Jama Al-Karim Mosque
GL GL1 .... 5 G7
JHP Business Centre
CIR GL7 .... 238 D3
John Blockley Gallery
CIR GL7 .... 238 D3
John Cabot City
Technology College
KGWD/HNM BS15 .... 337 L4
John Masefield High School
LED HR8 .... 19 M4
The John Milton Health Clinic
HNBRY/STHM BS10 .... 315 J8
The John M Museum
TEWK GL20 .... 48 F1
Jorrocks Estate
YATE/CS BS37 .... 319 L7
Joys Green CP School
MTCHDN GL17 .... 128 C6
Jubilee Public Baths
BRSG/KWL/STAPK BS4 .... 346 D1
Katerine Lady Berkeley School
WUE GL12 .... 277 H5
Kemble County
Primary School
CIR GL7 .... 261 H4
Kennedy Way Surgery
YATE/CS BS37 .... 320 A2
Kensington Business Centre
CHELT GL50 .... 2 C7
Keynsham County
Primary School
KEYN BS31 .... 347 M6
Keynsham Hospital
KEYN BS31 .... 348 D1

Keynsham Leisure Centre
KEYN BS31 .... 348 B6
Keynsham Rugby Club
KEYN BS31 .... 347 M4
Keynsham Town Football Club
KEYN BS31 .... 347 M4
King Edmund Community
School
YATE/CS BS37 .... 320 A2
Kingfisher Business Park
STROUD GL5 .... 233 G1
Kingham County
Primary School
CHNTN OX7 .... 104 C6
Kingham Hill School
CHNTN OX7 .... 104 D2
Kings Business Park
CBRISNE BS2 .... 336 E5
Kings Chase Shopping Centre
KGWD/HNM BS15 .... 337 M3
Kings Court Primary School
YATE/CS BS37 .... 320 A3
Kingsditch Retail Park
CHELTW GL51 .... 93 J6
Kingsdown Golf Club
COR/BOX SN13 .... 353 K8
Kingsdown Sports Centre
RDLND/MONT BS6 .... 335 L3
Kingsfield School
KGWD/HNM BS15 .... 338 C3
Kingsholm C of E
Primary School
GL GL1 .... 5 G3
Kings School
GL GL1 .... 4 E4
Kings Stanley C of E
Primary School
STNHO GL10 .... 207 J7
Kings Stanley County
Infant School
STNHO GL10 .... 207 J8
Kings Theatre
GL GL1 .... 5 G7
Kingsweston School
AVONM BS11 .... 324 C3
Kingswood Borough Council
MANG/FISH BS16 .... 327 M7
Kingswood County
Primary School
WUE GL12 .... 277 G6
Kingswood District Council
KGWD/HNM BS15 .... 337 M4
Kingswood Health Centre
KGWD/HNM BS15 .... 338 A3
Kingswood Leisure Centre
MANG/FISH BS16 .... 327 M8
Kirtlands Preparatory School
BDWAY WR12 .... 33 G3
Knightsbridge Business Centre
CHELTW GL51 .... 92 A1
Knowle Junior Mixed School
BRSG/KWL/STAPK BS4 .... 336 C8
Knowle Park Junior School
BRSG/KWL/STAPK BS4 .... 346 C2
Ladygrove Business Park
MTCHDN GL17 .... 130 E2
Lakers School
CLFD GL16 .... 151 L6
Lakeside Primary School
CHELTW GL51 .... 115 G4
The Lake Surgery
HNBRY/STHM BS10 .... 325 K4
Lansdown Industrial Estate
CHELTW GL51 .... 115 J2
Larkfield Infant School
VGL GL2 .... 113 G5
Larkhall Football Club
CBATH/BATHN BA1 .... 351 K8
Lawnwood Road
Industrial Estate
EVILLE/WHL BS5 .... 336 D3
Lawrence Hill Health Centre
CBRISNE BS2 .... 7 M2
Lawrence Hill Industrial Estate
EVILLE/WHL BS5 .... 336 E3
Lawrence Hill Industrial Park
EVILLE/WHL BS5 .... 336 D3
Lawrence Weston School
AVONM BS11 .... 324 D2
Lea C of E County
Primary School
RWYE HR9 .... 106 D3
Leckhampton Industrial Estate
CHELTS GL53 .... 115 M8
Leckhampton Primary School
CHELTS GL53 .... 115 L7
Leckhampton Surgery
CHELTS GL53 .... 115 L5
Leconfield Cheltenham College
CHELTS GL53 .... 2 D8
Ledbury Market Surgery
LED HR8 .... 19 M3
Ledbury Primary School
LED HR8 .... 19 M3
Ledbury Town Football Club
LED HR8 .... 19 L5
Leigh C of E School
HGHW SN6 .... 287 L6
Leigh Court Business Centre
CFTN/FAIL BS8 .... 334 C1
Leighterton County
Primary School
TET GL8 .... 279 L8
Leisure Centre
CLFD GL16 .... 151 L5
Leisure Centre
GL GL1 .... 5 G6
Leonard Stanley C of E
Primary School
STNHO GL10 .... 207 H7
Lewis Road Surgery
BMSTRD/HC/WWD BS13 .... 345 J3
Liberty Industrial Park
BMSTR BS3 .... 345 J2
Library, Museum & Art Gallery
CHELT GL50 .... 2 D4
Liddington Industrial Estate
CHELTS GL53 .... 115 M6

Linden Primary School
GL GL1 .... 135 M5
Linear Business Park
CIND GL14 .... 154 A4
Little Dean Hall
CIND GL14 .... 154 E4
Littledean Primary School
CIND GL14 .... 154 E3
Little Stoke Junior School
BRSTK/PCHW BS34 .... 316 F5
Llanthony Industrial Estate
VGL GL2 .... 4 A7
Llanthony Secunda Priory
VGL GL2 .... 4 B8
Lockleaze School
HORF/LLZ BS7 .... 326 E3
Lodge Causeway
Trading Estate
MANG/FISH BS16 .... 327 H8
London Road Medical Practice
GL GL1 .... 5 J4
Long Ashton Surgery
LGASH BS41 .... 344 B2
Longborough C of E
Primary School
MIM GL56 .... 79 K3
Longbrook Trading Estate
BMSTR BS3 .... 335 G8
Long Compton Junior &
Infant School
SHPSTR CV36 .... 61 H5
Longford Special School
VGL GL2 .... 112 D6
Longhope C of E
Primary School
MTCHDN GL17 .... 107 G7
Longhope Industrial Estate
MTCHDN GL17 .... 107 H8
Longlevens Primary School
VGL GL2 .... 112 E7
Longlevens R F C
VGL GL2 .... 112 D6
Longlevens Surgery
VGL GL2 .... 112 E7
Longney C of E
Primary School
VGL GL2 .... 157 L6
Longwell Green CP School
OLD/WMLY/WICK BS30 .... 338 B8
Lonsdale Business Centre
KGWD/HNM BS15 .... 337 L1
Lord Chancellors Department
CBRIS/FH BS1 .... 6 F3
Lord Chancellors Department
CFTN/FAIL BS8 .... 335 H4
Love Lane Industrial Estate
CIR GL7 .... 238 D5
Love Lane Trading Estate
CIR GL7 .... 238 D5
Luckwell Road School
BMSTR BS3 .... 335 J8
Lydbrook County
Primary School
MTCHDN GL17 .... 128 C8
Lydbrook Health Centre
MTCHDN GL17 .... 128 C7
Lydney C of E School
LYD GL15 .... 201 J8
Lydney Cricket Club
LYD GL15 .... 201 J8
Lydney & District Hospital
LYD GL15 .... 201 H8
Lydney Golf Club
LYD GL15 .... 225 L1
Lydney Health Centre
LYD GL15 .... 201 K8
Lydney Industrial Estate
LYD GL15 .... 225 M3
Lydney Rugby Football Club
LYD GL15 .... 201 K8
Lydney Yacht Club
LYD GL15 .... 226 A3
Lyntony House
Reading School
HORF/LLZ BS7 .... 325 M8
Lynworth Primary School
CHELTE/BC GL52 .... 3 L1
Madleaze Trading Estate
GL GL1 .... 4 C9
Maidenhill School
STNHO GL10 .... 207 H2
Malago Surgery
BMSTR BS3 .... 335 L8
Malago Vale Trading Estate
BMSTR BS3 .... 335 M8
The Mall Gallery
CFTN/FAIL BS8 .... 335 H4
The Mall
BRSTK/PCHW BS34 .... 315 M5
Malmesbury Business Park
MALM SN16 .... 303 H6
Malmesbury C of E
Primary School
MALM SN16 .... 303 H7
Malmesbury Cricket Club
MALM SN16 .... 303 J7
Malmesbury School
MALM SN16 .... 303 G8
Malmesbury Swimming Pool
MALM SN16 .... 303 G7
Malvern View Business Park
CHELTE/BC GL52 .... 71 M7
Mangotsfield School
MANG/FISH BS16 .... 328 D7
Mangotsfield United
Football Club
MANG/FISH BS16 .... 328 D6
Manor Brook School
THNB/SVB BS35 .... 273 L8
Manor C of E School
FRCTL/WBN BS36 .... 318 E5
Manor Farm Associated
Football Club
HNLZ/SM/SNYPK/WT BS9 .... 324 D6
Manor Park Business Centre
CHELTW GL51 .... 93 J6
Maritime Heritage Centre
CBRIS/FH BS1 .... 6 B6

Market
GL GL1 .... 4 E6
Market Theatre
LED HR8 .... 19 M3
Marling School
STROUD GL5 .... 208 B4
Marlwood School
THNB/SVB BS35 .... 293 H6
Marshfield Primary School
CHPMW/MSHF SN14 .... 342 C3
Martor Industrial Estate
CHPMW/MSHF SN14 .... 342 C1
Marybrook Medical Centre
BRKLY GL13 .... 227 G7
Matson Rugby Club House
GLE GL4 .... 136 E8
May Park Primary School
EVILLE/WHL BS5 .... 336 E1
Mead Lane Industrial Estate
LYD GL15 .... 225 H3
The Meadows Primary School
OLD/WMLY/WICK BS30 .... 348 F3
Mead Park Industrial Estate
CHELTS GL53 .... 115 M5
Medical Surgery
CIND GL14 .... 156 B3
Merchants Quay Shopping Centre
GL GL1 .... 4 C6
Merrywood School
BRSG/KWL/STAPK BS4 .... 346 B2
Meteor Business Park
BWTH/CHD GL3 .... 113 L2
Meysey Hampton
C of E School
CIR GL7 .... 241 K7
Midland Way Business Park
THNB/SVB BS35 .... 293 K3
The Milestone School
VGL GL2 .... 112 D6
Millcot Gallery
TEWK GL20 .... 47 M5
Millpond Primary School
EVILLE/WHL BS5 .... 336 C2
Minchinhampton Golf Club
TET GL8 .... 257 M1
Minsterworth School
VGL GL2 .... 134 B4
Minto Road Industrial Centre
RDLND/MONT BS6 .... 336 B1
Miserden C of E Primary School
RSTROUD/NAIL GL6 .... 187 J5
Mitcheldean Endowed
Primary School
MTCHDN GL17 .... 130 C2
Mitcheldean Surgery
MTCHDN GL17 .... 130 C1
Mitton Manor Primary School
TEWK GL20 .... 48 C3
The Moat Infant School
GLE GL4 .... 136 D7
Monk Meadow Dock
VGL GL2 .... 135 L4
Monkscroft Junior &
Infant School
CHELTW GL51 .... 115 G2
Monks Park School
HORF/LLZ BS7 .... 326 B2
Monks Park Surgery
HORF/LLZ BS7 .... 326 B3
Monmouthshire
County Council
CHEP NP16 .... 270 A3
Montpelier Health Centre
RDLND/MONT BS6 .... 336 A2
Montpellier Gallery
CHELT GL50 .... 2 A6
Moore Cottage Hospital
COTS GL54 .... 123 H5
Moore Health Centre
COTS GL54 .... 123 H4
Moreton-in-Marsh Hospital
MIM GL56 .... 58 C5
Moreton Wanderers
Football Club
MIM GL56 .... 58 E6
Mosque Centre
CHELTW GL51 .... 2 B3
The Mount
CBATH/BATHN BA1 .... 352 E6
Mount Zion School
RDLND/MONT BS6 .... 335 M2
Much Marcle C of E
Primary School
LED HR8 .... 40 B4
Museum
CBATH/BATHN BA1 .... 350 F7
Museum, Library & Art Gallery
GL GL1 .... 4 F6
Museum of Advertising &
Packaging
GL GL1 .... 4 D6
Naas House
LYD GL15 .... 225 M3
Nailsworth Mills Estate
RSTROUD/NAIL GL6 .... 232 E7
National Star Centre College
CHELTS GL53 .... 139 L5
National Waterways Museum
GL GL1 .... 4 C7
Natural Health Clinic
RDLND/MONT BS6 .... 335 K3
Naunton Downs Golf Club
COTS GL54 .... 99 J8
Naunton Park Primary School
CHELTS GL53 .... 116 A5
Newbridge Industrial Estate
BRSG/KWL/STAPK BS4 .... 336 F5
Newent Community School
NWNT GL18 .... 86 B4
Newent Sports Centre
NWNT GL18 .... 86 B4
Newent Town
Associated Football Club
NWNT GL18 .... 86 F3
Newent Town Council
NWNT GL18 .... 86 B3
New Fosseway School
HGRV/WHIT BS14 .... 346 D4

Newnham C of E School
CIND GL14 .... 155 J6
Newnham Surgery
CIND GL14 .... 155 H7
The New Olympus Theatre
GL GL1 .... 5 G8
New Siblands School
THNB/SVB BS35 .... 293 M2
Newtown Trading Estate
TEWK GL20 .... 48 E4
Northavon Business Centre
YATE/CS BS37 .... 309 L8
North Avon Magistrates Court
YATE/CS BS37 .... 320 A2
North Bristol Rugby
Football Club
ALMDB BS32 .... 306 C8
North Cerney Primary School
CIR GL7 .... 190 C6
Northleaze Primary School
LGASH BS41 .... 344 D1
North Nibley C of E
Primary School
DSLY GL11 .... 252 F6
Northridge Business Centre
YATE/CS BS37 .... 319 L1
North Road CP School
YATE/CS BS37 .... 309 K7
North Star Business Park
VGL GL2 .... 135 K8
Northville Family Practice
HORF/LLZ BS7 .... 326 D2
Northway County
Infant School
TEWK GL20 .... 49 G3
Northway Trading Estate
TEWK GL20 .... 49 G4
Northwick Business Centre
MIM GL56 .... 35 J5
North Wilts District Council
MALM SN16 .... 303 H7
Norton C of E School
VGL GL2 .... 90 E7
Novers Hill Trading Estate
BMSTR BS3 .... 345 L2
Novers Lane Jmi School
BRSG/KWL/STAPK BS4 .... 345 L4
Oakdene School
CIND GL14 .... 154 B3
Oakfield Business Park
KGWD/HNM BS15 .... 337 M4
Oak Hill Primary School
TEWK GL20 .... 51 L4
Oakridge Parochial School
RSTROUD/NAIL GL6 .... 210 E8
Oatley Trading Estate
KGWD/HNM BS15 .... 337 M2
Odeon Cinema
CBRIS/FH BS1 .... 6 F3
Odeon Cinema
CHELTE/BC GL52 .... 2 E5
Offas Mead CP School
CHEP NP16 .... 270 C2
Off Centre Gallery
BMSTR BS3 .... 335 M8
Old Bristolians Sports Club
CFTN/FAIL BS8 .... 334 B7
Oldbury Court Infant School
MANG/FISH BS16 .... 327 L4
Oldbury Court Jm School
MANG/FISH BS16 .... 327 L4
Oldbury-on-Severn
C of E School
THNB/SVB BS35 .... 272 D6
Old Coalyard Farm Estate
COTS GL54 .... 169 H1
Old Cryptians RFC
GLE GL4 .... 136 C7
The Old Estate Sawmill
Workshops
CIR GL7 .... 218 F4
Old Inchbrook School
RSTROUD/NAIL GL6 .... 232 C5
Oldland Surgery
OLD/WMLY/WICK BS30 .... 338 E8
The Old Mill Museum
COTS GL54 .... 123 G1
Old Print Gallery
BDWAY WR12 .... 32 F4
Old Quarries Industrial Estate
TET GL8 .... 282 A5
Old Sodbury County
Primary School
THNB/SVB BS35 .... 321 K3
Old Sucians R F C
CBATH/BATHN BA1 .... 350 F7
Old Wharf Industrial Estate
LED HR8 .... 19 L5
Olveston & Elberton
Primary School
THNB/SVB BS35 .... 292 C8
The Open University
CBRIS/FH BS1 .... 7 G5
Optimax Laser Eye Clinic
CBRIS/FH BS1 .... 6 E4
The Orchard Medical Centre
DSLY GL11 .... 229 H6
The Orchard Medical Centre
KGWD/HNM BS15 .... 337 M3
The Other Surgery
CFTN/FAIL BS8 .... 335 K2
Our Lady of Lourdes RC School
KGWD/HNM BS15 .... 338 A4
Our Lady of the Rosary
RC Primary School
AVONM BS11 .... 324 C3
Overbury First School
TEWK GL20 .... 28 B4
Overndale School
YATE/CS BS37 .... 321 J4
Overton Park Surgery
CHELT GL50 .... 2 B5
Oxstalls Community School
GL GL1 .... 112 C7
The Palace Theatre
CIND GL14 .... 154 C1
Parkend School
LYD GL15 .... 177 G7

The Park Primary School
STNHO GL10 .... 207 C
The Park School
KGWD/HNM BS15 .... 338 C
Park Surgery
CIR GL7 .... 238 C
Parkwall CP School
OLD/WMLY/WICK BS30 .... 338 C
Parkway Trading Estate
CBRISNE BS2 .... 336 C
Parliament School
STROUD GL5 .... 209 H
Parnall Road Industrial Estate
MANG/FISH BS16 327
Parson Street Primary School
BMSTR BS3 345
Parton Manor Infant School
BWTH/CHD GL3 .... 113 H
Parton Manor Junior School
BWTH/CHD GL3 .... 113 H
Patchway C of E
Primary School
BRSTK/PCHW BS34 .... 316 E
Patchway Health Clinic
BRSTK/PCHW BS34 .... 316 C
Patchway High School
ALMDB BS32 .... 316 D
Patchway Town Council
BRSTK/PCHW BS34 .... 316 E
Patchway Trading Estate
BRSTK/PCHW BS34 .... 315 M
Pates Grammar School
CHELT GL51 .... 93 C
Pauntley C of E Primary School
NWNT GL18 .... 64 C
Pavilion Business Park
CIND GL14 .... 129 M
Pebworth CP School
STRAT CV37 .... 8 A
Pembroke Junior &
Infant School
CHEP NP16 .... 270 A
Pembroke Road Surgery
CFTN/FAIL BS8 .... 335 J
Pendock C of E School
RTEWK/TIB GL19 .... 44 D
Pen Park School
HNBRY/STHM BS10 .... 325 M
Perry Court Junior &
Infant School
HGRV/WHIT BS14 .... 346 D
Petherton Road Infant School
HGRV/WHIT BS14 .... 346 D
Philblack Works
HNBRY/STHM BS10 .... 314 D
Phoenix Business Park
BMSTR BS3 .... 345 L
Phoenix NHS Trust
KGWD/HNM BS15 .... 337 L
Phoenix Surgery
CIR GL7 .... 238 C
Phoenix Surgery
CIR GL7 .... 263 H
Phoenix Trading Estate
STROUD GL5 .... 209 C
The Picture House
CBRIS/FH BS1 .... 7 C
Pillowell CP School
LYD GL15 .... 201 H
Pilning CP School
THNB/SVB BS35 .... 305 C
Pittville Comprehensive School
CHELTE/BC GL52 .... 94 B
Pittville Sports Centre
CHELTE/BC GL51 .... 93 H
Pixash Business Centre
KEYN BS31 .... 348 C
Playhouse Theatre
CHELT GL50 .... 2 D
Plump Hill County
Primary School
MTCHDN GL17 .... 130 D
Portrait Gallery
HORF/LLZ BS7 .... 326 E
Portway School
AVONM BS11 .... 324 A
Powells C of E School
CIR GL7 .... 238 E
The Practice
CFTN/FAIL BS8 .... 6 E
Prices Mill Surgery
RSTROUD/NAIL GL6 .... 232 C
Prim School
THNB/SVB BS35 .... 293 M
Primsdown Industrial Estate
CHNTN OX7 .... 83 L
Prinknash Abbey
GLE GL4 .... 161 M
Prior Park Preparatory School
HGHW SN6 .... 289 C
Priory Doctors Surgery
BRSG/KWL/STAPK BS4 .... 346 D
Priory Industrial Estate
TET GL8 .... 282 A
Priory Ruins
GL GL1 .... 4 E
The Priory Surgery
BRSG/KWL/STAPK BS4 .... 346 D
Pucklechurch C of E
Primary School
MANG/FISH BS16 .... 329 L
QEH Theatre
CFTN/FAIL BS8 .... 6 A
Quakers Friars
CBRIS/FH BS1 .... 7 H
Quedgeley Trading Estate East
STNHO GL10 .... 183 C
Quedgeley Trading Estate West
VGL GL2 .... 158 F
Queen Elizabeth Hospital
CFTN/FAIL BS8 .... 6 C
Queen Margaret County School
TEWK GL20 .... 48 A
Querns Business Centre
CIR GL7 .... 238 C
Querns School
CIR GL7 .... 238 C

ndwick C of E
Primary School
RSTROUD/NAIL GL6 .... 207 M1
ngeworthy C of E
Primary School
YATE/CS BS37 .... 309 H2
ysfield Infant School
YATE/CS BS37 .... 320 B3
ysfield Junior School
YATE/CS BS37 .... 320 B3
dbrook C of E
Primary School
MONM NP25 .... 174 B3
dcliffe College
GL GL1 .... 5 K4
dfield Edge Primary School
OLD/WMLY/WICK BS30 .... 338 F7
dfield Leisure Centre
EVILLE/WHL BS5 .... 336 E4
dgrave Theatre
CFTN/FAIL BS8 .... 335 H3
dhouse Primary School
BMSTRD/HC/WWD BS13 .... 345 J6
dland High Junior School
RDLND/MONT BS6 .... 335 L1
dland High School
RDLND/MONT BS6 .... 335 L1
d Maids Junior School
HNLZ/SM/SNYPK/WT BS9 .... 325 J5
d Maids School
HNLZ/SM/SNYPK/WT BS9 .... 325 J5
dmarley C of E
Primary School
RTEWK/TIB GL19 .... 43 J8
dnock
Comprehensive School
DSLY GL11 .... 253 J1
dwick & Northwick
C of E VC School
THNB/SVB BS35 .... 304 F1
gent Arcade
Shopping Centre
CHELT GL50 .... 2 D5
gent Gallery
CHELT GL50 .... 2 D5
gent Street Doctors Surgery
STNHO GL10 .... 207 G4
gimental Museum
GL GL1 .... 4 D6
gister Office
CBRIS/FH BS1 .... 7 G2
ndcomb College
CIR GL7 .... 190 B3
ston Hall Girls High School
GL GL1 .... 136 A6
chard Hagen Gallery
BDWAY WR12 .... 32 F4
e Richard Pate School
CHELTS GL53 .... 116 A8
e Ridge Junior School
YATE/CS BS37 .... 320 B1
dgeway Industrial Centre
EVILLE/WHL BS5 .... 337 G1
ding School
CIR GL7 .... 264 B7
dings High School
FRCTL/WBN BS36 .... 317 M5
gestate Industrial Estate
BRKLY GL13 .... 227 G6
verside Business Park
EVILLE/WHL BS5 .... 336 F5
verside Leisure Centre
CBRISNE BS2 .... 336 B3
verside Sports & Leisure Club
GL GL1 .... 4 C3
verside Surgery
BRSG/KWL/STAPK BS4 .... 337 H8
dborough CP School
STROUD GL5 .... 208 D5
dford CP School
YATE/CS BS37 .... 319 M4
dford Infant School
YATE/CS BS37 .... 319 L4
dmarton School
CIR GL7 .... 259 L3
mney Avenue Junior
Mixed School
HORF/LLZ BS7 .... 326 D5
mney House Surgery
TET GL8 .... 281 M4
sary RC Primary School
STROUD GL5 .... 208 D4
sebank Surgery
GL GL1 .... 136 A4
se Green Sports &
Leisure Centre
EVILLE/WHL BS5 .... 336 F2
se Hill School
WUE GL12 .... 297 M1
ses Theatre
TEWK GL20 .... 48 A4
ss-on-Wye Golf Club
RWYE HR9 .... 84 D2
othedean Trading Estate
CIND GL14 .... 154 A3
owanfield Infant School
CHELTW GL51 .... 93 H8
owanfield Primary School
CHELTW GL51 .... 115 H1
owcroft Medical Centre
STROUD GL5 .... 208 D4
oyal Crescent Surgery
CHELT GL50 .... 2 C5
oyal Navy & Royal Marines
CBRIS/FH BS1 .... 6 E3
oyal West of England Academy
CFTN/FAIL BS8 .... 6 B2
ruardean C of E
Primary School
MTCHDN GL17 .... 128 F4
spca & Dogs Home
BRSG/KWL/STAPK BS4 .... 7 K8
ussell Town Avenue
Industrial Centre
EVILLE/WHL BS5 .... 336 E4
yeford Industrial Estate
STNHO GL10 .... 207 K5

St Andrews C of E VC
Primary School
WUE GL12 .... 295 J2
St Andrews School
COTS GL54 .... 167 K8
St Annes C of E Primary School
OLD/WMLY/WICK BS30 .... 338 E8
St Annes Junior Mixed School
BRSG/KWL/STAPK BS4 .... 336 F6
St Annes Park JMI School
BRSG/KWL/STAPK BS4 .... 337 G6
St Apollonias Surgery
KEYN BS31 .... 348 A5
St Augustine of Canterbury RC
Primary School
MANG/FISH BS16 .... 328 A4
St Barnabas C of E VC
Junior Mixed Infant School
RDLND/MONT BS6 .... 336 B2
St Bedes RC School
AVONM BS11 .... 324 C1
St Benedicts Catholic High School
CHELTW GL51 .... 93 J8
St Bernadette RC School
HGRV/WHIT BS14 .... 346 E5
St Bernadettes RC Primary School
HGRV/WHIT BS14 .... 346 D5
St Bernards RC
Primary School
AVONM BS11 .... 324 A5
St Bonaventures RC School
RDLND/MONT BS6 .... 325 L7
St Brendans
Sixth Form College
BRSG/KWL/STAPK BS4 .... 347 H2
St Briavals Castle
LYD GL15 .... 198 F5
St Briavels Primary School
LYD GL15 .... 198 F6
St Briavels Surgery
LYD GL15 .... 199 G6
Saintbridge Sports Centre
GLE GL4 .... 136 D6
St Catherines Surgery
CHELT GL50 .... 2 D5
St Christophers C of E School
CIR GL7 .... 245 L2
St Davids Primary School
MIM GL56 .... 58 D6
St Dominics RC Primary School
STROUD GL5 .... 232 C1
St Edwards Junior School
CHELTE/BC GL52 .... 3 L9
St Edwards School
CHELTE/BC GL52 .... 3 K9
St Edwards School
CHELTS GL53 .... 116 B5
St Gabriels Business Park
EVILLE/WHL BS5 .... 336 D3
St George Health Centre
KGWD/HNM BS15 .... 337 J3
St Georges Business Park
CHELTW GL51 .... 115 J1
St George School
EVILLE/WHL BS5 .... 336 D3
St Georges Primary School
CFTN/FAIL BS8 .... 6 B5
St Gloucester Council
THNB/SVB BS35 .... 293 J2
St Gregorys RC School
CHELT GL50 .... 2 B4
St Helens C of E Primary School
THNB/SVB BS35 .... 293 J7
St James C of E Junior School
GL GL1 .... 5 H9
St James C of E Primary School
CHCAM GL55 .... 12 E8
St James Health Centre
VGL GL2 .... 159 H2
St James School
CHELT GL50 .... 115 K5
St James Trading Estate
GL GL1 .... 5 J9
St Johns Church & Old City Gate
CBRIS/FH BS1 .... 6 F3
St Johns C of E Primary School
KEYN BS31 .... 348 A6
St Johns C of E VC
Primary School
CFTN/FAIL BS8 .... 335 J1
St Johns Lane Health Centre
BMSTR BS3 .... 346 A1
St Johns Mead C of E VC
Primary School
YATE/CS BS37 .... 320 D2
St Johns on the Hill School
CHEP NP16 .... 270 B1
St Johns Primary School
CHELTE/BC GL52 .... 2 F6
St Johns School
CLFD GL16 .... 175 J1
St Josephs RC School
MANG/FISH BS16 .... 327 K8
St Katherines School
PTSHD/EG BS20 .... 324 A8
St Katherines Surgery
LED HR8 .... 19 M3
St Laurence C of E School
CIR GL7 .... 244 F8
St Marks C of E Junior School
CHELTW GL51 .... 114 F4
St Martins Surgery
BRSG/KWL/STAPK BS4 .... 346 D2
St Mary De Crypt
School & Church
GL GL1 .... 4 E6
St Mary Redcliffe
Primary School
BMSTR BS3 .... 7 G9
St Mary Redcliffe &
Temple C of E VA School
CBRIS/FH BS1 .... 7 H7
St Marys C of E Primary School
TET GL8 .... 281 M3
St Marys C of E Primary School
YATE/CS BS37 .... 320 A1
St Marys C of E School
TEWK GL20 .... 24 B6

St Marys C of E School
THNB/SVB BS35 .... 293 J1
St Marys Hospital
CFTN/FAIL BS8 .... 6 B3
St Marys RC Primary School
BDWAY WR12 .... 32 F3
St Marys RC Primary School
BWTH/CHD GL3 .... 113 H5
St Mary's Redcliff
CBRIS/FH BS1 .... 7 G6
St Marys Roman Catholic
Junior & Infant School
CHEP NP16 .... 270 A4
St Marys Rugby Club
ALMDB BS32 .... 317 H1
St Matthews School
STROUD GL5 .... 208 A4
St Michael on the Mount C of E
Primary School
CFTN/FAIL BS8 .... 6 D3
St Michaels C of E VC
Primary School
FRCTL/WBN BS36 .... 318 A5
St Michaels Hill Clinic
CBRISNE BS2 .... 6 D2
St Michaels Hospital
CBRISNE BS2 .... 6 D1
St Michaels Primary School
BRSTK/PCHW BS34 .... 317 G6
St Michaels Surgery
GL GL1 .... 4 E7
St Nicholas Market
CBRIS/FH BS1 .... 6 F4
St Nicholas RC Primary School
EVILLE/WHL BS5 .... 7 K1
St Oswald's Priory
GL GL1 .... 4 E3
St Patricks RC School
EVILLE/WHL BS5 .... 336 F4
St Pauls C of E Primary School
GL GL1 .... 4 D9
St Pauls RC Primary School
YATE/CS BS37 .... 320 A3
St Peter & St Paul School
RDLND/MONT BS6 .... 335 L3
St Peters Infant School
CIR GL7 .... 5 L5
St Peters RC Secondary School
GLE GL4 .... 160 A2
St Peters Road Surgery
CIR GL7 .... 238 C3
St Pius X RC Primary School
BMSTRD/HC/WWD BS13 .... 345 J6
St Roses Special School
STROUD GL5 .... 208 D4
St Sampsons Church of
England Junior School
HGHW SN6 .... 288 F3
St Sampsons County
Infants School
HGHW SN6 .... 288 F3
St Stephens Business Centre
OLD/WMLY/WICK BS30 .... 338 E6
St Stephens C of E VC
Junior School
KGWD/HNM BS15 .... 337 M1
St Teresas RC School
HORF/LLZ BS7 .... 326 A2
St Thomas More Primary
School
CHELTW GL51 .... 114 F1
St Thomas More RC School
HORF/LLZ BS7 .... 326 C8
St Ursulas High School
HNLZ/SM/SNYPK/WT BS9 .... 325 J5
St Vincents Trading Estate
CBRISNE BS2 .... 336 E5
St Whites School
CIND GL14 .... 154 B5
Salmon Springs Trading Estate
STROUD GL5 .... 208 D2
Salvation Army
BMSTR BS3 .... 6 D9
Sampson House Business Park
HNBRY/STHM BS10 .... 314 F4
Samuel Whites Infant School
KGWD/HNM BS15 .... 337 L6
Sandford Park Lido
CHELTS GL53 .... 2 F8
Sandford Park Trading Estate
CHELTS GL53 .... 2 E7
Sandford School
CHELTS GL53 .... 2 E9
Sandpits Clinic
DSLY GL11 .... 229 H8
Sapperton C of E School
CIR GL7 .... 211 M8
Saracens Rugby Club
HNBRY/STHM BS10 .... 315 H6
Satellite Business Park
EVILLE/WHL BS5 .... 336 F5
Saul C of E Primary School
VGL GL2 .... 181 H4
Saville Court Business Centre
CFTN/FAIL BS8 .... 335 J4
Sea Mills Infant School
HNLZ/SM/SNYPK/WT BS9 .... 324 E4
Sea Mills Junior School
HNLZ/SM/SNYPK/WT BS9 .... 324 D6
Sea Mills Surgery
HNLZ/SM/SNYPK/WT BS9 .... 324 D6
Sedbury Trading Estate
CHEP NP16 .... 270 D3
Sedgeberrow C of E
First School
EVE WR11 .... 30 C2
Seeba Gallery
CIR GL7 .... 244 E7
Sefton Park School
HORF/LLZ BS7 .... 326 B8
Severn Banks Primary School
LYD GL15 .... 201 L8
Severn Beach CP School
THNB/SVB BS35 .... 304 C5
Severn Sailing Club
TEWK GL20 .... 27 H4
Severnside Trading Estate
VGL GL2 .... 4 A6

Severnside Works
HNBRY/STHM BS10 .... 314 C1
Severn Vale Secondary School
VGL GL2 .... 159 G2
Severside Trading Estate
VGL GL2 .... 4 A7
Shaftesbury Industrial Estate
CHELTW GL51 .... 93 J5
Shambles Museum
NWNT GL18 .... 86 C5
Sharpness Primary School
BRKLY GL13 .... 226 F3
Sheene Court Industrial Estate
BMSTR BS3 .... 335 L8
Sheepscombe County
Primary School
RSTROUD/NAIL GL6 .... 186 A2
Sheilding Schools
THNB/SVB BS35 .... 293 J2
Shell House Gallery
LED HR8 .... 20 A3
Shipston Industrial Estate
SHPSTR CV36 .... 16 A4
Shipston Medical Centre
SHPSTR CV36 .... 16 B4
Shipston on Stour
Junior & Infant School
SHPSTR CV36 .... 16 B5
Shire Hall
GL GL1 .... 4 D5
Shirehampton Baths
AVONM BS11 .... 324 A5
Shirehampton Cricket Club
AVONM BS11 .... 324 B4
Shirehampton Health Centre
AVONM BS11 .... 324 A5
Showcase Cinema Bristol
CBRISNE BS2 .... 336 E6
The Shrubberies School
STNHO GL10 .... 207 G3
Shurdington Primary School
CHELTW GL51 .... 138 F2
Siddington C of E School
CIR GL7 .... 238 D7
Sikh Temple
EVILLE/WHL BS5 .... 336 E1
Silverhill School
FRCTL/WBN BS36 .... 318 A4
Simplex Trading Estate
OLD/WMLY/WICK BS30 .... 338 F7
Sir Bernard Lovell School
OLD/WMLY/WICK BS30 .... 338 E7
Sir Thomas Richs
Grammar School
VGL GL2 .... 112 F3
Sir William Romneys School
TET GL8 .... 282 A2
The Sisters of the Temple
CFTN/FAIL BS8 .... 335 H4
Slimbridge CP School
VGL GL2 .... 229 G1
Sneyd Park Surgery
HNLZ/SM/SNYPK/WT BS9 .... 325 G8
Soaphouse Industrial Estate
EVILLE/WHL BS5 .... 337 G3
The Soga Gallery
CFTN/FAIL BS8 .... 335 J5
Soudley CP School
CIND GL14 .... 178 C1
Soundwell College
CBRISNE BS2 .... 7 M4
Soundwell College
KGWD/HNM BS15 .... 338 A1
South Bristol College
BMSTRD/HC/WWD BS13 .... 345 M7
South Gloucestershire Council
BRSTK/PCHW BS34 .... 316 D8
South Gloucestershire Council
BRSTK/PCHW BS34 .... 316 B2
South Gloucestershire Council
MANG/FISH BS16 .... 328 D5
South Gloucestershire Council
YATE/CS BS37 .... 309 L7
South Gloucestershire Council
YATE/CS BS37 .... 320 B2
South Gloucestershire Council
YATE/CS BS37 .... 320 D2
South Gloucestershire
Magistrates Court
STROUD GL5 .... 208 E4
Southmead Health Centre
HNBRY/STHM BS10 .... 325 L1
Southmead Health
Services NHS Trust
HNBRY/STHM BS10 .... 325 M3
Southrop C of E
Primary School
CIR GL7 .... 220 C7
South Street Primary School
BMSTR BS3 .... 335 K8
South View Business Centre
MANG/FISH BS16 .... 328 A6
South View Business Park
MANG/FISH BS16 .... 328 A6
Southville Primary School
BMSTR BS3 .... 6 B9
Southville Surgery
BMSTR BS3 .... 6 D7
Spartans Rugby Club
GL GL1 .... 4 C2
Speedwell School
EVILLE/WHL BS5 .... 337 J2
Speedwell Swimming Baths
EVILLE/WHL BS5 .... 337 H2
Springfield Business Centre
STNHO GL10 .... 206 E3
Springfield School
RDLND/MONT BS6 .... 336 A1
Springhill Industrial Estate
BDWAY WR12 .... 33 M7
Spring Mill Industrial Estate
RSTROUD/NAIL GL6 .... 232 F8
Springwater Park
Trading Estate
EVILLE/WHL BS5 .... 337 G4
SS Great Britain
CBRIS/FH BS1 .... 6 B6

Stanbridge CP School
MANG/FISH BS16 .... 328 B5
Standish Hospital
STNHO GL10 .... 207 K1
Staple Hill Primary School
MANG/FISH BS16 .... 327 M7
Station Approach
Industrial Estate
BAD GL9 .... 323 J4
Station Industrial Estate
LED HR8 .... 19 M3
Station Industrial Estate
LED HR8 .... 20 A1
Station Road Industrial
Estate South
STROUD GL5 .... 232 C2
Station Road Trading Estate
STROUD GL5 .... 232 C2
Station Street Business Park
CIND GL14 .... 154 A3
Station Yard Industrial Estate
CHEP NP16 .... 270 B3
Staunton & Corse C of E
Aided School
RTEWK/TIB GL19 .... 66 E4
Staunton Court Business Park
RTEWK/TIB GL19 .... 66 C4
Steadings Business Centre
Maisemore Court
VGL GL2 .... 111 J3
Steam Mills School
CIND GL14 .... 129 M7
Stenders Business Centre
MTCHDN GL17 .... 130 B2
Stenders Business Park
MTCHDN GL17 .... 130 B1
Steps Gallery
CBRIS/FH BS1 .... 6 E3
Stockwood Green
Primary School
HGRV/WHIT BS14 .... 347 G7
Stoke Bishop C of E
Primary School
HNLZ/SM/SNYPK/WT BS9 .... 324 F6
Stoke Gifford Medical Centre
BRSTK/PCHW BS34 .... 317 G7
Stoke Lodge Infant School
BRSTK/PCHW BS34 .... 316 E3
Stokes Medical Centre
BRSTK/PCHW BS34 .... 316 E4
Stoke View Business Park
MANG/FISH BS16 .... 327 H7
Stonebury Day Hospital
LYD GL15 .... 201 H8
Stone Cricket Club
BRKLY GL13 .... 251 K5
Stonehill Business Centre
OLD/WMLY/WICK BS30 .... 338 A7
Stonehouse Health Clinic
STNHO GL10 .... 207 H4
Stone with Woodford
C of E Primary School
BRKLY GL13 .... 251 G7
Stour Valley Community School
SHPSTR CV36 .... 16 A5
Stover Trading Estate
YATE/CS BS37 .... 319 K2
Stow on the Wold
Primary School
COTS GL54 .... 102 B3
Stratton C of E Primary School
CIR GL7 .... 214 A7
Stroud College
RSTROUD/NAIL GL6 .... 232 B7
Stroud College
YATE/CS BS37 .... 320 A2
Stroud College of
Further Education
STROUD GL5 .... 208 C3
Stroud District Council
STROUD GL5 .... 207 M5
Stroud General Hospital
STROUD GL5 .... 208 F5
Stroud High School
STROUD GL5 .... 208 B4
Stroud Maternity Hospital
STROUD GL5 .... 208 F5
Stroud Rugby Club
STROUD GL5 .... 208 C5
Stroud Town Council
STROUD GL5 .... 208 E4
Stroud Valley Primary School
STROUD GL5 .... 208 E5
Stuckeys Furniture Gallery
HNLZ/SM/SNYPK/WT BS9 .... 335 J1
Stuckleys Pine Gallery
HORF/LLZ BS7 .... 326 A6
The Studio Gallery
WUE GL12 .... 277 K4
Sudbrook Trading Estate
GL GL1 .... 4 C8
Sudeley Castle
COTS GL54 .... 74 E7
Summerhill Infant School
EVILLE/WHL BS5 .... 337 G3
Sunday School
WUE GL12 .... 277 H7
Sun Life Sports Club
HNBRY/STHM BS10 .... 315 H7
Sussex Place Surgery
RDLND/MONT BS6 .... 336 B1
Swainswick School
CBATH/BATHN BA1 .... 351 K6
Swell Primary School
COTS GL54 .... 101 J4
Swimming Pool
CHCAM GL55 .... 34 E2
Swimming Pool
LYD GL15 .... 225 H2
Swindon Village
Primary School
CHELTW GL51 .... 93 K4
Taits Hill Industrial Estate
DSLY GL11 .... 228 E7
Temple County Primary School
KEYN BS31 .... 348 B5
Temple Guiting School
COTS GL54 .... 76 D7

Temple House Doctors Surgery
 KEYN BS31 .... 348 A6
Temple Industrial Estate
 CHELTE/BC GL52 .... 3 H2
The Temple
 MTCHDN GL17 .... 131 H1
Temple Trading Estate
 CBRISNE BS2 .... 336 D6
Ten Pin Alley
 GL GL1 .... 4 E7
Tetbury Gallery
 TET GL8 .... 282 A4
Tetbury Industrial Estate
 TET GL8 .... 282 B3
Tewkesbury Abbey School
 TEWK GL20 .... 48 A5
Tewkesbury Business Centre
 TEWK GL20 .... 48 E3
Tewkesbury C of E School
 TEWK GL20 .... 48 B5
Tewkesbury Cottage Hospital
 TEWK GL20 .... 48 A5
Tewkesbury Grant Maintained
 Comprehensive School
 TEWK GL20 .... 48 E4
Tewkesbury Museum
 TEWK GL20 .... 48 A5
Tewkesbury Rugby
 Football Club Ltd
 TEWK GL20 .... 48 A6
Tewkesbury Squash Club
 TEWK GL20 .... 48 D4
Teyfant Primary School
 BMSTRD/HC/WWD BS13 .... 346 A7
Thomas Keble School
 RSTROUD/NAIL GL6 .... 210 A6
Thornbury Health Centre
 THNB/SVB BS35 .... 293 L2
Thornbury Hospital
 THNB/SVB BS35 .... 293 L2
Thornbury Leisure Centre
 THNB/SVB BS35 .... 293 K4
Thornwell Junior School
 CHEP NP16 .... 270 B6
Thrupp Primary School
 STROUD GL5 .... 209 G8
Tibberton Primary School
 VGL GL2 .... 109 L2
Tirlebrook CP School
 TEWK GL20 .... 48 D5
Tockington Manor School
 ALMDB BS32 .... 306 E1
Toddington Primary School
 COTS GL54 .... 52 F6
Toll House Clinic
 YATE/CS BS37 .... 320 E2
Tortworth VC Primary School
 WUE GL12 .... 275 L4
Totterdown Bridge Estate
 CBRISNE BS2 .... 7 M8
Town Council
 MALM SN16 .... 303 J7
Towncrest Sports Club
 TEWK GL20 .... 48 B5
Transport Museum
 GL GL1 .... 4 D5
Tredworth Infant School
 GL GL1 .... 136 B4

Tredworth Junior School
 GL GL1 .... 136 B4
Trinity C of E School
 BAD GL9 .... 323 J5
Trinity College
 HNLZ/SM/SNYPK/WT BS9 .... 325 G7
TT Trading Estate
 YATE/CS BS37 .... 320 E2
Tuffley Primary School
 GLE GL4 .... 160 A2
Tuffley Trading Estate
 VGL GL2 .... 135 K7
Tufthorn Industrial Estate
 CLFD GL16 .... 175 L3
Tutshill Church of
 England School
 CHEP NP16 .... 246 B8
Twigworth C of E School
 VGL GL2 .... 112 B4
Two Mile Hill Junior &
 Infant School
 KGWD/HNM BS15 .... 337 K3
Twyford House Cricket Club
 AVONM BS11 .... 324 B4
Twyning CP School
 TEWK GL20 .... 26 C5
Tyning Junior & Mixed School
 HGRV/WHIT BS14 .... 346 C4
The Tynings CP School
 MANG/FISH BS16 .... 328 A7
Uley C of E Primary School
 DSLY GL11 .... 254 E2
United Bristol
 Healthcare NHS Trust
 CBRIS/FH BS1 .... 6 F2
University of Bristol
 CBRIS/FH BS1 .... 6 D3
University of Bristol
 CFTN/FAIL BS8 .... 6 C2
University of Bristol
 CFTN/FAIL BS8 .... 335 G6
University of Bristol
 HNLZ/SM/SNYPK/WT BS9 .... 325 H7
University of Bristol Childrens
 Hospital
 CFTN/FAIL BS8 .... 6 D1
University of the
 West of England
 CBRIS/FH BS1 .... 6 F4
University of the
 West of England
 MANG/FISH BS16 .... 327 G6
University of the
 West of England Bristol
 BMSTR BS3 .... 335 G6
University of the
 West of England Bristol
 MANG/FISH BS16 .... 326 F2
University of the
 West of England Bristol
 MANG/FISH BS16 .... 327 J6
University of the West of
 England Bristol
 RDLND/MONT BS6 .... 325 J8
Uplands CP School
 STROUD GL5 .... 208 E3
Upper Horfield Primary School
 HORF/LLZ BS7 .... 326 C3

Upton St Leonards
 C of E (C) School
 GLE GL4 .... 137 H8
Upton St Leonards
 Primary School
 GLE GL4 .... 161 G1
Venture Business Centre
 GL GL1 .... 4 B9
Victoria Park County
 Infant School
 BMSTR BS3 .... 336 A8
Victoria Rooms
 CFTN/FAIL BS8 .... 6 A2
Wadehurst Industrial Park
 CBRISNE BS2 .... 7 M3
Walcot Rugby Club
 CBATH/BATHN BA1 .... 350 E6
Wallis Estate
 CBRISNE BS2 .... 326 B8
Wallsworth Hall
 VGL GL2 .... 112 C1
Walmore Hill Primary School
 CIND GL14 .... 157 H1
Walton House Gallery
 COTS GL54 .... 101 M3
Wansdyke School
 HGRV/WHIT BS14 .... 346 B7
Warden Hill Primary School
 CHELTW GL51 .... 115 J3
Ward Industrial Estate
 LYD GL15 .... 225 J3
Warmley C of E School
 OLD/WMLY/WICK BS30 .... 338 E5
Watermoor C of E
 Controlled Primary School
 CIR GL7 .... 238 D4
Watershed Arts Complex
 CBRIS/FH BS1 .... 6 E5
Watledge Surgery
 TEWK GL20 .... 48 B5
Waycroft Primary School
 HGRV/WHIT BS14 .... 347 G6
Wellesley CP School
 YATE/CS BS37 .... 319 M5
Wellsway School
 KEYN BS31 .... 348 C6
Westbury Bazaar & Gallery
 HNLZ/SM/SNYPK/WT BS9 .... 325 J4
Westbury on Severn C of E Primary
 School
 CIND GL14 .... 156 B2
Westbury-on-Trym C of E
 Primary School
 HNLZ/SM/SNYPK/WT BS9 .... 325 J4
Westbury-on-Trym Practice
 HNLZ/SM/SNYPK/WT BS9 .... 325 H5
Westbury Park School
 RDLND/MONT BS6 .... 325 J8
Westbury Surgery
 CIND GL14 .... 156 A2
Westlands School
 CHELTW GL51 .... 115 J4
Westonbirt School
 TET GL8 .... 301 G3
Weston House Group Practice
 CHELT GL50 .... 2 C2
Weston Park Primary School
 AVONM BS11 .... 324 B3

Westpoint Trading Estate
 KGWD/HNM BS15 .... 337 M4
West Town Lane Infant School
 BRSG/KWL/STAPK BS4 .... 346 E2
West Town Lane Junior School
 BRSG/KWL/STAPK BS4 .... 346 E2
West Walk Surgery
 YATE/CS BS37 .... 320 A2
Westwing School
 THNB/SVB BS35 .... 293 G3
Whaddon Primary School
 CHELTE/BC GL52 .... 3 L3
Whimsey Industrial Estate
 CIND GL14 .... 153 M1
Whitchuch Health Centre
 HGRV/WHIT BS14 .... 346 C6
Whitchurch Parish Council
 HGRV/WHIT BS14 .... 346 E7
Whitchurch Primary School
 HGRV/WHIT BS14 .... 346 E7
Whitchurch VA School
 RWYE HR9 .... 126 E3
Whitecross Business Park
 LYD GL15 .... 225 J1
Whitecross School
 LYD GL15 .... 225 H1
Whitefield Fishponds School
 MANG/FISH BS16 .... 327 H7
Whitehall Primary &
 Infant School
 EVILLE/WHL BS5 .... 336 F2
Whitehall Trading Estate
 EVILLE/WHL BS5 .... 336 E3
White Knight Gallery
 CHELT GL50 .... 2 B9
Whiteladies Medical Group
 CFTN/FAIL BS8 .... 335 J2
Whiteshill Primary School
 RSTROUD/NAIL GL6 .... 184 B8
Whitminster Endowed
 Primary School
 VGL GL2 .... 182 A6
Whitminster Sports Club
 VGL GL2 .... 182 A6
Wick School
 OLD/WMLY/WICK BS30 .... 339 K5
Wick Surgery
 OLD/WMLY/WICK BS30 .... 339 M5
Wickwar Primary School
 WUE GL12 .... 296 D6
Wickwar Trading Estate
 WUE GL12 .... 296 D4
Wicliffe Industrial Centre
 STROUD GL5 .... 208 C5
Widden Infant School
 GL GL1 .... 5 H6
Widden Junior School
 GL GL1 .... 5 H7
Wildscreen @ Bristol
 CBRIS/FH BS1 .... 6 D5
Willersey Industrial Estate
 BDWAY WR12 .... 11 G6
Willersey School
 BDWAY WR12 .... 11 H7
William Budd Health Centre
 BRSG/KWL/STAPK BS4 .... 345 M3
Willow Green Infant School
 CBRISNE BS2 .... 336 C1

Willow Tree Surgery
 CLFD GL16 175
Wilverley Trading Estate
 BRSG/KWL/STAPK BS4 347
Winchcombe Business Centre
 COTS GL54 74
Winchcombe C of E Infant School
 COTS GL54 74
Winchcombe Junior School
 COTS GL54 74
Winchcombe School
 COTS GL54 74
Wincombe Trading Estate
 BRSG/KWL/STAPK BS4 7
Windmill Farm Business Centre
 BMSTR BS3 6
Windmill Hill City Farm
 BMSTR BS3 6
Winfield Hospital
 VGL GL2 112
Withington C of E School
 COTS GL54 142
Withington Primary School
 COTS GL54 142
Withywood School
 BMSTRD/HC/WWD BS13 345
Woodchester Endowed Primary
 School
 STROUD GL5 232
Woodfield Infants School
 DSLY GL11 229
Woodmancote CP School
 CHELTE/BC GL52 72
Wood Road Industrial Centre
 KGWD/HNM BS15 337
Woodside County Primary School
 MTCHDN GL17 129
Woodstock Special School
 KGWD/HNM BS15 338
Wotton Sports Centre
 WUE GL12 277
Wotton Under Edge Town Council
 WUE GL12 277
Wycliffe College
 STNHO GL10 207
Wyedean School
 CHEP NP16 270
Wynstones School
 GLE GL4 160
Yate Leisure Centre
 YATE/CS BS37 320
Yate Town Council
 YATE/CS BS37 320
Yate Town Football Club
 YATE/CS BS37 309
YHA
 CBRIS/FH BS1 6
YMCA
 BRSG/KWL/STAPK BS4 7
Yorkley County School
 LYD GL15 177
Yorkley Health Centre
 LYD GL15 177
Zhong Yi Clinic
 CFTN/FAIL BS8 335

Page 48

- Abbey Meadow

Page 72

- Bishops Meadow
- The Cloisters
- Cornfield Dr
- Foxmoor
- Little Orch
- Rosehip Wy
- Stanway Wood Dr
- Stonecroft Cl
- Tarlington Cl

- Buckland Cl
- Builders Paddock
- Fullar Cl
- Roberts Cl
- St John's Cl
- Shipway Ct
- Rowscombe Pk
- Streamside
- Willow Park Dr

- Wisnams Fld
- Combe Cl
- Robyfield La

- Birchfield Cl
- Rootenhay Rd
- Bares Cl
- Huntsmans Cl
- Owls End Rd
- Ward Cl

- Anderson Cl
- Coombe Meade
- Bares Ct
- East Gable
- Hawthorn Dr
- Hempsford Acre
- Lynghurst Ct
- Peakslbe Piece
- Woodmancote V

Page 93

- Blenheim Sq
- Bronwen Cl
- Hawthorn Rd
- Bechmere Rd

- Attwood Cl
- Patterdale Cl
- Summerfield Cl

- Aldridge Cl
- Bullingham Ct
- Carlton Pl
- Marsh Cl
- Midwinter Av
- Russell Pl
- Russell St
- Vine Ct
- White Hart Ms

- Pentathlon Wy

Page 94

- Corfe Cl
- Honeysuckle Cl
- Dry Bank
- Willowherb Cl

Page 112

- Fircroft Rd
- Stamp's Meadow
- Taurus Cl
- Teasel Cl
- Tewkesbury Rd

- Waders Gn
- Ashmead
- Ferndale Cl
- Firethorne Cl
- Foxcote
- Hornbeam Ms
- Longland Ct
- Oxtails Wy
- The Tulworths
- Wentworth Cl
- Oxstalls Wy
- Woodcote

- Crane Cl
- Clifford Cl
- Langdale Gdns
- Lea Crs
- Malet Cl
- Manley Gdns
- Mortimer Rd
- Mowberry Cl
- Saxon Cl
- Wedgwood Dr

Page 113

- Maple Ct

- Heathendan Rd

- Compton Cl
- Essex Cl
- St Vincent Wy
- Thomas Moore Ct
- Victory Cl

- Berryfield Gld
- Forsythia Cl
- Gardiners Ct
- Ilminster Ct

Page 115

- Amberley Rd
- St Aidans Cl
- Seacome Rd

- Cowper Rd
- Milton Av
- Wordsworth Av

- Chedworth Wy
- Cotgrove Cl
- Crssington Ct
- Sheepscombe Cl

- Harrington Dr
- Hatherley Brake
- Ullswater Rd
- Windermere Cl

(Page 48 grid index)

G5
1. Caernarvon Cl
2. Colwyn Dr
3. Glamorgan Rd
4. Haweswater Rd

G6
1. Arlingham
2. Ashcot Ms
3. Avsgarth Av
4. Beechmore Dr
5. Calverley Ms
6. Chasely Crs
7. Chyndhforoe Gv
8. Larchmere Gv
9. Meadow La
10. Pyrton Ms
11. Rowan Wy
12. Selworthy
13. Sevelm
14. Silverwood Wy
15. Swanscombe Pl
16. Thornhaugh Ms
17. Welwyn Ms
18. Withypool

H3
1. Church Rd
2. Finstock Cl
3. Granley Cl
4. Granley Dr
5. Greville Cl
6. Lansdown Castle Dr

H4
1. Bronte Cl
2. Browning Ms
3. Chapman Wy
4. Deacon Cl
5. Deans Ct
6. Grasmere Rd
7. Manse Gdns
8. Rolleston Wy

H5
1. Dover Hay
2. Warden Hill Cl

H6
1. Amaranth Wy
2. Barwick Rd
3. Cheriton Cl
4. Croft Thorne Cl
5. Crythan Wk
6. Ferndales Cl
7. Genista Wy
8. Glebe Farm Ct
9. Glenlea Gv
10. Greatfield La
11. The Greenings
12. Hawcombe Ms
13. Rothermere Cl

H7
1. Tayberry Gv

J1
1. Clevedon Sq

J2
1. Libertus Cl
2. Stow Ct

J3
1. Glencairn Ct
2. Lansdown Cl
3. Lansdown Lodge Dr
4. Skillicorne Ms

J6
1. Camellia Ct
2. David French Ct
3. Hampton Cl
4. Hidcote Av
5. Rochester Rd
6. St Albans Cl
7. Sissinghurst Cl

J7
1. Leckhampton Ga

K1
1. Millbrook Gdns
2. Old Millbrook Ter
3. Queen's Retreat
4. St George's Cl
5. Sterling Ct

K2
1. Wendover Gdns

K3
1. Thorncliffe Dr
2. Tivoli Wk

K4
1. Bakehouse La

L1
1. Devonshire St
2. Hereford Pl
3. Knapp La

L2
1. Fauconberg Rd
2. Overton Park Rd

M3
1. Bath Ville Ms
2. Belmore Pl
3. Eaton Pl
4. Glensands Ct
5. Montpellier Dr
6. Montpellier Retreat
7. Paragon Ter
8. Trafalgar St
9. Vittoria Wk

M4
1. Bath Ter
2. Bethesda St
3. Chapel La
4. Clare St
5. Exmouth St
6. Cratton St
7. Victoria Retreat

M5
1. Badminton Cl
2. Fairfield Park Rd
3. Fairfield St
4. Fairhaven Rd
5. Fairhaven St
6. Maida Vale Rd
7. Mornington Dr

M6
1. Charnwood Cl
2. Charnwood Rd
3. Duckworth Cl
4. Wychbury Cl

M8
1. Stoneleigh Cl

Page 116

A1
1. Albert Pl
2. Albion Pl
3. Back Albert Pl
4. Berkeley Av
5. Clarence Rd
6. Columbia St
7. Gloucester Pl
8. Jersey St
9. North Pl
10. Portland Pl
11. Portland Sq
12. Trinity La
13. Warwick Pl
14. Winchcombe St

A2
1. Albion St
2. Barratt's Mill La
3. Berkeley Ct
4. Berkeley Pl
5. Grosvenor Pl South
6. Grosvenor St
7. Grosvenor Ter
8. Hewlett Pl
9. Highbury La
10. St Anne's Rd
11. St James St
12. Tom Price Cl
13. Vernon Pl
14. Winchcombe St
15. Witcombe Pl

A5
1. All Saints' Villas Rd
2. Fairview Cl
3. Glenfall St
4. Pittville Circus
5. Pittville Circus Rd
6. St Anne's Ct
7. Whaddon Dr

B2
1. Brighton Rd
2. Fairview Rd
3. Victoria Pl
4. Westdown Gdns

B3
1. Oxford Cl

B5
1. Marlborough Cl
2. Randolph Cl

C4
1. Cirencester Cl
2. Hamilton St
3. Langton Grove Rd
4. Langton Pl
5. Oakland St
6. Overbury St

D1
1. Hill View Rd
2. Ibbourne Rd
3. Ladysmith Rd
4. Salamanca Rd
5. Whaddon Rd

D5
1. Acomb Crs
2. Courtfield Dr
3. Lawrence Cl
4. Porturet Wy
5. Reaburn Cl
6. Riverside Cl
7. Water La

D6
1. Cedar La
2. Church Piece
3. Clynrosa Rd
4. Little Herbert's Cl
5. New St

D7
1. Chatcombe Cl

E1
1. Kimberley Wk

E4
1. Carisbrooke Dr

E5
1. Farleigh Cl

E6
1. Balcarras Retreat
2. East End Rd
3. Peel Cl
4. Woodgate Cl

E7
1. Birch Cl
2. Willow Rd

Page 135

M1
1. Archdeacon Ct
2. Chester Wk
3. Church St
4. Jenner Wk
5. Oxford Pas
6. Rose & Crown Pas
7. Royal Oak Ms
8. St George's Pl

M2
1. Clarence Pde
2. Clarence St
3. College Pl
4. County Court Rd
5. High St
6. Imperial Cl
7. Imperial Sq
8. Oriel Rd
9. Ormond Pl
10. Post Office La
11. Promenade
12. Queen's Circ
13. Regent St
14. Royal Well Pl
15. Royal Well Rd

Page 136

A1
1. Bull La
2. Cross Keys La
3. Hare La
4. Market Pde
5. New Inn La
6. St Mary's St
7. Spread Eagle Rd
8. Station Rd

A2
1. Bell La
2. Brunswick Sq
3. Hampden Wy
4. Parliament St
5. St Michael's Sq
6. Southgate St
7. Whitfield St

A8
1. Beechwood Gv
2. Cherrywood Gdns
3. Coberley Rd

Page 154

B2
1. Edge Hills Cl
2. Ferndale Cl
3. Market St
4. Marshall's La
5. Moorland Cl
6. Mountjoy's La
7. Mountjoy's Lane End
8. Oakwood Cl

Page 159

G3
1. Ashleworth Gdns
2. Cheviot Cl
3. Coss Wood Cnr
4. Mendip Cl

Page 207

K1
1. Coombe Av
2. Kensington Cl
3. Orchard Gra

M3
1. Blackbird Cl
2. Cedar Gdns
3. Chaffinch Cl
4. Coates Gdns
5. Glen Ct
6. Goldcrest Ct
7. Greenstreet
8. Magpie Ct
9. Partridge Cl
10. Peasant Mead
11. Sherbourne Ct
12. Starling Ct

M3
1. Hawthorn Ri
2. Perry Orch
3. St Michael's La
4. Springfield Rd
5. The Wordens

Page 208

A3
1. Harper Rd
2. Moor Hall Pl
3. Park View Ct
4. Princes Rd

A4
1. Mosley Crs

E3
1. Birches Cl
2. The Circle
3. The Square
4. Upper Springfield Rd

E4
1. Bedford Cl
2. Fawkes Pl
3. Gloucester St
4. John St
5. Kendrick St
6. King St
7. Lime Gv
8. Locking Hl
9. Parliment Cl
10. Russell St
11. Ryeleaze Cl
12. Ryeleaze Rd
13. The Shambles
14. Streamside
15. Swan St
16. Threadneedle St

F3
1. John Bevan Cl
2. Shepherds Cl
3. Sycamore Dr
4. The Woodlands

F4
1. The Knoll
2. Wood St

F5
1. Churchfield Rd
2. Lower Churchfield Rd
3. Nursery Cl
4. Trinity Rd

F6
1. Weyhouse Cl

Page 233

H4
1. Burleigh Tor

H5
1. Dr Crawfords Wy
2. Southfield

K4
1. The Tynings

Page 238

B5
1. Foxes Bank Dr
2. Greyfriars Wk
3. Linacre Crs
4. Masefield Rd
5. Michaels Mead
6. Morestall Dr
7. Somerville Cl

C2
1. Black Jack St
2. Gosditch St
3. Hakeburn Rd
4. Park St
5. Silver St
6. West Market Pl

C4
1. Beaufort Ct
2. Garden Cl
3. Grantley Crs
4. Limes Ct
5. Martin Cl
6. St Michaels Rd
7. Whitworth Rd

D4
1. Bridge End
2. Mercian Cl
3. Sperringate
4. Watermoor Wy

D5
1. Bridge Cl

E4
1. The Smithy

Page 270

A3
1. Bank Sq
2. Beaufort Pl
3. Garden City Wy
4. Hardwick Av
5. High Vw
6. Middle St
7. Oxford St
8. Regent Wy
9. River Vw
10. Thomas St
11. Upper Nelson St

A6
1. Ash Cl
2. Holly Cl
3. Linden Cl
4. Mathern Wy

B6
1. Fisherman's Wk
2. Magnolia Cl
3. The Reddings
4. Sharps Wy
5. Warren Slade

Page 293

B7
1. Bishops Cl
2. Cidermill Cl
3. Fountain Wy
4. Lady Margaret Ct
5. Lewis Wy
6. Lord Eldon Dr
7. Preston Cl
8. Rougemont Gv
9. Summerhouse La
10. Thorn Tree Dr
11. Well Cl

C4
1. Maddocke Rd

Page 316

F1
1. Boursland Cl
2. Campion Dr
3. Foxborough Gdns
4. Perrys Lea
5. Primrose Cl
6. Teal Cl

F4
1. Blackthorn Dr
2. Garrett Dr
3. Kemperleve Wy
4. Penrose Dr
5. Shiels Dr
6. Somerby Cl

F6
1. Elming Down Cl
2. Olympus Cl

F7
1. Balmoral Cl
2. Chevening Cl
3. Holyrood Cl
4. Lancaster Cl
5. Osborne Cl

Page 317

G6
1. Cerimon Ga
2. Charbon Ga
3. Dighton Ga
4. Lysander Wk
5. Montague Cl
6. Roman Wk

Page 320

C2
1. Cherry Rd
2. Chestnut Dr
3. Meadow Rd
4. The Parade
5. River Rd
6. Streamside Wk
7. Wistaria Av

Page 324

B3
1. Broxholme Wk

C2
1. Burycourt Cl
2. Crokeswood Wk
3. Shortlands Rd

C3
1. Alderdown Cl
2. Rockingham Gdns

E1
1. Caldicot Cl
2. Chantry Gv
3. Gorham Cl
4. Hewland Ct
5. Jasmine Gv
6. Roman Farm Ct

E3
1. Bilberry Cl
2. Cranberry Wk
3. Drayton Rd
4. Mulberry Wk

E5
1. Failand Wk
2. Shirehampton Rd
3. Silklands Gv

E6
1. Abbeywood Dr
2. Ableton Wk
3. Druid Woods
4. Trymleaze

E7
1. Glenavon Pk
2. Hadrian Cl
3. Harbour Wall
4. Newcombe Dr
5. Pine Ridge Cl

F1
1. Kings Weston Rd

F4
1. Dinglewood Cl

F5
1. Ebenezer La
2. Poplar Av

F6
1. Ellibridge Cl
2. Halwyn Cl
3. Yeomans Cl

F8
1. Cook's Folly Rd

Page 325

G1
1. Dundas Cl
2. Gray's Cl
3. Henbury Rd

G4
1. Hammond Gdns

G5
1. Clifton Gv
2. Ebenezer La
3. Sunnyside

G7
1. Howcroft Ms

H2
1. Standish Cl

H3
1. Westover Gdns

H5
1. Stoke Hamlet
2. Stoke La

H7
1. Saville Gate Cl

Page 326

B5
1. Crofton Av

B6
1. Draycott Rd
2. Uphill Rd

B8
1. Hopetoun Rd
2. Osborne Av
3. St Bartholomew's Rd

C2
1. Cropthorne Rd

C3
1. Cropthorne Rd South
2. St Gregory's Wk
3. Thackeray Wk

C4
1. Masefield Wy
2. Rose Mead
3. Shearmore Cl
4. Taunton Wk

D2
1. Eleventh Av
2. Seventh Av

D3
1. Browning Ct

D4
1. Branwhite Cl

E1
1. Copley Gdns
2. Linnell Cl
3. Rowlandson Gdns
4. Stanfield Cl
5. Turner Gdns

D6
1. Haydon Gdns

E3
1. Bridge Rd
2. Kirtlington Rd
3. Tackley Rd

E5
1. Cameron Wk

E6
1. Baileys Mead Rd
2. Heath House La
3. Little Parr Cl

Page 327

E8
1. Chisbury St
2. Coleridge Rd
3. Freemantle Gdns
4. Freemantle Rd
5. Muller Rd

F5
1. Bryansons Cl
2. Countess Ms
3. Princess Gdns

F7
1. Fry's Cl
2. Wickham Vw

F9
1. Gloster Av
2. Herbert Crs
3. Queen St
4. Shamrock Rd

G5
1. Grove Vw
2. Kingfisher Gv
3. Redwing Gdns
4. Reedling Cl

G6
1. Blackberry Av
2. Cromwells Hide
3. Frome Ct
4. Glenside Pk
5. Stile Hay Cl
6. Lark's Fld
7. Pennyroyal Gv
8. Spires Vw

G7
1. Foxglove Cl
2. Honey Suckle La
3. Lower Grove Rd
4. Rosebay Mead

G8
1. Huyton Rd
2. Knowsles Rd
3. Marlborough Av
4. Marlborough St
5. Ridgeway Pde

H4
1. Broadways Dr

H5
1. Curlew Cl
2. Lapwing Gdns
3. Ronald Rd
4. Whinchat Gdns
5. Witherlies Rd

H7
1. Adelaide Pl
2. Albert Ter
3. Featherstone Rd
4. Langdale Rd
5. Wharf Rd

H8
1. Balaclava Rd
2. Drummond Rd
3. Halstock Av
4. Lodore Rd
5. Midland Ter
6. Stoke View Rd

J4
1. Blenman Cl
2. Probyn Cl
3. Scott Lawrence Cl
4. Stourden Cl

J6
1. Claverham Rd
2. College Av
3. Guinea La

J7
1. Hinton Rd
2. Hockey's La

J8
1. Acton Rd
2. Ivy La
3. Justice Rd
4. Poplar Pl

K2
1. Beaufort Rd
2. Berkeley Gn

K4
1. Churchside

K5
1. Lanaway Rd
2. Oldbury Court Dr

K6
1. Cunningham Gdns

K7
1. Bridges Cl
2. Chasefield La
3. Daws Ct
4. Parkhurst Av
5. Vicars Cl

K8
1. Fillwood Cl
2. William St

L2
1. Bryants Cl

L3
1. Beckspool Rd

L4
1. Quarry Rd
2. Tuckett La

L6
1. Pemberton Cl

L7
1. Edgeware Rd

Page 328

M7
1. Alexandra Dr
2. Kensington Rd
3. Nelson Rd
4. North Vw
5. Pendennis Av

M8
1. Beazer Cl
2. Colston Cl
3. Leicester Sq
4. Portland Pl
5. Wesley Cl

A8
1. Gladstone Cl
2. Gloucester Rd
3. St Stephens Cl
4. Wiltshire Cl
5. Woodchester

B3
1. Chantry Cl
2. Chepstow Pk
3. Goodwood Gdns
4. Haydock Ct
5. Plumpton Ct
6. Redcar Ct
7. Sedgefield Gdns
8. Wetherby Ct
9. Wincanton Cl

B3
1. Lytchet Dr
2. Rockside Gdns

B4
1. Boscombe Crs
2. Bowden Pl
3. Kimberley Cl
4. Westbourne Cl
5. Westerleigh Cl

B7
1. Bankside

C3
1. Meadowcroft

C5
1. Blackhorse Pl
2. Springfield Rd

C6
1. Balmoral Cl
2. Elmleigh Cl
3. Louise Av
4. Oaklands Rd
5. Westering Cl

D3
1. Youngs Ct

D4
1. Bromfield Rd
2. Cyrus Ct
3. Denton Patch
4. Howells Mead
5. Langley Mow
6. Pendock Ct

D6
1. Oaklands Cl
2. Shackel Hendy Ms

E4
1. Emersons Wy

E5
1. Paddock Cl

Page 335

G5
1. Bannerleigh La
2. Broad Oaks
3. Rownham Hl

G7
1. Rownham Cl

H3
1. Norland Rd

H4
1. Clifton Down Rd
2. Gloucester St
3. Westfield Cl

H5
1. Albemarle Rw
2. Cornwallis Av
3. Cumberland Rd
4. Dowry Sq
5. Freeland Pl
6. Glendale
7. Hopechapel Hl
8. Hope Sq
9. Hotwell Rd
10. Joy Hl
11. North Green St
12. Oxford Pl
13. The Paragon
14. Royal York Crs
15. South Green St
16. Victoria Ter
17. Windsor Ter

H6
1. Ashmead Wy
2. Brunswick Sq
3. Cumberland Rd
4. Grenville Pl
5. Little Caroline Pl

J1
1. Anglesea Pl
2. Belgrave Hl
3. Highland Crs
4. Highland Sq
5. Mornington Rd
6. Normanton Rd
7. Quarry Steps
8. Redland Ter
9. Richmond Cl
10. St Vincent's Hl
11. Westbury Rd
12. York St

J2
1. Beaconsfield Rd
2. Downside Rd
3. King's Parade Ms

J3
1. Buckingham Vs
2. Clifton Pk
3. Eaton Crs
4. Worcester Crs

J5
1. Ambra V
2. Ambra V South
3. Ambra V West
4. Camden Ter
5. Clifton Vale
6. Clifton Vale Cl
7. Cliftonwood Cr
8. Dowry Rd
9. Polygon Rd
10. Royal York Vls
11. St Vincent's Rd
12. Saville Pl

J6
1. Ashton Av
2. Dock Gate La
3. Oldfield Rd
4. Pembroke Pl
5. Pooles Wharf Ct
6. Rownham Mead
7. Sandford Rd

J7
1. Ashton Gate Ter
2. Baynton Rd
3. Leigh St
4. North Rd
5. St Francis Rd
6. Wells Rd

K1
1. East Shrubbery
2. Evans Rd
3. Hartington Pk
4. Luccombe Hl
5. Shrubbery Cottages
6. West Shrubbery
7. Woodland Ter

K2
1. Chantry Rd
2. Collingwood Rd
3. Cotham Gdns
4. Cotham Hl
5. Hampton Pk
6. Imperial Rd
7. King's Parade Av
8. Oakland Rd
9. Warwick Rd

K4
1. Berkley Av
2. Byron Pl
3. Queen's Av
4. Queen's Rd
5. Richmond Hill Av
6. Triangle South
7. Triangle West
8. Upper Byron Pl
9. Wetherell Pl

K5
1. Bellevue Cottages
2. Cliftonwood Crs
3. Gasferry Rd
4. Glentworth Rd
5. Gorse La
6. John Carr's Ter
7. St Edward's Rd
8. Southernhay
9. Southernhay Av

K6
1. Camden Rd
2. Gefle Cl
3. Hanover Pl
4. Mardyke Ferry Rd

K7
1. Dalston Rd
2. Earl St
3. King William St
4. Phipps St

K8
1. Crowther St
2. Dartmoor St
3. Dorset St
4. Jasper St
5. Lindrea St
6. Martin St
7. The Nursery
8. Parker St
9. Pembery Rd
10. Stanley St North
11. Thistle St
12. Upper Sydney St

L5
1. Bigwood La
2. Brandon Steep
3. Charlotte St South
4. College Sq
5. Culver St
6. Denmark Av
7. Frogmore St
8. Gaunt's La
9. Hobb's La
10. Lower College St
11. Lower Lamb St
12. Orchard Av
13. Orchard La
14. Partition St
15. Unity St
16. Upper Wells St
17. York Pl

L6
1. West End

L7
1. Argyle St
2. Dean St
3. Fairfield Rd
4. Kingston Rd
5. Merrywood Cl
6. Morley Rd
7. Mount Pleasant Ter
8. Murray St
9. Summer St

L8
1. Clifton St
2. Diamond St
3. Eaton St
4. Graham Rd
5. Hebron Rd
6. Kent St
7. New John St
8. Rowley St
9. St John's St
10. Sion Rd
11. Stanley St
12. Victoria Pl
13. Victor Rd
14. Wesley St

Page 336

M3
1. Barton St
2. Cherry La
3. Clevedon Ter
4. Cottage Pl
5. Earl St
6. Henrietta St
7. Hillgrove St North
8. King Sq
9. King Square Av
10. Lower Gay St
11. Marlborough Hill Pl
12. Montague Hl
13. Montague Hl South
14. Montague St
15. Princess Rw
16. Spring Hl
17. Terrell St
18. Whitson St

M4
1. All Saints' La
2. Bell La
3. Blackfriars
4. Bridewell St
5. Cannon St
6. Christmas St
7. Flennes Ct
8. High St
9. Host St
10. Lewins Mead
11. Nelson St
12. Pithay
13. Pithay Ct
14. Quay St
15. St Stephen's St
16. Silver St
17. Union St

M5
1. All Saints' La
2. Assembly Rooms La
3. Bridge St
4. Broad Quay
5. Clare St
6. Coronation Pl
7. Crow La
8. High St
9. King William Av
10. Marsh St
11. Middle Av
12. Queen Square Av
13. Rackhay
14. St Stephen's La
15. Telephone Av

M6
1. Barossa Pl
2. Challoner Ct
3. Draycot Pl
4. Farr's La
5. Grove Av
6. Jubilee Pl
7. Lower Guinea St
8. Redcliffe Pde East
9. Redcliffe Pde West

M7
1. Bedminster Pde
2. Boot La
3. Brook Rd
4. Clarke St
5. Dean Crs
6. Leicester St
7. Ludlow Cl
8. Regent Rd
9. St Paul's Rd
10. Southville Pl
11. Whitehouse La

M8
1. Brendon Rd
2. Church La
3. Hereford St
4. Porlock Rd
5. Stafford St

A1
1. Cheltenham La
2. Chesterfield Rd
3. Norfolk Av
4. St Andrew's Rd

A2
1. Armidale Av
2. Barnabas St
3. Bath Buildings
4. Dalrymple Rd
5. Drummond Rd
6. Norrisville Rd
7. Woodmancote Rd

A3
1. Backfields
2. Backfields La
3. Brunswick Sq
4. Chapter St
5. Cumberland St
6. Dalton Sq
7. Gloucester St
8. Hillgrove St
9. Little Bishop St
10. Norfolk Av
11. Pembroke St
12. Portland Sq
13. Thomas St
14. Wilder St

A4
1. Callowhill Ct
2. George Whitefield Ct
3. Hanover Ct
4. Marybush La
5. Meadow St
6. Old King Street Ct
7. Philadelphia Ct
8. Quakers' Friars
9. Wellington Rd
10. Whippington Ct

A5
1. Church St
2. Ferry St
3. Long Rw
4. Narrow Pln
5. The Streets East
6. Three Queens' La
7. Tower St

A6
1. Colston Pde
2. Mede Cl
3. Phippen St
4. Portwall La East
5. Somerset Sq

A7
1. Nicholas St
2. Sargent St

A8
1. Almorah Rd
2. Newport St
3. Orwell St
4. Paultow Av

B1
1. Ashley Court Rd
2. Ashley Grove Rd
3. Ashley Pde
4. Cumberland Gv
5. Fairlawn Rd
6. Falkland Rd
7. Milverton Gdns
8. Old Ashley Hl
9. Richmond Av
10. Richmond Rd
11. St Andrew's La
12. St Werburgh's Rd
13. Sommerville Rd South
14. York St

B2
1. Arley Cottages
2. Arley Pk
3. Elmgrove Pk
4. Fremantle La
5. Fremantle Rd
6. St Matthew's La
7. Southfield Rd
8. Victoria Gdns
9. Winsley Rd